CASES AND MATERIALS ON
MARIJUANA LAW

■ ■ ■

Howard Bromberg
Clinical Professor of Law
University of Michigan Law School

Mark K. Osbeck
Clinical Professor of Law
University of Michigan Law School

Michael Vitiello
Distinguished Professor of Law
University of the Pacific McGeorge School of Law

AMERICAN CASEBOOK SERIES®

WEST
ACADEMIC
PUBLISHING

American Casebook Series is a trademark registered in the U.S. Patent and Trademark Office.

© 2019 LEG, Inc. d/b/a West Academic
      444 Cedar Street, Suite 700
      St. Paul, MN 55101
      1-877-888-1330

West, West Academic Publishing, and West Academic are trademarks of West Publishing Corporation, used under license.

Printed in the United States of America

ISBN: 978-1-64242-245-0

To Samantha and Nate, as they explore
law, health, and business. —H.B.

To Betty, for always being there for me. —M.K.O.

To my friends Larry Levine and Michael Colatrella, who
persuaded me to make McGeorge Law School
a leader in Marijuana Law. —M.V.

ACKNOWLEDGMENTS

We would like to acknowledge the valuable assistance we received in research, proof-reading, obtaining copyright permissions, and assembling the manuscript from Kendall Fisher, Amy Gassner Seilliere, Dylan Marques, Megan Moore, Yana Nebuchina. Alison Southard, Olivia Wheeling, Laura Winterberger, and Wiemond Wu.

We would also like to thank the West production and publishing team—especially Daniel Buteyn, Louis Higgins, Laura Holle, and Greg Olson—for their professional support, suggestions, and guidance.

Finally, we would like to thank the following for permission to reproduce excerpts from their work in our casebook:

- Grinspoon, Lester & Bakalar, James B., *Marihuana: The Forbidden Medicine* (1997). Copyright © 1997 by Yale University. Reprinted by permission. All rights reserved.

- Jacobs, Leslie Gielow, *Regulating Marijuana Advertising and Marketing to Promote Public Health: Navigating the Constitutional Minefield* (2017). Copyright © 2017 by Lewis and Clark Law Review. Reprinted by permission. All rights reserved.

- Jacobs, Leslie Gielow, *Memo to Marijuana Regulators: The Expressions Hair Design Decision Does Not Limit Your Broad Authority to Restrict All Forms of Discounting* (2017). Copyright © 2017 by University of the Pacific Law Review. Reprinted by permission. All rights reserved.

- Mandiberg, Susan, *Marijuana Prohibition and the Shrinking Fourth Amendment* (2012). Copyright © 2012 by McGeorge Law Review. Reprinted by permission. All rights reserved.

- White, James Boyd, *Justice as Translation: An Essay in Cultural and Legal Criticism* (1990). Copyright © 1990 by University of Chicago Press. Reprinted by permission. All rights reserved.

- Hildy, John, *Fifth Amendment—Double Jeopardy and the Dangerous Drug Tax* (1995). Copyright © 1995 by Journal of Criminal Law and Criminology. Reprinted by permission. All rights reserved.

- Haas, Aaron, *Deportation and Double Jeopardy after Padilla* (2011). Copyright © 2011 by Geography Immigration Law Journal. Reprinted by permission. All rights reserved.

INTRODUCTION

A. What Is Marijuana Law?

When people think about marijuana law, they tend to think of one of three things. For some, "marijuana law" connotes the collection of various federal, state, and local laws that either prohibit and punish marijuana possession and distribution, or explicitly authorize such use. For others, marijuana law encompasses the various statutes and regulations that states have passed in setting up legalization schemes. And for still others, marijuana law brings to mind the policy debate between those who want marijuana legalized and those who prefer that it remain illegal.

As used in this book, "marijuana law" refers to all of those things—but also much more. Because it intersects with a number of different legal topics, marijuana law raises all kinds of theoretical as well as practical issues. At the theoretical level, it raises a number of issues related to federalism and the Constitution, including the extent to which the federal government can enforce its own laws within legalization states, whether federal law preempts state laws legalizing marijuana, and whether the federal government can require states to enforce federal laws in legalization states. And other important theoretical issues arise outside of the constitutional context. For example, certain international treaty obligations of the United States require it to criminalize marijuana possession and use, but more than half the states now allow medical use of marijuana, and ten states allow adult recreational use, and the federal government does not interfere. This raises the question whether the United States is fulfilling its obligations under these treaties. At the other end of the spectrum, there are theoretical issues pertaining to the conflict between state and local law, such as the extent to which localities may ignore or deviate from state laws regulating marijuana.

In addition to these theoretical issues, marijuana law raises a host of practical problems faced by users and distributors of the drugs in legalization states. For example, the conflict between state and federal law in legalization states has raised serious questions about the ability of marijuana-related businesses to obtain such things as banking services, adequate insurance coverage, bankruptcy court protection, and access to the federal courts. Marijuana-related businesses are also unable to deduct ordinary business expenses, unlike other types of businesses. Marijuana has also raised challenging issues regarding impaired driving because of the different ways marijuana and alcohol act in the human body, leading to difficulties for developing accurate roadside tests of marijuana impairment. In addition, marijuana law involves interesting issues related to family law and employment law. In family law, for example, the question arises as to what extent a spouse or parent's use of marijuana should have on divorce and/or child custody proceedings. And in employment law, the question arises whether employers should be able to enforce their zero-tolerance policies with respect to marijuana use outside the job with respect to employees who have valid medical marijuana licenses.

At bottom, all of these theoretical practical issues arise from conflict of law scenarios: most notably, the conflict between on the one hand, the Controlled Substances Act (which is the principal federal statute outlawing marijuana use), and, on the other, state/local laws legalizing marijuana. This conflict has created an uneasy truce between the United States and legalization states, whereby the federal government has opted not to interfere with state laws, provided they comply with certain enumerated federal priorities. But that could change at any time, since the federal government has simply chosen to refrain from enforcing federal laws that prohibit such schemes. And in fact, the Trump administration, reversing the policy of the Obama administration, has informed states that they should not rely on such forbearance, and it has empowered local U.S. attorneys to enforce federal laws to the extent they deem appropriate. Thus, the tension between federal law criminalizing the possession and distribution of marijuana and state laws that legalize it continues to simmer right below the surface of some of the most interesting marijuana law issues.

Of course, the subjects that most people think of when they hear the term "marijuana law" are also an important part of the field. Thus, in this case book we cover in depth the state and federal various laws that have traditionally criminalized marijuana possession and use. Marijuana has a significant presence in criminal law, both as to the number of marijuana arrests and convictions (marijuana is the most frequently used illicit drug), and in criminal law jurisprudence. In constitutional law, it can be argued that marijuana provoked the Supreme Court case affirming the furthest reach of the federal government under the commerce clause: *Gonzales v. Raich* (2005). Juxtaposed to the traditional criminalization of marijuana is recent state legalization. We discuss the detailed regulatory schemes that legalization states have enacted in order to set parameters on the legal use or distribution of marijuana, focusing in particular on California's regulatory scheme, since California is by far the largest state to have legalized recreational marijuana. And we also discuss the legal, medical and social issues that arise within the larger policy debate as to whether marijuana should be legalized, and if so, under what conditions.

Thus, far from being simply a niche area of the law, marijuana law is actually a rich, complicated discipline that raises numerous theoretical, practical and public policy considerations. In addition, it is a dynamic area of the law, morphing continuously as courts, legislatures, and regulatory agencies struggle to keep up with the changing social sentiment regarding marijuana. We find it to be a fascinating discipline, and we think that you will too.

B. Why a Casebook on Marijuana Law?

To begin with, ten states have legalized recreational marijuana. In addition twenty three states have legalized medical marijuana, with thirteen others authorizing some cannabis products for medical use. Members of the public, including those interested in entering the marijuana industry, read the headlines about marijuana's legalization and believe that they can smoke, produce and sell marijuana without legal reprisals. Many members of the public do not recognize a simple fact: nearly every use of marijuana, at least in theory, violates federal law.

Potential clients in states where marijuana is lawful are eager for legal advice. Product manufacturers want intellectual property for their trademarks, despite federal law that seems to prevent trademark protection for illegal products. Dispensary owners are trying to find ways around regulations preventing them from using traditional banking services. Members of the cannabis industry struggle to find a work-around of § 280E of the Internal Revenue Code, which prevents them from deducting ordinary business expenses. Many in the industry find out the hard way that insurance companies that accepted premiums to cover their crops or businesses will deny coverage when harm occurs.

Marijuana law affects those outside the marijuana industry as well. A common example is an employee who is suffering from chronic pain and has a doctor's recommendation to use marijuana in a state that has legalized medical marijuana. But the employer has a zero tolerance policy for drug use and fires the employee for failing a drug test. The fired employee is stunned to learn that the termination may be lawful.

Or consider members of a local medical physicians group debating whether they can recommend marijuana for their patients. They know that marijuana is still a Schedule I drug under the federal Controlled Substances Act and that prescribing marijuana may result in losing their right to prescribe medication. But some of the younger doctors insist that they should recommend marijuana to benefit their patients. They look to you to provide advice in the matter.

Imagine a lawyer considering specializing in marijuana law. She knows that the state where she practices has legalized recreational use of marijuana. When she studied professional responsibility, neither course material nor the lectures mentioned how the state bar viewed the ethics of a lawyer who helped business clients set up marijuana businesses. She wonders if doing so is legal, ethical and wise.

Organizations catering to the marijuana industry are growing rapidly. National conferences on cannabis products have multiplied in frequency and size. Entrepreneurs are pushing creative products relating to marijuana. Some entrepreneurs propose to sell cannabis infused wine and beer. Others hope to open restaurants with cannabis themed foods. Bar owners want to have cannabis space for customers. While some participants in the industry might rush ahead, more prudent individuals seek out counsel to help steer them through various levels of regulations.

Consider entrepreneurs in California, which, in 2016, legalized recreational marijuana. Over a year later, the state has promulgated hundreds of pages of regulations involving dozens of topics. Add to state regulations other regulations developed by county and city governments. Can those entrepreneurs open their restaurant with a cannabis infused menu?

And then there are old staples of marijuana law: criminal justice issues. Can a seriously ill person claim a medical necessity defense when charged with violating federal drug laws? Does an officer in a state that has legalized recreational marijuana have probable cause to arrest a person who has been smoking marijuana? With rapidly changing and at times conflicting laws, what defenses should criminal lawyers present on behalf of their clients? Should prosecutors devote scant resources to charge marijuana possession crimes?

The short discussion above highlights just a few of the many legal issues that arise in connection with marijuana. Quick reflection on these kinds of issues should explain why marijuana law is one of the fastest growing area of legal practice in states like California that have legalized marijuana.

The practice of marijuana law is also extremely complex. Lawyers interested in the field need to know about federalism, constitutional provisions bearing on marijuana law, employment issues, business organization questions and much more. Initially, a few law schools started teaching marijuana law five years ago. The number of schools offering marijuana law is proliferating, in part, in reaction to student interest in the topic and in light of inquiries from alums, some of whom wonder how they can get into this new specialized area of the law. All of this is occurring as a sizeable portion of the population, most importantly, perhaps, the Drug Enforcement Administration and other law enforcement officials, are opposed to relaxation of marijuana laws, a sentiment which is reflected in the near total federal prohibition of marijuana, going strong to this day.

All indications are that the practice of cannabis law will evolve, likely quite rapidly. Large capital flows into the industry, and changing public sentiment, create pressure on the federal government to accommodate states that have opted for marijuana. How will lawyers and law students develop a grounding in many of the complexities of marijuana law, and a familiarity with the public policy issues that inform the legalization debate?

Enter this casebook.

Although the primary audience for casebooks are law students, this casebook is also suitable for lawyers, policy makers, and anyone who wants a full knowledge of marijuana law. As is traditional for casebooks, we teach the law of marijuana through primary sources—primarily case law, from the U.S. and state supreme courts, but other courts as well. We also include the relevant statutory provisions and administrative regulations. We follow each primary document with *Notes and Questions*, highlighting important features to be discussed and supplementing the treatment of marijuana law and other legal issues. *Problems* are included to place the student in the position of a judicial authority, lawyer, or policy maker.

These materials teach not only how to extract legal principles and rules from cases, but also the workings of modern American codes and administrative law, which have come to dominate the legal landscape over the last century. For international law, we include excerpts from the major U.N. drug conventions. Where helpful we sprinkle in excerpts from commentators, academics, and institutional bodies. Hence we believe that this book will thoroughly ground the student in marijuana law, but also provide a focused but useful education in the following areas:

- interaction of state, federal, tribal, and international authorities in legal issues of shared concern
- federalism
- select issues in criminal and constitutional jurisprudence, especially the law of search and seizure
- the law of state constitutions and state administrative agencies
- certain canons of professional responsibility
- law of controlled substances
- international treaties
- tax law
- legal issues facing businesses in a controversial, growing, lucrative, and legally-complex industry.

Although our focus is on the law as it is—complex enough to understand—we also review how marijuana law has evolved and how it is likely to evolve in the future, including the highly-charged debate over legalization.

For all legal questions, a central issue is the law of which jurisdiction governs. Although we include the major federal and state cases illustrating principles of marijuana law, the casebook organizes material as much as possible according to jurisdictional criteria. For example, to illustrate state marijuana regulations in Chapter 5, we focus exclusively on California. For a question of preemption of state law in Chapter 7, we examine an Arizona Supreme Court decision and then an Arizona Court of Appeals case applying that decision. Chapter 17 on hemp focuses on the law of North and South Dakota. Whatever the grouping of cases, the student should keep in mind that a judicial decision or a statute is binding only in its own jurisdiction, although it may have persuasive value elsewhere. For a chart of marijuana law by jurisdiction, see the Appendix.

In our editing of cases, statutes, and regulations, we endeavor to retain as much of the text as necessary to allow for a procedural and substantive understanding of the materials, while focusing on the issues of marijuana law.

We have edited the legal materials in this casebook for relevance and readability. We indicate major omissions from the texts of these documents, including the judicial opinions, by asterisks (* * *) or brackets. Deletion of citations (including parenthetical explanation of cases), removal of section numbering and footnotes, reformatting of text and spacing, and other minor adjustments for the sake of readability, are not necessarily noted.

In this rapidly changing area of law, we emphasize recent materials, including newly published cases, significant FDA approval and DEA scheduling of cannabis extracts in September 2018, the marijuana ballot initiatives from the November 2018 elections, and the Hemp Farming Act, enacted in December 2018. Our notes bring marijuana law current through the end of 2018.

Finally, a note on terminology. The word "marijuana" is the term historically used in American law to refer to the cannabis plant and substances, constituents, and derivatives thereof. Hence it is the term we tend to use in the casebook. Federal law has historically spelled the term as "marihuana," and when so used in statutes and cases, we do not alter the spelling. When referring to scientific studies of the cannabis plant, as well as the international law of marijuana, we tend to use the term cannabis, as it is the botanical classification of the genus, and the legal term used most often in other nations.

SUMMARY OF CONTENTS

———

TABLE OF CONTENTS

TABLE OF CASES

The principal cases are in bold type.

_____

CASES AND MATERIALS ON
MARIJUANA LAW

CHAPTER 1

A Brief History of Marijuana Law in the United States

∎ ∎ ∎

The history of marijuana law in the United States is a fascinating one. Initially, it is closely intertwined with efforts to curb the use of dangerous drugs generally, which began in the late 19th century. Accordingly, when marijuana first made its appearance in the United States in the middle of the 19th century, it was an essentially unregulated substance, known primarily for its use in various patent medicines that were themselves unregulated. By the 1930s, however, marijuana had come to be regarded as a dangerous narcotic, and it was tightly controlled by both the states and the federal government. And in 1970, when Congress enacted the Controlled Substances Act, marijuana was included with those illegal drugs deemed most dangerous on Schedule I of the Act, which essentially precluded its use for any purpose, including medical. Since that time, the pendulum has swung back again, and it now appears that the country is moving more and more in the direction of full legalization, at least at the state level. This chapter gives an overview of how these movements transpired.

A. EARLY DRUG LAWS

Cultivation of the cannabis plant appears to have originated in central Asia several thousand years ago. It spread out from there into other parts of Asia, including the subcontinent of India, where marijuana and hashish have been used for many centuries for medicinal purposes. By the 10th century, cannabis was grown in many parts of the Islamic world as well. It is not clear when exactly hemp was first introduced to Europe, but we know it was widely cultivated there for its fiber during the Renaissance. It was then brought to the new world by early European colonists (probably first by the Spaniards), who used its fiber extensively for various purposes.

In America, cannabis was well-known from colonial times. For many years, hemp was legally grown as a cash crop; it was used for a variety of products, including rope, clothes, paint, paper, sails for boats, and birdseed. However, there is little or no evidence that cannabis was being grown during this time for its intoxicating effect.

By the middle of the 19th century, medical researchers in the United States and Europe began to study marijuana (the "drug" made from the flowers and leaves of the cannabis plant) for its therapeutic properties. And in 1870, marijuana was included in the United States Pharmacopeia, which is the country's official compendium of drug information (first published in 1820), establishing the accepted standards for medicines, drugs and related products. By that time, herbal marijuana was appearing frequently in patent medicines and other elixirs that were sold in drugstores to treat various medical conditions. It was then that the first laws regulating marijuana sales were passed.

These laws however, were less concerned with marijuana than with other drugs that had significant potential for harm, particularly opium and its derivatives, which were increasing in popularity in the late 19th century and proving to be quite destructive. For this reason, the history of marijuana regulation is best evaluated in the context of a more comprehensive societal crackdown on psychoactive substances generally— particularly the opiates and cocaine—including the movement to prohibit alcohol sales, which was beginning to gain ground in the late 19th century.

The first regulations affecting the sale of marijuana were state-enacted "poison laws" that imposed labeling and other requirements on patent medicines sold in pharmacies. At the urging of the American Medical Society, approximately two-thirds of the states enacted such laws in the period between 1870 and 1900. The concern motivating these laws was a lack of consumer awareness of the types of potentially harmful substances that were often contained in the patent medicines. These included a number of potentially harmful substances, such as strychnine, arsenic, and prussic acid, as well as psychoactive substances such as opiates, cocaine, marijuana, and alcohol. Patent medicines designed to help children sleep better, for example, might contain a significant amount of alcohol, or even an opiate, without indicating this on the package label. The state-enacted poison laws accordingly required labels listing each ingredient in the patent medicine, as well as visual warnings, such as a skull-and-cross-bones symbol or the word POISON prominently displayed upon the label, if the potion contained substances such as those listed above.

The federal government first became involved in regulating marijuana and other drugs when it followed the lead of the states and enacted the Pure Food and Drug Act in 1906. Similar to the state-enacted poison laws, the Pure Food and Drug Act prohibited misleading labeling, and it required the quantity of certain substances, including the opiates, cocaine, alcohol, and cannabis, to be identified on the label. The Act also established dose and purity standards for various drugs, based upon information in the United States Pharmacopeia.

While the state-enacted poison laws and the federal Pure Food and Drug Act were effective in helping to eliminate the veiled use of psychoactive drugs and other potentially harmful substances in patent medicines, they did not prevent public access to such substances. And by the last decade of the 19th century, state lawmakers were becoming increasingly concerned with the nonmedicinal, "recreational" use of these drugs. Much of this concern was focused on the smoking of opium, a practice that proliferated in the United States in the late 19th century. But much of it was also focused on the ready availability of narcotics such as cocaine and morphine, which were sold as medicines and generally obtainable without prescriptions. Legislators worried that the unrestricted access to such drugs would create a generation of addicts, and in fact it has been estimated that as much as 1% of the population in the United States was already addicted to morphine or opium by the turn of the 20th century. As a result, state legislatures began to modify their existing poison laws to prohibit the distribution of opiates and cocaine without a doctor's prescription. Accordingly, between 1890 and 1914, 29 states adopted statutes making it illegal to sell or distribute opiates without a prescription or other authorization, and most all states had similar restrictions on the distribution and sale of cocaine. The mere possession of these drugs, however, was still not a crime in most of these states.

At the federal level, Congress passed its first major anti-drug legislation, the Harrison Narcotics Tax Act of 1914. On its face, the Harrison Act was simply a taxing measure, requiring all persons who imported, produced or distributed opium, coca leaves, and their related derivatives to register with the federal government and pay a nominal occupational tax. But it also required them to file forms with the federal government describing all such transactions. Failure to do so was a criminal violation, subjecting the violator to fines, as well as up to five years imprisonment. The Act exempted patent medicines that contained very small amounts of opiates or cocaine. It also exempted physicians who prescribed these drugs, so long as they maintained adequate records of these prescriptions.

Although the Harrison Act did not directly apply to marijuana, its passage was significant with respect to marijuana regulation for two reasons. First, it served as the federal government's principal weapon against the non-medical use of opiates and cocaine prior to the passage of the Controlled Substances Act of 1970 (which remains the federal government's principal weapon against illegal drug use). Second, it established an important precedent for later federal regulation and control of illicit drugs. In fact, the constitutional authority upon which it relied, the Article I power of Congress to raise revenue through taxation, was later relied upon by Congress as the constitutional authority for the Marihuana Tax Act of 1937, which served as the federal government's principal weapon against marijuana distribution prior to Congress's enactment of the Controlled Substances Act.

In the following United States Supreme Court case, *United States v. Doremus*, 249 U.S. 86 (1919), the Court considered the constitutionality of the Harrison Act. The Court upheld the Act as a valid exercise of Congress' taxing authority. Four members of the Court, however, including the Chief Justice, dissented. In a terse summary opinion, they voted to strike down the Act as an unconstitutional attempt by Congress to exert a power not delegated to it by the United States Constitution: i.e., the reserved police power of the states.

United States v. Doremus

United States Supreme Court
249 U.S. 86 (1919)

Day, J.

Doremus was indicted for violating section 2 of the so-called Harrison Narcotic Drug Act. Act Dec. 17, 1914, c. 1, 38 Stat. 785 (6 U. S. Comp. Stat. 1916, § 6287g). Upon demurrer to the indictment the District Court held the section unconstitutional for the reason that it was not a revenue measure, and was an invasion of the police power reserved to the state. 246 Fed. 958. The case is here under the Criminal Appeals Act March 2, 1907, c. 2564, 34 Stat. 1246 (Comp. St. § 1704).

There are ten counts in the indictment. The first two were treated by the court below as sufficient to raise the constitutional question decided. The first count in substance charges that: Doremus, a physician, duly registered, and who had paid the tax required by the first section of the act, did unlawfully, fraudulently, and knowingly sell and give away and distribute to one Ameris a certain quantity of heroin, to wit, five hundred one-sixth grain tablets of heroin, a derivative of opium, the sale not being in pursuance of a written order on a form issued on the blank furnished for that purpose by the Commissioner of Internal Revenue.

The second count charges in substance that: Doremus did unlawfully and knowingly sell, dispense and distribute to one Ameris five hundred one-sixth grain tablets of heroin not in the course of the regular professional practice of Doremus and not for the treatment of any disease from which Ameris was suffering, but as was well known by Doremus, Ameris was addicted to the use of the drug as a habit, being a person popularly known as a 'dope fiend,' and that Doremus did sell, dispense, and distribute the drug, heroin, to Ameris for the purpose of gratifying his appetite for the drug as an habitual user thereof.

Section 1 of the act (section 6287g) requires persons who produce, import, manufacture, compound, deal in, dispense, sell, distribute, or give away opium or cocoa leaves or any compound, manufacture, salt, derivative or preparation thereof, to register with the collector of internal revenue of the district his name or style, place of business, and place or places where such business is to be carried on. At the time of such registry every person who produces, imports, manufactures, compounds, deals in, dispenses, sells, distributes, or gives away any of the said drugs is required to pay to the collector a special tax of $1 per annum. It is made unlawful for any person required to register under the terms of the act to produce, import, manufacture, compound, deal in, dispense, sell, distribute, or give away any of the said drugs without having registered and paid the special tax provided in the act.

Section 2 (section 6287h) provides in part:

'It shall be unlawful for any person to sell, barter, exchange, or give away any of the aforesaid drugs except in pursuance of a written order of the person to whom such article is sold, bartered, exchanged, or given, on a form to be issued in blank for that purpose by the Commissioner of Internal Revenue. Every person who shall accept any such order, and in pursuance thereof shall sell, barter, exchange, or give away any of the aforesaid drugs, shall preserve such order for a period of two years in such a way as to be readily accessible to inspection by any officer, agent, or employee of the Treasury Department duly authorized for that purpose, and the state, territorial, district, municipal, and insular officials named in section five of this act. Every person who shall give an order as herein provided to any other person for any of the aforesaid drugs shall, at or before the time of giving such order, make or cause to be made a duplicate thereof on a form to be issued in blank for that purpose by the Commissioner of Internal Revenue, and in case of the acceptance of such order, shall preserve such duplicate for a period of two years in such a way as to be readily accessible to inspection by the officers, agents, employees, and officials hereinbefore mentioned. Nothing contained in this section shall apply—

'(a) To the dispensing or distribution of any of the aforesaid drugs to a patient by a physician, dentist, or veterinary surgeon regularly registered under this act in the course of his professional practice only: Provided, that such physician, dentist, or veterinary surgeon shall keep a record of all such drugs dispensed or distributed, showing the amount dispensed or distributed, the date and the name and address of the patient to whom such drugs are dispensed or distributed, except such as may be dispensed or distributed to a patient upon whom such physician, dentist or veterinary surgeon shall personally attend; and such record shall be kept for a period of two years from the date of dispensing or distributing such drugs, subject to inspection, as provided in this act.

'(b) To the sale, dispensing, or distribution of any of the aforesaid drugs by a dealer to a consumer under and in pursuance of a written prescription issued by a physician, dentist, or veterinary surgeon registered under this act: Provided, however, that such prescription shall be dated as of the day on which signed and shall be signed by the physician, dentist, or veterinary surgeon who shall have issued the same: And provided further, that such dealer shall preserve such prescription for a period of two years from the day on which such prescription is filled in such a way as to be readily accessible to inspection by the officers, agents, employees, and officials hereinbefore mentioned.'

It is made unlawful for any person to obtain the drugs by means of the order forms for any purpose other than the use, sale or distribution thereof by him in the conduct of a lawful business in said drugs, or the legitimate practice of his profession.

It is apparent that the section makes sales of these drugs unlawful except to persons who have the order forms issued by the Commissioner of Internal Revenue, and the order is required to be preserved for two years in such way as to be readily accessible to official inspection. But it is not to apply (a) to physicians, etc., dispensing and distributing the drug to patients in the course of professional practice, the physician to keep a record thereof, except in the case of personal attendance upon a patient; and (b) to the sale, dispensing, or distributing of the drugs by a dealer upon a prescription issued by a physician, etc., registered under the act. Other exceptions follow which are unnecessary to the consideration of this case.

Section 9 (section 62870) inflicts a fine or imprisonment, or both, for violation of the act. This statute purports to be passed under the authority of the Constitution, article 1, § 8, which gives the Congress power 'To lay and collect taxes, duties, imposts, and excises to pay the debts and provide for the common defence and general welfare of the United States; but all duties, imposts, and excises shall be uniform throughout the United States.'

The only limitation upon the power of Congress to levy excise taxes of the character now under consideration is geographical uniformity throughout the United States. This court has often declared it cannot add others. Subject to such limitation Congress may select the subjects of taxation, and may exercise the power conferred at its discretion. Of course Congress may not in the exercise of federal power exert authority wholly reserved to the states. Many decisions of this court have so declared. And from an early day the court has held that the fact that other motives may impel the exercise of federal taxing power does not authorize the courts to inquire into that subject. If the legislation enacted has some reasonable relation to the exercise of the taxing authority conferred by the Constitution, it cannot be invalidated because of the supposed motives which induced it.

Nor is it sufficient to invalidate the taxing authority given to the Congress by the Constitution that the same business may be regulated by the police power of the state. The act may not be declared unconstitutional because its effect may be to accomplish another purpose as well as the raising of revenue. If the legislation is within the taxing authority of

Congress, that is sufficient to sustain it. The legislation under consideration was before us in a case concerning section 8 of the act, and in the course of the decision we said:

'It may be assumed that the statute has a moral end as well as revenue in view, but we are of opinion that the District Court, in treating those ends as to be reached only through a revenue measure and within the limits of a revenue measure, was right.

Considering the full power of Congress over excise taxation the decisive question here is: Have the provisions in question any relation to the raising of revenue? That Congress might levy an excise tax upon such dealers, and others who are named in section 1 of the act, cannot be successfully disputed. The provisions of section 2, to which we have referred, aim to confine sales to registered dealers and to those dispensing the drugs as physicians, and to those who come to dealers with legitimate prescriptions of physicians. Congress, with full power over the subject, short of arbitrary and unreasonable action which is not to be assumed, inserted these provisions in an act specifically providing for the raising of revenue. Considered of themselves, we think they tend to keep the traffic aboveboard and subject to inspection by those authorized to collect the revenue. They tend to diminish the opportunity of unauthorized persons to obtain the drugs and sell them clandestinely without paying the tax imposed by the federal law. This case well illustrates the possibility which may have induced Congress to insert the provisions limiting sales to registered dealers and requiring patients to obtain these drugs as a medicine from physicians or upon regular prescriptions. Ameris, being as the indictment charges, an addict may not have used this great number of doses for himself. He might sell some to others without paying the tax, at least Congress may have deemed it wise to prevent such possible dealings because of their effect upon the collection of the revenue.

We cannot agree with the contention that the provisions of section 2, controlling the disposition of these drugs in the ways described, can have nothing to do with facilitating the collection of the revenue, as we should be obliged to do if we were to declare this act beyond the power of Congress acting under its constitutional authority to impose excise taxes. It follows that the judgment of the District Court must be reversed.

Reversed.

The CHIEF JUSTICE dissents because he is of opinion that the court below correctly held the act of Congress, in so far as it embraced the matters complained of, to be beyond the constitutional power of Congress to enact because to such extent the statute was a mere attempt by Congress to exert a power not delegated, that is, the reserved police power of the states.

MR. JUSTICE MCKENNA, and MR. JUSTICE VAN DEVANTER and MR. JUSTICE MCREYNOLDS concur in this dissent.

NOTES AND QUESTIONS

1. **The federal government's constitutional authority to regulate drugs.** The apparent reason for Congress's reliance on its taxing authority as the constitutional basis for the Harrison Act was a widely shared view at the time that the federal government did not otherwise have the constitutional authority to regulate medical and pharmaceutical practices within the various states. *See Linder v. United States*, 268 U.S. 5, 18 (1925) ("Obviously, direct control of medical practice in the states is beyond the power of the federal government."). Congress would later rely on the *commerce clause* as its constitutional authority for enacting the Controlled Substances Act of 1970. But in 1914, the Supreme Court had not yet given the commerce clause the expansive reading it was to receive later in the century, so Congress chose to rely instead upon its uncontroverted authority to raise revenue through taxation. What do you think led Congress and the Supreme Court to change their understanding of the federal government's constitutional authority to enact anti-drug legislation during this period of time between 1914 and 1970? Was this change justified?

2. **Congress's taxing power.** Can you think of an important recent case in the area of health care law in which the Supreme Court upheld a federal statute's constitutionality based on Congress' taxing authority (or at least the deciding vote relied on this rationale), even though on its face the statute did not appear to be a tax provision?

3. **The Harrison Act as a criminal statute prohibiting illegal drugs.** The Harrison Act was clever in that it not only imposed a minor tax and administrative burden on would-be dealers in narcotics who wished to avoid violating the Act, thereby creating disincentives to deal in such drugs; it also created a kind of "catch-22" for illicit dealers of these drugs. Specifically, Section 5 of the Act provided that the federal government must make available to state law enforcement officials upon their request copies of the forms that registered distributors had filed with the I.R.S. By 1914, most of the states had prohibited the non-medical distribution of opiates, and nearly all the states had prohibited the non-medical distribution of cocaine, so illicit distributors of these drugs faced a serious dilemma. If they complied with federal law, registering, filing the proper forms, and paying the associated tax, they essentially admitted in writing to the commission of felonies under state law. On the other hand, if they failed to comply with the registration requirements of the Harrison Act, they faced under the Act itself penalties that included imprisonment for up to five years. Thus, the Harrison Act had the effect of criminalizing the non-medical sale and possession of narcotics, even if, on its face, it was merely a taxing provision.

B. THE CRIMINALIZATION OF MARIJUANA

Following enactment of the Harrison Narcotics Tax Act in 1914, the state legislatures began to ramp up their criminalization efforts with respect to drugs such as opiates and cocaine. Prior to this time, only a handful of states had made simple possession of these drugs illegal, concentrating instead on illegal sales and distribution. By 1931, however, 35 states had criminalized the mere possession of opiates, and 36 had criminalized the mere possession of cocaine. In addition, penalties for the sale and distribution of non-prescription opiates and cocaine were significantly increased.

It was also during this time that a majority of the states enacted laws prohibiting the non-medical use of marijuana. By 1929, 24 states had prohibited the non-medical use of marijuana, requiring a prescription for its use, and by 1933, another 9 states had followed suit. The impetus for outlawing the non-medical use of marijuana during this time was a wide-spread public perception that marijuana use was behind significant increases in crime and other social problems. While cannabis had been grown in the United States for centuries, the practice of smoking marijuana here appears to be much more recent, having apparently been introduced by immigrants and workers from Mexico in the western United States. Proponents of criminalization argued that marijuana was highly addictive, and that its regular use could lead to madness. As a result, many states legislatures enacted prohibitions on its use.

In 1930, Congress created the Federal Bureau of Narcotics under the auspices of the Treasury Department in order to consolidate enforcement of federal drug laws. It appointed Harry J. Anslinger as its first Commissioner, having previously served in the Treasury Department's Bureau of Prohibition. Anslinger is an important figure in the history of drug regulation in the United States. A strident anti-drug crusader, he served as Commissioner of the Bureau for 32 years, spanning five different administrations. In that role, he was instrumental in helping to formulate the first federal statute that directly regulated marijuana use: the Marihuana Tax Act of 1937. His first main agenda as Commissioner of the Bureau, however, was to push for the adoption of the Uniform Narcotic Drug Act, which was drafted by a commission appointed by Congress. The Uniform Narcotic Drug Act was a model statute designed to bring uniformity to state narcotic laws, and to encourage greater enforcement of such laws at the state level. The Commission approved the Act in 1932. And by 1937, after fairly intensive lobbying on the part of the Bureau, 37 states had enacted their own versions of it.

Commissioner Anslinger had initially pushed for the inclusion of marijuana within the coverage of the Uniform Narcotic Drug Act, describing the drug as a "national menace." And the issue was hotly debated through the five drafts of the Act. Ultimately, however, the

Commission decided to include a marijuana prohibition as a separate, optional provision. Thus, those states adopting versions of the Act could choose whether to include marijuana within the Act's prohibition on non-medical use of narcotics, along with the opiates and cocaine. Approximately two-thirds of the states that adopted the Act ultimately opted to include a marijuana prohibition. In addition, several other states that had not previously prohibited marijuana use enacted separate provisions criminalizing non-medical marijuana use. Therefore, by 1937, almost all the states had criminalized the non-medical use of marijuana in some manner. Furthermore, since medical use had declined significantly by this time, the effect was to eliminate almost all legal use of marijuana.

In 1937, the federal government weighed in again, when Congress enacted the Marihuana Tax Act. It did so notwithstanding the advice of Dr. Woodward, the spokesman for the American Medical Association, who testified that the purported dangers of marijuana were exaggerated.

Modeled after the Harrison Narcotics Tax Act, the Marihuana Tax Act of 1937 was ostensibly a revenue-generating statute, passed under Congress's constitutional taxing authority. Like the Harrison Act, it imposed a registration requirement on non-exempt producers and distributors of marijuana, the main exemptions being for physicians and pharmacists. And like the Harrison Act, it required these non-exempt producers and distributors to file forms and pay a tax ($1 per ounce) for each transaction they engaged in with registered persons. However, unlike the Harrison Act, it also imposed a hefty (in those days) $100 per ounce tax on sales to non-registered persons. And violators of these provisions faced fines of up to $2000 and imprisonment for up to five years.

The Marihuana Tax Act also contained a catch-22 provision, similar to the one in the Harrison Act, which provided that the federal government must make available to state law enforcement officials for a nominal fee copies of the forms that the registered distributors had filed with the federal government. Thus, the Act created a dilemma for nonexempt distributors. If they complied with the Act, registering, filing the proper forms, and paying the associated tax, but they were not authorized distributors under state law (e.g., they were street dealers), then they essentially admitted in writing to the commission of felonies under state law. On the other hand, if they failed to comply with the requirements of the Act in order to avoid such admissions, then they faced under the Act itself penalties that included imprisonment for up to five years. Thus, the Marihuana Tax Act had the effect of criminalizing the non-medical distribution of marijuana, even if, on its face, it was merely a taxing provision. Furthermore, under § 8 of the Act, a person's mere possession of marijuana without being able to produce the appropriate paperwork was presumptive evidence of guilt.

Congress passed the Marihuana Tax Act of 1937 with very little opposition. Some commentators attribute this to the Bureau of Narcotics' intense lobbying efforts to convince Congress that marijuana was a very dangerous substance, notwithstanding a lack of evidence to support that position:

> [T]he Act passed the Congress with little debate and even less public attention. Provoked almost entirely by the Federal Bureau of Narcotics and by a few hysterical state law enforcement agents hoping to get federal support for their activities, the law was tied neither to scientific study nor to enforcement need. The Marihuana Tax Act was hastily drawn, heard, debated and passed; it was the paradigm of the uncontroversial law.

Richard J. Bonnie & Charles H. Whitebread, II, *The Forbidden Fruit and the Tree of Knowledge: an Inquiry Into the Legal History of American Marijuana Prohibition*, 56 Va. L. Rev. 971, 1062 (1970). Nevertheless, the Marihuana Tax Act remained the federal government's principal tool for combating marijuana trafficking for decades, becoming obsolete only when the United States Supreme Court struck the statute down as unconstitutional in 1969.

The decade of the 1940's brought no major changes to marijuana law, except that, somewhat ironically, the federal government during the World War II years, actually encouraged the restricted cultivation of (hemp) cannabis in order to make up for a military shortage of rope. In the 1950's, however, societal fears of marijuana menace once again fueled federal legislation. Congress enacted the Boggs Act in 1951, in response to a widespread perception that narcotic drug use was spreading in society, particularly among America's youth. Predictably, the response of Congress to this perceived problem was to further ramp up penalties for possession and use of these drugs. Whereas the Marihuana Tax Act had provided for imprisonment "not more than five years," the Boggs Act imposed mandatory minimum sentences of two years for a first offense of simple possession, five years for second offense, and ten years for subsequent offenses. Five years later, Congress ramped up penalties for certain possession offense even higher when it enacted the Narcotics Control Act of 1956. Under this act, the mandatory minimum prison sentence for possession of marijuana known to have been brought into the United States illegally was set at 5 years. In addition, the Act eliminated the possibility of probation, suspension, and parole for most importation-related offenses.

Similar legislative changes took place at the state level. By 1956, the majority of the states had increased criminal penalties for the purchase and sale of marijuana. And by 1961, a majority had also imposed mandatory minimum sentences for these crimes. Accordingly, in some states, illegally selling marijuana could result in a decades-long prison sentence.

As the 1960s progressed, however, societal attitudes toward marijuana started changing rapidly. The practice of smoking marijuana became increasingly popular with America's youth, particularly on college campuses. By the late 1960s approximately half of the nation's college students had at least tried marijuana. And many were regular users. In addition, various scientific and medical groups began to cast serious doubt on the long-accepted narrative that marijuana was a highly addictive drug that led its victims to insanity and lives of crime.

As a result of this shift in societal attitudes, various states began to consider decreasing their penalties for marijuana possession. In the spring of 1969, Congress began extensive hearings on the issue of drug control. One of the main objectives of the hearings was to revisit the rationale for the harsh minimum sentence for marijuana possession imposed by the Boggs Act and the Narcotics Control Act in the 1950's. But Congress also wanted to streamline the patchwork system of statutes that governed the federal government's regulation of narcotics.

The tipping point for legal reform came in 1969 with the United States Supreme Court's decision in *Leary v. United States*, 395 U.S. 6 (1969). There the Court considered a challenge to the constitutionality of the Marihuana Tax Act of 1937 under the Fifth Amendment's right against self-incrimination. The *Leary* case involved Timothy Leary, a former Harvard psychology instructor who in the early 1960's experimented with using hallucinogenic drugs to treat certain mental illnesses. Leary later became a leading figure in the counterculture movement of the late 1960s, best known for advocating the use of LSD and other psychedelic drugs to expand consciousness.

In the case before the Supreme Court, Leary was arrested at the Mexican border in 1965 for possession of marijuana. He was convicted of transporting and concealing marijuana without paying the appropriate transfer tax imposed by the Marihuana Tax Act, and of knowingly transporting and concealing marijuana that had been illegally brought into the United States in violation of the Narcotic Drugs Import and Export Act. The Supreme Court reversed his conviction, holding with respect to the Marihuana Tax Act that the registration and tax requirements of the Act violated his Fifth Amendment right against self-incrimination.

LEARY V. UNITED STATES
United States Supreme Court
395 U.S. 6 (1969)

HARLAN, J.

This case presents constitutional questions arising out of the conviction of the petitioner, Dr. Timothy Leary, for violation of two federal statutes governing traffic in marihuana.

The circumstances surrounding petitioner's conviction were as follows. On December 20, 1965, petitioner left New York by automobile, intending a vacation trip to Yucatan, Mexico. He was accompanied by his daughter and son, both teenagers, and two other persons. On December 22, 1965, the party drove across the International Bridge between the United States and Mexico at Laredo, Texas. They stopped at the Mexican customs station and, after apparently being denied entry, drove back across the bridge. They halted at the American secondary inspection area, explained the situation to a customs inspector, and stated that they had nothing from Mexico to declare. The inspector asked them to alight, examined the interior of the car, and saw what appeared to be marihuana seeds on the floor. The inspector then received permission to search the car and passengers. Small amounts of marihuana were found on the car floor and in the glove compartment. A personal search of petitioner's daughter revealed a silver snuff box containing semi-refined marihuana and three partially smoked marihuana cigarettes.

Petitioner was indicted and tried before a jury in the Federal District for the Southern District of Texas, on three counts. First, it was alleged that he had knowingly smuggled marihuana into the United States, in violation of 21 U.S.C. § 176a. Second, it was charged that he had knowingly transported and facilitated the transportation and concealment of marihuana which had been illegally imported or brought into the United States, with knowledge that it had been illegally imported or brought in, all again in violation of § 176a. Third, it was alleged that petitioner was a transferee of marihuana and had knowingly transported, concealed, and facilitated the transportation and concealment of marihuana without having paid the transfer tax imposed by the Marihuana Tax Act, 26 U.S.C. § 4741 et seq., thereby violating 26 U.S.C. § 4744(a)(2).

After both sides had presented their evidence and the defense had moved for a judgment of acquittal, the District Court dismissed the first or smuggling count. The jury found petitioner guilty on the other two counts. He was tentatively sentenced to the maximum punishment, pending completion of a study and recommendations to be used by the District Court in fixing his final sentence. On appeal, the Court of Appeals for the Fifth Circuit affirmed. That court subsequently denied a petition for rehearing and rehearing en banc.

We granted certiorari to consider two questions: (1) whether petitioner's conviction for failing to comply with the transfer tax provisions of the Marihuana Tax Act violated his Fifth Amendment privilege against self-incrimination; (2) whether petitioner was denied due process by the application of the part of 21 U.S.C. § 176a which provides that a defendant's possession of marihuana shall be deemed sufficient evidence that the marihuana was illegally imported or brought into the United States, and that the defendant knew of the illegal importation or bringing in, unless the defendant explains his possession to the satisfaction of the jury. For reasons which follow, we hold in favor of the petitioner on both issues and reverse the judgment of the Court of Appeals.

I.

We consider first petitioner's claim that his conviction under the Marihuana Tax Act violated his privilege against self-incrimination.

A.

Petitioner argues that reversal of his Marihuana Tax Act conviction is required by our decisions of last Term in *Marchetti v. United States,* 390 U.S. 39 (1969); *Grosso v. United States*, 390 U.S. 62 (1968), and *Haynes v. United States*, 390 U.S. 85, 88 (1968). In *Marchetti*, we held that a plea of the Fifth Amendment privilege provided a complete defense to a prosecution for failure to register and pay the occupational tax on wagers, as required by 26 U.S.C. §§ 4411–4412. We noted that wagering was a crime in almost every State, and that 26 U.S.C. § 6107 required that lists of wagering taxpayers be furnished to state and local prosecutors on demand. We concluded that compliance with the statute would have subjected petitioner to a "real and appreciable" risk of self-incrimination. We further recognized that the occupational tax was not imposed in "an essentially non-criminal and regulatory area * * *," 390 U.S. at 57, but was 'directed to a 'selective group inherently suspect of criminal activities." We found that it would be inappropriate to impose restrictions on use of the information collected under the statute—a course urged by the Government as a means of removing the impact of the statute upon the privilege against self-incrimination—because of the evident congressional purpose to provide aid to prosecutors. We noted that, unlike the petitioner in *Shapiro v. United States*, 335 U.S. 1 (1948), Marchetti was not required to supply information which had a 'public aspect' or was contained in records of the kind he customarily kept.

In Grosso, we held that the same considerations required that a claim of the privilege be a defense to prosecution under 26 U.S.C. § 4401, which imposes an excise tax on proceeds from wagering. And in Haynes we held for the same reasons that assertion of the Fifth Amendment privilege provided a defense to prosecution for possession of an unregistered weapon under the National Firearms Act, 26 U.S.C. § 5851, despite the fact that in 'uncommon' instances registration under the statute would not be incriminating.

B.

In order to understand petitioner's contention that compliance with the Marihuana Tax Act would have obliged him to incriminate himself within the meaning of the foregoing decisions, it is necessary to be familiar with the statutory scheme. The Marihuana Tax Act has two main subparts. The first imposes a tax on transfers of marihuana, the second an occupational tax upon those who deal in the drug. It is convenient to begin with the occupational tax provisions, 26 U.S.C. §§ 4751–4753.

Section 4751 provides that all persons who 'deal in' marihuana shall be subject to an annual occupational tax. Subsections require that specified categories of persons, such as importers, producers, physicians, researchers, and millers pay varying rates of tax per year. See §§ 4751(1)–(4), (6). Persons who 'deal in' marihuana but do not fall into any of the specified categories are required to pay $3 per year. See § 4751(5). Section 4753 provides that at the time of paying the tax the taxpayer must 'register his name or style and his place or places of business' at the nearest district office of the Internal Revenue Service.

The first of the transfer tax provisions, 26 U.S.C. § 4741, imposes a tax 'upon all transfers of marihuana which are required by section 4742 to be carried out in pursuance of written order forms.' Section 4741 further provides that on transfers to persons registered under § 4753 the tax is $1 per ounce, while on transfers to persons not so registered the tax is $100 per ounce. The tax is required to be paid by the transferee 'at the time of securing each order form.' With certain exceptions not here relevant, § 4742 makes it unlawful for any person, 'whether or not required to pay a special tax and register under sections 4751 to 4753,' to transfer marihuana except pursuant to a written order form to be obtained by the transferee. A regulation, 26 CFR § 152.69, provides that the order form must show the name and address of the transferor and transferee; their § 4753 registration numbers, if they are registered; and the quantity of marihuana transferred. Another regulation, 26 CFR § 152.66, requires the transferee to submit an application containing these data in order to obtain the form. Section 4742(d) of the Act requires the Internal Revenue Service to 'preserve' in its records a duplicate copy of each order form which it issues.

Another statutory provision, 26 U.S.C. § 4773, assures that the information contained in the order form will be available to law enforcement officials. That section provides that the duplicate order forms required to be kept by the Internal Revenue Service shall be open to inspection by Treasury personnel and state and local officials charged with enforcement of marihuana laws, and that upon payment of a fee such officials shall be furnished copies of the forms.

Finally, 26 U.S.C. § 4744(a) makes it unlawful for a transferee required to pay the § 4741(a) transfer tax either to acquire marihuana without having paid the tax or to transport, conceal, or facilitate the transportation or concealment of, any marihuana so acquired. Petitioner was convicted under § 4744(a). He conceded at trial that he had not obtained an order form or paid the transfer tax.

C.

If read according to its terms, the Marihuana Tax Act compelled petitioner to expose himself to a 'real and appreciable' risk of self-incrimination, within the meaning of our decisions in *Marchetti, Grosso,* and *Haynes*. Sections 4741–4742 required him, in the course of obtaining an order form, to identify himself not only as a transferee of marihuana but as a transferee who had not registered and paid the occupational tax under ss 4751–4753. Section 4773 directed that this information be conveyed by the Internal Revenue Service to state and local law enforcement officials on request.

Petitioner had ample reason to fear that transmittal to such officials of the fact that he was a recent, unregistered transferee of marihuana 'would surely prove a significant 'link in a chain' of evidence tending to establish his guilt' under the state marihuana laws then in effect. When petitioner failed to comply with the Act, in late 1965, possession of any quantity of marihuana was apparently a crime in every one of the 50 States, including New York, where petitioner claimed the transfer occurred, and Texas, where he was arrested and convicted. It is true that almost all States, including New York and Texas, had exceptions making lawful, under specified conditions, possession of marihuana by: (1) state-licensed manufacturers and wholesalers; (2) apothecaries; (3) researchers; (4) physicians, dentists, veterinarians, and certain other medical personnel; (5) agents or employees of the foregoing persons or common carriers; (6) persons for whom the drug had been prescribed or to whom it had been given by an authorized medical person; and (7) certain public officials. However, individuals in the first four of these classes are among those compelled to register and pay the occupational tax under §§ 4751–4753; in consequence of having registered, they are required to pay only a $1 per ounce transfer tax under § 4741(a)(1). It is extremely unlikely that such persons will remain unregistered, for failure to register renders them liable not only to an additional $99 per ounce transfer tax but also to severe criminal penalties. Persons in the last three classes mentioned above appear to be wholly exempt from the order form and transfer tax requirements.

Thus, at the time petitioner failed to comply with the Act those persons who might legally possess marihuana under state law were virtually certain either to be registered under § 4753 or to be exempt from the order form requirement. It follows that the class of possessors who were both unregistered and obliged to obtain an order form constituted a 'selective group inherently suspect of criminal activities.' Since compliance with the transfer tax provisions would have required petitioner unmistakably to identify himself as a member of this 'selective' and 'suspect' group, we can only decide that when read according to their terms these provisions created a 'real and appreciable' hazard of incrimination.

* * *

D.

We cannot accept the Government's argument, for we find that Congress did intend that a non-registrant should be able to obtain an order form and prepay the transfer tax. This congressional intent appears both from the language of the Act and from its legislative history.

We begin with the words of the statute. Section 4741(a), when read in conjunction with § 4742, imposes a tax upon every transfer of marihuana, with a few exceptions not here relevant. Section 4741(a)(1) states that the tax on registrants shall be $1 per ounce and § 4741(a)(2) that the tax on transfers to nonregistrants shall be $100 per ounce. Section 4741(b) states that (s)uch tax shall be paid by the transferee at the time of securing each order form and shall be in addition to the price of such form.' (Emphasis added.) Since § 4741(b) makes no distinction between the s 4741(a)(1) tax on transfers to registrants and the § 4741(a)(2) tax on transfers to nonregistrants, it seems clear that Congress contemplated that nonregistrant as well as registrant transferees should be able to obtain order forms and prepay the tax.

The legislative history also strongly indicates that the Act was intended merely to impose a very high tax on transfers to nonregistrants and not to prohibit such transfers entirely. As a taxing measure, the bill of course originated in the House of Representatives. At the start of the first hearing on the bill, before the House Ways and Means Committee, the committee chairman announced that he had introduced the bill at the request of the Secretary of the Treasury. The transfer provisions of the bill then read essentially as they do now. The first witness to appear before the Committee was the Treasury Department's Assistant General Counsel, Clinton M. Hester. He began by stating that the bill's purpose was 'not only to raise revenue from the marihuana traffic, but also to discourage the current and widespread undesirable use of marihuana by smokers and drug addicts * * *.' He stated that in form the bill was a 'synthesis' of the Harrison Narcotics Act, now 26 U.S.C. § 4701 et seq., and the National Firearms Act, now 26 U.S.C. § 5801 et seq. Both of these statutes compelled dealers in the respective goods to register and pay a special tax. Both prohibited transfer except in pursuance of a written form and imposed a transfer tax. However, the transfer provisions differed in that the Narcotics Act provided that no one except a registrant could legally obtain an order form, see 26 U.S.C. § 4705(g), while the Firearms Act merely imposed a $200 tax upon each transfer of a firearm covered by the Act.

* * *

The foregoing shows that at the time petitioner acquired marihuana he was confronted with a statute which on its face permitted him to acquire the drug legally, provided he paid the $100 per ounce transfer tax and gave incriminating information, and simultaneously with a system of regulations which, according to the Government, prohibited him from acquiring marihuana under any conditions. We have found those regulations so out of keeping with the statute as to be ultra vires. Faced with these conflicting commands, we think petitioner would have been justified in giving precedence to the higher authority: the statute. "(L)iteral and full compliance' with all the statutory requirements' would have entailed a very substantial risk of self-incrimination. See supra, at 1537–1539.

The United States has not urged us, as it did in *Marchetti*, *Grosso*, and *Haynes*, to avoid this constitutional difficulty by placing restrictions upon the use of information gained under the transfer provisions. We declined to impose use restrictions in those cases because we found that the furnishing of information to interested prosecutors was a 'significant element of Congress' purposes in adopting' the statute there involved. The text and legislative history of the Marihuana Tax Act plainly disclose a similar congressional purpose. As has been noted, 26 U.S.C. § 773 requires that copies of order forms be kept available for inspection by state and local officials, and that copies be furnished to such officials on request. The House and Senate reports both state that one objective of the Act was 'the development of an adequate means of publicizing dealings in marihuana in order to tax and control the traffic effectively.' In short, we think the conclusion inescapable that the statute was aimed at bringing to light transgressions of the marihuana laws. Hence, as in last Term's cases, we decline to impose use restrictions and are obliged to conclude that a timely and proper assertion of the privilege should have provided a complete defense to prosecution under § 4744(a)(2).

          * * *

For the reasons stated in Part I of this opinion we reverse outright the judgment of conviction on Count 3 of the indictment. For the reasons stated in Part II, we reverse the judgment of conviction on Count 2 and remand the case to the Court of Appeals for further proceedings consistent with this opinion. We are constrained to add that nothing in what we hold today implies any constitutional disability in Congress to deal with the marihuana traffic by other means.

Reversed and remanded.

NOTES AND QUESTIONS

1.   **Self-incrimination under the Marihuana Tax Act.** In *Leary*, the Court essentially held that the "clever" catch-22 the Act created for illicit users through its mandatory registration and tax-form requirements also rendered it unconstitutional. This is because the Marihuana Tax Act essentially required illicit dealers to identify themselves as such when they filled out the required forms under the Act—forms that were expressly made available to

state law enforcement officials for inspection. Thus, in order to comply with the Act, non-exempt users were effectively required to admit to violations of state criminal laws, since marijuana was illegal in every state by 1965. Accordingly, the Supreme Court held, "we think the conclusion inescapable that the statute was aimed at bringing to light transgressions of the [state] marihuana laws," and therefore it violated the defendant's Fifth-Amendment right against self-incrimination. 395 U.S. at 27. Why do you think Congress set up the statute the way it did? What would have been the result if instead Congress had left out the provision requiring that access to the forms be made available to state law-enforcement officials?

2. Early marijuana statutes. It appears that the early impetus for criminalization of marijuana was due in large part to a racist narrative. Newspaper accounts of the time, particularly in the western states, provide accounts of crazed Mexican men, under the influence of this new drug, committing all sorts of violent acts. As Professors Bonnie and Whitebread describe it:

> Geometric increases in Mexican immigration after the turn of the century naturally resulted in the formation of sizeable Mexican-American minorities in each western state. It was thought then and is generally assumed now that use of marijuana west of the Mississippi was limited primarily to the Mexican segment of the population. We do not find it surprising, therefore, that sixteen of these states prohibited sale or possession of marijuana before 1930. Whether motivated by outright prejudice or simple discriminatory disinterest, the result was the same in each legislature—little if any public attention, no debate, pointed references to the drug's Mexican origins, and sometimes vociferous allusion to the criminal conduct inevitably generated when Mexicans ate "the killer weed."

Richard J. Bonnie & Charles H. Whitebread, II, *The Forbidden Fruit and the Tree of Knowledge: an Inquiry Into the Legal History of American Marijuana Prohibition*, 56 Va L. Rev. 971, 1012 (1970).

3. Public sentiment and the law. A striking example of a controversial case contributing to changing public sentiment and a partial relaxation of marijuana laws in the late 1960s and early 1970s is that of *People v. Sinclair* (1972). John Sinclair was politically active in Ann Arbor and Detroit, Michigan in the late 1960s. He was a co-founder of the "White Panthers" (later renamed Rainbow People's Party), which was established to support the Black Panther party, and he promoted various other radical objectives. His political activities and involvement in the countercultural movement brought him to the attention of law enforcement officials, both federal and local. In 1967, the Detroit Police Department arranged a sting operation at a Detroit commune, the Artists' Workshop, which Sinclair ran, and where he was residing at the time. After several weeks of infiltration, two undercover police officers persuaded Sinclair to give them two marijuana joints. Sinclair was subsequently arrested and charged with the sale and possession of marijuana in violation of Michigan law. He remained on bail for two years until his trial, at which he was convicted, and sentenced by the trial judge to 9 ½ to 10 years in prison.

This harsh sentence brought national attention to Sinclair's plight, especially within the student community and the countercultural movement. Sinclair helped manage the campaign from prison. Among other protests, a highly publicized "John Sinclair Freedom Rally" concert was held in Ann Arbor. (The counterculture movement, marijuana, and protest music were closely linked at that time; in fact, Sinclair himself managed the proto-punk-rock Detroit band, the MC5, before his imprisonment.) The concert was headlined by John Lennon and his wife, Yoko Ono, as well as a number of other well-known musicians (including Stevie Wonder, Commander Cody, and Bob Seger), poet Allen Ginsberg, and political activists such as Jerry Rubin and Bobby Seale. At the climax of the concert, Lennon sang a song he wrote for the event, called "John Sinclair." The concert attracted national attention, and within a few days, the Michigan Supreme Court issued an order freeing Sinclair from prison. Three months later, in March 1972, the court issued its per curiam opinion on the matter, striking down the Michigan statute under which Sinclair had been convicted as violative of the United States and the Michigan constitutions. *See People v. Sinclair*, 194 N.W.2d 878 (1972) [set out and discussed further in Chapter 21]. The Michigan Supreme Court's decision illustrated the shift in many states toward more lenient policies as to marijuana use in the early 1970s.

C. THE ENACTMENT OF THE CONTROLLED SUBSTANCES ACT AND ITS AFTERMATH

Several months after the Court in *Leary* rendered its decision, Congress enacted the Controlled Substances Act of 1970. The Controlled Substances Act ("CSA") was a comprehensive scheme that has remained the cornerstone of federal drug-control policy to the present time. The enactment of the CSA ushered in a new paradigm for marijuana regulation in the United States. After 1970 federal law would basically remain fixed with respect to marijuana possession and distribution. But many states and municipalities increasingly diverged over time from the rigid federal standards, moving more and more in the direction of legalization.

The Controlled Substances Act itself reflected America's conflicting views on marijuana at this time. On the one hand, the Controlled Substances Act took a more lenient approach toward mere possession or use of marijuana, and narcotic drugs generally, eliminating the harsh mandatory minimum sentences first imposed by the Boggs Act in 1951. On the other hand, Congress elected to include marijuana within the list of the Act's most highly regulated "Schedule I" drugs. The Act designated five different schedules of drugs, classified on the bases of their potential for harm and abuse, as well as their potential for efficacious medical use. Schedule I, which included drugs such as heroin, LSD, and, notably, marijuana, was for drugs that were deemed to have no medical use, in addition to having a high potential for abuse, and a lack of a proven safety record. (Curiously, cocaine received a Schedule II designation, along with drugs such as morphine, because Congress believed that cocaine, unlike marijuana, had some medical value.) Thus, marijuana retained its status as a strictly outlawed drug under the Controlled Substances Act.

Meanwhile, at the state level, a number of state legislatures began easing the penalties for simple marijuana possession, making it a minor misdemeanor rather than a high misdemeanor or felony. By 1973, all but 6 of the states had reduced the crime of possessing small amounts of marijuana for personal use to minor misdemeanor status.

During this time, there was also a movement toward decriminalizing marijuana, that is, to making possession a mere civil infraction rather than a criminal violation. In fact, when the Marijuana Commission that Congress created when it enacted the Controlled Substances Act issued its report in 1972, it recommended the elimination of criminal penalties for the possession of small amounts of marijuana for personal use. Not surprisingly, that recommendation spurred a lot of opposition, even though it had received the support of the American Bar Association. Most importantly, President Nixon adamantly opposed the Commission's recommendation, even though he had appointed nine of its thirteen members (Congress appointed the other four). As a result, Congress never acted upon the Commission's proposal.

Decriminalization received a more favorable reception at the state and local level, however. The Oregon legislature decriminalized marijuana possession in 1973, passing legislation that made marijuana possession for personal use merely a civil infraction with a $100 fine. By 1979, the legislatures of 8 additional states decriminalized personal possession of small amounts of marijuana, either by making it a mere civil infraction, or by eliminating the possibility of imprisonment for a violation. And in Alaska, the state's supreme court effectively decriminalized possession of marijuana for personal use in *Ravin v. State,* 537 P.2d 494 (Alaska 1975). There the court held that the Alaska Constitution contains an implicit right to privacy that protects possession of small amounts of marijuana kept in the home for personal use.

A few municipalities also decriminalized simple marijuana possession during this time, beginning with Ann Arbor, Michigan. The newly freed activist John Sinclair helped to rally support for decriminalization, and in 1972, the city council enacted an ordinance reducing marijuana possession to a civil infraction, and making the penalty for its violation a mere $5 fine. While that initial ordinance was subsequently struck down by a state trial court as an improper exercise of local authority, a similar city charter amendment was passed by the voters in 1974 and was subsequently upheld by the courts. Several other municipalities passed decriminalization measures in the late 1970's as well, including Madison, Wisconsin, in 1977 (reducing the penalty for simple possession to a $100 fine), and Berkeley, California, in 1979) (which passed an ordinance making enforcement of marijuana prohibitions the lowest police priority).

Thus, it looked by the end of the 1970's that the liberalization of marijuana laws was gaining momentum. Marijuana use reached its apex among high school and college students at this time, and it appeared to be only a matter of time until decriminalization would become the norm.

The momentum shifted quickly, however, after Ronald Reagan was elected as the 40th President of the United States. The Reagan administration ushered in a new era of political conservatism, and the country's attitudes toward drug policy followed suit. This was reflected in the First Lady's "Just Say No" campaign beginning in the early 1980s. That campaign sought to combat drug abuse among America's youth, and received widespread publicity. It even led to the creation of "Just Say No" clubs within thousands of schools and youth organizations across the country.

In keeping with this shift in public sentiment, Congress enacted several significant acts in the 1980's that tamped down the movement toward liberalization of marijuana laws. The two most significant were the Comprehensive Crime Control Act of 1984 and the Anti-Drug-Abuse Act of 1986. The former created the United States Sentencing Commission, which formulated mandatory sentencing guidelines for federal judges. This had the effect of significantly reducing judicial discretion in sentencing. The Act also increased the penalties for transfer and possession of large quantities of marijuana. The 1986 Act targeted narcotic trafficking generally, imposing stiff mandatory minimum sentences for various offenses. With respect to marijuana, possession of 100 and more kilograms of marijuana subjected the individual defendant to a minimum of five years imprisonment, along with a fine up to $2 million. And possession of 1000 or more kilograms of marijuana subjected the individual defendant to a minimum of 10 years imprisonment along with a fine of up to $4 million. These mandatory minimum sentences helped set in motion the trend toward a dramatically expanding prison population in the United States over the next several decades.

For the most part, state laws respecting marijuana did not change a great deal during the 1980s, although some states imposed additional restrictions on marijuana trafficking. For example, in the wake of a crack cocaine epidemic, a number of states, following the federal lead, imposed drug-free zones around schools, and imposed harsh penalties for marijuana possession in those zones. No additional states decriminalized marijuana during this time, tracking the nation's increasing intolerance of drug abuse.

D. THE MARCH TOWARD LEGALIZATION

By the beginning of the 1990s, therefore, marijuana reformers were becoming somewhat discouraged, since the advances they had made toward decriminalization in the 1970s seemed to be reversing course. Additionally, marijuana use declined significantly, at least among young people, during the 1980s. According to a study by the Institute for Social Research at the University of Michigan, for example, marijuana use among high school seniors dropped from 50% in 1978 to 12% in 1991.

In fact, however, the 1990s turned out to be an important decade for the push toward legalization. It was during this decade that many states and municipalities began passing laws legalizing the use of marijuana for medical purposes. The first of these was a result of a ballot initiative in San Francisco in 1991. Subsequently, various other municipalities began to follow suit. Then, in 1996, California became the first state to legalize marijuana for medical use, and two years later several other states passed such measures as well. By 2014, 23 states and the District of Columbia had enacted laws to legalize the medical use of marijuana, and by the end of 2018, the number was 33. Some of these laws were passed by state legislatures, and some were enacted by ballot measures. These laws vary significantly among the various states, both as to the amount that the medical marijuana user may possess, as well as the manner in which the marijuana can be obtained and consumed. Some states, for example, allowed the creation of medical marijuana dispensaries, some allowed merely the private growing of medical marijuana for personal use or by caregivers, and some were silent as to how marijuana used for medical purposes could be obtained. State laws also vary significantly with respect to the types of medical conditions that come within the scope of the law. Some states limited the ability to obtain a medical license to persons with just a few serious conditions, while other states were significantly less restrictive. California is among the least restrictive, allowing doctors to recommend marijuana for any conditions they think it will help, including such common conditions as anxiety, chronic pain, and insomnia. [*See* Chapter 5 for a more detailed discussion of California law.]

In addition to these states that have enacted medical marijuana laws, a number of other states in the past several years have passed legislation that permits the use of low-THC cannabis or a cannabis extract for the treatment of certain limited conditions, such as seizure disorder or cancer. Some of these also limit the distribution of such drugs, requiring, for example, that they be dispensed only by a major research university's medical center.

In the year 2000, a conservative Republican president, George W. Bush, was elected to the White House. Based on the aggressive policies previous Republican administrations had adopted with respect to illegal drugs, it was reasonable to expect that the new millennium would see a retrenchment in the continuing movement toward liberalization of marijuana laws in the states. In fact, however, that did not take place. As discussed above, the first decade of the new millennium witnessed a number of states adopting medical marijuana statutes. And while the federal government made a number of arrests in connection with abuses of these laws, it did not shut the programs down.

In addition, state and local governments renewed their decriminalization efforts. In 2001, Nevada became the first state in 23 years to decriminalize possession of small amounts of marijuana for personal use. By 2015, 20 states plus the District of Columbia had enacted laws decriminalizing possession of small amounts of marijuana for personal use (including states that had fully legalized it), and about a dozen more states were expected to consider such legislation in the near future. In most of these states, possession of small amounts of marijuana for personal use is reduced to a civil infraction with a fine; in a few of them, such possession is still technically a crime, but only minor misdemeanor, with no possibility of imprisonment for a violation, at least for a first offense.

Decriminalization also picked up steam at the local level. In certain states that had not yet decriminalized marijuana, voters in marijuana-friendly pockets of the states championed local initiatives that made possession of small amounts of marijuana for personal use merely civil infractions. In Michigan and Wisconsin alone, approximately two dozen municipalities had passed laws decriminalizing simple possession by 2016. It is likely that this trend will continue across a number of the states that have not decriminalized marijuana possession statewide.

The final frontier for marijuana liberalization has been the legalization of adult recreational-use, and since 2012, ten states, plus the District of Columbia, have crossed that historic divide. These states allow full "recreational" use of marijuana within certain limits, such as restrictions on possession by those under age 21, restrictions on the amount of marijuana that can be possessed, and restrictions on public use.

The first two states to fully legalize marijuana were Colorado and Washington, which both passed ballot initiatives in 2012. Of these two, Colorado was the first to implement its ballot initiative, enacting a regulatory scheme in 2013, and opening the first recreational marijuana dispensaries (which are rather similar to liquor stores) in January 2014. In doing so, Colorado became the model for states who wanted to legalize and regulate marijuana for adult use. Under Colorado law, local municipalities are not *required* to allow marijuana dispensaries within their jurisdiction; rather it is optional with the municipality. Interestingly, the majority of the municipalities chose not to allow dispensaries. But most of the larger cities did allow them, so a substantial majority of state citizens live in or near a municipality that has recreational dispensaries, and can therefore obtain recreational marijuana without much difficulty. The State of Washington lagged behind Colorado a bit in terms of implementing regulations, opening licensed dispensaries in July 2014. Later that same year, two additional states, Oregon and Alaska, along with the District of Columbia, adopted measures legalizing recreational marijuana use. In November 2016, four additional states legalized recreational marijuana use, including the nation's most populous state, California, as well as Nevada, Maine, and Massachusetts. In addition, legislators in a handful of other states introduced pending legislation seeking to legalize the recreational use of marijuana; in January 2018, Vermont became the first state to legalize adult-use marijuana via the legislative process. Michigan is the most recent state to have legalized recreational use, having done so by voter initiative in November 2018.

The federal response to state-enacted recreational marijuana laws has largely been restrained to date. The Obama administration took the position that states should be able to decide for themselves on the issue of legalization, subject to certain to certain broad restrictions. Accordingly, the Justice Department issued a series of memoranda, beginning in 2012, the centerpiece of which were the so-called Ogden and Cole Memos, which outlined the priorities the states had follow if they wanted to avoid having the federal government interfere with their marijuana legalization schemes. To date, the states that have legalized marijuana have largely complied with the federal government's enumerated priorities. Thus, the potential conflict between state and local law has not thus far created an insuperable problem for the marijuana industry in the states that have chosen to legalize it, although the lingering uncertainty of prosecution under the Trump administration definitely creates consternation for marijuana-related businesses. In January 2018, for example, the Justice Department announced that it was retracting the policy set out in the Cole Memo, leaving open the possibility that the Trump administration would take a more hard-lined approach to enforcing the CSA, perhaps even taking steps (such as arresting owners of marijuana-related businesses) to shut the burgeoning industry down. But to date, nothing has significantly changed with respect to the federal government's enforcement priorities.

Thus, the slow and halting march toward full legalization in the United States appears to be continuing apace. However, the future of legalization efforts will depend in large part on how the federal government resolves the conflict between state laws legalizing marijuana use and federal laws prohibiting it. The Trump administration (or a future administration) could adopt a more aggressive approach towards states that allow recreational use or even medical use. Conversely, Congress could enact a measure (several such bills have been introduced in the last few years) that expressly allows the states to decide the matter for themselves. Or it could even decide to remove marijuana from the CSA altogether. Thus, while the future of marijuana prohibition is far from clear, one thing seems highly likely: the next few years should provide another interesting chapter in the history of marijuana law.

NOTES AND QUESTIONS

1. **Non-enforcement of federal law.** The conflict between state and federal law has been the most challenging legal problem facing the states that have legalized medical and/or adult-use marijuana. The Controlled Substances Act's prohibition on marijuana allows no exception for valid state-sanctioned use of marijuana. Thus, a strong argument can be made that the supremacy clause of the United States Constitution empowers the federal government to shut down medical marijuana programs within the states, notwithstanding the fact that individual states have chosen to legalize marijuana use for medical or recreational purposes. The issue of the federal government's authority to do so was addressed by the United States Supreme Court in the 2005 case *Gonzales v. Raich*, 545 U.S. 1 (2005). There the Court ruled in favor of the federal government, holding that Congress had the power under the commerce clause to regulate activities that are purely intrastate, if those activities have a substantial effect on interstate commerce. The Court found that intrastate production of medical marijuana would have such an interstate effect, and thus it fell within Congress' power to regulate even homegrown marijuana. Subsequent to the *Raich* decision, however, the federal government has, for the most part, chosen not to exercise this authority, leaving state legalization schemes alone as long as they complied with certain enumerated requirements. Do you think it is appropriate for the executive branch to limit the enforcement of federal statutes in this way? [*See* Chapter 21 for a more extensive discussion of this issue.]

2. **The profitability of the marijuana industry.** As discussed in Chapter 15, the conflict between state and federal law in legalization states has created a variety of problems for marijuana-related businesses such as growers and dispensaries. Among other things, marijuana-related businesses have found it difficult, if not impossible, to obtain essential services such as banking, adequate insurance, and protection in federal bankruptcy court. They also are not allowed to take normal business tax deductions, such as their rent, under federal law. In addition, sales of marijuana are heavily taxed by the states and often by local authorities as well. Thus, the popular conception of marijuana-related businesses as money generating machines may not always be accurate.

PROBLEM 1-1

State X has legalized marijuana use for both medical and recreational purposes. State Y adjoins state X. Since the time state X's legalization scheme went into effect, the flow of marijuana into state Y has doubled due to the illegal smuggling of marijuana legally purchased in state X into state Y. State Y has now filed a lawsuit in federal court against state X, seeking to recover, among other things, the increased law enforcement costs it has incurred as a result of state X's legalization efforts. Does state Y have a plausible cause of action against state X?

PROBLEM 1-2

Do you think the federal government has the constitutional authority to crack down on state legalization schemes, as the Trump administration has asserted it does, or do you think such action would violate the Constitution's reservation of police powers to the individual states? And even if the federal government does have such authority, can it compel state and local law enforcement officials to assist it in enforcing federal drug laws?

CHAPTER 2

DEFINING AND CLASSIFYING MARIJUANA

■ ■ ■

While virtually everyone knows what marijuana is, defining and classifying "marijuana" and related terms for purposes of the Controlled Substances Act and other state and federal statutes regulating marijuana has sometimes raised challenging legal issues. With respect to the issue of *definitions*, the Controlled Substances Act provides a statutory definition of "marijuana," but disputes have arisen as to what exactly is included within this definition (e.g., hemp), and disputes have arisen under other state and federal statutes as to the meaning of related terms (e.g., what constitutes a marijuana "plant".)With respect to the issue of marijuana's *classification* in relation to other substances, its inclusion under Schedule I of the Controlled Substances Act has been the primary obstacle to scientists trying to thoroughly research marijuana's medical benefits and risks, since that classification restricts greatly scientists' ability to access marijuana for use in studies. This chapter explores these types of issues, after first providing an overview of marijuana and its use as an intoxicating drug.

A. BACKGROUND ON MARIJUANA

The word "marijuana" (sometimes spelled "marihuana") refers to the herbal substance made from the crushed leaves and flower buds of the *Cannabis* plant. The term "marijuana" is principally used in North America. It was coined in Mexico, and Americans later adopted it from Mexican immigrants, who introduced the drug to the western United States around the end of the 19th century. In Europe and many other parts of the world, marijuana is referred to instead as "herbal cannabis." (Of course, marijuana is also known by numerous slang terms as well in various parts of the world.) Some proponents of legalization prefer to use the term "cannabis" rather than "marijuana" when referring to the substance, in large part because of certain negative racial stereotypes associates with the latter term, but "marijuana" continues to be the term used by the Controlled Substances Act and most other statutes that regulate the substance.

"Cannabinoids" refers to the various unique chemical compounds (the most important being THC) that are found in the *Cannabis* plant. Different cannabinoids have different effects, and they interact with each other in complex ways to alter the psychoactive effects of the plant.

The most recognized cannabinoid is tetrahydrocannabinol, or "THC." It is the chemical primarily responsible for marijuana's intoxicating effect. THC is mainly found in the flowers of the *Cannabis* plant (especially the resin-producing trichomes within the flower); the leaves contain some THC, and the stem and seeds very little. Thus, a batch of marijuana made exclusively from flowering buds will have a higher THC content than one that is comprised of the same buds mixed with leaves and stems.

THC is only one of several dozen other cannabinoids found in marijuana, however, and the mix of these compounds varies among different genetic strains of marijuana. The most plentiful cannabinoid in marijuana other than THC is cannabidiol, or "CBD.' Many marijuana users claim that marijuana with more CBD and less THC makes them less anxious than marijuana with a high THC content and low CBD content. In addition, CBD is being studied extensively for a variety of possible medical uses, including treatment of some seizure disorders that are resistant to other treatment. In fact, the FDA recently approved a pharmaceutical drug comprised of CBD, called "Epidiliox," for treatment of certain childhood seizure disorders. CBD oil is also becoming increasingly popular as a dietary supplement and as a type of holistic medicine.

The cannabinoids besides THC do not by themselves produce an intoxicating "high," but they do interact with THC to produce its varying psychoactive effects. Thus, different batches of marijuana can affect the user differently, depending on the mix of cannabinoids. This has enabled commercial growers to tinker with the cannabinoid mix in order to produce marijuana strains with the desired effects, thereby catering to the varying tastes of consumers.

"Hemp" can refer either to a strain of the *Cannabis* plant that is very low in THC and cultivated for its fibers, rather than for its intoxicating effect, or it can refer to the fibers themselves, which are derived from the stalk and the stems of the cannabis plant. These fibers have a long history of commercial use. Prior to the invention of nylon, hemp fiber was the principal source for rope. In addition, its fibers could be woven into a sturdy fabric, which was used for a variety of purposes, including sails for ships, tents, clothes, etc. Hemp fibers were also used to make paper, and hemp seed was used extensively as birdfeed at one time. Hemp is now being used again as a food supplement, and its rich oil is being used as a cooking oil, as well as an ingredient in body lotions. Industrial-grade hemp is made from *Cannabis* strains that have been bred over time to be taller and sturdier than strains of the plant used to produce marijuana. These strains are also significantly lower in THC than the *Cannabis* plants used to produce marijuana, and thus they lack their intoxicating potential.

Hemp was reportedly grown in the earliest English colonies, and it has a long commercial history throughout large parts of the United States. Commercial production peaked around the mid-nineteenth century, centering in the area around Kentucky and in the Great Lakes states. However, it appears that the hemp plant was not widely grown in the United States as a means to produce the intoxicating marijuana herb from its flowering buds. In the latter half of the 19th century, production began to fall off due to commercial substitutes, and the hemp industry was completely shut down by the late 1930's due to legal restrictions. However, production was allowed temporarily during World War II because hemp had various military uses, such as rope production.

Prior to the 1960s, marijuana was often classified as a "narcotic," which encompasses a group of drugs—most notably opioids, such as morphine and heroin—that depress the central nervous system, dulling the senses and inducing sleep. In the 1960s, however, marijuana began to develop a much wider following, particularly among young people, and proponents began espousing the drug for its "consciousness expanding" properties. At that time it was thought of as a mild hallucinogen, without the potential for addiction that the opioids had.

Neither of these descriptions is entirely accurate, however, as marijuana has a fairly unique psychoactive effect. It is neither a true stimulant, nor a true depressant. And while it has some hallucinogenic properties, particularly at high doses, most of its users do not use it primarily for that effect, as would users of LSD, peyote, or Mescaline. Marijuana's active ingredients, its cannabinoids, have a complex effect, interacting with nerve receptors in a way that is different from these other types of drugs. Thus, it is probably best understood as being in its own separate class of drugs. In addition, the psychoactive effects also very significantly, depending not only on the dose received, but also on the mix of cannabinoids within any particular batch of marijuana.

Because the psychoactive effects of marijuana are complex and vary among individuals, there is no one reason people take the drug. For one thing, marijuana, like alcohol, has sometimes been described as a "social drug." And many users report that it enhances sociability, promotes tolerance, gives users a greater appreciation of humor and music, and all-around contributes to a pleasurable experience. Additionally, people claim to enjoy marijuana because it relaxes them, relieves their anxiety, or helps them sleep better. Some advocates of marijuana go further, claiming that marijuana heightens sensory awareness and even enhances creativity, and still others claim that it enhances spiritual awareness, giving then a fuller understanding of the nature of reality. To date, however, there has been very little research to see whether these effects are consistently observed across various groups of users.

Marijuana can be consumed in a number of different ways. And in legalization states, users of marijuana have a variety of options. Dispensaries, in addition to selling a variety of different strains of herbal marijuana for smoking, also sell various edible products, including cookies, brownies, and candies that contain single or multiple "doses" of the drug, as well as marijuana-infused beverages, tinctures, and concentrated extract oils that can be used in vaporizers. Vaporizers (i.e. "vapes") have become increasingly popular because they are discreet, portable, and allow the user to inhale the cannabinoids without the by-products of combustion.

Determining the precise scope of marijuana use in the United States is not easy because it relies for the most part on self-reporting, and there is evidence that users significantly under-report. Nevertheless, some statistics are available. It is estimated that at least 30 million Americans use marijuana at least occasionally, and approximately 20 million use it at least once per month. Usage is highest among young people between the ages of 18 and 25 years. Many younger adolescents have tried marijuana as well. According to some sources, close to half of all high school seniors in recent years have tried the drug at least once; over 20% use the drug at least monthly, and 6% of these students use marijuana nearly every day. Among all Americans, over 40% have tried marijuana at least once. At least 5 million use it nearly every day. Not surprisingly, marijuana use varies significantly across different areas the country. The states with the highest marijuana use per capita include Alaska, Colorado, Oregon, and Vermont (all of which have legalized recreational adult use), and the states with the lowest marijuana use per capita include Alabama, Kansas, and Louisiana.

Marijuana's medicinal value has been extolled for centuries in areas such as India, China, and northern Africa. And by 1870, marijuana was included in the United States' Pharmacopoeia, which is the country's official compendium of medical drugs. During this time, marijuana was available as an herb, and marijuana extracts were also frequently included in patent medicines that were sold widely in pharmacies. The availability of these medicines dried-up as the states and the federal government began to regulate psychoactive drugs in the early years of the 20th century. Thus, to a great extent, the criminalization of marijuana in the 20th century prevented the medical and scientific communities from being able to adequately research the potential medical benefits and risks of marijuana. This was particularly so after Congress enacted the Controlled Substances Act of 1970 (or "CSA"). Under the CSA, which still controls federal law, marijuana was designated a Schedule I drug, meaning that Congress deemed it to be a drug with significant potential for abuse, an inability to be prescribed safely, and no recognized medical value. This designation has significantly hampered the ability of scientists to research the medical benefits of marijuana. The federal government controls all access to legal sources of marijuana for purposes of testing, and it tightly controls who is allowed to undertake research on it.

Notwithstanding this information deficit, a majority of states have moved forward in efforts to legalize the medical use of marijuana, even though it remains illegal for all purposes under federal law. The first state to do so was California in 1996. Today, 33 states, in addition to the District of Columbia, have enacted statutes authorizing the medical use of marijuana, and a number of other states have enacted statutes that allow CBD and/or marijuana strains or extracts that are very low in THC content to be used for medicinal purposes under certain circumstances.

Since the beneficial effects of medical marijuana have not been rigorously tested, claims of its efficacy are still somewhat speculative. Nevertheless, proponents of medical marijuana claim that there is significant evidence—both anecdotal evidence as well as evidence from studies done abroad—that indicate marijuana has therapeutic value for a variety of conditions. But opponents of medical marijuana argue that marijuana's medicinal benefits are unproven, and that it has adverse side effects that make it unsuitable for medical use. For one thing, it is now generally agreed that marijuana is addictive, and that approximately 10% of people who use it regularly develop a dependence. (The withdrawal symptoms associated with removal of the drug, however, are not nearly as severe as they are for the opioids or even alcohol.) Opponents of medical marijuana also argue that better alternatives already exist for the medical conditions in question. At this point in time, due to the lack of thorough, FDA-approved research studies, it is difficult to draw firm conclusions about either the medical benefits or the adverse effects of marijuana.

NOTES AND QUESTIONS

1.   **Introduction of marijuana into European culture.** The use of cannabis as a drug (as opposed to its use for making hemp fibers) debuted in Europe in the first half of the 19th century. As one commentator has noted, however, its medical and recreational uses took separate paths:

> In France, interest centered on the nonmedical application of the psychoactive effects, whereas in England the interest was primarily medical. During the Napoleonic invasion of Egypt in 1798, De Sacy and Rouyer, two French scholars who accompanied the army, described the plant, and the practice and effects of hashish smoking, and they collected samples of the material to take back to France for further study. The famous French psychiatrist Moreau de Tours made further observations of its effects on mood during his North African travels in the 1830s. . . .In Paris, the Club des Haschichins flourished in the 1850s, with such members as the poets and authors Baudelaire, Gautier and Dumas. They served as subjects for Moreau's experiments and popularized hashish in their writings as a claimed route to esthetic self-realization. . . .

> In the United Kingdom, on the other hand, interest in cannabis was aroused by the medical and scientific writings of O'Shaughnessy, a British physician working in India as Professor of Chemistry and Materia Medica in Calcutta. He observed the use of cannabis in Indian traditional medicine for the treatment of spastic and

convulsive disorders such as hydrophobia (rabies), tetanus, cholera and delirium tremens. He sent supplies of the material to a pharmaceutical firm in London for analysis and clinical trials. The extracts of cannabis were adopted into the British Pharmacopoeia and later into the American Pharmacopeia, and were widely used in the English-speaking world as sedative, hypnotic and anticonvulsant agents in the late 19th and early 20th centuries.

Harold Kalant, *Medicinal Use of Cannabis: History and Current Status*, 6 Pain Research & Management 80, 81 (2001).

2. Scientific evidence. While scientific research regarding marijuana's risks and benefits has been hampered by its classification as a Schedule I drug, a significant amount of empirical information has been accumulating over the years. In 2017, the National Academies of Science, Engineering and Medicine issued a comprehensive report entitled *The Health Effects of Cannabis and Cannabinoids: The Current State of Evidence and Recommendations for Research*, which analyzed the state of existing research. It summarizes nearly 100 conclusions and offers recommendations designed to inform public health decisions. Among other things, the report concludes that marijuana has therapeutic benefit for the treatment of chronic pain, the treatment of nausea, and the treatment of certain seizure disorders.

B. DEFINING "MARIJUANA" AND RELATED STATUTORY TERMS

As is true with any statutory scheme, determining the scope and coverage of the CSA and other federal and state marijuana prohibitions requires the courts to engage in statutory interpretation. The CSA itself defines "marijuana" as follows:

> [A]ll parts of the plant Cannabis sativa L., whether growing or not; the seeds thereof; the resin extracted from any part of such plant; and every compound, manufacture, salt, derivative, mixture, or preparation of such plant, its seeds or resin. Such term does not include the mature stalks of such plant, fiber produced from such stalks, oil or cake made from the seeds of such plant, any other compound, manufacture, salt, derivative, mixture, or preparation of such mature stalks (except the resin extracted therefrom), fiber, oil, or cake, or the sterilized seed of such plant which is incapable of germination.

21 U.S.C. § 802(16).

Although this definition seems comprehensive, disputes have still arisen both as to the CSA's extension to other cannabis-related substances, such as hemp. And disputes have risen with respect to the meaning of marijuana-related terms.

The following case from the Supreme Court of Pennsylvania, *Commonwealth v. Burnsworth,* concerns the latter issue. In *Burnsworth,* the court considered the meaning of the word "plant" in a state statute that conditions the degree of criminal penalty on the number of live plants in the defendant's possession. The court found for the Commonwealth, holding that plants connected by a common root system are nevertheless separate plants for purposes of the Pennsylvania statute.

COMMONWEALTH V. BURNSWORTH

Supreme Court of Pennsylvania
543 Pa. 18 (1995)

MONTEMURO, J.

Appellant, the Commonwealth of Pennsylvania, appeals from a judgment of sentence entered by the Erie County Court of Common Pleas in which the common pleas court sentenced Appellee, Mark Allen Burnsworth, to six to twelve months imprisonment, followed by forty-eight months of probation. In fashioning such a sentence, the common pleas court refused to impose a minimum mandatory sentence as required by our legislature. Instead, the sentencing court declared that the mandatory sentencing provisions of 18 Pa.C.S. § 7508(a)(1)(i), (ii), and (iii), relating to "live plants," were unconstitutional.

Burnsworth was charged with two counts of unlawful manufacturing of marijuana and two counts of possession with intent to deliver marijuana plants in violation of 35 P.S. § 780–113(a)(30). On May 11, 1994, Burnsworth appeared for trial. Nevertheless, after consultation with his attorney, and after being notified that the Commonwealth would be seeking the application of the mandatory sentencing provisions set forth in 18 Pa.C.S. § 7508(a)(1)(i) and (iii), Burnsworth pled guilty to the offenses. As a specific condition of his plea agreement, Burnsworth retained the right to contest the application of the mandatory sentence provisions, specifically with respect to the number of marijuana plants confiscated.

During the July 8, 1994 sentencing hearing, the Commonwealth presented the testimony of Officer Edward Podpora of the Girard Police Department. Officer Podpora, present when the marijuana plants were confiscated, testified that with respect to Count 2738, sixteen "live" marijuana plants were found at Burnsworth's residence. He stated that the plants were four to five feet high, and that "a majority of them were planted in five gallon pails . . . [and that t]here were also a few planted into the ground at the residence." Officer Podpora also testified that in regard to Count 2739, he was again present when sixty-one marijuana plants were confiscated from a nearby fenced-in area.

At the conclusion of Officer Podpora's testimony, Burnsworth introduced the testimony of Dr. Larry Gauriloff, an assistant professor of biology at Mercyhurst College. Dr. Gauriloff testified that in addition to propagation by seed, marijuana will often germinate by a lateral root system, meaning that lateral shoots come up from the roots. The following testimony ensued between defense counsel and Dr. Gauriloff:

Q: Would the collectivity of these lateral roots and stems shooting up from the roots, is that defined as one plant or multiple plants?

A: That would define as a plant arising from a single seed, so you would consider it one plant. Many people counting them, certainly if they were pulled out of the ground, would count them as individual plants.

Q: Is there anything in the literature, in your expertise—would you view this as a plant, a tap system with multiple stems, would you view it as one plant or multiple plants?

A: From a research point of view as a single plant.

Dr. Gauriloff also offered testimony in regard to the weight of the plants at issue in this case:

Q: Can you form an opinion based on the collectivity of 61 plants with the description that Officer Podpora gave as to how much wet weight there would be?

A: Total?

Q: Yes.

[At this point, the Commonwealth objected on the basis that the testimony would be speculative. The sentencing court overruled the objection.]

A: Wet weight on 61 plants, like I said, probably 18 inches tall, the whole plant?

Q: Yes.

A: Figure about 4 grams per plant, you're looking at 240 grams roughly, divided by 28 in terms of ounces.

Q: So could you extrapolate that into pounds?

A: Pounds, you're looking at what, maybe 7, 8 ounces; half a pound.

The court further inquired whether Dr. Gauriloff had an opinion on the weight of the sixteen plants. Dr. Gauriloff responded: "Probably in terms of total weight I would say— I'll give them six, probably seven grams. Yeah, they are real sparse looking. But probably about six, seven grams of wet weight" which would correspond to about "four ounces, three ounces, three, three and a half."

Based upon the evidence presented, the sentencing court declared that the mandatory sentencing provisions of 18 Pa.C.S. § 7508(a)(1) were unconstitutional as:

> vague and overbroad and fail to take into account, among other things, the difference in size, maturity and intoxicating productivity of the plants, fail to define what constitutes a plant in terms of height, sex, percent of intoxicating cannabis, or root system and that there is a great disparity which has been pointed out in court by Dr. Gauriloff in the mandatory sentencing statute in the comparison between the amount of marijuana in pounds and the weight of marijuana in plant form. And this Court finds that such appears to be totally discretionary with no logical reasonable, or scientific basis for comparison. Therefore, the plant portion of the mandatory sentencing is fundamentally unfair, particularly in comparison with the mandatory sentencing by weight.

Moreover, the sentencing court determined that no rational basis existed for the disparity between the statute's weight and "live" plant provisions. The Commonwealth appealed.

We begin by noting that when confronted with the interpretation of a statute, we are guided by the principles of the Statutory Construction Act, Act of December 6, 1972, P.L. 1339, No. 290, 1 Pa.C.S. §§ 1901–1991. Moreover, it is well established that all legislation enacted by the General Assembly carries a strong presumption of constitutionality, and any party challenging a statute's constitutionality bears a heavy burden to demonstrate that the legislation clearly, palpably and plainly violates the terms of the constitution.

With that in mind, we shall commence our discussion of this case by addressing the sentencing court's opinion that the term "plant," as used by the legislature in 18 Pa.C.S. § 7508, is unconstitutionally vague and overbroad.

It is well settled that when the language of a statute is clear and unambiguous, the statute must be interpreted in accordance with its plain and common usage. *Commonwealth v. Corporan,* 531 Pa. 348, 351, 613 A.2d 530, 531 (1992). Our legislature specifically has provided that "[w]ords and phrases shall be construed according to rules of grammar and according to their common and approved usage . . .," 1 Pa.C.S. § 1903(a), and furthermore, that only technical words are to be construed according to their peculiar meaning. *Id.*

Herein, the legislature adopted the following sentencing requirements:

Drug trafficking sentencing and penalties

(a) **General rule**—Notwithstanding any other provisions of this or any other act to the contrary, the following provisions shall apply:

(1) A person who is convicted of violating section 13(a)(14), (30) or (37) of the act of April 14, 1972 (P.L. 233, No. 64), known as The Controlled Substance, Drug, Device and Cosmetic Act, where the controlled substance is marijuana shall, upon conviction, be sentenced to a mandatory minimum term of imprisonment and a fine as set forth in this subsection:

(i) when the amount of marijuana involved is a least two pounds, but less than ten pounds, **or at least ten live plants but less than 21 live plants;** one year in prison and a fine of $5,000 . . .;

(ii) when the amount of marijuana involved is at least ten pounds, but less than 50 pounds, **or at least 21 live plants but less than 51 live plants;** three years in prison and a fine of $15,000 . . .;

(iii) when the amount of marijuana involved is at least 50 pounds, **or at least 51 live plants;** five years in prison and a fine of $50,000. . . .

(emphasis supplied).

We believe that this language is clear and unambiguous, and as such, that we should construe the term "plant" according to its common usage. Even Dr. Gauriloff testified that while, from a biological and research point of view, lateral roots and stems could be considered as a single plant, "[m]any people counting them, certainly if they were pulled out of the ground, would count them as individual plants." Dr. Gauriloff also stated:

The lateral roots are quite fragile, the main body of the root being underneath each new shoot. As long as they were attached by a lateral root, they would be considered a single plant, but when torn from the ground, the lateral root would break. In fact, he opined that once the "plant" is torn from the earth, the identity of whether it was a single plant or a shoot from one plant's lateral root structure essentially would be indeterminable.

While not controlling, we find the opinion of the United States Court of Appeals for the Tenth Circuit in *United States v. Eves*, 932 F.2d 856 (10th Cir.1991), to be instructive. In that case, a very similar argument to the one raised in this case was lodged against a similar federal sentencing statute. From eight parent plants, the defendant grew over 1000 cuttings. The defendant argued that in order to determine if a "plant" was actually a plant, it was necessary to engage in a viability analysis. The Tenth Circuit Court of Appeals disagreed. Instead, the court opined that Congress intended the term "marijuana plant" to include those cuttings accompanied by root balls. Whether the plant could survive on its own would not be an issue; if it looks like a "plant"—that is, if it has a reasonable root system—it will be considered a "plant." No expert need testify, no experiment with instrumentation to monitor whether gaseous exchange is occurring need be conducted, no elaborate trimester or viability system need be established. If a cutting has a root ball attached, it will be considered a plant. *Id.* at 860. Accordingly, the federal appeals court determined that as a matter of statutory interpretation, the word "plant" should be interpreted consistent with its commonplace meaning, and in so ruling, specifically rejected defendant's argument that a more scientific definition should be applied. *Id.* at 857. Furthermore, in *United States v. Robinson,* 35 F.3d 442 (9th Cir.1994), the United States Court of Appeals for the Ninth Circuit recognized that an organism should have three readily apparent characteristics in order to be classified as a "plant" pursuant to the ordinary meaning of that word—roots, stems and leaves. *Id.* at 446. As we have already indicated, we agree that such a commonsensical definition of the term "plant" should be applied in this instance.

Another precept of statutory construction is that the legislature cannot be presumed to intend a result that is absurd, impossible of execution or unreasonable. 1 Pa.C.S. § 1922(1). The legislature originally enacted this particular section in an attempt to curb drug trafficking. By adding language to trigger the terms of the mandatory sentence when the marijuana involved is a specified number of plants, it is clear that the legislature intended to deter the growing of marijuana. To conclude, as Burnsworth would have us do, that one "plant" could produce an indefinite number of shoots, thereby providing a large quantity of marijuana for harvest, but yet be considered only one plant so as to evade the reach of the statute, would be directly contrary to the obvious intent of the legislature. Accordingly, we do not agree with the Erie County Court of Common Pleas that 18 Pa.C.S. § 7508(a)(1)(i), (ii) and (iii) are unconstitutionally vague.

* * *

Accordingly, the opinion of the Erie County Court of Common Pleas is reversed and the case is remanded for sentencing consistent with this opinion.

NOTES AND QUESTIONS

1. **Reliance on ordinary language.** In *Burnsworth,* the court relied primarily upon a principle of statutory construction that looks to the common and ordinary meaning of the statutory term "plant," and rejected the defendant's argument that various stocks of marijuana connected by a common root system are all one plant. Do you think it is appropriate for the court to construe the statute in this manner, in accordance with the ordinary meaning of the term "plant," even if there is scientific testimony to the contrary? Does

the fact that it was the Commonwealth that drafted the criminal statute—rather than the defendant—favor interpreting any ambiguity in favor of the defendant?

2.   **Other marijuana-related terms.** "Plant" is not the only marijuana related term the courts of been called upon to interpret in connection with statutory prohibitions on marijuana. One noteworthy example is the meaning of the word "hemp" and the extent to which hemp falls within the prohibitions of the Controlled Substances Act. In *Monson v. DEA*, 552 F.Supp.2d 1188 (N.D.N.D. 2007), for example, the court considered whether the CSA's statutory definition of "marijuana" extended to cannabis that qualified as "industrial hemp" under a North Dakota statute legalizing such hemp production, where the North Dakota statute explicitly limited the THC content in "industrial hemp" to a very small (.3%) amount. The plaintiffs argued that because the CSA specifically excludes the fiber-rich stalks of the cannabis plant (from which hemp is made) from its definition of "marijuana," the low-THC cannabis they were growing was outside of the reach of the statute. The court, however, in keeping with the decisions of other federal courts, rejected that argument because the CSA's definition of "marijuana" covered all varieties of cannabis, regardless of their THC content. And since the plaintiff was growing whole plants (it would presumably be impossible to grow only stalks and seeds), such plants came within the CSA's statutory definition of "marijuana" and were therefore illegal. (However, in 2014, Congress passed legislation allowing low THC industrial hemp production by the states pursuant to federally approved "pilot programs," thereby essentially overruling *Monson* by statute.)

C. CLASSIFYING MARIJUANA FOR PURPOSES OF THE CSA

Perhaps the most controversial aspect of the Controlled Substances Act ("CSA") is its inclusion of marijuana within the category of Schedule I controlled substances. When Congress passed the CSA in 1970, it created five schedules of controlled substances. The most tightly controlled substances are on Schedule I, which includes drugs such as heroin, LSD, and opium. Congress determined that these substances have (1) a high potential for abuse, (2) no medically accepted use, and (3) are unsafe even under medical supervision. Access to such substances is strictly limited, even for purposes of medical research, and the penalties for illegal possession are the harshest among the various controlled substances.

In the following case, *National Organization for the Reform of Marijuana Laws (NORML) v. Bell*, the United States District Court for the District of Columbia considered a constitutional challenge to the CSA on the part of NORML, an organization dedicated to the reform of marijuana laws. The court rejected the challenge, however, concluding that the relief NORML sought was ultimately a political issue that Congress needed to address, not a constitutional issue for the courts to resolve.

NATIONAL ORGANIZATION FOR THE REFORM
OF MARIJUANA LAWS (NORML) v. BELL

United States District Court, District of Columbia
488 F.Supp. 123 (D.D.C. 1980)

TAMM, J.

In this action, the National Organization for The Reform of Marijuana Laws (NORML or plaintiff) challenges the provisions of the Controlled Substances Act, 21 U.S.C. ss 801–904 (1976) (CSA or Act), that prohibit the private possession and use of marijuana. Plaintiff asserts that the Act violates the Constitution's guarantees of privacy and equal protection and its prohibition against cruel and unusual punishment. Finding the Act to be a reasonable congressional attempt to deal with a difficult social problem, we must reject this challenge and leave NORML to seek redress through political channels.

I. The Litigation

NORML filed this action October 10, 1973, seeking a declaratory judgment that the CSA and District of Columbia Uniform Narcotic Drug Act, D.C. Code ss 33–401 to 425 (1973), are unconstitutional in prohibiting the private possession and use of marijuana and requesting a permanent injunction enjoining enforcement of those statutes. This court stayed the proceedings for a year while NORML tried to obtain administrative relief through a proceeding to reclassify marijuana. After the stay was vacated, the parties battled over preliminary motions for two years. Finally, in June 1978, this court heard five days of evidentiary hearings before Judge Aubrey Robinson. Both sides presented live and documentary evidence concerning the effects of marijuana. Shortly thereafter, the parties submitted proposed findings of fact on the effects of marijuana and legal arguments for the court's consideration.

II. The Controlled Substances Act

Congress passed the Comprehensive Drug Abuse Prevention and Control Act of 1970 (DAPCA), 21 U.S.C. ss 801–966 (1976), to fight this nation's growing drug problem. The act was designed to

> deal in a comprehensive fashion with the growing menace of drug abuse in the United States (1) through providing authority for increased efforts in drug abuse prevention and rehabilitation of users, (2) through providing more effective means for law enforcement aspects of drug abuse prevention and control, and (3) by providing for an overall balanced scheme of criminal penalties for offenses involving drugs. It ended the patchwork federal effort against drug abuse and signaled a national commitment to deal with this problem by committing federal funds for rehabilitation programs.

In addition to the rehabilitation programs, DAPCA also revised completely the federal drug laws dealing with drug control. Title II, called the Controlled Substances Act (CSA), establishes five schedules for classifying controlled substances according to specified criteria. Two criteria the potential for abuse and the medical applications of a drug are the major bases for classification, along with certain social and medical information. 21 U.S.C. §§ 811(c), 812(b). Congress, on the basis of information gathered from extensive hearings, made the initial classifications. Recognizing that scientific information concerning controlled substances would change, Congress empowered the Attorney General to hear petitions for the reclassification or removal of drugs from the schedules. Id. § 811.

Congress also has revamped the penalties for distribution or possession of controlled substances. Heavy penalties up to fifteen years and a $25,000 fine are authorized for violators who manufacture or distribute Schedule I or II narcotic drugs. 21 U.S.C. § 841(b)(1)(A). The manufacture or distribution of a nonnarcotic Schedule I or II substance, or a Schedule III drug, carries a possible five year and $15,000 penalty. Id. § 841(b)(1)(B). The penalties for violations involving Schedules IV and V are correspondingly lower. Penalties double for second offenses.

In setting the penalties, Congress sought to reduce drug abuse by deterring suppliers through stiff penalties for drug distribution. Section 848 of DAPCA contains a special minimum term of ten years and a possible fine of $100,000 for anyone convicted of engaging in a "continuing criminal enterprise" involving five or more people in a series of drug violations. These heavier penalties for distribution, combined with strict registration requirements for manufacturers and researchers of Schedule I and II substances are designed to reduce trafficking in dangerous drugs.

Penalties for possession are not so severe. Possession of any controlled substance carries a maximum sentence of one year and a $5,000 fine, with no distinctions being drawn among drugs in different schedules. These penalties again double for a second offense. None of these penalties are mandatory, however, and this flexibility lets a judge impose a sentence that takes account of individual circumstances. In addition, a court may place first offenders on probation for one year; upon successful completion of probation, court proceedings are dismissed without an adjudication of guilt, and the conviction is not placed on the individual's record. A special provision places those dealing in a small amount of marijuana for no compensation under the possession penalties; thus, someone giving small amounts to friends is not subject to the stiff penalties for distribution.

III. Marijuana

Marijuana (cannabis sativa L.) is a psychoactive drug made of the leaves, flowers, and stems of the Indian Hemp plant. It derives its psychoactive properties from delta-9-tetrahydrocannabinol (THC), which exists in varying concentrations in the plant, depending on its origin, growing conditions, and cultivation. Marijuana and Health: A Report to the Congress from the Secretary, Department of Health, Education, and Welfare 13–14 (1971) (hereinafter cited as 1971 HEW Report). The concentration of THC within the sections of the plant also varies widely. The resin contains the greatest concentration of THC; smaller amounts are found, respectively, in the flowers, the leaves, and the stems. The most potent form of the drug, hashish, is prepared from the resins of the flowers and contains 5–12% THC. Marijuana generally found in the United States is weaker, with around 1% THC.

The drug produces a number of physiological and psychological effects. The short-term physiological effects have been well documented. They are reddening of the whites of the eye, dryness in the mouth, increased pulse rate, and impaired motor responses. The short-term psychological effects are equally well known:

At low, usual "social" doses, the intoxicated individual may experience an increased sense of well-being; initial restlessness and hilarity followed by a dreamy, carefree state of relaxation; alteration of sensory perceptions including expansion of space and time; and a more vivid sense of touch, sight, smell, taste, and sound; a feeling of hunger, especially a craving for sweets; and subtle changes in thought formation and expression. To an unknowing observer, an individual in this state of consciousness would not appear noticeably different from his normal state.

At higher, moderate doses, these same reactions are intensified . . . . The individual may experience rapidly changing emotions, changing sensory imagery, dulling of attention, more altered thought formation and expression such as fragmented thought, flight of ideas, impaired immediate memory, disturbed associations, altered sense of self-identity and, to some, a perceived feeling of enhanced insight.

At very high doses, psychotomimetic phenomena may be experienced. These include distortions of body image, loss of personal identity, sensory and mental illusions, fantasies and hallucinations. The intensity of these reactions depends on dosage, method of use, metabolism, attitude and setting, tolerance, duration of use, and pattern of use.

Experiences under marijuana intoxication are usually pleasurable, but negative reactions are not infrequent. These negative reactions include distortion of body image, depersonalization, acute panic anxiety reaction, nausea, and, more rarely, psychosis. These reactions may be caused or exaggerated by pre-existing psychological problems.

The long-term effects of marijuana are less well known. Studies have dispelled many of the myths about the drug: marijuana is not a narcotic, not addictive, and generally not a stepping-stone to other, more serious drugs. Furthermore, it causes neither aggressive behavior nor insanity.

Despite these findings, questions about long-term use remain. Studies have indicated that marijuana may affect adversely the lungs and the endocrine, the immunity, and the cardiovascular systems. Some of these studies are disputed, but an examination of these adverse findings illustrates the important questions still remaining about marijuana use.

Smoking marijuana may contribute to lung disorders in the same way as tobacco. Marijuana smoke contains more tar than tobacco smoke, and the typical user inhales this smoke in his lungs and holds it there to derive the greatest effect from the THC. The smoke irritates the lung tissue, and with heavy long-term use, may impair lung functions.

Marijuana may also affect the levels of the male sex hormone testosterone and other pituitary hormones. Several studies have found lower levels of testosterone after marijuana use. Even where lower testosterone levels were found, they were still within acceptable limits, but the possibility of damage from long-term, heavy use still exists. Researchers are particularly concerned about marijuana's effects on pubertal males, males with impaired sexual functioning, and pregnant women.

In a 1974 study, scientists found evidence that marijuana use impaired the functioning of the immunity system, causing a reduction in the white blood cell count. Later studies reached similar conclusions, while others have found no such reduction. More study of this question is needed, but conducting research in this and other areas involving physiological changes from marijuana is extremely difficult, for researchers cannot even agree on appropriate procedures.

Marijuana affects the cardiovascular system by accelerating the heart rate. Studies also indicate that it may weaken temporarily contractions of heart muscle, posing dangers for smokers with heart disease or abnormalities. Studies on healthy young men have revealed no cardiovascular effects, but those with heart problems may experience pain due to less efficient delivery of oxygen in the blood. The long-range consequences of these temporary changes in the cardiovascular system are difficult to assess, but they may be significant and require further study.

In addition to these problems, other tests have found negative aspects to marijuana use. Amotivational difficulties and changes in brain cells, chromosomes, and cell metabolism have been noted in various studies. These findings have not been corroborated, however, and other research has reached contradictory conclusions. As with the other areas, these questions demand further scientific study to determine conclusively the long-term effects of marijuana. Although we now know that marijuana is not the "killer" drug, as branded in the past, its long-term effects are still an open question and must be approached as unresolved. These lingering questions must be kept in mind in considering the legal issues.

* * *

B. Equal Protection

NORML further contends that the CSA violates the equal protection component of the due process clause. First, it argues that the classification of marijuana, a relatively harmless drug, as a controlled substance violates equal protection. Second, NORML believes that, even if marijuana may be controlled, its classification as a Schedule I drug is infirm: placement in Schedule I is both underinclusive in failing to include as a controlled substance drugs such as alcohol and nicotine, which satisfy Schedule I criteria, and overinclusive for establishing the same penalties for possession of marijuana as for all other controlled substances and for including marijuana in Schedule I with the more dangerous narcotics and opiates. For the reasons stated below, this court rejects these contentions.

Legislation that does not affect a "fundamental" right or a "suspect" class need only bear a rational relationship to a legitimate state interest. The distinctions drawn by a challenged statute must bear some rational relationship to a legitimate state end and will be set aside as violative of the Equal Protection Clause only if based on reasons totally unrelated to the pursuit of that goal. Legislatures are presumed to have acted constitutionally even if source materials normally resorted to for ascertaining their grounds for action are otherwise silent, and their statutory classification will be set aside only if no grounds can be conceived to justify them. This standard of judicial review gives legislatures wide discretion and permits them to attack problems in any rational manner. "In an equal protection case of this type . . ., those challenging the legislative judgment must convince the court that the legislative facts on which the classification is apparently based could not reasonably be conceived to be true by the governmental decision-maker." *Vance v. Bradley*, 440 U.S. 93, 111 (1979). The classification will be upheld unless "the varying treatment of different groups or persons is so unrelated to the achievement of any combination of legitimate purposes that (a court) can only conclude that the legislature's actions were irrational." Id. at 97. "In short, the judiciary may not sit as a superlegislature to judge the wisdom or desirability of legislative policy determinations made in areas that neither affect fundamental rights nor proceed along suspect lines. . . ." *New Orleans v. Dukes*, 427 U.S. 297, 303 (1976).

1. Classification as a Controlled Substance

The inclusion of marijuana as a controlled substance under the CSA easily satisfies this deferential rationality standard. Congress gave the

CSA provisions concerning marijuana considerable attention. It recognized that much of the information regarding marijuana was inaccurate and that bias and ignorance had perpetuated many myths about the consequences and dangers of marijuana use. Despite all the concern over the drug, few reliable scientific studies existed that could give accurate information to the legislators. Representative Cohelan acknowledged this lack of accurate information on marijuana during the House discussion of the bill: "Much remains to be done to find out the effects of marijuana. Assertions from both sides are not hard to find, but there is precious little hard clinical data on this subject." 116 Cong.Rec. 33658 (1970). Unsure of marijuana's effects, Congress placed marijuana in Schedule I, with its program of strict controls, until it could obtain more scientific information on the drug's effects. In so doing, Congress followed the recommendation of the Department of Health, Education, and Welfare, which had suggested classification in Schedule I until further tests could be completed.

Inclusion of marijuana as a controlled substance in 1970 certainly was rational. The information then available indicated that marijuana might well have substantial detrimental effects, and Congress thus reasonably could decide to include the drug as a controlled substance rather than leave it unregulated. NORML argues that, although classification of marijuana as a controlled substance in 1970 might have been rational, the scientific evidence available today establishes that "private possession and use of marijuana by adults (do) not pose any significant danger to the public health, safety or welfare." Brief for Plaintiff at 18. NORML therefore asserts the classification of marijuana as a controlled substance is no longer rational and invokes *United States v. Carolene Products Co.*, 304 U.S. 144, 153 (1938): "the constitutionality of a statute predicated upon a particular state of facts may be challenged by a showing to the court that those facts have ceased to exist."

The record, however, is not so clear as NORML contends. Experts still strongly disagree about the safety of marijuana, and its long-term effects remain an open question. Studies indicate that marijuana may impair the circulatory, the endocrine, and the immunity systems of the body, alter chromosomes, and change cell metabolism. Although many dispute these findings, this contradictory evidence demonstrates that important questions about marijuana use persist.

Given the continuing debate over marijuana, this court must defer to the legislature's judgments on disputed factual issues. In the *Carolene Products* decision on which NORML relies, the Supreme Court recognized the importance of this policy of judicial restraint:

> (I)nquiries, where the legislative judgment is drawn in question, must be restricted to the issue whether any state of facts either known or which could reasonably be assumed affords support for (the classification). Here the demurrer challenges the

validity of the statute on its face and it is evident from all the considerations presented to Congress, and those of which we may take judicial notice, that the question is at least debatable. As that decision was for Congress, neither the findings of a court arrived at by weighing the evidence, nor the verdict of a jury can be substituted for it.

The classification need not change continually as more information becomes available. Congressional action must be upheld as long as a rational basis still exists for the classification. The continuing questions about marijuana and its effects make the classification rational.

Furthermore, judicial deference is appropriate when difficult social, political, and medical issues are involved. Courts should not step in when legislators have made policy choices among conflicting alternatives. That this court might resolve the issues differently is immaterial. "When Congress undertakes to act in areas fraught with medical and scientific uncertainties, legislative options must be especially broad and courts should be cautious not to rewrite legislation, even assuming, arguendo, that judges with more direct exposure to the problem might make wiser choices." Thus, this court should not substitute its judgment for the reasonable determination made by Congress to include marijuana under the CSA.

2. Classification in Schedule I

In a related equal protection challenge, NORML argues that classification of marijuana in Schedule I is irrational as being both underinclusive and overinclusive. The CSA does not regulate alcohol and tobacco, which are more harmful than marijuana, and it places marijuana in the same schedule with such dangerous substances as heroin and other narcotics. Thus, even if the classification of marijuana as a controlled substance is rational, the plaintiff believes that the legislation nonetheless is unconstitutional because marijuana's treatment within the Act is irrational in relation to other controlled substances.

a. Underinclusiveness

"Underinclusive classifications do not include all who are similarly situated with respect to a rule, and thereby burden less than would be logical to achieve the intended government end." L. Tribe, American Constitutional Law, § 16–4, at 997 (1978). To be successful in a challenge based on underinclusiveness, plaintiff must show that the governmental choice is " 'clearly wrong, a display of arbitrary power, not an exercise of judgment,' " Mathews v. de Castro, 429 U.S. 181, 185 (1976). Few challengers can sustain such a heavy burden of proof. Courts have recognized the very real difficulties under which legislatures operate difficulties that arise due to the nature of the legislative process and the society that legislation attempts to reshape. As Professor Tribe has explained: "underinclusive" or "piecemeal legislation is a pragmatic means of effecting needed reforms, where a demand for completeness may lead to total paralysis . . . ." L. Tribe, supra § 16–4, at 997.

Legislatures have wide discretion in attacking social ills. "A State may 'direct its law against what it deems the evil as it actually exists without covering the whole field of possible abuses, and it may do so none the less that the forbidden act does not differ in kind from those that are allowed.'" *Hughes v. Superior Court*, 339 U.S. 460, 468 (1950). Failure to address a certain problem in an otherwise comprehensive legislative scheme is not fatal to the legislative plan.

> A legislature traditionally has been allowed to take reform "one step at a time, addressing itself to the phase of the problem which seems most acute to the legislative mind," *Williamson v. Lee Optical of Oklahoma, Inc.*, 348 U.S. 483, 489 (1955); and a legislature need not run the risk of losing an entire remedial scheme simply because it failed, through inadvertence or otherwise, to cover every evil that might conceivably have been attacked.

McDonald v. Board of Election Commissioners, 394 U.S. at 809.

Given this policy of legislative freedom in confronting social problems, the exclusion of alcohol and tobacco from the CSA does not render the scheme unconstitutional. Different legislative schemes control the sale and distribution of alcohol and tobacco, see, e. g., 26 U.S.C. §§ 5661(b), 5681, 5683, 5686 (1976). The specific exemption of alcohol and tobacco from the provisions of the CSA, 21 U.S.C. § 802(6) (1976), reflects Congress's view that other regulatory schemes are more appropriate for alcohol and tobacco. That alcohol and tobacco may have adverse effects on health does not mean the CSA is the only proper means of regulating these drugs, nor does it mean that marijuana should be treated identically. As a Presidential commission on drug abuse pointed out, "While alcoholism constitutes a major social problem, surely it is not valid to justify the adoption of a new abuse on the basis that it is no worse than a presently existing one. The result could only be added social damage from a new source." Task Force Report: Narcotics, Marijuana, and Dangerous Drugs (1969), reprinted in 115 Cong.Rec. 25454, 25456 (1969). Congress, having the power to deal with drug abuse in any reasonable manner, decided to exclude alcohol and tobacco from the CSA. This court will not disturb that judgment.

b.   Overinclusiveness

A law also may be challenged for including within a prohibited class an item that does not rationally belong with the other members of that class. NORML once again draws its support from the Carolene Products decision:

(T)he constitutionality of a statute, valid on its face, may be assailed by proof of facts tending to show that the statute as applied to a particular article is without support in reason because the article, although within the (particular) class, is so different from others of the class as to be without the reason for the prohibition.

United States v. Carolene Products Co., 304 U.S. at 153–5. The plaintiff here argues that penalties for possession of marijuana should be lower than those authorized for other, more dangerous Schedule I drugs. Moreover, NORML contends marijuana's classification in Schedule I is impermissible because the drug does not fit the statutory criteria for placement in that schedule.

* * *

2. Classification in Schedule I

NORML argues that marijuana does not belong in Schedule I, for it does not satisfy that schedule's statutory criteria high potential for abuse, no medically accepted use, and no safe use of the drug even under medical supervision. 21 U.S.C. § 812(b)(1) (1976). The Government disagrees and contends that all three criteria are met. It claims the drug has a "high potential for abuse," in that millions of Americans use marijuana on their own initiative rather than on the basis of medical advice. While tests have indicated that marijuana may have therapeutic uses in the treatment of glaucoma and cancer, the Food and Drug Administration does not currently accept it for any form of medical treatment. Finally, the Government claims that marijuana cannot be used safely due to the differing concentrations of THC in cannabis.

Even assuming, arguendo, that marijuana does not fall within a literal reading of Schedule I, the classification still is rational. Placing marijuana in Schedule I furthered the regulatory purposes of Congress. The statutory criteria of section 812(b)(1) are guides in determining the schedule to which a drug belongs, but they are not dispositive. Indeed, the classifications at times cannot be followed consistently, and some conflict exists as to the main factor in classifying a drug potential for abuse or possible medical use. The district court in *United States v. Maiden*, 355 F.Supp. 743 (D.Conn.1973), discussed this problem in rejecting the identical claim raised here by NORML:

(The statutory classifications) cannot logically be read as cumulative in all situations. For example finding (B) for Schedule I requires that "The drug or other substance has no currently accepted medical use in treatment in the United States." Finding (B) for the other four schedules specifies that the drug has a currently accepted medical use. At the same time, finding (A) requires that the drug has a "high potential for abuse" for placement in Schedule I, but a "potential for abuse less than the drugs or other substances in Schedules I and II" for placement in Schedule III. If the findings are really cumulative, where would one place a drug that has no accepted medical use but also has a potential for abuse less than the drugs in Schedules I and II? According to finding (A) for Schedule III it belongs in Schedule III, but finding (B) for that schedule precludes Schedule III; according to finding (B) for Schedule I it belongs in Schedule I, but finding (A) for that schedule appears to preclude Schedule I.

The legislative history also indicates the statutory criteria are not intended to be exclusive. The House report states that "(a)side from the criterion of actual or relative potential for abuse, subsection (c) of section 201 (21 U.S.C. s 811(c)) lists seven other criteria ... which must be considered in determining whether a substance meets the specific requirements specified in section 202(b) (21 U.S.C. s 812(b)) for inclusion in particular schedules ...." 1970 House Report, supra at 35. The criteria listed in section 811(c) include the state of current knowledge, the current pattern of abuse, the risk to public health, and the significance of abuse. These more subjective factors significantly broaden the scope of issues to be considered in classifying a drug. Given these other concerns, Congress might well want marijuana in Schedule I for regulatory purposes. Such a classification carries heavier penalties for sale, distribution, and importation, thus aiding law enforcement officials in their effort to reduce the supply of marijuana.

In addition, Congress itself made the initial classifications, 21 U.S.C. s 812(c), and established a procedure for reclassifying drugs and controlled substances: "Schedules I, II, III, IV, and V shall, unless and until amended pursuant to section 811 of this title (21 U.S.C. s 811), consist of the following drugs and other substances ...." 21 U.S.C. s 812(c) (emphasis added). In making the initial determination, Congress placed marijuana in Schedule I. The clear meaning of section 812(c) is that Congress intended marijuana to remain in Schedule I until such time as it might be reclassified by the Attorney General on the basis of more complete scientific information about the drug. In such a reclassification hearing, the statutory criteria would be the guides to determining the most appropriate schedule for marijuana. By providing for periodic review and constant revision of drug classifications, Congress enacted a sensible mechanism for scrutinizing the classification of marijuana. As Judge Feinberg stated in *United States v. Kiffer*:

> (T)he very existence of the statutory scheme indicates that, in dealing with the "drug" problem, Congress intended flexibility and receptivity to the latest scientific information to be the hallmarks of its approach. This ... is the very antithesis of the irrationality (plaintiff) attributes to Congress.

477 F.2d 349 at 357.

The legislative scheme under section 811 offers a flexible means of reclassifying controlled substances, and the Attorney General may reclassify marijuana pursuant to that scheme. The propriety of any administrative determination on the reclassification of marijuana is not before this court. The constitutional legitimacy of the classification of marijuana in Schedule I is challenged, however, and this court concludes that the classification is constitutionally permissible. Thus, plaintiff's equal protection challenge must be rejected.

* * *

V.   Final Considerations

In this case, NORML has asked this court to overturn the CSA prohibition on private possession of marijuana. In so doing, NORML misdirects its efforts. This challenge presents the difficult social questions that legislatures are especially adept at resolving, and we do not sit to second-guess their judgments. Under our system of checks and balances, it is the court's duty to examine legislation and to determine the legality or illegality of that legislation within the confines of the law. It is the responsibility of the court "to construe and enforce the Constitution and laws of the land as they are and not to legislate social policy on the basis of . . . personal inclinations" or other non-legal considerations. *Evans v. Abney*, 396 U.S. 435, 447 (1970). The legislative system may not always work efficiently, or fairly, but we have staked our fortunes on it, and our history would support the wisdom of our forefathers' judgment. As Justice Frankfurter once noted:

> (T)here is not under our Constitution a judicial remedy for every political mischief, for every undesirable exercise of legislative power. . . . Appeal must be to an informed civically militant electorate. In a democratic society like ours, relief must come through an aroused popular conscience that sears the conscience of the people's representatives.

Baker v. Carr, 369 U.S. 186, 270 (1962) (Frankfurter, J., dissenting).

NORML's efforts have seared the conscience of many representatives. Eleven states have decriminalized possession of marijuana, and efforts to decriminalize are continuing in many others. The legislative branch, and not the judicial, is the proper battleground for the fight to decriminalize the possession of marijuana. The people, and not the courts, must decide whether the battle will be won or lost.

NOTES AND QUESTIONS

1.   **The CSA's three-part test for Schedule I substances.** The court in *NORML* declined to strike down the Schedule I classification of marijuana

on constitutional grounds, deferring to the executive and legislative branches of government with respect to the appropriateness of that classification as a matter public policy. In your view, does marijuana satisfy the 3-part test for inclusion in Schedule I, given what you know about the state of current scientific knowledge? In other words, does it: (1) lack any accepted medical use in the United States, (2) have a high potential for abuse, and (3) lack the ability to be prescribed safely? Does marijuana's classification in Schedule I make sense in light of the Schedule II classification of some seemingly more dangerous substances, such as prescription opiates and cocaine? Do you think that the court is right to defer to the other branches of government as to this question?

2.   **Epidiolex and CBD oil.** As discussed in Chapter 1, the marijuana plant contains a number of different cannabinoids, the most predominant of which are THC and CBD. Both substances are subject to the prohibitions of Schedule I, including the oil derived from CBD, which has become popular in many legalization states. Recently, however, the FDA approved a pharmaceutical drug called "Epidiolex," whose active ingredient is CBD, for the treatment of certain seizure disorders. That drug was included on Schedule V of the Controlled Substances Act—the least restrictive category. Does it make sense for the essentially same substance—CBD—to be included in the most restrictive category, Schedule I, if it is sold as CBD oil by generic manufacturers, while the pharmaceutical version of a CBD extract is included in Schedule V, the least restrictive category? What are the possible rationales from the perspective of the federal government?

3.   **Rescheduling marijuana.** Many commentators, including some politicians who favor the federal legalization of marijuana, at least for medical use, advocate rescheduling marijuana by moving it from Schedule I to one of the lower schedules. Some see this as a way to make marijuana itself available as a prescription drug. But rescheduling alone would not enable doctors to prescribe marijuana as a prescription drug; there would be other significant hurdles that marijuana would have to clear first, such as FDA approval. And what about adult recreational use? Would rescheduling automatically remove marijuana from the specter of federal criminal prosecution and resolve the conflict with state legalization, given that criminal penalties are attached to the nonmedical use of drugs on lower schedules (e.g., cocaine and most opiates) as well?

4.   **DEA control of research.** In August 2017, the Drug Enforcement Administration (DEA) loosened the controls on marijuana research somewhat by announcing that it would accept applications from growers to supply marijuana for DEA-approved research projects. Prior to that time, the DEA had only issued a single license for the cultivation of marijuana for research, to the University of Mississippi, which then provided marijuana to all approved researchers under tightly controlled conditions. Presumably this change indicates a willingness on the part of the DEA to expand federally approved research on the medical benefits and risks of marijuana.

PROBLEM 2-1

As noted above, the federal FDA recently approved the pharmaceutical drug called "Epidiolex" for the treatment of certain types of childhood epilepsy. The active ingredient in Epidiolex is CBD, which is a (relatively) non-psychoactive cannabinoid. In order for Epidiolex to be legally prescribed, the DEA had to classify Epidiolex as a Schedule II or lower drug, meaning that, among other things, it has an accepted medical use in the United States. It chose to place Epidiolex in Schedule V, the least restrictive category. Given that the Controlled Substances Act includes within the definition of "marijuana" all "compounds" and "derivatives" of the cannabis plant, will Congress also have to change the definition of "marijuana" in the CSA to accommodate the DEA's rescheduling of Epidiolex?

CHAPTER 3

STATUS UNDER FEDERAL LAW

■ ■ ■

As developed in Chapter 1, by 1969, marijuana use was widespread on college campuses. *Leary v. United States* seemed to signal a Court sympathetic to liberalization of marijuana laws. The late 1960s were a high water mark for legislative efforts to reform marijuana laws. That was about to change.

Leary struck down the Marihuana Tax Act of 1937, leaving a void in federal criminal law. In 1970, Congress repealed the 1937 law and replaced it with a more comprehensive drug law, the Controlled Substances Act of 1970 (the CSA). The new law reflected the societal differences over drug use.

The CSA eliminated harsh minimum sentences for possession or use of marijuana and narcotic drugs that had been mandatory under the Boggs Act, the law in effect since its passage in 1951. Initially, in 1971, marijuana was provisionally made a Schedule I drug. As developed below, Schedule I drugs are ones have that little or no medical use, high potential for abuse, and no proven safety record. In theory, Congress included marijuana as a Schedule I drug provisionally to give time for an assessment of the science relating to marijuana.

While many groups, individuals and legislators favored liberalization of marijuana laws, not all Americans shared that view. Notably, President Richard Nixon opposed liberalization. As demonstrated by Nixon's recorded conversations, he and members of his White House staff saw an attack on marijuana use as a way to punish antiwar activists. He organized The National Commission on Marihuana and Drug Abuse (or the Shafer Commission as it became known) to marshal support for marijuana's placement in Schedule I.

In 1972, the Shafer Commission concluded that marijuana was as safe as alcohol and recommended adoption of a public health approach to marijuana use. By the time of the report, the Federal Bureau of Narcotics had merged into the Department of Justice, a process begun at the end of Lyndon Johnson's presidency. That placed the agency under Attorney General John Mitchell's control. Mitchell, Nixon's close ally, maintained marijuana in Schedule I. As discussed below, efforts to reschedule marijuana have failed, in part, because of aggressive efforts by federal authorities.

Nixon also introduced powerful anti-drug rhetoric. He described drug abuse as "Enemy Number One," and proclaimed the "War on Drugs." Some commentators have pointed out that Nixon did not increase criminal sentences for marijuana use, despite leading efforts to keep it as a Schedule I substance. President Ronald Reagan's administration led to an even more aggressive war on drugs.

First Lady Nancy Reagan's "Just Say No" campaign symbolized the new federal approach to drug use. Schools and youth organizations around the country created "Just Say No" clubs. Congress took a punitive approach to drugs. The Comprehensive Crime Control Act of 1984 created the United States Sentencing Commission, which reduced judicial sentencing discretion by formulating what were thought to be mandatory sentencing guidelines. The Anti-Drug Abuse Act of 1986 imposed severe mandatory minimum sentences for various offenses. For example, possession of 100 kilograms or more resulted in a minimum term of five years in prison and a fine up to $2 million. The 1980s were a low point for proponents of marijuana legalization, with aggressive law enforcement efforts to eradicate marijuana use and a Supreme Court willing to uphold many aggressive policing tactics.

Events took place in the 1990s that resulted in dramatic changes, the kinds of changes that make the study of marijuana law worthwhile today. But those changes are the subject of later chapters. For now, this chapter focuses on the status of marijuana as a Schedule I drug and efforts to change that characterization.

A. PROVISIONS OF THE CONTROLLED SUBSTANCES ACT

This section includes the important provisions of the CSA. Support for the CSA was overwhelming in Congress. The vote in the House of Representatives was 342 to 7, with 82 members not voting. The vote was 54–0 in the Senate, with 46 not voting. President Nixon signed the bill into law in October 1970 as Title II of the Comprehensive Drug Abuse Prevention and Control Act of 1970.

As reflected in the discussion above, drug policy divides Americans. Perhaps not surprisingly, the CSA is both a public health measure and a criminal statute. Thus, CSA appears in 21 U.S.C., Food and Drug Acts. Many of its enforcement provisions appear in Title 18: Crimes and Criminal Procedure.

As you read the provisions of the CSA, consider the breadth of the law. Is any use of marijuana illegal? What about the possession of a single marijuana cigarette?

21 U.S.C. § 801. Congressional findings and declarations: controlled substances

The Congress makes the following findings and declarations:

(1) Many of the drugs included within this subchapter have a useful and legitimate medical purpose and are necessary to maintain the health and general welfare of the American people.

(2) The illegal importation, manufacture, distribution, and possession and improper use of controlled substances have a substantial and detrimental effect on the health and general welfare of the American people.

(3) A major portion of the traffic in controlled substances flows through interstate and foreign commerce. Incidents of the traffic which are not an integral part of the interstate or foreign flow, such as manufacture, local distribution, and possession, nonetheless have a substantial and direct effect upon interstate commerce because—

(A) after manufacture, many controlled substances are transported in interstate commerce,

(B) controlled substances distributed locally usually have been transported in interstate commerce immediately before their distribution, and

(C) controlled substances possessed commonly flow through interstate commerce immediately prior to such possession.

(4) Local distribution and possession of controlled substances contribute to swelling the interstate traffic in such substances.

(5) Controlled substances manufactured and distributed intrastate cannot be differentiated from controlled substances manufactured and distributed interstate. Thus, it is not feasible to distinguish, in terms of controls, between controlled substances manufactured and distributed interstate and controlled substances manufactured and distributed intrastate.

(6) Federal control of the intrastate incidents of the traffic in controlled substances is essential to the effective control of the interstate incidents of such traffic.

(7) The United States is a party to the Single Convention on Narcotic Drugs, 1961, and other international conventions designed to establish effective control over international and domestic traffic in controlled substances.

21 U.S.C. § 802. Definitions

(16) The term "marihuana" means all parts of the plant Cannabis sativa L., whether growing or not; the seeds thereof; the resin extracted from any part of such plant; and every compound, manufacture, salt, derivative,

mixture, or preparation of such plant, its seeds or resin. Such term does not include the mature stalks of such plant, fiber produced from such stalks, oil or cake made from the seeds of such plant, any other compound, manufacture, salt, derivative, mixture, or preparation of such mature stalks (except the resin extracted therefrom), fiber, oil, or cake, or the sterilized seed of such plant which is incapable of germination.

21 U.S.C. § 812(c). Initial schedules of controlled substances

Schedules I, II, III, IV, and V shall, unless and until amended pursuant to section 811 of this title, consist of the following drugs or other substances, by whatever official name, common or usual name, chemical name, or brand name designated:

21 U.S.C. § 812. Schedules of controlled substances: Sched. I(c)(10), (17);

Unless specifically excepted or unless listed in another schedule, any material, compound, mixture, or preparation, which contains any quantity of the following hallucinogenic substances, or which contains any of their salts, isomers, and salts of isomers whenever the existence of such salts, isomers, and salts of isomers is possible within the specific chemical designation:

* * *

(10) Marihuana.

* * *

(17) Tetrahydrocannabinols.

21 U.S.C. § 841(a)(1). Prohibited acts A

(a)   Unlawful acts

Except as authorized by this subchapter, it shall be unlawful for any person knowingly or intentionally—

(1)   to manufacture, distribute, or dispense, or possess with intent to manufacture, distribute, or dispense, a controlled substance * * *

21 U.S. C. § 844. Penalties for simple possession

(a)   Unlawful acts; penalties

It shall be unlawful for any person knowingly or intentionally to possess a controlled substance unless such substance was obtained directly, or pursuant to a valid prescription or order, from a practitioner, while acting in the course of his professional practice, or except as otherwise authorized by this subchapter or subchapter II.

21 C.F.R. § 1308.11, Sched. I(23, 31, 58)

(d)   Hallucinogenic substances. Unless specifically excepted or unless listed in another schedule, any material, compound, mixture, or preparation, which contains any quantity of the following hallucinogenic substances, or which contains any of its salts, isomers, and salts of isomers whenever the existence of such salts, isomers, and salts of isomers is possible within the specific chemical designation (for purposes of this paragraph only, the term "isomer" includes the optical, position and geometric isomers):

(23) Marihuana * * *

(31) Tetrahydrocannabinols * * *

Meaning tetrahydrocannabinols naturally contained in a plant of the genus Cannabis (cannabis plant), as well as synthetic equivalents of the substances contained in the cannabis plant, or in the resinous extractives of such plant, and/or synthetic substances, derivatives, and their isomers with similar chemical structure and pharmacological activity to those substances contained in the plant, such as the following:

1 cis or trans tetrahydrocannabinol, and their optical isomers

6 cis or trans tetrahydrocannabinol, and their optical isomers

3, 4 cis or trans tetrahydrocannabinol, and its optical isomers

(Because nomenclature of these substances is not internationally standardized, compounds of these structures, regardless of numerical designation of atomic positions covered.) * * *

(58) Marihuana Extract * * *

Meaning an extract containing one or more cannabinoids that has been derived from any plant of the genus Cannabis, other than the separated resin (whether crude or purified) obtained from the plant.

NOTES AND QUESTIONS

1.   **Scope of the CSA.** Does the CSA recognize a federal authority to regulate purely intrastate and personal use or possession? Are local law enforcement officers obligated under the CSA to seize marijuana from someone who is acting in accordance with state law?

2.   **Limitations on financial backing.** What problems might a marijuana dispensary encounter when seeking financial backing? What concerns would a banking institution consider before agreeing to assist a dispensary?

3.   **Ethical issues.** Are there ethical issues that an attorney would face in rendering legal advice to a cannabis business?

B. AUTHORITY AND SCOPE OF CONTROLLED SUBSTANCES ACT

In *Gonzales v. Raich*, 545 U.S. 1 (2005), the Court faced constitutional challenges to enforcing the Controlled Substances Act against two medical marijuana users in California. The most serious challenge was that enforcement against them violated the Commerce Clause. The discussion of that challenge appears in Chapter 8, Constitutional Issues. The following section of the *Raich* opinion provides the historical background leading to adoption of the CSA.

GONZALES V. RAICH
United States Supreme Court
545 U.S. 1 (2005)

STEVENS, J.

[For the facts of the case, see Chapter 8, Constitutional Issues]

II

Shortly after taking office in 1969, President Nixon declared a national "war on drugs." As the first campaign of that war, Congress set out to enact legislation that would consolidate various drug laws on the books into a comprehensive statute, provide meaningful regulation over legitimate sources of drugs to prevent diversion into illegal channels, and strengthen law enforcement tools against the traffic in illicit drugs. That effort culminated in the passage of the Comprehensive Drug Abuse Prevention and Control Act of 1970.

This was not, however, Congress' first attempt to regulate the national market in drugs. Rather, as early as 1906 Congress enacted federal legislation imposing labeling regulations on medications and prohibiting the manufacture or shipment of any adulterated or misbranded drug traveling in interstate commerce. Aside from these labeling restrictions, most domestic drug regulations prior to 1970 generally came in the guise of revenue laws, with the Department of the Treasury serving as the Federal Government's primary enforcer. For example, the primary drug control law, before being repealed by the passage of the CSA, was the Harrison Narcotics Act of 1914 (repealed 1970). The Harrison Act sought to exert control over the possession and sale of narcotics, specifically cocaine and opiates, by requiring producers, distributors, and purchasers to register with the Federal Government, by assessing taxes against parties so registered, and by regulating the issuance of prescriptions.

Marijuana itself was not significantly regulated by the Federal Government until 1937 when accounts of marijuana's addictive qualities and physiological effects, paired with dissatisfaction with enforcement efforts at state and local levels, prompted Congress to pass the Marihuana Tax Act (repealed 1970). Like the Harrison Act, the Marihuana Tax Act did not outlaw the possession or sale of marijuana outright. Rather, it imposed registration and reporting requirements for all individuals importing, producing, selling, or dealing in marijuana, and required the payment of annual taxes in addition to transfer taxes whenever the drug changed hands. Moreover, doctors wishing to prescribe marijuana for medical purposes were required to comply with rather burdensome administrative requirements. Noncompliance exposed traffickers to severe federal penalties, whereas compliance would often subject them to prosecution under state law. Thus, while the Marihuana Tax Act did not declare the drug illegal per se, the onerous administrative requirements, the prohibitively expensive taxes, and the risks attendant on compliance practically curtailed the marijuana trade.

Then in 1970, after declaration of the national "war on drugs," federal drug policy underwent a significant transformation. A number of noteworthy events precipitated this policy shift. First, in *Leary v. United States*, 395 U.S. 6 (1969), this Court held certain provisions of the Marihuana Tax Act and other narcotics legislation unconstitutional. Second, at the end of his term, President Johnson fundamentally reorganized the federal drug control agencies. The Bureau of Narcotics, then housed in the Department of the Treasury, merged with the Bureau of Drug Abuse Control, then housed in the Department of Health, Education, and Welfare (HEW), to create the Bureau of Narcotics and Dangerous Drugs, currently housed in the Department of Justice. Finally, prompted by a perceived need to consolidate the growing number of piecemeal drug laws and to enhance federal drug enforcement powers, Congress enacted the Comprehensive Drug Abuse Prevention and Control Act.

Title II of that Act, the CSA, repealed most of the earlier antidrug laws in favor of a comprehensive regime to combat the international and interstate traffic in illicit drugs. The main objectives of the CSA were to conquer drug abuse and to control the legitimate and illegitimate traffic in controlled substances. Congress was particularly concerned with the need to prevent the diversion of drugs from legitimate to illicit channels.

To effectuate these goals, Congress devised a closed regulatory system making it unlawful to manufacture, distribute, dispense, or possess any controlled substance except in a manner authorized by the CSA. The CSA categorizes all controlled substances into five schedules. The drugs are grouped together based on their accepted medical uses, the potential for abuse, and their psychological and physical effects on the body. Each schedule is associated with a distinct set of controls regarding the manufacture, distribution, and use of the substances listed therein. The CSA and its implementing regulations set forth strict requirements regarding registration, labeling and packaging, production quotas, drug security, and recordkeeping.

In enacting the CSA, Congress classified marijuana as a Schedule I drug. This preliminary classification was based, in part, on the recommendation of the Assistant Secretary of HEW "that marihuana be retained within schedule I at least until the completion of certain studies now underway." Schedule I drugs are categorized as such because of their high potential for abuse, lack of any accepted medical use, and absence of any accepted safety for use in medically supervised treatment. These three factors, in varying gradations, are also used to categorize drugs in the other four schedules. For example, Schedule II substances also have a high potential for abuse which may lead to severe psychological or physical dependence, but unlike Schedule I drugs, they have a currently accepted medical use. By classifying marijuana as a Schedule I drug, as opposed to listing it on a lesser schedule, the manufacture, distribution, or possession of marijuana became a criminal offense, with the sole exception being use of the drug as part of a Food and Drug Administration preapproved research study.

The CSA provides for the periodic updating of schedules and delegates authority to the Attorney General, after consultation with the Secretary of Health and Human Services, to add, remove, or transfer substances to, from, or between schedules. Despite considerable efforts to reschedule marijuana, it remains a Schedule I drug.

NOTES AND QUESTIONS

1. **Keeping marijuana a Schedule I drug.** As Justice Stevens indicated in *Raich*, the CSA's classification of marijuana as a Schedule I drug was preliminary until completion of scientific studies underway at that time. As indicated above, President Nixon opposed rescheduling marijuana. Because the Federal Bureau of Narcotics had become part of the Justice Department, Nixon's Attorney General John Mitchell was able to keep marijuana as a Schedule I drug.

2. **Marijuana's long history as medicine.** Is marijuana properly characterized as a Schedule I drug? Proponents of medical marijuana argue that history provides ample support that marijuana has effective medical uses. They point to mention of marijuana for medical uses as early as 2737 B.C. in China when "it was recommended . . . for female weaknesses, beriberi, constipation, absent mindedness and surgical anesthesia." In reviewing medical literature from the nineteenth century alone, the Subcommittee on Alcoholism & Narcotics, U.S. Dep't of Health, Educ., and Welfare, 92d Cong., Report on Marijuana and Health 53–54 (1971) [hereinafter Report on Marijuana and Health] cited numerous therapeutic uses for marijuana. As summarized in Michael Vitiello, *Proposition 215: De Facto Legalization of Pot and the Shortcomings of Democracy,* 31 U. Mich. J. L. Reform 707, 749 (1998), "Marijuana was officially listed in the *United States Pharmacopoeia* in 1850, and it was routinely prescribed until the late 1930s. Before the 1937 Marihuana Tax Act was passed, physicians could prescribe 28 pharmaceutical preparations containing cannabis."

More recent reports add increasing support to proponents' claims of health benefits. We revisit the health benefits in Chapter 18 Medical Issues. For now, understanding that marijuana appears to have medical benefits and that it is nonetheless a Schedule I drug is important, as developed immediately below.

3. Procedure to reschedule. As indicated above, initially including marijuana as a Schedule I drug was provisional. The expectation was that further study would determine whether it belonged in Schedule I. The Nixon administration kept it in Schedule I. That raises an important legal question: how does a drug get rescheduled? The following notes pick up some of the issues that have arisen in litigation aimed at rescheduling marijuana.

4. Specific procedures to reschedule. Marijuana might be rescheduled in one of two ways. Congress might simply change the law making it a Schedule I drug. The other way in which marijuana might be rescheduled would be by the Drug Enforcement Agency.

5. Specific efforts to reschedule. In *Marijuana Law in a Nutshell*, Mark K. Osbeck and Howard Bromberg summarized legislative efforts to reschedule marijuana:

> Since 1981 numerous bills have been introduced to Congress, mostly in the House of Representatives, to reschedule marijuana; all died quietly in committee. Recently, however rescheduling bills have been introduced into the Senate, a more significant step. For example in 2015 Senator Bernie Sanders introduced Senate Bill 2237, "Ending Marijuana Prohibition" Act. This is a far-reaching bill, as it proposes removing marijuana from any of the five CSA schedules. The bill received no-cosponsors and is unlikely ever to move forward. (This was also the position of Gary Johnson, who was the Libertarian Party candidate for president in 2016.)

> The Compassionate Access, Research Expansion, and Respect States Act (CARERS Act), S. 683; H.R. 1538 is the most important marijuana reform legislation introduced in Congress. Besides strong bipartisan support, it emphasized the therapeutic value of marijuana—clearly the most popular tack and the most likely area of reform: legitimating state legalization of medical marijuana.

> The CARERS Act was introduced in March 2015 by three senators across the political spectrum, Cory Booker and Kirsten Gillibrand, Democrats, and Rand Paul, Republican as S. 683. Accompanying legislation was introduced into the House as H.R. 1538. As of June 2016, the House bill had 36 co-sponsors, reflecting a broad coalition, geographically and ideologically.

> The aim of the CARERS Act is to "extend the principle of federalism to State drug policy, provide access to medical marijuana, and enable research into the medical properties of marijuana." It transfers marijuana from Schedule I to Schedule II status. It codifies the Department of Justice non-enforcement memoranda,[1] in that it

---

[1] Memorandum for Selected U.S. Attorneys from David W. Ogden, Deputy Att'y Gen., Re: Investigations and Prosecutions in States Authorizing the Medical Use of Marijuana 1–3 (Oct. 19, 2009), *available at* https://www.justice.gov/sites/default/files/opa/legacy/2009/10/19/medical-

forbids enforcement of the CSA against persons who act in compliance with state marijuana laws. It prohibits regulators from punishing federally chartered banks for conducting marijuana-related business. It expands research opportunities and allows VA physicians to provide access to marijuana for veterans. Finally, it removes cannabidiol (CBD) as a controlled substance if containing less than 0.3% of THC—which would allow use of the medically promising, non-intoxicating oil sold under such brands as "Charlotte's Web."

Whatever the fate of the CARERS Act, it indicates the manner in which Congress is most likely to reform marijuana law: by allowing the states to serve as "laboratories of social change" as to medical and recreational marijuana, removing onerous federal restrictions on legal marijuana businesses, expanding access to marijuana by researchers, and allowing veterans with post-traumatic stress disorder access to medical marijuana options in the Veterans Administration health system.

Marijuana Law in a Nutshell (West 2017) at 473–75.

6. Modern efforts to reschedule. A more limited version of the bill was introduced in June, 2017 as the CARERS Act of 2017, S. 1374; H.R. 2920. While the 2017 version would still shield those who act in accordance with state law, it does not contain the banking and rescheduling provisions found in the previous Act. The co-sponsors of the House bill, nine Republicans and ten Democrats, reflect the continued bipartisan support for reform.

7. Changing attitudes about medicinal benefits. While the CARERS Act has yet to become law, it reflects a changing political climate surrounding legalization of marijuana. What has changed, say, since the Reagan years and the War on Drugs that his administration waged? Why has the CARERS Act not become law yet? Why does CARERS Act draw bipartisan support in a period when Congress divides along party lines on most issues?

8. Efficacy of rescheduling. From the perspective of individuals supporting legalization of marijuana generally, what is the advantage of the CARERS Act over mere rescheduling of marijuana from Schedule I, say to Schedule II? Framed differently, if efforts to reschedule marijuana are successful, would that mean individuals who want to purchase marijuana be able to do so?

9. DEA and hardball. The second method for rescheduling marijuana is through the executive branch. Specifically, the DEA has the authority to make an administrative decision to reschedule marijuana. The effort to convince the DEA to reschedule marijuana is a fascinating topic worth

---

marijuana.pdf; Memorandum for All U.S. Attorneys from James M. Cole, Deputy Att'y Gen., Re: Guidance Regarding Marijuana Enforcement 2–3 (Aug. 29, 2013), *available at* https://www.justice.gov/iso/opa/resources/3052013829132756857467.pdf.

extensive consideration. We cover early efforts to do so in the next subsection and more recent efforts in Chapter 10.

10. Attorney General Sessions and marijuana. In January 2018, Attorney General Sessions announced that the federal government would no longer follow the Cole Memorandum issued during the Obama Presidency. That sent shockwaves through the marijuana industry. Many members of Congress have begun to push back, often for the first time expressing support for efforts to legalize medical marijuana. Here is one of many articles describing changes in the politics surrounding the federal ban on marijuana. Alexandra Oliveira & Alison Spann, *Republican Lawmakers Optimistic About Passing Cannabis Legislation in 2018,* http://thehill.com/video/lawmaker-interviews/371854-republican-lawmakers-optimistic-about-passing-cannabis-legislation.

C. SCHEDULING MARIJUANA

Many observers of our legal system are surprised to learn that the agency in charge of enforcing drug laws has the authority to decide how it should schedule a particular drug. Some scholars and lawyers are critical of the DEA's power over not only enforcement but also scheduling. Seemingly, it sets up a conflict of interest: the DEA has benefitted from the War on Drugs, adding billions to its budget over the many years of that war. Rescheduling marijuana seemingly reduces the need for some of the DEA's enforcement capacity. In addition, the very agency members who have argued for the need to enforce marijuana laws because it causes social harm seem ill-equipped to rethink their position. Nevertheless, that is within the DEA's prerogative.

Under federal law, the Attorney General makes the decision to reschedule a drug listed in the CSA. But federal law also gives the Attorney General the authority to delegate the rescheduling decision to the DEA. It has done so. See 21 U.S.C. § 871(a), 28 C.F.R. § 0.100(b). Interested parties may petition the DEA to reschedule marijuana, at which point, the agency refers the matter to Health and Human Services. The matter is referred to the Food and Drug Administration for its input. The FDA provides medical input and refers the matter back to the DEA. It then evaluates all relevant data to determine whether to reschedule marijuana.

Federal courts play a role in the process as well. As with the administrative scheme, the role of the courts is complicated. That is explained more fully in the cases below and in the notes following those cases. The first significant litigation began on May 18, 1972, when the National Organization for the Reform of Marijuana Law (NORML) petitioned to have marijuana removed from Schedule I. It asked that no restriction be imposed or alternatively that it be rescheduled and placed in Schedule V, allowing only minimal control. The Director of the DEA's predecessor, the Bureau of Narcotics and Dangerous Drugs, even refused to accept the petition. That set the stage for protracted litigation.

NAT'L ORG. FOR THE REFORM OF MARIJUANA LAWS V. INGERSOLL
United States Court of Appeals for the D.C. Circuit
497 F.2d 654 (D.C. Cir. 1974)

LEVENTHAL, J.

This case is before us on a petition for review of the rejection of a petition which sought to initiate a rule-making proceeding looking toward a change in the control applicable to marihuana under the Controlled Substances Act.

The rule-making petition was filed May 18, 1972, by The National Organization for the Reform of Marijuana Laws (NORML) and other organizations concerned with the Federal Government's treatment of the marihuana problem. The petitioners requested that respondent remove marihuana from control under the Act, or in the alternative, transfer marihuana from Schedule I to Schedule V in the control scheme established by that Act.

The rule-making petition was filed with, and the petition in this court named as respondent, the Director of the Bureau of Narcotics and Dangerous Drugs, to whom the Attorney General had delegated his authority under the Act. We remand for further proceedings.

A.   The Rejection of the Rule-making Petition

The response to the petition reflects some official confusion. We are asked to review the decision dated September 1, 1972, published in the Federal Register of September 7 that the petition was not accepted for filing on the ground that respondent 'was not authorized to institute proceedings for the rule requested.' He specified in this connection the provisions of the Act and its legislative history which he relied upon as the basis for his opinion; namely, that by virtue of Section 201(d) of the Act, 21 U.S.C. § 811(d), he was required to establish the controls appropriate to carry out obligations under the Single Convention on Narcotic Drugs, 1961, 18 U.S.T. 1407 (1967) ('Single Convention') and that these obligations insofar as marihuana is concerned precluded consideration of either removing marihuana from all schedules or transferring it from Schedule I to Schedule V.

The petition in this court was filed on September 12.

B.   Basic Authority to Decontrol Substances or Transfer to Different Schedules

The Act's classification scheme was a cardinal feature of the effort by Congress to rationalize the Federal Government's control programs for dangerous drugs. The Act's five Schedules define classes of drugs and substances pursuant to criteria set in terms of dangers and benefits of the drugs. Differences in consequences and sanctions attach to the differences in classification. For example, the offense of distribution is a felony as to Class I drugs, a misdemeanor as to Class V drugs.

Congress contemplated that the classification set forth in the Act as originally passed would be subject to continuing review by the executive officials concerned, notably in the Department of Justice and the Department of Health, Education and Welfare. Provision was made for further consideration, one taking into account studies and data not available to Congress when the Act was passed in 1970. Section 202 of the CSA, 21 U.S.C. § 812, establishing the schedules of controlled substances, provides that 'such schedules shall initially consist of the substances listed.' Subsection (c) provides 'Schedules I, II, III, IV and V shall, unless and until amended pursuant to (21 U.S.C. § 811) consist of the following drugs . . . .' In subsection (a) of § 201 of the Act, 21 U.S.C. § 811, Congress provides that the Attorney General shall apply the provisions of the Act to the controlled substances listed in the schedules (in § 202) and other drugs added to such schedule, and 'may, by rule,' add substances to a schedule, transfer them between schedules, or 'remove any drug or other substance from the schedules.'

Section 201(a) of the Act, 21 U.S.C. § 811(a), provides that such rules shall be made on the record after opportunity for hearing, pursuant to the rulemaking procedures prescribed by 5 U.S.C. ch. 5, subch. II. It further provides that proceedings for adding, transferring, or deleting substances may be initiated by the Director on his own motion, at the request of the Secretary of Health, Education, and Welfare, or on the petition of any interested party. The Act provides that the Attorney General, before initiating proceedings to either control a substance or to remove one from the schedules, shall 'request from the Secretary (of HEW) a scientific and medical evaluation, and his recommendations'. The Secretary is directed to consider certain factors listed in § 201(c) pharmacological effect, risk to the public health, psychic or psychological dependence. He is also directed to consider any scientific or medical considerations involved in other listed factors—such as actual or relative potential for abuse; history and current pattern of abuse; scope, duration and significance of abuse. The statute provides that the Secretary's recommendations 'shall be binding on the Attorney General as to such scientific and medical matters, and if the Secretary recommends that a drug or other substance not be controlled, the Attorney General shall not control the drug or other substance.' § 201(b) CSA, 21 U.S.C. § 811(b).

Put in larger setting, the provisions for modification of Schedules betoken the same approach of ongoing research, study, and supplemental consideration that characterize other provisions. The Controlled

Substances Act is the short title for Title II (Controls and Enforcement) of the Comprehensive Drug Abuse Prevention and Control Act of 1970. Other provisions of the legislation provided for studies and researches by HEW or contracting agencies, for coordination of ongoing studies and programs in the White House under the Special Action Office for Drug Abuse, and for establishment. The House Report recommending that marihuana be listed in Schedule I notes that this was the recommendation of HEW 'at least until the completion of certain studies now under way,' and projects that the Presidential Commission's recommendations 'will be of aid in determining the appropriate disposition of this question in the future.' H.R.Rep.No. 91-1444 (Part 1), 91st Cong., 2d Sess. (1970) at p. 13.

The Executive is aware of its general authority under the Act to modify the classification initially set by Congress, and indeed has exercised that authority, as in the transfer of amphetamines from Schedule III to Schedule II.

The Executive has a corollary responsibility to give appropriate consideration to petitions for reclassification. And, indeed, certain petitions have been designated for official consideration. The respondent's action in declining to accept the petition filed May 18, 1972, does not confront us with a supposed prerogative to reject any petitions before considering them. The action was based on the ground that outstanding treaty commitments preclude any executive relief, and that becomes the crucial question before the court.

We pass by a subsidiary contention that even if there are current treaty obligations, the executive officials have a duty to consider the petition toward the objective of possible modification of legislative or treaty action. However, even this issue is one that should not be determined prior to a focusing on the major issue, the nature of treaty obligations.

C.   The Issue of the Requirement of Treaty Obligations

Government counsel say that unless marihuana is subject to the restrictions imposed by § 306 of the Act (21 U.S.C. § 826), applicable only to Schedules I and II substances, the United States will be unable to carry out its obligations under Article 21 and related provisions of the Convention. As we point out later, this was not made the subject of focused discussion and consideration in respondent's decision.

Petitioners assert that the treaty, the Single Convention on Narcotic Drugs, does not regulate marihuana as such, that it regulates 'cannabis' and 'cannabis resin,' and these are carefully defined so as to be inapplicable to the leaves of the cannabis plant. They say that the question of removing the leaves from the controls of the Act should be referred to the Secretary of Health, Education and Welfare and that rule-making proceedings should be instituted.

The convention does not specify any mandatory controls the parties must adopt as to the leaves. The petitioners claim that the official commentary makes clear that the Convention permits use of the leaves for recreational purposes.

Government counsel say that respondent did not deal with the 'leaves' question presented to this court by petitioners, and that this court should affirm respondent's action with permission to petitioners to file a new application under the Act. The Government's brief says the application sought only the removal or transfer of 'marihuana' as that term is defined in the Act. We have some difficulties with this procedural approach. It is not at all unusual for persons seeking governmental action—from any of the branches—to pray for the maximum desired, or such other relief as may be deemed appropriate. To say that this may act as a disqualification from obtaining more limited relief is to strain ordinary conceptions of fair procedure, in the absence of an express warning or alert.

Moreover, we are uneasy that respondent's own unorthodox procedural devices may have contributed to a procedural impasse and a non-responsive discussion on different planes of discourse.

Respondent refused to accept the petition for filing. The outright rejection of the filing of a petition is an executive or administrative action that has only a narrow role. A 'rejection' of a party's filing is a 'peremptory' action, soundly used only in 'the clear case of a filing that patently is either deficient in form or a substantive nullity.' *Municipal Light Boards v. FPC*, 146 U.S.App.D.C. 294, 298 (1971).

In this case there is no procedural defect or failure to comply with a clear-cut requirement of law. What accounted for respondent's action is his conclusion on the merits that the petition sought action inconsistent with treaty commitment. Even if we accept the argument now put forward by Government counsel as to the relationship between Article 21 of the Treaty and § 306 of the CSA, the point is not obvious or clear-cut, but requires a reflective consideration and analysis. That kind of determination should have been reflected in an action denying the petition on the merits, an action that can be taken without convoking a formal rule-making proceeding when issues of law are decisive and can be decided without taking testimony or hearing the views of others involved. The matter is not critical so far as judicial review is concerned, as appears from our order * * * designating the case as one pending before us on a petition to review a 'final decision,' filed under § 507 of the Act. But if this had been handled properly by respondent as a decision on the merits, petitioners could have refined their alternative position in the light of respondent's decision.

Instead they considered respondent's 'rejection' of even a filing to signal short shrift for a serious presentation. It was not the kind of agency action that promoted the kind of interchange and refinement of views that is the lifeblood of a sound administrative process.

More difficult of analysis is the assertion in the Government brief that the 'leaves' argument is an 'academic after-thought.' The petition filed with the Department of Justice in May 1972 was certainly primarily concerned with marihuana in the large. It was filed within two months after the release of Marihuana: A Signal of Misunderstanding, the title given to the First Report by the National Commission on Marihuana and Drug Abuse, chaired by Governor Shafer. It relied on that report in good measure, in some respects relying less on the Shafer Report itself than on what petitioners called 'the more objective Appendix' for 'an accurate picture of the scientific evidence.' The contention was that marihuana does not meet the criteria in the Act for Schedules I and II substances, that, e.g., it has neither an actual nor relative 'high potential for abuse.'

The respondent took the petition as addressed to all marihuana plant material as used, including the flowers, and his decision quoted from the petition as follows: 'In summary, the plant material of what is commonly called marihuana in the United States consists of a mixture of crushed leaves, flowers and twigs of the Indian Hemp plant, an annual belonging to the single species of Cannabis sativa.'

This sentence appears in the petition in passing, as a preliminary to discussion of the state of current knowledge on marihuana. It does not fairly indicate that petitioners were implacably limited in terms of relief sought to the plant as a whole. When the respondent set forth his position on treaty obligation, he did not say one word about the presentation in the petition on the international obligations issue, where the petition expressly points out that leaves are not covered by the treaty and adds: 'The narrow definition of marihuana and the attendant limitations on mandatory regulations, are significant since it is the leaves of the marihuana plant that are commonly used in the United States.'

Obviously, this court is in no position to decide this case in its present posture. Having in mind our doubts as to the propriety of the respondent's action in rejecting even the filing of the petition, we think the optimum course, in the interest of justice, 28 U.S.C. § 2106, and a sound disposition, is to remand the case to respondent for further consideration, to be denominated a consideration on the merits. This consideration will embrace the subject of removal or transfer of control of the leaves of the plant.

On the remand, respondent will also supply findings that will sharpen and clarify the issue whether control under Schedules I and II is required as to the flowers. The decision under review rightly refers to § 201(d) of the Act as establishing a basis for control under the Act if required by treaty obligations. But the decision seems to go further and say that if some control is required by treaty then the decision of which Schedule is appropriate is a matter for the exclusive decision of the respondent as the delegee of the Attorney General. This is a matter that gives us pause. The respondent seems to be saying that even though the treaty does not require more control than schedule V provides, he can on his own say-so and without any reason insist on Schedule I. We doubt that this was the intent of Congress.

On appeal to this court, Government counsel argue that the structures of the treaty (Art. 21) and pertinent statutes (CSA § 306) are such that the only way to satisfy treaty obligations is by control under Schedule I. But this is argument of counsel, which cannot take the place of reasoned decision-making by the official or agency concerned. And petitioners join issue on the meaning of the Treaty and the nature of the required mechanics.

The matter is not one on which the expertise of respondent is exclusive, and it would seem appropriate for the court to have the benefit of the views of sources in the State Department and the international organizations involved. If it should develop, as petitioners suggest, that there is latitude in treaty obligations depending on the country's assessment of the health aspects of the problem involved, a substantial question would arise whether the Department of Justice may insist on making these determinations without obtaining the appraisal of the Department of Health, Education and Welfare.

Our conclusion that such a remand is appropriate is fortified by the reorganization and redelegation of authority within the Department of Justice, under which the pertinent functions of the Attorney General now have been transferred to the Director of the Drug Enforcement Administration, an official who can provide a new look and a hard look at the questions raised by the petition.

The case is remanded for further proceedings not inconsistent with this opinion.

So ordered.

NOTES AND QUESTIONS

1. **The government's early position on rescheduling.** What do you think of the government's position on the merits? The substantive argument focused on whether rescheduling marijuana would be consistent with obligations under the 1961 Single Convention on Narcotic Drugs. For an in depth discussion of that issue, see Chapter 6 Status under International Law.

2. **More on the government's early position on rescheduling.** What do you think of the government's procedural position? That is, it rejected the petition. From the court's perspective, what was wrong with the government's proposed procedural disposition of the case? Did the court's response surprise you? If not, can you see reasons why the government might proceed as it did?

3.   **Ongoing litigation.** What would you expect the litigants to do next? Would you expect NORML to continue its efforts to reschedule marijuana?

NAT'L ORG. FOR THE REFORM OF MARIJUANA LAWS V. DRUG ENFORCEMENT ADMIN.

United States Court of Appeals for the D.C. Circuit
559 F.2d 735 (D.C. Cir. 1977)

J. SKELLY WRIGHT, J.

The present case represents yet another phase in the ongoing controversy between petitioner National Organization for the Reform of Marijuana Laws (NORML) and respondent Drug Enforcement Administration (DEA), an agency within the Department of Justice. NORML has been seeking to effect a change in the controls applicable to marihuana under the Controlled Substances Act of 1970 (CSA or Act). Respondent DEA has resisted those efforts by citing United States treaty obligations under the Single Convention on Narcotic Drugs, opened for signature March 30, 1961. A brief overview of the pertinent portions of those laws is necessary to a meaningful discussion of the background of this litigation.

[Part I of the opinion reviewed the history of the CSA, tracking the discussion in *Nat'l Org. for the Reform of Marijuana Laws v. Ingersoll*. Part II discussed the 1961 Single Convention on Narcotic Drugs.]

III. HISTORY OF THE LITIGATION

A.   The first court case

On May 18, 1972 petitioner NORML and two other interested parties petitioned the Director of the Bureau of Narcotics and Dangerous Drugs (BNDD) to initiate proceedings to remove marihuana from control under the CSA or, alternatively, to transfer the substance from Schedule I to Schedule V. On September 1, 1972 the Director, as delegee of the Attorney General, refused to accept the petition for filing. He stated that decontrol or reclassification of marihuana would violate United States treaty obligations under the Single Convention. He concluded that Section 201(d), 21 U.S.C. § 811(d), gave him sole authority over the scheduling of substances controlled by treaty, without regard to the referral and rulemaking procedures specified in Section 201(a)–(c).

NORML filed a petition for review with this court and, on January 15, 1974, the court reversed and remanded for consideration on the merits. *National Organization for Reform of Marijuana Laws (NORML) v. Ingersoll*, 162 U.S.App.D.C. 67 (1974). The court's opinion inveighed against an agency's outright rejection of the filing of a petition, except in narrowly circumscribed situations:

In this case there is no procedural defect or failure to comply with a clear-cut requirement of law. What accounted for respondent's action is his conclusion on the merits that the petition sought action inconsistent with treaty commitment. That kind of determination should have been reflected in an action denying the petition on the merits. *Id.* at 72.

In delineating the areas of interest to be addressed on remand, the court indicated that, in view of the treaty's exclusion of separated leaves from the terms "cannabis" and "cannabis resin," the agency should separately consider rescheduling the leaves of the marihuana plant. In addition, the court suggested that the proceeding on remand be divided into two phases:

> In the first phase, the Department of Justice could consider whether there is any latitude (to reschedule) consistent with treaty obligations, and herein receive expert testimony limited to this treaty issue. The second phase would arise only if some latitude were found, and would consider how the pertinent executive discretion should be exercised. *Id.* at 661 n.17.

In connection with this "second phase" the court commented on the Director's argument that under Section 201(d) scheduling of marihuana was a matter entrusted to his sole discretion as delegee of the Attorney General:

> This is a matter that gives us pause. The respondent seems to be saying that even though the treaty does not require more control than Schedule V provides, he can on his own say-so and without any reason insist on schedule I. We doubt that this was the intent of Congress. *Id.* at 73–74.

B.   The proceedings on remand.

On June 26, 1974 DEA published a notice in the Federal Register announcing that the agency was prepared to hold a hearing to determine the regulatory controls necessary to satisfy the Single Convention. In response to this notice NORML and the American Public Health Association requested a "phase one" hearing on this issue. They specifically asked that the hearing include an inquiry as to whether separated leaves and/or seeds of the marihuana plant could be removed from CSA Schedule I.

From January 28 through January 30, 1975 a hearing was held before Administrative Law Judge (ALJ) Parker. NORML called two witnesses, Mr. Lawrence Hoover and Dr. Joel Fort, both of whom qualified as experts on the obligations imposed by the Single Convention. Respondent called two chemists, Mr. Philip Porto and Dr. Carlton Turner, as well as DEA's Chief Counsel, Mr. Donald Miller, who qualified as an expert on the treaty issue. The parties introduced numerous exhibits.

On May 21, 1975 ALJ Parker issued his report. He held that, consistent with the Single Convention, "cannabis" and "cannabis resin" as defined by the treaty could be rescheduled to CSA Schedule II, cannabis leaves could be rescheduled to CSA Schedule V, and cannabis seeds and "synthetic cannabis" could be decontrolled. He rejected respondent's interpretation of Section 201(d) and held that in the second phase of the rescheduling proceeding the agency should follow the referral and hearing procedures set forth in Section 201(a)–(c).

On appeal from ALJ Parker's order, DEA's Acting Administrator, Henry S. Dogin, denied NORML's petition for rescheduling "in all respects." 40 Fed.Reg. 44164, 44168 (1975). Turning first to the issue of United States treaty commitments, he held that cannabis and cannabis resin could be rescheduled to CSA Schedule II, separated cannabis leaves could be rescheduled to CSA Schedule III or IV, synthetic tetrahydrocannabinol (or THC) and seeds incapable of germination need not be controlled, but seeds capable of germination could not be decontrolled. He failed to specify the schedule that would satisfy the Single Convention with respect to seeds capable of germination. He did hold, however, that neither cannabis seeds incapable of germination nor synthetic THC were at issue in the proceeding.

After outlining the latitude within which various parts of the marihuana plant could be rescheduled, the Acting Administrator proceeded to determine how to exercise his discretion to reschedule. He examined a letter of April 14, 1975 from Dr. Theodore Cooper, Acting Assistant Secretary for Health. The letter, which was introduced at oral argument before ALJ Parker, states that there "is currently no accepted medical use of marihuana in the United States" and that there "is no approved New Drug Application" for marihuana on file with the Food and Drug Administration of HEW. Relying on this letter, the Acting Administrator concluded that marihuana could not be removed from CSA Schedule I. He stated that Schedule I "is the only schedule reserved for drugs without a currently accepted medical use in treatment in the United States." *Id.* at 44167. Because the letter from Dr. Cooper established that marihuana has no medical use, "no matter the weight of the scientific or medical evidence which petitioners might adduce, the Attorney General could not remove marihuana from Schedule I." *Id.*

Turning finally to the controversy over the interpretation of Section 201(d), the Acting Administrator stated:

> It is unnecessary to decide whether Section 201(d) requires the Attorney General to seek the views of HEW on a substance included in an international treaty. In the instance of marihuana he has done so and he has received a reply. *Id.* at 44165.42

C.   The present lawsuit.

On October 22, 1975 NORML filed with this court a petition for review of the Acting Administrator's order. Petitioner urges the court to reverse and remand the case for further proceedings to include referral of the rescheduling petition to the Secretary of HEW pursuant to Section 201(b)–(c) of the CSA. NORML agrees with ALJ Parker's conclusions as to the scheduling options left open by the Single Convention, except to the extent that he ruled out rescheduling cannabis and cannabis resin below CSA Schedule II.

Respondent proffers alternative arguments in defense of the Acting Administrator's decision to deny NORML's rescheduling petition and thereby perpetuate placement of marihuana in CSA Schedule I. Respondent alleges first that by virtue of Section 201(d) the referral and hearing procedures of Section 201(a)–(c) do not apply to drugs subject by treaty to international control. Accordingly, the decision whether to reschedule marihuana is entrusted to the Acting Administrator, as delegee of the Attorney General, and the only question open on review is whether his decision not to reschedule the drug is based on substantial evidence. Alternatively, respondent suggests that the Acting Administrator satisfied the referral and hearing requirements by basing his rescheduling decision on the letter from Dr. Cooper. Finally, although conceding in its brief and at oral argument that filing of a petition to reschedule synthetic THC would "require consideration by DEA." Respondent contends that reclassification of synthetic THC is not an issue in this proceeding.

IV. SCHEDULING DECISIONS UNDER SECTION 201

A.   Statutory construction of Section 201(d).

[Judge Wright rejected the DEA's Acting Administrator's argument that the United States' treaty obligations prevented it from rescheduling marijuana. For a further discussion, see Status under International Law, Chapter 6]

B.   Satisfaction of the referral and hearing procedures of Section 201(a)–(c).

As an alternative argument respondent contends and the Acting Administrator held that whatever the proper interpretation of Section 201(d), Dr. Cooper's letter satisfied the Section 201(b)–(c) requirement that the Acting Administrator refer the petition to the Secretary of HEW for medical and scientific findings and recommendations. The Acting Administrator premised his conclusion on the assumption that placement in CSA Schedule I is automatically required if the substance has no currently accepted medical use in the United States. Our analysis of the Act compels us to reject his finding.

The CSA makes clear that, upon referral by the Attorney General, the Secretary of HEW is required to consider a number of different factors in making his evaluations and recommendations. Section 201(b)–(c) specifies that the Secretary must consider "scientific evidence of (the substance's) pharmacological effect, if known"; "the state of current scientific knowledge regarding the drug or other substance"; "what, if any, risk there is to the public health"; the drug's "psychic or physiological dependence liability"; "whether the substance is an immediate precursor of a substance already controlled under this subchapter"; and any scientific or medical factors relating to the drug's "actual or relative potential for abuse," its "history and current pattern of abuse," and "scope, duration, and significance of abuse." The provision does not in any way qualify the Secretary's duty of evaluation. If, as respondent contends, a determination that the substance has no accepted medical use ends the inquiry, then presumably Congress would have spelled that out in its procedural guidelines. Its failure to do so indicates an intent to reserve to HEW a finely tuned balancing process involving several medical and scientific considerations. By shortcutting the referral procedures of Section 201(b)–(c) the Acting Administrator precluded the balancing process contemplated by Congress.

Admittedly, Section 202(b), 21 U.S.C. § 812(b), which sets forth the criteria for placement in each of the five CSA schedules, established medical use as the factor that distinguishes substances in Schedule II from those in Schedule I. However, placement in Schedule I does not appear to flow inevitably from lack of a currently accepted medical use. Like that of Section 201(c), the structure of Section 202(b) contemplates balancing of medical usefulness along with several other considerations, including potential for abuse and danger of dependence. To treat medical use as the controlling factor in classification decisions is to render irrelevant the other "findings" required by Section 202(b). The legislative history of the CSA indicates that medical use is but one factor to be considered, and by no means the most important one.

Moreover, DEA's own scheduling practices support the conclusion that substances lacking medical usefulness need not always be placed in Schedule I. At the hearing before ALJ Parker DEA's Chief Counsel, Donald Miller, testified that several substances listed in CSA Schedule II, including poppy straw, have no currently accepted medical use. He further acknowledged that marihuana could be rescheduled to Schedule II without a currently accepted medical use. Neither party offered any contrary evidence.

More importantly, even if lack of medical use is dispositive of a classification decision, we do not think the finding in this case was established in conformity with the statute. Dr. Cooper's letter is addressed to a member of DEA's legal staff, in response to the latter's inquiry; the letter was not solicited by the Acting Administrator, and it can hardly take the place of the elaborate referral machinery contemplated by Congress. The one-page letter makes conclusory statements without providing a basis for or explanation of its findings. It is unclear what Dr. Cooper means when he writes that marihuana has no currently accepted medical use. As a legal conclusion, his statement cannot be doubted: Placement in Schedule I creates a self-fulfilling prophecy because the drug can be used only for research purposes, and therefore is barred from general medical use. But if Dr. Cooper's statement is meant to reflect a scientific judgment as to the medicinal potential of marihuana, then the basis for his evaluation should be elaborated. Recent studies have yielded findings to the contrary: HEW's Fifth Annual Report to the U.S. Congress, Marihuana and Health (1975), devotes a chapter to the therapeutic aspects of marihuana, discovered through medical research. *Id.* ch. 9, at 117–127. Possible uses of marihuana include treatment of glaucoma, asthma, and epilepsy, and provision of "needed relief for cancer patients undergoing chemotherapy." *Id.* at 117. These promising findings were discussed by Dr. Fort in his testimony before ALJ Parker. Only a formal referral and hearing will allow due weight to be given to such findings. Accordingly, recognizing that it is our obligation as a court to ensure that the agency acts within statutory bounds, we hold that Dr. Cooper's letter was not an adequate substitute for the procedures enumerated in Section 201(a)–(c). The case must be remanded for further proceedings consistent with those statutory requirements.

NOTES AND QUESTIONS

1. **Critique of the government's position.** What was wrong with the government's position, according to Judge Wright? Is the government's position consistent with a commitment to a fair hearing process?

2. **A look back at the history of how marijuana got on Schedule I.** Think back to the discussion of how marijuana ended up as a Schedule I drug. During the legislative process that resulted in adoption of the CSA, marijuana ended up as a Schedule I drug as a compromise awaiting publication of the Shafer Commission report. It recommended decriminalizing marijuana possession. President Nixon ignored the recommendation. As developed below, marijuana has remained a Schedule I drug despite the historical accident that it ended up in that Schedule.

MARIJUANA SCHEDULING PETITION; DENIAL OF PETITION; REMAND

Drug Enforcement Administration
57 Fed. Reg. 10499 (March 22, 1992)

BONNER, ADMINISTRATOR.

SUMMARY: This is a final order of the Administrator of the Drug Enforcement Administration (DEA) concluding the plant material marijuana has no currently accepted medical use and denying the petition of the National Organization for Reform of Marijuana Laws (NORML) to reschedule marijuana from Schedule I to Schedule II of the Controlled Substances Act. * * *

Background

On December 21, 1989, the former Administrator of DEA, following rulemaking on the record, which included a hearing before an administrative law judge, issued a final order concluding the plant material marijuana has no currently accepted medical use, and denying the petition of NORML to reschedule marijuana from Schedule I to Schedule II of the Controlled Substances Act. 54 FR 63767. On April 26, 1991, the United States Court of Appeals for the District of Columbia Circuit remanded the matter to the Administrator for clarification of DEA's interpretation of the term "currently accepted medical use in treatment in the United States." *Alliance for Cannabis Therapeutics v. DEA*, 930 F.2d 936.

Following a review of the entire record in this matter, and a comprehensive re-examination of the relevant statutory standard, I conclude that marijuana has no currently accepted medical use and must remain in Schedule I. Further hearings are unnecessary since the record is extraordinarily complete, all parties had ample opportunity and wide latitude to present evidence and to brief all relevant issues, and the narrow question on remand centers exclusively on this Agency's legal interpretation of a statutorily-created standard.

Summary of the Decision

Does the marijuana plant have any currently accepted medical use in treatment in the United States, within the meaning of the Federal Controlled Substances Act, 21 U.S.C. 801, et seq.? Put simply, is marijuana good medicine for illnesses we all fear, such as multiple sclerosis (MS), glaucoma and cancer?

The answer might seem obvious based simply on common sense. Smoking causes lung cancer and other deadly diseases. Americans take their medicines in pills, solutions, sprays, shots, drops, creams and sometimes in suppositories, but never by smoking. No medicine prescribed for us today is smoked.

With a little homework, one can learn that marijuana has been rejected as medicine by the American Medical Association, the National Multiple Sclerosis Society, the American Glaucoma Society, the American Academy of Ophthalmology the American Cancer Society. Not one American health association accepts marijuana as medicine.

For the last half century, drug evaluation experts at the United States Food and Drug Administration (FDA) have been responsible for protecting

Americans from unsafe and ineffective new medicines. Relying on the same scientific standards used to judge all other drugs, FDA experts repeatedly have rejected marijuana for medical use.

Yet claims persist that marijuana has medical value. Are these claims true? What are the facts?

Between 1987 and 1988, DEA and NORML, under the guidance of an administrative law judge, collected all relevant information on this subject. Stacked together it stands nearly five feet high. Is there reliable scientific evidence that marijuana is medically effective, If it has medical value, do its benefits outweigh its risks? What do America's top medical and scientific experts say? Would they prescribe it for their patients, their families, their friends?

As the current Administrator of Drug Enforcement, and as a former United States District Judge, I have made a detailed review of the evidence in this record to find the answers.

There are significant short-term side effects and long-term risks linked to smoking marijuana. Marijuana is likely to be more cancer-causing than tobacco; damages brain cells; causes lung problems, such as bronchitis and emphysema; may weaken the body's antibacterial defenses in the lungs; lowers overall blood pressure, which could adversely affect the supply of blood to the head; causes sudden drops in blood pressure (orthostatic hypotension), rapid heart beat (tachycardia), and heart palpitations; suppresses luteinizing hormone secretion in women, which affects the production of progesterone, an important female hormone; causes anxiety and panic in some users because of its mind-altering effects; produces dizziness, trouble with thinking, trouble with concentrating, fatigue, and sleepiness; and impairs motor skills.

As a plant, marijuana can contain bacteria capable of causing serious infections in humans, such as salmonella enteritidis, Klebsiella pneumoniae, group D Streptoccoccus and pathogenic aspergillus. Several of these risks stand out. The immune systems of cancer patients are weakened by radiation and chemotherapy, leaving them susceptible to infection. If they experiment with marijuana to control nausea, they risk weakening their immune systems further and exposing themselves to the infection-causing bacteria in the plant. It is estimated, for example, that at Memorial Sloan-Kettering Cancer Center 60 patients die each year from pathogenic aspergillus infections.

Glaucoma patients face possible blindness caused by very high fluid pressures within their eyes. If they experiment with marijuana to lower their eye fluid pressure, it can cause dramatic drops in their blood pressure and reduce the blood supply to their heads. Glaucoma experts testified this reduced the blood supply to the optic nerves and could speed up, rather than slow down, their loss of eyesight.

MS, glaucoma and cancer patients who have undiagnosed heart problems risk heart palpitations, very rapid heart beats and sudden dramatic drops in blood pressure if they experiment with marijuana. For MS and glaucoma patients who must take medications for the rest of their lives, experimenting with marijuana poses the additional risks of lung cancer, emphysema, bladder cancer and leukemia.

Many risks remain unknown. Marijuana contains over 400 separately identified chemicals. No one knows all the effects of burning these chemicals together and inhaling the burnt mix. Are these risks outweighed by medical benefits?

There are scientific studies showing pure THC (Delta-9-Tetrahydrocannabinol), one of the many chemicals found in marijuana, has some effect in controlling nausea and vomiting. Pure THC is pharmaceutically made in a clean capsule form, called Marinol, and is available for use by the medical community.

Since marijuana contains THC, you might think marijuana also would be effective. However, the effect of taking a drug in combination with other chemicals is seldom the same as taking just the pure drug. As already noted, marijuana contains over 400 other chemicals, not just THC. There are no reliable scientific studies that show marijuana to be significantly effective in controlling nausea and vomiting. People refer to the Sallan study as proving marijuana's effectiveness. They are mistaken. The Sallan study involved pure THC, not marijuana. People refer to the Chang study to support marijuana's effectiveness. They also are mistaken. Doctor Chang tested the combination of pure THC and marijuana to treat nausea and vomiting. The preliminary results he got were probably due to the THC, not the marijuana. Because he tested the combination, we cannot tell just what effects can be attributed to marijuana alone. People cite a third study, done by Doctor Levitt, as proof marijuana is effective. They are mistaken. Doctor Levitt compared marijuana to THC in controlling nausea and vomiting, and he concluded that THC was the more effective drug.

During the 1970's and 1980's, a number of states set up research programs to give marijuana to cancer and glaucoma patients, on the chance it might help. Some people point to these programs as proof of marijuana's usefulness. Unfortunately, all research is not necessarily good scientific research. These state programs failed to follow responsible scientific methods. Patients took marijuana together with their regular medicines, so it is impossible to say whether marijuana helped them. Observations or results were not scientifically measured. Procedures were so poor that much critical research data were lost or never recorded. Although these programs were well-intentioned, they are not scientific proof of anything.

Those who say there are reliable scientific studies showing marijuana is an effective drug for treating nausea and vomiting are wrong. No such studies exist.

Our nation's top cancer experts reject marijuana for medical use. Doctor David S. Ettinger, a professor of oncology at the Johns Hopkins University School of Medicine, an author of over 100 scholarly articles on cancer treatment, and a nationally respected cancer expert, testified:

There is no indication that marijuana is effective in treating nausea and vomiting resulting from radiation treatment or other causes. No legitimate studies have been conducted which make such conclusions.

Doctor Richard J. Gralla, a professor of medicine at Cornell University Medical College, an associate attending physician at the Memorial Sloan-Kettering Cancer Center, and an expert in cancer research, testified:

Most experts would say, and our studies support, that the cannabinoids in general are not very effective against the major causes of nausea and vomiting.

Doctor Gralla added:

I have found that because of the negative side effects and problems associated with marijuana, most medical oncologists and researchers have little interest in marijuana for the treatment of nausea and vomiting in their patients.

Doctor John Laszlo, Vice President of Research for the American Cancer Society, an expert who has spent 37 years researching cancer treatments, and who has written a leading textbook on the subject, "Antiemetics and Cancer Chemotherapy," testified there is not enough scientific evidence to justify using marijuana to treat nausea and vomiting. Not one nationally-recognized cancer expert could be found to testify on marijuana's behalf.

[A discussion of studies relating to glaucoma is omitted].

No scientific studies have shown marijuana can reduce eye pressure over long periods of time.

No scientific studies have shown marijuana can save eyesight.

America's top glaucoma experts reject marijuana as medicine. Doctor Keith Green is a professor of Ophthalmology who serves, or has served, on the editorial boards of eight prestigious eye journals [and] has conducted extensive basic and clinical research using marijuana and THC to treat glaucoma patients. He has authored over 200 books or research articles in ophthalmology and is a highly respected expert on this subject. Doctor Green testified:

There is no scientific evidence that indicates that marijuana is effective in regulating the progression of symptoms associated with glaucoma. It is clear that there is no evidence that marijuana use prevents the progression of visual loss in glaucoma. The quantities of the drug required to reduce intraocular pressure in glaucoma sufferers are large, and would require the inhalation of at least six marijuana cigarettes each day. Smoking is not a desirable form of treatment for many reasons. (M)arijuana . . . has little potential future as a glaucoma medication.

Amputees and victims of MS can suffer from extreme muscle spasms. It is claimed marijuana is useful in treating spasticity. Three unusually small, inconclusive studies have tried using pure THC, not marijuana, to treat spasticity.

No scientific studies exist which test marijuana to relieve spasticity.

National experts on MS reject marijuana as medicine.

At this time, I am not aware of any legitimate medical research in which marijuana was used to treat the symptoms of multiple sclerosis. To conclude that marijuana is therapeutically effective without conducting rigorous testing would be professionally irresponsible.

[A discussion of experts testifying that marijuana does benefit MS patients is omitted]

The only favorable evidence that could be found by NORML and DEA consists of stories by marijuana users who claim to have been helped by the drug. Scientists call these stories anecdotes. They do not accept them as reliable proofs. The FDA's regulations, for example, provide that in deciding whether a new drug is a safe and effective medicine, "isolated case reports will not be considered." 21 CFR 314.126(e). Why do scientists consider stories from patients and their doctors to be unreliable?

First, sick people are not objective scientific observers, especially when it comes to their own health. We all have heard of the placebo effect. Patients have a tendency to respond to drugs as they believe is expected of them. Imagine how magnified this placebo effect can be when a suffering person experiments on himself, praying for some relief. Many stories no doubt are due to the placebo effect, not to any real medical effects of marijuana.

Second, most of the stories come from people who took marijuana at the same time they took prescription drugs for their symptoms. For example, Robert Randall claims marijuana has saved his sight, yet he has taken standard glaucoma drugs continuously since 1972. There is no objective way to tell from these stories whether it is marijuana that is helpful, or the proven, traditional medicines. Even these users can never know for sure. Third, any mind-altering drug that produces euphoria can make a sick person think he feels better. Stories from patients who claim marijuana helps them may be the result of the mind-altering effects of the drug, not the results of improvements in their conditions.

Fourth, long-time abusers of marijuana are not immune to illness. Many eventually get cancer, glaucoma, MS and other diseases. People who become dependent on mind-altering drugs tend to rationalize their behavior. They invent excuses, which they can come to believe, to justify their drug dependence. Stories of marijuana's benefits from sick people with a prior history of marijuana abuse may be based on rationalizations caused by drug dependence, not on any medical benefits caused by the drug. Robert Randall, for example, admits under oath to becoming a regular user in 1968, four years before he showed the first signs of, and was diagnosed as having, glaucoma. Since then he has smoked marijuana 8 to 10 times every day.

A century ago many Americans relied on stories to pick their medicines, especially from snake oil salesmen. Thanks to scientific advances and to the passage of the Federal Food, Drug and Cosmetic Act (FDCA) in 1906, 21 U.S.C. 301 et seq., we now rely on rigorous scientific proof to assure the safety and effectiveness of new drugs. Mere stories are not considered an acceptable way to judge whether dangerous drugs should be used as medicines.

There are doctors willing to testify that marijuana has medical uses. NORML found over a dozen to testify in this case. We have a natural tendency to believe doctors. We assume their opinions are entitled to respect. But what if a doctor is giving an opinion beyond his professional competence? Evaluating the safety and effectiveness of drugs is a specialized area. Does the doctor have this specialized expertise? Is he familiar with all the published scientific studies? Or is he improperly basing his opinion on mere stories or anecdotal evidence? Does he really know what he is talking about? Does he have a personal motive to exaggerate or lie? Questions like these led the United States Supreme Court, in 1973, to warn about the opinions of doctors concerning the value of drugs as medicine, when not supported by rigorous scientific testing,

(I)mpressions or beliefs of physicians, no matter how fervently held, are treacherous.

Nearly half the doctors who testified for NORML are psychiatrists. They do not specialize in treating or researching cancer, glaucoma or MS. One is a general practitioner who works as a wellness counselor at a health spa. Under oath he admits to using every illegal, mind-altering drug he has ever studied, and he prides himself on recommending drugs that would never be recommended by medical schools or reputable physicians. Another is a general practitioner who quit practicing in 1974. He admits he has not kept up on new medical and scientific information about marijuana for 18 years.

Only one of the doctors called by NORML is a nationally-recognized expert. Doctor John C. Merritt is a board-certified ophthalmologist and researcher who has authored articles on the use of marijuana and cannabinoids to reduce eye pressure. He is in private practice and sees mostly children who suffer from glaucoma. Doctor Merritt testified, "(M)arijuana is a highly effective IOP-lowering drug which may be of critical value to some glaucoma patients who, without marijuana, would progressively go blind." The last scientific study using marijuana in glaucoma patients, published by Doctor Merritt in 1979, concluded:

It is because of the frequency and severity with which the untoward events occurred that marijuana inhalation is not an ideal therapeutic modality for glaucoma patients.

One year later, in 1980, Doctor Merritt gave the following testimony, under oath, before the United States Congress, House Select Committee on Narcotics Abuse and Control:

For me to sit here and say that the lowering pressure effects occurred repeatedly, day in and day out, I have no data, and neither does anyone else, and that is the real crux of the matter. When we are talking about treating a disease like glaucoma, which is a chronic disease, the real issue is, does the marijuana repeatedly lower the intraocular pressure? I have shown you no studies, and to my knowledge there is no data to that effect.

Doctor Merritt was unable to explain, under oath, the contradictory positions he has taken on this subject.

Each of NORML's doctors testified his opinion is based on the published scientific studies. With one exception, none of them could identify under oath the scientific studies they swore they relied on. Only one had enough knowledge to discuss the scientific technicalities involved. Eventually, each one admitted he was basing his opinion on anecdotal evidence, on stories he heard from patients, and on his impressions about the drug.

Sadly, Doctor Ivan Silverberg, an oncologist from San Francisco, exaggerated while on the witness stand. At first he swore "there is voluminous medical research which shows marijuana is effective in easing nausea and vomiting." Pushed on cross-examination to identify this voluminous research, Doctor Silverberg replied, "Well, I'm going to have to back off a little bit from that." How far would Doctor Silverberg back off? Was he aware, at least, of the approximate number of scientific studies that have been done using marijuana to treat nausea? Under oath, he replied, "I would doubt very few. But, no, I'm not."

Beyond doubt, the claims that marijuana is medicine are false, dangerous and cruel.

Sick men, women and children can be fooled by these claims and experiment with the drug. Instead of being helped, they risk serious side effects. If they neglect their regular medicines while trying marijuana, the damage could be irreversible. It is a cruel hoax to offer false hope to desperately ill people.

Those who insist marijuana has medical uses would serve society better by promoting or sponsoring more legitimate scientific research, rather than throwing their time, money and rhetoric into lobbying, public relations campaigns and perennial litigation.

Clarification of Currently Accepted Medical Use

The Controlled Substances Act of 1970 divides the universe of all drugs of abuse into five sets or schedules. Drugs in Schedule I are subject to the most severe controls, because they have a high potential for abuse and no currently accepted medical use in treatment in the United States. 21 U.S.C. 812 (b)(1). Drugs of abuse which have currently accepted medical use in treatment in the United States are placed in Schedules II, III, IV and V. Regrettably, the Controlled Substances Act does not speak directly to what is meant by "currently accepted medical use." * * *

By 1969, Congress had developed detailed Federal statutory criteria under the [Food, Drug and Cosmetic Act, the FDCA] to determine whether drugs are acceptable for medical use.

In enacting the Controlled Substances Act in 1970, could Congress have intended to create a totally new Federal standard for determining whether drugs have accepted medical uses? Or did Congress intend to rely on standards it had developed over the prior 64 years under the FDCA? There is nothing in the Controlled Substances Act, its legislative history, or its purposes that would indicate Congress intended to depart radically from existing Federal law. * * *

The pattern of initial scheduling of drugs in the Controlled Substance Act, viewed in light of the prior legal status of these drugs under the FDCA, convinces me that Congress equated the term "currently accepted medical use in treatment in the United States" as used in the Controlled Substances Act with the core FDCA standards for acceptance of drugs for medical use. * * *

These same core FDCA criteria served as the basis for an eight-point test used by my predecessor as Administrator to describe drugs with currently accepted medical uses. 54 FR 53783 (December 29, 1989):

1.   Scientifically determined and accepted knowledge of its chemistry;

2.   The toxicology and pharmacology of the substance in animals;

3.   Establishment of its effectiveness in humans through scientifically designed clinical trials;

4.   General availability of the substance and information regarding the substance and its use;

5.   Recognition of its clinical use in generally accepted pharmacopeia, medical references, journals or textbooks;

6.   Specific indications for the treatment of recognized disorders;

7.   Recognition of the use of the substance by organizations or associations of physicians; and

8.   Recognition and use of the substance by a substantial segment of the medical practitioners in the United States.

Some uncertainty remains over the precise meaning and application of parts of this test. Therefore, the Court of Appeals for the District of Columbia Circuit remanded these proceedings for a further explanation. In addition to addressing those parts of the test that concerned the Court of Appeals, it would be useful to clarify the entire test, pinpoint its origins, and identify which elements are both necessary and sufficient to establish a prima facie case of currently accepted medical use. This is not an effort to change the substantive law. The statutory meaning of currently accepted medical use remains the same as enacted by Congress in 1970. My purpose simply is to clarify this Agency's understanding of the law.

* * *

To summarize, the five necessary elements of a drug with currently accepted medical use in treatment in the United States are:

(i) The Drug's Chemistry Must Be Known and Reproducible

The substance's chemistry must be scientifically established to permit it to be reproduced into dosages which can be standardized. The listing of the substance in a current edition of one of the official compendia, as defined by section 201(j) of the Food, Drug and Cosmetic Act, 21 U.S.C. 321(j), is sufficient generally to meet this requirement.

(ii) There Must Be Adequate Safety Studies

There must be adequate pharmacological and toxicological studies done by all methods reasonably applicable on the basis of which it could fairly and responsibly be concluded, by experts qualified by scientific training and experience to evaluate the safety and effectiveness of drugs, that the substance is safe for treating a specific, recognized disorder.

(iii) There Must Be Adequate and Well-Controlled Studies Proving Efficacy

There must be adequate, well-controlled, well-designed, well-conducted and well-documented studies, including clinical investigations, by experts qualified by scientific training and experience to evaluate the safety and effectiveness of drugs on the basis of which it could fairly and responsibly be concluded by such experts, that the substance will have its intended effect in treating a specific, recognized disorder.

(iv) The Drug Must Be Accepted by Qualified Experts

The drug must have a New Drug Application (NDA) approved by the Food and Drug Administration, pursuant to the Food, Drug and Cosmetic Act. 21 U.S.C. 355. Or, a consensus of the national community of experts, qualified by scientific training and experience to evaluate the safety and effectiveness of drugs, must accept the safety and effectiveness of the substance of use in treating a specific, recognized disorder. A material conflict of opinion among experts precludes a finding of consensus.

(v) The Scientific Evidence Must Be Widely Available

In the absence of NDA approval, information concerning the chemistry, pharmacology, toxicology and effectiveness of the substance must be reported, published, or otherwise widely available in sufficient detail to permit experts, qualified by scientific training and experience to evaluate the safety and effectiveness of drugs, to fairly and responsibly conclude the substance is safe and effective for use in treating a specific, recognized disorder.

Together these five elements constitute prima facie evidence that a drug has currently accepted medical use in treatment in the United States. In the interest of total clarity, let me emphasize those proofs that are irrelevant to the determination of currently accepted medical use, and that will not be considered by the Administrator:

(i)   Isolated case reports;

(ii)   Clinical impressions of practitioners;

(iii)   Opinions of persons not qualified by scientific training and experience to evaluate the safety and effectiveness of the substance at issue;

(iv)   Studies or reports so lacking in detail as to preclude responsible scientific evaluation;

(v)   Studies or reports involving drug substances other than the precise substance at issue;

(vi)   Studies or reports involving the substance at issue combined with other drug substances;

(vii)   Studies conducted by persons not qualified by scientific training and experience to evaluate the safety and effectiveness [sic] of the substance at issue;

(viii) Opinions of experts based entirely on unrevealed or unspecified information;

(ix)   Opinions of experts based entirely on theoretical evaluations of safety or effectiveness.

Bad Medicine By Any Standard

My predecessor as DEA Administrator developed and relied upon an eight-point test to determine whether marijuana has accepted medical uses. 54 FR 53783 (December 29, 1989):

1. Scientifically determined and accepted knowledge of its chemistry;

2. The toxicology and pharmacology of the substance in animals;

3. Establishment of its effectiveness in humans through scientifically designed clinical trials;

4. General availability of the substance and information regarding the substance and its use;

5. Recognition of its clinical use in generally accepted pharmacopeia, medical references, journals or textbooks;

6. Specific indications for the treatment of recognized disorders;

7. Recognition of the use of the substance by organizations or associations of physicians; and

8. Recognition and use of the substance by a substantial segment of the medical practitioners in the United States.

The Court of Appeals remanded the decision of my predecessor for clarification of what role factors (4), (5) and (8) of the initial eight-point test played in his reasoning. For ease of discussion, these factors can be divided as follows:

(4)(a) General availability of the substance * * *;

(4)(b) General availability of * * * information regarding the substance and its use;

(5) Recognition of its clinical use in generally accepted pharmacopeia, medical references, journals or textbooks;

(8)(a) Recognition * * * of the substance by a substantial segment of the medical practitioners in the United States; and

(8)(b) (U)se of the substance by a substantial segment of the medical practitioners in the United States.

I have found no evidence indicating initial factors (4)(a) or (8)(b) played any role in my predecessor's decision. In light of my understanding of the legal standard involved, these factors are irrelevant to whether marijuana has a currently accepted medical use.

My predecessor emphasized the lack of scientific evidence of marijuana's effectiveness, and the limited data available on its risks, as reflected in the published scientific studies. He also emphasized the importance of this data to the conclusions reached by experts concerning the drug. 54 FR 53783. I take this to mean that, under initial factor (4)(b), he believed the information available to experts is insufficient for them responsibly and fairly to conclude the marijuana is safe and effective for use as medicine.

Marijuana is not recognized as medicine in generally accepted pharmacopeia, medical references and textbooks, as noted by my predecessor. 54 FR 53784. I take this to mean, under initial factor (5), that he determined that marijuana's chemistry is neither known, nor reproducible, as evidenced by its absence from the official pharmacopeia.

Finally, my predecessor concluded, under initial factor (8)(a), that the vast majority of physicians do not accept marijuana as having medical use. 54 FR 53784. Along the way, he found that highly respected oncologists and antiemetic researchers reject marijuana for use in controlling nausea and vomiting, 54 FR 53777, that experts experienced in researching glaucoma medications reject marijuana for use in treating glaucoma, 54 FR 53779, and that noted neurologists who specialize in treating and conducting research in spasticity reject marijuana for use by MS patients, 54 FR 53780. I take this to mean my predecessor found no national consensus of qualified experts accepts marijuana's value as medicine.

Certainly I cannot know my predecessor's unstated reasoning. However, I have reviewed the entire record de novo, and I am convinced that his application of the initial eight-point test to this record correctly resulted in the conclusion that marijuana has no currently accepted medical use in treatment in the United States. Therefore, I adopt in their entirety the findings of facts and conclusions of law reached by the former Administrator in his final order of December 21, 1989, 54 FR 53767.

Pursuant to the remand of the Court of Appeals, I have condensed and clarified the initial standard into a five-point test. My application of the refined, five-point test to this record is set out briefly below.

First, marijuana's chemistry is neither fully known, nor reproducible. Thus far, over 400 different chemicals have been identified in the plant. The proportions and concentrations differ from plant to plant, depending on growing conditions, age of the plant, harvesting and storage factors. THC levels can vary from less than 0.2% to over 10%. It is not known how smoking or burning the plant material affects the composition of all these chemicals. It is not possible to reproduce the drug in dosages which can be considered standardized by any currently accepted scientific criteria. Marijuana is not recognized in any current edition of the official compendia. 21 U.S.C. 321(j).

Second, adequate safety studies have not been done. All reasonably applicable pharmacological and toxicological studies have not been carried out. Most of the chronic animal studies have been conducted with oral or intravenous THC, not with marijuana. Pharmacological data on marijuana's bioavailability, metabolic pathways and pharmacokinetics is inadequate. Studies in humans are too small and too few. Sophisticated epidemiological studies of marijuana use in large populations are required, similar to those done for tobacco use. Far too many questions remain unknown for experts fairly and responsibly to conclude marijuana is safe for any use.

Third, there are no adequate, well-controlled scientific studies proving marijuana is effective for anything.

Fourth, marijuana is not accepted for medical use in treatment by even a respectable minority, much less a consensus, of experts trained to evaluate drugs. The FDA's expert drug evaluators have rejected marijuana for medical use. No NDA has been approved by FDA for marijuana. The testimony of nationally recognized experts overwhelmingly rejects marijuana as medicine, compared to the scientifically empty testimony of the psychiatrists, a wellness counselor and general practitioners presented by NORML.

Fifth, given my conclusions on points one, two and three, it follows that the published scientific evidence is not adequate to permit experts to fairly and responsibly conclude that marijuana is safe and effective for use in humans.

A failure to meet just one of the five points precludes a drug from having a currently accepted medical use. Marijuana fails all five points of the test.

NORML has argued, unsuccessfully, that the legal standard for currently accepted medical use should be whether a respectable minority of physicians accepts the drug. The key to this medical malpractice defense is that the minority opinion must be recognized as respectable, as competent, by members of the profession.

In the absence of reliable evidence adequately establishing marijuana's chemistry, pharmacology, toxicology and effectiveness, no responsible physician could conclude that marijuana is safe and effective for medical use. To quote Doctor Kenneth P. Johnson, Chairman of the Department of Neurology at the University of Maryland, and the author of over 100 scientific and medical articles on MS: "To conclude that marijuana is therapeutically effective without conducting rigorous testing would be professionally irresponsible."

By any modern scientific standard, marijuana is no medicine.

Under the authority vested in the Attorney General by section 201(a) of the Controlled Substances Act, 21 U.S.C. 811(a), and delegated to the Administrator of the Drug Enforcement Administration by regulations of the Department of Justice, 28 CFR 0.100(b), the Administrator hereby orders that marijuana remain in Schedule I as listed in 21 CFR 1308.11(d)(14).

NOTES AND QUESTIONS

1.   **The scientific literature.** The Administrator's opinion ended the litigation approximately 20 years after its inception. What do you think about the Administrator's review of the scientific literature? Have you read about more recent studies involving the health benefits and harms of marijuana?

2.   **Quality of the science.** Before and after the NORML litigation ended, numerous books were published questioning the accuracy of the Administrator's conclusions. See, e.g., Lynn Zimmer & John P. Morgan,

Marijuana Myths, Marijuana Facts (1997); Lester Grinspoon & Jazmes B. Bakalar, *Marihuana: The Forbidden Medicine* (1997).

3.   **Catch 22.** Do you see a problem faced by plaintiffs in litigation like the litigation discussed above? How, for example, does the plaintiff establish that adequate safety studies have been conducted? How does the plaintiff demonstrate that a respectable minority, even short of a consensus, of the medical community accept marijuana's medical use? Although technically possible to study marijuana, critics point to roadblocks that researchers have faced. For example, Dr. Grinspoon and his co-author Bakalar have observed:

> Despite the obstructionism of the federal government, a few patients have been able to obtain marihuana legally for therapeutic purposes. State governments began to respond in a limited way to pressure from patients and physicians in the 1970s. In 1978, New Mexico enacted the first law designed to make marihuana available for medical use. * * * [By 1994, thirty-five states had followed suit].

> But the laws proved difficult to implement. Because marihuana is not recognized as a medicine under federal law, states can dispense it only by establishing formal research programs and getting FDA approval for an Investigational New Drug (IND) application. Many states gave up as soon as the officials in charge of the programs confronted the regulatory nightmare of the relevant federal laws. Nevertheless, between 1978 and 1984, seventeen states received permission to establish programs for the use of marihuana in treating glaucoma and the nausea induced by cancer chemotherapy. Each of these programs have fallen into abeyance because of the many problems involved.

Lester Grinspoon & Jazmes B. Bakalar, *Marihuana: The Forbidden Medicine*, 18–19 (1997).

4.   **California's medical marijuana law.** In States' Regulatory Schemes, Chapter 5, we pick up with a discussion of how California bucked the trend when its voters adopted Proposition 215, dealing with medical marijuana. As developed there, Proposition 215 became a game-changer over the past twenty plus years.

5.   **Agency review.** Despite criticism of the Administrator's position, courts have limited ability to overturn the Administrator's refusal to reschedule marijuana. That is so because a court must defer to findings by the Attorney General as long as they are supported by substantial evidence.

6.   **Future of rescheduling.** We take up the future of rescheduling in Chapter 10 Rescheduling. For now, as you work through the material, consider whether rescheduling is worth the cost at this point. At a minimum, rescheduling marijuana does not solve many of the problems that proponents identify in the current administration of federal law. Grace Wallack & John Hudak, *Marijuana Rescheduling: A Partial Prescription for Policy Change*, 14 Ohio St. J. Crim. L. 207, 211 (2016).

CHAPTER 4

OVERVIEW OF STATE AND LOCAL LAW

■ ■ ■

The history of state and local marijuana law took a significant and interesting turn after the passage of the Controlled Substances Act in 1970. Prior to that time, the various states all criminalized marijuana possession and distribution, but there was a fair amount of variance among the different states' laws. In 1970, however, at the urging of the Nixon administration, the Uniform Law Commission issued the Uniform Controlled Substances Act ("UCSA"). This had the effect of harmonizing legislation among the various states, as states began conforming more closely to federal law. And while the UCSA provided a model for state legislation that tracked the federal CSA, it also allowed for some flexibility on the part of the states to alter the CSA's rescheduling scheme, and to modify penalties for violations of each state's laws. As a result, a substantial majority of the states adopted versions of the USCA in the years following Congress' enactment of the CSA. By 1979, 44 states as well as the District of Columbia had adopted versions of the UCSA.

Even so, there were some early signs of dissent. In 1973, for example, Oregon became the first state to decriminalize marijuana. It did away with criminal penalties for simple marijuana possession and replaced them with a $100 civil fine. Thus began one of the major trends in state law: decriminalizing possession of small amounts of marijuana held for personal use, either by substituting civil penalties for criminal penalties, or by eliminating the possibility of jail time for a first offense. A second trend emerged somewhat later: in 1996, California became the first state to legalize (on a limited basis) marijuana for medical use, starting a trend that has now been followed by nearly two-thirds of the states. The third major trend in state marijuana law has been the legalization of marijuana for recreational (i.e., adult) use. This trend started in 2012, when Colorado and Washington first adopted comprehensive schemes to legalize and regulate the adult recreational use of marijuana. To date, ten states, plus the District of Columbia, have legalized adult recreational use.

In a nutshell, therefore, the story of marijuana at the state and local level is one of initial conformity shortly after the passage of the CSA and the UCSA, followed by increasing diversity as the states increasingly distanced themselves from federal law with respect to marijuana possession and distribution. In the sections that follow, these three major trends are discussed in more detail. Section A discusses the movement toward decriminalization, Section B the adoption of medical marijuana laws, and Section C, the movement toward full recreational use. The final section of this chapter, Section D, looks at some trends in local (i.e., municipal) law, beginning with the city of Ann Arbor's decriminalization of marijuana in 1973.

A. DECRIMINALIZATION STATES

As noted above, in 1973, Oregon became the first state to decriminalize marijuana. This followed the release of the report of the Shafer Commission in 1972, which concluded that marijuana criminalization was unnecessary, given that marijuana did not constitute a health risk, was not a gateway drug, and did not constitute a danger to public safety. Not long after Oregon decriminalized possession of small amounts of marijuana for personal use, the Supreme Court of Alaska in 1975 effectively decriminalized marijuana possession of small amounts of marijuana in the home, finding a constitutional right to privacy encompassed such use. By 1979, 10 other states had decriminalized marijuana possession as well, and it looked as though more states would soon follow suit.

During the Reagan years of the 1980s, however, decriminalization came to a halt, as the country became more conservative with respect to drug laws. Thus, for the next two decades, no additional states decriminalized marijuana possession. But in 2001, Nevada became the first state since the 1970s to do so, and the trend renewed course. Thus, at the present time, a majority of the states have either enacted laws legalizing or decriminalizing simple possession. Those that have decriminalized simple possession have done so either by substituting civil fines for criminal penalties, or by eliminating the possibility of jail time for the crime of possession. Decriminalization is accordingly something of a hybrid between traditional criminalization and legalization. Like criminalization, it discourages the use of marijuana, but it does so without imposing harsh penalties on personal use.

In the following case, *Ravin v. Alaska*, the Supreme Court of Alaska was called upon to decide whether the right to privacy under the Alaska Constitution protects marijuana possession in the home. The court concluded that it does, but only as to small amounts held for personal use in the home, and subject to certain restrictions. As you read the following opinion, think about what this right to privacy in the state constitution is based upon.

RAVIN V. ALASKA

Supreme Court of Alaska
537 P.2d 494 (Alaska 1975)

RABINOWITZ, C.J.

The constitutionality of Alaska's statute prohibiting possession of marijuana is put in issue in this case. Petitioner Ravin was arrested on December 11, 1972 and charged with violating AS 17.12.010. Before trial Ravin attacked the constitutionality of AS 17.12.010 by a motion to dismiss in which he asserted that the State had violated his right of privacy under both the federal and Alaska constitutions, and further violated the equal protection provisions of the state and federal constitutions. Lengthy hearings on the questions were held before District Court Judge Dorothy D. Tyner, at which testimony from several expert witnesses was received. Ravin's motion to dismiss was denied by Judge Tyner. The superior court then granted review and after affirmance by the superior court, we, in turn, granted Ravin's petition for review from the superior court's affirmance.

Here Ravin raises two basic claims: first, that there is no legitimate state interest in prohibiting possession of marijuana by adults for personal use, in view of the right to privacy; and secondly, that the statutory classification of marijuana as a dangerous drug, while use of alcohol and tobacco is not prohibited, denies him due process and equal protection of law.

We first address petitioner's contentions that his constitutionally protected right to privacy compels the conclusion that the State of Alaska is prohibited from penalizing the private possession and use of marijuana. Ravin's basic thesis is that there exists under the federal and Alaska constitutions a fundamental right to privacy, the scope of which is sufficiently broad to encompass and protect the possession of marijuana for personal use. Given this fundamental constitutional right, the State would then have the burden of demonstrating a compelling state interest in prohibiting possession of marijuana. In light of these controlling principles, petitioner argues that the evidence submitted below by both sides demonstrates that marijuana is a relatively innocuous substance, at least as compared with other less-restricted substances, and that nothing even approaching a compelling state interest was proven by the State.

Ravin's arguments necessitate a close examination of the contours of the asserted right to privacy and the scope of this court's review of the legislature's determination to criminalize possession of marijuana.

We have previously stated the tests to be applied when a claim is made that state action encroaches upon an individual's constitutional rights. In *Breese v. Smith*, 501 P.2d 159 (Alaska 1972), we had before us a school hair-length regulation which encroached on what we determined to be the individual's fundamental right to determine his own personal appearance. There we stated:

> Once a fundamental right under the constitution of Alaska has been shown to be involved and it has been further shown that this constitutionally protected right has been impaired by governmental action, then the government must come forward and meet its substantial burden of establishing that the abridgement in question was justified by a compelling governmental interest.

This standard is familiar federal law as well. As stated by the United States Supreme Court:

> Where there is a significant encroachment upon personal liberty, the State may prevail only upon showing a subordinating interest which is compelling.

The law must be shown "necessary, and not merely rationally related, to the accomplishment of a permissible state policy."

When, on the other hand, governmental action interferes with an individual's freedom in an area which is not characterized as fundamental, a less stringent test is ordinarily applied. In such cases our task is to determine whether the legislative enactment has a reasonable relationship to a legitimate governmental purpose. Under this latter test, which is sometimes referred to as the "rational basis" test, the State need only demonstrate the existence of facts which can serve as a rational basis for belief that the measure would properly serve the public interest.

In our recent opinion in *Lynden Transport, Inc. v. State,* 532 P.2d 700 (Alaska 1975), we recognized the existence of considerable dissatisfaction with the fundamental right-compelling state interest test. There we said:

> It has been suggested that there is mounting discontent with the rigid two-tier formulation of the equal protection doctrine, and that the United States Supreme Court is prepared to use the clause more rigorously to invalidate legislation without expansion of "fundamental rights" or "suspect" categories and the concomitant resort to the "strict scrutiny" tests. We are in agreement with the view that the Supreme Court's recent equal protection decisions have shown a tendency towards less speculative, less deferential, more intensified means-to-end inquiry when it is applying the traditional rational basis test, and we approve of this development.

This court has previously applied a test different from the rigid two-tier formulation to state regulations. In *State v. Wylie,* we tested durational residency requirements for state employment by both the compelling state interest test and a test which examined whether the means chosen suitably furthered an appropriate governmental interest. It is appropriate in this case to resolve Ravin's privacy claims by determining whether there is a proper governmental interest in imposing restrictions on marijuana use and whether the means chosen bear a substantial relationship to the legislative purpose. If governmental restrictions interfere with the individual's right to privacy, we will require that the relationship between means and ends be not merely reasonable but close and substantial.

Thus, our undertaking is two-fold: we must first determine the nature of Ravin's rights, if any, abridged by AS 17.12.010, and, if any rights have been infringed upon, then resolve the further question as to whether the statutory impingement is justified.

As we have mentioned, Ravin's argument that he has a fundamental right to possess marijuana for personal use rests on both federal and state law, and centers on what may broadly be called the right to privacy. This "right" is increasingly the subject of litigation and commentary and is still a developing legal concept.

In Ravin's view, the right to privacy involved here is an autonomous right which gains special significance when its situs is found in a specially protected area, such as the home. Ravin begins his privacy argument by citation of and reliance upon *Griswold v. Connecticut,* in which the Supreme Court of the United States struck down as unconstitutional a state statute effectively barring the dispensation of birth control information to married persons. Writing for five members of the Court, Mr. Justice Douglas noted that rights protected by the Constitution are not limited to those specifically enumerated in the Constitution. In order to secure the enumerated rights, certain peripheral rights must be recognized. In other words, the "specific guarantees in the Bill of Rights have penumbras, formed by emanations from those guarantees that help give them life and substance." Certain of these penumbral rights create "zones of privacy", for example, First Amendment rights of association, Third and Fourth Amendment rights pertaining to the security of the home, and the Fifth Amendment right against self-incrimination. The Supreme Court of the United States then proceeded to find a right to privacy in marriage which antedates the Bill of Rights and yet lies within the zone of privacy created by several fundamental constitutional guarantees. It was left unclear whether this particular right to privacy exists independently, or comes into being only because of its connection with fundamental enumerated rights.

The next important Supreme Court opinion regarding privacy is *Stanley v. Georgia,* in which a state conviction for possession of obscene matter was overturned as violative of the First and Fourteenth Amendments. The Supreme Court had previously held that obscenity is not protected by the First Amendment. But in *Stanley* the Count made a distinction between commercial distribution of obscene matter and the private enjoyment of it at home. The Constitution, it said, protects the fundamental right to receive information and ideas, regardless of their worth. Moreover, the Supreme Court said, in the context of this case—a prosecution for mere possession of printed or filmed matter in the privacy of a person's own home—that right takes on an added dimension. For also fundamental is the right to be free, except in very limited circumstances, from unwanted governmental intrusions into one's privacy.

The Supreme Court concluded that the First Amendment means a state has no business telling a man, sitting alone in his own home, what books he may read or what films he may watch. The Court took care to limit its holding to mere possession of obscene materials by the individual in his own home. It noted that it did not intend to restrict the power of the state or federal government to make illegal the possession of items such as narcotics, firearms, or stolen goods.

The Stanley holding was subsequently refined by a series of cases handed down in 1973. In *Paris Adult Theatre I v. Slaton,* the Supreme Court rejected the claim of a theater owner that his showing of allegedly obscene films was protected by *Stanley* because his films were shown only to consenting adults. The Court explicitly rejected the comparison of a theater to a home and found a legitimate state interest in regulating the use of obscene matter in local commerce and places of public accommodation. It apparently found no fundamental right involved in viewing obscene matter under these conditions, for it noted that the right to privacy guaranteed by the Fourteenth Amendment extends only to fundamental rights. The protection offered by *Stanley,* the Supreme Court stated, was restricted to the home, and it explicitly refused to say that all activities occurring between consenting adults were beyond the reach of the government.

These Supreme Court cases indicate to us that the federal right to privacy arises only in connection with other fundamental rights, such as the grouping of rights which involve the home. And even in connection with the penumbra of home-related rights, the right of privacy in the sense of immunity from prosecution is absolute only when the private activity will not endanger or harm the general public.

The view is confirmed by the Supreme Court's abortion decision, *Roe v. Wade.* There appellant claimed that her right to decide for herself concerning abortion fell within the ambit of a right to privacy flowing from the federal Bill of Rights. The Court's decision in her favor makes clear that only personal rights which can be deemed "fundamental" or "implicit in the concept of ordered liberty" are protected by the right to privacy. The Supreme Court found this right "broad enough to encompass a woman's decision whether or not to terminate her pregnancy," but it rejected the idea that a woman's right to decide is absolute. At some point, the state's interest in safeguarding health, maintaining medical standards, and protecting potential life becomes sufficiently compelling to sustain regulations. One does not, the Supreme Court said, have an unlimited right to do with one's body as one pleases.

The right to privacy which the Court found in *Roe* is closely akin to that in *Griswold*; in both cases the zone of privacy involves the area of the family and procreation, more particularly, a right of personal autonomy in relation to choices affecting an individual's personal life.

In Alaska this court has dealt with the concept of privacy on only a few occasions. One of the most significant decisions in this area is *Breese v. Smith,* where we considered the applicability of the guarantee of "life, liberty, the pursuit of happiness" found in the Alaska Constitution, to a school hair-length regulation. Noting that hairstyles are a highly personal matter in which the individual is traditionally autonomous, we concluded that governmental control of personal appearance would be antithetical to the concept of personal liberty under Alaska's constitution. Since the student would be forced to choose between controlling his own personal appearance and asserting his right to an education if the regulations were upheld, we concluded that the constitutional language quoted above embodied an affirmative grant of liberty to public school students to choose their own hairstyles, for "at the core of [the concept of liberty] is the notion of total personal immunity from government control: the right 'to be let alone.'" That right is not absolute, however; we also noted that this "liberty" must yield where it "intrude[s] upon the freedom of others."

Subsequent to our decision in *Breese,* a right to privacy amendment was added to the Alaska Constitution. Article I, section 22 reads:

> The right of the people to privacy is recognized and shall not be infringed. The legislature shall implement this section.

The effect of this amendment is to place privacy among the specifically enumerated rights in Alaska's constitution. But this fact alone does not, in and of itself, yield answers concerning what scope should be accorded to this right of privacy. We have suggested that the right to privacy may afford less than absolute protection to "the ingestion of food, beverages or other substances". For any such protection must be limited by the legitimate needs of the State to protect the health and welfare of its citizens.

Although a number of other jurisdictions have considered the privacy issue as it applies to marijuana prosecutions, they provide little help in defining the scope of article I, section 22 of Alaska's constitution. In Hawaii, whose constitution also contains an express guarantee of the right to privacy, the supreme court has faced a similar issue. In *State v. Kantner,* the Supreme Court of Hawaii upheld a conviction for possession of marijuana by a 3–2 vote, with one member of the majority concurring only because he thought the constitutional issue had not been properly raised.

A majority rejected the claim that application of the statute violated guarantees of equal protection and due process, and two members of the court rejected the claim of violation of "fundamental liberty" based on *Griswold*. In dissent, Justice Levinson emphasized the guarantees of privacy and personal autonomy which he found in both the Hawaii Constitution and the due process clause of the Fourteenth Amendment to the United States Constitution. He found that the right to privacy "guarantees to the individual the full measure of control over his own personality consistent with the security of himself and others." The experiences generated by use of marijuana are mental in nature, he wrote, and thus among the most personal and private experiences possible. So long as conduct does not produce detrimental results, the right of privacy protects the individual's conduct designed to affect these inner areas of the personality. The state failed to show, he found, any harm to the user or others from the private, personal use of marijuana, and so the statute infringed on the right to personal autonomy.

In a Michigan case the same year, a conviction for possession of marijuana was overturned by a unanimous court, though for a variety of reasons. One of the justices in *People v. Sinclair,* Justice T.G. Kavanagh, rested his opinion squarely on the basic right of the individual to be free from government intrusions. He found the marijuana possession statute to be "an impermissible intrusion on the fundamental rights to liberty and the pursuit of happiness, and is an unwarranted interference with the right to possess and use private property." He noted the basic freedom of the individual to be free to do as he pleases so long as his actions do not interfere with the rights of his neighbor or of society. ". . . 'Big Brother' cannot, in the name of *Public* health, dictate to anyone what he can eat or drink or smoke in the *privacy* of his own home."

Generally, however, privacy as a constitutional defense in marijuana cases has not met with much favor. It was rejected, for instance, by the Massachusetts Supreme Judicial Court in *Commonwealth v. Leis,* where the court held that there was no constitutional right to smoke marijuana, that smoking marijuana was not fundamental to the American scheme of justice or necessary to a regime of ordered liberty, and that smoking marijuana was not locatable in any "zone of privacy". Furthermore, the court said, there is no constitutional right to become intoxicated.

Assuming this court were to continue to utilize the fundamental right-compelling state interest test in resolving privacy issues under article I, section 22 of Alaska's constitution, we would conclude that there is not a fundamental constitutional right to possess or ingest marijuana in Alaska. For in our view, the right to privacy amendment to the Alaska Constitution cannot be read so as to make the possession or ingestion of marijuana itself a fundamental right. Nor can we conclude that such a fundamental right is shown by virtue of the analysis we employed in *Breese*. In that case, the student's traditional liberty pertaining to autonomy in personal appearance was threatened in such a way that his constitutionally guaranteed right to an education was jeopardized. Hairstyle, as emphasized in *Breese,* is a highly personal matter involving the individual and his body. In this sense this aspect of liberty-privacy is akin to the significantly personal areas at stake in *Griswold* and *Eisenstadt v. Baird.* Few would believe they have been deprived of something of critical importance if deprived of marijuana, though they would if stripped of control over their personal appearance. And, as mentioned previously, a discrete federal right of privacy separate from the penumbras of specifically enumerated constitutional rights has not as yet been articulated by the Supreme Court of the United States. Therefore, if we were employing our former test, we would hold that there is no fundamental right, either under the Alaska or federal constitutions, either to possess or ingest marijuana.

The foregoing does not complete our analysis of the right to privacy issues. For in *Gray* we stated that the right of privacy amendment of the Alaska Constitution "clearly it shields the ingestion of food, beverages or other substances", but that this right may be held to be subordinate to public health and welfare measures. Thus, Ravin's right to privacy contentions are not susceptible to disposition solely in terms of answering the question whether there is a general fundamental constitutional right to possess or smoke marijuana. This leads us to a more detailed examination of the right to privacy and the relevancy of where the right is exercised. At one end of the scale of the scope of the right to privacy is possession or ingestion in the individual's home. If there is any area of human activity to which a right to privacy pertains more than any other, it is the home. The importance of the home has been amply demonstrated in constitutional law. Among the enumerated rights in the federal Bill of Rights are the guarantee against quartering of troops in a private house in peacetime (Third Amendment) and the right to be "secure in their . . . houses . . . against unreasonable searches and seizures . . ." (Fourth Amendment). The First Amendment has been held to protect the right to "privacy and freedom of association in the home." The Fifth Amendment has been described as providing protection against all governmental invasions "of the sanctity of a man's home and the privacies of life." The protection of the right to receive birth control information in *Griswold* was predicated on the sanctity of the marriage relationship and the harm to this fundamental area of privacy if police were allowed to "search the sacred precincts of marital bedrooms." And in *Stanley v. Georgia,* the Court emphasized the home as the situs of protected "private activities". The right to receive information and ideas was found in *Stanley* to take on an added dimension precisely because it was a prosecution for possession in the home: "For also fundamental is the right to be free, except in very limited circumstances, from unwanted governmental intrusions into one's privacy." In a later case, the Supreme Court noted that *Stanley* was not based on the notion that the obscene matter was itself protected by a constitutional penumbra of privacy, but rather was a "reaffirmation that 'a man's home is his castle.'" [At the same time the Court noted, "the Constitution extends special safeguards to the privacy of the home, just as it protects other special privacy rights such as those of marriage, procreation, motherhood, child rearing, and education." And as the Supreme Court pointed out, there exists a "myriad" of activities which may be lawfully conducted within the privacy and confines of the home, but may be prohibited in public.

In Alaska we have also recognized the distinctive nature of the home as a place where the individual's privacy receives special protection. This court has consistently recognized that the home is constitutionally protected from unreasonable searches and seizures, reasoning that the home itself retains a protected status under the Fourth Amendment and Alaska's constitution distinct from that of the occupant's person. The privacy amendment to the Alaska Constitution was intended to give recognition and protection to the home. Such a reading is consonant with the character of life in Alaska. Our territory and now state has traditionally been the home of people who prize their individuality and who have chosen to settle or to continue living here in order to achieve a measure of control over their own lifestyles which is now virtually unattainable in many of our sister states.

The home, then, carries with it associations and meanings which make it particularly important as the situs of privacy. Privacy in the home is a fundamental right, under both the federal and Alaska constitutions. We do not mean by this that a person may do anything at anytime as long as the activity takes place within a person's home. There are two important limitations on this facet of the right to privacy. First, we agree with the Supreme Court of the United States, which has strictly limited the *Stanley* guarantee to possession for purely private, noncommercial use in the home. And secondly, we think this right must yield when it interferes in a serious manner with the health, safety, rights and privileges of others or with the public welfare. No one has an absolute right to do things in the privacy of his own home which will affect himself or others adversely. Indeed, one aspect of a private matter is that it *is* private, that is, that it does not adversely affect persons beyond the actor, and hence is none of their business. When a matter does affect the public, directly or indirectly, it loses its wholly private character, and can be made to yield when an appropriate public need is demonstrated.

Thus, we conclude that citizens of the State of Alaska have a basic right to privacy in their homes under Alaska's constitution. This right to privacy would encompass the possession and ingestion of substances such as marijuana in a purely personal, non-commercial context in the home unless the state can meet its substantial burden and show that proscription of possession of marijuana in the home is supportable by achievement of a legitimate state interest.

This leads us to the second facet of our inquiry, namely, whether the State has demonstrated sufficient justification for the prohibition of possession of marijuana in general in the interest of public welfare; and further, whether the State has met the greater burden of showing a close and substantial relationship between the public welfare and control of ingestion or possession of marijuana in the home for personal use.

* * *

But one way in which use of marijuana most clearly does affect the general public is in regard to its effect on driving. All of which brings us to the opposite (from the home) end of the scale of the right to privacy in the context of ingestion or possession of marijuana, namely, when the individual is operating a motor vehicle. Recent research has produced increasing evidence of significant impairment of the driving ability of persons under the influence of cannabis. Distortion of time perception, impairment of psychomotor function, and increased selectivity in attentiveness to surroundings apparently can combine to lower driver ability. In this regard, Ravin points out that marijuana usually produces passivity and inactivity, in contrast to alcohol, which increases aggressiveness and is likely to result in overconfidence in one's driving ability. Although a person under the influence of marijuana may be less likely to attempt to drive than a person under the influence of alcohol, there exists the potential for serious harm to the health and safety of the general public.

In view of the foregoing, we believe that at present, the need for control of drivers under the influence of marijuana and the existing doubts as to the safety of marijuana, demonstrate a sufficient justification for the prohibition found in AS 17.12.010 as an exercise of the state's police power for the public welfare. Given the evidence of the effect of marijuana on driving an individual's right to possess or ingest marijuana while driving would be subject to the prohibition provided for in AS 17.12.010. However, given the relative insignificance of marijuana consumption as a health problem in our society at present, we do not believe that the potential harm generated by drivers under the influence of marijuana, standing alone, creates a close and substantial relationship between the public welfare and control of ingestion of marijuana or possession of it in the home for personal use. Thus we conclude that no adequate justification for the state's intrusion into the citizen's right to privacy by its prohibition of possession of marijuana by an adult for personal consumption in the home has been shown. The privacy of the individual's home cannot be breached absent a persuasive showing of a close and substantial relationship of the intrusion to a legitimate governmental interest. Here, mere scientific doubts will not suffice. The state must demonstrate a need based on proof that the public health or welfare will in fact suffer if the controls are not applied.

The state has a legitimate concern with avoiding the spread of marijuana use to adolescents who may not be equipped with the maturity to handle the experience prudently, as well as a legitimate concern with the problem of driving under the influence of marijuana. Yet these interests are insufficient to justify intrusions into the rights of adults in the privacy of their own homes. Further, neither the federal or Alaska constitution affords protection for the buying or selling of marijuana, nor absolute protection for its use or possession in public. Possession at home of amounts of marijuana indicative of intent to sell rather than possession for personal use is likewise unprotected.

In view of our holding that possession of marijuana by adults at home for personal use is constitutionally protected, we wish to make clear that we do not mean to condone the use of marijuana. The experts who testified below, including petitioner's witnesses, were unanimously opposed to the use of any psychoactive drugs. We agree completely. It is the responsibility of every individual to consider carefully the ramifications for himself and for those around him of using such substances. With the freedom which our society offers to each of us to order our lives as we see fit goes the duty to live responsibly, for our own sakes and for society's. This result can best be achieved, we believe, without the use of psychoactive substances.

We briefly address Ravin's second assertion of error, namely that AS 17.12.010 denies him due process and equal protection of the law. The argument is two-fold. First, Ravin asserts, the proscription denies equal protection because the other commonly used "recreational" drugs, alcohol and tobacco, are not proscribed, though they inflict far more damage on the user than does marijuana. We reject, however, the assumption that the legislature must apply equal controls to equal threats to the public health. Assuming some degree of control of marijuana use is permissible, it does not follow that the political obstacles to placing controls on alcohol and tobacco should render the legislature unable to regulate other substances equally or less harmful. It is not irrational for the legislature to regulate those public health areas where it can do so, when there exists other areas where controls are less feasible.

Ravin also attacks as irrational the classification of marijuana with the other drugs covered by AS 17.12.150(3) ("depressant, stimulant, or hallucinogenic"). He may be correct that marijuana is the least harmful of the drugs covered by AS 17.12.150(3), but that alone is not sufficient to make the classification irrational. In a number of cases the classification of marijuana either as or with narcotic drugs has been struck down as irrational in view of the relative harmlessness of marijuana. In other cases, courts have deferred to the legislative finding of facts implicit in the classification. However, in every case in which statutes have been struck down, the statutory scheme classified marijuana with, or subject to equal sanctions with, the most dangerous proscribed drugs. In Alaska, however, "hard" drugs are in a completely different category from marijuana, with substantially greater penalties for misuse. The drugs with which marijuana is grouped in AS 17.12.150(3) are not so different from marijuana that yet another classification must be set up for marijuana alone. We find no merit to Ravin's contention on this point.

One other facet of this petition remains for discussion. Ravin urges us to recognize that whatever harm results from marijuana use is far outweighed by the negative aspects of enforcement. Over 400,000 persons were arrested for marijuana-related crimes in 1973; 81% of them had no previous criminal records. Using these statistics, and asserting that marijuana use does not pose a substantial public health threat, Ravin questions the wisdom of AS 17.12.010. We note that the Alaska Bar Association, American Bar Association, National Conference of Commissioners on Uniform State Laws, National Advisory Commission on Criminal Justice Standards and Goals and the Governing Board of the American Medical Association have recommended decriminalization of possession of marijuana. The National Commission on Marihuana and Drug Abuse has recommended that private possession for personal use no longer be an offense. A Canadian study has arrived at similar results. And at least one state, Oregon, has already decriminalized possession of small amounts of marijuana.

In opposition, the State argues that under Alaska's constitutional system of separate but equal branches of government the issue is a "political controversy over the State's fundamental policy toward the drug marijuana". Thus, the "issue should be properly determined by the people's elected representatives". We agree that determination of the wisdom of a particular legislative enactment is more properly the subject of investigation and resolution by the legislature rather than the judiciary.

The record does not disclose any facts as to the situs of Ravin's arrest and his alleged possession of marijuana. In view of these circumstances, we hold that the matter must be remanded to the district court for the purpose of developing the facts concerning Ravin's arrest and circumstances of his possession of marijuana. Once this is accomplished, the district court is to consider Ravin's motion to dismiss in conformity with this opinion.

Remanded for further proceedings consistent with this opinion.

NOTES AND QUESTIONS

1. **The right to privacy.** The *Ravin* decision relied upon a right to privacy under the Alaska constitution that, under the court's holding, prohibits the State of Alaska from criminalizing the possession of small amounts of marijuana in the home kept for personal use. Why did the court rely on the

Alaska constitution rather than the United States Constitution? Do the United States Constitution and the Alaska constitution differ with respect to the right to privacy? And why does the court limit the protected zone of privacy to the home?

2.   Legislative decriminalization. Alaska was unusual among decriminalization states in that the decriminalization effort was the result of a court decision rather than a legislative decision. Typically, states that have decriminalized simple possession have done so via legislation that either substitutes civil fines for criminal penalties, or eliminates the possibility of imprisonment for simple possession. Among the states that impose civil fines, the amount of the fines ranges from a maximum of $100 in some states, such as Maryland and California, to a maximum of $600 in Maine.

3.   Subsequent history of *Ravin*. In 2009, the Alaska Supreme Court was asked to reconsider its holding in *Ravin* with respect to its reliance on a constitutional right to privacy. *See State v. ACLU of Alaska*, 204 P. 3d 364 (Alaska 2009). In that case, the ACLU argued that the court should strike down a 2006 state statute that imposed a criminal fine for possession of small amounts of marijuana, without making an exception for home use. The ACLU argued that the statute violated the Alaska constitution's right to privacy, as interpreted by *Ravin*. The court declined to hear that case on ripeness grounds, however, leaving that substantive question unresolved.

4.   Current status in Alaska. In 2015, voters in Alaska approved a ballot initiative amending the state's constitution to allow the recreational use of marijuana. That measure permits adults 21 or older to possess up to 1 ounce of marijuana and to grow up to six plants for personal use. Thus, technically speaking, Alaska is currently a recreational-use state rather than a decriminalization state. Does that render the *Ravin* decision moot?

5.   Limits of decriminalization. It is important to keep in mind that decriminalization, in all states, applies only to "simple possession": that is, to possession of small amounts of marijuana for personal use. Possession of larger amounts of marijuana, as well as trafficking in illicit marijuana, remain crimes in every state. Thus, even though the state of Washington has legalized possession of up to 1 ounce of marijuana for personal use, the sale or distribution of marijuana by a non-licensed person is a felony that can be punished by a term of imprisonment of up to five years.

B. MEDICAL MARIJUANA STATES

In 1996, California adopted its Compassionate Use Act (Proposition 215), thereby becoming the first state in the country to legalize marijuana (on a limited basis) for medical use. In order to use medical marijuana legally, patients had to obtain a doctor's recommendation and a state-issued license. Doctors cannot actually prescribe marijuana because medical prescriptions are subject to the oversight of the federal DEA. (*See also* the discussion in Chapter 5 on California's Proposition 215.)

In the years since California broke the legalization barrier, a majority of states have gradually followed suit. In 2018, Oklahoma, Utah, and Missouri became the most recent states to legalize medical marijuana use, joining 30 other states and the District of Columbia. And it is likely that one or more additional states will legalize medical marijuana in the near future. In addition, most of the states that have not yet legalized medical marijuana now allow limited use of CBD oil for therapeutic purposes.

The individual states vary widely with regard to the medical conditions that qualify a patient to use medical marijuana. In Louisiana, for example, medical use of marijuana's is limited to three conditions: "glaucoma, symptoms resulting from administration of chemotherapy cancer treatment, and spasticity quadriplegia." La. Act No. 261(1)(A). In Illinois, on the other hand, a qualifying (i.e., "debilitating") condition is broadly defined to encompass a host of medical disorders:

> (h) "Debilitating medical condition" means one or more of the following:

> > (1) cancer, glaucoma, positive status for human immunodeficiency virus, acquired immune deficiency syndrome, hepatitis C, amyotrophic lateral sclerosis, Crohn's disease, agitation of Alzheimer's disease, cachexia/wasting syndrome, muscular dystrophy, severe fibromyalgia, spinal cord disease, including but not limited to arachnoiditis, Tarlov cysts, hydromyelia, syringomyelia, Rheumatoid arthritis, fibrous dysplasia, spinal cord injury, traumatic brain injury and post-concussion syndrome, Multiple Sclerosis, Arnold-Chiari malformation and Syringomyelia, Spinocerebellar Ataxia (SCA), Parkinson's, Tourette's, Myoclonus, Dystonia, Reflex Sympathetic Dystrophy, RSD (Complex Regional Pain Syndromes Type I), Causalgia, CRPS (Complex Regional Pain Syndromes Type II), Neurofibromatosis, Chronic Inflammatory Demyelinating Polyneuropathy, Sjogren's syndrome, Lupus, Interstitial Cystitis, Myasthenia Gravis, Hydrocephalus, nail-patella syndrome, residual limb pain, seizures (including those characteristic of epilepsy), post-traumatic stress disorder (PTSD), or the treatment of these conditions;

> > (1.5) terminal illness with a diagnosis of 6 months or less; if the terminal illness is not one of the qualifying debilitating medical conditions, then the physician shall on the certification form identify the cause of the terminal illness; or

> > (2) any other debilitating medical condition or its treatment that is added by the Department of Public Health by rule as provided in Section 45.

10 I.L.C.S. 130/10(h). And in the states that allow only CBD oil, the majority of such states limit the use of CBD oil to intractable epilepsy/seizure disorders. Thus, medical marijuana is much more widely available in some states than in others, depending on what counts as a qualifying condition.

Individual state laws differ in other respects as well. For example, state laws sometimes differ as to how and where medical marijuana can legally be consumed. In the following case, *Arizona v. Maestas*, the Arizona Supreme Court considered an appeal by a student at Arizona State University who had been arrested for possession of marijuana in his dorm room, even though the student had a valid medical marijuana license. The student had been charged pursuant to a state statute that made it illegal to possess marijuana on college campuses. The court held for the student, finding that the criminal statute violated the state's constitution because it amounted to an improper amendment by the legislature of Arizona's Medical Marijuana Act.

ARIZONA V. MAESTAS

Arizona Supreme Court
No. CR-0193-PR (Ariz. 2018)

PERLANDER, J.

The Arizona Medical Marijuana Act ("AMMA"), enacted by voters as Proposition 203 in 2010, generally permits qualified AMMA cardholders to possess a limited amount of marijuana and, with certain exceptions and limitations, immunizes their AMMA-compliant possession or use from "arrest, prosecution or penalty in any manner." A.R.S. § 36–2811(B). Among its limitations, the AMMA prohibits the possession or use of medical marijuana at certain specified locations. A.R.S. § 36–2802(B). In 2012, the Arizona Legislature added another location by enacting a statute under which "a person, including [a qualified AMMA cardholder], may not lawfully possess or use marijuana on the campus of any public university, college, community college or postsecondary educational institution." A.R.S. § 15–108(A). Because that statute violates Arizona's Voter Protection Act ("VPA") with respect to AMMA-compliant marijuana possession or use, we hold it unconstitutional as applied to the university student/cardholder in this case.

I.   BACKGROUND

In March 2014, an Arizona State University police officer arrested Andre Lee Juwaun Maestas after the officer observed Maestas sitting in a road near Maestas's dormitory on the university campus. The officer searched Maestas and found a valid AMMA registry identification card in Maestas's wallet. After Maestas admitted that he had marijuana in his dorm room, the officer obtained a search warrant, searched Maestas's dorm room, and found two envelopes containing 0.4 grams of marijuana. (The AMMA provides that an "[a]llowable amount of marijuana" is "[t]wo-and-one-half ounces of usable marijuana." A.R.S. § 36–2801(1)(a)(i). Maestas's 0.4 grams of marijuana is roughly equivalent to 0.014 ounces.)

The State charged Maestas with obstructing a public thoroughfare and possession of marijuana. Before trial, Maestas moved to dismiss the marijuana-possession charge, arguing that his possession was AMMA-compliant and he was therefore immune from prosecution under § 36–2811(B). The State opposed the motion, arguing that Maestas's AMMA-compliant possession of marijuana was nevertheless unlawful under § 15–108(A), which prohibits even AMMA cardholders from possessing marijuana on public college and university campuses. The superior court denied Maestas's motion, convicted him on both counts after a bench trial, imposed a fine on the marijuana-possession charge, and placed him on probation for one year.

The court of appeals vacated Maestas's conviction for possession of marijuana and held that § 15–108(A) is unconstitutional under the VPA. *State v. Maestas*, 242 Ariz. 194, 198 (App. 2017). As a threshold matter, the court ruled that the constitutionality of § 15–108(A) is a justiciable question because the political question doctrine is inapplicable here. *Id.* at 196–97. On the merits, the court reasoned that the VPA's requirements apply to § 15–108(A) because the statute amends the AMMA by re-criminalizing AMMA "cardholders' marijuana possession on college and university campuses." The court further concluded that § 15–108(A) violates the VPA because the AMMA's purpose is to protect AMMA "cardholders from criminal and other penalties," *id.* and § 15–108(A) does not further that purpose but rather "eliminates some of [the AMMA's] protections," *id.*

We granted review because § 15–108(A)'s validity presents a recurring legal question of statewide importance. We have jurisdiction under article 6, section 5(3), of the Arizona Constitution and A.R.S. § 12–120.24.

II. DISCUSSION

We review the constitutionality of a statute de novo. *Biggs v. Betlach*, 243 Ariz. 256, 258 (2017). "When the statute in question involves no fundamental constitutional rights or distinctions based on suspect classifications, we presume the statute is constitutional and will uphold it unless it clearly is not." *Cave Creek Unified Sch. Dist. v. Ducey*, 233 Ariz. 1, 5 (2013).

A.

The State first contends that the constitutionality of § 15–108(A) under the VPA is a non-justiciable political question because the AMMA "authorizes universities to restrict and penalize cardholders to protect federal funding, and the necessity of such measures" is delegated to the legislature. We disagree.

"The Arizona Constitution entrusts some matters solely to the political branches of government, not the judiciary." *Ariz. Indep. Redistricting Comm'n v. Brewer*, 229 Ariz. 347, 351 (2012); see also Ariz. Const. art. 3 (providing that the three departments of Arizona's government "shall be separate and distinct, and no one of such departments shall exercise the powers properly belonging to either of the others").

Flowing from "the basic principle of separation of powers," a non-justiciable political question is presented when "there is a textually demonstrable constitutional commitment of the issue to a coordinate political department; or a lack of judicially discoverable and manageable standards for resolving it." *Kromko v. Ariz. Bd. of Regents*, 216 Ariz. 190, 192 (2007). Neither aspect of this test is present here.

The State argues that there is a "textually demonstrable constitutional commitment of the issue" to the legislature, *Kromko*, 216 Ariz. at 192, because the Arizona Constitution commits to that branch the power to establish and maintain "a general and uniform public school system," which includes universities, Ariz. Const. art. 11, § 1(A)(6). But the legislature's power to maintain universities is limited by the VPA.

As relevant here, the Arizona Constitution was amended in 1998 when voters approved the VPA to expressly limit the legislature's "authority to amend measures approved by voters in initiative elections." *Ariz. Early Childhood Dev. & Health Bd. v. Brewer*, 221 Ariz. 467, 469 (2009); see also Ariz. Const. art. 4, pt. 1, § 1(6)(C) (providing that the legislature may only amend a voter initiative if "the amending legislation furthers the purposes of such measure and at least three-fourths of the members of each house of the legislature vote to amend such measure"). Adopting the State's argument would mean that, notwithstanding the VPA's limitations on the legislature's power, courts could not adjudicate any VPA challenge to a law enacted in a subject area over which the legislature exercised power given to it by the constitution. Such an interpretation would render the VPA meaningless. Accordingly, there is not a "textually demonstrable constitutional commitment of the issue" presented here, i.e., whether § 15–108(A) is constitutional under the VPA, to "a coordinate political department." *Kromko*, 216 Ariz. at 192.

In addition, there is not "a lack of judicially discoverable and manageable standards for resolving" this issue. Id. We have ruled on VPA challenges in the past, see, e.g., *Cave Creek Unified Sch. Dist.*, 233 Ariz. at 4–8; *Brewer*, 221 Ariz. at 469–72, and no legal obstacle prevents us from resolving the challenge raised here. Accordingly, we conclude that the issue presented is justiciable.

B.

The State next contends that the VPA's requirements do not apply to § 15–108(A) because the legislature did not amend the AMMA when it enacted § 15–108(A). The State reasons that the AMMA "expressly authorizes restrictions for cardholders on university campuses" and "expressly authorizes penalties in order to assure continued access to federal funding." Alternatively, the State argues that even if the VPA's requirements apply to § 15–108(A), the legislature complied with those requirements because at least three-fourths of the members of each chamber voted to enact § 15–108(A), and that law is consistent with the AMMA when the statutory scheme is viewed as a whole. We disagree.

The VPA limits the legislature's power to amend, repeal, or supersede voter initiatives. See Ariz. Const. art. 4, pt. 1, § 1(6)(B)–(C), (14). A threshold question, therefore, is whether the legislature amended, repealed, or superseded the AMMA when it enacted § 15–108(A). It is undisputed that § 15–108(A) did not repeal or supersede the AMMA, but the parties disagree about whether § 15–108(A) amends it.

The AMMA specifies the circumstances under which the legislature may impose "civil, criminal or other penalties" when a person, including a qualified AMMA cardholder, possesses or uses marijuana. A.R.S. § 36–2802(B). Specifically, the AMMA "does not authorize any person" to possess or use marijuana in the following locations: "[o]n a school bus," "[o]n the grounds of any preschool or primary or secondary school," and "[i]n any correctional facility." § 36–2802(B)(1)–(3). In general, when the legislature (or voters) expressly prescribes a list in a statute (or initiative), "we assume the exclusion of items not listed." *State v. Ault*, 157 Ariz. 516, 519 (1988). Because the AMMA sets forth a list of locations where the legislature may impose "civil, criminal or other penalties" when a person possesses or uses marijuana, § 36–2802, and because that list does not include college and university campuses (unlike pre-, primary-, and secondary-school grounds), we assume that the voters did not intend to criminalize AMMA-compliant possession or use of marijuana on public college and university campuses.

By its terms, § 15–108(A) amends the AMMA by adding a location to the AMMA's list of specified locations where the legislature may impose "civil, criminal or other penalties" for a person's possession or use of marijuana otherwise allowed under the AMMA. § 36–2802. Indeed, § 15–108(A) begins by stating that "[i]n addition to the limitations prescribed in" § 36–2802(B), a person "may not lawfully possess or use marijuana on the campus of any public university, college, community college or postsecondary educational institution." Consequently, the legislature amended the AMMA when it enacted § 15–108(A) because that statute makes AMMA-compliant possession or use of marijuana on public college and university campuses criminal.

Although this conclusion is apparent from the statute's terms, it is also bolstered by § 15–108's legislative history. When that proposed law was introduced in the legislature as House Bill 2349, the Bill Summary noted that it would "require the affirmative vote of at least three-fourths of the members of each house of the Legislature" to be enacted. Ariz. H.B. Summary for H.B. 2349, 50th Leg., 2d Reg. Sess. (Jan. 23, 2012). With one exception that is inapplicable here, see Ariz. Const. art. 9, § 22(A) (requiring three-fourths vote of legislature to override governor's veto of revenue-raising act), such a requirement applies only when a legislative enactment is subject to the VPA. Accordingly, when House Bill 2349 was introduced, the bill's sponsor presumably understood that its provisions would amend the AMMA if enacted.

For the foregoing reasons, we conclude that the VPA's restrictions apply to the legislature's enactment of § 15–108(A) because it amends the AMMA. We next turn to whether the legislature complied with the VPA's requirements when it enacted § 15–108(A).

To comply with the VPA, the legislature may constitutionally amend a voter initiative only if "the amending legislation furthers the purposes of such measure and at least three-fourths of the members of each house of the legislature vote to amend such measure." Ariz. Const. art. 4, pt. 1, § 1(6)(C). Here, "at least three-fourths of the members of each house of the legislature" voted to enact § 15–108(A). Id. The dispositive question, therefore, is whether § 15–108(A) "furthers the purposes" of the AMMA. Id. It does not.

The AMMA "permits those who meet statutory conditions to [possess and] use medical marijuana." *Reed-Kaliher v. Hoggatt*, 237 Ariz. 119, 122 (2015). "Because marijuana possession and use are otherwise illegal in Arizona, the drafters [of the AMMA] sought to ensure that those using marijuana pursuant to [the] AMMA would not be penalized for such use." Id. Indeed, this purpose is made explicit in the AMMA's voter initiative statements. See Proposition 203 § 2(G) (2010) (stating that the purpose of the AMMA "is to protect patients with debilitating medical conditions from arrest and prosecution, [and] criminal and other penalties if such patients engage in the medical use of marijuana"). Criminalizing AMMA-compliant marijuana possession or use on public college and university campuses plainly does not further the AMMA's primary purpose as expressed in those statements supporting the voter initiative. Section 15–108(A) does not "protect" qualifying AMMA cardholders from criminal penalties arising from AMMA-compliant marijuana possession or use on public college and university campuses, but rather subjects them to such penalties. Therefore, because § 15–108(A) does not further the purpose of the AMMA, we hold that § 15–108(A) violates the VPA as applied to AMMA-compliant marijuana possession or use.

In so holding, we disagree with the State that the AMMA's anti-discrimination provision, A.R.S. § 36–2813(A), authorizes the legislature to criminalize AMMA-compliant marijuana possession or use on public college and university campuses to preserve federal funding. Section 36–2813(A) provides that a "school" may "penalize a person solely for his status as a cardholder" only if "failing to do so would cause the school to lose a monetary or licensing related benefit under federal law or regulations."

By its terms, § 36–2813(A) does not authorize the legislature to criminalize AMMA-compliant marijuana possession or use on public college and university campuses for two reasons. First, § 36–2813(A) authorizes a "school" to penalize a cardholder to preserve federal funding. But a school is not authorized to enact criminal laws. Therefore, any authority that is vested in a school under this statute does not extend to criminalizing AMMA-compliant marijuana possession or use.

Second, even if § 36–2813(A) did authorize the legislature to take some action to preserve federal funding, criminalizing AMMA-compliant marijuana possession or use is impermissible because it is unnecessary to achieve the statute's purpose. The State has not shown that failing to "penalize a person solely for his status as a cardholder would cause" a school to lose federal funding. § 36–2813(A) (emphasis added). A university can comply with federal funding requirements by adopting and implementing "a program to prevent the use of illicit drugs." 20 U.S.C. § 1011i(a). The program must prohibit "the unlawful possession of illicit drugs," id. § 1011i(a)(1)(A), and describe "the applicable legal sanctions under local, State, or Federal law for the unlawful possession of illicit drugs," id. § 1011i(a)(1)(B), which may include "referral for prosecution," id. § 1011i(a)(1)(E). But a university does not have to guarantee prosecution for violations of its programs. And it can refer violations of its programs to the federal prosecutor. The State has not shown that a university would lose (or has lost) federal funding if a state prosecutor did not prosecute violations of the university's program. Consequently, we conclude that A.R.S. § 36–2813(A) does not authorize the legislature to criminalize AMMA-compliant marijuana possession or use on public university and college campuses to preserve federal funding.

III. CONCLUSION

For the reasons stated above, we vacate Maestas's conviction for possession of marijuana. We also vacate the court of appeals' opinion.

NOTES AND QUESTIONS

1. **Scope of the court's holding.** The *Maestas* decision strikes down a state statute that criminalized the possession of marijuana on college campuses, finding that the statute violated Arizona's Voter Protection Act because it improperly amended Arizona's Medical Marijuana Act, which was passed by voter initiative. Specifically, the court found, the statute improperly

added a location to the Arizona Medical Marijuana Act's list of specified locations where the legislature was allowed to impose criminal penalties for possession of marijuana, i.e., college campuses. Would the court's decision also prohibit the legislature from imposing *civil penalties* for possession of marijuana on college campuses?

2.   Medical marijuana states. By the end of 2018, 33 states plus the District of Columbia had enacted statutes legalizing medical marijuana use. In addition, 13 additional states that did not allow medical marijuana *per se* had passed legislation allowing CBD oil to be used for treatment of certain disorders, e.g., seizure disorders. Thus, there now remain only a handful of states that have not approved the medical use of at least some marijuana-derived products. However, as noted above, the state statutes vary significantly with respect to such things as (1) which medical conditions qualify a patient to obtain a medical license, (2) the permissible manner of ingestion (e.g., a few legalization states require medical marijuana patients to take an extract or pill, rather than smoking), (3) the amount of marijuana the patient is allowed to possess, and (4) the manner in which medical marijuana can be distributed (e.g., dispensaries versus caregivers).

3.   Federal legislation. Since 2015, Congress has annually passed appropriations acts (i.e., spending bills) that prohibit the United States Department of Justice from using federal funds to prevent states from implementing their own medical marijuana laws. *See, e.g.,* Consolidated Appropriations Act, Pub. L. No. 114-113 § 542, 129 Stat. 2242, 2332–33 (2015). Thus, state-enacted medical marijuana laws would appear to have a degree of protection from federal interference that is lacking in the case of state-enacted recreational marijuana laws, as discussed further in the following section.

4.   Medical marijuana as a bridge to recreational marijuana. Some commentators have argued that state legalization of medical marijuana eased the way legally to state legalization of recreational marijuana:

> This article suggests five ways in which the passage and implementation of medical marijuana laws smoothed the transition to nonmedical legalization in the United States: (a) they demonstrated the efficacy of using voter initiatives to change marijuana supply laws, (b) enabled the psychological changes needed to destabilize the "war on drugs" policy stasis, (c) generated an evidence base that could be used to downplay concerns about nonmedical legalization, (d) created a visible and active marijuana industry, and (e) revealed that the federal government would allow state and local jurisdictions to generate tax revenue from marijuana.

Beau Kilmer and Robert J. MacCoun, *How Medical Marijuana Smoothed the Transition to Marijuana Legalization in the United States*, 13 Ann. Rev. L. & Social Sciences 181, 181 (2017).

PROBLEM 4-1

State X has legalized medical marijuana; state Y has not. Is it legal for residents of State X that have legally purchased marijuana there to bring it into state Y and consume it? May residents of state Y buy marijuana in state X and legally consume it there? May residents of state Y go into state X, purchase marijuana legally there, and then bring it back to state Y?

C. RECREATIONAL (ADULT USE) STATES

In 2012, Colorado and Washington became the first states in the country to legalize marijuana (in limited amounts) for adult recreational use. In both states, voters approved ballot initiatives that amended the states' constitutions to legalize the adult recreational use of marijuana, essentially requiring the states to regulate and tax marijuana sales in a manner similar to the way the states regulated and taxed alcohol. (Note that sales of recreational marijuana are generally taxed at a higher rate than sales of medical marijuana in states that have legalized both.) Both states set up detailed regulatory schemes that limited the amounts and manner of marijuana sales, and created a licensing system for producers, processors, and retailers of recreational marijuana. Recreational sales began in January 2014 in Colorado, and in July 2014 in Washington.

Since that time, eight additional states (Alaska, California, Maine, Massachusetts, Michigan, Nevada, Oregon, and Vermont) plus the District of Columbia have legalized recreational use. Of these, only Vermont did so via legislation; the others did so via ballot initiatives.

The laws in the states that have legalized recreational use vary fairly significantly. In Colorado and Washington, for example, it is legal for adults age 21 and over to purchase up to 1 ounce of marijuana, whereas in Oregon dispensaries are only allowed to sell up to ¼ ounce of marijuana to adults 21 and older. And in the District of Columbia, because Congress blocked the city Council's attempt to implement regulatory scheme that would have licensed dispensaries, it is legal for adults to grow marijuana at home, but it is not legal for them to buy or sell it.

Set out below is Article 18, section 16 of the Colorado Constitution, which was enacted by the voters' approval of Amendment 64 in November 2012. The amendment establishes (in subsection 3) that the personal possession of up to 1 ounce of marijuana is no longer unlawful in the State of Colorado, and it provides (in subsection 4) for the cultivation and sale of marijuana in such amounts to the public. The amendment also (in subsection 5) directs the state to set up a regulatory scheme for the cultivation and sale of recreational marijuana, including licensing. And it addresses (in subsection 6) certain other miscellaneous issues, such as preventing use by minors, prohibiting driving under the influence of marijuana, and establishing that employers do not need to condone marijuana possession or use at the place of employment.

The text to Amendment 64, set out below, is instructive because it provided a model for other states that have sought to legalize recreational marijuana through ballot initiatives. As you review it, think about whether the Amendment provides adequate guidance to the Colorado Legislature and the Colorado Department of Revenue in setting up a regulatory scheme for legalizing sales of marijuana to the public.

AMENDMENT 64 TO C.R.S.A. CONST. ART. 18, § 16

§ 16.   Personal use and regulation of marijuana

(1) Purpose and findings.

(a)   In the interest of the efficient use of law enforcement resources, enhancing revenue for public purposes, and individual freedom, the people of the state of Colorado find and declare that the use of marijuana should be legal for persons twenty-one years of age or older and taxed in a manner similar to alcohol.

(b)   In the interest of the health and public safety of our citizenry, the people of the state of Colorado further find and declare that marijuana should be regulated in a manner similar to alcohol so that:

(I)   Individuals will have to show proof of age before purchasing marijuana;

(II) Selling, distributing, or transferring marijuana to minors and other individuals under the age of twenty-one shall remain illegal;

(III) Driving under the influence of marijuana shall remain illegal;

(IV) Legitimate, taxpaying business people, and not criminal actors, will conduct sales of marijuana; and

(V) Marijuana sold in this state will be labeled and subject to additional regulations to ensure that consumers are informed and protected.

(c)   In the interest of enacting rational policies for the treatment of all variations of the cannabis plant, the people of Colorado further find and declare that industrial hemp should be regulated separately from strains of cannabis with higher delta-9 tetrahydrocannabinol (THC) concentrations.

(d)   The people of the state of Colorado further find and declare that it is necessary to ensure consistency and fairness in the application of this section throughout the state and that, therefore, the matters addressed by this section are, except as specified herein, matters of statewide concern.

(2) Definitions. As used in this section, unless the context otherwise requires,

* * *

(3) Personal use of marijuana. Notwithstanding any other provision of law, the following acts are not unlawful and shall not be an offense under Colorado law or the law of any locality within Colorado or be a basis for seizure or forfeiture of assets under Colorado law for persons twenty-one years of age or older:

(a) Possessing, using, displaying, purchasing, or transporting marijuana accessories or one ounce or less of marijuana.

(b) Possessing, growing, processing, or transporting no more than six marijuana plants, with three or fewer being mature, flowering plants, and possession of the marijuana produced by the plants on the premises where the plants were grown, provided that the growing takes place in an enclosed, locked space, is not conducted openly or publicly, and is not made available for sale.

(c) Transfer of one ounce or less of marijuana without remuneration to a person who is twenty-one years of age or older.

(d) Consumption of marijuana, provided that nothing in this section shall permit consumption that is conducted openly and publicly or in a manner that endangers others.

(e) Assisting another person who is twenty-one years of age or older in any of the acts described in paragraphs (a) through (d) of this subsection.

(4) Lawful operation of marijuana-related facilities. Notwithstanding any other provision of law, the following acts are not unlawful and shall not be an offense under Colorado law or be a basis for seizure or forfeiture of assets under Colorado law for persons twenty-one years of age or older:

(a) Manufacture, possession, or purchase of marijuana accessories or the sale of marijuana accessories to a person who is twenty-one years of age or older.

(b) Possessing, displaying, or transporting marijuana or marijuana products; purchase of marijuana from a marijuana cultivation facility; purchase of marijuana or marijuana products from a marijuana product manufacturing facility; or sale of marijuana or marijuana products to consumers, if the person conducting the activities described in this paragraph has obtained a current, valid license to operate a retail marijuana store or is acting in his or her capacity as an owner, employee or agent of a licensed retail marijuana store.

(c) Cultivating, harvesting, processing, packaging, transporting, displaying, or possessing marijuana; delivery or transfer of marijuana to a marijuana testing facility; selling marijuana to a marijuana cultivation facility, a marijuana product manufacturing facility, or a retail marijuana store; or the purchase of marijuana from a marijuana cultivation facility, if the person conducting the activities described in this paragraph has obtained a current, valid license to operate a marijuana cultivation facility or is acting in his or her capacity as an owner, employee, or agent of a licensed marijuana cultivation facility.

(d)   Packaging, processing, transporting, manufacturing, displaying, or possessing marijuana or marijuana products; delivery or transfer of marijuana or marijuana products to a marijuana testing facility; selling marijuana or marijuana products to a retail marijuana store or a marijuana product manufacturing facility; the purchase of marijuana from a marijuana cultivation facility; or the purchase of marijuana or marijuana products from a marijuana product manufacturing facility, if the person conducting the activities described in this paragraph has obtained a current, valid license to operate a marijuana product manufacturing facility or is acting in his or her capacity as an owner, employee, or agent of a licensed marijuana product manufacturing facility.

(e)   Possessing, cultivating, processing, repackaging, storing, transporting, displaying, transferring or delivering marijuana or marijuana products if the person has obtained a current, valid license to operate a marijuana testing facility or is acting in his or her capacity as an owner, employee, or agent of a licensed marijuana testing facility.

(f)   Leasing or otherwise allowing the use of property owned, occupied or controlled by any person, corporation or other entity for any of the activities conducted lawfully in accordance with paragraphs (a) through (e) of this subsection.

(5)   Regulation of marijuana.

(a)   Not later than July 1, 2013, the department shall adopt regulations necessary for implementation of this section. Such regulations shall not prohibit the operation of marijuana establishments, either expressly or through regulations that make their operation unreasonably impracticable. Such regulations shall include:

     * * *

(6)   Employers, driving, minors and control of property.

(a)   Nothing in this section is intended to require an employer to permit or accommodate the use, consumption, possession, transfer, display, transportation, sale or growing of marijuana in the workplace or to affect the ability of employers to have policies restricting the use of marijuana by employees.

(b)   Nothing in this section is intended to allow driving under the influence of marijuana or driving while impaired by marijuana or to supersede statutory laws related to driving under the influence of marijuana or driving while impaired by marijuana, nor shall this section prevent the state from enacting and imposing penalties for driving under the influence of or while impaired by marijuana.

(c) Nothing in this section is intended to permit the transfer of marijuana, with or without remuneration, to a person under the age of twenty-one or to allow a person under the age of twenty-one to purchase, possess, use, transport, grow, or consume marijuana.

(d) Nothing in this section shall prohibit a person, employer, school, hospital, detention facility, corporation or any other entity who occupies, owns or controls a property from prohibiting or otherwise regulating the possession, consumption, use, display, transfer, distribution, sale, transportation, or growing of marijuana on or in that property.

(7) Medical marijuana provisions unaffected. Nothing in this section shall be construed:

(a) To limit any privileges or rights of a medical marijuana patient, primary caregiver, or licensed entity as provided in section 14 of this article and the Colorado Medical Marijuana Code;

(b) To permit a medical marijuana center to distribute marijuana to a person who is not a medical marijuana patient;

(c) To permit a medical marijuana center to purchase marijuana or marijuana products in a manner or from a source not authorized under the Colorado Medical Marijuana Code;

(d) To permit any medical marijuana center licensed pursuant to section 14 of this article and the Colorado Medical Marijuana Code to operate on the same premises as a retail marijuana store; or

(e) To discharge the department, the Colorado Board of Health, or the Colorado Department of Public Health and Environment from their statutory and constitutional duties to regulate medical marijuana pursuant to section 14 of this article and the Colorado Medical Marijuana Code.

(8) Self-executing, severability, conflicting provisions. All provisions of this section are self-executing except as specified herein, are severable, and, except where otherwise indicated in the text, shall supersede conflicting state statutory, local charter, ordinance, or resolution, and other state and local provisions.

(9) Effective date. Unless otherwise provided by this section, all provisions of this section shall become effective upon official declaration of the vote hereon by proclamation of the governor, pursuant to section 1(4) of article V.

NOTES AND QUESTIONS

1. **Statutory interpretation.** As discussed in Chapter 15, many employers have zero-tolerance policies for drug use, including marijuana, and many of them have random drug-testing programs. Looking at the language of subsection 6(a) of Amendment 64, could a Colorado employer terminate an employee for testing positive for marijuana on a random drug test, if the employee consumed legally consumed marijuana while on vacation and was never impaired while at work?

2. **Department of Justice policies.** Under the Obama administration, the Department of Justice took a largely hands-off approach to state legalization of marijuana. As set out in the so-called Cole and Ogden memos (see Chapter 1(D)), the Department made it clear that would not prioritize enforcement of the Controlled Substances Act as against states that have enacted legalization schemes, provided these schemes complied with certain enumerated criteria, such as prohibiting use by minors and preventing illegal drug cartels from infiltrating the industry. In January 2018, however, Attorney General Sessions announced a change in policy. The Attorney General made it clear that under the Trump administration's policies, the Department, while not prioritizing interference with state legalization schemes, was leaving its options open with regard to all sales or other distributions of marijuana that were in violation of federal law. (And since federal law prohibits all such distributions, all dispensary sales would be subject to prosecution.) Specifically, each United States Attorney was authorized to enforce federal law to the extent that the U.S. Attorney deemed appropriate. As a result, the marijuana industry in legalization states appears to be in a rather more precarious position under the Trump administration than it was under the Obama administration, although thus far the Department of Justice has not exercised its discretion to crack down on recreational use in legalization states.

3. **Challenges by other states.** In December 2014, Nebraska and Oklahoma filed a motion with the United States Supreme Court, seeking leave to file a complaint against Colorado. The states alleged that Colorado's Amendment 64 facilitated violation of federal drug laws, and had increased trafficking and transportation of Colorado-sourced marijuana into their states, requiring them to expend significant law enforcement resources to combat the increased trafficking in marijuana. The states sought a preliminary injunction barring implementation of Amendment 64. In March 2016, however, a majority of the Supreme Court denied the motion without rendering a written opinion. Justice Thomas, joined by Justice Alito, issued a dissenting opinion, which argued that the complaint, on its face, presented a controversy between two or more states that the Supreme Court alone had the authority to adjudicate, and that the states had alleged significant harms to their sovereign interest caused by another state. Thus, the dissenters would have granted Nebraska and Oklahoma's motion for leave to file a complaint.

4. **Concerns about crime.** Some critics of recreational marijuana legalization have been concerned about the possible effect of such legalization

on crime rates. Professors Maier, Mannes, and Kloppenhofer argue that this fear is unfounded, based on their review of the limited data available at this point:

> There is no significant difference in drug abuse arrest violations in states where marijuana has been decriminalized compared to states where it has not, and drug arrest rates were significantly lower in states where medical marijuana has been legalized and operationalized. Results also show the arrest rates for possession of opiates, synthetic drugs, or other drugs were not different based on state classification of marijuana laws. This contradicts the assumption that legalizing or decriminalizing marijuana will lead to increased arrest for other drugs (presumably due to increased use). Finally, there appears to be no relationship between state classification of marijuana laws and property crime rate, violet crime rate, arrests for opiate, synthetics, or other drug possession. . . .

Shana L. Maier, Suzanne Mannes & Emily L. Koppenhofer, *The Implications of Marijuana Decriminalization and Legalization on Crime in the United States*, 44 Cont. Drug Prob. 125 (2017).

PROBLEM 4-2

In state Z, which has legalized recreational marijuana, municipalities are allowed to choose whether to have dispensaries operating within their city limits. City M does not allow marijuana dispensaries or any marijuana sales within its limits. Is it nevertheless legal for residents of city M to buy marijuana in other cities and bring it back to their homes in the city M? What about nonresidents of city M: is it legal for them to bring marijuana purchased legally elsewhere with them into city M and consume it within city limits?

D. LOCAL LAWS REGULATING MARIJUANA

As discussed in section A above, various states began decriminalizing the personal use of marijuana in the early 1970s, starting with an Oregon statute that made possession of small amounts of marijuana held for personal use a mere civil infraction with a $100 fine. At the same time, in states that were not pursuing decriminalization, certain municipalities pursued their own versions of decriminalization. The first was Ann Arbor, Michigan, which passed an ordinance in 1972 that reduced marijuana possession to a civil infraction, the violation of which resulted in a mere $5 fine. This provision was later struck down by local court, but two years later the voters of Ann Arbor amended the city's charter to reenact the provision, and it remains in effect to this day (although the amount of the fine was later raised to $25 for a first offense, $50 for a second offense, and $100 for subsequent offenses). Other municipalities that passed decriminalization measures in the 1970s included Berkeley, California, and Madison, Wisconsin.

In recent years, local decriminalization efforts have picked up again within states that continued to maintain criminal penalties for personal marijuana possession. In Michigan and Wisconsin alone, for example, more than two dozen municipalities had passed decriminalization provisions by 2016, including Milwaukee and Detroit. Other large cities in the United States that have passed decriminalization measures include Chicago and Philadelphia. And in New York, a local ordinance was passed giving police the discretion to issue civil infractions for marijuana possession in lieu of criminal sanctions. Of course, many of these local laws have or will become moot as the states in which the municipalities are located decriminalize or legalize recreational marijuana use themselves.

While most municipalities that enacted marijuana laws did so in order to create local zones of decriminalization within states that had not yet criminalized simple marijuana possession, a few municipalities have sought to impose local laws that are *more* restrictive than state laws in states that have legalized medical marijuana. For example. in the following case, *Ter Beek v. City of Wyoming*, the Michigan Supreme Court considered a medical marijuana patients' challenge to a local ordinance that essentially made it illegal to use medical marijuana within the municipality. The court struck down the ordinance, finding that it was preempted by the Michigan Medical Marijuana Act because it permitted the municipality to penalize medical marijuana patients for state-compliant medical marijuana use.

TER BEEK V. CITY OF WYOMING

Supreme Court of Michigan
495 Mich. 1, 846 N.W.2d 531 (2014)

MCCORMACK, J.

The Michigan Medical Marihuana Act (MMMA), MCL 333.26421 *et seq.,* enacted pursuant to a voter initiative in November 2008, affords certain protections under state law for the medical use of marijuana in the state of Michigan. Among them is § 4(a) of the MMMA, which immunizes registered qualifying patients from "penalty in any manner" for specified MMMA-compliant medical marijuana use. MCL 333.26424(a). At issue here is the relationship between this immunity, the federal prohibition of marijuana under the controlled substances act (CSA), 21 USC 801 *et seq.,* and a local zoning ordinance adopted by the city of Wyoming which prohibits and subjects to civil sanction any land "[u]ses that are contrary to federal law." City of Wyoming Code of Ordinances, § 90–66. As set forth below, we agree with the Court of Appeals that the ordinance directly conflicts with, and is preempted by, § 4(a) of the MMMA, and that § 4(a) is not preempted by the federal CSA. Accordingly, we affirm the Court of Appeals' judgment.

I.   FACTUAL AND PROCEDURAL BACKGROUND

In 2010, approximately two years after the MMMA went into effect, defendant, the city of Wyoming (the City), adopted an ordinance (the Ordinance) amending the zoning chapter of the Wyoming city code to add the following provision:

Uses not expressly permitted under this article are prohibited in all districts. Uses that are contrary to federal law, state law or local ordinance are prohibited.

City of Wyoming Code of Ordinances, § 90–66. Under the city code, violations of the Ordinance constitute municipal civil infractions punishable by "civil sanctions, including, without limitation, fines, damages, expenses and costs," City of Wyoming Code of Ordinances, § 1–27(a) to (b), and are also subject to injunctive relief, City of Wyoming Code of Ordinances, § 1–27(g).

Plaintiff, John Ter Beek, lives in the City and is a qualifying patient under the MMMA who possesses a state-issued registry identification card. Upon the City's adoption of the Ordinance, Ter Beek filed the instant lawsuit in circuit court. Ter Beek alleges that he wishes to grow, possess, and use medical marijuana in his home in accordance with the MMMA. The Ordinance, however, by its incorporation of the CSA's federal prohibition of marijuana, prohibits and penalizes such conduct. This, Ter Beek contends, impermissibly contravenes § 4(a) of the MMMA, which provides that registered qualifying patients "shall not be subject to arrest, prosecution, or penalty in any manner . . . for the medical use of marihuana in accordance with" the MMMA. Accordingly, Ter Beek seeks a declaratory judgment that the Ordinance is preempted by the MMMA and a corresponding injunction prohibiting the City from enforcing the Ordinance against him for the medical use of marijuana in compliance with the MMMA.

The parties filed cross-motions for summary disposition pursuant to MCR 2.116(C)(10), disputing whether the Ordinance is preempted by the MMMA and whether the MMMA is preempted by the CSA. The circuit court granted summary disposition in favor of the City, concluding that the MMMA is preempted by the CSA. Ter Beek appealed by right in the Court of Appeals, which reversed the circuit court's grant of summary disposition in favor of the City and remanded the case for entry of summary disposition in favor of Ter Beek. *Ter Beek v. Wyoming,* 297 Mich.App. 446 (2012). The Court of Appeals first concluded that the Ordinance directly conflicts with, and is thus preempted by, § 4(a) of the MMMA, because it purports to penalize the medical use of marijuana in contravention of § 4(a)'s grant of immunity from such penalties. The Court of Appeals then concluded that § 4(a) is not preempted by the federal CSA, reasoning that it is possible to comply with both statutes simultaneously and that § 4(a)'s state-law immunity for certain medical marijuana patients does not stand as an obstacle to the CSA's federal regulation of marijuana use or to the federal enforcement of same. The City sought leave to appeal, which we granted, to address the questions of state and federal preemption.

II. STANDARD OF REVIEW

Whether § 4(a) of the MMMA preempts the Ordinance, and whether the CSA preempts § 4(a), are questions of law which we review de novo. *Detroit v. Ambassador Bridge Co.,* 481 Mich. 29, 35, 748 N.W.2d 221 (2008). We also review de novo the decision to grant or deny summary disposition, *Spiek v. Dep't of Transp.,* 456 Mich. 331, 337 (1998), and review for clear error factual findings in support of that decision, *Ambassador Bridge,* 481 Mich. at 35.

As we have recently explained, the intent of the electors governs the interpretation of voter-initiated statutes such as the MMMA, just as the intent of the Legislature governs the interpretation of legislatively enacted statutes. *People v. Bylsma,* 493 Mich. 17, 26 (2012). The first step when interpreting a statute is to examine its plain language, which provides the most reliable evidence of intent. If the statutory language is unambiguous, no further judicial construction is required or permitted because we must conclude that the electors intended the meaning clearly expressed. *Id.*

III. ANALYSIS

A. KEY PROVISIONS OF THE MMMA, THE CSA, AND THE ORDINANCE

The questions of state and federal preemption in this case arise from the differing treatment of medical marijuana use under the MMMA and the CSA. As noted, § 4(a) of the MMMA provides, in relevant part:

A qualifying patient who has been issued and possesses a registry identification card shall not be subject to arrest, prosecution, or penalty in any manner, or denied any right or privilege, including but not limited to civil penalty or disciplinary action by a business or occupational or professional licensing board or bureau, for the medical use of marihuana in accordance with this act. . . . [MCL 333.26424(a).]

The MMMA defines "medical use" as "the acquisition, possession, cultivation, manufacture, use, internal possession, delivery, transfer, or transportation of marihuana or paraphernalia relating to the administration of marihuana to treat or alleviate a registered qualifying patient's debilitating medical condition or symptoms associated with the debilitating medical condition." MCL 333.26423(f).

The CSA, meanwhile, contains no such immunity. Rather, it makes it "unlawful for any person knowingly or intentionally . . . to manufacture, distribute, or dispense, or possess with intent to manufacture, distribute, or dispense, a controlled substance." 21 USC 841(a)(1). The CSA classifies marijuana as a Schedule I controlled substance, 21 USC 812(c)(c)(10), and thus largely prohibits its manufacture, distribution, or possession.

The parties do not dispute that the Ordinance, by prohibiting all "[u]ses that are contrary to federal law," incorporates the CSA's prohibition of marijuana and makes certain violations of that prohibition both punishable by civil sanctions and subject to injunctive relief. Thus, an individual whose medical use of marijuana falls within the scope of § 4(a)'s immunity from "penalty in any manner" may nonetheless be subject to punishment under the Ordinance for that use.

B.   THE CSA DOES NOT PREEMPT § 4(a) OF THE MMMA

As noted, the circuit court rejected Ter Beek's challenge to the Ordinance because it held that § 4(a) of the MMMA is preempted by the CSA. The Court of Appeals disagreed. Although raised under the particular circumstances of this case as a defense, we address this question first, and hold that the CSA does not preempt § 4(a).

* * *

C.   THE ORDINANCE IS PREEMPTED
BY § 4(a) OF THE MMMA

Having found that the CSA does not preempt § 4(a) of the MMMA, we turn next to whether the Ordinance, as applied to Ter Beek, is preempted by § 4(a). We agree with the Court of Appeals that it is. The required analysis on this point is not complex.

Under the Michigan Constitution, the City's "power to adopt resolutions and ordinances relating to its municipal concerns" is "subject to the constitution and the law." Const. 1963, art. 7, § 22. As this Court has previously noted, "[w]hile prescribing broad powers, this provision specifically provides that ordinances are subject to the laws of this state, i.e., statutes." *AFSCME v. Detroit*, 468 Mich. 388, 410, 662 N.W.2d 695 (2003). The City, therefore, "is precluded from enacting an ordinance if . . . the ordinance is in direct conflict with the state statutory scheme, or . . . if the state statutory scheme preempts the ordinance by occupying the field of regulation which the municipality seeks to enter, to the exclusion of the ordinance, even where there is no direct conflict between the two schemes of regulation." *People v. Llewellyn*, 401 Mich. 314, 322 (1977) (footnotes omitted). A direct conflict exists when "the ordinance permits what the statute prohibits or the ordinance prohibits what the statute permits." Here, the Ordinance directly conflicts with the MMMA by permitting what the MMMA expressly prohibits—the imposition of a "penalty in any manner" on a registered qualifying patient whose medical use of marijuana falls within the scope of § 4(a)'s immunity.

The City disputes this characterization of the Ordinance, noting that while it permits the imposition of civil sanctions, it does not require them;

instead, a violation of the Ordinance can be enforced through equitable relief such as a civil injunction. We agree with the Court of Appeals, however, that enjoining a registered qualifying patient from engaging in MMMA-compliant conduct unambiguously falls within the scope of penalties prohibited by § 4(a). For § 4(a) makes clear that individuals who satisfy the statutorily specified criteria "shall not be subject to . . . penalty in any manner," a prohibition which expressly includes "civil penalt[ies]." As the Court of Appeals noted, the MMMA does not define "penalty," but that term is commonly understood to mean a "punishment imposed or incurred for a violation of law or rule . . . something forfeited." *Random House Webster's College Dictionary* (2000). Under the Ordinance, individuals are subject to civil punishment for engaging in the medical use of marijuana in accordance with the MMMA; by the plain terms of § 4(a), the manner of that punishment—be it requiring the payment of a monetary sanction, or denying the ability to engage in MMMA-compliant conduct— is not material to the MMMA's immunity from it.

Nor do we agree with the City that our decision in *Michigan v. McQueen,* 493 Mich. 135 (2013), mandates a different outcome. In *McQueen,* this Court held that, because the defendants' business, a medical marijuana dispensary, was not being operated in accordance with the MMMA, it was properly enjoined as a public nuisance under MCL 600.3801. The City contends that, because the growth and cultivation of marijuana is a violation of the Ordinance, and violations of zoning ordinances constitute nuisances per se under the Michigan Zoning Enabling Act (MZEA), *McQueen* permits the City's regulation through injunction. *McQueen,* however, affirmed the injunction of the defendants' business not simply because it was a nuisance, but because it was a nuisance that fell outside the scope of conduct permitted under the MMMA. *McQueen* does not, as the City contends, authorize a municipality to enjoin a registered qualifying patient from engaging in medical use of marijuana in compliance with the MMMA, simply by characterizing that conduct as a zoning violation.

Furthermore, contrary to the City's suggestion, the fact that the Ordinance is a local zoning regulation enacted pursuant to the MZEA does not save it from preemption. The City stresses that the MZEA affords local municipalities a broad grant of authority to use their zoning powers to advance local interests, such as "public health, safety, and welfare." The MMMA, however, provides in no uncertain terms that "[t]he medical use of marihuana is allowed under state law to the extent that it is carried out in accordance with" the MMMA, MCL 333.26427(a), and that "[a]ll other acts and parts of acts inconsistent with [the MMMA] do not apply to the medical use of marihuana." The City contends that the MMMA does not express a sufficiently clear intent to supersede the MZEA, but we see no ambiguity in the MMMA's plain language to this effect. It is well accepted that when two legislative enactments seemingly conflict, the specific provision prevails over the more general provision. Accordingly, the City cannot look to the MZEA to authorize or excuse the Ordinance's contravention of the specific immunity for medical marijuana use provided under § 4(a) of the MMMA.

The City also points to *Riverside v. Inland Empire Patients Health & Wellness Ctr., Inc.,* 56 Cal.4th 729 (2013), in support of its position. In that case, the California Supreme Court found certain state medical marijuana laws did not preempt a local zoning ordinance. *Riverside,* however, is beside the point. At issue there was whether a local zoning ordinance prohibiting medical marijuana dispensaries within city limits was preempted by California's Compassionate Use Act (CUA) and Medical Marijuana Program Act (MMP). The California Supreme Court concluded that there was no preemption, as the CUA and MMP offered only a limited immunity from sanction under certain specified state criminal and nuisance statutes, thereby "signal[ing] that the *state* declines to regard the described acts as nuisances or criminal violations, and that the *state's* enforcement mechanisms will thus not be available against these acts." *Id.* at 762. As such, these "limited provisions" were found to "neither expressly or impliedly restrict or preempt the authority of individual local jurisdictions to choose otherwise for local reasons, and to prohibit collective or cooperative medical marijuana activities within their own borders." *Id.* The scope of § 4(a)'s immunity, however, is not similarly circumscribed; in prohibiting certain individuals from being "subject to . . . penalty in any manner," § 4(a) draws no distinction between state and local laws or penalties. We thus do not find *Riverside's* reasoning instructive.

Lastly, the City stresses that the MMMA does not create an absolute right to grow and distribute marijuana. Correct. Ter Beek, however, does not seek to assert any such general or absolute right. Nor does our conclusion recognize one. The Ordinance directly conflicts with the MMMA not because it generally pertains to marijuana, but because it permits registered qualifying patients, such as Ter Beek, to be penalized by the City for engaging in MMMA-compliant medical marijuana use. Section 4(a) of the MMMA expressly prohibits this. As such, the MMMA preempts the Ordinance to the extent of this conflict.

IV. CONCLUSION

For the foregoing reasons, we hold that the Ordinance is preempted by § 4(a) of the Michigan Medical Marijuana Act, which in turn is not preempted by the federal controlled substances act. Accordingly, we affirm the judgment of the Court of Appeals, reverse the circuit court's grant of summary disposition in favor of the City, and remand for entry of summary disposition in favor of Ter Beek.

NOTES AND QUESTIONS

1.   **Preemption doctrine.** The court in *Ter Beek* struck down a municipal ordinance that prohibited medical marijuana use in the municipality; it also upheld the Michigan Medical Marijuana Act. The court ruled that the City of Wyoming ordinance was preempted by the Michigan Medical Marijuana Act, and was thus invalid, while the Act itself was not preempted by the federal Controlled Substances Act, and was thus valid. On what basis did the court ground this distinction with respect to the preemption doctrine? Do you agree with the court's rationale? (*See also* Chapter 7 on federal preemption.)

2.   **Zoning restrictions.** Attempts by municipalities such as the City of Wyoming to enact zoning provisions that impose restrictions on state medical marijuana laws have raised some thorny issues with the courts. In one such case, the Supreme Court of Washington upheld a local ordinance that prohibited medical marijuana "collective gardens" within a municipality, even though such gardens (which allowed medical marijuana users to share responsibility for growing and producing marijuana) were explicitly provided for by the state's Medical Use of Cannabis Act. *See Cannabis Action Coalition v. City of Kent*, 351 P.3d 151 (Wash. 2015). The Cannabis Coalition had argued that the Act preempted the ordinance because the two were in direct conflict. The court rejected this argument, however, finding that the zoning restriction was a permissible land-use measure under the Act.

3.   **Local regulations.** Within legalization states, municipalities have enacted a variety of local laws that deal with a number of issues not discussed above. For example, state laws legalizing medical and recreational marijuana use frequently give municipalities the discretion whether to allow dispensaries within their limits or not (but not to outlaw marijuana use, as the Ciy of Wyoming attempted to do in *Ter Beek*). In addition, municipalities have broad discretion to regulate matters such as zoning, licensing, and health/safety issues, and so municipalities commonly enact zoning provisions that restrict where dispensaries may operate, that restrict their hours of operation, or that limit the size of their operations. Municipalities have attempted to enact other types of provisions as well, such as Denver Initiative 300, which city voters enacted in November 2016. It created a pilot program that allowed businesses to obtain licenses to operate "designated consumption areas," in which customers could consume cannabis, notwithstanding a prohibition in state law against all public consumption. However, the state significantly restricted the scope initiative 300 shortly after it was enacted by prohibiting businesses that serve alcohol from obtaining licenses to operate as designated consumption areas. Thus, it seems that Denver residents now have to make a vexing choice before they go to a bar or nightclub, as they cannot legally consume both cannabis and alcohol in the same establishment.

CHAPTER 5

STATE REGULATORY SCHEMES

■ ■ ■

The previous chapter focused on several themes relating to the regulation and deregulation of marijuana at the state level. This chapter highlights developments in California. California is worth special attention for a number of reasons. It played a pivotal role in advancing the interest in medical marijuana. The adoption of Proposition 215 has been essential towards legitimizing medical marijuana and moving the country closer to a national solution on that front. Beyond that, California has been at the vortex of the move towards acceptance of recreational marijuana. Although not the first state to legalize recreational marijuana (Colorado was), California has legalized recreational marijuana through the initiative process. As California comes online with its regulations, increased production and capacity to serve a much larger market than the state market, California should interest anyone involved in the industry or regulation of that industry.

Section A provides a brief history of the adoption of Proposition 215 (the Compassionate Use Act), which ushered medical marijuana into California. Section B explores some of the ambiguity in the Compassionate Use Act, some of which was intentional. It develops some of the California legislature's efforts to clarify the law and the state supreme court's response to some of those changes. Section C discusses California's first ballot initiative, Proposition 19, which would have legalized recreational marijuana. It considers how the failure of that proposition may have provided other states a blue print for drafting successful initiatives. Section D highlights provisions of Proposition 64, the initiative that brought legal recreational marijuana to California and hints at some of the competing policy choices that California faces as it rolls out its recreational marijuana licenses. Finally, Section E provides some of the regulations that California state agencies have put in place to implement its new law.

A. MEDICAL MARIJUANA COMES TO CALIFORNIA: A BRIEF HISTORY

Anyone familiar with the spread of marijuana across college campuses during the 1960s is aware of California's role in popularizing marijuana as a drug of choice. Less well known is its role in beginning the modern march towards the acceptance of medical marijuana:

California was one of the first states to outlaw marijuana, preceding federal efforts to regulate marijuana by over twenty years. California also led efforts to legalize medical use. * * *

By the late 1960s, Californians began a serious study of marijuana. In 1968, the California legislature established a state research advisory panel to investigate the effects of marijuana and hallucinogenic drugs. Health and Safety Code section 11481 (formerly codified under section 11655.6) gave the panel authority to approve and review annually research projects on marijuana. In 1979, Senate Bill 184 added a requirement that the Research Advisory Panel establish an additional panel to research marijuana's medicinal uses.

SB 184 received widespread support from mainline medical organizations like the American Cancer Society, the Board of Osteopathic Examiners, and Stanford's Children's Hospital and from the print media. Published opposition was slim. The only outspoken opponent of the bill was a representative of the DEA, who argued that marijuana had no recognized medical use. In addition to mandating research, SB 184 instructed the Research Advisory Panel to establish a study program on marijuana's utility for cancer patients. The law exempted program participants from prosecution for possession and distribution of marijuana.

Michael Vitiello, *Proposition 215: De Facto Legalization of Pot and the Shortcomings of Direct Democracy*, 31 U. Mich. J. L. Reform 707, 758–60 (1998).

When the FDA approved Marinol, many of the physicians involved in the process lost interest in the continued study of marijuana. But average Californians continued to push for access to marijuana for medicinal purposes. That was particularly true in communities like Santa Cruz. There, for example, in 1992, 75% of the local electorate voted for Measure A, which supported efforts to legalize medicinal marijuana and instructed the board of supervisors to ask local law enforcement to follow the spirit of the ordinance. So too did AID activists. For example, doctors like Donald Abrams were working on the front lines of the AIDS crisis in San Francisco and began noticing benefits for patients suffering from HIV/AIDS. Anecdotally, they saw increases in some patients' longevity that they associated with the use of marijuana. Some activists began pushing for legislative reform.

In 1994 and again in 1995, the legislature passed bills intended to move towards legalizing marijuana for medicinal purposes. In 1994, Senate Bill 1364 sought to have marijuana rescheduled as a Schedule II drug, one for which there are recognized medical uses. Then Governor Pete Wilson, involved in a heated race for re-election, vetoed the bill as part of his toughest-on-crime position in the race. Wilson's veto letter explained that federal law would preempt state law. In 1995, Assembly Bill 1529 created a defense for a seriously ill person charged with possession of marijuana. Such an approach avoided the preemption question.

AB 1529 specified a narrow set of conditions for which a person could use marijuana. Further, the bill had wide support from diverse groups. Again, Wilson vetoed the bill and stated that the bill would "for all intent [sic] and purposes legalize possession and cultivation in California." He also expressed concern that AB 1529 would unduly complicate law enforcement's efforts and noted that "[t]he FDA concluded that marijuana has no recognized medical use." Letter from Pete Wilson, Governor of California, to the California Assembly (May 3, 1996).

Given the inability to get legislation passed, proponents of medical marijuana (joined by proponents of marijuana generally) turned to the initiative process. As you saw in Chapter 4, some states have carefully focused medical marijuana statutes, narrowly describing conditions for which marijuana is appropriate. Not so in California. Drafters of Proposition 215 did not demonstrate the same restraint as did members of the legislature in California or the legislatures in other states. Here are some of the key provisions of Proposition 215, codified as the Compassionate Use Act of 1996 § 11362.5 of the Health & Safety Code:

(b) (1)   The people of the State of California hereby find and declare that the purposes of the Compassionate Use Act of 1996 are as follows:

(A)   To ensure that seriously ill Californians have the right to obtain and use marijuana for medical purposes where that medical use is deemed appropriate and has been recommended by a physician who has determined that the person's health would benefit from the use of marijuana in the treatment of cancer, anorexia, AIDS, chronic pain, spasticity, glaucoma, arthritis, migraine, or *any other illness for which marijuana provides relief.*

(B)   To ensure that patients and *their primary caregivers* who obtain and use marijuana for medical purposes upon the recommendation of a physician are not subject to criminal prosecution or sanction. * * *

(d)   Section 11357, relating to the possession of marijuana, and Section 11358, relating to the cultivation of marijuana, shall not apply to a patient, or to a patient's primary caregiver, who possesses or cultivates marijuana for the personal medical purposes of the patient upon the written or oral recommendation or approval of a physician.

The initiative included some intentionally broad language, inviting de facto legalization of marijuana for those willing to get a doctor's recommendation. Indeed, some of those involved in drafting Proposition 215 admitted that they hoped that the open-ended language in the initiative would lead to *de facto* legalization of marijuana. The late marijuana advocate Dennis Peron contended that all use of marijuana is medical. Under the Compassionate Use Act, virtually anyone has an "illness for which marijuana provides relief." Among conditions for which marijuana might be appropriate, according to supporters of Proposition 215, are pain, stress and insomnia.

The drafters included a provision requiring a doctor's recommendation, not a prescription, to avoid conflict with federal law. Because marijuana is a Schedule I drug (one with no recognized medical use), a doctor cannot prescribe marijuana and would lose her license to prescribe drugs if she prescribed marijuana. As developed in Chapter 8, Constitutional Issues, the Court of Appeals for the Ninth Circuit found that the First Amendment protected a doctor's discussion and recommendation of marijuana to a patient. *Conant v. Walters,* 309 F.3d 629 (9th Cir. 2002).

Whether intentional or not, Proposition 215 created any number of problems. The courts solved some of the problems; the legislature attempted to solve others. A few of those are raised in the following problems.

PROBLEM 5-1

Defendant is a medical marijuana activist and a medical marijuana user in California. She has pooled her resources with other advocates and opened a medical marijuana dispensary. She has examined the statute and is aware of some of the events that led to passage of Proposition 215. Many voters, for example, were swayed to vote for the initiative in reaction to aggressive police raids of medical marijuana dispensaries. As a result, she was stunned when the police raided her dispensary and have charged her with violating § 11360 of the California Health & Safety Code (making certain marijuana offenses felonies at that time). She has consulted with you and asked whether she is not a "primary caregiver," as provided in § 11362.5(b)(1)(B). Discuss how the court should interpret that language as applied to Defendant.

PROBLEM 5-2

Defendant suffers from chronic pain and asked her doctor for a recommendation to allow her to purchase marijuana for her personal use. After receiving her doctor's recommendation, Defendant purchased a pound of marijuana from a medical marijuana dispensary. During a lawful police investigation, Officer found Defendant's pound of marijuana. She showed the Officer her doctor's recommendation but Officer said that was a matter for trial. The prosecutor has charged Defendant with felony possession of marijuana. Later she learned that the prosecutor decided to pursue criminal charges because of the large amount of marijuana that she possessed. She has asked you for advice on two questions: one, doesn't the Compassionate Use Act give her immunity from prosecution? As a result, can she get an injunction to prevent her prosecution? Two, she wonders how much marijuana a patient may possess under the Compassionate Use Act. Discuss your advice to your client.

PROBLEM 5-3

After receiving his doctor's recommendation, Defendant picked up a small amount of marijuana from a medical dispensary. During a lawful traffic stop, Officer saw the marijuana on the front seat of Defendant's vehicle. She arrested Defendant for the transportation of marijuana. The prosecutor has charged Defendant with that offense, found in § 11360 subd. (a) of the Health & Safety Code. Startled, Defendant asks you, his attorney, what possible argument the prosecutor could make that he is not protected under the Compassionate Use Act. Discuss.

NOTES AND QUESTIONS

1. **Gaps in the law.** These problems demonstrate some gaps in the Compassionate Use Act. For a particularly thorough opinion discussing the issues posed above and citing other cases interpreting the Compassionate Use Act, *see People v. Urziceanu,* 132 Cal. App. 4th 747 (3d Dist. 2005).

2. **The importance of Proposition 215.** As one author noted, Proposition 215 in California "got the ball rolling in Colorado" and Amendment 19 was put on Colorado's ballot in 1998 but failed. The same proponents tried again in 2000 and Coloradans approved Amendment 20, making Colorado the first state to legalize medical marijuana in its constitution. William Breathes, *The history of cannabis in Colorado. . .or how the state went to pot*, Westwold (Nov. 1, 2012), https://www.westword.com/news/the-history-of-cannabis-in-coloradoor-how-the-state-went-to-pot-5118475.

B. AMENDING THE COMPASSIONATE USE ACT

The discussion in the previous section and the problems posed there demonstrate a few of the problems created by the Compassionate Use Act. In some instances, the open-ended drafting was intentional, a way to create *de facto* legalization of marijuana. In other instances, almost certainly, the confusion was an unintended consequence of the drafting process, which included a number of marijuana advocates who were not lawyers. As developed in the next case, the California legislature recognized the problems created by the Compassionate Use Act. It attempted to resolve many of those issues in 2003 when it enacted the Medical Marijuana Program. As you can see in *People v. Kelly,* 222 P. 3d 186 (CA 2010), that effort was only partially successful.

PEOPLE v. KELLY

Supreme Court of California
222 P. 3d 186 (CA 2010)

GEORGE, C.J.

Health and Safety Code section 11362.77, which is part of the Medical Marijuana Program (MMP) (§ 11362.7 et seq.), prescribes a specific amount of marijuana that a "qualified patient" may possess or cultivate. We granted review to determine whether this aspect of section 11362.77 is invalid under California Constitution, article II, section 10, subdivision (c), insofar as it amends, without approval of the electorate, the Compassionate Use Act (CUA) (§ 11362.5), an initiative measure adopted by the voters as Proposition 215 in 1996. We conclude, consistently with the decision of the Court of Appeal below (and with the position of both parties in the present litigation), that insofar as section 11362.77 burdens a defense under the CUA to a criminal charge of possessing or cultivating marijuana, it impermissibly amends the CUA and in that respect is invalid under article II, section 10, subdivision (c). We also conclude, consistently with the views of both parties in the present litigation, that the Court of Appeal erred in concluding that section 11362.77 must be severed from the MMP and hence voided.

I.

In 1996, the California electorate approved Proposition 215 and adopted the CUA, which provides: "Section 11357, relating to the possession of marijuana, and Section 11358, relating to the cultivation of marijuana, shall not apply to a patient, or to a patient's primary caregiver, who possesses or cultivates marijuana for the personal medical purposes of the patient upon the written or oral recommendation or approval of a physician." § 11362.5, subd. (d).) By this and related provisions, the CUA provides an affirmative defense to *prosecution* for the crimes of possession and cultivation. The CUA does not grant immunity from *arrest* for those crimes, however. So long as the authorities have probable cause to believe that possession or cultivation has occurred, law enforcement officers may arrest a person for either crime regardless of the arrestee's having a physician's recommendation or approval.

Nor does the CUA specify an amount of marijuana that a patient may possess or cultivate; it states instead that the marijuana possessed or cultivated must be for the patient's *"personal medical purposes."* (§ 11362.5, subd. (d), An early decision construed this provision of the CUA as establishing "that the *quantity possessed* by the patient or the primary caregiver, and the form and manner in which it is possessed, *should be reasonably related to the patient's current medical needs."* (*People v. Trippet* (1997) 56 Cal.App.4th 1532, 1549).

Despite—or, perhaps, because of—this judicial construction of the CUA, questions persisted for both qualified medical marijuana patients and for law enforcement officers relating to enforcement of and arrest for possession, cultivation, and other related marijuana offenses. In 2003, the Legislature found that "reports from across the state have revealed problems and uncertainties in the [CUA] that have impeded the ability of law enforcement officers to enforce its provisions as the voters intended and, therefore, have prevented qualified patients and designated primary caregivers from obtaining the protections afforded by the act." (Stats.2003, ch. 875, § 1, subd. (a)(2).) In response, the Legislature enacted the MMP (§ 11362.7 et seq.) to "[c]*larify the scope of the application of the [CUA] and facilitate the prompt identification of qualified patients and their designated primary caregivers in order to avoid unnecessary arrest and prosecution of these individuals and provide needed guidance to law enforcement officers.*" (Stats.2003, ch. 875, § 1, subd. (b)(1).

Although the MMP did not literally amend the statute that established the CUA (that is, § 11362.5), the MMP did add 18 new code sections that address the general subject matter covered by the CUA. At the heart of the MMP is a voluntary "identification card" scheme that, unlike the CUA— which, as noted, provides only an *affirmative defense* to a charge of possession or cultivation—*provides protection against arrest* for those and related crimes. Under the MMP, a person who suffers from a "serious medical condition," and the designated "primary caregiver" of that person, may register and receive an annually renewable identification card that, in turn, can be shown to a law enforcement officer who otherwise might arrest the program participant or his or her primary caregiver. Section 11362.71, subdivision (e) of the MMP provides in full: "No person or designated primary caregiver in possession of a valid identification card shall be subject to arrest for possession, transportation, delivery, or cultivation of medical marijuana *in an amount established pursuant to this article* [that is, the 18 new sections comprising the MMP], unless there is reasonable cause to believe that the information contained in the card is false or falsified, the card has been obtained by means of fraud, or the person is otherwise in violation of the provisions of the article."

The "amount established pursuant to this article" is addressed in section 11362.77, the statute at issue in this case. That section does two things: (1) it establishes *quantity limitations,* and (2) it sets forth a "safe harbor" by authorizing possession of specific amounts of medical marijuana within those specific limits.

Subdivision (a) of section 11362.77 provides that a "qualified patient" or primary caregiver may "*possess* no more than eight ounces of dried marijuana," and may, "[i]n addition . . . *maintain* no more than six mature or 12 immature marijuana plants." The next two subdivisions of the same section provide qualified exceptions for even greater amounts. Subdivision

(b) specifies that a patient may "possess an amount of marijuana consistent with the patient's needs," on condition that the patient "has a doctor's recommendation" stating that the quantity set out in subdivision (a) is insufficient for the patient's medical needs. Subdivision (c) specifies that cities or counties may retain or enact guidelines allowing greater quantities than those set out in subdivision (a). These aspects of section 11362.77 evidently were designed to provide an objective, bright-line standard in lieu of the subjective, highly individualized reasonable-amount standard set forth in the CUA as construed by *Trippet,* 56 Cal.App.4th at page 1549, thereby providing law enforcement officers with uniform standards, and providing patients who meet those standards (and their primary caregivers) with predictability.

The MMP's safe harbor provision, subdivision (f) of section 11362.77, authorizes possession of certain amounts of medical marijuana. It provides that a "qualified patient or a person holding a valid identification card, or the designated primary caregiver of that qualified patient or person, may possess amounts of marijuana consistent with this article [that is, as provided in subdivisions (a)–(c) of section 11362.77]." By its terms, this safe harbor provision, which is not directly implicated on the facts of this case, would apply not only to those who hold MMP identification cards, but also to qualified patients or their primary caregivers—those persons who are entitled to the protections of the CUA but who do not obtain a program identification card that may provide protection against arrest.

As alluded to above and further explained below, subdivision (a) of section 11362.77, by its terms, does not confine its specific quantity limitations to those persons who voluntarily register with the program and obtain identification cards that protect them against arrest. It also restricts individuals who are entitled, under the CUA, to possess or cultivate any quantity of marijuana reasonably necessary for their current medical needs, thereby burdening a defense that might otherwise be advanced by persons protected by the CUA. Moreover, although subdivision (b) of section 11362.77 allows *possession* of a quantity "consistent with the patient's needs" that is greater than the amount set out in subdivision (a), it affords this protection only if a physician so recommends—a qualification not found in the CUA.

II.

[Defendant suffered from severe medical conditions. A doctor employed by a physician-owned entity that evaluated patients interested in a recommendation of marijuana for medical purposes. The doctor provided a recommendation that did not include a recommended dosage. Further, defendant did not register under the MMP.]

[Unable to afford marijuana from a dispensary, defendant grew his own. He consumed between one and two ounces each week.]

[Acting on a confidential informant's tip, police developed probable cause to believe that defendant was engaged in the illegal production and sale of marijuana. A search of defendant's property revealed "seven potted marijuana plants and additional marijuana plants growing in the soil outside the garage in the backyard of defendant's home. They also discovered seven plastic bags, most of which were vacuum sealed, each containing one to two ounces of dried marijuana, along with a small amount of marijuana in a jar. In total, deputies seized slightly more than 12 usable ounces of dried marijuana. Deputies also recovered a scale and a loaded firearm from a nightstand in the master bedroom. No other traditional indicia of sales—such as pagers, cell phones, "pay-owe sheets," cash money in bills, "nickel and dime bags" (bags used to hold small amounts of marijuana, to be sold for $5 or $10), safes, or sophisticated growing systems—were found during the search."]

[The dispute revolved around whether the MMP controlled.]

Prior to trial, defendant moved to bar the prosecution from eliciting testimony concerning the quantity limitations set out in section 11362.77, on the ground that the statute, in that regard, constitutes an impermissible amendment of the CUA. After an extensive hearing the trial court denied the motion. The court explained that it would instruct the jury pursuant to CALCRIM No. 2370, which, as the court observed, "doesn't mention [specific] amounts," and provides instead that the amount possessed or cultivated must be reasonably related to the patient's current medical needs. Nevertheless, the trial court ruled that the prosecutor would be permitted to question witnesses concerning section 11362.77 and also argue to the jury, consistently with this statute, that defendant possessed more than eight ounces of dried marijuana and yet lacked a physician's recommendation for possessing more than that amount. In that regard, the trial court ruled: "I think the Legislature has a right to—I don't really [think] it changed the [CUA]. I think it further defined it. So, that's my ruling." * * *

The jury deliberated for approximately 90 minutes and found defendant guilty of "possessing more than 28.5 grams [one ounce] of marijuana (§ 11357, subd. (c))"—a lesser offense of the charged count of possessing marijuana for sale (§ 11359). The jury also found defendant guilty as charged of cultivating marijuana (§ 11358). The trial court placed defendant on three years' probation under various terms and conditions, including that he serve two days in jail, less credit for two days already served.

III.

The Court of Appeal held, first, that section 11362.77 of the MMP, insofar as it limits the amount of medical marijuana that a person protected by the CUA may possess, constitutes an amendment of the CUA in violation of California Constitution, article II, section 10, subdivision (c), which precludes legislative amendment of an initiative measure unless the measure explicitly permits such an amendment. Second, the Court of Appeal held that section 11362.77 is "unconstitutional" in its entirety—and "must be severed from the MMP."

Third and finally, addressing an issue concerning which we did not grant review, the Court of Appeal determined that although the trial court properly instructed the jury under the CUA that defendant could possess an amount of marijuana reasonably related to his current medical needs, the court improperly permitted the prosecutor to elicit testimony indicating that the quantity limitations set out in section 11362.77 applied to defendant and to his defense under the CUA—and to extensively so argue to the jury. In other words, the Court of Appeal concluded that the jury was informed, in essence, that the quantity limitations set out in section 11362.77 overrode the CUA's guarantee that a qualified patient is permitted to possess and cultivate any amount reasonably necessary for his or her medical needs. This, the Court of Appeal held, constituted prejudicial error: "We cannot conclude that the jury found defendant guilty because [it] believed the amount of marijuana he possessed and cultivated was not reasonably related to his medical needs, as opposed to believing defendant was guilty because he had more marijuana than section 11362.77 says he may have. Defendant therefore is entitled to a reversal of the judgment."

* * * [W]e agree with the Court of Appeal's first determination—that section 11362.77 is unconstitutional insofar as it burdens a defense, provided by the CUA, to charges of possessing or cultivating marijuana. But, as explained in part V. below, we disagree with the Court of Appeal's second conclusion—that section 11362.77 is wholly invalid, and that it "must be severed from the MMP."

IV.

We first address the Court of Appeal's conclusion that section 11362.77 of the MMP, insofar as that statute establishes quantity limitations, constitutes an amendment of the CUA, in violation of California Constitution, article II, section 10, subdivision (c). That provision (quoted in full *ante,* fn. 15) states in relevant part: "The Legislature . . . may amend or repeal an initiative statute by another statute that becomes effective only when approved by the electors unless the initiative statute permits amendment or repeal without their approval."

Significantly, as alluded to earlier, section 11362.77 of the MMP does not confine the reach of its quantity limitations to those persons who voluntarily elect to register with the program and obtain identification cards, but instead extends its reach to "qualified patient[s]" and their "primary caregiver[s]." The term qualified patient is defined by the MMP as "*a person who is entitled to the protections of Section 11362.5 [the CUA],* but who *does not have an identification card* issued pursuant to this article [that is, the MMP]." (§ 11362.7, subd. (f).) The term primary caregiver is defined by the MMP as an "individual, designated by a qualified patient or by a person with an identification card, who has consistently assumed responsibility for the housing, health, or safety of that patient or person." (§ 11362.7, subd. (d).) In other words, section 11362.77, on its face, sets quantity limitations *not only* for those persons who voluntarily register under the MMP and hold a valid identification card that provides protection against arrest. The statute also applies to and sets limits for all those "qualified patient[s]" and "primary caregiver[s]" who are entitled under the CUA to possess or cultivate any amount reasonably necessary for the patient's current medical needs. We proceed to consider whether, in this respect, section 11362.77 constitutes an amendment of the CUA, in violation of California Constitution, article II, section 10, subdivision (c).

A.

We begin with the observation that "[t]he purpose of California's constitutional limitation on the Legislature's power to amend initiative statutes is to 'protect the people's initiative powers by precluding the Legislature from undoing what the people have done, without the electorate's consent.' " * * *

At the same time, despite the strict bar on the Legislature's authority to amend initiative statutes, judicial decisions have observed that this body is not thereby precluded from enacting laws addressing the general subject matter of an initiative. The Legislature remains free to address a " 'related but distinct area' " (*County of San Diego v. San Diego NORML* (2008) 165 Cal.App.4th 798, 830, 81 Cal.Rptr.3d 461.) * * *

C.

The Court of Appeal's analysis began with a review of the voters' intent in enacting the CUA. The court observed: "The CUA does not quantify the marijuana a patient may possess. Rather, the only 'limit' on how much marijuana a person falling under the CUA may possess is" that it must be " 'reasonably related to the patient's current medical needs.' " (Quoting *Trippet, supra,* 56 Cal.App.4th 1532, 1549.) The appellate court continued: "Ballot materials make clear that this is the only 'limitation' on how much marijuana a person under the CUA may possess. . . . According to these ballot statements, the CUA does not place a numeric cap on how much marijuana is sufficient for a patient's personal medical use. Section 11362.77, however, does just that. It specifies that a qualified patient may possess eight ounces of dried marijuana [and may maintain] six mature or 12 immature marijuana plants. (§ 11362.77, subd. (a).) A qualified patient may possess a greater quantity if the patient has a doctor's recommendation that the quantity in subdivision (a) does not meet the qualified patient's medical needs. (§ 11362.77, subd. (b).) In other words, section 11362.77 . . . has clarified what is a reasonable amount for a patient's personal medical use, namely, eight ounces of dried marijuana [or a greater quantity if a physician so recommends, plus cultivation of six mature or 12 immature marijuana plants]. But clarifying the limits of 'reasonableness' is amendatory."

[The Court of Appeal noted that the legislature itself recognized that the quantity limitation exceeded the legislature's bounds but that the governor vetoed legislation that would have removed that limitation.]

D.

In this court, both parties essentially agree with the foregoing conclusion reached by the Court of Appeal. The Attorney General, who petitioned for this court's review of the appellate decision, states at the outset of his opening brief: "Respondent does not contest the Court of Appeal's conclusion that section 11362.77 is unconstitutionally amendatory insofar as it limits an in-court CUA defense." The Attorney General subsequently concludes that "application of section 11362.77's limits to the in-court CUA defense exceeds the boundaries of legislative power under article II, section 10, subdivision (c) . . . by replacing the CUA's 'reasonableness' standard with specified, numeric guidelines." Defendant, unsurprisingly, agrees with Attorney General in these respects.

* * * [W]e return to the Court of Appeal's threshold determination that section 11362.77 of the MMP, insofar as it places a specific limitation upon the amount of medical marijuana that a person protected by the CUA may possess and cultivate, constitutes an amendment of the CUA in violation of California Constitution, article II, section 10, subdivision (c). As observed earlier, this constitutional provision specifies that the Legislature may amend an initiative measure solely "by another statute that becomes effective only when approved by the electors"—unless "the initiative statute permits" such amendment explicitly.

In the present case, the CUA—unlike many other initiative measures in recent decades—did not grant the Legislature authority to amend. Nor did the Legislature merely propose the MMP and submit it to the electorate for approval. Instead, the Legislature adopted that scheme on its own, without seeking ratification by the electorate.

* * * [W]e conclude that section 11362.77, by imposing quantity limitations upon "qualified patients" and "primary caregivers," amends the CUA. Under the CUA as adopted by Proposition 215, these individuals are not subject to any specific limits and do not require a physician's recommendation in order to exceed any such limits; instead they may possess an amount of medical marijuana reasonably necessary for their, or their charges', personal medical needs. By extending the reach of section 11362.77's quantity limitations beyond those persons who voluntarily register under the MMP and obtain an identification card that provides protection against arrest—and by additionally restricting the rights of all "qualified patients" and "primary caregivers" who fall under the CUA—the

challenged language of section 11362.77 effectuates a change in the CUA that takes away from rights granted by the initiative statute. In this sense, section 11362.77's quantity limitations conflict with—and thereby substantially restrict—the CUA's guarantee that a qualified patient may possess and cultivate *any amount of marijuana reasonably necessary for his or her current medical condition.* In that respect, section 11362.77 improperly amends the CUA in violation of the California Constitution.

V.

* * * [A]fter the Court of Appeal concluded that section 11362.77 (together with its quantity limitations) is unconstitutional insofar as this statute burdens a defense otherwise available under the CUA, that court further held that section 11362.77 "must be severed from the MMP" and hence voided in its entirety.* * *

The Court of Appeal provided no reason for its conclusion that section 11362.77 must be severed from the MMP and hence voided in its entirety—and we discern no principled basis for doing so. A determination that section 11362.77 is unconstitutional insofar as it might be applied in a manner that burdens a defense authorized by the CUA does not, in and of itself, require invalidation of the remaining aspects of this statute; there is no operational or functional reason for such a conclusion. Section 11362.77 continues to have legal significance, and can operate as part of the MMP, even if it cannot constitutionally restrict a CUA defense. * * *

Accordingly, although we disallow the invalid application of section 11362.77—that is, insofar as the terms of the statute purport to burden a defense otherwise available to qualified patients or primary caregivers under the CUA—we conclude that the Court of Appeal erred in holding that section 11362.77 must be severed from the MMP and hence voided in its entirety.

VI.

Whether or not a person entitled to register under the MMP elects to do so, that individual, so long as he or she meets the definition of a patient or primary caregiver under the CUA, retains all the rights afforded by the CUA. Thus, such a person may assert, as a defense in court, that he or she possessed or cultivated an amount of marijuana reasonably related to meet his or her current medical needs (see *Trippet, supra,* 56 Cal.App.4th 1532, 1549, 66 Cal.Rptr.2d 559), without reference to the specific quantitative limitations specified by the MMP.

We conclude as follows: To the extent section 11362.77 (together with its quantitative limitations) impermissibly amends the CUA by burdening a defense that would be available pursuant to that initiative statute, section 11362.77 is invalid under California Constitution article II, section 10, subdivision (c). Nevertheless, it would be inappropriate to sever section 11362.77 from the MMP and hence void that provision in its entirety. To the extent the judgment of the Court of Appeal purports to sever section 11362.77 from the MMP and to void this statute in its entirety, the judgment is reversed. In all other respects, the judgment is affirmed.

NOTES AND QUESTIONS

1. **Chaos in California.** Obviously, the California legislature attempted to bring more order to California medical marijuana business. As indicated in *People v. Kelly*, the Compassionate Use Act created problems for law enforcement agencies and medical marijuana users. Here is a more complete overview of some of the problems created by the Compassionate Use Act and ways that various stakeholders reacted:

> Not surprisingly, courts and the legislature have been left to clean up the problems created by the initiative. California courts have had to resolve many of the all-too-obvious issues created by the law. For example, Proposition 215 gave qualifying patients an affirmative defense to the crimes of possessing marijuana and cultivating marijuana. It failed, however, to provide a defense for transporting marijuana. Lower appellate courts divided on the issue, and before the California Supreme Court could decide the question, the legislature created an affirmative defense to the crime of transporting marijuana for individuals otherwise covered by Proposition 215.

> Courts have had to decide various other legal issues created by the proposition. For example, they have had to define the meaning of a physician's "recommendation" or "approval" of marijuana for the patient, the illnesses that qualify under the catchall provision in the law, the meaning of "caregiver," and the status of cannabis clubs or cooperatives. Additionally, courts had to settle procedural issues, including whether the law creates an affirmative defense or immunity from prosecution and whether a person who presents a card identifying him- or herself as a medical marijuana user may nonetheless be arrested for marijuana offenses. In addition, courts have struggled with how much marijuana a qualifying patient may possess.

> In 2004, the legislature attempted to resolve some ongoing issues. For example, the Medical Marijuana Program Act (MMP) addressed some of the problems that had troubled law enforcement and medical marijuana users and suppliers. The MMP set out limits on the amount of marijuana a qualifying patient may possess. It granted local governments the power to approve regulations permitting possession of larger amounts of marijuana, while also directing the Department of State Health Services to establish a voluntary medicinal marijuana registry and to issue identification cards. The MMP also attempted to clarify the status of marijuana dispensaries It provided that "[q]ualified patients, persons with valid identification cards, and the designated primary caregivers of

qualified patients . . . who associate within the State of California in order collectively or cooperatively to cultivate marijuana for medical purposes, shall not solely on the basis of that fact be subject to state criminal sanctions."

The MMP defined key terms, including "attending physician," "qualified patient," and "primary caregiver." My impression is that the MMP, although not without some ambiguity, has reduced litigation by providing some greater clarity. But it has hardly ended uncertainty. Further, the state's supreme court found one provision of the MMP unconstitutional because of the law's imposition of a quantity limitation on all qualified patients, not just those who voluntarily registered. That requirement, inconsistent with the initiative, violated the provision of the state constitution allowing the legislature to amend an initiative "only when approved by the electors unless the initiative statute permits amendment or repeal without their approval."

Other government officials have also helped to clarify the law governing medical marijuana. For example, in 2007, the Board of Equalization clarified the state's policy on taxing the medical marijuana trade and imposed a requirement that those in the marijuana trade secure a seller's permit. In 2008, then-Attorney General Jerry Brown released guidelines on how law enforcement should deal with medical marijuana cooperatives, caregivers, and patients. Published twelve years after the passage of Proposition 215, the memorandum finally provides guidance in a number of areas that marijuana providers, patients, and law enforcement should have had years ago. Most importantly, the memorandum includes guidelines to regulate dispensaries.

Between 1996 and [2012] * * *, cities * * * struggled with how to regulate medical marijuana. Even since the 2008 guidelines, cities around the state continue to struggle with zoning issues. Individuals interested in getting into the medical marijuana business have had to act at their own risk because of the lack of clear guidance. According to news reports, police have targeted some bona fide medical marijuana users. Some police departments have demonstrated a settled policy to frustrate Proposition 215. The absence of clear guidelines has also allowed other individuals to use marijuana illegally or to set up an illegal drug enterprise under the guise of serving medical marijuana clientele.

Michael Vitiello, *Why the Initiative Process Was the Wrong Way to Go: Lessons We Should Have Learned from Proposition 215,* 43 McGeorge L. Rev. 63, 67–70 (2012). Once again, a comparison with Colorado's medical marijuana law demonstrates the more careful drafting of Colorado's Amendment 20. For example, Colorado Amendment 20 defined primary care-giver as "a person, other than the patient and the patient's physician, who is eighteen years of age or older and has significant responsibility for managing the well-being of a patient who has a debilitating medical condition." Colo. Const. art. XVII § 14(1)(f).

2. **MMP's failure.** According to *People v. Kelly,* why did the Medical Marijuana Program fail? Is the court's reasoning sound?

3. **Regulating "medical" marijuana.** Apart from the unique aspects of California law, what should the law be regarding medical marijuana patients? That is, would it make sense to require medical marijuana patients to have a card to demonstrate that they have complied with state law? Would it make sense to place a limit on the amount of marijuana that one might possess for medical purposes? What are the competing policies? Although the opinion above is heavily edited, the edited discussion suggests some of those competing policies. Colorado created far more certainty than did California. For example, in order to be protected with a defense to state prosecution for possession of marijuana a patient must designate a caregiver and receive a medical user card. Sam Kamin, *Medical Marijuana in Colorado and the Future of Marijuana Regulation in the United States*, 43 U. Pac. L. Rev. 147, 148 (2013). Indeed, Colorado's Amendment 20 limited medical marijuana possession to up to 2 ounces of marijuana in usable form. Colo. Const. art. XVIII, § 14(2)(b).

4. **Law enforcement and medical marijuana.** Chief Justice George's opinion in *Kelly* refers to some of the law enforcement issues created by the Compassionate Use Act. Beyond that, state and federal law enforcement agencies cooperated in aggressive actions against medical marijuana dispensaries and growers in California and elsewhere. Peter Hecht's *Weed Land* (2014) provides a view of some of those activities, including raids on medical marijuana cooperatives. Publicity generated by some of the more aggressive raids gained national attention. Indeed, then-candidate Barrack Obama made those raids a campaign issue in 2008. He promised a more tolerant approach, allowing states where medical marijuana was lawful to regulate their own industry.

5. **Comparing Colorado and California.** Although Colorado's Amendment 20, which legalized medical marijuana, is widely recognized as more carefully drafted than was Proposition 215, it included ambiguities. For example, one point that was ambiguous was the patient-caregiver relationship. The State Department of Public Health created a rule allowing only five patients to be associated with a caregiver, making wide-scale distribution of medical marijuana almost impossible. *See*, Sam Kamin, *Medical Marijuana in Colorado and the Future of Marijuana Regulation in the United States*, 43 U. Pac. L. Rev. 147, 148 (2013).

6. **The Obama approach to medical marijuana.** In 2009, President Obama's Department of Justice published a memorandum explaining how Obama's campaign promise would be implemented. The Ogden memorandum, first published in October 2009, laid out federal law enforcement priorities. In effect, the government assured states that complied with those priorities room to regulate their own industries.

7.   California: the Wild West? What followed the Ogden memorandum seemed to boomerang. As summarized in one law review article:

> [W]hat followed seems like a U-turn in administration policy. Notably, in California, marijuana providers opened hundreds of dispensaries, often in central business locations. The Obama administration reacted forcefully. Under his administration, there have been more raids on marijuana dispensaries in California than there were under the Bush administration. Federal government agents have threatened landlords with forfeiture of their property if they lease to dispensaries. They have invoked federal drug laws that heighten penalties when drug dealers sell drugs within proximity to schools.

Michael Vitiello, *Joints or the Joint: Colorado and Washington Square Off Against the United States,* 91 Or. L. Rev. 1009, 1018–19 (2013). As it turned out, the federal government's aggressive conduct in California was a reaction to its unregulated industry. Elsewhere, in states like Colorado that had in place strict regulations of the industry, the federal government honored the Ogden memorandum's promise of a more tolerant approach. The next section picks up with developments after the Ogden memorandum and the push towards legalization of recreational marijuana.

C. FROM PROPOSITION 19 TO PROPOSITION 64

California's adoption of the Compassionate Use Act increased interest in medical marijuana initiatives around the country. A number of states adopted medical marijuana laws in the late 1990s and early 2000s. Some, like Colorado, provided for careful monitoring of marijuana from seed to sale. The success of businesses in such states, including red states like Montana, generated interest among investors. The Ogden memorandum gave additional confidence to investors.

Unlike Colorado, California did not demonstrate the same commitment to careful regulation of the industry, as discussed above. As described above, that led to continued aggressive enforcement of marijuana laws in California. Despite that, marijuana proponents qualified a ballot initiative for the mid-term election in 2010, Proposition 19, which would have legalized recreational marijuana in California. As discussed below, the initiative failed; at the same time, it was a learning experience for proponents of marijuana advocates.

According to the ballot summary of Proposition 19, the proposition:

> Allows people 21 years old or older to possess, cultivate, or transport marijuana for personal use. Permits local governments to regulate and tax commercial production and sale of marijuana to people 21 years old or older. Permits people from possessing marijuana on school grounds, using it in public, smoking it while minors are present, or providing it to anyone under 21 years old.

Maintains prohibitions current prohibitions against driving while impaired.

Official Summary of Proposition 19, the "Regulate, Control and Tax Cannabis Act of 2010.

Despite conflicting polling data, the initiative failed, with about 56% of voters opposing the proposition. Opposition came from some of the predictable groups opposing reforming drug laws. But some centrist organizations and individuals also opposed it. A Sacramento Bee editorial opposed the law, noting "The Nov. 2 ballot is full of worrisome loopholes and ambiguities that would create a chaotic nightmare for law enforcement, local governments and businesses. It is so poorly drafted, in fact, that it almost makes you wonder: What were they smoking?" Sacramento Bee, "Proposition 19 deserves to go up in smoke," October 1, 2010. Other commentators argued that, despite proponents' claims that the proposition would raise $1.4 billion per year in tax revenues, the initiative did not include provisions explaining how the state would tax marijuana at all.

Choosing a midterm election year to advance legalization proved to be another mistake. Typically, younger voters, who are far more likely than older voters to favor legalization, do not vote in midterm elections in large numbers. That proved to be the case in 2010.

Marijuana proponents in other states were watching what happened in California. Buoyed by the Ogden memorandum and by the federal government's less aggressive enforcement efforts in Colorado, proponents in Colorado and Washington drafted more tightly constructed laws than did Proposition 19's authors. They also qualified their initiatives in 2012, a presidential election year. Those choices proved to be a winning strategy with both states adopting recreational marijuana laws. As summarized in an introduction to a symposium on marijuana law, marijuana advocates awaited the Obama administration's response to those ballot initiatives:

> An aggressive law enforcement response to Washington and Colorado's legalization efforts would almost certainly have been a major setback for legalization proponents. Few producers would sign up for licenses, few sellers would comply with a host of regulations, and few investors would risk capital if the federal government might shut them down for violating federal law. That did not happen.

> Similar to the Ogden memo, a newly published memorandum, authored by Department of Justice Deputy Attorney General James Cole, laid out guidelines for businesses in states that wanted to legalize recreational use of marijuana. Some critics pointed out that the memorandum seemed to say very little of substance and, more to the point, that it did not have the full force

of law. A new administration could end the Obama administration's tolerance of marijuana businesses at the stroke of a pen.

Despite those realities, the Cole memo created a brave new world for marijuana businesses. One commentator suggested that James Cole has had a bigger impact on the marijuana industry than any other individual. His memo was a green light to the industries in Colorado and Washington. With some fits and starts, the marijuana business in those states is now a growth industry, and both states are seeing increasing tax revenue from it.

Encouraged by the Obama administration's tolerance of the industry, marijuana proponents have pushed through legal reforms in a number of other states, including Alaska, California, Maine, Massachusetts, Nevada, and Oregon. Like Colorado and Washington, Oregon, which now has an industry up-and-running, has exceeded its early projections on tax revenues.

Not only did the Obama administration give states room to experiment with recreational use of marijuana, but it invited investment in the industry. Accurate predictions about the size of the marijuana market are difficult to make, but plenty of mainstream media have published stories about the potential growth of the industry. Naturally, most advisers warn of the risks inherent in investing in the industry, but that has not stopped capital from flowing in. Finding stories about creative efforts to invest in the industry is not difficult; for example, one creative entrepreneur is attempting to create marijuana real estate investment trusts to allow producers to invest their capital in creating the product, while investors share the risks and profits by buying the land for production.

Michael Vitiello, Introduction, *Symposium—Regulating Marijuana at Home and Abroad*, 49 U. Pac. L. Rev. 1, 6–8 (2017).

As indicated, the success in Colorado and Washington led to California's marijuana proponents qualifying Proposition 64 in time for another presidential election year. California's marijuana proponents learned a lesson from Colorado and Washington and drafted a much more carefully created initiative than did Proposition 19's drafters. The next section turns to the key elements of Proposition 64.

Before this chapter turns to Proposition 64, it makes a brief stop for a look at two important interim developments in California's march towards legalization of recreational marijuana. Taking a lead on the issue, then-Lieutenant Governor Gavin Newsom assembled a commission to study issues raised by legalizing marijuana. That report provides a balanced and thoughtful view of many of the complex issues involved in the debate. That report, entitled Blue Ribbon Commission Report, Pathways may be found at https://www.safeandsmartpolicy.org/wp-content/uploads/2015/07/BRC PathwaysReport.pdf.

The second interim development was the passage of the California Medical Cannabis Regulation and Safety Act, Assemb. B. 266, 2015–2016 Sess. (Cal. 2015); Assemb. B. 243, 2015–2016 Sess. (Cal. 2015); S.B. 643, 2015–2016 Sess. (Cal. 2015) (known collectively as the Medical Cannabis Regulation and Safety Act)(MCRSA). The extended drought in California brought front and center the impact that illegal marijuana production had on the state's environment. Legislative committees conducted joint hearings on the environmental impact of marijuana production. Witnesses testified illegal diversion of water, off-label use of agricultural chemicals that ended up in streams and other waterways, fouling the environment. Despite estimates of about 50,000 marijuana growing operations in the state, the State Water Resources Control Board representative admitted that the agency had no way to regulate water use. Other witnesses testified concerning significant damage in pristine wilderness areas. For a more detailed discussion, *see* Michael Vitiello, *Legalizing Marijuana and Abating Environmental Harm: An Overblown Promise?* 50 U.C. Davis L. Rev. 773 (2016).

The hearings led to the passage of the California Medical Cannabis Regulation and Safety Act. Some commentators wondered why the legislature acted when it did in light of the fact that members knew that a ballot initiative might moot the act. But MCRSA was significant.

The act created a framework for licensing and regulating marijuana cultivation. It instructed state agencies to develop regulations of pesticides and of illegal water diversion, among other topics. It also mandated a host of other regulations of health and safety standards and protected local governments from having to buy into the statewide system. Indeed, after almost 20 years since passage of Proposition 215, California put in place a comprehensive regulatory structure for the state's multibillion dollar industry. The process required agreement among many of the stakeholders, including law enforcement, local governmental entities, unions and some members of the marijuana industry. With that background, enter Proposition 64.

D. PROPOSITION 64

The final version of Proposition 64 exceeded 60 pages. It can be found at this site: https://www.oag.ca.gov/system/files/initiatives/pdfs/15-0103% 20(Marijuana)_1.pdf.

In addition, you may find another source worth reviewing. Ballotpedia included an overview of Proposition 64 that you can find here: https:// ballotpedia.org/California_Proposition_64,_Marijuana_Legalization_(2016).

Here are some of the main provisions of the law, as adopted by the voters of California in November 2016:

SECTION 1. TITLE.

This measure shall be known as the Control, Regulate and Tax Adult Use of Marijuana Act ("the Adult Use of Marijuana Act"). * * *

SECTION 3. PURPOSE AND INTENT.

The purpose of the Adult Use of Marijuana Act is to establish a comprehensive system to legalize, control and regulate the cultivation, processing, manufacture, distribution, testing, and sale of nonmedical marijuana, including marijuana products, for use by adults 21 years and older, and to tax the commercial growth and retail sale of marijuana. It is the intent of the People in enacting this Act to accomplish the following:

(a) Take nonmedical marijuana production and sales out of the hands of the illegal market and bring them under a regulatory structure that prevents access by minors and protects public safety, public health, and the environment.

(b) Strictly control the cultivation, processing, manufacture, distribution, testing and sale of nonmedical marijuana through a system of state licensing, regulation, and enforcement.

(c) Allow local governments to enforce state laws and regulations for nonmedical marijuana businesses and enact additional local requirements for nonmedical marijuana businesses, but not require that they do so for a nonmedical marijuana business to be issued a state license and be legal under state law.

(d) Allow local governments to ban nonmedical marijuana businesses as set forth in this Act.

(e) Require track and trace management procedures to track nonmedical marijuana from cultivation to sale.

(f) Require nonmedical marijuana to be comprehensively tested by independent testing services for the presence of contaminants, including mold and pesticides, before it can be sold by licensed businesses.

(g) Require nonmedical marijuana sold by licensed businesses to be packaged in child-resistant containers and be labeled so that consumers are fully informed about potency and the effects of ingesting nonmedical marijuana.

(h) Require licensed nonmedical marijuana businesses to follow strict environmental and product safety standards as a condition of maintaining their license.

(i) Prohibit the sale of nonmedical marijuana by businesses that also sell alcohol or tobacco.

(j) Prohibit the marketing and advertising of nonmedical marijuana to persons younger than 21 years old or near schools or other places where children are present.

(k) Strengthen the state's existing medical marijuana system by requiring patients to obtain by January 1, 2018, a new recommendation from their physician that meets the strict standards signed into law by the Governor in 2015, and by providing new privacy protections for patients who obtain medical marijuana identification cards as set forth in this Act.

(l) Permit adults 21 years and older to use, possess, purchase and grow nonmedical marijuana within defined limits for use by adults 21 years and older as set forth in this Act.

(m) Allow local governments to reasonably regulate the cultivation of nonmedical marijuana for personal use by adults 21 years and older through zoning and other local laws, and only to ban outdoor cultivation as set forth in this Act.

(n) Deny access to marijuana by persons younger than 21 years old who are not medical marijuana patients.

(o) Prohibit the consumption of marijuana in a public place unlicensed for such use, including near K-12 schools and other areas where children are present.

(p) Maintain existing laws making it unlawful to operate a car or other vehicle used for transportation while impaired by marijuana.

(q) Prohibit the cultivation of marijuana on public lands or while trespassing on private lands.

(r) Allow public and private employers to enact and enforce workplace policies pertaining to marijuana.

(s) Tax the growth and sale of marijuana in a way that drives out the illicit market for marijuana and discourages use by minors, and abuse by adults.

(t) Generate hundreds of millions of dollars in new state revenue annually for restoring and repairing the environment, youth treatment and prevention, community investment, and law enforcement.

(u) Prevent illegal production or distribution of marijuana.

(v) Prevent the illegal diversion of marijuana from California to other states or countries or to the illegal market.

(w) Preserve scarce law enforcement resources to prevent and prosecute violent crime.

(x) Reduce barriers to entry into the legal, regulated market.

(y) Require minors who commit marijuana-related offenses to complete drug prevention education or counseling and community service.

(z) Authorize courts to resentence persons who are currently serving a sentence for offenses for which the penalty is reduced by the Act, so long as the person does not pose a risk to public safety, and to redesignate or dismiss such offenses from the criminal records of persons who have completed their sentences as set forth in this Act.

(aa) Allow industrial hemp to be grown as an agricultural product, and for agricultural or academic research, and regulated separately from the strains of cannabis with higher delta-9 tetrahydrocannabinol concentrations.

SECTION 4. PERSONAL USE.

Sections 11018 of the Health and Safety Code is hereby amended, and Sections 11018.1 and 11018.2 of the Health and Safety Code are hereby added to read:

11362.1. [Personal Possession & Cultivation]

(a) Subject to Sections <u>11362.2. [Personal Cultivation Restrictions]</u>, <u>11362.3. [Personal Use Restrictions]</u>, and <u>11362.4. [Punishment for Violations]</u>, but notwithstanding any other provision of law, it shall be lawful under state and local law, and shall not be a violation of state or local law, for persons 21 years of age or older to:

(1) Possess, process, transport, purchase, obtain, or give away to persons 21 years of age or older without any compensation whatsoever, not more than 28.5 grams of marijuana not in the form of concentrated cannabis;

(2) Possess, process, transport, purchase, obtain, or give away to persons 21 years of age or older without any compensation whatsoever, not more than eight grams of marijuana in the form of concentrated cannabis, including as contained in marijuana products;

(3) Possess, plant, cultivate, harvest, dry, or process not more than six living marijuana plants and possess the marijuana produced by the plants;

(4) Smoke or ingest marijuana or marijuana products; and

(5) Possess, transport, purchase, obtain, use, manufacture, or give away marijuana accessories to persons 21 years of age or older without any compensation whatsoever.

* * *

11362.2. [Personal Cultivation Restrictions]

(a) Personal cultivation of marijuana under paragraph <u>(3)</u> of subdivision <u>(a)</u> of Section <u>11362.1. [Personal Possession & Cultivation]</u> is subject to the following restrictions:

(1) A person shall plant, cultivate, harvest, dry, or process plants in accordance with local ordinances, if any, adopted in accordance with subdivision <u>(b)</u> of this section.

(2)   The living plants and any marijuana produced by the plants in excess of 28.5 grams are kept within the person's private residence, or upon the grounds of that private residence (e.g., in an outdoor garden area), are in a locked space, and are not visible by normal unaided vision from a public place.

(3)   Not more than six living plants may be planted, cultivated, harvested, dried, or processed within a single private residence, or upon the grounds of that private residence, at one time.

(1)   A city, county, or city and county may enact and enforce reasonable regulations to reasonably regulate the actions and conduct in paragraph (3) of subdivision (a) of Section 11362.1. [Personal Possession & Cultivation].

(2)   Notwithstanding paragraph (1) no city, county, or city and county may completely prohibit persons engaging in the actions and conduct under paragraph (3) of subdivision (a) of Section 11362.1. [Personal Possession & Cultivation] inside a private residence, or inside an accessory structure to a private residence located upon the grounds of a private residence that is fully enclosed and secure.

(3)   Notwithstanding paragraph (3) of subdivision (a) of Section 11362.1. [Personal Possession & Cultivation], a city, county, or city and county may completely prohibit persons from engaging in actions and conduct under paragraph (3) of subdivision (a) of Section 11362.1. [Personal Possession & Cultivation] outdoors upon the grounds of a private residence.

* * *

11362.3. [Personal Use Restrictions]

(a)   Nothing in Section 11362.1. [Personal Possession & Cultivation] shall be construed to permit any person to:

(1)   Smoke or ingest marijuana or marijuana products in any public place, except in accordance with Section 26200. [Local Limits / Pot Lounges] of the Business and Professions Code.

(2)   Smoke marijuana or marijuana products in a location where smoking tobacco is prohibited.

(3)   Smoke marijuana or marijuana products within 1,000 feet of a school, day care center, or youth center while children are present at such a school, day care center, or youth center, except in or upon the grounds of a private residence or in accordance with Section 26200. [Local Limits / Pot Lounges] of the Business and Professions Code or **Chapter 3.5 of Division 8 of the** Business and Professions Code and only if such smoking is not detectable by others on the grounds of such a school, day care center, or youth center while children are present.

(4) Possess an open container or open package of marijuana or marijuana products while driving, operating, or riding in the passenger seat or compartment of a motor vehicle, boat, vessel, aircraft, or other vehicle used for transportation.

(5) Possess, smoke or ingest marijuana or marijuana products in or upon the grounds of a school, day care center, or youth center while children are present.

(6) Manufacture concentrated cannabis using a volatile solvent, unless done in accordance with a license under **Chapter 3.5 of Division 8** or Division 10. Marijuana of the Business and Professions Code.

(7) Smoke or ingest marijuana or marijuana products while driving, operating a motor vehicle, boat, vessel, aircraft, or other vehicle used for transportation.

(8) Smoke or ingest marijuana or marijuana products while riding in the passenger seat or compartment of a motor vehicle, boat, vessel, aircraft, or other vehicle used for transportation except as permitted on a motor vehicle, boat, vessel, aircraft, or other vehicle used for transportation that is operated in accordance with 26200.of the Business and Professions Code and while no persons under the age of 21 years are present.

* * *

11362.4. [Punishment for Violations]

(a) A person who engages in the conduct described in paragraph (1) of subdivision (a) of Section 11362.3. [Personal Use Restrictions] is guilty of an infraction punishable by no more than a one hundred dollar ($100) fine; provided, however, that persons under the age of 18 shall instead be required to complete four hours of a drug education program or counseling, and up to 10 hours of community service, over a period not to exceed 60 days once the drug education program or counseling and community service opportunity are made available to the person.

(b) A person who engages in the conduct described in paragraphs (2) through (4) of subdivision (a) of Section 11362.3. [Personal Use Restrictions] shall be guilty of an infraction punishable by no more than a two hundred and fifty dollar ($250) fine, unless such activity is otherwise permitted by state and local law; provided, however, that persons under the age of 18 shall instead be required to complete four hours of drug education or counseling, and up to 20 hours of community service, over a period not to exceed 90 days once the drug education program or counseling and community service opportunity are made available to the person.

(c) A person who engages in the conduct described in paragraph (5) of subdivision (a) of Section 11362.3. [Personal Use Restrictions] shall be subject to the same punishment as provided under subdivisions (c) or (d) of 11357. Possession.

(d)   A person who engages in the conduct described in paragraph (6) of subdivision (a) of Section 11362.3. [Personal Use Restrictions] shall be subject to punishment under **Section 11379.6**.

(e)   A person who violates the restrictions in subdivision (a) of Section 11362.2. [Personal Cultivation Restrictions] is guilty of an infraction punishable by no more than a two hundred and fifty dollar ($250) fine.

* * *

SECTION 5. USE OF MARIJUANA FOR MEDICAL PURPOSES.

Sections 11362.712, 11362.713, 11362.84 and 11362.85 are added to the Health and Safety Code, and 11362.755 of the Health and Safety Code is amended to read:

11362.712. [Recommendation Requirements]

(a)   Commencing on January 1, 2018, a qualified patient must possess a physician's recommendation that complies with **Article 25 (commencing with Section 2525) of Chapter 5 of Division 2** of the **Business and Professions Code**. Failure to comply with this requirement shall not, however, affect any of the protections provided to patients or their primary caregivers by **Section 11362.5**.

(b)   A county health department or the county's designee shall develop protocols to ensure that, commencing upon January 1, 2018, all identification cards issued pursuant to **Section 11362.71** are supported by a   physician's   recommendation   that   complies   with   **Article   25 (commencing with Section 2525) of Chapter 5 of Division 2** of the **Business and Professions Code**.

* * *

SECTION 6. MARIJUANA REGULATION AND SAFETY.

Division 10 is hereby added to the Business and Professions Code to read as follows:

Division 10. Marijuana

Chapter 1. General Provisions and Definitions

26000. [Purpose & Intent]

(a)   The purpose and intent of this division is to establish a comprehensive system to control and regulate the cultivation, distribution, transport, storage, manufacturing, processing, and sale of nonmedical marijuana and marijuana products for adults 21 years of age and over.

(b)   In the furtherance of subdivision (a), this division expands the power and duties of the existing state agencies responsible for controlling and regulating the medical cannabis industry under **Chapter 3.5 of Division 8** to include the power and duty to control and regulate the commercial nonmedical marijuana industry.

(c)   The Legislature may, by majority vote, enact laws to implement this division, provided such laws are consistent with the purposes and intent of the Control, Regulate and Tax Adult Use of Marijuana Act.

Chapter 2. Administration

26010. [Bureau of Marijuana Control]

(a)   The Bureau of Medical Marijuana Regulation established in Section 19302 in **Chapter 3.5 of Division 8** is hereby renamed the Bureau of Marijuana Control. The director shall administer and enforce the provisions of this division in addition to the provisions of **Chapter 3.5 of Division 8**. The director shall have the same power and authority as provided by subdivisions and (c) of Section 19302.1 for purposes of this division.

(b)   The bureau and the director shall succeed to and are vested with all the duties, powers, purposes, responsibilities, and jurisdiction vested in the Bureau of Medical Marijuana Regulation under **Chapter 3.5 of Division 8**.

(c)   In addition to the powers, duties, purposes, responsibilities, and jurisdiction referenced in subdivision (b), the bureau shall heretofore have the power, duty, purpose, responsibility, and jurisdiction to regulate commercial marijuana activity as provided in this division.

(d)   Upon the effective date of this section, whenever "Bureau of Medical Marijuana Regulation" appears in any statute, regulation, or contract, or in any other code, it shall be construed to refer to the bureau.

Chapter 3. Enforcement

26030. [Grounds for Discipline]

Grounds for disciplinary action include:

(a)   Failure to comply with the provisions of this division or any rule or regulation adopted pursuant to this division.

(b)   Conduct that constitutes grounds for denial of licensure pursuant to Chapter 3 (commencing with **Section 490**) of Division 1.5.

(c)   Any other grounds contained in regulations adopted by a licensing authority pursuant to this division.

(d)   Failure to comply with any state law including, but not limited to, the payment of taxes as required under the Revenue and Taxation Code, except as provided for in this division or other California law.

(e)   Knowing violations of any state or local law, ordinance, or regulation conferring worker protections or legal rights on the employees of a licensee.

(f)   Failure to comply with the requirement of a local ordinance regulating commercial marijuana activity.

(g) The intentional and knowing sale of marijuana or marijuana products by a licensee to a person under the legal age to purchase or possess.

* * *

Chapter 6. Licensed Cultivation Sites

26060. [Agency Jurisdictions]

(a) Regulations issued by the Department of Food and Agriculture governing the licensing of indoor, outdoor, and mixed-light cultivation sites shall apply to licensed cultivators under this division.

(b) Standards developed by the Department of Pesticide Regulation, in consultation with the Department of Food and Agriculture, for the use of pesticides in cultivation, and maximum tolerances for pesticides and other foreign object residue in harvested cannabis shall apply to licensed cultivators under this division.

(c) The Department of Food and Agriculture shall include conditions in each license requested by the Department of Fish and Wildlife and the State Water Resources Control Board to ensure that individual and cumulative effects of water diversion and discharge associated with cultivation do not affect the instream flows needed for fish spawning, migration, and rearing, and the flows needed to maintain natural flow variability, and to otherwise protect fish, wildlife, fish and wildlife habitat, and water quality.

(d) The regulations promulgated by the Department of Food and Agriculture under this division shall, at a minimum, address in relation to commercial marijuana activity, the same matters described in subdivision (e) of Section 19332 of **Chapter 3.5 of Division 8**.

(e) The Department of Pesticide Regulation, in consultation with the State Water Resources Control Board, shall promulgate regulations that require that the application of pesticides or other pest control in connection with the indoor, outdoor, or mixed light cultivation of marijuana meets standards equivalent to Division 6 (commencing with **Section 11401**) of the Food and Agricultural Code and its implementing regulations.

* * *

Chapter 7. Retailers and Distributors

26070. Retailers and Distributors

(a) State licenses to be issued by the Department of Consumer Affairs are as follows:

(1) "Retailer," for the retail sale and delivery of marijuana or marijuana products to customers.

(2) "Distributor," for the distribution of marijuana and marijuana products. A distributor licensee shall be bonded and insured at a minimum level established by the licensing authority.

(3) "Microbusiness," for the cultivation of marijuana on an area less than 10,000 square feet and to act as a licensed distributor, Level 1 manufacturer, and retailer under this division, provided such licensee complies with all requirements imposed by this division on licensed cultivators, distributors, Level 1 manufacturers, and retailers to the extent the licensee engages in such activities. Microbusiness licenses that authorize cultivation of marijuana shall include conditions requested by the Department of Fish and Wildlife and the State Water Resources Control Board to ensure that individual and cumulative effects of water diversion and discharge associated with cultivation do not affect the instream flows needed for fish spawning, migration, and rearing, and the flow needed to maintain flow variability, and otherwise protect fish, wildlife, fish and wildlife habitat, and water quality.

(b) The bureau shall establish minimum security and transportation safety requirements for the commercial distribution and delivery of marijuana and marijuana products. The transportation safety standards established by the bureau shall include, but not be limited to, minimum standards governing the types of vehicles in which marijuana and marijuana products may be distributed and delivered and minimum qualifications for persons eligible to operate such vehicles.

(c) Licensed retailers and microbusinesses, and licensed nonprofits under Section 26070.5 [Non-Profit Feasibility Study], shall implement security measures reasonably designed to prevent unauthorized entrance into areas containing marijuana or marijuana products and theft of marijuana or marijuana products from the premises. These security measures shall include, but not be limited to, all of the following:

(1) Prohibiting individuals from remaining on the licensee's premises if they are not engaging in activity expressly related to the operations of the dispensary.

(2) Establishing limited access areas accessible only to authorized personnel.

(3) Other than limited amounts of marijuana used for display purposes, samples, or immediate sale, storing all finished marijuana and marijuana products in a secured and locked room, safe, or vault, and in a manner reasonably designed to prevent diversion, theft, and loss.

* * *

Chapter 11. Quality Assurance, Inspection, and Testing

26110. Quality Assurance

(a) All marijuana and marijuana products shall be subject to quality assurance, inspection, and testing.

(b) All marijuana and marijuana products shall undergo quality assurance, inspection, and testing in the same manner as provided in Section 19326 in **Chapter 3.5 of Division 8** except as otherwise provided in this division or by law.

Chapter 12. Packaging and Labeling

26120. [Labeling & Warnings]

(a) Prior to delivery or sale at a retailer, marijuana and marijuana products shall be labeled and placed in a resealable, child resistant package.

(b) Packages and labels shall not be made to be attractive to children.

(c) All marijuana and marijuana product labels and inserts shall include the following information prominently displayed in a clear and legible fashion in accordance with the requirements, including font size, prescribed by the bureau or the Department of Public Health:

(1) Manufacture date and source.

(2) The following statements, in bold print:

(A) For marijuana: "GOVERNMENT WARNING: THIS PACKAGE CONTAINS MARIJUANA, A SCHEDULE I CONTROLLED SUBSTANCE. KEEP OUT OF REACH OF CHILDREN AND ANIMALS. MARIJUANA MAY ONLY BE POSSESSED OR CONSUMED BY PERSONS 21 YEARS OF AGE OR OLDER UNLESS THE PERSON IS A QUALIFIED PATIENT. MARIJUANA USE WHILE PREGNANT OR BREASTFEEDING MAY BE HARMFUL. CONSUMPTION OF MARIJUANA IMPAIRS YOUR ABILITY TO DRIVE AND OPERATE MACHINERY. PLEASE USE EXTREME CAUTION."

(B) For marijuana products: "GOVERNMENT WARNING: THIS PRODUCT CONTAINS MARIJUANA, A SCHEDULE I CONTROLLED SUBSTANCE. KEEP OUT OF REACH OF CHILDREN AND ANIMALS. MARIJUANA PRODUCTS MAY ONLY BE POSSESSED OR CONSUMED BY PERSONS 21 YEARS OF AGE OR OLDER UNLESS THE PERSON IS A QUALIFIED PATIENT. THE INTOXICATING EFFECTS OF MARIJUANA PRODUCTS MAY BE DELAYED UP TO TWO HOURS. MARIJUANA USE WHILE PREGNANT OR BREASTFEEDING MAY BE HARMFUL. CONSUMPTION OF MARIJUANA PRODUCTS IMPAIRS YOUR ABILITY TO DRIVE AND OPERATE MACHINERY. PLEASE USE EXTREME CAUTION."

(3)   For packages containing only dried flower, the net weight of marijuana in the package.

(4)   Identification of the source and date of cultivation, the type of marijuana or marijuana product and the date of manufacturing and packaging.

(5)   The appellation of origin, if any.

(6)   List of pharmacologically active ingredients, including, but not limited to, tetrahydrocannabinol (THC), cannabidiol (CBD), and other cannabinoid content, the THC and other cannabinoid amount in milligrams per serving, servings per package, and the THC and other cannabinoid amount in milligrams for the package total, and the potency of the marijuana or marijuana product by reference to the amount of tetrahydrocannabinol and cannabidiol in each serving.

(7)   For marijuana products, a list of all ingredients and disclosure of nutritional information in the same manner as the federal nutritional labeling requirements in **21 C.F.R. section 101.9.**

(8)   A list of any solvents, nonorganic pesticides, herbicides, and fertilizers that were used in the cultivation, production, and manufacture of such marijuana or marijuana product.

(9)   A warning if nuts or other known allergens are used.

(10) Information associated with the unique identifier issued by the Department of Food and Agriculture.

(11) Any other requirement set by the bureau or the Department of Public Health.

(d)   Only generic food names may be used to describe the ingredients in edible marijuana products.

(e)   In the event the bureau determines that marijuana is no longer a schedule I controlled substance under federal law, the label prescribed in subdivision (c) shall no longer require a statement that marijuana is a schedule I controlled substance.

* * *

SECTION 7. MARIJUANA TAX.

Part 14.5 (commencing with Section 34010) is added to Division 2 of the Revenue and Taxation Code, to read:

Part 14.5. Marijuana Tax

* * *

34011. [Excise Tax]

(a)   Effective January 1, 2018, a marijuana excise tax shall be imposed upon purchasers of marijuana or marijuana products sold in this state at the rate of fifteen percent (15%) of the gross receipts of any retail sale by a dispensary or other person required to be licensed pursuant to **Chapter 3.5 of Division 8** of the Business and Professions Code or a retailer, microbusiness, nonprofit, or other person required to be licensed pursuant to <u>Division 10. Marijuana</u> of the Business and Professions Code to sell marijuana and marijuana products directly to a purchaser.

(b)   Except as otherwise provided by regulation, the tax levied under this section shall apply to the full price, if non-itemized, of any transaction involving both marijuana or marijuana products and any other otherwise distinct and identifiable goods or services, and the price of any goods or services, if a reduction in the price of marijuana or marijuana products is contingent on purchase of those goods or services.

(c)   A dispensary or other person required to be licensed pursuant to **Chapter 3.5 of Division 8** of the Business and Professions Code or a retailer, microbusiness, nonprofit, or other person required to be licensed pursuant to <u>Division 10. Marijuana</u> of the Business and Professions Code shall be responsible for collecting this tax and remitting it to the board in accordance with rules and procedures established under law and any regulations adopted by the board.

(d)   The excise tax imposed by this section shall be in addition to the sales and use tax imposed by the state and local governments.

(e)   Gross receipts from the sale of marijuana or marijuana products for purposes of assessing the sales and use tax under Part 1 of this division shall include the tax levied pursuant to this section.

(f)   No marijuana or marijuana products may be sold to a purchaser unless the excise tax required by law has been paid by the purchaser at the time of sale.

(g)   The sales and use tax imposed by Part 1 of this division shall not apply to retail sales of medical cannabis, medical cannabis concentrate, edible medical cannabis products or topical cannabis as those terms are defined in **Chapter 3.5 of Division 8** of the Business and Professions Code when a qualified patient (or primary caregiver for a qualified patient) provides his or her card issued under **Section 11362.71** of the Health and Safety Code and a valid government issued identification card.

34012. [Cultivation Tax]

(a)   Effective January 1, 2018, there is hereby imposed a cultivation tax on all harvested marijuana that enters the commercial market upon all persons required to be licensed to cultivate marijuana pursuant to **Chapter 3.5 of Division 8** of the Business and Professions Code or <u>Division 10. Marijuana</u> of the Business and Professions Code. The tax shall be due after the marijuana is harvested.

(1) The tax for marijuana flowers shall be nine dollars and twenty-five cents ($9.25) per dryweight ounce.

(2) The tax for marijuana leaves shall be set at two dollars and seventy-five cents ($2.75) per dry-weight ounce.

(b) The board may adjust the tax rate for marijuana leaves annually to reflect fluctuations in the relative price of marijuana flowers to marijuana leaves.

(c) The board may from time to time establish other categories of harvested marijuana, categories for unprocessed or frozen marijuana or immature plants, or marijuana that is shipped directly to manufacturers. These categories shall be taxed at their relative value compared with marijuana flowers.

(d) The board may prescribe by regulation a method and manner for payment of the cultivation tax that utilizes tax stamps or state-issued product bags that indicate that all required tax has been paid on the product to which the tax stamp is affixed or in which the marijuana is packaged.

(e) The tax stamps and product bags shall be of the designs, specifications and denominations as may be prescribed by the board and may be purchased by any licensee under **Chapter 3.5 of Division 8** of the Business and Professions Code or under Division 10. Marijuana of the Business and Professions Code.

(f) Subsequent to the establishment of a tax stamp program, the board may by regulation provide that no marijuana may be removed from a licensed cultivation facility or transported on a public highway unless in a state-issued product bag bearing a tax stamp in the proper denomination.

(g) The tax stamps and product bags shall be capable of being read by a scanning or similar device and must be traceable utilizing the track and trace system pursuant to Section 26170. [Seed-to-Sale Tracking] of the Business and Professions Code.

(h) Persons required to be licensed to cultivate marijuana pursuant to **Chapter 3.5 of Division 8** of the Business and Professions Code or Division 10. Marijuana of the Business and Professions Code shall be responsible for payment of the tax pursuant to regulations adopted by the board. No marijuana may be sold unless the tax has been paid as provided in this part.

(i) All marijuana removed from a cultivator's premises, except for plant waste, shall be presumed to be sold and thereby taxable under this section.

(j) The tax imposed by this section shall be imposed on all marijuana cultivated in the state pursuant to rules and regulations promulgated by the board, but shall not apply to marijuana cultivated for personal use under Section 11362.1. [Personal Possession & Cultivation] of the Health and Safety Code or cultivated by a qualified patient or primary caregiver in accordance with the Compassionate Use Act.

(k) Beginning January 1, 2020, the rates set forth in subdivisions (a), (b), and (c) shall be adjusted by the board annually thereafter for inflation.

34013. [Tax Collection]

(a) The board shall administer and collect the taxes imposed by this part pursuant to the Fee Collection Procedures Law (Part 30 (commencing with **Section 55001**) of Division 2 of the Revenue and Taxation Code). For purposes of this part, the references in the Fee Collection Procedures Law to "fee" shall include the tax imposed by this part, and references to "fee payer" shall include a person required to pay or collect the tax imposed by this part.

(b) The board may prescribe, adopt, and enforce regulations relating to the administration and enforcement of this part, including, but not limited to, collections, reporting, refunds, and appeals.

(c) The board shall adopt necessary rules and regulations to administer the taxes in this part. Such rules and regulations may include methods or procedures to tag marijuana or marijuana products, or the packages thereof to designate prior tax payment.

(d) The board may prescribe, adopt, and enforce any emergency regulations as necessary to implement, administer and enforce its duties under this division. Any emergency regulation prescribed, adopted, or enforced pursuant to this section shall be adopted in accordance with Chapter 3.5 (commencing with **section 11340**) of Part 1 of Division 3 of Title 2 of the Government Code, and, for purposes of that chapter, including **Section 11349.6** of the Government Code, the adoption of the regulation is an emergency and shall be considered by the Office of Administrative Law as necessary for the immediate preservation of the public peace, health and safety, and general welfare. Notwithstanding any other provision of law, the emergency regulations adopted by the board may remain in effect for two years from adoption.

(e) Any person who fails to pay the taxes imposed under this part shall, in addition to owing the taxes not paid, be subject to a penalty of at least one-half the amount of the taxes not paid, and shall be subject to having its license revoked pursuant to Section 26031. [License Suspension] of the Business and Professions Code or pursuant to **Chapter 3.5 of Division 8** of the Business and Professions Code.

(f) The board may bring such legal actions as are necessary to collect any deficiency in the tax required to be paid, and, upon the board's request, the Attorney General shall bring the actions.

* * *

NOTES AND QUESTIONS

1.   **Implementing Proposition 64's goals.** Review the section of Proposition 64 stating the "Purpose and Intent" of the law. Can you see problems with implementing all of those purposes?

2.   **Reining in the illegal market.** California has an extremely large illegal marijuana market, including thousands of marijuana growers. Do any of the stated goals of Proposition 64 deter illegal producers from entering the legal market? What should the state do to assure that illegal producers enter the legal market?

3.   **More on the hope for reining in the illegal market.** The Emerald Triangle is the name of a three county area in Northern California known for marijuana production. By some estimates, between 25–50% of all residents in Humboldt County rely on marijuana for their incomes. Many of the marijuana producers sought refuge in remote regions of the Emerald Triangle as a way to avoid detection. Not surprisingly, they are producing marijuana far from major highways and markets. Some marijuana investors are buying up land in regions closer, say, to Sacramento and San Francisco, to reduce costs of transportation. What will happen to efforts to eliminate the black market if producers in the Emerald Triangle do not enter the legal market? For a discussion of some of the relevant problems, *see* Michael Vitiello and Rosemary Deck, *Legalizing Marijuana: A View From Among the Weeds*, 69 Hastings L. J. 961 (2018).

4.   **California's slow start.** At least early reports from California indicated that very few growers signed up for licenses because the licenses were too expensive and regulations too prohibitive. *See* Robert Gauthier, *California Gov. Jerry Brown's new budget says pot revenue is 'slower than anticipated'*, CNBC (May 11, 2018, 2:08 PM), https://www.cnbc.com/2018/05/ 10/california-gov-brown-could-slash-cannabis-tax-revenue-forecasts.html.

5.   **Corporation domination of the market.** Many marijuana proponents expressed concern about Big Tobacco or Big Weed entering the market and squeezing out small producers. That raises serious policy concerns. How does Proposition 64 deal with that risk?

6.   **Mop up legislation.** Six months after California adopted Proposition 64, the legislature passed a budget trailer bill, Senate Bill 94. The bill, the Medicinal and Adult-Use Cannabis Regulation and Safety Act (MAUCRSA) integrated Proposition 64 (Adult Use of Marijuana Act [AUMA]) and Medical Cannabis Regulation and Safety Act (MCRSA), described above.

7.   **More on Proposition 64.** For a discussion of background to Proposition 64: Marchini, Gage and Parino, Brian (2016) "Proposition 64: Marijuana Legalization," *California Initiative Review* (CIR) Vol. 2016, Article 15.   https://scholarlycommons.pacific.edu/cgi/viewcontent.cgi?article=1014& context=california-initiative-review.

E. PROPOSITION 64'S REGULATORY SCHEME

Despite Proposition 64's necessary length, the initiative left the development of implementation to regulatory agencies. Some of Proposition 19's critics pointed to its lack of detail, for example, leaving uncertain how state taxation would work. In 2012, drafters in Colorado and Washington off-loaded responsibility for writing specific regulations implementing their initiatives. Proposition 64's drafters followed suit.

California initially drafted interim regulations. More recently, permanent regulations have become effective. Those regulations number in the hundreds of pages. What follows are some of the key regulations. Interspersed are notes and questions about specific regulations.

CALIFORNIA CODE OF REGULATIONS
TITLE 16
DIVISION 42.   BUREAU OF CANNABIS CONTROL
Chapter 1. ALL BUREAU LICENSEES

§ 5017. Substantially Related Offenses and Criteria for Rehabilitation

(a) For the purpose of license denial, convictions that are substantially related to the qualifications, functions, or duties of the business for which the application is made include:

(1) A violent felony conviction, as specified in subdivision (c) of section 667.5 of the Penal Code.

(2) A serious felony conviction, as specified in subdivision (c) of section 1192.7 of the Penal Code.

(3) A felony conviction involving fraud, deceit, or embezzlement.

(4) A felony conviction for hiring, employing, or using a minor in transporting, carrying, selling, giving away, preparing for sale, or peddling, any controlled substance to a minor; or selling, offering to sell, furnishing, offering to furnish, administering, or giving any controlled substance to a minor.

(5) A felony conviction for drug trafficking with enhancements pursuant to Health and Safety Code section 11370.4 or 11379.8.

(b) Except as provided in subsections (4) and (5) of subsection (a) and notwithstanding Chapter 2 (commencing with Section 480) of Division 1.5 of the Business and Professions Code, a prior conviction, where the sentence, including any term of probation, incarceration, or supervised release, is completed, for possession of, possession for sale, sale, manufacture, transportation, or cultivation of a controlled substance is not considered substantially related, and shall not be the sole ground for denial of a license. Conviction for any controlled substance felony subsequent to licensure shall be grounds for revocation of a license or denial of the renewal of a license.

(c)   When evaluating whether an applicant who has been convicted of a criminal offense that is substantially related to the qualifications, functions, or duties of the business for which the application is made should be issued a license, the Bureau shall consider the following criteria of rehabilitation:

(1)   The nature and severity of the act or offense;

(2)   Whether the person has a felony conviction based on possession or use of cannabis or cannabis products that would not be a felony if the person was convicted of the offense on the date of the person's application;

(3)   The applicant's criminal record as a whole;

(4)   Evidence of any act committed subsequent to the act or offense under consideration that could be considered grounds for denial, suspension, or revocation of a commercial cannabis activity license;

(5)   The time that has elapsed since commission of the act or offense;

(6)   The extent to which the applicant has complied with any terms of parole, probation, restitution, or any other sanctions lawfully imposed against the applicant;

(7)   If applicable, evidence of dismissal under Penal Code sections 1203.4, 1203.4(a), 1203.41 or another state's similar law;

(8)   If applicable, a certificate of rehabilitation obtained under Penal Code section 4852.01 or another state's similar law; and

(9)   Other evidence of rehabilitation submitted by the applicant.

* * *

NOTES AND QUESTIONS

1.   **Proposition 64's goals and the regulations.** Review Section 3 of Proposition 64, the section on Purpose and Intent. What are the goal of § 5017? As you consider the other regulations below, consider how other regulations may be at odds with the goals of § 5017.

2.   **Racial disparity in arrests and Proposition 64's aspirations.** Numerous studies and books focus on the racial disparity in the administration of marijuana and other drug laws. Perhaps most famous among those works is Professor Michelle Alexander's *The New Jim Crow* (2010). Some proponents of legalizing marijuana do so, in part, to reduce this disparate impact on minorities. Early studies suggest that legalization in states like Colorado and Washington have failed to remedy the problem. Instead, the disparity has even

increased in some areas. *See* Steve W. Bender, *The Colors of Cannabis: Race and Marijuana* 50 U.C, Davis L. Rev. 689, 700–704 (2016). Some local governments in California are working on ways to increase minority access to the legal market. *See Overview of California City Equity Programs,* Bureau of Cannabis Control (Feb. 26, 2018), https://bcc.ca.gov/about_us/meetings/materials/20180301_equ_overview.pdf.

   3.   Qualifying for a license. Section 5018 addresses "Additional Grounds for Denial of a License." The grounds are fairly typical of licensing regulations. Thus, one might not receive a license if her premises do not comply with the regulations, the applicant refused access to regulators, or the applicant failed to pay taxes as required by the state code.

   4.   The burden of regulation. The following regulation deals with the kinds of activities on a commercial marijuana site.

---

§ 5025. Premises

(a) Each license shall have a designated premises for the licensee's commercial cannabis activity, which is subject to inspection by the Bureau.

(b) The Bureau may allow a licensee to conduct both adult-use and medicinal commercial cannabis activity on the same licensed premises if all of the following criteria are met:

   (1) The licensee holds both an A-designation and M-designation on the license for the identical type of commercial cannabis activity; and

   (2) The licensee only conducts one type of commercial cannabis activity on the premises.

(c) Retailers and microbusinesses authorized to conduct retail activities shall only serve customers who are within the licensed premises, or at a delivery address that meets the requirements of this division.

   (1) The sale and delivery of cannabis goods shall not occur through a pass-out window or a slide-out tray to the exterior of the premises.

   (2) Retailers or microbusinesses shall not operate as or with a drive-in or drive-through at which cannabis goods are sold to persons within or about a motor vehicle.

   (3) No cannabis goods shall be sold and/or delivered by any means or method to any person within a motor vehicle.

(d) Alcoholic beverages as defined in Business and Professions Code section 23004 shall not be stored or consumed on a premises.

(e) Any premises that is adjacent to another premises engaging in manufacturing or cultivation shall be separated from those premises by walls, and any doors leading to the cultivation or manufacturing premises shall remain closed.

* * *

[Article 4, dealing with displaying one's license, and Article 5, dealing with security measures, have been edited out of this casebook.]

NOTES AND QUESTIONS

1.   Proposition 64's goals and the regulations. Review Section 3 of Proposition 64, the section on Purpose and Intent. What are the goals of § 5025?

2.   Stoned drivers and Proposition 64. One obvious concern reflected in § 5025 is to keep marijuana out of the hands of drivers. Proposition 64 earmarked funds for the California Highway Patrol to study ways to detect drivers who are under the influence of marijuana. On one hand, traces of marijuana remain in the blood well past the point of intoxication. On the other, current methods of detection focus on an officer's subjective observations of a driver. Critics raise concern about the exercise of such subjective judgments. *See* Andrea Roth, *The Uneasy Case for Marijuana as Chemical Impairment Under a Science-Based Jurisprudence of Dangerousness*, 103 Calif. L. Rev. 841, 890 (2015).

3.   More regulations and more regulations. The following provisions focus on measuring the amount of marijuana that a person produces or sells.

Article 6.   Track and Trace Requirements

§ 5048. Track and Trace System

(a) A licensee shall create and maintain an active and functional account within the track and trace system prior to engaging in any commercial cannabis activity, including the purchase, sale, test, packaging, transfer, transport, return, destruction, or disposal, of any cannabis goods.

(b) A licensee shall designate one individual owner as the track and trace system account manager. The account manager may authorize additional owners or employees as track and trace system users and shall ensure that each user is trained on the track and trace system prior to its access or use.

(1) The account manager shall attend and successfully complete all required track and trace system training, including any orientation and continuing education.

(2) If the account manager did not complete the required track and trace system training prior to receiving their annual license, the account manager shall sign up for and complete state mandated training, as prescribed by the Bureau, within five business days of license issuance.

(c)   The account manager and each user shall be assigned a unique log-on, consisting of a username and password. The account manager or each user accessing the track and trace system shall only do so under his or her assigned log-on, and shall not use or access a log-on of any other individual. No account manager or user shall share or transfer his or her log-on, username, or password, to be used by any other individual for any reason.

(d)   The account manager shall maintain a complete, accurate, and up-to-date list of all track and trace system users, consisting of their full names and usernames.

(e)   A licensee shall monitor all compliance notifications from the track and trace system, and timely resolve the issues detailed in the compliance notification.

> (1)   A licensee shall keep a record, independent of the track and trace system, of all compliance notifications received from the track and trace system, and how and when compliance was achieved.

> (2)   If a licensee is unable to resolve a compliance notification within three business days of receiving the notification, the licensee shall notify the Bureau immediately.

(f)   A licensee is accountable for all actions its owners or employees take while logged into or using the track and trace system, or otherwise while conducting track and trace activities.

§ 5049. Track and Trace Reporting

(a)   A licensee shall record in the track and trace system all commercial cannabis activity, including:

> (1)   Packaging of cannabis goods.

> (2)   Sale of cannabis goods.

> (3)   Transportation of cannabis goods to a licensee.

> (4)   Receipt of cannabis goods.

> (5)   Return of cannabis goods.

> (6)   Destruction and disposal of cannabis goods.

> (7)   Laboratory testing and results.

> (8)   Any other activity as required pursuant to this division, or by any other licensing authority.

(b)   The following information shall be recorded for each activity entered in the track and trace system:

> (1)   Name and type of the cannabis goods.

> (2)   Unique identifier of the cannabis goods.

> (3)   Amount of the cannabis goods, by weight or count.

(4) Date and time of the activity or transaction.

(5) Name and license number of other licensees involved in the activity or transaction.

(6) If the cannabis goods are being transported:

(A) The licensee shall transport pursuant to a shipping manifest generated through the track and trace system, that includes items (1) through (5) of this subsection, as well as:

(i) The name, license number, and premises address of the originating licensee.

(ii) The name, license number, and premises address of the licensee transporting the cannabis goods.

(iii) The name, license number, and premises address of the destination licensee receiving the cannabis goods into inventory or storage.

(iv) The date and time of departure from the licensed premises and approximate date and time of departure from each subsequent licensed premises, if any.

(v) Arrival date and estimated time of arrival at each licensed premises.

(vi) Driver license number of the personnel transporting the cannabis goods, and the make, model, and license plate number of the vehicle used for transport.

(B) Upon pick-up or receipt of cannabis goods for transport, storage, or inventory, a licensee shall ensure that the cannabis goods received are as described in the shipping manifest, and shall record acceptance and acknowledgment of the cannabis goods in the track and trace system.

(C) If there are any discrepancies between the type or quantity specified in the shipping manifest and the type or quantity received by the licensee, the licensee shall record and document the discrepancy in the track and trace system and in any relevant business record.

(7) If cannabis goods are being destroyed or disposed of, the licensee shall record in the track and trace system the following additional information:

(A) The name of the employee performing the destruction or disposal.

(B) The reason for destruction or disposal.

(C) The name of the entity being used to collect and process cannabis waste, pursuant to section 5055 of this division.

(8) Description for any adjustments made in the track and trace system, including, but not limited to:

(A) Spoilage or fouling of the cannabis goods.

(B) Any event resulting in exposure or compromise of the cannabis goods.

(9) Any other information as required pursuant to this division, or by any other applicable licensing authorities.

(c) Unless otherwise specified, all transactions must be entered into the track and trace system within 24 hours of occurrence.

(d) Licensees shall only enter and record complete and accurate information into the track and trace system, and shall correct any known errors entered into the track and trace system immediately upon discovery.

NOTES AND QUESTIONS

1. **The importance of track and trace.** Review Section 3, Purpose and Intent of Proposition 64. Why have the regulators included these rather detailed provisions for track and trace?

2. **Workable rules?** Apart from why track and trace requirements are built into the law, is the system workable? Do you see any conflict between the policies supporting track and trace and other policies implemented by the California voters? For an article about Colorado's tracking procedures, *see* Sam Kamin & Joel Warner, *"Blazing a Trail"*, Slate (Dec. 12, 2013, 10:33 AM), http://www.slate.com/articles/news_and_politics/altered_state/2013/12/colorado_pot_legalization_how_much_can_the_state_learn_from_the_end_of_prohibition.html.

3. **Colorado as a model.** Some states like Colorado have effective track and trace regulations in place. One obvious goal of an effective track and trace system is to be sure that the state and local governments are receiving tax revenues promised by legalization proponents. Colorado's tax revenues have generally exceeded earlier projected estimates.

4. **Complex issues surrounding taxation of marijuana.** Consider how a state should tax marijuana. Should it be based on the net weight of the product sold? On the THC content of the product? On the sales price of the product? What are the advantages and disadvantages of each of these (or other) approaches? For a discussion of this problem, *see* George Theofanis, *The Golden State's 'High' Expectations: Will California Realize the Fiscal Benefits of Cannabis Legalization?* 49 U. Pac. L. Rev. 155 (2017).

5. **Still more regulations.** The following provisions deal with various regulations of retail businesses.

———————

Chapter 3.   RETAILERS

§ 5402. Retail Area

(a)   Individuals shall be granted access to the retail area to purchase cannabis goods only after the retailer or an employee of the retailer has confirmed that the individual is at least 21 years of age and has a valid proof of identification, or that the individual is at least 18 years of age and has valid proof of identification and a valid physician's recommendation for himself or herself or for a person for whom he or she is a primary caregiver.

(b)   Acceptable forms of identification include the following:

(1)   A document issued by a federal, state, county, or municipal government, or a political subdivision or agency thereof, including, but not limited to, a valid motor vehicle operator's license, that contains the name, date of birth, physical description, and photo of the person;

(2)   A valid identification card issued to a member of the Armed Forces that includes a date of birth and a photo of the person; or

(3)   A valid passport issued by the United States or by a foreign government.

(c)   A valid proof of identification must clearly indicate the age or birthdate of the individual.

(d)   The retailer or at least one employee shall be physically present in the retail area at all times when individuals who are not employees of the retailer are in the retail area.

§ 5404. Retail Customers

(a)   A retailer shall only sell adult-use cannabis goods to individuals who are at least 21 years of age, and medicinal cannabis goods to individuals at least 18 years of age who possess a valid physician's recommendation for himself or herself or a person for whom he or she is a primary caregiver.

(b)   A retailer shall confirm the identity and age, and physician's recommendation if applicable, of a customer as required by section 5402(a) of this division.

§ 5406. Cannabis Goods for Sale

A retailer shall not make any cannabis goods available for sale or delivery to a customer unless:

(a)   The cannabis goods were received from a licensed distributor;

(b)   The retailer has verified that the cannabis goods have not exceeded their expiration or sell-by date if one is provided; and

(c) In the case of manufactured cannabis products, the product complies with all requirements of Business and Professions Code section 26130 and all other relevant laws.

§ 5409. Daily Limits

(a) A retailer shall not sell more than the following amounts to a single adult-use cannabis customer in a single day:

(1) 28.5 grams of non-concentrated cannabis.

(2) 8 grams of concentrated cannabis as defined in Business and Professions Code section 26001, including concentrated cannabis contained in cannabis products.

(3) 6 immature cannabis plants.

(b) A retailer shall not sell more than the following amounts to a single medicinal cannabis patient, or to a patient's primary caregiver purchasing medicinal cannabis on behalf of the patient, in a single day:

(1) 8 ounces of medicinal cannabis as defined in section 11362.77 of the Health and Safety Code.

(2) 12 immature cannabis plants.

(c) If a valid physician's recommendation contains a different amount than the limits listed in this section, the medicinal cannabis customer may purchase an amount of medicinal cannabis consistent with the patient's needs as recommended by a physician.

[Section 5410, dealing with customer return of cannabis goods has been edited out of the casebook.]

NOTES AND QUESTIONS

1. **Proposition 64's goals and the regulations.** Review Section 3, Purpose and Intent of Proposition 64. Why have the regulators included these provisions governing retail businesses?

2. **Regulations and frustration of the legal market?** Apart from whether these provisions achieve the goals of the voters in adopting Proposition 64, what problems can you anticipate might arise under these provisions?

3. **Predictions about the future in California.** Will participants in black market sales sign up for licenses? Will licensed dealers comply with such detailed regulations? Compliance with detailed regulations comes with a significant cost. How can the state deter black market sellers or licensed dealers who cheat? Enforcement comes with significant costs as well. For a discussion of some of these tensions, *see* Michael Vitiello, *Legalizing Marijuana: California's Pot of Gold?*, 2009 Wis. L. Rev. 1349 (2009).

4. **Microbusinesses.** Section 5500, Chapter 4, deals with microbusinesses. The creation of special licensing requirements for microbusinesses reflect the hope that smaller producers will be able to enter the legal market. The state charges less for a microbusiness license and creates a bit more flexibility in regulating such businesses. Whether that approach will succeed in creating a good business climate for smaller producers is very much up in the air.

5. **More regulations.** The next section deals with requirements for testing the quality of marijuana offered to consumers.

Chapter 6. TESTING LABORATORIES

§ 5726. Certificate of Analysis (COA)

(a) The laboratory shall generate a COA only for each representative sample that the laboratory analyzes.

(b) The laboratory shall, within 1 business day of completing analyses of a sample, both enter the COA information into the track and trace system and provide a copy of the COA to the requester.

(c) The COA shall contain, at minimum, the following information:

(1) Laboratory's name, address, and license number;

(2) Distributor's name, address, and license number;

(3) Cultivator's, manufacturer's, or microbusiness' name, address, and license number;

(4) Batch number of the batch from which the sample was obtained;

(5) Sample identifying information, including matrix type and unique sample identifiers;

(6) Sample history, including the date collected, the date received by the laboratory, and the date(s) of sample analyses and corresponding testing results;

(7) For cannabis samples, the total weight, in grams, of both the representative sample and the total batch size;

(8) For cannabis product samples, the total unit count of both the representative sample and the total batch size;

(9) The identity of the analytical methods used and corresponding Limits of Detection (LOD) and Limits of Quantitation (LOQ); and

(10) Analytes detected during the analyses of the sample that are unknown, unidentified, or injurious to human health if consumed, if any.

(d)   The laboratory shall report test results for each representative sample on the COA as follows:

(1)   Indicate an overall "pass" or "fail" for the entire batch;

(2)   When reporting qualitative results for each analyte, the laboratory shall indicate "pass" or "fail";

(3)   When reporting quantitative results for each analyte, the laboratory shall use the appropriate units of measurement as required under this chapter;

(4)   When reporting results for each test method, the laboratory shall indicate "pass" or "fail";

(5)   For representative samples obtained from a cannabis or cannabis product batch to which a content label is affixed at the time of sampling, the laboratory shall report the following on the COA:

(A)   The cannabinoid content and terpenoid content as printed or written on the label that is affixed to the cannabis or cannabis product batch;

(B)   The cannabinoid profile and the terpenoid profile of the representative sample as determined by the laboratory as required under section 5724 and section 5725 of this chapter, respectively; and

(C)   The difference, in percentage, between the cannabinoid content and terpenoid content as printed or written on the label and the cannabinoid profile and the terpenoid profile of the representative sample, if any, as determined by the laboratory;

(6)   When reporting results for any analytes that were detected below the analytical method LOQ, indicate "<LOQ";

(7)   When reporting results for any analytes that were not detected or detected below the LOD, indicate "ND"; and

(8)   Indicate "NT" for any test that the laboratory did not perform.

(e)   The laboratory supervisory or management employee shall validate the accuracy of the information contained on the COA and sign and date the COA.

Article 7.   Laboratory Quality Assurance and Quality Control

§ 5729. Laboratory Quality Assurance (LQA) Program

(a)   The laboratory shall develop and implement a LQA program to assure the reliability and validity of the analytical data produced by the laboratory. The LQA program shall, at minimum, include a written LQA manual that addresses the following:

(1)   Quality control procedures;

(2) Laboratory organization and employee training and responsibilities;

(3) LQA objectives for measurement data;

(4) Traceability of data and analytical results;

(5) Instrument maintenance, calibration procedures, and frequency;

(6) Performance and system audits;

(7) Steps to change processes when necessary;

(8) Record retention;

(9) Test procedure standardization; and

(10) Method validation.

(b) The supervisory or management laboratory employee shall annually review, amend if necessary, and approve the LQA program and manual both when they are created and when there is a change in methods, laboratory equipment, or the supervisory or management laboratory employee.

§ 5730. Laboratory Quality Control (LQC) Samples

(a) The laboratory shall use LQC samples in the performance of each analysis according to the following specifications.

(b) The laboratory shall analyze LQC samples in the same manner as the laboratory analyzes cannabis and cannabis product samples.

(c) The laboratory shall use negative and positive controls for microbial testing.

(d) The laboratory shall prepare and analyze at least one of each of the following LQC samples for each analytical batch within each set of 20 samples for the following LQC samples:

(1) Method blank;

(2) Continuing calibration verification (CCV);

(3) Laboratory replicate sample; and

(4) Matrix spike sample or matrix spike duplicate sample.

(e) If the result of the analyses is outside the specified acceptance criteria in the following table, the laboratory shall determine the cause and take steps to remedy the problem until the result is within the specified acceptance criteria.

Laboratory Quality Control Sample	Acceptance Criteria
Method blank sample for chemical analysis	Not to exceed LOQ
Reference material and certified reference material for chemical analysis	Percent recovery 80%–120%
Laboratory replicate sample	RPD no greater than 20%
Matrix spike or matrix spike duplicate sample for chemical analysis	Percent recovery between 80% to 120%
CCV for chemical analysis	Percent recovery between 80% to 120%

(f)   The laboratory shall generate a LQC sample report for each analytical batch that includes LQC parameters, measurements, analysis date, and matrix.

[Further testing requirements are found in § 5731. Limits of Detection (LOD) and Limits of Quantitation (LOQ) for Quantitative Analyses. They have been edited out of this casebook.]

§ 5732. Data Package

(a)   The laboratory shall generate a data package for each batch of samples that the laboratory analyzes. At a minimum, the data package shall contain the following:

   (1)   The name and address of the laboratory that performed the analytical procedures;

   (2)   The names, functions, and signatures of the laboratory employees that performed the sample preparation, analyses, and reviewed and approved the data;

   (3)   All batch sample results and batch LQC sample results;

   (4)   Raw data, including instrument raw data, for each sample, if any;

   (5)   Instrument test method with parameters, if any;

   (6)   Instrument tune report, if any;

   (7)   Instrument calibration data, if any;

   (8)   LQC sample report with worksheets, forms, or copies of laboratory notebook pages containing pertinent information related to the identification and traceability of all reagents, reference materials, and standards used for analysis;

(9) Analytical batch sample sequence, if any;

(10) The field sample log and the COC form; and

(11) The COA created as required under this chapter.

(b) After the data package is compiled, the supervisory or management laboratory employee shall do the following:

(1) Review the analytical results for technical correctness and completeness;

(2) Verify that the results of each analysis carried out by the laboratory are reported accurately, clearly, unambiguously, and objectively; and

(3) Approve the laboratory results by signing and dating the data package prior to release of the data by the laboratory.

(c) The data package shall be kept for a minimum of 7 years and shall be made available upon request by the Bureau.

[Further testing and auditing requirements are found in §§ 5733–5736. Those sections include detailed specifications, including rules governing the qualifications of laboratory employees. Those sections have been edited out of this casebook.]

NOTES AND QUESTIONS

1. **Proposition 64's goals and the regulations.** Review Section 3, Purpose and Intent of Proposition 64. Why have the regulators included these provisions governing testing and packaging?

2. **Too many regulations?** As with other detailed provisions, what are the risks of including detailed testing provisions and package detail provisions?

3. **Private testing labs and a conflict of interest?** An issue raised by some critics of California's implementation of Proposition 64 is whether its testing scheme will work. As you can see, the state allows private businesses to test product quality. Some have advocated state testing laboratories; but involvement of the state implicates important questions about federal preemption. Critics of California's scheme question whether laboratories have sufficient incentive to report accurate test results. The primary concern expressed is that a marijuana producer will not continue to have a laboratory test its cannabis if the laboratory routinely finds the product out of compliance with the strict standards set out in the regulations. The jury is out on whether the system will work.

4. **Sanctions.** Some of the questions above focused on whether black market sellers or even licensed businesses would have enough incentive to comply with detailed regulations. The following regulations deal with failure of licensed businesses to comply with the published regulations.

Chapter 7. ENFORCEMENT

§ 5800. Right of Access

(a) The Bureau, and its authorized representatives, shall have full and immediate access to inspect and:

(1) Enter onto any premises licensed by the Bureau.

(2) Test any vehicle or equipment possessed by, in control of, or used by a licensee or their agents and employees for the purpose of conducting commercial cannabis activity.

(3) Test any cannabis goods or cannabis-related materials or products possessed by, in control of, or used by a licensee or their agents and employees for the purpose of conducting commercial cannabis activity.

(4) Copy any materials, books, or records of any licensee or their agents and employees.

(b) Failure to cooperate with and participate in any Bureau investigation pending against the licensee may result in a licensing violation subject to discipline. This subsection shall not be construed to deprive a licensee of any privilege guaranteed by the Fifth Amendment to the Constitution of the United States, or any other constitutional or statutory privileges. This subsection shall not be construed to require a licensee to cooperate with a request that would require the licensee to waive any constitutional or statutory privilege or to comply with a request for information or other matters within an unreasonable period of time in light of the time constraints of the licensee's business. Any constitutional or statutory privilege exercised by the licensee shall not be used against the licensee in a regulatory or disciplinary proceeding against the licensee.

(c) The Bureau, and its authorized representatives, shall have the rights of immediate access under subsection (a), during any inspection, investigation, review, or audit, or as otherwise allowed by law.

(d) Prior notice of an inspection, investigation, review, or audit is not required.

(e) Any inspection, investigation, review, or audit of a licensed premises shall be conducted anytime the licensee is exercising privileges under the license, or as otherwise agreed to by the Bureau and the licensee or its agents, employees, or representatives.

(f) If the premises is not accessible because access is only available by going through another licensed premises and the licensee occupying the other premises denies the Bureau access, the licensees shall both be held responsible and subject to discipline.

§ 5802. Citations; Orders of Abatement; Administrative Fines

(a) The Bureau may issue citations containing orders of abatement and fines against a licensee, or an unlicensed person, for any acts or omissions which are in violation of any provision of the Act or any regulation adopted pursuant thereto.

(b) The Bureau may issue a citation under this section to a licensee for a violation of a term or condition contained in a decision placing that licensee on probation.

(c)   Each citation:

(1)   Shall be in writing.

(2) Shall describe with particularity the nature of the violation, including a reference to the law or regulation determined to have been violated.

(3) May contain an assessment of an administrative fine of up to $5,000, and/or an order of abatement fixing a reasonable time for abatement of the violation;

(4)   Shall be served personally or by certified mail; and

(5) Shall inform the licensee or person that he or she may request an informal conference, or contest the citation, or both, pursuant to section 5803.

(d)   Failure to pay a fine within 30 calendar days of the date of assessment, unless the citation is being contested, may result in further action being taken by the Bureau including, but not limited to, suspension or revocation of a license. If a citation is not appealed and the fine is not paid, the full amount of the assessed fine shall be added to the fee for renewal of the license. A license shall not be renewed without the payment of the renewal fee and fine.

(e)   The amount of any fine to be levied by the Bureau shall take into consideration the factors listed in subdivision (b)(3) of Section 125.9 of the Business and Professions Code.

(f)   Nothing in this section shall be deemed to prevent the Bureau from filing an accusation to suspend or revoke a license where grounds for such suspension or revocation exist.

§ 5804. Citation Compliance

(a)   The time to abate or correct a violation as provided for in an order of abatement may be extended for good cause. If a cited licensee or person who has been issued an order of abatement is unable to complete the correction within the time set forth in the citation because of conditions beyond his or her control after the exercise of reasonable diligence, the licensee or person cited may request an extension of time from the Bureau in which to complete the correction. Such a request shall be in writing and shall be made within the time set forth for abatement.

(b) When a citation is not contested, or if it is appealed and the person cited does not prevail, failure to abate the violation within the time allowed or pay a fine that was imposed shall constitute a violation and a failure to comply with the citation or order of abatement.

(c) Failure to timely comply with an order of abatement or pay a fine that was imposed may result in further action being taken by the Bureau, including, but not limited to, suspension or revocation of a license, or further administrative or civil proceedings.

§ 5808. Additional Grounds for Discipline

The following include, but are not limited to, additional grounds that constitute a basis for disciplinary action:

(a) Failure to pay a fine imposed by the Bureau or agreed to by the licensee.

(b) Failure to take reasonable steps to correct objectionable conditions on the licensed premises, including the immediately adjacent area that is owned, leased, or rented by the licensee, that constitute a nuisance, within a reasonable time after receipt of notice to make those corrections, under Section 373a of the Penal Code.

(c) Failure to take reasonable steps to correct objectionable conditions that occur during operating hours on any public sidewalk abutting a licensed premises and constitute a nuisance, within a reasonable time after receipt of notice to correct those conditions from the Bureau. This subsection shall apply to a licensee only upon written notice to the licensee from the Bureau. The Bureau shall issue this written notice upon its own determination, or upon a request from the local law enforcement agency in whose jurisdiction the premises is located, that is supported by substantial evidence that persistent objectionable conditions are occurring on the public sidewalk abutting the licensed premises. For purposes of this subsection:

> (1) "Any public sidewalk abutting a licensed premises" means the publicly owned, pedestrian-traveled way, not more than 20 feet from the premises, that is located between a licensed premises, including any immediately adjacent area that is owned, leased, or rented by the licensee, and a public street

> (2) "Objectionable conditions that constitute a nuisance" means disturbance of the peace, public intoxication, drinking alcoholic beverages in public, smoking or ingesting cannabis or cannabis products in public, harassment of passersby, gambling, prostitution, loitering, public urination, lewd conduct, drug trafficking, or excessive loud noise.

(3) "Reasonable steps" means all of the following:

(A) Calling the local law enforcement agency. Timely calls to the local law enforcement agency that are placed by the licensee, or his or her agents or employees, shall not be construed by the Bureau as evidence of objectionable conditions that constitute a nuisance.

(B) Requesting those persons engaging in activities causing objectionable conditions to cease those activities, unless the licensee, or his or her agents or employees, feel that their personal safety would be threatened in making that request.

(C) Making good faith efforts to remove items that facilitate loitering, such as furniture, except those structures approved or permitted by the local jurisdiction. The licensee shall not be liable for the removal of those items that facilitate loitering.

(4) When determining what constitutes "reasonable steps," the Bureau shall consider site configuration constraints related to the unique circumstances of the nature of the business.

(d) Notwithstanding that the licensee corrects the objectionable conditions that constitute a nuisance, the licensee has a continuing obligation to meet the requirements of subsections (a) and (b), and failure to do so shall constitute grounds for disciplinary action.

(e) If a licensee has knowingly permitted the illegal sale, or negotiations for the sales, of controlled substances or dangerous drugs upon his or her licensed premises. Successive sales, or negotiations for sales, over any continuous period of time shall be deemed evidence of permission. As used in this section, "controlled substances" shall have the same meaning as is given that term in Article 1 (commencing with Section 11000) of Chapter 1 of Division 10 of the Health and Safety Code, and "dangerous drugs" shall have the same meaning as is given that term in Article 2 (commencing with Section 4015) of Chapter 9 of Division 2 of the Business and Professions Code.

(f) If the licensee has employed or permitted any persons to solicit or encourage others, directly or indirectly, to buy such persons cannabis goods in the licensed premises under any commission, percentage, salary, or other profit-sharing plan, scheme, or conspiracy.

§ 5813. Enforcement Costs

(a) In any order in resolution of a disciplinary proceeding for suspension or revocation of a license, the Bureau may request the administrative law judge to direct a licensee found to have committed a violation or violations of the Act, or any regulation adopted pursuant to the Act, to pay a sum not to exceed the reasonable costs of the investigation and enforcement of the case.

(b) A certified copy of the actual costs, or a good faith estimate of costs where actual costs are not available, signed by the Bureau's designated representative shall be prima facie evidence of reasonable costs of investigation and prosecution of the case. The costs shall include the amount of investigative and enforcement costs up to the date of the hearing, including, but not limited to, charges imposed by the Attorney General.

(c) The administrative law judge shall make a proposed finding of the amount of reasonable costs of investigation and prosecution of the case when requested pursuant to subsection (a). The Bureau may reduce or eliminate the cost award, or remand to the administrative law judge where the proposed decision fails to make a finding on costs requested pursuant to subsection (a).

(d) Where an order for recovery of costs is made and timely payment is not made as directed in the decision, the Bureau may enforce the order for repayment in any appropriate court. This right of enforcement shall be in addition to any other rights the Bureau may have as to any licensee to pay costs.

(e) In any action for recovery of costs, proof of the decision shall be conclusive proof of the validity of the order of payment and the terms for payment.

(f) Except as provided in subsection (g) of this section, the Bureau shall not renew or reinstate any license of any licensee who has failed to pay all of the costs ordered under this division.

(g) Notwithstanding subsection (f) of this section, the Bureau may, in its discretion, conditionally renew or reinstate for a maximum of one year the license of any licensee who demonstrates financial hardship and who enters into a formal agreement with the Bureau for reimbursement within that one-year period for the unpaid costs.

(h) Nothing in this section shall preclude the Bureau from including the recovery of the costs of investigation and enforcement of a case in any stipulated settlement.

NOTES AND QUESTIONS

1. **Right-sizing sanctions?** The regulations above deal with enforcement of the law against licensed participants in the cannabis market. Participants in the black market remain subject to criminal penalties that pre-existed Proposition 64. That provides some incentive for members of the black market to sign up for the legal market.

2. **Fourth Amendment problems?** Section 5800 allows representatives of the bureau in charge of enforcement to gain access to licensed businesses. The representative does not need to make any showing of cause. For example, she does not have to allege probable cause or other level

of suspicion that the business does not comply with the statute or regulations. Does that comport with the Fourth Amendment's prohibition against unreasonable searches? Compare *Camara v. Municipal Court,* 387 U.S. 523 (1967) with *New York v. Burger*, 482 U.S. 691 (1987).

3.   **Stacking licenses.** Even before the publication of final regulations, the California Department of Food and Agriculture, the agency in charge of promulgating regulations for cannabis cultivation, allowed businesses to secure more than one license. As described in an article in the Marijuana Business Journal, a small handful of growers have been able to secure a disproportionate number of license already issued. That article appears here: https://mjbizdaily.com/chart-handful-growers-hold-hundreds-cultivation-licenses-california-legal-marijuana-market/.

4.   **More on stacking licenses.** What are the competing arguments concerning "stacking" of licenses as described in the article in the previous note? Think back to the several purposes and intents of the drafters of Proposition 64 and the likely purposes and intents of the voters. Is stacking consistent with those purposes and intents? Are some goals advanced by stacking and some frustrated by stacking? If so, which ones?

5.   **Litigation to block stacking licenses.** The California Growers Association, a cannabis industry trade group, filed suit to block the regulations put in place by the California Department of Food and Agriculture. For a story about the background to that suit, *see* https://www.mendovoice.com/2018/01/cga-acreage-suit/.

6.   **The black market in Colorado and Washington.** Although not without some debate, many observers believe that Colorado and Washington have begun to reduce the number of black market producers and sellers. The amount of tax revenue in both states has exceeded expectations at a time when overall marijuana use has not increased dramatically. That suggests that more buyers prefer the safer, more reliable environment of legal businesses than they do seeking out an illegal seller. Whether California experiences a similar reasonably orderly process towards a regulated market is an open question.

7.   **Colorado: a template for California?** Consider obvious differences between Colorado and California. Colorado's climate is far less conducive to growing marijuana outdoors than is California's. Many growers in Colorado have gone into business after medical and then recreational marijuana became legal there. They have established indoor facilities, more secure than outdoor grows, especially because of weather conditions there. California has a well-established illegal market in rural regions of the state, like Humboldt County. It has a climate far more conducive to growing marijuana than does almost any other state. How does this factor into California's prospects for developing a well-regulated market?

8.   **The size of the "Pot of Gold."** Estimating the amount of marijuana grown in California or the value of the crop involves many difficult assumptions. Illegal producers do not often file reports detailing their output. One can find estimates that the value of marijuana grown in California exceeds

$14 billion a year. Some estimate that California produces between 8 to 10 times more marijuana than can be consumed by Californians. What are the implications of those facts for California's hoped-for Pot of Gold?

9.   **A business plan?** The primary focus of this chapter has not been on business planning. Nonetheless, the following question helps bring together a number of themes in this chapter.

PROBLEM 5-4

You are a lawyer practicing in California. One of your clients has made an appointment to discuss entering the marijuana business. She explains that she has sold a successful business in San Francisco for several million dollars. Many of her friends have urged her to look for opportunities in the burgeoning marijuana field. She asks you for your advice on whether that seems like a good investment. Your thoughts?

CHAPTER 6

INTERNATIONAL LAW

■ ■ ■

The debate over marijuana regulation in the United States is dominated by domestic considerations. Yet in many ways international law is the essential framework for understanding the genesis of federal marijuana prohibition in the United States, and how this prohibition might change in the future.

The 1961 Single Convention on Narcotic Drugs (Single Convention) obligates participating nations to prohibit cannabis use except for limited scientific and medical purposes, which are to be strictly controlled by government agencies. The United States was a major proponent of these international drug treaties and is a party. The Single Convention remains the overarching framework for the international, and to a large extent domestic, regulation of cannabis use. This prohibition of cannabis was consolidated in the 1971 Convention on Psychotropic Substances and the 1988 United Nations Convention against Illicit Traffic in Narcotic Drugs and Psychotropic Substances.

The U.S. Controlled Substances Act of 1970 (CSA) implemented the Single Convention, employing its system of schedules to control drugs (cannabis is controlled in the most prohibitive schedules in both the Single Convention and the CSA), and incorporating features of the international drug conventions.

The DEA has cited obligations under the international treaties to oppose legalizing or decriminalizing marijuana at both the federal and state level. For example, DEA has asserted the requirements of international law as its primary argument against transferring marijuana to less restrictive schedules of the CSA.

As states have legalized marijuana over the last twenty-two years, two important questions have surfaced as to U.S. obligations under the international drug treaties. First, does state legalization—recreational, and even medical—represent a dereliction of national obligations under the drug conventions? Second, what would be the implications of the federal government further relaxing federal enforcement of its marijuana laws, to the point of rescheduling marijuana?

In Section A, we examine DEA interpretation of the international treaties. In Section B, we see how the treaties continue to guide administrative decisions on marijuana law. In Section C, we examine the implications of state legalization and federal relaxation of enforcement under international law.

A. SINGLE CONVENTION AND THE CSA

The Single Convention, which enacts an international framework for prohibiting drugs, including cannabis, is not self-enforcing. Nations that are parties enact specific laws to effect the broad prohibitions of international law. The United States complied with the Single Convention by enacting the CSA. The DEA is the administrative agency tasked under the CSA as the government entity that decides the scheduling of marijuana. DEA has repeatedly ruled that the international treaties dictate scheduling of marijuana under the CSA.

PLACEMENT IN SCHEDULE V OF CERTAIN FDA-APPROVED DRUGS CONTAINING CANNABIDIOL

Drug Enforcement Administration
83 Fed. Reg. 48950 (September 28, 2018)

Dhillon, Acting Administrator.

SUMMARY:

With the issuance of this final order, the Acting Administrator of the Drug Enforcement Administration places certain drug products that have been approved by the Food and Drug Administration (FDA) and which contain cannabidiol (CBD) in schedule V of the Controlled Substances Act (CSA). Specifically, this order places FDA-approved drugs that contain CBD derived from cannabis and no more than 0.1 percent tetrahydrocannabinols in schedule V. This action is required to satisfy the responsibility of the Acting Administrator under the CSA to place a drug in the schedule he deems most appropriate to carry out United States obligations under the Single Convention on Narcotic Drugs, 1961. Also consistent therewith, DEA is adding such drugs to the list of substances that may only be imported or exported pursuant to a permit.

SUPPLEMENTARY INFORMATION:

Background and Legal Authority

The United States is a party to the Single Convention on Narcotic Drugs, 1961 (Single Convention), and other international conventions designed to establish effective control over international and domestic traffic in controlled substances. 21 U.S.C. 801(7). The Single Convention entered into force for the United States on June 24, 1967, after the Senate gave its advice and consent to the United States' accession. See Single Convention, 18 U.S.T. 1407. The enactment and enforcement of the Controlled Substances Act (CSA) are the primary means by which the

United States carries out its obligations under the Single Convention[1]. Various provisions of the CSA directly reference the Single Convention. One such provision is 21 U.S.C. 811(d)(1), which relates to scheduling of controlled substances.

As stated in subsection 811(d)(1), if control of a substance is required "by United States obligations under international treaties, conventions, or protocols in effect on October 27, 1970, the Attorney General shall issue an order controlling such drug under the schedule he deems most appropriate to carry out such obligations, without regard to the findings required by [subsections 811(a) or 812(b)] and without regard to the procedures prescribed by [subsections 811(a) and (b)]." This provision is consistent with the Supremacy Clause of the U.S. Constitution (art. VI, sec. 2), which provides that all treaties made under the authority of the United States "shall be the supreme Law of the Land." In accordance with this constitutional mandate, under section 811(d)(1), Congress directed the Attorney General (and the Administrator of DEA, by delegation) to ensure that compliance by the United States with our nation's obligations under the Single Convention is given top consideration when it comes to scheduling determinations.

Section 811(d)(1) is relevant here because, on June 25, 2018, the Food and Drug Administration (FDA) announced that it approved a drug that is subject to control under the Single Convention. Specifically, the FDA announced that it approved the drug Epidiolex for the treatment of seizures associated with two rare and severe forms of epilepsy, Lennox-Gastaut syndrome and Dravet syndrome, in patients two years of age and older. Epidiolex is an oral solution that contains cannabidiol (CBD) extracted from the cannabis plant. This is the first FDA-approved drug made from the cannabis plant. Now that Epiodiolex has been approved by the FDA, it has a currently accepted medical use in treatment in the United States for purposes of the CSA. Accordingly, Epidiolex no longer meets the criteria for placement in schedule I of the CSA. DEA must therefore take the appropriate scheduling action to remove the drug from schedule I.

In making this scheduling determination, as section 811(d)(1) indicates, it is necessary to assess the relevant requirements of the Single Convention. Under the treaty, cannabis, cannabis resin, and extracts and tinctures of cannabis are listed in Schedule I.[2] The cannabis plant contains

---

[1] See S. Rep. No. 91-613, at 4 (1969) ("The United States has international commitments to help control the worldwide drug traffic. To honor those commitments, principally those established by the Single Convention on Narcotic Drugs of 1961, is clearly a Federal responsibility."); Control of Papaver Bracteatum, 1 Op. O.L.C. 93, 95 (1977) ("[A] number of the provisions of [the CSA] reflect Congress' intent to comply with the obligations imposed by the Single Convention.").

[2] It should also be noted that the schedules of the Single Convention operate somewhat differently than the schedules of the CSA. Unlike the CSA, the Single Convention imposes additional restrictions on drugs listed in Schedule IV that go beyond those applicable to drugs listed in Schedule I. All drugs in Schedule IV of the Single Convention are also in Schedule I of the

more than 100 cannabinoids. Among these are tetrahydrocannabinols (THC) and CBD. Material that contains THC and CBD extracted from the cannabis plant falls within the listing of extracts and tinctures of cannabis for purposes of the Single Convention. Thus, such material, which includes, among other things, a drug product containing CBD extracted from the cannabis plant, is a Schedule I drug under the Single Convention.

Parties to the Single Convention are required to impose a number of control measures with regard to drugs listed in Schedule I of the Convention. These include, but are not limited to, the following:

- Limiting exclusively to medical and scientific purposes the production, manufacture, export, import, distribution of, trade in, use and possession of such drugs. Article 4.

- Furnishing to the International Narcotics Control Board (INCB) annual estimates of, among other things, quantities of such drugs to be consumed for medical and scientific purposes, utilized for the manufacture of other drugs, and held in stock. Article 19.

- Furnishing to the INCB statistical returns on the actual production, utilization, consumption, imports and exports, seizures, and stocks of such drugs during the prior year. Article 20.

- Requiring that licensed manufacturers of such drugs obtain quotas specifying the amounts of such drugs they may manufacture to prevent excessive production and accumulation beyond that necessary to satisfy legitimate needs. Article 29.

- Requiring manufacturers and distributors of such drugs to be licensed. Articles 29 & 30.

- Requiring medical prescriptions for the dispensing of such drugs to patients. Article 30.

- Requiring importers and exporters of such drugs to be licensed and requiring each individual importation or exportation to be predicated on the issuance of a permit. Article 31.

- Prohibiting the possession of such drugs except under legal authority. Article 33.

- Requiring those in the legitimate distribution chain (manufacturers, distributors, scientists, and those who lawfully dispense such drugs) to keep records that show the

---

Convention. Cannabis and cannabis resin are among the drugs listed in Schedule IV of the Single Convention.

quantities of such drugs manufactured, distributed, dispensed, acquired, or otherwise disposed of during the prior two years. Article 34.

Because the CSA was enacted in large part to satisfy United States obligations under the Single Convention, many of the CSA's provisions directly implement the foregoing treaty requirements. None of the foregoing obligations of the United States could be satisfied for a given drug if that drug were removed entirely from the CSA schedules. At least one of the foregoing requirements (quotas) can only be satisfied if the drug that is listed in Schedule I of the Single Convention is also listed in schedule I or II of the CSA because, as 21 U.S.C. 826 indicates, the quota requirements generally apply only to schedule I and II controlled substances.

The permit requirement warrants additional explanation. As indicated above, the Single Convention obligates parties to require a permit for the importation and exportation of drugs listed in Schedule I of the Convention. This permit requirement applies to a drug product containing CBD extracted from the cannabis plant because, as further indicated above, such a product is a Schedule I drug under the Single Convention. However, under the CSA and DEA regulations, the import/export permit requirement does not apply to all controlled substances. Rather, a permit is required to import or export any controlled substance in schedule I and II as well as certain controlled substances in schedules III, IV, and V. See 21 U.S.C. 952 and 953; 21 CFR 1312.11, 1312.12, 1312.21, 1312.22. Thus, in deciding what schedule is most appropriate to carry out the United States' obligations under the Single Convention with respect to the importation and exportation of Epidiolex, I conclude there are two options:

(i) Control the drug in schedule II, which will automatically require an import/export permit under existing provisions of the CSA and DEA regulations or

(ii) control the drug in schedule III, IV, or V, and simultaneously amend the regulations to require a permit to import or export Epidiolex.

It bears emphasis that where, as here, control of a drug is required by the Single Convention, the DEA Administrator "shall issue an order controlling such drug under the schedule he deems most appropriate to carry out such obligations, without regard to the findings required by [21 U.S.C. 811 (a) or 812(b)] and without regard to the procedures prescribed by [21 U.S.C. 811 (a) or (b)]." 21 U.S.C. 811(d)(1). Thus, in such circumstances, the Administrator is not obligated to request a medical and scientific evaluation or scheduling recommendation from the Department of Health and Human Services (HHS) (as is normally done pursuant to section 811(b)). Nonetheless, DEA did seek such an evaluation and recommendation from HHS with respect to the Epidiolex formulation. In responding to that request, HHS advised DEA that it found the Epidiolex formulation to have a very low potential for abuse and, therefore, recommended that, if DEA concluded that control of the drug was required under the Single Convention, Epidiolex should be placed in schedule V of the CSA. Although I am not required to consider this HHS recommendation when issuing an order under section 811(d)(1), because I believe there are two legally viable scheduling options (listed above), both of which would satisfy the United States' obligations under the Single Convention, I will exercise my discretion and choose the option that most closely aligns to the HHS recommendation. Namely, I am hereby ordering that the Epidiolex formulation (and any future FDA-approved generic versions of such formulation made from cannabis) be placed in schedule V of the CSA.

As noted, this order placing the Epidiolex formulation in schedule V will only comport with section 811(d)(1) if all importations and exportations of the drug remain subject to the permit requirement. Until now, since the Epidiolex formulation had been a schedule I controlled substance, the importation of the drug from its foreign production facility has always been subject to the permit requirement. To ensure this requirement remains in place (and thus to prevent any lapse in compliance with the requirements of the Single Convention), this order will amend the DEA regulations (21 CFR 1312.30) to add the Epidiolex formulation to the list of nonnarcotic schedule III through V controlled substances that are subject to the import and export permit requirement.

Finally, a brief explanation is warranted regarding the quota requirement in connection with the Single Convention. As indicated above, for drugs listed in Schedule I of the Convention, parties are obligated to require that licensed manufacturers of such drugs obtain quotas specifying the amounts of such drugs they may manufacture. The purpose of this treaty requirement is to prevent excessive production and accumulation beyond that necessary to satisfy legitimate needs. Under this scheduling order, the United States will continue to meet this obligation because the bulk cannabis material used to make the Epidiolex formulation (as opposed to the FDA-approved drug product in finished dosage form) will remain in schedule I of the CSA and thus be subject to all applicable quota provisions under 21 U.S.C. 826.

NOTES AND QUESTIONS

1. **Epidiolex.** Epidiolex is the first and so far the only drug made from the cannabis plant to be approved by FDA and placed on a Schedule less restrictive than Schedule 1. Epidiolex contains an isomer of Cannabidiol (CBD). CBD remains a Schedule I substance.

2. **Single Convention.** The United Nations codified a half-century of international agreements as to regulating drugs in the Single Convention of

1961.[3] The United States ratified the Single Convention in 1967; as of 2018, 186 states are parties to the treaty. Whereas earlier international agreements were largely administrative in nature, requiring nations to keep statistical information about narcotics production and restrict exports, the Single Convention added explicit prohibitions, which the party nations were required to enforce. The Single Convention controls over 160 specific narcotics; cannabis is one of a handful of drugs subject to the most rigorous controls. For a history of the Single Convention, see William McAllister, *Drug Diplomacy in the Twentieth Century* (Routledge 1992). For an analysis of the move from trade regulations to a punitive approach, see Chantal Thomas, *Disciplining Globalization: International Law, Illegal Trade, and the Case of Narcotics*, 24 Mich. J. of Int'l L. 549 (2003).

3.   **Treaties and CSA.** According to article VI, section 2 of the U.S. Constitution "all Treaties made, or which shall be made, under the Authority of the United States, shall be the supreme Law of the Land." Thus the Single Convention is binding to the same extent as federal law. However, the Single Convention is not self-executing law. See *Medellin v. Texas*, 552 U.S. 491, 505 (2008). In other words, the Single Convention is binding on the U.S., as it is on all parties, but domestic laws must be enacted to enforce its provisions within each nation. As DEA states, Congress enacted many of the provisions of the CSA to comply with the Single Convention. Party nations are prohibited from enacting domestic laws contrary to the Single Convention, although permitted to enact more stringent controls. However, nations in fashioning their legislation, are accorded a great deal of flexibility.

4.   **Cannabis restrictions.** The Single Convention "limit[s] exclusively to medical and scientific purposes the production, manufacture, export, import, distribution of, trade in, use and possession of drugs." Art. 4(c). As to the permitted purposes of "medical and scientific," it establishes controls based on the efficacy and hazards of drugs, as classified under four schedules. Cannabis and cannabis resin are placed in the most stringent schedule.

5.   **Cannabis definitions.** Neither the Single Convention nor CSA adopt a pharmacological definition of cannabis, but a legal definition. The Single Convention defines cannabis as:

> the flowering or fruiting tops of the cannabis plant (excluding the seeds and leaves when not accompanied by the tops) from which the resin has not been extracted, by whatever name they may be designated.

Art. 1(b). It defines "Cannabis resin" as the "separated resin, whether crude or purified, obtained from the cannabis plant." Art. 1(d).

---

[3]   Single Convention on Narcotic Drugs, *opened for signature*, Mar. 30, 1961, 18 U.S.T. 1407, 520 U.N.T.S. 151, 14 I.L.M. 302, *entered into force*, Dec. 13, 1964, *as amended by* Protocol Amending the Single Convention on Narcotic Drugs, 1961, *opened for signature* Mar. 25, 1972, 26 U.S.T. 1439, 976 U.N.T.S. 3, 11 I.L.M. 804, *entered into force*, Aug. 8. 1975.

The CSA definition of "marihuana," includes all parts of the cannabis plant except for the mature stalks, sterilized seeds, oil from the seeds, and certain derivatives and extracts thereof. 21 U.S.C. 802(16) (58).

6. CSA scheduling of marijuana. "The DEA Administrator is obligated under section 811(d) to control marijuana in the schedule that he deems most appropriate to carry out the U.S. obligations under the Single Convention." DEA states that marijuana must be scheduled in either CSA Schedule I or II to satisfy Single Convention controls such as import and export permits and quota recordkeeping. DEA asserts it need not request any data from HHS or FDA or hold any hearings before an administrative law judge to do so.

7. Controls. The controls mandated by the Single Convention for Schedule I drugs include

- Authorization for imports and exports

- Licensing of manufacturers/distributors

- Recordkeeping

- Prescriptions required for medical use

- Annual estimate of needs

- Quotas

- No accumulation of stocks

- Security and inspection

- Annual statistical reporting

The National Institute on Drug Abuse (NIDA) fulfills the requirement of a government agency to report data on marijuana and safeguard cultivation for research purposes.

PROBLEM 6-1

A petition is filed to reschedule marijuana from Schedule I. 21 U.S.C. section 811(b) requires DEA (on delegation from the Attorney General) to request necessary data from FDA (on delegation from HHS) in assessing the petition. However under section 811(d)(1), DEA is required to control drugs under the schedule most appropriate to satisfy the Single Convention without regards to FDA evaluations of the drug or other administrative procedures. Citing § 811(d)(1), DEA peremptorily denies the petition, claiming no procedures or findings are necessary. Petitioner claims that § 811(d)(1) does not obviate the need to initiate such proceedings, only that DEA can override FDA to the extent necessary to correspond to the obligations of the Single Convention. What result?

PROBLEM 6-2

Same Scenario as in Problem 6-2. Petitioner claims sections 811(a) and 812(b) also require DEA proceedings and findings as to rescheduling separated cannabis leaves, separated cannabis seeds capable of germination, and separated cannabis seeds incapable of germination. None of these is included in the Single Convention definition of marijuana but the Single Convention does include the following articles:

"The Parties shall adopt such measures as may be necessary to prevent the misuse of, and illicit traffic in, the leaves of the cannabis plant." Art. 28, para 3. [Consumption of the leaves was not prohibited because they were considered less psychoactive than the flowers.]

"The Parties shall use their best endeavors to apply to substances which do not fall under this Convention, but which may be used in the illicit manufacture of drugs." Art. 2, paragraph 8.

Again, citing § 811(d)(1), DEA peremptorily denies the petition, claiming no other procedures or findings are necessary. Again, Petitioner claims that 811(d)(1) doesn't obviate the need to initiate such proceedings for rescheduling separated cannabis leaves, separated cannabis seeds capable of germination, and separated cannabis seeds incapable of germination. What result? Can separated cannabis leaves, separated cannabis seeds capable of germination, or separated cannabis seeds incapable of germination be controlled in Schedules less restrictive than Schedules I or II, or even decontrolled, without violating the Single Convention? What additional factors would you need to know to reach a decision. [For a fuller consideration of these issues, see *NORML v. DEA*, 559 F.2d 735 (D.C. Cir. 1977) discussed in Chapter 3.]

B. SCHEDULING CANNABIS UNDER THE SINGLE CONVENTION

In the last section, we saw the DEA interpret the Single Convention to require that marijuana be controlled at a minimum in Schedule II. In Problems 6-1 and 6-2, we saw that the Single Convention makes distinctions among cannabis constituents. If DEA desires that the CSA more closely match international treaties, should DEA create new categories to approximate international definitions?

FINAL RULE: ESTABLISHMENT OF A NEW DRUG CODE FOR MARIHUANA EXTRACT

Drug Enforcement Administration
81 Fed. Reg. 90194 (Dec. 14, 2016)

Rosenberg, Acting Administrator.

[After explaining the background of establishment of the new code, DEA explains the impetus for its creation in the requirements of the Single Convention.]

Why a New Code Number Is Needed.

The United Nations Conventions on international drug control treats extracts from the cannabis plant somewhat differently than marihuana or tetrahydrocannabinols. The creation of a new drug code in the DEA regulations for marihuana extracts will allow for more appropriate accounting of such materials consistent with treaty provisions.

The Single Convention on Narcotic Drugs, 1961 ("Single Convention") and the 1971 Convention on Psychotropic Substances ("Psychotropic Convention") provide for the international control of marihuana constituents. Many of the CSA's provisions were drafted to comply with these Conventions. The CSA includes schemes of drug scheduling and procedures for adding, removing, and transferring drugs among the schedules that are similar, in some ways, to those in the Single Convention. With respect to those drugs that are subject to control under the Single Convention, the CSA mandates that DEA control such drugs in a manner that will ensure the United States meets its obligations under the Single Convention. 21 U.S.C. 811(d)(1).

Somewhat similar to the CSA, the Single Convention lists substances in four schedules. However, under the Single Convention, the drugs that are subject to the most stringent controls are in Schedule IV. Another difference between the CSA and the Single Convention is that, under the latter, a drug can be listed in more than one schedule. Cannabis and cannabis resin are listed in both Schedule IV and Schedule I of the Single Convention. Schedule I controls under the Single Convention include: Requirements for import and export authorization, licensing of manufacturers/distributors, recordkeeping requirements, a requirement for prescriptions for medical use, annual estimate of needs, quotas, annual statistical reporting, and a requirement that use be limited to medical and scientific purposes. Schedule II of the Single Convention is similar in controls to Schedule I with a few exceptions, and Schedule III is less restrictive. All substances listed in Schedule IV are also listed in Schedule I under the Single Convention in order to encompass the requirements mentioned above. In addition, as indicated, the Single Convention imposes certain heightened measures of control with respect to Schedule IV drugs. The placing of a drug into both Schedule I and Schedule IV, therefore imposes the most stringent controls under the Single Convention. Although cannabis and cannabis resin are listed in Schedules I and IV of the Single Convention, cannabis extracts are listed only in Schedule I. * * *

As discussed in the NPRM [Notice of Proposed Rule Making], a new drug code is necessary in order to better account for these materials in accordance with treaty obligations. The Single Convention placed "cannabis" and "cannabis resin" under both Schedule I and IV of the Convention, the most stringent level of control under the Convention. While "cannabis resin" is extracted from "cannabis," the Single Convention specifically controls "extracts" separately. Extracts of cannabis are controlled only under Schedule I of the Convention, which is a lower level of control than "cannabis resin."

Accordingly, it is the DEA's intent to define the term "marihuana extract" so as to exclude material referenced as "cannabis resin" under the Single Convention on Narcotics. "Cannabis resin" (regulated under the CSA as a resin of marihuana) contains a variety of "cannabinoids" and will continue to be regulated as marihuana under drug code 7360. The new drug code for marihuana extracts under 21 CFR 1308.11(d)(58) will exclude the resin. Cannabis resin and marihuana resin remain captured under the drug code for marihuana (drug code 7360), thus differentiating this material from marihuana extracts (new drug code 7350). This will maintain compliance with the Single Convention.

Final Action

After careful consideration of all comments, the DEA is hereby amending 21 CFR 1308.11(d) to include a new subparagraph (58) which creates a new code number in Schedule I as follows:

"(58) Marihuana Extract—7350

"Meaning an extract containing one or more cannabinoids that has been derived from any plant of the genus Cannabis, other than the separated resin (whether crude or purified) obtained from the plant."

The creation of this new drug code in the DEA regulations for marihuana extracts allows for more appropriate accounting of such materials consistent with treaty provisions.* * *

NOTES AND QUESTIONS

1. **Single Convention schedules.** As explained in the above Final Rule, the schedules of the Single Convention guide scheduling in the CSA, but they are not identical. It is perhaps helpful to think of the Single Convention as maintaining three schedules (I–III), with a sub-schedule of schedule I (Schedule IV). Schedules I–III are listed in order of stringent controls. Drugs on Schedule I have potential therapeutic uses but are liable to significant abuse and hence are subject to the most controls. Drugs in schedule II are liable to lower abuse and thus are less strictly controlled. Drugs in Schedule III are subject to the lightest controls. However a special category of Schedule I drugs is carved out for certain drugs whose liability to abuse "is not offset by substantial therapeutic advantages." Nations are encouraged to impose maximal controls for Schedule I drugs also listed in Schedule IV. There are a limited number of such drugs, including cannabis and cannabis resin.

2. **Drug codes.** Drug codes are an essential aspect of the system of controls implemented by the CSA. As provided in 21 CFR 1308.03, controlled substances are assigned four-digit Administration Controlled Substance Code

Numbers ("Code number" or "drug code") that are employed to track quantities of controlled substance imported and exported to and from the United States. Code numbers are also used to establish aggregate production quotas as required by 21 U.S.C. § 826 for substances controlled in Schedules I and II.

3. A New code. DEA first proposed this rule on July 5, 2011. 76 Fed Reg. 9039. In the New Rule, DEA states that for marijuana extracts "a new drug code is necessary in order to better account for these materials in accordance with treaty obligations." What reasons are given by the DEA for this claim? Are they compelling? Is there any indication why this new code was not proposed until 2011?

4. Marijuana extracts. DEA defines extracts as concentrates of chemicals obtained by a physical or chemical process. As the Final Rule indicates, the "United Nations Conventions on international drug control treats extracts from the cannabis plant somewhat differently than marihuana or tetrahydrocannabinols." Whereas cannabis and cannabis resin are also listed in Schedule IV, extracts and tinctures of marijuana are listed only in the less restrictive Schedule I, which presupposes "potential therapeutic uses." If the goal of the DEA is to more closely align marijuana extract codes with the Single Convention, should it schedule marijuana extracts in Schedule II of the CSA, which allows medical use?

5. Hemp Industries Ass'n v. DEA. In response to issuance of this Final Rule, Hemp Industries Association, an international trade group, filed suit claiming that DEA was opposing recent legislation of Congress, such as the Pilot Hemp Program (section 7606 of the 2014 Farm Bill), which allows some cultivation of non-psychoactive marijuana compounds. The petition for review was denied by the Ninth Circuit Court of Appeals. *Hemp Industries Ass'n v. Drug Enforcement Administration*, No. 17-70162 (9th Cir. 2018). Nevertheless DEA issued a clarification to the Final Rule, explaining that the new extracts code did not apply to products derived from parts of the cannabis plant not included in the CSA definition of marijuana. See *Clarification of the New Drug Code (7350) for Marijuana Extract* (March 14, 2017).

PROBLEM 6-3

As we have seen, the CSA sets a minimum floor by which U.S. drug laws must satisfy international obligations but also mandates more stringent controls by defining marijuana broadly, prohibiting medical use, and banning hemp cultivation. A member of Congress intends to introduce a bill amending the CSA so as to comply with international obligations but not be any more restrictive than the Single Convention itself. What amendments to the CSA and associated DEA regulations would you recommend to meet this objective?

C. NON COMPLIANCE

In the first two sections of this chapter we have seen how constraining the DEA holds international drug laws. Beginning with California medical legalization in 1996, many states have not felt so constrained. Does state legalization violate international law, even if federal prohibitions stay in place? In light of the federal government's own partial relaxation of federal enforcement of the CSA, and its forbearance of state legalization, can the United States still maintain that it is in compliance with the Single Convention?

To explore these questions, we begin with some excerpts from the major U.N. drug conventions, relating to scope of treaties, penalties for cannabis abusers, accommodation to a nation's constitutional structure, and consequences for nations that fail to enforce.

SINGLE CONVENTION ON NARCOTIC DRUGS, 1961
United Nations
18 U.S.T. 1407, 520 U.N.T.S. 151

Article 4: GENERAL OBLIGATIONS

The parties shall take such legislative and administrative measures as may be necessary:

a) To give effect to and carry out the provisions of this Convention within their own territories.* * *

Article 14: MEASURES BY THE BOARD TO ENSURE THE EXECUTION OF PROVISIONS OF THE CONVENTION

1. a) If, on the basis of its examination of information submitted by Governments to the Board [International Narcotics Control Board], under the provisions of this Convention, or of information communicated by United Nations organs or by specialized agencies or, provided that they are approved by the Commission on the Board's recommendation, by either, other intergovernmental organizations or international non-governmental organizations which have direct competence in the subject matter and which are in consultative status with the Economic and Social Council under Article 71 of the Charter of the United Nations or which enjoy a similar status by special agreement with the Council, the Board has objective reasons to believe that the aims of this Convention are being seriously endangered by reason of the failure of any Party, country or territory to carry out the provisions of this Convention, the Board shall have the right to propose to the Government concerned the opening of consultations or to request it to furnish explanations. * * *

Article 36: PENAL PROVISIONS

1. (a) Subject to its constitutional limitations, each Party shall adopt such measures as will ensure that cultivation, production, manufacture, extraction, preparation, possession, offering, offering for sale, distribution, purchase, sale, delivery on any terms whatsoever, brokerage, dispatch, dispatch in transit, transport, importation and exportation of drugs contrary to the provisions of this Convention, and any other action which

in the opinion of such Party may be contrary to the provisions of this Convention, shall be punishable offences when committed intentionally, and that serious offences shall be liable to adequate punishment particularly by imprisonment or other penalties of deprivation of liberty.

(b) Notwithstanding the preceding subparagraph, when abusers of drugs have committed such offences, the Parties may provide, either as an alternative to conviction or punishment or in addition to conviction or punishment, that such abusers shall undergo measures of treatment, education, after-care, rehabilitation and social reintegration in conformity with paragraph 1 of article 38.

THE CONVENTION ON PSYCHOTROPIC SUBSTANCES OF 1971

United Nations
32 U.S.T. 543, 1019 U.N.T.S. 175

Article 19: MEASURES BY THE BOARD TO ENSURE THE EXECUTION OF THE PROVISIONS OF THE CONVENTION

1. (a) If, on the basis of its examination of information submitted by governments to the Board or of information communicated by United Nations organs, the Board has reason to believe that the aims of this Convention are being seriously endangered by reason of the failure of a country or region to carry out the provisions of this Convention, the Board shall have the right to ask for explanations from the Government of the country or region in question.* * *

Article 22: PENAL PROVISIONS

1. a)   Subject to its constitutional limitations, each Party shall treat as a punishable offence, when committed intentionally, any action contrary to a law or regulation adopted in pursuance of its obligations under this Convention and shall ensure that serious offences shall be liable to adequate punishment, particularly by imprisonment or other penalty of deprivation of liberty.

UNITED NATIONS CONVENTION AGAINST ILLICIT TRAFFIC IN NARCOTIC DRUGS AND PSYCHOTROPIC SUBSTANCES, 1988

United Nations
1582 U.N.T.S. 95

Article 3: OFFENCES AND SANCTIONS

1.   Each Party shall adopt such measures as may be necessary to establish as criminal offences under its domestic law, when committed intentionally:

a) i) The production, manufacture, extraction; preparation, offering, offering for sale, distribution, sale, delivery on any terms whatsoever, brokerage, dispatch, dispatch in transit, transport, importation or exportation of any narcotic drug or any psychotropic substance contrary to the provisions of the 1961 Convention, the 1961 Convention as amended or the 1971 Convention;

ii)   The cultivation of opium poppy, coca bush or cannabis plant for the purpose of the production of narcotic drugs contrary to the provisions of the 1961 Convention and the 1961 Convention as amended;

iii) The possession or purchase of any narcotic drug or psychotropic substance for the purpose of any of the activities enumerated in i) above;
* * *

c)   Subject to its constitutional principles and the basic concepts of its legal system:

[A Party shall adopt a criminal offence under its domestic law prohibiting]

iii) Publicly inciting or inducing others, by any means, to commit any of the offences established in accordance with this article or to use narcotic drugs or psychotropic substances illicitly;

iv) Participation in, association or conspiracy to commit, attempts to commit and aiding, abetting, facilitating and counselling the commission of any of the offences established in accordance with this article.

2.   Subject to its constitutional principles and the basic concepts of its legal system, each Party shall adopt such measures as may be necessary to establish as a criminal offence under its domestic law, when committed intentionally, the possession, purchase or cultivation of narcotic drugs or psychotropic substances for personal consumption contrary to the provisions of the 1961 Convention, the 1961 Convention as amended or the 1971 Convention.

VIENNA CONVENTION ON THE LAW OF TREATIES, 1969
United Nations
1115 U.N.T.S. 331

Article 27. INTERNAL LAW AND OBSERVANCE OF TREATIES:

A party may not invoke the provisions of its internal law as justification for its failure to perform a treaty.

Article 29. TERRITORIAL SCOPE OF TREATIES:

Unless a different intention appears from the treaty or is otherwise established, a treaty is binding upon each party in respect of its entire territory.

NOTES AND QUESTIONS

1. **U.N. Drug Conventions.** The Single Convention was supplemented by two treaties that complete the international framework for controlling drugs. As of 2018, 184 nations are parties to the Convention on Psychotropic Substances of 1971[4] (Psychotropic Convention), which added over 100 prescription, synthetic, and hallucinogenic drugs to the list of controlled substances. Most notably as it relates to cannabis, it added Tetrahydrocannabinol (THC) to Schedule 1. (Dronabinol, a synthetic cannabinoid of THC, was later transferred to Schedule II—See chapter 10.) In reaction to a worldwide increase in drug manufacture, 190 Parties are parties to the Trafficking Convention the United Nations Convention Against Illicit Traffic in Narcotic Drugs and Psychotropic Substances of 1988[5] (Trafficking Convention). This treaty provided for international cooperation to combat organized drug trafficking and drug money laundering. These two treaties imposed stricter criminal sanctions for personal use, in addition to curtailing supply. (The Single Convention allowed treatment as an alternative to punishment.) The United States is a party to all three treaties. Although the United States has not ratified the 1969 Vienna Convention on the Law of Treaties[6] (VCLT), it considers many of its provisions to constitute customary international law and binding in that manner.

2. **Competent authorities.** The U.N. Drug Conventions create several organizations as competent authorities to monitor implementation and compliance. The Commission on Narcotic Drugs (CND) makes policy for drug regulation. It schedules drugs based on the recommendation of the World Health Organization (WHO). The International Narcotics Control Board (INCB), an independent body created by the conventions, monitors treaty compliance. The U.N. Office on Drugs and Crime (UNODC) assists member countries in fighting drug crimes and publishes an annual report on illegal drug activity.

3. **States compliance with the Conventions?** Is the United States in compliance with the international drug treaties? The majority of states have legalized marijuana for medical purposes. Although the treaties allow for use of marijuana for medical purposes, they do so only with strict controls applied. These controls were satisfied by DEA administration and by NIDA as the single entity controlling the entire supply of medical marijuana in the nation. Most commentators agree that the various state medical marijuana legalization regimes do not satisfy the strict controls required for drugs listed on Schedule I of the Single Convention. As to recreational legalization, the situation is even clearer. As Warner Sipp, the president of the INCB, stated at

---

[4] *Opened for signature*, Feb. 21 1971, 32 U.S.T. 543, 1019 U.N.T.S. 175, 10 I.L.M. 261, *entered into force*, Aug. 16 1976.

[5] *Opened for signature*, Dec. 20, 1988, 1582 U.N.T.S. 95, 28 I.L.M. 493, *entered into force*, Nov. 11, 1990.

[6] *Opened for signature*, May 23, 1969, 1155 U.N.T.S. 331, 8 I.L.M. 679, *entered into force*, Jan. 27, 1980.

the 59th Session of the CND (March 14, 2016), "there is no flexibility for allowing and regulating any kind of non-medical use."

4.   Federal compliance with the Conventions? Since 2013, the INCB has warned the United States that it is falling out of compliance with the drug treaties. For example, examine the penal provisions above in the three drug treaties: Single Convention, Art. 36(1)(a); Psychotropic Convention, Art. 22(1)(a); Trafficking Convention, Art. 3(1). What in federal enforcement of marijuana law in the United States might constitute non compliance? As to responsibility of the United States for state legalization, examine VCLT articles 27 and 29 above.

5.   Defenses to treaty non compliance. Because of the flexible terms in which many of the treaty provisions are written, nations can present various defenses to ostensible treaty violations. Uruguay formally legalized adult use cannabis in 2013, arguing that cannabis use is a human right which overrides specific treaty terms. Although Uruguay has not been sanctioned by the INCB, U.S. Banks, citing the Patriot Act, which prohibits U.S. financial institutions from doing business with illicit distributors of controlled substances, cut ties with Uruguayan banks. In 2000, Portugal decriminalized possession of illegal substances for personal use. The INCB responded that removing criminal sanctions for drug possession was "not in line with the international drug control treaties." See Alexander Henderson, *Portuguese Defiance: Analysing the Strenuous Relationship Between Drug Decriminalization and International Law*, 24 Mich. St. Int'l L. Rev. 725 (2015). Canada legalized cannabis in October 2018. For an assessment of Canadian legalization under international law, see Roojin Habibi. & Steven Hoffman, *Legalizing Cannabis Violates the UN Drug Control Treaties, But Progressive Countries Like Canada Have Options*, 49 (2) Ott. L. Rev. ___ (2018).

An important feature of the drug conventions is that they make many treaty terms subject to the "constitutional principles" and "basic concepts of its legal system." Are there "constitutional principles" and "basic concepts of its legal system," that can demonstrate compliance of U.S. marijuana law?

6.   Changing treaty terms. Parties can also act to change the terms of their obligations under the treaty, although these are complicated procedures. All three U.N. drug conventions provide for terms to be modified.

Amendments. Amending the treaty is a time consuming, consensus building procedure. Any nation can register an objection to the amendment, which, if it garners support, can derail the amendment.

Rescheduling. WHO can make a rescheduling recommendation, as it did with rescheduling dronabinol in 1989 and 1990. However, as demonstrated by the refusal to reschedule dronabinol in 2007 (See chapter 10), CND is not strictly bound by WHO recommendations. (In April, 2018, WHO announced a review of the classification of cannabis under the treaties and solicited input from member nations. FDA in turn solicited input from U.S. "interested parties" before submitting its comments to WHO. 83 Fed. Reg. 15155, April 9, 2018). However rescheduling or decontrolling cannabis is particularly difficult

.e its prohibitions are imbedded directly in the articles of the drug
.ntion articles, and not just in the Schedules (see e.g. Single Convention,
. 28).

.ter Se Modification. Parties can agree to modify treaty terms among
.hemselves ("inter se"). Although such modification is an accepted principle of
international law, it is not explicitly provided for in the treaties. For a
discussion of inter se modification in the cannabis context, see Martin Jelsma,
Neil Boister, David Bewley-Taylor, Malgosia Fitzmaurice, and John Walsh,
*Balancing Treaty Stability and Change: Inter se modification of the UN drug
control conventions to facilitate cannabis regulation*, The Policy Report 7 (The
Global Drug Policy Observatory, March 2018).

Denunciation. A party can withdraw from a treaty (termed a "denunciation"
under treaty provisions), freeing itself from treaty obligations (although the
United Nations may treat the nation as still bound by international drug law).
Such an action could lead to pariah status and refusal of other nations to
cooperate with the denouncing party on international drug measures.
Denunciation by as significant a presence on the world stage as the United
States would be a dramatic step.

Reaccession with Reservations. Parties can join treaties with reservations. The
United States has no such reservation significantly affecting cannabis law.
However a party can denounce a treaty and then reaccede (re-join) the treaty,
with a reservation as to the use of a controlled drug. Bolivia, for example,
withdrew from the Single Convention in 2011, and reacceded in 2013 with
reservation as to legal use of coca among its indigenous tribes. This maneuver
was met with hostility and was almost defeated, despite the indigenous tribes
undisputed traditional consumption of coca leaves. The United States would
seem to have a minuscule chance of being allowed to denounce and reaccede
with the reserved right to allow marijuana use.

7.   **Future of treaty obligations.** For recent articles on U.S.
obligations and international treaties see Brian Blumenfeld, *Pacta Sunt
Servanda: State Legalization of Marijuana and Subnational Violations of
International Treaties: A Historical Perspective*, 46 Pepp. L. Rev. 69 (2018);
Mike Tackeff, *Constructing a Creative Reading: Will US State Cannabis
Legislation Threaten the Fate of the International Drug Control Treaties?* 51
Vand. J. of Transnat'l L. 247 (2018).

PROBLEM 6-4

The drug treaties allow the INCB to demand an explanation if a nation
appears to be in dereliction of its treaty obligations. See above, Single
Convention, Art. 14(1)(a); Psychotropic Convention, Art.19 (1)(a). (The treaties
do have sanctioning provisions at the end of the examining process but for the
most part they amount to publicly naming a nation as a treaty violator.) The
INCB has asked the United States to explain its current marijuana law and
policies. You have been asked to prepare a defense for the United States. The
following three questions relate to this scenario.

A.   INCB cites the following provision of the Psychotropic Convention:

1) c) Subject to its constitutional principles and the basic concepts of its legal system [parties shall adopt measures prohibiting]:

* * *

iii)   Publicly inciting or inducing others, by any means, to commit any of the offences established in accordance with this article or to use narcotic drugs or psychotropic substances illicitly;

iv)   Participation in, association or conspiracy to commit, attempts to commit and aiding, abetting, facilitating and counselling the commission of any of the offences established in accordance with this article.

The Commission demands to know why the federal government and states have not enforced these provisions of the Psychotropic Convention against advocates of marijuana use and legalization. What "constitutional principles" and "basic concepts of its legal system" can you assert to maintain United States compliance?

B.   INCB claims that the U.S. is noncompliant because the United States has allowed states to legalize marijuana for medical and recreational purposes, in violation of articles 27 and 29 of the VCLT. What "constitutional principles" and "basic concepts of its legal system" can you assert to maintain U.S. compliance? How would an objective observer nation (one of the standards mentioned in the treaties) assess the situation?

C.   Assuming that by 2022 every state in the United States will have legalized medical marijuana, and the most populous states will have legalized recreational marijuana, what do you recommend as the best long-term strategy for the United States in terms of complying with international law?

CHAPTER 7

PREEMPTION AND STATE LEGALIZATION

■ ■ ■

A fundamental question of marijuana law is whether state legalization of marijuana is preempted by federal prohibition of marijuana. As federal law is the supreme law of the land, are states allowed to legalize marijuana within their borders, and if so in what manner? Regardless of their own particular marijuana laws, are states required to enforce the federal prohibition? And are these questions answered by general constitutional principles or by the text of the Controlled Substances Act itself?

Three major legal doctrines govern the interplay of federal and state drug laws: *federalism*—the simultaneous exercise of legal authority by the federal government and by the 50 states; 2) *preemption*—when federal law, as the supreme law of the land preempts, that is renders void, state law; and 3) *anti-commandeering*—the constitutional principle that the federal government cannot compel the states, as sovereign entities in their own right, to enforce federal law.

This chapter covers these doctrines by focusing on two controversies: 1) whether states can immunize users of medical marijuana from penalty or can zone for medical marijuana dispensaries despite federal marijuana prohibition; and 2) whether the CSA "immunity provision," § 885(d), allows state law enforcement officials to return confiscated marijuana.

A. CONFLICT PREEMPTION

Conflict preemption is a general principle of federalism which states that under the Supremacy Clause of the U.S. Constitution, state laws are preempted if they conflict with federal law. Are state laws legalizing marijuana in conflict and thus void?

REED-KALIHER V. HOGGATT

Supreme Court of Arizona
237 Ariz. 119, 347 P.3d 136 (AZ 2015)

BERCH, J.

Keenan Reed-Kaliher pleaded guilty to possession of marijuana for sale and attempted possession of a narcotic drug for sale. A superior court judge sentenced him to 1.5 years in prison on the marijuana count and suspended the sentence on the narcotic drug count, imposing three years' probation. One of the conditions of his probation required him to "obey all laws."

While Reed-Kaliher was serving his prison term, the people of Arizona passed Proposition 203, the Arizona Medical Marijuana Act ("AMMA"). AMMA permits "a person who has been diagnosed by a physician as having a debilitating medical condition" to apply for a card identifying the possessor as a "registered qualifying patient." A.R.S. § 36–2801(13), (14). The definition of "debilitating medical condition" includes a "chronic. . .medical condition. . .that produces. . .severe and chronic pain." *Id.* § 36–2801(3)(b). Reed-Kaliher suffers chronic pain resulting from a fractured hip. After AMMA became state law, Reed-Kaliher obtained a "registry identification card" from the Arizona Department of Health Services that identifies him as a "registered qualifying patient" under AMMA, so that he might obtain medical marijuana to ease his pain.

During the term of Reed-Kaliher's probation, his probation officer added a new condition to his probation, specifying that he "not possess or use marijuana for any reason." Reed-Kaliher opposed this condition and sought relief in the superior court. He claimed that AMMA's immunity provision, A.R.S. § 36–2811(B), shields him from prosecution, revocation of probation, or other punishment for his possession or use of medical marijuana. That provision specifies that "[a] registered qualifying patient . . .is not subject to arrest, prosecution or penalty in any manner, or denial of any right or privilege. . .[f]or. . .medical use of marijuana pursuant to [AMMA]," as long as the patient complies with statutory limits on quantity and location of marijuana use. Reed-Kaliher asked the court to amend his probation conditions to delete the "no marijuana" term. The court denied the motion.

Reed-Kaliher filed a special action in the court of appeals. That court granted relief, holding that a qualifying patient cannot "be deprived of the privilege of probation solely based on his medical use of marijuana" within the limitations on quantity and location provided by AMMA, and "a condition of probation threatening to revoke his privilege for such use cannot be enforced lawfully and is invalid." *Reed-Kaliher v. Hoggatt* (State), 332 P.3d 587, 590 (App. 2014). We granted review because the scope of immunity under AMMA is a question of statewide importance.

I.   DISCUSSION

We review questions of statutory interpretation de novo. "Our primary objective in construing statutes adopted by initiative is to give effect to the intent of the electorate." *State v. Gomez*, 212 Ariz. 55, 57, 127 P.3d 873, 875 (2006)

A.   AMMA's Application to Probationers

AMMA permits those who meet statutory conditions to use medical marijuana. Because marijuana possession and use are otherwise illegal in

Arizona, A.R.S. § 13–3405(A), the drafters sought to ensure that those using marijuana pursuant to AMMA would not be penalized for such use. They therefore included an immunity provision that protects users from being "subject to arrest, prosecution or penalty in any manner, or denial of any right or privilege" as long as their use or possession complies with the terms of AMMA. A.R.S. § 36–2811(B).

AMMA broadly immunizes qualified patients, carving out only narrow exceptions from its otherwise sweeping grant of immunity against "penalty in any manner, or denial of any right or privilege." *Id.* It does not allow qualified patients to use medical marijuana "in any correctional facility," in public places, or while driving or performing other tasks that must be undertaken with care, nor does it immunize possession of marijuana in excess of the quantity limitations provided by the Act. But it does not expressly prohibit those who have been convicted of drug offenses from using medical marijuana pursuant to AMMA. The immunity expressly applies to any "registered qualifying patient." The State does not contest that Reed-Kaliher is such a patient. Thus, the immunity provision by its terms would include rather than exclude him.

AMMA precludes people who have committed "excluded felony offense[s]" from serving as "designated caregiver[s]" or "medical marijuana dispensary agent [s]." *Id.* § 36–2801(5)(c), (10). But even such offenders are not disqualified from being "qualifying patient[s]." *Id.* § 36–2801(13). The "excluded felony offense[s]" include violent crimes and recent drug offenses, except "conduct that would be immune" under AMMA. *Id.* § 36–2801(7). Thus, AMMA does not deny even those convicted of violent crimes or drug offenses (so long as they are not incarcerated) access to medical marijuana if it could alleviate severe or chronic pain or debilitating medical conditions. *Id.* §§ 36–2801(3), –2802(B)(3). We therefore conclude that the immunity provision of AMMA does not exclude probationers.

B. Conditioning Probation on Abstention from AMMA-Compliant Marijuana Use

Probation is a privilege. Revocation of probation is a penalty. Under AMMA, if the state extends a plea offer that includes probation, it cannot condition the plea on acceptance of a probationary term that would prohibit a qualified patient from using medical marijuana pursuant to the Act, as such an action would constitute the denial of a privilege. Nor may a court impose such a condition or penalize a probationer by revoking probation for such AMMA-compliant use, as that action would constitute a punishment. In this case, an Arizona statute, AMMA, precludes the court from imposing any penalty for AMMA-compliant marijuana use. A.R.S. § 36–2811(B)(1).

The State nonetheless argues that prohibiting one convicted of a drug crime from using marijuana should be permitted because it is a reasonable and necessary condition of probation. Our job here, however, is not to determine the appropriateness of the term, but rather to determine its legality. While the State can and should include reasonable and necessary terms of probation, it cannot insert illegal ones. The State observes that probation conditions can prohibit a wide range of behaviors, even those that are otherwise legal, such as drinking alcohol or being around children. While the court can condition probation on a probationer's agreement to abstain from lawful conduct, it cannot impose a term that violates Arizona law.

We therefore hold that any probation term that threatens to revoke probation for medical marijuana use that complies with the terms of AMMA is unenforceable and illegal under AMMA.

C.   Harmonizing AMMA's Immunity Provision with Statutes Prohibiting Marijuana Use

The court of appeals' dissent reasoned that an existing statute banning possession or use of narcotic drugs "requires defendants convicted of enumerated drug offenses and placed on probation to be 'prohibited from using any marijuana'" during the term of probation. *Reed-Kaliher*, 235 Ariz. at 370, 332 P.3d at 596 (Espinosa, J., dissenting) (quoting A.R.S. § 13–3408(G)). The dissent maintained that this provision conflicts with the immunity provision and that "we could give meaning to both the AMMA and the more specific drug-sentencing statutes by interpreting the AMMA's silence [regarding] probationers [as] assent to the long-standing limitations on drug use by those convicted of drug-related offenses." *Id.* Just as AMMA provides immunity for charges of violating § 13–3405, which would otherwise subject a person to criminal prosecution for marijuana use, AMMA also provides immunity for charges of violating § 13–3408(G), which might otherwise subject a person to revocation of probation for marijuana use.

Section 13–3408(G) prohibits the use of marijuana or narcotic or prescription drugs except as "lawfully administered by a health care practitioner," a phrase that suggests that the legislature intended to distinguish between illicit use and lawful medicinal use of such drugs. Medical marijuana use pursuant to AMMA is lawful under Arizona law. Thus, we harmonize § 13–3408(G) with AMMA by interpreting the former as barring probationers from illegally using drugs while nonetheless permitting legal medicinal uses of such drugs, which seems to be the intent of the statutes.

D.   Preemption

[The] State argues that the probation condition requiring Reed-Kaliher to "obey all laws" requires compliance with federal laws, including federal drug laws. Although a court may require compliance with federal law as a condition of probation, federal law does not require the court to do so. Cf. *Printz v. United States*, 521 U.S. 898, 935 (1997) ("Congress cannot compel the States to enact or enforce a federal regulatory program.").

AMMA, an Arizona law, now precludes Arizona courts from conditioning probation on the probationer's abstention from medical marijuana use pursuant to AMMA. Federal law does not require our courts to enforce federal law, and Arizona law does not permit them to do so in contravention of AMMA. Thus, while the court can impose a condition that probationers not violate federal laws generally, it must not include terms requiring compliance with federal laws that prohibit marijuana use pursuant to AMMA.

The State suggests that AMMA conflicts with federal law, and because state officers cannot simultaneously follow both laws, they should enforce the federal proscriptions on marijuana use pursuant to the Controlled Substances Act ("CSA"), 21 U.S.C. §§ 801–971, even if doing so requires them to violate state law. The State is correct in this assertion only if the CSA preempts AMMA. A federal law can preempt a state law if (1) the federal law contains "an express preemption provision," (2) Congress has determined it must exclusively govern the field, or (3) the federal and state law conflict to such an extent that compliance with both is "a physical impossibility" or the state law "stands as an obstacle to the accomplishment and execution of the full purposes and objectives of Congress." *Arizona v. United States*, 567 U.S. 387 (2012). "In preemption analysis, courts should assume that 'the historic police powers of the States' are not superseded 'unless that was the clear and manifest purpose of Congress.' " *Id.*

Congress itself has specified that the CSA does not expressly preempt state drug laws or exclusively govern the field:

> No provision of [the subchapter on control and enforcement of United States drug laws] shall be construed as indicating an intent on the part of the Congress to occupy the field. . .to the exclusion of any State law on the same subject matter which would otherwise be within the authority of the State, unless there is a positive conflict between that provision. . .and that State law so that the two cannot consistently stand together.

21 U.S.C. § 903. There is no such conflict here. By not including a prohibition against AMMA-compliant marijuana use, or in this case by removing the condition upon Reed-Kaliher's request, the trial court would not be authorizing or sanctioning a violation of federal law, but rather would be recognizing that the court's authority to impose probation conditions is limited by statute.

We find persuasive the analysis of the Michigan Supreme Court, which held that the CSA does not preempt a Michigan statute that is substantially identical to AMMA. *See Ter Beek v. City of Wyoming*, 846 N.W.2d 531, 536–41 (Mich.2014). That court reasoned that the statute does not prevent federal authorities from enforcing federal law-it merely provides "a limited state-law immunity." See *id.* at 537. The manifest purpose of the CSA was "to conquer drug abuse and to control the legitimate and illegitimate traffic in controlled substances." *Gonzales v. Raich* (2005). A state law stands as an obstacle to a federal law "[i]f the purpose of the [federal law] cannot otherwise be accomplished-if its operation within its chosen field else must be frustrated and its provisions be refused their natural effect." *Crosby v. Nat'l. Foreign Trade Council*, 530 U.S. 363, 373 (2000).

The state-law immunity AMMA provides does not frustrate the CSA's goals of conquering drug abuse or controlling drug traffic. Like the people of Michigan, the people of Arizona "chose to part ways with Congress only regarding the scope of acceptable medical use of marijuana." *Ter Beek*, 846 N.W.2d at 539. Possession and use of marijuana not in compliance with AMMA remain illegal under Arizona law.

Nor does the oath of office taken by state officers require them to condition probation on abstention from AMMA-compliant marijuana use. All state officers and employees in Arizona, including judges and prosecutors, swear to "support the Constitution of the United States and the Constitution and laws of the State of Arizona." A.R.S. § 38–231(E)–(F). Under the Supremacy Clause, laws made pursuant to the federal constitution are part of "the Supreme Law of the Land" and "Judges in every State shall be bound thereby." U.S. Const. art. 6, cl. 2. But, as noted above, nothing in federal law purports to require state judges to include a prohibition on the use of medical marijuana pursuant to AMMA as a condition of probation. Because AMMA prohibits such a condition and federal law does not require it, a state judge does not violate the oath of office by omitting such a condition. * * *

II. CONCLUSION

For the foregoing reasons, we affirm the opinion of the court of appeals.

NOTES AND QUESTIONS

1. Medical marijuana and probation. The Arizona Marijuana "Immunity" Provision states:

> A registered qualifying patient or registered designated caregiver is not subject to arrest, prosecution or penalty in any manner, or denial of any right or privilege, including any civil penalty or disciplinary action by a court or occupational or professional licensing board or bureau. . . .

Arizona Revised Statutes Title 36. Public Health and Safety Section 36–2811(B).

Most states that have legalized medical marijuana allow courts to prohibit its use as a condition of probation. See e.g. Cal. Health & Safety Code § 11362.795(a); *California v. Leal*, 210 Cal. App. 4th 827, 837–45 (Cal. Ct. App. 2012). The state of Washington, one of the first recreational marijuana states, even bans by statute marijuana use by probationers. Rev. Code Wash.

§ 69.51A.010(19)(b). Does Arizona differ from these other states solely because of its "immunity clause," which protects medical users from "denial of any right or privilege?" How does this immunity clause create a different situation than other commonly-imposed restrictions of legal activities on probationers, "such as drinking alcohol or being around children"?

2.   Statutory construction. As the court recounts in Section I.C., the court of appeals' dissent below cited A.R.S. § 13–3408(G), which prohibits drug offenders on probation "from using any marijuana, dangerous drug, narcotic drug or prescription-only drug except as lawfully administered by a health care practitioner." The dissent reasoned that the concurrent existence of this provision indicated that it was not the intent of AMMA to allow drug offenders on probation to use marijuana. *Reed-Kaliher*, 332 P.3d at 596. The Arizona Supreme Court replied that the AMMA "also provides immunity for charges of violating § 13–3408(G), which might otherwise subject a person to revocation of probation for marijuana use." What reasoning does the court apply to reach this conclusion and is it a plausible harmonizing of the two statutes?

Why does the Court in section I.A. find that "the immunity provision by its terms would include rather than exclude Reed-Kaliher"? The court also reasons that because AMMA explicitly excludes certain categories of people from its "sweeping grant of immunity," by the canons of statutory construction, it does not exclude probationers. However can the opposite be argued: that since the statute does not specifically include probationers, they are excluded in light of A.R.S. § 13–3408(G)?

3.   Preemption. In assessing consumption of marijuana by probationers, the Arizona Supreme Court addresses the issue of when federal law preempts state legalization. What reasons does the court give for deciding that AMMA is not preempted? One of the court's explanations is that allowing probationers to take medical marijuana "does not frustrate the CSA's goal of conquering drug abuse or controlling drug traffic." Can this be supported if the CSA prohibits the consumption of marijuana for any purpose, even by registered individuals for medical reasons? How does it strengthen the argument against preemption for the Court to point to a presumption against superseding "the historic police powers of the state?"

Preemption is addressed more fully in the following case, *White Mountain Center v. County of Maricopa* (2016).

4.   Anti-commandeering. The court cites the *Printz* case for the proposition that "Congress cannot compel states to enact or enforce a federal regulatory program." This is the anti-commandeering (or non-commandeering) doctrine which derives from the Tenth Amendment to the U.S. Constitution: "The powers not delegated to the United States by the Constitution, nor prohibited by it to the states, are reserved to the states respectively, or to the people." Under this doctrine, states cannot be compelled to enact a federal regulatory scheme, *New York v. United States*, 505 U.S. 144, 188 (1992); state law enforcement officials cannot be compelled to enforce federal legislation, *Printz v. United States*, 521 U.S. 898, 935 (1997); and the federal government cannot employ its Article I spending power so as to "unduly coerce" states to enact or enforce federal law through withholding of essential federal funds. *National Federation of Independent Business v. Sebelius*, 567 U.S. 519, 574–84 (2012); *see also South Dakota v. Dole*, 483 U.S. 203, 205–06, 211–12 (1987).

———————

The Arizona Court of Appeals applied the *Reed-Kaliher* decision the following year in *White Mountain Center v. County of Maricopa*, extending the discussion of possible preemption of AMMA. *Maricopa* revolves around the legality of Arizona municipalities applying zoning regulations to exclude marijuana dispensaries in their communities. Discussion of the zoning issues and much of the court's lengthy citations of the *Reed-Kaliher* and *Ter Beek* (see Chapter 4) cases are omitted to focus on the constitutional question of preemption.

WHITE MOUNTAIN CENTER V. COUNTY OF MARICOPA
Arizona Court of Appeals
241 Ariz. 230, 386 P.3d 416 (2016)

KESSLER, J.

In 2012, White Mountain Health Center, Inc. ("White Mountain") sought county zoning approval to establish a medical marijuana dispensary ("MMD") pursuant to the Arizona Medical Marijuana Act ("AMMA"), Arizona Revised Statutes ("A.R.S.") sections 36–2801 to –2819 (2014 and Supp. 2015). Maricopa County refused to issue the necessary zoning documents and White Mountain filed suit. Appellants seek reversal of the superior court's partial summary judgment for White Mountain and denial of the Appellants' motions for summary judgment, in which the court held that the Controlled Substances Act ("CSA"), 21 U.S.C. §§ 801 to 971, does not preempt the AMMA.* * *

For the reasons that follow, we affirm the superior court's rulings except the sanctions imposed against the County. First, the CSA does not preempt the AMMA to the extent the AMMA requires the County to pass reasonable zoning regulations for MMDs and process papers concerning zoning compliance or requires the State to issue documents to allow MMDs to operate.* * *

FACTUAL AND PROCEDURAL HISTORY

I.   Background A.

AMMA and Regulations

In 2010, Arizona voters passed Proposition 203, now codified as the AMMA. Ariz. Sec'y of State, State of Arizona Official Canvass at 15 (2010). The AMMA decriminalizes and provides protections against discrimination under state law for the medical use and possession, cultivation, and sale of marijuana under the circumstances described in the AMMA. The AMMA granted the Arizona Department of Health Services ("ADHS") rulemaking authority to promulgate regulations in order to implement and administer the AMMA. Those regulations are found in the Arizona Administrative Code ("A.A.C.") at sections R9–17–101 to R9–17–323. No party challenges the validity or construction of the ADHS regulations.

The AMMA also empowers ADHS to establish the system to register MMDs throughout the state and track compliance with statutory requirements. A.R.S. § 36–2803. * * *

II. White Mountain's Complaint

White Mountain filed a complaint in superior court against the County, ADHS, and its Director in his official capacity, alleging that White Mountain could not obtain the necessary zoning documentation because the County refused to issue it. The State stipulated that "the only deficiency in [White Mountain's] application [was] the lack of documentation from Maricopa County." White Mountain attached to its complaint a copy of a letter from the Maricopa County Attorney's Office that stated:

> [T]he County is not issuing zoning verification for [MMDs] due to the fact that doing so would potentially subject the County and its employees to prosecution under federal law. . .the County will not be accepting any further applications for [MMDs] or cultivation sites, further processing any pending applications, or issuing any certificates, permits or other authorizations or justification for [MMDs] or cultivation sites until the threat of federal prosecution is conclusively removed.
>
> * * *

III. The Preliminary Injunction

In response to White Mountain's request for injunctive relief, the superior court entered a preliminary injunction enjoining ADHS from withdrawing or denying White Mountain's application based on White Mountain's failure to provide the zoning verification. The State did not seek appellate relief from the injunction.

IV. Motions for Summary Judgment

Federal Preemption

White Mountain then moved for partial summary judgment seeking, among other things, a court order directing the County to issue the zoning documentation. The County filed a cross-motion for summary judgment, asserting "the relief sought [was] preempted by the laws of the United States" and that the court could not order declaratory relief to "compel" a public lawyer, here the Maricopa County Attorney, to give a "certain legal opinion." It maintained that a mandatory injunction requiring compliance with the AMMA "would require county employees to subject themselves to the risk of criminal prosecution by the United States" and specifically that County employees "could be held liable as aiders or abettors" under the CSA. Ultimately, the County argued that (1) because the County and its employees could not comply with both the AMMA and the CSA, the relief sought was preempted ("impossibility preemption"); and (2) the AMMA was preempted because it created an obstacle to enforcement of the CSA ("obstacle preemption"). The State intervened, counterclaimed for declaratory relief, and moved for summary judgment, arguing White Mountain's requested relief was preempted by the CSA. It asserted all relevant provisions of the AMMA authorizing the running of MMDs were barred by obstacle preemption.

The parties agreed the CSA neither expressly preempts state law nor occupies the whole field. The superior court determined neither obstacle preemption nor impossibility preemption applied, but the court limited relief to simply ordering the County to issue zoning documentation stating that either no relevant zoning requirements existed or White Mountain had complied with them. * * *

DISCUSSION

I.   Preemption Appeal

In the Preemption Appeal, Appellants contend the CSA preempts all provisions of the AMMA. However, the only issue raised in the superior court, and the only issue we will address, is whether the actions the AMMA required the State and the County to take in this case—for the County, approving zoning for specific areas for MMDs, processing zoning documents, and taking action pursuant to zoning laws to ensure MMDs meet other zoning requirements, and for the State, processing White Mountain's application to operate an MMD—are impliedly preempted because such relief allegedly conflicts with the CSA. *See County of San Diego v. San Diego NORML*, 81 Cal.Rptr.3d 461 (2008). * * *

A.   Standard of Review and Burdens of Proof

Although we defer to the superior court's factual findings and review grants of injunctive and mandamus relief for an abuse of discretion, the rest of our review is de novo. Appellants bear a heavy burden to show preemption. "Statutes are presumed constitutional and the burden of proof is on the opponent of the statute to show it infringes upon a constitutional guarantee or violates a constitutional principle." *State v. Wagstaff*, 164 Ariz. 485, 494 (1990); Similarly, "[t]he party claiming preemption bears the burden of demonstrating that federal law preempts state law," and "must overcome the assumption that a federal law does not supersede the historic police powers of the states."*E. Vanguard Forex, Ltd. v. Ariz. Corp. Comm'n*, 206 Ariz. 399, 405 (App. 2003).

B.   General Preemption Principles

State and federal governments have "elements of sovereignty the other is bound to respect," *Arizona v. United States,* 132 S.Ct. 2492, 2500 (2012), and states have "vast residual powers" reserved by the Tenth Amendment to the United States Constitution. One of these is the states' historical police power to provide for the health, safety, and welfare of their citizens, including the power to define criminal offenses and sanctions, prosecute crimes, and regulate land use and medical practices. *See, e.g., Qualified Patients Ass'n v. City of Anaheim,* 115 Cal.Rptr.3d 89 (2010) ("[R]egulation of medical practices and state criminal sanctions for drug possession are historically matters of state police power").

Of course, "[f]rom the existence of two sovereigns follows the possibility that laws can be in conflict or at cross-purposes." *Arizona,* 132 S.Ct. at 2500. In such a case, the Supremacy Clause provides that federal law prevails because "state action cannot circumscribe Congress' plenary commerce power." *Raich,* 545 U.S. at 29. Thus, "the States possess sovereignty concurrent with that of the Federal Government, subject only to limitations imposed by the Supremacy Clause." *Tafflin v. Levitt,* 493 U.S. 455, 458 (1990). Indeed, federalism is one of the beauties of the American system of government, permitting states to act as laboratories of democracy consistent with the Tenth Amendment and the Supremacy Clause. *New State Ice Co. v. Liebmann,* 285 U.S. 262, 311 (1932) (Brandeis, J., dissenting) ("It is one of the happy incidents of the federal system that a single courageous state may, if its citizens choose, serve as a laboratory; and try novel social and economic experiments without risk to the rest of the country.").

In general, federal preemption is conceptualized as either express or implied. Express preemption occurs when Congress explicitly defines the extent of preemption. Implied preemption occurs by: (1) federal occupation of the field ("field preemption"); or (2) a conflict between the state and federal law that either (a) creates an obstacle to federal law ("obstacle preemption"), or (b) makes it physically impossible to comply with both state and federal law ("impossibility preemption").

As an initial matter, Appellants do not and cannot successfully argue that Congress expressly preempted all state drug law or occupied the entire field by enacting the CSA. As our supreme court noted in *Reed-Kaliher,* Congress "specified that the CSA does not expressly preempt state drug laws or exclusively govern the field." 347 P.3d 136. The CSA states: "No provision of this subchapter shall be construed as indicating an intent on the part of the Congress to occupy the field. . .unless there is a positive conflict" between a provision of the CSA and "State law so that the two cannot consistently stand together." 21 U.S.C. § 903; *see also Oregon,* 546 U.S. at 251 ("The CSA explicitly contemplates a role for the States in regulating controlled substances, as evidenced by its pre-emption provision."). Thus, express preemption and field preemption do not apply. Instead, Appellants argue that conflict preemption applies; the State contends the CSA preempts the AMMA using obstacle analysis, and the County uses both obstacle and impossibility analyses.

C.   Conflict Preemption

1.   Obstacle Preemption. *Reed-Kaliher*

We gain substantial guidance from our supreme court's recent decision, *Reed-Kaliher v. Hoggatt*. Reed-Kaliher was an AMMA patient who sought amendment of a probation condition banning marijuana use or possession "for any reason." He asserted the AMMA protected him from "arrest, prosecution or penalty in any manner, or denial of any right or privilege . . . [f]or. . .medical use of marijuana pursuant to [AMMA]." The State claimed the CSA preempted the AMMA under conflict analysis, but the court rejected its argument, pointedly holding there was "no such conflict here." Relying on *Ter Beek v. City of Wyoming*, 495 Mich. 1, 846 N.W.2d 531, 536–41 (2014), the court explained that the AMMA does not prevent the United States from enforcing federal law, but instead provides a limited state-law immunity. *Reed-Kaliher*, 237 Ariz. At 124, 347 P.3d 136. As such, the AMMA does not stand as an obstacle to the CSA. State law conflicts with federal law on obstacle preemption only if the purpose of the federal law cannot otherwise be accomplished.

In light of *Reed-Kaliher*, we conclude Appellants have not met their burden to show the AMMA is preempted by the CSA under conflict analyses. In supplemental briefs, Appellants attempt to distinguish *Reed-Kaliher* from this case, arguing: (1) *Reed-Kaliher* does not address the same federal preemption issue or conclusively determine the outcome here because it is limited to its facts; and (2) the AMMA requires the State and County to "affirmatively authorize" violations of the CSA, unlike in *Reed-Kaliher*.

We disagree with Appellants' argument that *Reed-Kaliher* is limited to its facts for several reasons. First, in applying *Reed-Kaliher*, we must look to what was "central to the [supreme court's] analysis" when interpreting precedent. *State v. Gear*, 239 Ariz. 343, 346 (2016). The rationale of *Reed-Kaliher* applies to this situation as well as to probationary terms prohibiting use of medical marijuana under the AMMA. The essence of *Reed-Kaliher* is that Arizona voters' approval of medical marijuana under a regulated state law system in no way conflicts as an obstacle with federal enforcement of the CSA. As the court explained, nothing in the AMMA precludes the United States from enforcing the CSA; the AMMA "chose to part ways with congress only regarding the scope of acceptable medical use of marijuana. Possession and use of marijuana not in compliance with AMMA remain illegal under Arizona law." *Reed-Kaliher*, 237 Ariz. at 124–25. The federal government is free to enforce the

CSA in Arizona and cannot require the state to enforce the CSA. *Id.* at 123–24.* * *

We also find support for our conclusion from *County of San Diego v. San Diego NORML*, 165 Cal.App.4th 798 (2008). In *San Diego NORML*, various California counties challenged the state's medical marijuana program. They argued in part that the CSA preempted the program because the program required them to issue identification cards identifying the person as authorized to possess, transport, deliver, or cultivate marijuana under California's medical marijuana laws. The court rejected that argument, first concluding that preemption under 21 U.S.C. § 903 of the CSA was limited to positive conflicts between the CSA and state law, meaning impossibility preemption rather than obstacle preemption. Alternatively, the court reasoned that even if obstacle preemption applied to the identification card provisions, the cards did not pose a significant obstacle to specific federal objectives under the CSA. Instead, the cards merely allowed qualified citizens to obtain identification that would facilitate protection from prosecution under state law. The court also rejected the counties' impossibility preemption argument, concluding the program only required counties to process applications for the cards and the CSA was silent by not banning such cards.

Authorization Versus Decriminalization

Appellants argue *Reed-Kaliher* is distinguishable because the AMMA requires the State and County to "affirmatively authorize" violations of the CSA rather than merely decriminalizing them. Although the State maintains that "[i]dentifying a person who is not subject to arrest or prosecution under state law is certainly within the State's power to decriminalize activities for purposes of its own laws," it cites four provisions of the AMMA to support its argument that the AMMA "expressly authorizes" activities that violate the criminal enforcement provisions in the CSA. Similarly, the County argues the AMMA goes "beyond mere decriminalization" to "affirmatively authorize" violations of the CSA.

We disagree with Appellants. As we understand the Appellants' arguments, if the AMMA had merely decriminalized the manufacture, distribution, and sale of medical marijuana, the AMMA would not be preempted by the CSA any more than decriminalization of growth and possession for personal use would have been preempted. However, because the State decided to regulate MMDs, that regulation is preempted. The logic of that distinction escapes us.

We also fail to see a principled basis for the State's distinction between Arizona's identification system to determine whether a patient is exempt from criminal sanction (i.e., for possession) and its system to determine whether an MMD is exempt (i.e., for possession and distribution). The State does not explain why any arguable differences in registering MMDs and patients under Arizona law somehow amount to authorizing federal crimes in one instance but not the other. Appellants have not shown that the AMMA or portions thereof go "beyond decriminalization," or that authorization/decriminalization is even a valid distinction for purposes of Arizona law. However, even assuming the validity of the distinction and its applicability here, Appellants have not shown how the AMMA creates "significant and unsolvable obstacles to the enforcement" of the CSA. * * *

Appellants' argument relies on *Emerald Steel Fabricators, Inc. v. Bureau of Labor and Industries*, 348 Or. 159, 230 P.3d 518 (2010), but this reliance is misplaced. In *Emerald Steel*, the Oregon Supreme Court held that the CSA preempted Oregon's medical marijuana act insofar as it authorized marijuana use by a patient in violation of the CSA. By construing the terms "may engage" and "authorized to engage" in the Oregon medical marijuana act, the court determined the Oregon act affirmatively authorized marijuana use in violation of the CSA and was thus preempted. We fail to see how *Emerald Steel* supports Appellants' positions. The ultimate question is whether the AMMA creates an obstacle so that the CSA cannot otherwise be enforced, *Reed-Kaliher*, 237 Ariz. at 124, 347 P.3d 136, that is, whether the AMMA's requirement that the State and County process MMD applications and permit MMDs under zoning ordinances creates "significant and unsolvable obstacles to the enforcement" of the CSA, *Ter Beek*, 846 N.W.2d at 539. We fail to see how having a state regulatory scheme to permit MMD operation consistent with the AMMA creates significant and unsolvable obstacles to the enforcement of the CSA. *See Garcia v. Tractor Supply Co.*, 154 F.Supp.3d 1225, 1229–30 (D. N.M. 2016) (noting that cases holding state medical marijuana laws are not preempted by the CSA for exempting persons from prosecution under state law are distinguishable from *Emerald Steel*, which dealt with interpretation of state discrimination laws requiring employers to accommodate use of medical marijuana under state law).

We also decline to adopt *Emerald Steel's* distinction between decriminalization and authorization of medical marijuana use. The authorization/decriminalization distinction itself seems to be primarily semantic and ultimately results in a circular analysis. See *Emerald Steel*, 230 P.3d at 538–39 (Walters, J., dissenting) (stating the state medical marijuana act's words of authorization "serve only to make operable the exceptions to and exemptions from state prosecution [and] do not grant permission that would not exist if those words were eliminated or replaced with words of exception or exclusion"). As stated by the dissent in *Emerald Steel*, even if the state law "did not use words of permission, [it] would permit, for purposes of [state] law, the conduct that it does not punish." Indeed, the AMMA's decriminalization of patients' production, possession, and use of marijuana within the terms of the AMMA is no less an authorization to produce, possess, and use marijuana than authorizing MMDs to operate by producing, possessing, and selling marijuana within the terms of the AMMA. Authorization, in this context, is merely another term for the absence of penalties or criminal sanctions under state law. *See Reed-Kaliher*, 237 Ariz. at 124 (holding that by permitting an AMMA-compliant marijuana use for probationers, a court would "not be authorizing or sanctioning a violation of federal law, but rather would be recognizing that the court's authority to impose probation conditions is limited by statute.").

Finally, the State argues A.R.S. § 36–2811(B)–(G) provides protection from arrest and prosecution for AMMA activities that exceed state authority. It asserts "[t]hese provisions do not limit the prohibition to state tribunals . . . [and] the State cannot stop federal officers or courts from enforcing federal law." We find this argument unpersuasive. Not only are these provisions not at issue in this case, but we read them to be limited to prosecution under state law, particularly since the AMMA does not otherwise purport to shield anyone or any act from federal prosecution. We have a duty to construe our statutes "to avoid conflict with the United States Constitution and federal statutes." *U.S. W. Commc'ns*, 201 Ariz. at 246, 34 P.3d 351.

2.   Impossibility Analysis

In addition to Appellants' other conflict preemption arguments, the County argues the CSA preempts the AMMA using an impossibility analysis. The County asserts it is impossible to comply with both the CSA and the AMMA, and that by issuing the necessary zoning documents pursuant to the AMMA, County officials might face criminal prosecution for aiding and abetting MMDs' violations of the CSA. We find this argument unpersuasive for several reasons.

First, *Reed-Kaliher* rejected a similar argument as it applied to state court judges. The court held that by permitting an AMMA-compliant marijuana use for probationers, a court would "not be authorizing or sanctioning a violation of federal law, but rather would be recognizing that the court's authority to impose probation conditions is limited by statute." 237 Ariz. at 124. Similarly, the County by issuing zoning documents would "not be authorizing or sanctioning a violation of federal law," but rather would be recognizing that the County had a duty to issue such documents by statute. Furthermore, the court also held that by allowing use of medical marijuana consistent with the AMMA as part of probation, state officers or employees, including prosecutors, would not violate their oath of office to "support the Constitution of the United States and the Constitution and laws of the State of Arizona" because

> nothing in federal law purports to require state judges to include a prohibition on the use of medical marijuana pursuant to AMMA as a condition of probation. Because AMMA prohibits such a condition and federal law does not require it, a state judge does not violate the oath of office by omitting such a condition.

Id. at 125. This impliedly rejects an impossibility argument because the CSA does not expressly prohibit a county official from abiding by the AMMA in issuing zoning documents, and the state law requires such conduct. Second, we cannot accept the County's aiding and abetting argument. 18 U.S.C. § 2 provides that:

> (a) Whoever commits an offense against the United States or aids, abets, counsels, commands, induces or procures its commission, is punishable as a principal.

> (b) Whoever willfully causes an act to be done which if directly performed by him or another would be an offense against the United States, is punishable as a principal.

However, the CSA provides that subject to exceptions relating to search warrants,

> no civil or criminal liability shall be imposed by virtue of this subchapter upon any duly authorized Federal officer lawfully engaged in the enforcement of this subchapter, or upon any duly authorized officer of any State, territory, political subdivision thereof, the District of Columbia, or any possession of the United States, who shall be lawfully engaged in the enforcement of any law or municipal ordinance relating to controlled substances.

21 U.S.C. § 885(d). Our supreme court found that § 885(d) provides immunity from federal prosecution to sheriffs who follow court orders to return medical marijuana to lawful possessors. *Okun*, 296 P.3d 998 (citing 21 U.S.C. § 885(d)). Although the County contends that such a statute is limited to law enforcement personnel, the Ninth Circuit Court of Appeals has held that state or local officials who enforce state medical marijuana statutes are entitled to immunity under that provision. Here, County officials are "engaged in the enforcement" of state statutes by processing applications for the zoning permits and promulgating reasonable regulations to permit MMDs pursuant to state law.

Additionally, to prove aiding and abetting under federal law, "it is necessary that a defendant in some sort associate himself with the venture, that he participate in it as in something that he wishes to bring about, that he seek by his action to make it succeed." *Nye & Nissen v. United States*, 336 U.S. 613, 619 (1949). As the California Court of Appeal held in Garden Grove, state law enforcement officials acting pursuant to state law in returning medical marijuana to a person authorized by state law to possess it cannot be liable for violating the CSA as aiders and abettors. 157 Cal.App.4th at 368. This is because to aid and abet, a person "must associate himself with the venture and participate in it as in something that he wishes to bring about and seeks by his actions to make it succeed." If police officers actually returning marijuana to possessors cannot be liable as aiders and abettors, we fail to see how County officials who obey state law in passing a zoning ordinance consistent with the AMMA or processing applications for zoning clearance under the AMMA can be liable as aiders or abettors.

Third, the County rationalizes its fear of prosecution by relying on past statements of federal prosecutors, who themselves are limited in deciding what cases to prosecute. *See* 28 U.S.C. § 542 ("Each assistant United States attorney is subject to removal by the President."). However, no evidence of a credible threat of prosecution substantiates the County's impossibility preemption argument.

As White Mountain notes, this fear of prosecution has now become even less credible or immediate, if not moot, given acts by Congress since entry of the judgment here. On December 18, 2015, Congress passed the Consolidated Appropriations Act. Consolidated Appropriations Act, 2016, Pub. L. No. 114–113, 129 Stat. 2242 (2015). Pursuant to that act, the Department of Justice may not use any of its funding "with respect to. . .Arizona. . .to prevent [it] from implementing [its] own laws that authorize the use, distribution, possession, or cultivation of medical marijuana." *Id.* at § 542, 2332–33. The Ninth Circuit Court of Appeals has held that the Appropriations Act prohibits the Department of Justice from interfering with the implementation of such laws not simply by suing states with medical marijuana laws but by prosecuting private individuals under the CSA when those individuals are compliant with the state medical marijuana law in their jurisdiction. *United States v. McIntosh*, 833 F.3d 1163, 1176–78 (9th Cir. 2016). This development vitiates Appellants' argument that at this time they might be subject to federal criminal prosecution under the CSA for aiding and abetting violations of that act if they acted in compliance with the AMMA.

In sum, the County does not show how the relief ordered here makes it impossible to comply with the AMMA due to a risk of prosecution under federal law and specifically the CSA. The County's broad contention that any act which is in any way related to fulfilling duties mandated by the AMMA is somehow criminal under federal law, does not persuade us that the AMMA is preempted. "Impossibility pre-emption is a demanding defense," and the County has not carried its burden. *Wyeth v. Levine*, 555 U.S. 555, 573 (2009).

We heed the Supreme Court's warning that "[p]re-emption analysis should not be a freewheeling judicial inquiry into whether a state statute is in tension with federal objectives, but an inquiry into whether the ordinary meanings of state and federal law conflict." *Id.* at 588. Appellants have not established that the relief granted here relating to the AMMA is an obstacle to effectuating Congress' commerce goals embodied by the CSA or poses a "positive conflict" with the CSA such that state and federal law cannot "consistently stand together." 21 U.S.C. § 903.

[In the remainder of the opinion, the Court addressed the Zoning Appeal and the Attorney's Fee Appeal.]

For the reasons stated above, we affirm all of the judgments entered for White Mountain.

NOTES AND QUESTIONS

1. **Federalism.** Federalism is integral to American law. It fosters two systems of law, federal and state, both sovereign within their own sphere. States have broad authority to enact legislation for the health, safety, and welfare of its residents; the federal government has only the authority delegated to it under the Constitution. When these two spheres overlap, as they frequently do in modern times, federal law is supreme.

Although the federal government may be able to exercise exclusive powers in what is called competitive federalism, federal laws and state laws more often coexist in cooperative federalism. The CSA was deliberately drafted as a cooperative regulatory scheme of federal and state law. As the Court points out, Congress explicitly disclaimed an intent "to occupy the field" of regulating controlled substances. CSA § 903. The CSA contemplated concurrent state laws, which in fact were rapidly enacted by states, modeled on the Uniform Controlled Substances Act (USCA). Under this joint regulatory scheme, federal law enforcement traditionally concentrated on drug trafficking, and state law enforcement focused on individual marijuana consumption, which constitutes the vast majority of marijuana arrests in the United States.

The *Maricopa* court cites the famous quote of Justice Brandeis that it "is one of the happy incidents of the federal system that a single courageous state may, if its citizens choose, serve as a as a laboratory; and try novel social and economic experiments without risk to the rest of the country." States are experimenting with marijuana legalization; transgression of federal law would be the risk, leading to the question of whether state legalization is preempted. See Mikos, Robert A., *On the Limits of Supremacy: Medical Marijuana and the States' Overlooked Power to Legalize Federal Crime*, 62 Vand. L. Rev. 1421 (2009).

2. **Preemption as a constitutional doctrine.** As the Court notes, a state statute can be preempted if Congress has passed legislation encompassing the entire field of relevant law, or if the state statute interferes with the implementation of federal law. As Congress in § 903 of the CSA expressly disavows the intent "to occupy the field" of controlled substances regulation, the question becomes whether state laws interfere with the federal regulatory scheme set out by the CSA. The CSA frames such interference as to whether there is a "positive conflict" between the CSA and state law "so that the two cannot consistently stand together. "Constitutional doctrine classifies "positive conflict" as either "obstacle" or "impossibility" preemption, and the *Maricopa* court so analyzes this question.

If the CSA explicitly states the calculus for determining whether state drug laws are preempted in the text of § 903, is there a need to resort to traditional constitutional law doctrines of express and implied preemption, field and conflict preemption, and obstacle and impossibility preemption?

The *Maricopa* court quotes the U.S. Supreme Court that "[p]re-emption analysis should not be a freewheeling judicial inquiry into whether a state statute is in tension with federal objectives, but an inquiry into whether the ordinary meanings of state and federal law conflict." How would an inquiry into the "ordinary meanings" of whether state and federal law conflict differ from a "free-wheeling inquiry" into federal objectives?

Using these doctrinal principles, most courts have found that state legalization of marijuana is not preempted by the CSA. *See e.g. Cty of San Diego v. San Diego NORML.,* 165 Cal. App. 4th 798 (2008); *Qualified Patients Association v. City of Anaheim*, 187 Cal. App. 4th 734 (Cal. Ct. App. 4th Dis. 2010); *Tracy v. USAA Cas. Ins. Co.*, No. 11-00487, 2012 WL 928186, at *11–*13 (D. Haw. Mar. 16, 2012); *Kirby v. County of Fresno*, 195 Cal. Rptr. 3d 815, 831–32 (Ct. App. 2015). By and large these courts have found that there is no impossibility preemption because state legalization does not prevent the federal government from enforcing federal prohibition of marijuana if it so chooses. Likewise there is no obstacle preemption so long as states do not enact legislation that would shield their residents from federal enforcement of the CSA. *See also*, Lea Brilmayer, *A General Theory of Preemption: With Comments on State Decriminalization of Marijuana*, 58 B.C.L Rev. 895 (2017); Robert A. Mikos, *Preemption Under the Controlled Substances Act*, 16 J. Health Care L. & Pol'y 5 (2013).

In contrast, in *Emerald Steel Fabricators, Inc. v. BOLI*, 348 Or. 159, 230 P.3d 518, 528–29 (Or. 2010), the Oregon Supreme Court rejected an employee's claim that he was protected under Oregon's medical marijuana law, and held that Oregon's issuing a registry identification card to medical patients "affirmatively" authorized the use of marijuana and thus was preempted by the CSA. However, the following year, in *Willis v. Winters*, 350 Or 299, 253 P3d. 1053 (2011), the same court limited *Emerald* to holding that because marijuana use is a federal crime, employers in Oregon do not have to accommodate employee's medical use, rejecting the rule that "any state law that can be viewed as 'affirmatively authorizing' what federal law prohibits is preempted." (Is that the "free-wheeling" analysis?)

The U.S. Supreme Court has not yet decided a marijuana preemption case, but it has denied certiorari in court cases rejecting preemption of state legalization. In addition, the Court declined without opinion to hear a lawsuit Nebraska and Oklahoma filed against Colorado in which the two states contended that Colorado's legalization of marijuana conflicts with, and hence is preempted, by the CSA. *Nebraska v. Colorado*, 136 S.Ct. 1034 (2016). Justices Thomas, joined by Justice Alito, dissented, writing that

> The complaint, on its face, presents a "controvers[y] between two or more States" that this Court alone has authority to adjudicate. 28 U. S. C. § 1251(a). The plaintiff States have alleged significant harms to their sovereign interests caused by another State. Whatever the

merit of the plaintiff States' claims, we should let this complaint proceed further rather than denying leave without so much as a word of explanation.

The Justice Department has not sued to preempt any state legalization schemes; to the contrary, it joined Colorado in the *Nebraska v. Colorado* lawsuit, also arguing against preemption.

Does it make a difference in considering preemption that, as the *Maricopa* court quotes, "regulation of medical practices and state criminal sanctions for drug possession are historically matters of state police power"?

3.   No threat of prosecution? In finding no preemption, the Court also discounts the possibility of state officials being charged with aiding and abetting a federal crime for issuing zoning certificates for MMDs. As the Court points out, at the time the federal government itself had largely disclaimed prosecution of marijuana crimes in legalizing states. Recent congressional appropriation bills have denied funding to the Justice Department to interfere with state legalization regimes by lawsuit or prosecuting individuals in compliance with those regimes. See the Court's discussion of Consolidated Appropriations Act. Consolidated Appropriations Act, 2016, Pub. L. No. 114–113, 129 Stat. 2242 (2015). Likewise the Justice Department, in a series of memoranda, dated October 19, 2009; June 29, 2011; August 29, 2013; February 14, 2014, and October 28, 2014, announced that it would not enforce the CSA prohibition against marijuana in states that decriminalized marijuana use, so long as the states maintained robust enforcement mechanisms to safeguard these federal priorities. The memoranda listed eight federal enforcement priorities to guide the states: 1) preventing distribution of marijuana to minors; 2) preventing revenue from sale of marijuana going to criminal enterprises; 3) preventing diversion of marijuana from states where it is legal to other states; 4) preventing marijuana activity from being used as a cover for trafficking of illegal drugs; 5) preventing violence and the use of firearms in marijuana activity; 6) preventing marijuana-impaired driving and other adverse public health consequences; 7) preventing growing of marijuana on public lands; and 8) preventing marijuana possession and use on federal property.

(Although not relevant to understanding this case, it is important to note that on January 4, 2018, the Department of Justice revoked these memoranda, but it is possible the Department will act on the same principles underlying the revoked memoranda.)

However, neither the congressional appropriations bill nor the DOJ memoranda amended the criminalization of marijuana under the CSA or removed at least a theoretical risk of federal prosecution. *See e.g. United States v. Washington*, 887 F. Supp. 2d. 1077 (D. Mont. 2012). Is this theoretical possibility sufficient to support the county's argument that it cannot subject its employees to possible federal prosecution? The discussion of liability of state officers is the central focus of Section B of this Chapter.

4.   A matter of semantics? The Court writes that "the authorization/decriminalization distinction itself seems to be primarily semantic and ultimately results in a circular analysis." What is the circular analysis the court is referring to? The proposition that there is no meaningful difference for the purposes of preemption analysis between a state's undoubted right not to pass any legislation relating to marijuana, and a statute regulating and taxing marijuana sale and consumption, has found wide acceptance in both the courts and academic commentary. See e.g. Erwin Chemerinsky et al., *Cooperative Federalism and Marijuana Regulation*, 62 UCLA L. Rev. 74, 113 (2015) ("For the same reasons that states may repeal any and all state marijuana laws, they may remove some or even all criminal penalties and impose a state system to regulate marijuana activity instead."). Nevertheless, it seems that a state system taxing and licensing marijuana use might well have an impact on the goals and purposes of the federal prohibition, if only for the expressive message of state regulation. See e.g. *Pack v. Superior Court*, 132 Cal. Rptr. 3d 633, 654 (Ct. App. 2011) ("There is a distinction, in law, between not making an activity unlawful and making the activity lawful. . .The City's ordinance, however, goes beyond decriminalization into authorization. . .A law which 'authorizes [individuals] to engage in conduct that the federal Act forbids'. . .stands as an obstacle to the accomplishment and execution of the full purposes and objectives of Congress' and is therefore preempted.").

Is the authorization/decriminalization distinction semantical or substantial?

5. State activity. If authorization does not create a conflict with federal law, commentators have speculated as to what might create such a conflict, and thus be preempted. These possibilities include the state shielding marijuana users from employment discrimination, guaranteeing a right to housing or benefits despite a marijuana conviction, the state offering economic incentives to encourage marijuana businesses, or the state itself manufacturing or distributing marijuana. See e.g. *Garcia v. Tractor Supply Co.*, 154 F. Supp. 3d 1225, 1229–30 (D.N.M. 2016) (holding that requiring employers to accommodate an employee's state-compliant medical marijuana use would be preempted by the CSA).

PROBLEM 7-1

State X has a comprehensive health insurance plan using state and federal funds to ensure that all of its residents have access to medicines prescribed by a physician. State X has also legalized marijuana for medical purposes. As State X legislature has determined that indigent residents cannot afford high-quality medical marijuana, State X is considering several solutions, all of which would include operating the medical marijuana program under strictly controlled circumstances, including physician oversight and certification of the indigent status of the resident.

Which of the following solutions do you believe would be preempted by the CSA and thus void?

1. State X allows tax deductions and tax credits for the purchase of medical marijuana.

2.   State X-employed physicians provide free services to indigent patients and recommend the use of medical marijuana for certain medical conditions.

3.   State X covers the expenses of marijuana under its indigent patient insurance program.

4.   State X directly reimburses indigent patients for the cost of marijuana.

5.   State X owns and operates dispensaries that distribute medical marijuana at reduced prices to indigent patients under strictly-regulated conditions.

PROBLEM 7-2

State Y has legalized marijuana for medical purposes. The federal government has a long-standing program which contributes funds, under the U.S. Constitution Spending Clause, for state infrastructure projects in neighborhoods that meet federal criteria for classification as economically depressed regions. For State Y, the percentage of the federal contribution to these infrastructure projects averages about 75%. In 2018, the federal government redesigned this program to forbid states from contracting out infrastructure work to any company that fails to test workers for marijuana use, and that fails to prohibit marijuana-users from working on these federally-supported projects. A marijuana medical card holder, long employed by State Y on these infrastructure programs, claims that application of the marijuana prohibition to the state infrastructure projects constitutes federal coercion of state sovereignty, in violation of the Tenth Amendment. What are the doctrinal criteria for adjudicating her claim? *See South Dakota v. Dole*, 483 U.S. 203, 205–06, 211–12 (1987); *National Federation of Independent Business v. Sebelius*, 567 U.S. 519, 574–84 (2012); Samuel R. Bagenstos, *The Anti-Leveraging Principle and the Spending Clause After NFIB*, 101 Geo. L. J. 861, 864–65 (2013).

B. RETURN OF CONFISCATED MARIJUANA

If the police confiscate marijuana from a defendant, and the marijuana is later found to be legally possessed under the state's legalization statute, can the police return the seized marijuana, as they would with other property, or would this return itself constitute a violation of the CSA?

PEOPLE V. CROUSE
Supreme Court of Colorado
388 P.3d 39 (2017)

EID, J.

The state's medical marijuana amendment, article XVIII, section 14(2)(e) of the Colorado Constitution, requires law enforcement officers to return medical marijuana seized from an individual later acquitted of a state drug charge. The federal Controlled Substances Act ("CSA") prohibits the distribution of marijuana, with limited exceptions. 21 U.S.C. §§ 801–971 (2012). The question in this case is whether the return provision of section 14(2)(e) is preempted by the federal CSA. In a split decision, the court of appeals held that the return provision was not preempted by the CSA on the ground that § 885(d) of the CSA exempts those officers who are "lawfully engaged" in the enforcement of laws relating to controlled substances. According to the appellate court, officers returning marijuana pursuant to section 14(2)(e) are acting "lawfully" and the exemption thus resolves any conflict between the CSA and the return provision. *People v. Crouse*, 2013 COA 174.

We granted certiorari and now reverse. The CSA does not preempt state law on the same subject matter "unless there is a positive conflict between [a] provision of [the CSA] and that State law so that the two cannot consistently stand together." 21 U.S.C. § 903 (2012). The return provision requires law enforcement officers to return, or distribute, marijuana. Distribution of marijuana, however, remains unlawful under federal law. Thus, compliance with the return provision necessarily requires law enforcement officers to violate federal law. This constitutes a "positive conflict" between the return provision and the CSA's distribution prohibition such that "the two cannot consistently stand together."

Moreover, the exemption relied upon by the court of appeals does not resolve this conflict. Section 885(d) of the CSA immunizes only those officers who are "lawfully engaged in the enforcement of any law. . .relating to controlled substances." 21 U.S.C. § 885(d) (2012). This court has held that an act is "lawful" only if it complies with both state and federal law. *Coats v. Dish Network*, LLC, 350 P.3d 849, 851 (2015). The officers here could not be "lawfully engaged" in law enforcement activities given that their conduct would violate federal law. We thus conclude that, because section 14(2)(e) "positive[ly] conflicts" with the CSA, and because § 885(d) does not protect officers acting unlawfully under federal law, the return provision is preempted and rendered void.

I.

On May 5, 2011, the Colorado Springs Police Department arrested Robert Crouse for cultivating and possessing marijuana with intent to manufacture in violation of state law. The police seized drug paraphernalia, fifty-five marijuana plants, and approximately 2.9 kilograms of marijuana product from Crouse's home. He was charged with one felony count of cultivation of more than thirty marijuana plants and one felony count of possession of between five and one hundred pounds of marijuana with intent to distribute. At trial, Crouse asserted that he was a registered medical marijuana patient, and that state law authorized his cultivation and possession of medical marijuana. The jury acquitted him of both charges.

After trial, Crouse requested that the district court order the police to return the seized marijuana plants and marijuana pursuant to article XVIII, section 14(2)(e) of the Colorado Constitution. Under this provision, "marijuana and paraphernalia seized by state or local law enforcement officials from a patient. . .in connection with the claimed medical use of marijuana shall be returned immediately upon. . . the dismissal of charges, or acquittal." Colo. Const. art. XVIII, § 14(2)(e). The People opposed the motion, arguing that the return provision of section 14(2)(e) conflicts with and is therefore preempted by the federal Controlled Substances Act. The People argued that the return of marijuana and related property would require them to "distribute" marijuana, in violation of the CSA. The district court rejected the People's argument and ordered the return of the seized property.

The People appealed, arguing that the return provision of section 14(2)(e) conflicted with the CSA. In a split opinion, the court of appeals affirmed the district court's decision, holding that the return of the marijuana would not violate the CSA due to the statute's express immunity for law enforcement officers "lawfully engaged in the enforcement of any law. . .relating to controlled substances." 21 U.S.C. § 885(d). Because law enforcement officers would be enforcing section 14(2)(e), the court of appeals reasoned, the officers would be acting lawfully under § 885(d), and therefore no conflict exists. *People v. Crouse*, 2013 COA 174.

We granted review of the court of appeals' opinion and now reverse. Compliance with the return provision necessarily requires law enforcement officers to violate federal law. We therefore conclude that the return provision of 14(2)(e) "positive[ly] conflicts" with the CSA such that "the two cannot consistently stand together." Moreover, the exemption relied upon by the court of appeals does not resolve this conflict. Section 885(d) immunizes only those officers who are "lawfully engaged in the enforcement of any law. . .relating to controlled substances." 21 U.S.C. § 885(d). This court has held that an act is "lawful" only if it complies with both state and federal law. *Coats*, 350 P.3d at 851. Here, the officers could not be "lawfully engaged" in law enforcement activities given that such conduct would violate federal law. We therefore hold that, because section 14(2)(e) "positive[ly] conflicts" with the CSA, and because § 885(d) does not protect officers acting unlawfully under federal law, the return provision is preempted and rendered void.

II.

We review de novo the question of whether the return provision of article XVIII, section 14(2)(e) of the Colorado Constitution is preempted by the federal Controlled Substances Act.

In 2000, the Colorado Constitution was amended to allow persons "suffering from debilitating medical conditions" to use "medical marijuana." Colo. Const. art. XVIII, § 14. Here we consider only section 14(2)(e) of article XVIII. Section 14(2)(e) provides that if marijuana is seized pursuant to an arrest, "such property shall be returned immediately upon an acquittal."

Conversely, the CSA prohibits the distribution and possession of marijuana for nearly all uses. Under federal law, marijuana is classified as a Schedule I controlled substance, meaning that it has no acceptable medical use and cannot be legally prescribed. 21 U.S.C. § 812(c)[(Sched. I)](c)(10) (2012); see also 21 U.S.C. § 812(b)(1)(A)–(C) (2012). There is no exception for marijuana use for medical purposes, nor is there an exception for use in compliance with state law. *See Gonzales v. Raich*, 545 U.S. 1, 14 (2005). The CSA states that "it shall be unlawful for any person knowingly or intentionally to manufacture, distribute, or dispense, or possess with intent to manufacture, distribute, or dispense, a controlled substance." 21 U.S.C. § 841(a)(1) (2012).

However, § 885(d) provides an exemption under the CSA for law enforcement officers in certain situations. Section 885(d) states that "no civil or criminal liability shall be imposed by virtue of this subchapter. . .upon any duly authorized officer of any State, territory, political subdivision thereof, the District of Columbia, or any possession of the United States, who shall be lawfully engaged in the enforcement of any law or municipal ordinance relating to controlled substances."

Under the Supremacy Clause of the United States Constitution, the "Constitution, and the laws of the United States. . .shall be the supreme law of the land. . .anything in the constitution or laws of any state to the contrary notwithstanding." U.S. Const. art. VI, cl. 2. "Under this principle, Congress has the power to preempt state law." *Arizona v. United States*, 132 S.Ct. 2492, 2500 (2012). The CSA includes its own preemption language. Section 903 of the CSA states that the CSA will not preempt state law on the same subject matter "unless there is a positive conflict between [a] provision of [the CSA] and that State law so that the two cannot consistently stand together." 21 U.S.C. § 903. We thus must determine whether a "positive conflict" exists between the CSA and the return provision in section 14(2)(e) such that "the two cannot consistently stand together."

Section 14(2)(e) requires law enforcement officers to return seized marijuana and marijuana products to medical marijuana patients after an acquittal. The CSA, however, prohibits the distribution of marijuana without regard to whether state law permits its use for medical purposes. 21 U.S.C. § 841. The CSA defines "distribute" to mean "to deliver a controlled substance or a listed chemical." 21 U.S.C. § 802(11) (2012). The CSA further defines "deliver" to mean "the actual, constructive, or attempted transfer of a controlled substance." 21 U.S.C. § 802(8) (2012). An officer returning marijuana to an acquitted medical marijuana patient will be delivering and transferring a controlled substance. Therefore, based on the CSA definition, when law enforcement officers return marijuana in compliance with section 14(2)(e), they distribute marijuana in violation of the CSA. Because compliance with one law necessarily requires noncompliance with the other, there is a "positive conflict" between section 14(2)(e) and the CSA such that the two cannot consistently stand together.

We also must consider whether § 885(d) resolves this conflict. The § 885(d) exemption immunizes only those officers who are "lawfully" engaged in the enforcement of a law relating to controlled substances. The court of appeals suggested that because the return provision requires law enforcement officers to return marijuana, their actions in compliance with that law are "lawful." We disagree.

In construing undefined statutory terms we look to the language of the statute itself "with a view toward giving the statutory language its commonly accepted and understood meaning." *People v. Schuett*, 833 P.2d 44, 47 (Colo. 1992). The term "lawful" as it relates to conduct permitted by state law but prohibited under federal law has already been considered by this court. In *Coats v. Dish Network, LLC*, 350 P.3d 849, 852, we considered how Colorado's medical marijuana law interacted with section 24–34–402.5, C.R.S. (2014), which prohibits an employer from terminating an employee for his or her "lawful" outside of work activities. In that case, the plaintiff was terminated when he tested positive for marijuana in violation of his employer's drug use policy. The plaintiff argued that the termination was improper because his marijuana use was "lawful" under Colorado medical marijuana laws. We disagreed, concluding that "the commonly accepted meaning of the term 'lawful' is that which is permitted by law or, conversely, that which is not contrary to, or forbidden by law." Applying this definition, we held that "an activity such as medical marijuana use that is unlawful under federal law is not a 'lawful' activity under section 24–34–402.5."

The term "lawful" is not defined in the CSA. However, we look to the plain meaning of a term in interpreting a federal statute just as we would look at the plain meaning of a term in interpreting a state statute. As we stated in *Coats*, the plain meaning of "lawful" is "that which is permitted by law or, conversely, that which is not contrary to, or forbidden by law." Consistent with our holding in *Coats*, then, we again find that conduct is "lawful" only if it complies with both federal and state law. Because compliance with the return provision necessarily requires law enforcement officers to violate federal law, officers complying with that provision cannot be said to be acting "lawfully" and thus are not protected by § 885(d)'s exemption.

We therefore hold that the return provision of section 14(2)(e) is in positive conflict with and thus preempted by the federal Controlled Substances Act. The exemption relied upon by the court of appeals protects only those officers acting lawfully under both state and federal law and is thus inapplicable here.

For the reasons stated above, we reverse the decision of the court of appeals.

GABRIEL, J., dissenting.

The majority concludes that the federal Controlled Substances Act ("CSA"), 21 U.S.C. §§ 801–904 (2012), expressly preempts section 14(2)(e) of article XVIII of the Colorado Constitution, which requires the immediate return of marijuana seized by state or local law enforcement officials from a patient upon the determination that the patient was entitled to use the marijuana for medical purposes in accordance with the Colorado Constitution, as evidenced by, among other things, a decision not to prosecute, the dismissal of charges, or an acquittal.

Because I believe that the plain language of § 885(d) of the CSA, 21 U.S.C. § 885(d), immunizes federal and state officers from civil and criminal liability in the circumstances at issue here, I perceive no conflict between the CSA and section 14(2)(e) of article XVIII of the Colorado Constitution, nor do I believe that it is impossible to comply with both the CSA and the Colorado Constitution, as the majority implicitly and the People expressly contend. Accordingly, I do not agree that the CSA preempts section 14(2)(e) of article XVIII of the Colorado Constitution, and therefore, I respectfully dissent.* * *

Here, I believe that § 885(d) of the CSA is unambiguous. That section provides:

> Except as provided in sections 2234 and 2235 of Title 18, no civil or criminal liability shall be imposed by virtue of this subchapter upon any duly authorized Federal officer lawfully engaged in the enforcement of this subchapter, or upon any duly authorized officer of any State, territory, political subdivision thereof, the District of Columbia, or any possession of the United States, who shall be lawfully engaged in the enforcement of any law or municipal ordinance relating to controlled substances.

"Lawfully engaged" plainly means taking part in, pursuant to and within the scope of one's legitimate authority. Thus, a police officer who sells drugs to a target as part of an undercover sting is lawfully engaged in performing his or her duties. A police officer who sells drugs while off duty to supplement his or her income is not lawfully engaged in performing his or her duties. "Enforcing," in turn, means "giving force to." And "any law or municipal ordinance relating to controlled substances" assuredly includes section 14(2)(e) of article XVIII of the Colorado Constitution.

Applying these definitions here, I believe that in returning Crouse's medical marijuana pursuant to section 14(2)(e) of article XVIII of the Colorado Constitution, the state officers would be acting within the scope of their legitimate authority (indeed, pursuant to a court order) and would unquestionably be giving force to section 14(2)(e). Accordingly, in my view, in carrying out the district court's order, the officers would be lawfully engaged in enforcing a law relating to controlled substances pursuant to § 885(d) of the CSA. For these reasons, I agree with the division's conclusion that § 885(d) of the CSA would immunize the officers' conduct.

For two reasons, I am not persuaded otherwise by the majority's determination that because section 14(2)(e) of article XVIII of the Colorado Constitution is unlawful under federal law, law enforcement officers complying with that provision cannot be said to be acting lawfully.

First, in making this determination, the majority simply assumes its conclusion, namely, that section 14(2)(e) is preempted. This analysis strikes me as backwards. Specifically, in my view, we must first determine what "lawfully engaged" means because, as I explain more fully below, the definition of that phrase necessarily informs the preemption analysis.

Second, the majority's analysis leads to absurd results. The majority defines "lawful" with reference to the CSA's prohibition on distribution of controlled substances and states that when law enforcement officers return marijuana in compliance with section 14(2)(e) of article XVIII of the Colorado Constitution, they are distributing marijuana in violation of the CSA. Under this same reasoning, however, when a law enforcement officer provides marijuana to a target in a sting operation, the officer is also distributing marijuana in violation of the CSA, clearly an absurd result.

Perhaps having anticipated the flaws in the analysis that the majority ultimately adopts, the People advance a somewhat different argument, namely, that "lawfully engaged" requires the officers to carry out the purposes of the CSA. For several reasons, however, this argument, too, is unpersuasive. First, for the reasons set forth above, the plain meaning of the term "lawfully engaged" does not support this interpretation. Nor does the plain language of § 885(d), which makes no reference to any purpose of the CSA.

Second, the People's interpretation defines the CSA's purpose by referring to the CSA provisions precluding the distribution of controlled substances. In doing so, however, the People overlook the fact that § 885(d), which allows the "distribution" of controlled substances in certain circumstances, is also part of the CSA and thus must be considered in determining the CSA's purposes. In my view, doing so reveals not only an intention to prohibit the distribution of controlled substances but also an intention to allow officers to act to enforce both the CSA and, as pertinent here, any law relating to controlled substances.

I likewise am unpersuaded by the People's argument that "enforcement" within the meaning of § 885(d) means compelling someone to comply with the law. Although in certain circumstances, "enforcement" can involve compulsion, I do not believe that it must do so or that "compulsion" captures the plain and ordinary meaning of the term "enforcement."

Having thus concluded that § 885(d) would immunize state officers who are ordered to return Crouse's medical marijuana to him pursuant to the Colorado Constitution, the question remains whether, in light of that conclusion, the CSA preempts section 14(2)(e) of article XVIII of the Colorado Constitution. Unlike the majority, I would conclude that it does not.

By immunizing state officers from criminal and civil liability in the circumstances at issue here, § 885(d) of the CSA effectively sanctions the return of medical marijuana pursuant to state law. Accordingly, the CSA and section 14(2)(e) of article XVIII of the Colorado Constitution can consistently stand together, and the simultaneous compliance with both is not at all impossible. For the same reason, I fail to see how the return of Crouse's medical marijuana pursuant to both the Colorado Constitution and an enforceable state court order would in any way pose an obstacle to the accomplishment and execution of the purposes and objectives of the CSA. As noted above, the CSA effectively allows the return of Crouse's medical marijuana through its grant of immunity to state officers. Accordingly, returning such marijuana is consistent with the CSA. Moreover, I do not perceive how the return of Crouse's medical marijuana in the limited and seemingly unusual circumstances at issue here would materially hinder the federal government's enforcement of any applicable federal drug laws.

For these reasons, I would affirm the judgment of the court of appeals. Accordingly, I respectfully dissent.

NOTES AND QUESTIONS

1. **Definition of lawful.** 21 U.S.C. Section 885(d) of the CSA exempts from criminal liability "any duly authorized officer of any State. . .who shall be lawfully engaged in the enforcement of any law or municipal ordinance relating to controlled substances." The crucial question in deciding whether the police are required to return marijuana later found to be legal under state law is apparently the definition of "lawfully engaged" in the "enforcement of any law. . .relating to controlled substances." What are the definitions of "lawfully," "engaged" and "enforcement"? *Reed-Kaliher* found that for legally registered marijuana users on probation, "lawfully" referred only to state law. The majority in *Crouse* held that police actions must be lawful under both state and federal law. The dissent in *Crouse* found "lawfully engaged" to mean any actions within police authority. If a broader definition of "law" is to be

preferred, do the actions also have to be legal under municipal ordinances (also mentioned in § 885(d))? Under international law?

2. Absurd results? The *Crouse* dissent suggests that a strictly literal reading of § 885(d) of the CSA would lead to absurd results. For example, a police officer who distributes marijuana as part of a sting operation would be guilty of violating the CSA. The majority replies that this result is avoided by looking at the purpose of the CSA. In a way this disagreement reflects the perennial debate of interpreting a statute by its plain meaning or by its underlying purpose. In this context, which is the better method of interpreting § 885(d)?

3. Dissent. The dissent claims that the majority "assumes its conclusion." In what way? The dissent also suggests that a law enforcement officer who provides marijuana in a sting operation and a police officer who returns seized marijuana are equally engaged in the "enforcement" of law. Is that correct?

4. Intent to distribute. The Defendant in this case was arrested with drug paraphernalia, fifty-five marijuana plants, and approximately 2.9 kilograms of marijuana product, and was charged, in addition to possession, with counts of cultivation and with possession with intent to distribute, although acquitted. Is it possible that the Court prohibits return of confiscated marijuana, because it suspects that, in this and similar cases, the defendant is possessed of an excessive amount of marijuana, and may actually be engaged in trafficking?

5. Other states. State courts have split on the question of whether state laws requiring return of confiscated marijuana are preempted by the CSA. Finding no preemption, and hence return of confiscated marijuana, *see e.g. State v. Okun*, 296 P.3d 998, 1001–02 (Ariz. Ct. App. 2013) (§ 885(d) immunizes law enforcement for complying with a court order to return defendant's marijuana); *in accord, City of Garden Grove v. Superior Court (Kha)*, 68 Cal. Rptr. 3d 656, 681 (Cal. Ct. App. 2007); *Oregon v. Kama*, 39 P.3d 866, 868 (Or. Ct. App. 2002). Finding such statutes in conflict with the CSA and thus preempted, and hence no return of confiscated marijuana, *see e.g. Oregon v. Ehrensing*, 255 Or App 402, 415, 296 P3d 1279 (2013) (return of property only permitted if lawfully possessed; marijuana cannot be lawfully possessed under federal law); *in accord, United States v. Rosenthal*, 454 F.3d 943, 948 (9th Cir. 2006); Opinion Mich. Att'y Gen., No. 7262 (Nov. 10, 2011); Opinion Or. Att'y Gen., No. OP-2012-1 (Jan. 19, 2012).

PROBLEM 7-3

In State Z, a state which has legalized medical marijuana, a marijuana medical dispensary is burglarized. The police recover from the robbers a large amount of cash representing the stores weekly profits from marijuana sales, office equipment such as cell phones, a computer, cash register, and a credit card reader, marijuana paraphernalia, and 19 kilograms of marijuana. State Z has a law requiring the police to return recovered stolen material to the victim.

Which if any of the recovered items do you think return would be preempted by the CSA: a) the cash; b) the office equipment; c) the marijuana paraphernalia; d) the 19 kilograms of marijuana?

CHAPTER 8

CONSTITUTIONAL ISSUES

■ ■ ■

As developed in Chapter 3, litigants have attempted to compel the federal government to reschedule marijuana. Despite increasing support for legalization of marijuana for medical purposes, efforts to compel the rescheduling of marijuana have failed. Marijuana advocates have also raised constitutional challenges to marijuana restrictions. Those lawsuits and related constitutional questions issues are the focus of this chapter.

This chapter reviews the following constitutional challenges: Does the CSA exceed the federal government's power under the Commerce Clause of the United States Constitution when the CSA is enforced against a person growing and using marijuana for medical purposes entirely within the borders of a state that has legalized the medical use of marijuana? Do laws regulating drug paraphernalia violate a person's right to free speech? Does the First Amendment protect an adolescent's right to advocate for marijuana? Does the First Amendment give a physician the right to recommend marijuana, despite the fact that marijuana has no recognized medical use? Does the First Amendment's guarantee of the free exercise of one's religion prevent the federal government from enforcing the CSA against someone who claims the right to use marijuana for religious purposes? Federal law bans a person who uses marijuana from possessing a firearm. Does such a ban violate the Second Amendment to the Constitution?[1]

By way of introduction, litigants pursuing constitutional challenges to marijuana laws have not done particularly well. They have won an occasional victory in lower federal courts; the Supreme Court has not been receptive to their claims. Interspersed in this chapter are some speculations about whether any of the constitutional challenges may fare better in the future.

A. COMMERCE CLAUSE

The Commerce Clause provides that Congress has the authority "to regulate Commerce . . . among the several States . . ." U.S. Const. art. 1,

---

[1] In Chapter 4, Status under State and Local Law, you also saw that some state courts have upheld challenges based on the Constitution. Notably, some courts have found that a person has a right to privacy broad enough to allow the possession of a small amount of marijuana. Some courts have found that the treatment of marijuana under specific state laws violates the equal protection clause of the Constitution.

§ 8, cl. 3. As developed in Chapter 3, prior to the enactment of the 1906 Pure Food and Drug Act, the federal government had not regulated drug use within the states. Contemporary thinking was that matters of health and welfare were within the Tenth Amendment, beyond the reach of federal power. The 1906 act was within Commerce Clause power because it regulated labeling of drugs shipped in interstate commerce. The Harrison Act of 1914, which did regulate certain narcotic drugs (but not marijuana), was upheld under Congress's taxing authority. Even that conclusion was closely contested in *United States v. Doremus*, 249 U.S. 86 (1919), a 5–4 decision upholding the act. Congress expanded its regulation of drugs to include marijuana in the Marihuana Tax Act of 1937. Like the Harrison Act, the Marijuana Tax Act was justified under Congress's taxing authority, not under the Commerce Clause. But the scope of the Commerce Clause was about to change.

Students of constitutional law are familiar with the expansion of the Commerce Clause during the 1930s and 1940s. Consistent with earlier case law that gave a narrow reading to the Commerce Clause, the Supreme Court struck down a number of New Deal statutes that were aimed at alleviating the effects of the Depression. According to many legal historians, the Court began to rethink its narrow Commerce Clause case law in 1937 in reaction to President Franklin Delano Roosevelt's 1936 court-packing scheme. In 1937, Justice Owen Roberts joined the liberal wing of the Court in upholding a progressive law in reliance on the Commerce Clause. As one commentator quipped, "a switch in time saved nine."

Decided in 1942, *Wickard v. Filburn*, 317 U.S. 111 (1942), may represent the broadest Commerce Clause decision. There, a small farmer sought an injunction to prevent enforcement of the Agricultural Adjustment Act of 1938 against him. He contended that the federal government lacked the power to enforce the law's penalties against him for exceeding his allotment of wheat because the government lacked power under the Commerce Clause to regulate purely local activity. According to the record, most of the farmer's wheat was consumed on his farm. The Court found that the provision was constitutional despite the fact that the farmer's activity alone could hardly affect interstate commerce. That was so because, in the aggregate, were many farmers to raise wheat for home consumption, their conduct would affect total supply for interstate use. The possibility of such an effect on interstate commerce was sufficient to constitutionalize the federal law.

The Court also relied on the Commerce Clause in upholding some of the important Civil Rights legislation of the 1960s. Congress enacted laws like the Civil Rights Act of 1964 and sections of the Fair Housing Act of 1968 under the Commerce Clause. The Court relied on the Commerce Clause in finding that the Civil Rights Act of 1964 was constitutional.

The Reagan Presidency seemed to give promise to states' rights advocates who saw the broad reading of the Commerce Clause as an intrusion on states' rights. Indeed, the Federalist Society, which began and came of age during the Reagan administration, sought a narrower interpretation of the Commerce Clause. For a brief moment in history, that seemed to be the case. In *United States v. Lopez*, 514 U.S. 549 (1995), the Court found that the Gun-Free School Zones Act of 1990 (preventing knowing possession of a firearm within a school zone) exceeded Congress's power under the Commerce Clause. In *United States v. Morrison*, 529 U.S. 598 (2000), the Court found that a provision of the Violence Against Women Act of 1994 exceeded Congress's power under the Commerce Clause. Specifically, the provision at issue created a private right of action for a woman against someone who committed an act of gender-based violence against her. With that background, consider the issue in the next case.

At issue in *Gonzales v. Raich*, 545 U.S. 1 (2005) was whether the Rehnquist Court's new federalism case law signaled a new approach to the Commerce Clause. At this point, review the excerpt from *Gonzales v. Raich* in Chapter 3. That excerpt dealt with the facts and the history of the CSA. What follows is the Court's discussion of the Commerce Clause, including the dissenting opinions.

GONZALES V. RAICH

United States Supreme Court
545 U.S. 1 (2005)

STEVENS, J.

California is one of at least nine States that authorize the use of marijuana for medicinal purposes. The question presented in this case is whether the power vested in Congress by Article I, § 8, of the Constitution "[t]o make all Laws which shall be necessary and proper for carrying into Execution" its authority to "regulate Commerce with foreign Nations, and among the several States" includes the power to prohibit the local cultivation and use of marijuana in compliance with California law.

I

California has been a pioneer in the regulation of marijuana. In 1913, California was one of the first States to prohibit the sale and possession of marijuana, and at the end of the century, California became the first State to authorize limited use of the drug for medicinal purposes. In 1996, California voters passed Proposition 215, now codified as the Compassionate Use Act of 1996. The proposition was designed to ensure that "seriously ill" residents of the State have access to marijuana for medical purposes, and to encourage Federal and State Governments to take steps toward ensuring the safe and affordable distribution of the drug to patients in need. The Act creates an exemption from criminal prosecution for physicians, as well as for patients and primary caregivers who possess or cultivate marijuana for medicinal purposes with the recommendation or approval of a physician. A "primary caregiver" is a person who has consistently assumed responsibility for the housing, health, or safety of the patient.

Respondents Angel Raich and Diane Monson are California residents who suffer from a variety of serious medical conditions and have sought to avail themselves of medical marijuana pursuant to the terms of the Compassionate Use Act. They are being treated by licensed, board-certified family practitioners, who have concluded, after prescribing a host of conventional medicines to treat respondents' conditions and to alleviate their associated symptoms, that marijuana is the only drug available that provides effective treatment. Both women have been using marijuana as a medication for several years pursuant to their doctors' recommendation, and both rely heavily on cannabis to function on a daily basis. Indeed, Raich's physician believes that forgoing cannabis treatments would certainly cause Raich excruciating pain and could very well prove fatal.

Respondent Monson cultivates her own marijuana, and ingests the drug in a variety of ways including smoking and using a vaporizer. Respondent Raich, by contrast, is unable to cultivate her own, and thus relies on two caregivers, litigating as "John Does," to provide her with locally grown marijuana at no charge. These caregivers also process the cannabis into hashish or keif, and Raich herself processes some of the marijuana into oils, balms, and foods for consumption.

On August 15, 2002, county deputy sheriffs and agents from the federal Drug Enforcement Administration (DEA) came to Monson's home. After a thorough investigation, the county officials concluded that her use of marijuana was entirely lawful as a matter of California law. Nevertheless, after a 3-hour standoff, the federal agents seized and destroyed all six of her cannabis plants.

Respondents thereafter brought this action against the Attorney General of the United States and the head of the DEA seeking injunctive and declaratory relief prohibiting the enforcement of the federal Controlled Substances Act (CSA), 84 Stat. 1242, 21 U.S.C. § 801 *et seq.*, to the extent it prevents them from possessing, obtaining, or manufacturing cannabis for their personal medical use. In their complaint and supporting affidavits, Raich and Monson described the severity of their afflictions, their repeatedly futile attempts to obtain relief with conventional medications, and the opinions of their doctors concerning their need to use marijuana. Respondents claimed that enforcing the CSA against them would violate the Commerce Clause, the Due Process Clause of the Fifth Amendment, the Ninth and Tenth Amendments of the Constitution, and the doctrine of medical necessity.

The District Court denied respondents' motion for a preliminary injunction. Although the court found that the federal enforcement interests "wane[d]" when compared to the harm that California residents would suffer if denied access to medically necessary marijuana, it concluded that respondents could not demonstrate a likelihood of success on the merits of their legal claims. *Raich v. Ashcroft*, 248 F.Supp.2d 931 (N.D.Cal.2003).

A divided panel of the Court of Appeals for the Ninth Circuit reversed and ordered the District Court to enter a preliminary injunction. The court found that respondents had "demonstrated a strong likelihood of success on their claim that, as applied to them, the CSA is an unconstitutional exercise of Congress' Commerce Clause authority." *Id.,* at 1227. The Court of Appeals distinguished prior Circuit cases upholding the CSA in the face of Commerce Clause challenges by focusing on what it deemed to be the "*separate and distinct class of activities*" at issue in this case: "the intrastate, noncommercial cultivation and possession of cannabis for personal medical purposes as recommended by a patient's physician pursuant to valid California state law." *Id.,* at 1228. * * *

The obvious importance of the case prompted our grant of certiorari. The case is made difficult by respondents' strong arguments that they will suffer irreparable harm because, despite a congressional finding to the contrary, marijuana does have valid therapeutic purposes. The question before us, however, is not whether it is wise to enforce the statute in these circumstances; rather, it is whether Congress' power to regulate interstate markets for medicinal substances encompasses the portions of those markets that are supplied with drugs produced and consumed locally. Well-settled law controls our answer. The CSA is a valid exercise of federal power, even as applied to the troubling facts of this case. We accordingly vacate the judgment of the Court of Appeals.

III

Respondents in this case do not dispute that passage of the CSA, as part of the Comprehensive Drug Abuse Prevention and Control Act, was well within Congress' commerce power. Nor do they contend that any provision or section of the CSA amounts to an unconstitutional exercise of congressional authority. Rather, respondents' challenge is actually quite limited; they argue that the CSA's categorical prohibition of the manufacture and possession of marijuana as applied to the intrastate manufacture and possession of marijuana for medical purposes pursuant to California law exceeds Congress' authority under the Commerce Clause.

In assessing the validity of congressional regulation, none of our Commerce Clause cases can be viewed in isolation. As charted in considerable detail in *United States v. Lopez,* our understanding of the reach of the Commerce Clause, as well as Congress' assertion of authority thereunder, has evolved over time. The Commerce Clause emerged as the Framers' response to the central problem giving rise to the Constitution itself: the absence of any federal commerce power under the Articles of Confederation. For the first century of our history, the primary use of the Clause was to preclude the kind of discriminatory state legislation that had once been permissible. Then, in response to rapid industrial development and an increasingly interdependent national economy, Congress "ushered in a new era of federal regulation under the commerce power," beginning with the enactment of the Interstate Commerce Act in 1887, 24 Stat. 379, and the Sherman Antitrust Act in 1890, 26 Stat. 209, as amended, 15 U.S.C. § 2 *et seq.*

Cases decided during that "new era," which now spans more than a century, have identified three general categories of regulation in which Congress is authorized to engage under its commerce power. First, Congress can regulate the channels of interstate commerce. Second, Congress has authority to regulate and protect the instrumentalities of interstate commerce, and persons or things in interstate commerce. Third, Congress has the power to regulate activities that substantially affect interstate commerce. Only the third category is implicated in the case at hand.

Our case law firmly establishes Congress' power to regulate purely local activities that are part of an economic "class of activities" that have a substantial effect on interstate commerce. *Wickard v. Filburn,* 317 U.S. 111, 128–129 (1942). As we stated in *Wickard,* "even if appellee's activity be local and though it may not be regarded as commerce, it may still, whatever its nature, be reached by Congress if it exerts a substantial economic effect on interstate commerce." *Id.,* at 125. We have never required Congress to legislate with scientific exactitude. When Congress decides that the " 'total incidence' " of a practice poses a threat to a national market, it may regulate the entire class. * * *

Our decision in *Wickard,* is of particular relevance. In *Wickard,* we upheld the application of regulations promulgated under the Agricultural Adjustment Act of 1938, 52 Stat. 31, which were designed to control the volume of wheat moving in interstate and foreign commerce in order to avoid surpluses and consequent abnormally low prices. The regulations established an allotment of 11.1 acres for Filburn's 1941 wheat crop, but he sowed 23 acres, intending to use the excess by consuming it on his own farm. Filburn argued that even though we had sustained Congress' power to regulate the production of goods for commerce, that power did not authorize "federal regulation [of] production not intended in any part for commerce but wholly for consumption on the farm." Justice Jackson's opinion for a unanimous Court rejected this submission. He wrote:

> "The effect of the statute before us is to restrict the amount which may be produced for market and the extent as well to which one may forestall resort to the market by producing to meet his own needs. That appellee's own contribution to the demand for wheat

may be trivial by itself is not enough to remove him from the scope of federal regulation where, as here, his contribution, taken together with that of many others similarly situated, is far from trivial." *Id.,* at 127–128, 63 S.Ct. 82.

Wickard thus establishes that Congress can regulate purely intrastate activity that is not itself "commercial," in that it is not produced for sale, if it concludes that failure to regulate that class of activity would undercut the regulation of the interstate market in that commodity.

The similarities between this case and *Wickard* are striking. Like the farmer in *Wickard,* respondents are cultivating, for home consumption, a fungible commodity for which there is an established, albeit illegal, interstate market. Just as the Agricultural Adjustment Act was designed "to control the volume [of wheat] moving in interstate and foreign commerce in order to avoid surpluses . . ." and consequently control the market price, a primary purpose of the CSA is to control the supply and demand of controlled substances in both lawful and unlawful drug markets. In *Wickard,* we had no difficulty concluding that Congress had a rational basis for believing that, when viewed in the aggregate, leaving home-consumed wheat outside the regulatory scheme would have a substantial influence on price and market conditions. Here too, Congress had a rational basis for concluding that leaving home-consumed marijuana outside federal control would similarly affect price and market conditions.

More concretely, one concern prompting inclusion of wheat grown for home consumption in the 1938 Act was that rising market prices could draw such wheat into the interstate market, resulting in lower market prices. The parallel concern making it appropriate to include marijuana grown for home consumption in the CSA is the likelihood that the high demand in the interstate market will draw such marijuana into that market. While the diversion of homegrown wheat tended to frustrate the federal interest in stabilizing prices by regulating the volume of commercial transactions in the interstate market, the diversion of homegrown marijuana tends to frustrate the federal interest in eliminating commercial transactions in the interstate market in their entirety. In both cases, the regulation is squarely within Congress' commerce power because production of the commodity meant for home consumption, be it wheat or marijuana, has a substantial effect on supply and demand in the national market for that commodity. * * *

In assessing the scope of Congress' authority under the Commerce Clause, we stress that the task before us is a modest one. We need not determine whether respondents' activities, taken in the aggregate, substantially affect interstate commerce in fact, but only whether a "rational basis" exists for so concluding. Given the enforcement difficulties that attend distinguishing between marijuana cultivated locally and marijuana grown elsewhere, 21 U.S.C. § 801(5), and concerns about diversion into illicit channels, we have no difficulty concluding that Congress had a rational basis for believing that failure to regulate the intrastate manufacture and possession of marijuana would leave a gaping hole in the CSA. * * *

IV

To support their contrary submission, respondents rely heavily on two of our more recent Commerce Clause cases. In their myopic focus, they overlook the larger context of modern-era Commerce Clause jurisprudence preserved by those cases. Moreover, even in the narrow prism of respondents' creation, they read those cases far too broadly.

Those two cases, of course, are *Lopez* and *Morrison.* As an initial matter, the statutory challenges at issue in those cases were markedly different from the challenge respondents pursue in the case at hand. Here, respondents ask us to excise individual applications of a concededly valid statutory scheme. . . .

Unlike those at issue in *Lopez* and *Morrison,* the activities regulated by the CSA are quintessentially economic. "Economics" refers to "the production, distribution, and consumption of commodities." Webster's Third New International Dictionary 720 (1966). The CSA is a statute that regulates the production, distribution, and consumption of commodities for which there is an established, and lucrative, interstate market. Prohibiting the intrastate possession or manufacture of an article of commerce is a rational (and commonly utilized) means of regulating commerce in that product. Such prohibitions include specific decisions requiring that a drug be withdrawn from the market as a result of the failure to comply with regulatory requirements as well as decisions excluding Schedule I drugs entirely from the market. Because the CSA is a statute that directly regulates economic, commercial activity, our opinion in *Morrison* casts no doubt on its constitutionality. * * *

It is so ordered.

SCALIA, J., concurring in the judgment.

* * *

Our cases show that the regulation of intrastate activities may be necessary to and proper for the regulation of interstate commerce in two general circumstances. Most directly, the commerce power permits Congress not only to devise rules for the governance of commerce between States but also to facilitate interstate commerce by eliminating potential obstructions, and to restrict it by eliminating potential stimulants. That is why the Court has repeatedly sustained congressional legislation on the ground that the regulated activities had a substantial effect on interstate commerce. *Lopez* and *Morrison* recognized the expansive scope of Congress's authority in this regard: "[T]he pattern is clear. Where economic activity substantially affects interstate commerce, legislation regulating that activity will be sustained." *Lopez, supra,* at 560.

* * *

Unlike the power to regulate activities that have a substantial effect on interstate commerce, the power to enact laws enabling effective regulation of interstate commerce can only be exercised in conjunction with congressional regulation of an interstate market, and it extends only to those measures necessary to make the interstate regulation effective. As *Lopez* itself states, and the Court affirms today, Congress may regulate noneconomic intrastate activities only where the failure to do so "could . . . undercut" its regulation of interstate commerce. See *Lopez, supra,* at 561. This is not a power that threatens to obliterate the line between "what is truly national and what is truly local." *Lopez, supra,* at 567–568. . . .

And there are other restraints upon the Necessary and Proper Clause authority. As Chief Justice Marshall wrote in *McCulloch v. Maryland,* even when the end is constitutional and legitimate, the means must be "appropriate" and "plainly adapted" to that end. Moreover, they may not be otherwise "prohibited" and must be "consistent with the letter and spirit of the constitution." *Ibid.* These phrases are not merely hortatory. * * *

The application of these principles to the case before us is straightforward. In the CSA, Congress has undertaken to extinguish the interstate market in Schedule I controlled substances, including marijuana. The Commerce Clause unquestionably permits this. The power to regulate interstate commerce "extends not only to those regulations which aid, foster and protect the commerce, but embraces those which prohibit it." *Darby,* 312 U.S., at 113. To effectuate its objective, Congress has prohibited almost all intrastate activities related to Schedule I substances-both economic activities (manufacture, distribution, possession with the intent to distribute) and noneconomic activities (simple possession). See 21 U.S.C. §§ 841(a), 844(a). That simple possession is a noneconomic activity is immaterial to whether it can be prohibited as a necessary part of a larger regulation. Rather, Congress's authority to enact all of these prohibitions of intrastate controlled-substance activities depends only upon whether they are appropriate means of achieving the legitimate end of eradicating Schedule I substances from interstate commerce.

By this measure, I think the regulation must be sustained. * * *

O'CONNOR, J., dissenting.

We enforce the "outer limits" of Congress' Commerce Clause authority not for their own sake, but to protect historic spheres of state sovereignty from excessive federal encroachment and thereby to maintain the distribution of power fundamental to our federalist system of government. *United States v. Lopez,* 514 U.S. 549, 557. One of federalism's chief virtues, of course, is that it promotes innovation by allowing for the possibility that "a single courageous State may, if its citizens choose, serve as a laboratory; and try novel social and economic experiments without risk to the rest of the country." *New State Ice Co. v. Liebmann,* 285 U.S. 262, 311 (1932).

This case exemplifies the role of States as laboratories. The States' core police powers have always included authority to define criminal law and to protect the health, safety, and welfare of their citizens. Exercising those powers, California (by ballot initiative and then by legislative codification) has come to its own conclusion about the difficult and sensitive question of whether marijuana should be available to relieve severe pain and suffering. Today the Court sanctions an application of the federal Controlled Substances Act that extinguishes that experiment, without any proof that the personal cultivation, possession, and use of marijuana for medicinal purposes, if economic activity in the first place, has a substantial effect on interstate commerce and is therefore an appropriate subject of federal regulation. * * *

Even assuming that economic activity is at issue in this case, the Government has made no showing in fact that the possession and use of homegrown marijuana for medical purposes, in California or elsewhere, has a substantial effect on interstate commerce. Similarly, the Government has not shown that regulating such activity is necessary to an interstate regulatory scheme. Whatever the specific theory of "substantial effects" at issue (*i.e.,* whether the activity substantially affects interstate commerce, whether its regulation is necessary to an interstate regulatory scheme, or both), a concern for dual sovereignty requires that Congress' excursion into the traditional domain of States be justified. * * *

There is simply no evidence that homegrown medicinal marijuana users constitute, in the aggregate, a sizable enough class to have a discernable, let alone substantial, impact on the national illicit drug market-or otherwise to threaten the CSA regime. Explicit evidence is helpful when substantial effect is not "visible to the naked eye." See *Lopez,* 514 U.S., at 563. And here, in part because common sense suggests that medical marijuana users may be limited in number and that California's Compassionate Use Act and similar state legislation may well isolate activities relating to medicinal marijuana from the illicit market, the effect of those activities on interstate drug traffic is not self-evidently substantial.

In this regard, again, this case is readily distinguishable from *Wickard.* To decide whether the Secretary could regulate local wheat farming, the Court looked to "the actual effects of the activity in question upon interstate commerce." Critically, the Court was able to consider "actual effects" because the parties had "stipulated a summary of the economics of the wheat industry." After reviewing in detail the picture of the industry provided in that summary, the Court explained that consumption of homegrown wheat was the most variable factor in the size of the national wheat crop, and that on-site consumption could have the effect of varying the amount of wheat sent to market by as much as 20 percent. With real numbers at hand, the *Wickard* Court could easily conclude that "a factor of such volume and variability as home-consumed wheat would have a substantial influence on price and market conditions" nationwide.

* * *

THOMAS, J., dissenting.

Respondents Diane Monson and Angel Raich use marijuana that has never been bought or sold, that has never crossed state lines, and that has had no demonstrable effect on the national market for marijuana. If Congress can regulate this under the Commerce Clause, then it can regulate virtually anything-and the Federal Government is no longer one of limited and enumerated powers.

Respondents' local cultivation and consumption of marijuana is not "Commerce . . . among the several States." U.S. Const., Art. I, § 8, cl. 3. By holding that Congress may regulate activity that is neither interstate nor commerce under the Interstate Commerce Clause, the Court abandons any attempt to enforce the Constitution's limits on federal power. The majority supports this conclusion by invoking, without explanation, the Necessary and Proper Clause. Regulating respondents' conduct, however, is not "necessary and proper for carrying into Execution" Congress' restrictions on the interstate drug trade. Art. I, § 8, cl. 18. Thus, neither the Commerce Clause nor the Necessary and Proper Clause grants Congress the power to regulate respondents' conduct.

As I explained at length in *United States v. Lopez,* the Commerce Clause empowers Congress to regulate the buying and selling of goods and services trafficked across state lines. The Clause's text, structure, and history all indicate that, at the time of the founding, the term " 'commerce' consisted of selling, buying, and bartering, as well as transporting for these purposes." * * *

Monson and Raich neither buy nor sell the marijuana that they consume. They cultivate their cannabis entirely in the State of California-it never crosses state lines, much less as part of a commercial transaction. Certainly no evidence from the founding suggests that "commerce" included the mere possession of a good or some purely personal activity that did not involve trade or exchange for value. In the early days of the Republic, it would have been unthinkable that Congress could prohibit the local cultivation, possession, and consumption of marijuana.

On this traditional understanding of "commerce," the Controlled Substances Act (CSA), 21 U.S.C. § 801 *et seq.,* regulates a great deal of marijuana trafficking that is interstate and commercial in character. The CSA does not, however, criminalize only the interstate buying and selling of marijuana. Instead, it bans the entire market-intrastate or interstate, noncommercial or commercial-for marijuana. Respondents are correct that the CSA exceeds Congress' commerce power as applied to their conduct, which is purely intrastate and noncommercial. . . .

More difficult, however, is whether the CSA is a valid exercise of Congress' power to enact laws that are "necessary and proper for carrying into Execution" its power to regulate interstate commerce. Art. I, § 8, cl. 18. The Necessary and Proper Clause is not a warrant to Congress to enact any law that bears some conceivable connection to the exercise of an enumerated power. Nor is it, however, a command to Congress to enact only laws that are absolutely indispensable to the exercise of an enumerated power.

* * *

On its face, a ban on the intrastate cultivation, possession, and distribution of marijuana may be plainly adapted to stopping the interstate flow of marijuana. Unregulated local growers and users could swell both the supply and the demand sides of the interstate marijuana market, making the market more difficult to regulate. But respondents do not challenge the CSA on its face. Instead, they challenge it as applied to their conduct. The question is thus whether the intrastate ban is "necessary and proper" as applied to medical marijuana users like respondents.

Respondents are not regulable simply because they belong to a large class (local growers and users of marijuana) that Congress might need to reach, if they also belong to a distinct and separable subclass (local growers and users of state-authorized, medical marijuana) that does not undermine the CSA's interstate ban. The Court of Appeals found that respondents' "limited use is clearly distinct from the broader illicit drug market," because "th[eir] medicinal marijuana . . . is not intended for, nor does it enter, the stream of commerce." *Raich v. Ashcroft,* 352 F.3d 1222, 1228 (C.A.9 2003). If that is generally true of individuals who grow and use marijuana for medical purposes under state law, then even assuming Congress has "obvious" and "plain" reasons why regulating intrastate cultivation and possession is necessary to regulating the interstate drug trade, none of those reasons applies to medical marijuana patients like Monson and Raich.

In sum, neither in enacting the CSA nor in defending its application to respondents has the Government offered any obvious reason why banning medical marijuana use is necessary to stem the tide of interstate drug trafficking. Congress' goal of curtailing the interstate drug trade would not plainly be thwarted if it could not apply the CSA to patients like Monson and Raich. That is, unless Congress' aim is really to exercise police power of the sort reserved to the States in order to eliminate even the intrastate possession and use of marijuana. * * *

Here, Congress has encroached on States' traditional police powers to define the criminal law and to protect the health, safety, and welfare of their citizens. Further, the Government's rationale-that it may regulate the production or possession of any commodity for which there is an interstate market-threatens to remove the remaining vestiges of States' traditional police powers. This would convert the Necessary and Proper Clause into precisely what Chief Justice Marshall did not envision, a "pretext . . . for the accomplishment of objects not intrusted to the government."

* * *

NOTES AND QUESTIONS

1. **Local Production.** Which of the justices has the best argument? In considering that question, consider the implications of upholding application of the CSA to local production of marijuana. Would that undercut federal policy reflected in the CSA? Since the Court's decision in *Raich,* Justice Scalia died and Justice Kennedy retired. One prominent commentator, Ohio State Professor Doug Berman, raised the question whether it may be time for marijuana proponents to challenge *Raich.* Since his appointment, Justice Gorsuch, according to Berman, might vote for a plaintiff like Raich. President Trump's next appointment might do so as well. See http://lawprofessors.type pad.com/marijuana_law/2018/06/with-justice-kennedy-now-retiring-and-precedents-being-reversed-is-it-time-for-marijuana-advocates-t.html?utm_ source=feedburner&utm_medium=email&utm_campaign=Feed%3A+ MarijuanaLaw+-Marijuana+Law'+Policy+%26+Reform.

2. **Dissents.** What if Justice O'Connor or Justice Thomas won the argument? Can you think of other federal programs that might be at risk of exceeding Commerce Clause power?

3. **ACA Mandate.** If you favored Justice O'Connor or Justice Thomas' view of the Commerce Clause, what are your thoughts about whether the individual mandate (the requirement that all individuals have health care coverage) in the Affordable Care Act violated the Commerce Clause? If you are interested in how the Court resolved that question, examine *National Federation of Independent Business v. Sebelius*, 567 U.S. 519 (2012).

4. **Death with Dignity Act.** Oregon became the first state to enact a Death with Dignity Act (allowing physician-assisted suicide) in 1994. The George W. Bush Administration attempted to prevent implementation of the law, eventually losing in the Supreme Court. See *Gonzales v. Oregon*, 546 U.S. 243 (2006). The parties debated whether the act violated the Controlled Substances Act and did not turn on the application of the Commerce Clause. (Certainly, the Bush Administration, which tended to take a narrow view of the Commerce Clause, would have argued for a broad reading of the Commerce Clause.) How should the Commerce Clause apply to a Death with Dignity Act?

5.   Legal scholarship. *Gonzales v. Raich* produced a significant amount of scholarship. Fairly predictably, some scholars were critical of the decision on federalism grounds. *See, e.g.,* Randy Barnett, Foreword, *Federalism after Gonzales v. Raich,* 9 Lewis & Clark L. Rev. 743 (2005); Ilva Somin, *Gonzales v. Raich: Federalism as a Casualty to the War on Drugs,* 15 Cornell J. of L. & Pub. Policy 507 (2006). Other authors took different perspectives on the case, less critical of the holding. *See, e.g.,* George D. Brown, *Counterrevolution?—National Criminal Law after Raich,* 66 Ohio St. L. J. 947 (2005); John T. Parry, *"Society Must Be [Regulated]": Biopolitics and the Commerce Clause in Gonzales v. Raich,* 9 Lewis & Clark L. Rev. 853 (2005).

6.   A journalist's view. For an excellent journalistic account of the litigants in this case and the battles over marijuana in California, see Peter Hecht, *Weed Land: Inside Marijuana's Epicenter and How Pot Went Legit* (2014).

7.   Anti-commandeering. Another possible Tenth Amendment issue may arise in some states or cities in states where the state has legalized medical or recreational marijuana. According to an article in the Los Angeles Times, "State lawmakers in Washington and Colorado also considered sanctuary-like bills this year that would have barred local law enforcement and other public employees from assisting in federal crackdowns on people engaging in the marijuana activities the state had authorized. Colorado's bill died amid concerns that it could make it too difficult to conduct joint investigations into marijuana operations that were suspected of violating state laws in addition to federal ones. Washington's bill was spiked because of worries that it might antagonize and provoke the federal government—a fear echoed by the California League of Cities and other groups." See *No Sanctuary for Marijuana in California,* http://www.latimes.com/opinion/editorials/la-ed-marijuana-sanctuary-20170516-story.html. In the fall of 2017, several legislators in California proposed a bill that would have prevented state law enforcement authorities from cooperating with federal drug enforcement efforts. That bill did not pass. That bill may be found here: https://leginfo.legislature.ca.gov/faces/billNavClient.xhtml?bill_id=201720180AB1578. If states or local governments were to enact such statutes or ordinances, the states might raise an objection under a doctrine developed by the Supreme Court in *Printz v. United States,* 521 U.S. 898 (1997). There, the Court held that provisions of the Brady Bill that required state law enforcement officials to collect data on behalf of the federal government violated the Tenth Amendment. State and local governmental entities cannot frustrate federal law enforcement, but they cannot be compelled to act on behalf of the federal government. For an additional discussion of *Printz,* see Federal Preemption, Chapter Seven.

8.   Other arguments. In the district court, the respondents raised two other arguments: one was a substantive due process claim; the other was a medical necessity defense. The Court did not reach those claims because the Ninth Circuit did not reach those claims. You will find a discussion of substantive due process in Chapter 18, dealing with health effects of marijuana. Chapter 9 includes a discussion of the medical necessity defense.

B. FREE SPEECH

The First Amendment provides that Congress shall make no law abridging the freedom of speech. U.S. Const. amend. I. The First Amendment protects individuals' freedom of speech from government action that are considered "overbroad" in nature. Government action that is "overbroad" has a chilling effect on free speech.

I. SPEECH IN MARIJUANA COMMERCE

In the 1970s, local governments started to enforce licensing requirements on business owners who designed, marketed, and sold items for the use of illegal cannabis and drugs. The government feared that, without regulation, sellers of such products would be promoting illegal drug use. The following case, *Hoffman Estates, Inc. v. The Flipside*, is an example of this kind of regulation. What exactly is the "speech" at issue in the following case? Is the regulation overbroad and inconsistent with the First Amendment?

Not only have local governments imposed such restrictions, but also the Controlled Substances Act criminalizes marijuana paraphernalia, including "national and local advertising concerning [marijuana's] use." See 21 U.S.C. § 863(e). Clearly such provisions implicate some free speech rights. But do such provisions violate the First Amendment?

HOFFMAN ESTATES, INC. V. THE FLIPSIDE
United States Supreme Court
455 U.S. 489 (1982)

MARSHALL, J.

This case presents a pre-enforcement facial challenge to a drug paraphernalia ordinance on the ground that it is unconstitutionally vague and overbroad. The ordinance in question requires a business to obtain a license if it sells any items that are "designed or marketed for use with illegal cannabis or drugs." Village of Hoffman Estates Ordinance No. 969–1978. The United States Court of Appeals for the Seventh Circuit held that the ordinance is vague on its face. We noted probable jurisdiction, and now reverse.

I

For more than three years prior to May 1, 1978, appellee The Flipside, Hoffman Estates, Inc. (Flipside), sold a variety of merchandise, including phonographic records, smoking accessories, novelty devices, and jewelry, in its store located in the village of Hoffman Estates, Ill. (village). On

February 20, 1978, the village enacted an ordinance regulating drug paraphernalia, to be effective May 1, 1978. The ordinance makes it unlawful for any person "to sell any items, effect, paraphernalia, accessory or thing which is designed or marketed for use with illegal cannabis or drugs, as defined by Illinois Revised Statutes, without obtaining a license therefor." The license fee is $150. A business must also file affidavits that the licensee and its employees have not been convicted of a drug-related offense. Moreover, the business must keep a record of each sale of a regulated item, including the name and address of the purchaser, to be open to police inspection. No regulated item may be sold to a minor. A violation is subject to a fine of not less than $10 and not more than $500, and each day that a violation continues gives rise to a separate offense. A series of licensing guidelines prepared by the Village Attorney define "Paper," "Roach Clips," "Pipes," and "Paraphernalia," the sale of which is required to be licensed.

After an administrative inquiry, the village determined that Flipside and one other store appeared to be in violation of the ordinance. The Village Attorney notified Flipside of the existence of the ordinance, and made a copy of the ordinance and guidelines available to Flipside. Flipside's owner asked for guidance concerning which items were covered by the ordinance; the Village Attorney advised him to remove items in a certain section of the store "for his protection," and he did so. The items included, according to Flipside's description, a clamp, chain ornaments, an "alligator" clip, key chains, necklaces, earrings, cigarette holders, glove stretchers, scales, strainers, a pulverizer, squeeze bottles, pipes, water pipes, pins, an herb sifter, mirrors, vials, cigarette rolling papers, and tobacco snuff. On May 30, 1978, instead of applying for a license or seeking clarification via the administrative procedures that the village had established for its licensing ordinances, Flipside filed this lawsuit in the United States District Court for the Northern District of Illinois.

The complaint alleged, *inter alia*, that the ordinance is unconstitutionally vague and overbroad, and requested injunctive and declaratory relief and damages. The District Court, after hearing testimony, declined to grant a preliminary injunction. The case was tried without a jury on additional evidence and stipulated testimony. The court issued an opinion upholding the constitutionality of the ordinance, and awarded judgment to the village defendants.

The Court of Appeals reversed on the ground that the ordinance is unconstitutionally vague on its face. The court reviewed the language of the ordinance and guidelines and found it vague with respect to certain conceivable applications, such as ordinary pipes or "paper clips sold next to *Rolling Stone* magazine." It also suggested that the "subjective" nature of the "marketing" test creates a danger of arbitrary and discriminatory enforcement against those with alternative lifestyles. Finally, the court determined that the availability of administrative review or guidelines cannot cure the defect. Thus, it concluded that the ordinance is impermissibly vague on its face.

II

In a facial challenge to the overbreadth and vagueness of a law, a court's first task is to determine whether the enactment reaches a substantial amount of constitutionally protected conduct. If it does not, then the overbreadth challenge must fail. The court should then examine the facial vagueness challenge and, assuming the enactment implicates no constitutionally protected conduct, should uphold the challenge only if the enactment is impermissibly vague in all of its applications. A plaintiff who engages in some conduct that is clearly proscribed cannot complain of the vagueness of the law as applied to the conduct of others. A court should therefore examine the complainant's conduct before analyzing other hypothetical applications of the law.

The Court of Appeals in this case did not explicitly consider whether the ordinance reaches constitutionally protected conduct and is overbroad, nor whether the ordinance is vague in all of its applications. Instead, the court determined that the ordinance is void for vagueness because it is unclear in *some* of its applications to the conduct of Flipside and of other hypothetical parties. Under a proper analysis, however, the ordinance is not facially invalid.

III

We first examine whether the ordinance infringes Flipside's First Amendment rights or is overbroad because it inhibits the First Amendment rights of other parties. Flipside makes the exorbitant claim that the village has imposed a "prior restraint" on speech because the guidelines treat the proximity of drug-related literature as an indicium that paraphernalia are "marketed for use with illegal cannabis or drugs." Flipside also argues that because the presence of drug-related designs, logos, or slogans on paraphernalia may trigger enforcement, the ordinance infringes "protected symbolic speech."

These arguments do not long detain us. First, the village has not directly infringed the noncommercial speech of Flipside or other parties. The ordinance licenses and regulates the sale of items displayed "with" or "within proximity of" "literature encouraging illegal use of cannabis or illegal drugs,". . . but does not prohibit or otherwise regulate the sale of literature itself. Although drug-related designs or names on cigarette papers may subject those items to regulation, the village does not restrict speech as such, but simply regulates the commercial marketing of items that the labels reveal may be used for an illicit purpose. The scope of the ordinance therefore does not embrace noncommercial speech.

Second, insofar as any *commercial* speech interest is implicated here, it is only the attenuated interest in displaying and marketing merchandise in the manner that the retailer desires. We doubt that the village's restriction on the manner of marketing appreciably limits Flipside's communication of information—with one obvious and telling exception. The ordinance is expressly directed at commercial activity promoting or encouraging illegal drug use. If that activity is deemed "speech," then it is speech proposing an illegal transaction, which a government may regulate or ban entirely. Finally, it is irrelevant whether the ordinance has an overbroad scope encompassing protected commercial speech of other persons, because the overbreadth doctrine does not apply to commercial speech.

IV

A

A law that does not reach constitutionally protected conduct and therefore satisfies the overbreadth test may nevertheless be challenged on its face as unduly vague, in violation of due process. To succeed, however, the complainant must demonstrate that the law is impermissibly vague in all of its applications. Flipside makes no such showing.

The standards for evaluating vagueness were enunciated in *Grayned v. City of Rockford*, 408 U.S. 104, 108–109 (1972):

> Vague laws offend several important values. First, because we assume that man is free to steer between lawful and unlawful conduct, we insist that laws give the person of ordinary intelligence a reasonable opportunity to know what is prohibited, so that he may act accordingly. Vague laws may trap the innocent by not providing fair warning. Second, if arbitrary and discriminatory enforcement is to be prevented, laws must provide explicit standards for those who apply them. A vague law impermissibly delegates basic policy matters to policemen, judges, and juries for resolution on an *ad hoc* and subjective basis, with the attendant dangers of arbitrary and discriminatory applications.

These standards should not, of course, be mechanically applied. The degree of vagueness that the Constitution tolerates—as well as the relative importance of fair notice and fair enforcement—depends in part on the nature of the enactment. Thus, economic regulation is subject to a less strict vagueness test because its subject matter is often more narrow, and because businesses, which face economic demands to plan behavior carefully, can be expected to consult relevant legislation in advance of action. Indeed, the regulated enterprise may have the ability to clarify the meaning of the regulation by its own inquiry, or by resort to an administrative process. The Court has also expressed greater tolerance of enactments with civil rather than criminal penalties because the consequences of imprecision are qualitatively less severe. And the Court has recognized that a scienter requirement may mitigate a law's vagueness, especially with respect to the adequacy of notice to the complainant that his conduct is proscribed.

Finally, perhaps the most important factor affecting the clarity that the Constitution demands of a law is whether it threatens to inhibit the exercise of constitutionally protected rights. If, for example, the law interferes with the right of free speech or of association, a more stringent vagueness test should apply.

B

This ordinance simply regulates business behavior and contains a scienter requirement with respect to the alternative "marketed for use" standard. The ordinance nominally imposes only civil penalties. However, the village concedes that the ordinance is "quasi-criminal," and its prohibitory and stigmatizing effect may warrant a relatively strict test. Flipside's facial challenge fails because, under the test appropriate to either a quasi-criminal or a criminal law, the ordinance is sufficiently clear as applied to Flipside.

The ordinance requires Flipside to obtain a license if it sells "any items, effect, paraphernalia, accessory or thing which is designed or marketed for use with illegal cannabis or drugs, as defined by the Illinois Revised Statutes." Flipside expresses no uncertainty about which drugs this description encompasses; as the District Court noted, Illinois law clearly defines cannabis and numerous other controlled drugs, including cocaine. On the other hand, the words "items, effect, paraphernalia, accessory or thing" do not identify the type of merchandise that the village desires to regulate. Flipside's challenge thus appropriately focuses on the language "designed or marketed for use." Under either the "designed for use" or "marketed for use" standard, we conclude that at least some of the items sold by Flipside are covered. Thus, Flipside's facial challenge is unavailing.

1.   "Designed for use"

The Court of Appeals objected that "designed . . . for use" is ambiguous with respect to whether items must be inherently suited only for drug use; whether the retailer's intent or manner of display is relevant; and whether the intent of a third party, the manufacturer, is critical, since the manufacturer is the "designer." For the reasons that follow, we conclude that this language is not unconstitutionally vague on its face.

The Court of Appeals' speculation about the meaning of "design" is largely unfounded. The guidelines refer to "paper of colorful design" and to other specific items as conclusively "designed" or not "designed" for illegal use. A principal meaning of "design" is "[t]o fashion according to a plan."

Webster's New International Dictionary of the English Language 707 (2d ed. 1957). It is therefore plain that the standard encompasses at least an item that is principally used with illegal drugs by virtue of its objective features, *i.e.*, features designed by the manufacturer. A business person of ordinary intelligence would understand that this term refers to the design of the manufacturer, not the intent of the retailer or customer. It is also sufficiently clear that items which are principally used for nondrug purposes, such as ordinary pipes, are not "designed for use" with illegal drugs. Moreover, no issue of fair warning is present in this case, since Flipside concedes that the phrase refers to structural characteristics of an item. . . .

2. *"Marketed for use"*

Whatever ambiguities the "designed . . . for use" standard may engender, the alternative "marketed for use" standard is transparently clear: it describes a retailer's intentional display and marketing of merchandise. The guidelines refer to the display of paraphernalia, and to the proximity of covered items to otherwise uncovered items. A retail store therefore must obtain a license if it deliberately displays its wares in a manner that appeals to or encourages illegal drug use. The standard requires scienter, since a retailer could scarcely "market" items "for" a particular use without intending that use.

Under this test, Flipside had ample warning that its marketing activities required a license. Flipside displayed the magazine High Times and books entitled Marijuana Grower's Guide, Children's Garden of Grass, and The Pleasures of Cocaine, physically close to pipes and colored rolling papers, in clear violation of the guidelines. As noted above, Flipside's co-operator admitted that his store sold "roach clips," which are principally used for illegal purposes. Finally, in the same section of the store, Flipside had posted the sign, "You must be 18 or older to purchase any head supplies."

* * *

Accordingly, the judgment of the Court of Appeals is reversed, and the case is remanded for further proceedings consistent with this opinion.

It is so ordered.

STEVENS, J. took no part in the consideration or decision of this case.

WHITE, J., concurring in the judgment [but believed that the Court did not need to address the overbreadth problem.] * * *

NOTES AND QUESTIONS

1. **The Court's clear signal.** Once you read the following sentence in Justice Marshall's opinion, did you have any doubt about the result in *Hoffman Estates*?: "A plaintiff who engages in some conduct that is clearly proscribed

cannot complain of the vagueness of the law as applied to the conduct of others." Is the result correct?

2. **Rethinking Hoffman Estates.** In 1982, when the Court decided *Hoffman Estates*, marijuana was illegal in virtually every state in the United States. How would a court resolve similar issues as raised in *Hoffman Estates* today in a state where medical or recreational marijuana does not violate state law?

3. **More on rethinking Hoffman Estates.** Proposition 64, which legalized recreational marijuana in California, included an unusual provision: it allows for advertising of marijuana related products, but a broadcast must be to an audience that is expected to have at least 71.6% of its viewership consist of adults 21 years or older. That became a contentious issue during the election campaign in 2016. Opponents, including California's Senator Dianne Feinstein, contended that would lead to advertising in prime time to audiences including children and eroding restrictions on tobacco advertisements. Proponents of Proposition 64 argued, consistently with cases like *Hoffman Estates*, that as long as marijuana remains a Schedule I drug, marijuana advertisements remain unlikely. See Gage Marchini and Brian Parino, *Proposition 64: Marijuana Legalization,* http://www.mcgeorge.edu/Documents/ Publications/prop64_CIR2016.pdf.

4. **An added level of complexity.** For a broader look at the commercial speech implications of marijuana advertising, see Leslie Gielow Jacobs, *Regulating Marijuana Advertising and Marketing to Promote Public Health: Navigating the Constitutional Minefield,* 21 Lewis & Clark L. Rev. 1081 (2017) (suggesting that overly broad restrictions on advertising marijuana may violate the First Amendment). As Professor Jacobs argued there:

> The First Amendment of the United States Constitution prohibits governments at all levels from "abridging the freedom of speech." This guarantee is not absolute, even with respect to core political speech. The Supreme Court has interpreted the First Amendment's protection to extend to commercial advertising. Some boundaries of this protection are in flux. A critical aspect of the Court's interpretation that is not likely to change is that First Amendment protection for an advertisement applies only if it promotes a "lawful" product or service. Marijuana is not lawful at the federal level. One court and some commentators have concluded that this means that the federal Constitution's free speech guarantee does not protect marijuana advertising in states where it is legal.

> It is not at all clear, however, that other courts will agree. In *Bigelow v. Virginia*, the Supreme Court held that a Virginia statute making it a misdemeanor to encourage the procurement of an abortion violated the First Amendment when the statute was applied to a Virginia newspaper editor who had published an advertisement from a New York abortion referral service regarding legal abortions in New

York. Courts have read this holding as articulating "a strong position against the constitutionality of a prohibition by one locality . . . on advertising regarding activities lawful in another locality." These courts have "interpreted *Bigelow* to mean that an activity is 'lawful' under the *Central Hudson* test so long as it is lawful where it will occur." *Bigelow*, which deals with different judgments about the lawfulness of an activity by coequal sovereigns, does not fully address the jurisprudential status of selling marijuana where the activity is simultaneously lawful under state law but unlawful under federal law in the place "where it will occur." As a matter of enforcement authority, the federal judgment that the activity is unlawful clearly prevails. But as a matter of constitutional free speech protection, where the Court has been ratcheting up protections for advertisements and condemning restrictions that keep consumers "in the dark" to promote government policies, it seems unlikely that it, the ultimate arbiter, would allow a state that has legalized the sale of marijuana to regulate by suppressing speech that, according to the Court, consumers very much need and value highly. Lower courts, which will issue the first interpretations, may reasonably read the Court's precedent in this way. At the very least, litigants will raise the federal constitutional issue and argue it strenuously, imposing costs on regulators and causing delays. Moreover, many state constitutions have similar free speech guarantees that protect advertising. Colorado and California, two states that have legalized the sale of marijuana, have constitutions that protect advertisements at least as much as the constitutional free speech guarantee. California's Supreme Court has explicitly likened its methodology in interpreting the state constitutional commercial speech protection to the tests and categories articulated by the United States Supreme Court. Additionally, marijuana could become lawful, at least in some respects, under federal law, which would mean that advertisements would certainly receive First Amendment protection. For all of these reasons, regulators should assume that United States Supreme Court commercial speech precedent will guide the analysis of marijuana marketing and advertising restrictions.

21 Lewis & Clark L. Rev. at 1095–98.

5.   **Another view of the issue.** See also, Leslie Gielow Jacobs, *Memo to Marijuana Regulators: The* Expressions Hair Design *Decision Does Not Limit Your Broad Authority to Restrict All Forms of Discounting*, 49 Univ. Pac. L. Rev. 67 (2017) (reviewing First Amendment implications of regulations of marijuana sellers online efforts to increase demand).

PROBLEM 8-1

Weed-finder is a company in a state that has legalized recreational and medical marijuana sales. The state has not licensed companies like Weed-finder. Weed-finders' business involves hosting a website where it lists dispensaries around the state and includes links to sites of companies that deliver marijuana. It makes money from ads and from businesses listed on its website. The state agency in charge of regulating marijuana has sent notice to Weed-finder that its business is not in compliance with state law. A representative of Weed-finder has contacted you and asked whether Weed-finder should file an action to prevent the state from enforcing state law against it. The representative believes that the First Amendment right to free speech protects Weed-finder's activities. Discuss fully.

II. MARIJUANA ADVOCACY IN SCHOOLS

Morse v. Frederick, 551 U.S. 393 (2007) is another Supreme Court case involving marijuana and First Amendment rights. There, as the Olympic Torch Relay passed through Juneau, Alaska, high school students unfurled a banner with the phrase "BONG HiTS 4 JESUS." Only student Joseph Frederick did not comply with the principal's demand to take down the banner. She demanded that the student do so because she believed that the banner encouraged illegal drug use. The student was suspended. He then filed a § 1983 claim against school board members and the principal on the grounds that his suspension violated his First Amendment free speech rights. Initially, the Court agreed with the principal's interpretation of the banner as taking a pro-drug use position in violation of school policy. The Court concluded, "The question thus becomes whether a principal may, consistent with the First Amendment, restrict student speech at a school event, when that speech is reasonably viewed as promoting illegal drug use. We hold that she may." The Court recognized that the First Amendment does not stop at the school house door, as it made clear in *Tinker v. Des Moines Independent Community School Dist.*, 393 U.S. 503. The Court relied on other cases demonstrating that students' constitutional rights are not enforced to the same degree as it would enforce adults' rights or as would students' rights be enforced outside of the school context. Most importantly, the case turned on the state's compelling interest to deter drug use by schoolchildren.

Justice Thomas concurred, observing: "...in the earliest public schools, teachers taught, and students listened. Teachers commanded, and students obeyed. Teachers did not rely solely on the power of ideas to persuade; they relied on discipline to maintain order." He expressed a willingness to overrule *Tinker*.

Justice Alito, joined by Justice Kennedy, concurred and stated: "I join the opinion of the Court on the understanding that (1) it goes no further than to hold that a public school may restrict speech that a reasonable observer would interpret as advocating illegal drug use and (2) it provides no support for any restriction of speech that can plausibly be interpreted as commenting on any political or social issue, including speech on issues such as "the wisdom of the war on drugs or of legalizing marijuana for medicinal use." "

Justice Breyer concurred but saw the First Amendment issue as a difficult one. Instead, he thought that the Court should resolve the question on the ground that the principal had a winning qualified immunity in the § 1983 action.

Justice Stevens dissented and was joined by Justices Souter and Ginsburg. Although he agreed with Justice Breyer's position on the available immunity, he argued that, "I would hold, however, that the school's interest in protecting its students from exposure to speech 'reasonably regarded as promoting illegal drug use,'... cannot justify disciplining Frederick for his attempt to make an ambiguous statement to a television audience simply because it contained an oblique reference to drugs. The First Amendment demands more, indeed, much more."

Given the division within the Court, Justice Alito's description of the Court's holding is critical. Without Justices Alito and Kennedy's votes, the Chief Justice would have lacked a majority.

NOTES AND QUESTIONS

1. **The First Amendment enters public schools.** As the opinions in *Morse* make clear, *Tinker* held that Tinker's high school violated the First Amendment when it prohibited students from wearing black armbands to protest the Vietnam War. Does that decision seem radical? As Justice Thomas indicates, *Tinker* was a radical departure from traditional First Amendment case law in 1969 when it was decided.

2. **The different judicial views.** Which justice has the best argument about the First Amendment and its application in the high school setting? Does a school's primary mission of educating students outweigh students' interests in voicing their views? In Part II of his dissent, Justice Stevens questioned the majority's conclusion that the banner advocated for the illegal use of drugs.

3. **More complicated questions.** Consider the various opinions and how the justices might resolve the following hypothetical case: what if instead of wearing a t-shirt with the slogan BONG HITS 4 JESUS, the student held a sign stating, "Alaska should legalize marijuana!"? Would the result be the same? Is the difference meaningful? Is the line easy to draw?

4. **Scholars' views of Morse.** Scholars disagree about the soundness of *Morse*. Professor (now Dean) Erwin Chemerinsky raised questions about the decision and suggested that the case could not be justified under existing First Amendment principles, even while he recognized that the case was consistent with post-*Tinker* decisions, eroding its holding. *How Will Morse v. Frederick Be Applied?*, 12 Lewis & Clark 17 (2008). One student commentator supported the decision's limitations on speech in the school setting. See Shannon L. Noder, Morse v. Frederick: *Students' First Amendment Rights Restricted Again*, 43 Val. U. L. Rev. 859 (2009). Professor Scott A. Moss argued that, despite the "prevailing narrative" that decisions like *Morse* sweepingly altered the legal landscape, it had only modest real-world impact on the law and on the lives of

the litigants. Scott A. Moss, *The Overhyped Path From Tinker to Morse: How the Student Speech Cases Show the Limits of Supreme Court Decisions—for the Law and the Litigants*, 63 Fla. L. Rev. 1407 (2011).

III. MARIJUANA SPEECH BY REGULATED PROFESSIONALS

Yet another First Amendment issue has arisen in the marijuana realm. As discussed in Chapter 3 Status Under Federal Law, under the Controlled Substance Act, a physician cannot prescribe a Schedule I drug. After all, the federal government has determined that such drugs have no recognized medical use. How then can a person in a state that authorizes medical marijuana get a doctor's approval for a person to use marijuana? The following case deals with the way in which California's Proposition 215 developed a work-around of Schedule I.

CONANT V. WALTERS
United States Court of Appeals for the Ninth Circuit
309 F.3d 629 (9th Cir. 2002)

SCHROEDER, C.J.

This is an appeal from a permanent injunction entered to protect First Amendment rights. The order enjoins the federal government from either revoking a physician's license to prescribe controlled substances or conducting an investigation of a physician that might lead to such revocation, where the basis for the government's action is solely the physician's professional "recommendation" of the use of medical marijuana. The district court's order and accompanying opinion are at *Conant v. McCaffrey*, 2000 WL 1281174 (N.D. Cal. Sept. 7, 2000). The history of the litigation demonstrates that the injunction is not intended to limit the government's ability to investigate doctors who aid and abet the actual distribution and possession of marijuana. The government has not provided any empirical evidence to demonstrate that this injunction interferes with or threatens to interfere with any legitimate law enforcement activities. Nor is there any evidence that the similarly phrased preliminary injunction that preceded this injunction, which the government did not appeal, interfered with law enforcement. The district court, on the other hand, explained convincingly when it entered both the earlier preliminary injunction and this permanent injunction, how the government's professed enforcement policy threatens to interfere with expression protected by the First Amendment. We therefore affirm.

I.   The Federal Marijuana Policy

The federal government promulgated its policy in 1996 in response to initiatives passed in both Arizona and California decriminalizing the use of marijuana for limited medical purposes and immunizing physicians from prosecution under state law for the "recommendation or approval" of using marijuana for medical purposes. The federal policy declared that a doctor's "action of recommending or prescribing Schedule I controlled substances is not consistent with the 'public interest' (as that phrase is used in the federal Controlled Substances Act)" and that such action would lead to revocation of the physician's registration to prescribe controlled substances. The policy relies on the definition of "public interest" contained in 21 U.S.C. § 823(f), which provides:

> In determining the public interest, the following factors shall be considered: (1) The recommendation of the appropriate State licensing board or professional disciplinary authority. (2) The applicant's experience in dispensing, or conducting research with respect to controlled substances. (3) The applicant's conviction record under Federal or State laws relating to the manufacture, distribution, or dispensing of controlled substances. (4) Compliance with applicable State, Federal, or local laws relating to controlled substances. (5) Such other conduct which may threaten the public health and safety.

The policy also said that the DOJ and the HHS would send a letter to practitioner associations and licensing boards informing those groups of the policy. The federal agencies sent a letter two months later to national, state, and local practitioner associations outlining the Administration's position ("Medical Leader Letter"). The Medical Leader Letter cautioned that physicians who "intentionally provide their patients with oral or written statements in order to enable them to obtain controlled substances in violation of federal law . . . risk revocation of their DEA prescription authority."

II. Litigation History

Plaintiffs are patients suffering from serious illnesses, physicians licensed to practice in California who treat patients with serious illnesses, a patient's organization, and a physician's organization. The patient organization is Being Alive: People with HIV/AIDS Action Coalition, Inc. The physician's organization is the Bay Area Physicians for Human Rights. Plaintiffs filed this action in early 1997 to enjoin enforcement of the government policy insofar as it threatened to punish physicians for communicating with their patients about the medical use of marijuana. The case was originally assigned to District Judge Fern Smith, who entered . . . a temporary restraining order and then a preliminary injunction. * * *

[The preliminary injunction] provided that the government "may not take administrative action against physicians for recommending marijuana unless the government in good faith believes that it has substantial evidence" that the physician aided and abetted the purchase, cultivation, or possession of marijuana or engaged in a conspiracy to cultivate, distribute, or possess marijuana. Judge Smith specifically enjoined the "defendants, their agents, employees, assigns, and all persons acting in concert or participating with them, from threatening or prosecuting physicians, [or] revoking their licenses . . . based upon conduct relating to medical marijuana that does not rise to the level of a criminal offense." The preliminary injunction covered not only "recommendations," but also "non-criminal activity related to those recommendations, such as providing a copy of a patient's medical chart to that patient or testifying in court regarding a recommendation that a patient use marijuana to treat an illness."

The government did not appeal the preliminary injunction, and it remained in effect after the case was transferred more than two years later to Judge Alsup on August 19, 1999. [Judge Alsup entered a permanent injunction]. * * * The permanent injunction appears to be functionally the same as the preliminary injunction that Judge Smith originally entered. It provides that the government is permanently enjoined from:

> (i) revoking any physician class member's DEA registration merely because the doctor makes a recommendation for the use of medical marijuana based on a sincere medical judgment and (ii) from initiating any investigation solely on that ground. The injunction should apply whether or not the doctor anticipates that the patient will, in turn, use his or her recommendation to obtain marijuana in violation of federal law.

In explaining his reasons for entering the injunction, Judge Alsup pointed out that there was substantial agreement between the parties as to what doctors could and could not do under the federal law. The government agreed with plaintiffs that revocation of a license was not authorized where a doctor merely discussed the pros and cons of marijuana use. The court went on to observe that the plaintiffs agreed with the government that a doctor who actually prescribes or dispenses marijuana violates federal law. The fundamental disagreement between the parties concerned the extent to which the federal government could regulate doctor-patient communications without interfering with First Amendment interests. This appeal followed.

III. Discussion

* * *

The dispute in the district court in this case focused on the government's policy of investigating doctors or initiating proceedings against doctors only because they "recommend" the use of marijuana. While the government urged that such recommendations lead to illegal use, the district court concluded that there are many legitimate responses to a recommendation of marijuana by a doctor to a patient. There are strong examples in the district court's opinion supporting the district court's conclusion. For example, the doctor could seek to place the patient in a

federally   approved,   experimental   marijuana-therapy   program.
Alternatively, the patient upon receiving the recommendation could
petition the government to change the law. By chilling doctors' ability to
recommend marijuana to a patient, the district court held that the
prohibition compromises a patient's meaningful participation in public
discourse. The district court stated:

> Petitioning Congress or federal agencies for redress of a grievance
> or a change in policy is a time-honored tradition. In the
> marketplace of ideas, few questions are more deserving of free-
> speech protection than whether regulations affecting health and
> welfare are sound public policy. In the debate, perhaps the status
> quo will (and should) endure. But patients and physicians are
> certainly entitled to urge their view. To hold that physicians are
> barred from communicating to patients sincere medical
> judgments would disable patients from understanding their own
> situations well enough to participate in the debate. As the
> government concedes, . . . many patients depend upon discussions
> with their physicians as their primary or only source of sound
> medical information. Without open communication with their
> physicians, patients would fall silent and appear uninformed. The
> ability of patients to participate meaningfully in the public
> discourse would be compromised.

On appeal, the government first argues that the "recommendation"
that the injunction may protect is analogous to a "prescription" of a
controlled substance, which federal law clearly bars. We believe this
characterizes the injunction as sweeping more broadly than it was
intended   or   than   as   properly   interpreted.   If,   in   making   the
recommendation, the physician intends for the patient to use it as the
means for obtaining marijuana, as a prescription is used as a means for a
patient to obtain a controlled substance, then a physician would be guilty
of aiding and abetting the violation of federal law. That, the injunction is
intended to avoid. Indeed the predecessor preliminary injunction spelled
out what the injunction did not bar; it did not enjoin the government from
prosecuting physicians when government officials in good faith believe that
they have "probable cause to charge under the federal aiding and abetting
and/or conspiracy statutes."

The plaintiffs themselves interpret the injunction narrowly, stating in
their brief before this Court that, "the lower court fashioned an injunction
with a clear line between protected medical speech and illegal conduct."
They characterize the injunction as protecting "the dispensing of
information," not the dispensing of controlled substances, and therefore
assert that the injunction does not contravene or undermine federal law.

As Judge Smith noted in the preliminary injunction order, conviction
of aiding and abetting requires proof that the defendant "associate[d]

himself with the venture, that he participate[d] in it as something that he wishe[d] to bring about, that he [sought] by his actions to make it succeed." This is an accurate statement of the law. We have explained that a conviction of aiding and abetting requires the government to prove four elements: "(1) that the accused had the specific intent to facilitate the commission of a crime by another, (2) that the accused had the requisite intent of the underlying substantive offense, (3) that the accused assisted or participated in the commission of the underlying substantive offense, and (4) that someone committed the underlying substantive offense." The district court also noted that conspiracy requires that a defendant make "an agreement to accomplish an illegal objective and [that he] knows of the illegal objective and intends to help accomplish it."

The government on appeal stresses that the permanent injunction applies "whether or not the doctor anticipates that the patient will, in turn, use his or her recommendation to obtain marijuana in violation of federal law," and suggests that the injunction thus protects criminal conduct. A doctor's anticipation of patient conduct, however, does not translate into aiding and abetting, or conspiracy. A doctor would aid and abet by acting with the specific intent to provide a patient with the means to acquire marijuana. Similarly, a conspiracy would require that a doctor have knowledge that a patient intends to acquire marijuana, agree to help the patient acquire marijuana, and intend to help the patient acquire marijuana. Holding doctors responsible for whatever conduct the doctor could anticipate a patient might engage in after leaving the doctor's office is simply beyond the scope of either conspiracy or aiding and abetting.

The government also focuses on the injunction's bar against "investigating" on the basis of speech protected by the First Amendment and points to the broad discretion enjoyed by executive agencies in investigating suspected criminal misconduct. The government relies on language in the permanent injunction that differs from the exact language in the preliminary injunction. The permanent injunction order enjoins the government "from initiating any investigation solely on" the basis of "a recommendation for the use of medical marijuana based on a sincere medical judgment." The preliminary injunction order provided that "the government may not take administrative action against physicians for recommending marijuana unless the government in good faith believes that it has substantial evidence of [conspiracy or aiding and abetting]."

The government, however, has never argued that the two injunctive orders differ in any material way. Because we read the permanent injunction as enjoining essentially the same conduct as the preliminary injunction, we interpret this portion of the permanent injunction to mean only that the government may not initiate an investigation of a physician solely on the basis of a recommendation of marijuana within a bona fide doctor-patient relationship, unless the government in good faith believes that it has substantial evidence of criminal conduct. Because a doctor's recommendation does not itself constitute illegal conduct, the portion of the injunction barring investigations solely on that basis does not interfere with the federal government's ability to enforce its laws.

The government policy does, however, strike at core First Amendment interests of doctors and patients. An integral component of the practice of medicine is the communication between a doctor and a patient. Physicians must be able to speak frankly and openly to patients. That need has been recognized by the courts through the application of the common law doctor-patient privilege.

The doctor-patient privilege reflects "the imperative need for confidence and trust" inherent in the doctor-patient relationship and recognizes that "a physician must know all that a patient can articulate in order to identify and to treat disease; barriers to full disclosure would impair diagnosis and treatment." *Trammel v. United States*, 445 U.S. 40, 51 (1980). The Supreme Court has recognized that physician speech is entitled to First Amendment protection because of the significance of the doctor-patient relationship.

* * *

Being a member of a regulated profession does not, as the government suggests, result in a surrender of First Amendment rights. To the contrary, professional speech may be entitled to "the strongest protection our Constitution has to offer." Even commercial speech by professionals is entitled to First Amendment protection. Attorneys have rights to speak freely subject only to the government regulating with "narrow specificity."

In its most recent pronouncement on regulating speech about controlled substances, the Supreme Court found that provisions in the Food and Drug Modernization Act of 1997 that restricted physicians and pharmacists from advertising compounding drugs violated the First Amendment. The Court refused to make the "questionable assumption that doctors would prescribe unnecessary medications" and rejected the government's argument that "people would make bad decisions if given truthful information about compounded drugs." The federal government argues in this case that a doctor-patient discussion about marijuana might lead the patient to make a bad decision, essentially asking us to accept the same assumption rejected by the Court in *Thompson*. We will not do so. Instead, we take note of the Supreme Court's admonition in *Thompson*: "If the First Amendment means anything, it means that regulating speech must be a last—not first—resort. Yet here it seems to have been the first strategy the Government thought to try."

The government's policy in this case seeks to punish physicians on the basis of the content of doctor-patient communications. Only doctor-patient conversations that include discussions of the medical use of marijuana trigger the policy. Moreover, the policy does not merely prohibit the discussion of marijuana; it condemns expression of a particular viewpoint, i.e., that medical marijuana would likely help a specific patient. Such condemnation of particular views is especially troubling in the First Amendment context. "When the government targets not subject matter but particular views taken by speakers on a subject, the violation of the First Amendment is all the more blatant." Indeed, even content-based restrictions on speech are "presumptively invalid." The government's policy is materially similar to the limitation struck down in *Legal Services Corp. v. Velazquez*, 531 U.S. 533 (2001), that prevented attorneys from "present[ing] all the reasonable and well-grounded arguments necessary for proper resolution of the case." In *Velazquez*, a government restriction prevented legal assistance organizations receiving federal funds from challenging existing welfare laws. Like the limitation in *Velazquez*, the government's policy here "alter[s] the traditional role" of medical professionals by "prohibit[ing] speech necessary to the proper functioning of those systems." * * *

To survive First Amendment scrutiny, the government's policy must have the requisite "narrow specificity." Throughout this litigation, the government has been unable to articulate exactly what speech is proscribed, describing it only in terms of speech the patient believes to be a recommendation of marijuana. Thus, whether a doctor-patient discussion of medical marijuana constitutes a "recommendation" depends largely on the meaning the patient attributes to the doctor's words. This is not permissible under the First Amendment. In *Thomas*, the court struck down a state statute that failed to make a clear distinction between union membership, solicitation, and mere "discussion, laudation, [or] general advocacy." The distinction rested instead on the meaning the listeners attributed to spoken words. The government's policy, like the statute in *Thomas*, leaves doctors and patients "no security for free discussion." As Judge Smith appropriately noted in granting the preliminary injunction, "when faced with the fickle iterations of the government's policy, physicians have been forced to suppress speech that would not rise to the level of that which the government constitutionally may prohibit."

Our decision is consistent with principles of federalism that have left states as the primary regulators of professional conduct. We must "show respect for the sovereign States that comprise our Federal Union. * * *

For all of the foregoing reasons, we affirm the district court's order entering a permanent injunction.

AFFIRMED.

NOTES AND QUESTIONS

1.   **Key distinctions.** Does a physician have a First Amendment right to prescribe marijuana?

2.   More line drawing. Does a physician know that recommending marijuana results in a violation of the Controlled Substances Act? As such, is the doctor's recommendation a federal crime? For example, would the doctor be guilty of aiding and abetting a violation of the CSA?

3.   A view from the Supreme Court. Is Judge Schroeder's opinion convincing? *Conant* and cases coming to a similar conclusion have been important in states where the state authorizes medical marijuana. Apart from the pragmatic effect of the decision (giving physicians some assurances that they can discuss marijuana with patients), are you convinced by the court's reasoning? While the Supreme Court has still not addressed the precise issue in *Conant*, language in *National Institute of Family and Life Advocates v. Becerra,* 585 U.S. ___ (2018), the Court held that the First Amendment limits what states can tell doctors and other health care providers that they can and cannot say. Justice Thomas' rhetoric was quite powerful, "As with other kinds of speech, regulating the content of professionals' speech 'pose[s] the inherent risk that the Government seeks not to advance a legitimate regulatory goal, but to suppress unpopular ideas or information.'" He pointed to instances when, during the Cultural Revolution in China, the government forced physicians to convince peasants to use contraceptives. During the 1930s, the Soviet government forced physicians to reject medical leave for patients so that their patients, who were working on the Siberian railroad construction, would not miss work. He also cited the example of Nazi Germany, where "the Third Reich systematically violated the separation between state ideology and medical discourse."

4.   More on *Conant's* holding. Judge Schroeder's opinion sets out the traditional elements that the government must prove to establish a person's liability as an accomplice to an underlying offense: "(1) that the accused had the specific intent to facilitate the commission of a crime by another, (2) that the accused had the requisite intent of the underlying substantive offense, (3) that the accused assisted or participated in the commission of the underlying substantive offense, and (4) that someone committed the underlying substantive offense." Which element is missing, according to Judge Schroeder?

5.   Physicians run afoul of *Conant*. In considering the previous questions, do a Google search for "medical marijuana doctor," or similar terms. You will come up with any number of websites, many advertising that the doctors at their facilities will perform an exam and can provide a recommendation to allow the patient to procure medical marijuana. Does that alter your view of the court's analysis in *Conant v. Walters*?

PROBLEM 8-2

Dr. Greta Green is a co-owner of Cannabis Health, a medical marijuana dispensary in a state that has authorized doctors to recommend medical marijuana to qualified patients. Cannabis Health aggressively advertises marijuana's many medical uses, including stress relief and relief from pain. Its ads state that a person can bring medical records but absent proof of existing conditions, the ads explain that a person can get a doctor's recommendation upon completion of questionnaire about that person's health history. The ads explain that a personal appearance is usually required, absent some physical limitation that prevents a person from coming to Cannabis Health. The ads explain further that the cost of the examination is $50. Dr. Green has issued over a thousand recommendations, which she provides in writing so that the person seeking medical marijuana can submit the letter as proof of compliance with state law. Recently, a local police officer applied for a recommendation and was able to get it online with little explanation for why he needed medical marijuana other than the occasional experience of stress. The officer believes that Cannabis Health is a scam and that Dr. Green is an accomplice to the illegal distribution of marijuana under state law. After her arrest for disturbing marijuana in violation of state law, Dr. Green has hired you as her attorney. She explains that she believed that her conduct was lawful under the *Conant* case. Discuss fully whether she has a valid defense under *Conant*.

C. FREE EXERCISE OF RELIGION

As indicated in the previous section, litigants have had little success in raising First Amendment speech claims in cases involving marijuana. But can one have a valid claim that she uses marijuana as part of her religion? The cases in this section involve the interface between the First Amendment's Free Exercise clause and the Religious Freedom Restoration Act of 1993, 42 U.S.C. § 2000bb et. seq. (RFRA). Technically, RFRA provides a litigant who makes a Free Exercise claim with added protection against action by the federal government. As described below, when the government acts in a way that impairs the exercise of religion, RFRA forces the government to meet a heightened standard of scrutiny to justify its regulation of a religious practice; or as the court in *United States v. Quaitance* stated: RFRA "forbids the federal government from substantially burdening sincere religious exercises absent a countervailing compelling governmental interest."

Marijuana proponents have at times argued that the Supreme Court's decision in *Gonzales v. O Centro Espirita Beneficente Uniao do Vegetal*, 546 U.S. 418 (2006) provides support for their cause. In *O Centro*, a religious sect with origins in the Amazon Rainforest that uses a hallucinogenic drug as part of its communion successfully challenged the federal government's seizure of its ceremonial tea, despite the government's contention that the tea violated the Controlled Substances Act. The Supreme Court found for the religious sect. But the precedent provides marijuana users little support in most cases: the government conceded that the practice was "a sincere exercise of religion," often at issue in other cases. In addition, the case was not based on a Free Exercise challenge. Instead, the Court found that the government had not met its burden of the Religious Freedom Restoration Act of 1993, 42 U.S.C. § 2000bb et. seq.

The following case is more typical of cases in which litigants have attempted to claim that their use of marijuana is part of their religious

·ices, thereby protected under federal law. The following case may be
·cial importance because its author, then Judge Neil Gorsuch, is now
·ate Justice Gorsuch.

UNITED STATES V. QUAINTANCE

United States Court of Appeals for the Tenth Circuit
608 F.3d 717 (10th Cir. 2010)

GORSUCH, J.

Danuel and Mary Quaintance responded to their indictment for
conspiracy and possession with intent to distribute marijuana with a
motion to dismiss. They didn't deny their involvement with the drug, but
countered that they are the founding members of the Church of
Cognizance, which teaches that marijuana is a deity and sacrament. As a
result, they submitted, any prosecution of them is precluded by the
Religious Freedom Restoration Act ("RFRA"), which forbids the federal
government from substantially burdening sincere religious exercises
absent a countervailing compelling governmental interest.

After taking extensive evidence, the district court denied the motion
to dismiss. It held, as a matter of law, that the Quaintances' professed
beliefs are not religious but secular. In addition and in any event, the
district court found, as a matter of fact, that the Quaintances don't
sincerely hold the religious beliefs they claim to hold, but instead seek to
use the cover of religion to pursue secular drug trafficking activities.

After this ruling, the Quaintances pled guilty to the charges against
them but reserved their right to appeal the district court's denial of their
motion to dismiss. They do that now. Because we conclude the district court
did not err in finding the Quaintances insincere in their beliefs, we affirm
its judgment.

* * *

In due course, the Quaintances moved to dismiss the indictment under
RFRA, 42 U.S.C. § 2000bb *et seq*. They explained that they are members of
the Church of Cognizance, which Mr. Quaintance founded in 1991. The
church is organized around the teaching that marijuana is a deity and
sacrament. The Quaintances claimed that they sincerely hold this belief
and that possession (and consumption) of marijuana is essential to their
religious exercise. Accordingly, they argued the prosecution against them
unduly burdened their religious beliefs and thus could not stand under
RFRA.

RFRA allows religious adherents to challenge government activities
that encroach on their beliefs. To make out a prima facie RFRA defense, a
criminal defendant must show by a preponderance of the evidence that
government action (1) substantially burdens (2) a religious belief, not
merely a philosophy or way of life, (3) that the defendant sincerely holds.

If a defendant makes that showing, it falls to the government to show that the challenged action is justified as the least restrictive means of furthering a compelling governmental interest. Here, the government conceded that criminal punishment for the charged crimes constitutes a substantial burden, leaving the Quaintances to prove the religiosity and sincerity prongs of their prima facie defense.

The Quaintances sought and received an evidentiary hearing in connection with their motion to dismiss. That hearing eventually consumed approximately three days, during which the district court received live testimony from ten witnesses as well as argument and briefing from counsel. At the end of it all, the district court issued an extensive 38-page opinion denying the motion to dismiss and concluding that the Quaintances had failed to establish either of the remaining elements of their prima facie case.

In the district court's view, the Quaintances failed to show that their beliefs about marijuana qualify as "religious" within the meaning of RFRA. Even if they had succeeded on that score, the court added, they couldn't show that they sincerely held their professed religious beliefs, rather than simply used them as cover for secular drug activities.

* * *

Under our precedents, sincerity of religious beliefs "is a factual matter," and so, "as with historical and other underlying factual determinations, we defer to the district court's findings, reversing only if those findings are clearly erroneous." That is, we may disturb the district court's finding of insincerity "only if the court's finding is without factual support in the record or if, after reviewing all the evidence, we are left with a definite and firm conviction that a mistake has been made." *Aquila, Inc. v. C.W. Mining,* 545 F.3d 1258, 1263 (10th Cir. 2008). To be clearly erroneous, "a finding must be more than possibly or even probably wrong; the error must be pellucid to any objective observer." *Watson v. United States,* 485 F.3d 1100, 1108 (10th Cir. 2007).

As the district court noted, numerous pieces of evidence in this case strongly suggest that the Quaintances' marijuana dealings were motivated by commercial or secular motives rather than sincere religious conviction.

First, the Quaintances' colleague and putative fellow church member, Mr. Kripner, testified that the Quaintances considered themselves in the marijuana "business." According to Mr. Kripner, the Quaintances bought marijuana from him about once every two weeks. The quantities involved ranged from a half pound to a pound, while the prices ran from $350 to $600, which the Quaintances paid in cash, mostly in $100 and $20 bills. The Quaintances indicated to Mr. Kripner that they were reselling the marijuana, sometimes telling him "it went really fast," other times saying "they were still sitting on some of it." At one point they complained to Mr.

Kripner that he'd sold them "bad weed," saying they "couldn't get rid of it" and it "was going to hurt their business."

②   Second, that business was apparently integral to the particular marijuana transaction resulting in the Quaintances' arrest. As the district court noted, Mr. Butts's arrest and consequent need for $100,000 bail gave the Quaintances a powerful motive "to undertake a large drug transaction for monetary, as opposed to religious, purposes." *Quaintance,* 471 F.Supp.2d at 1173. And they made it clear to Mr. Kripner that bail money was precisely the goal of the "job" they recruited him to perform. To that end, they coordinated a fairly intricate process whereby Mr. Kripner, together with the Quaintances, was to meet up with backpack runners in the New Mexico desert, collect his marijuana cargo, and then transport the load to California. There, Mr. Kripner would park his car at a hotel, where the Quaintances had arranged for someone to take the car, remove the marijuana, and replace it with $100,000 for Mr. Kripner to return to the Quaintances. Had the whole plan not been short-circuited at the initial pick-up, two more trips were scheduled to follow, ultimately resulting in a $35,000 payday for Mr. Kripner. So it is that the very transaction at issue here was part of a lucrative scheme to raise money for a secular purpose.

③   Third, the Quaintances hastily inducted Mr. Kripner into the Church of Cognizance the night before he was to pick up the first load of marijuana for them. The Quaintances had previously suggested Mr. Kripner join their church, promising that it would legalize his marijuana use, but he had declined the offer. On the eve of his scheduled pick-up, though, he joined, signing a church membership pledge and receiving a certificate designating him an authorized church courier. But the Quaintances never had him read the pledge or asked if he shared their beliefs. And Mr. Kripner never considered marijuana a deity or sacrament. Rather, he testified that he joined the Church of Cognizance just so he could "do the load" the Quaintances hired him to transport. The timing and circumstances of all this, the district court found, tended to suggest that the Quaintances, too, "were acting for the sake of convenience, *i.e.,* because they believed the church would cloak Mr. Kripner with the protection of the law." *Quaintance,* 471 F.Supp.2d at 1174. That is, they inducted Mr. Kripner because they thought it might insulate their drug transactions from confiscation, "not because they had a sincere religious belief that marijuana is a sacrament and deity." *Id.*

④   Fourth, Mr. Kripner testified that he sold the Quaintances cocaine along with their marijuana purchases. He shared cocaine with Ms. Quaintance, then later started selling the Quaintances a quarter-ounce of the drug about once a month. The fact that the Quaintances bought cocaine for recreational purposes, the district court explained, tends to "undermine," though not foreclose, their assertion that they used another illegal drug (marijuana) for religious rather than secular purposes. *Quaintance,* 471 F.Supp.2d at 1174.

These four considerations convincingly support the district court's finding that the Quaintances' professed beliefs were not sincerely held.

* * *

Because the district court's finding of insincerity stands, it is unnecessary for us to address the district court's alternative holding that the Quaintances' proffered beliefs were not even religious in nature. Without the essential element of sincerity, their RFRA defense must fail. The judgment of the district court is affirmed.

NOTES AND QUESTIONS

1. **The smell test?** Does the defendants' claim seem plausible? What if the court allowed such a claim? What effect would it have on the federal government's policies reflected in the Controlled Substances Act?

2. **Similar cases.** Other cases have come to similar results. See, e.g., *Religion of Jesus Church THC v. Ashcroft,* No. 04-CV-200 (D. Haw. 2004); *Olsen v. DEA,* 878 F. 2d 1458 (D.C. Cir. 1989).

3. **RFRA and the First Amendment.** Like *O Centro, Quaintance* involved the application of RFRA, not a direct First Amendment free exercise claim. Can you see why a litigant would not have any better chance under the First Amendment than under RFRA?

4. **Second guessing sincerity of beliefs.** In a strongly worded dissent in *Burwell v. Hobby Lobby Stores, Inc.,* 134 S.Ct. 2751 (2014), Justice Ginsburg questioned whether courts should be in the business of evaluating the sincerity of asserted religious beliefs. *Id.* at 2805. Two commentators questioned whether that argument is sound: although courts have no business evaluating underlying religious truths, they routinely make factual determinations whether a person asserting to hold those beliefs is truthful. See, Ben Adams and Cynthia Barmore, *Questioning Sincerely: The Role for Courts after Hobby Lobby,* 67 Stanford L. Rev. Online 59 (2014). Who has the better argument, Justice Ginsburg or Adams and Barmore?

D. RIGHT TO BEAR ARMS

Federal law prohibits a person who uses marijuana from possessing a firearm or ammunition. See 18 U.S.C. §§ 922(g)(3), 929(1)–(2); C.F.R. § 478.11 (2016). The Bureau of Alcohol, Tobacco, Firearms and Explosives (ATF) enforces the rule, in part, with a question on the form that determines eligibility to buy a firearm. A false answer is punishable as a federal crime, with a maximum possible term of five years in prison. The ATF has made clear that the rule applies in states that have legalized medical or recreational marijuana. The federal statute and the ATF's position on the issue obviously raise a Second Amendment question: to what extent does the ban on gun ownership violate the Second Amendment? Not surprisingly, courts have had to resolve that question. The next decision is a leading case on point.

WILSON V. LYNCH

United States Court of Appeals for the Ninth Circuit
835 F.3d 1083 (9th Cir. 2016)

RAKOFF, J.

Plaintiff-Appellant S. Rowan Wilson acquired a Nevada medical marijuana registry card. She then sought to purchase a firearm, but the firearms dealer knew that Wilson held a registry card. Consistent with a letter issued by the Bureau of Alcohol, Tobacco, Firearms, and Explosives ("ATF"), the dealer refused to sell Wilson a firearm because of her registry card. Wilson sued, challenging the federal statutes, regulations, and guidance that prevented her from buying a gun. The district court dismissed Wilson's complaint, and Wilson appealed. We affirm.

BACKGROUND

Marijuana is classified as a Schedule I controlled substance under the Controlled Substances Act, 21 U.S.C. § 812. As a Schedule I controlled substance, marijuana, under federal law, is deemed to have "no currently accepted medical use in treatment[, and] [t]here is a lack of accepted safety for use of the . . . substance under medical supervision." *Id.* § 812(b)(1)(B) & (C).

This, however, is not the view of the State of Nevada. Although Nevada law criminalizes the possession of marijuana, Nevada's Constitution was amended in 2000 to provide for medical marijuana use. Under a statutory scheme enacted pursuant to this constitutional amendment, a holder of a valid marijuana registration ID card (a "registry card") is exempt from state prosecution for marijuana-related crimes. To acquire a registry card, an applicant must provide documentation from an attending physician affirming that the applicant has a chronic or debilitating medical condition, that the medical use of marijuana may mitigate the symptoms of the condition, and that the physician has explained to the applicant the risks and benefits of the medical use of marijuana. Cardholders must also comply with certain ongoing requirements, including limitations on the amount of marijuana they have at one time, as well as the requirement that they "[e]ngage in . . . the medical use of marijuana in accordance with the provisions of this chapter as justified to mitigate the symptoms or effects of a person's chronic or debilitating medical condition." A registry card is valid for one year and may be renewed annually by submitting updated written documentation from a physician.

Turning to federal firearms provisions, under 18 U.S.C. § 922(g)(3) no person "who is an unlawful user of or addicted to any controlled substance" may "possess . . . or . . . receive any firearm or ammunition." In addition, it is unlawful for "any person to sell or otherwise dispose of any firearm or ammunition to any person knowing or having reasonable cause to believe that such person . . . is an unlawful user of or addicted to any controlled substance." *Id.* § 922(d)(3).

The ATF has promulgated regulations implementing § 922 and defining a person "who is an unlawful user of or addicted to any controlled substance." *See* 27 C.F.R. § 478.11. The ATF has also developed Form 4473, which confirms eligibility for gun ownership under § 922. Prospective purchasers of firearms fill out Form 4473 when they seek to buy a firearm. Form 4473 includes Question 11.e., which asks "Are you an unlawful user of, or addicted to, marijuana or any depressant, stimulant, narcotic drug, or any other controlled substance?" *See* Firearms Transaction Record Part I—Over-the-Counter ("Form 4473"), https://www.atf.gov/file/61446/download. If the answer is "yes," the putative transaction is prohibited.

On September 21, 2011, the ATF issued an "Open Letter to All Federal Firearms Licensees" (the "Open Letter") that stated the following:

> [A]ny person who uses or is addicted to marijuana, regardless of whether his or her State has passed legislation authorizing marijuana use for medicinal purposes, is an unlawful user of or addicted to a controlled substance, and is prohibited by Federal law from possessing firearms or ammunition. Such persons should answer "yes" to question 11.e. on ATF Form 4473 . . . and you may not transfer firearms or ammunition to them. Further, if you are aware that the potential transferee is in possession of a card authorizing the possession and use of marijuana under State law, then you have "reasonable cause to believe" that the person is an unlawful user of a controlled substance. As such, you may not transfer firearms or ammunition to the person, even if the person answered "no" to question 11.e. on ATF Form 4473.

It was against this regulatory and statutory context that appellant Wilson, on May 12, 2011, was issued a marijuana registry card by the State of Nevada. A few months later, on October 4, 2011, Wilson sought to purchase a firearm from Custom Firearms & Gunsmithing in the small community of Moundhouse, Nevada. As Wilson began to fill out Form 4473, the owner of the store, Frederick Hauser, stopped her from completing Question 11.e, which asked whether Wilson was an unlawful user of a controlled substance. Hauser explained that, because (as Hauser already knew) Wilson held a marijuana registry card, Wilson was deemed an unlawful user of a controlled substance and therefore someone to whom he could not sell a firearm without jeopardizing his federal firearms license. Wilson handed Hauser Form 4473 with Question 11.e. left blank. Hauser, who had received the ATF Open Letter three days earlier, nonetheless refused to sell her a firearm. Wilson alleges that Hauser's refusal to sell her a firearm was a direct consequence of Hauser's receipt of the Open Letter.

On October 18, 2011, Wilson filed the present action against the Government and, on December 17, 2012, filed a First Amended Complaint (the "FAC"). Wilson asserted five causes of action: (1) violation of the Second Amendment, (2) violation of the Equal Protection Clause of the Fifth Amendment, (3) violation of the procedural Due Process Clause of the Fifth Amendment, (4) violation of the substantive Due Process Clause of the Fifth Amendment, and (5) violation of the First Amendment. Wilson sought declarations that 18 U.S.C. § 922(g)(3) and (d)(3), as well as all derivative regulations, such as 27 C.F.R. § 478.11, and the Open Letter, were unconstitutional. Wilson also sought a permanent injunction barring enforcement of § 922(g)(3) and (d)(3), all derivative regulations, and the Open Letter. Finally, Wilson sought compensatory and punitive damages, costs, fees, and expenses.

On January 31, 2013, the Government filed a motion to dismiss the FAC. In her opposition to Defendants' motion to dismiss, Wilson asserted that the Open Letter also violated the Administrative Procedure Act ("APA"). On March 11, 2014, the district court granted the Government's motion to dismiss the FAC. The district court also denied Wilson leave to amend the FAC to raise an APA claim, concluding that amendment would be futile. Wilson timely appealed.

DISCUSSION

* * *

Wilson's first constitutional challenge to 18 U.S.C. § 922(d)(3), 27 C.F.R. § 478.11, and the Open Letter purportedly rests on the Second Amendment. Specifically, Wilson claims that these provisions unconstitutionally burden her individual right to bear arms. The district court concluded, however, that Wilson's Second Amendment challenge failed under our decision in *United States v. Dugan*, 657 F.3d 998 (9th Cir. 2011). In *Dugan*, we held that the Second Amendment does not protect the rights of unlawful drug users to bear arms, in the same way that it does not protect the rights of "felons and the mentally ill," The Government argues that if the Second Amendment does not protect the rights of unlawful drug users to bear arms, it must not protect any possible rights of unlawful drug users to purchase firearms or of firearm dealers to sell to unlawful drug users. Therefore, were Wilson an unlawful drug user, she would be beyond the reach of the Second Amendment, and her claims would fail categorically.

However, taking Wilson's allegations as true, as we must on an appeal from a motion to dismiss, she is not actually an unlawful drug user. Instead, she alleges that, although she obtained a registry card, she chose not to use medical marijuana for various reasons, such as the difficulties of acquiring medical marijuana in Nevada, as well as a desire to make a political statement. Regardless of her motivations, we agree that Wilson's claims do not fall under the direct scope of *Dugan*.

This does not mean that her Second Amendment claim succeeds. We have adopted a two-step inquiry to determine whether a law violates the Second Amendment. We ask (1) "whether the challenged law burdens conduct protected by the Second Amendment and (2) if so . . . apply an appropriate level of scrutiny." *United States v. Chovan*, 735 F.3d 1127, 1136 (9th Cir. 2013). Following this approach, we apply intermediate scrutiny and uphold 18 U.S.C. § 922(d)(3), 27 C.F.R. § 478.11, and the Open Letter.

i.   Whether 18 U.S.C. § 922(d)(3), 27 C.F.R. § 478.11, and the Open Letter Burden Protected Conduct

At *Chovan*'s first step, we ask "whether the challenged law burdens conduct protected by the Second Amendment, based on a historical understanding of the scope of the [Second Amendment] right, or whether the challenged law falls within a well-defined and narrowly limited category of prohibitions that have been historically unprotected." *Jackson v. City & County of San Francisco*, 746 F.3d 953, 960 (9th Cir. 2014) With respect to Wilson, this inquiry is straightforward: because Wilson insists that she is not an unlawful drug user, a convicted felon, or a mentally-ill person, she is not a person historically prohibited from possessing firearms under the Second Amendment. Accordingly, by preventing Wilson from purchasing a firearm, 18 U.S.C. § 922(d)(3), 27 C.F.R. § 478.11, and the Open Letter directly burden her core Second Amendment right to possess a firearm, and we proceed to *Chovan*'s second step.

ii.   Which Level of Scrutiny Applies to 18 U.S.C. § 922(d)(3), 27 C.F.R. § 478.11, and the Open Letter

The appropriate level of scrutiny for laws that burden conduct protected by the Second Amendment "depend[s] on (1) how close the law comes to the core of the Second Amendment right and (2) the severity of the law's burden on the right." *Chovan*, 735 F.3d at 1138. Application of the first prong is guided by "*Heller*'s holding that the Second Amendment has 'the core lawful purpose of self-defense,' and that 'whatever else it leaves to future evaluation, [the Second Amendment] surely elevates above all other interests the right of law-abiding, responsible citizens to use arms in defense of hearth and home.'" *Jackson*, 746 F.3d at 961. Here, as previously stated, 18 U.S.C. § 922(d)(3), 27 C.F.R. § 478.11, and the Open Letter burden the core of Wilson's Second Amendment right because they prevent her from purchasing a firearm under certain circumstances and thereby impede her right to use arms to defend her "hearth and home." *Id.*

With respect to the second prong of the second *Chovan* step,

> laws which regulate only the *manner* in which persons may exercise their Second Amendment rights are less burdensome

than those which bar firearm possession completely. Similarly, firearm regulations which leave open alternative channels for self-defense are less likely to place a severe burden on the Second Amendment right than those which do not. *Id.*

The burden on Wilson's core Second Amendment right is not severe. Title 18 U.S.C. § 922(d)(3), 27 C.F.R. § 478.11, and the Open Letter bar only the sale of firearms to Wilson—not her possession of firearms. Wilson could have amassed legal firearms before acquiring a registry card, and 18 U.S.C. § 922(d)(3), 27 C.F.R. § 478.11, and the Open Letter would not impede her right to keep her firearms or to use them to protect herself and her home. In addition, Wilson could acquire firearms and exercise her right to self-defense at any time by surrendering her registry card, thereby demonstrating to a firearms dealer that there is no reasonable cause to believe she is an unlawful drug user.

Because 18 U.S.C. § 922(d)(3), 27 C.F.R. § 478.11, and the Open Letter do not place a severe burden on Wilson's core right to defend herself with firearms, we apply intermediate scrutiny to determine whether these laws and guidance pass constitutional muster.

iii. Applying Intermediate Scrutiny to 18 U.S.C. § 922(d)(3), 27 C.F.R. 478.11, and the Open Letter

Intermediate scrutiny "require[s] (1) the government's stated objective to be significant, substantial, or important; and (2) a reasonable fit between the challenged regulation and the asserted objective." *Chovan*, 735 F.3d at 1139. Wilson concedes that the Government had a substantial interest in enacting § 922(d)(3) to prevent gun violence. However, she argues that the fit between 27 C.F.R. § 478.11 and the Open Letter, on the one hand, and violence prevention, on the other, is not reasonable because 27 C.F.R. § 478.11 and the Open Letter deprive so many non-violent people, such as Wilson, who hold registry cards for political reasons, of their Second Amendment rights.

The Government argues that empirical data and legislative determinations support a strong link between drug use and violence. As to the first, studies and surveys relied on in similar cases suggest a significant link between drug use, including marijuana use, and violence. While it would have been helpful for the Government to provide the studies in this case, Wilson has not challenged their methodology. We therefore have no occasion to evaluate the reliability of the studies and surveys, and instead accept them as probative.

Moreover, legislative determinations also support the link between drug use and violence. In particular, Congress enacted 18 U.S.C. § 922(g)(3), which bars unlawful drug users from possessing firearms, "to keep firearms out of the hands of presumptively risky people." *Dickerson v. New Banner Inst., Inc.*, 460 U.S. 103, 112 (1983). It is beyond dispute that illegal drug users, including marijuana users, are likely as a consequence of that use to experience altered or impaired mental states that affect their judgment and that can lead to irrational or unpredictable behavior. They are also more likely to have negative interactions with law enforcement officers because they engage in criminal activity. Finally, they frequently make their purchases through black market sources who themselves frequently resort to violence.

It may be argued that medical marijuana users are less likely to commit violent crimes, as they often suffer from debilitating illnesses, for which marijuana may be an effective palliative. They also may be less likely than other illegal drug users to interact with law enforcement officers or make purchases through illicit channels. But those hypotheses are not sufficient to overcome Congress's reasonable conclusion that the use of such drugs raises the risk of irrational or unpredictable behavior with which gun use should not be associated.

By citing to the link between unlawful drug users and violence in this case, however, the Government incorrectly conflates registry cardholders with unlawful drug users. While these two categories of people overlap, they are not identical. The Government's showings of the link between drug use and violence would be sufficient were we applying intermediate scrutiny to 18 U.S.C. § 922(g)(3), which bars unlawful drug users from possessing firearms. But Wilson flatly maintains that she is not an unlawful drug user and is instead challenging a set of laws that bar non-drug users from purchasing firearms if there is only reasonable cause to believe that they are unlawful drug users, for instance, if they hold a registry card. Wilson correctly points out that the degree of fit between these laws and the ultimate aim of preventing gun violence is not as tight as the fit with laws like 18 U.S.C. § 922(g)(3), which affect only illegal drug users.

Nonetheless, the degree of fit between 18 U.S.C. § 922(d)(3), 27 C.F.R. § 478.11, and the Open Letter and the aim of preventing gun violence is still reasonable, which is sufficient to survive intermediate scrutiny. The connection between these laws and that aim requires only one additional logical step: individuals who firearms dealers have reasonable cause to believe are illegal drug users are more likely actually to be illegal drug users (who, in turn, are more likely to be involved with violent crimes). With respect to marijuana registry cards, there may be some small population of individuals who—although obtaining a marijuana registry card for medicinal purposes—instead hold marijuana registry cards only for expressive purposes. But it is eminently reasonable for federal regulators to assume that a registry cardholder is much more likely to be a marijuana user than an individual who does not hold a registry card.

Because the degree of fit between 18 U.S.C. § 922(d)(3), 27 C.F.R. § 478.11, and the Open Letter and their purpose of preventing gun violence is reasonable but not airtight, these laws will sometimes burden—albeit minimally and only incidentally—the Second Amendment rights of individuals who are reasonably, but erroneously, suspected of being unlawful drug users. However, the Constitution tolerates these modest collateral burdens in various contexts, and does so here as well. For instance, the Fourth Amendment allows an officer to burden an individual's right to be free from searches when the officer has "reason to believe" the person is armed and dangerous, *see Terry v. Ohio*, 392 U.S. 1, 27 (1968), a standard comparable to the "reasonable cause to believe" standard of § 922(d). Moreover, as previously noted, there are various ways for individuals in Wilson's position to minimize or eliminate altogether the burdens that 18 U.S.C. § 922(d)(3), 27 C.F.R. § 478.11, and the Open Letter place on their Second Amendment rights. Accordingly, 18 U.S.C. § 922(d)(3), 27 C.F.R. § 478.11, and the Open Letter survive intermediate scrutiny, and the district court did not err in dismissing Wilson's Second Amendment claims.

* * *

NOTES AND QUESTIONS

1.   **The Ninth Circuit's approach.** Does the court's holding surprise you? If so, why does it?

2.   **Expanded gun rights.** As a matter of history, when did Congress adopt the rules preventing a person who uses marijuana from possessing firearms or ammunition? At that time, what was the Supreme Court's view of Second Amendment? Prior to *District of Columbia v. Heller*, 554 U.S. 570 (2008) (upholding as a personal right, an individual's right to own a weapon), and *McDonald v. Chicago*, 561 U.S. 742 (2010) (holding that the Second Amendment applied to the states), the Court's case law on the Second Amendment was extremely limited. In its only major pronouncement on the meaning of the Second Amendment, the Court held in *United States v. Miller*, 307 U.S. 174 (1939) that a law criminalizing the possession of a sawed-off shotgun did not violate the Second Amendment. Advocates on both sides of the gun debate argue about the meaning of the case, but it can be read to mean that the right to bear arms relates to the need for a well-regulated militia, not a private right to possess a firearm.

3.   **Rethinking marijuana users.** When did the Court adopt the view that the Second Amendment creates a personal right to possess firearms? See *Heller* and *McDonald*, cited above. When Congress adopted the limitation on a marijuana user's right to bear arms, what might members of Congress thought about individuals who used marijuana? Is it possible for courts to rethink the question before the court in *Wilson v. Lynch?*

PROBLEM 8-3

Assume that Rowan Wilson's attorney contacted you after the court found against him. Wilson's attorney asks you whether applying for the writ of certiorari would be worthwhile. Specifically, the attorney asks what arguments you might make if you were able to argue the merits of the case to the Supreme Court. Discuss.

PROBLEM 8-4

Assume that well-designed studies demonstrate that states where recreational marijuana is available legally, violent crime rates have consistently declined. Further, assume that those studies demonstrate that marijuana users commit less violent crime than non-marijuana users. Armed with those studies, Plaintiff has filed a declaratory judgment action in which she claims that federal law preventing her from gun-ownership violates her Second Amendment right to bear arms. Discuss how the court should rule on her claim.

CHAPTER 9

AFFIRMATIVE DEFENSES, EXEMPTIONS, AND IMMUNITY

■ ■ ■

A. NECESSITY DEFENSE

The Comments to the Model Penal Code described the defense of necessity as follows: "[The defense] reflects the judgment that such a qualification on criminal liability, like the general requirements of culpability, is essential to the rationality of the criminal law. . ." American Law Institute, Model Penal Code and Commentaries, Comment to § 3.02 (1985). The same commentary offered the following examples of the defense: ". . . property may be destroyed to prevent the spread of fire. A speed limit may be violated in pursuing a suspected criminal. . . Mountain climbers lost in a storm may take refuge in a house or may appropriate provisions." While some states follow a narrow rule, requiring that the source of the necessity be a natural disaster, other states' necessity defense and that of the Model Penal Code are more general. Instead, provisions like § 3.02 balance the harm caused by a violation of the law with the harm to be avoided by that violation. If the harm of violating the law is less than the harm avoided, an offender is justified in violating the law. So destroying a home to prevent the spread of a fire that might otherwise destroy five homes is the morally and legally right decision.

Congress has not codified the defense of necessity. But the Supreme Court recognized the defense in *United States v. Bailey,* 444 U.S. 394 (1980).

Does a person who uses marijuana for medical purposes have a medical necessity defense? A person making such a defense would argue that she faces debilitating pain without using marijuana; balanced against that is the violation of the Controlled Substances Act. On balance, the defendant would argue, the violation of the CSA is minor by comparison to the suffering that the offender would experience without violating the law. Especially if the case got to a jury, such a defense might seem worthwhile.

As attractive as the defense might seem in such cases, a bit more careful look at the typical elements of the defense suggest why marijuana advocates may have been too optimistic in advancing the marijuana necessity argument. Typically, an offender must show a clear and imminent danger. While a marijuana user might be able to show a causal relationship between the violation of the law and an abatement of the harm (e.g., chronic pain), the offender must also show the absence of an effective legal way to avert the harm. In addition, measuring the balance of harms is often challenging: what counts as a social harm when one violates the law? And who (judge or jury) measures such harms? With those elements in mind, consider the following case:

I. FEDERAL LAW

UNITED STATES V. OAKLAND CANNABIS BUYERS' COOPERATIVE, ET AL.

United States Supreme Court
532 U.S. 483 (2001)

THOMAS, J. delivered the opinion of the Court.

The Controlled Substances Act prohibits the manufacture and distribution of various drugs, including marijuana. In this case, we must decide whether there is a medical necessity exception to these prohibitions. We hold that there is not.

I

In November 1996, California voters enacted an initiative measure entitled the Compassionate Use Act of 1996. Attempting "[t]o ensure that seriously ill Californians have the right to obtain and use marijuana for medical purposes," Cal. Health & Safety Code Ann. § 11362.5 (West Supp.2001), the statute creates an exception to California laws prohibiting the possession and cultivation of marijuana. These prohibitions no longer apply to a patient or his primary caregiver who possesses or cultivates marijuana for the patient's medical purposes upon the recommendation or approval of a physician. In the wake of this voter initiative, several groups organized "medical cannabis dispensaries" to meet the needs of qualified patients. *United States v. Cannabis Cultivators Club*, 5 F.Supp.2d 1086, 1092 (N.D.Cal.1998). Respondent Oakland Cannabis Buyers' Cooperative is one of these groups.

The Cooperative is a not-for-profit organization that operates in downtown Oakland. A physician serves as medical director, and registered nurses staff the Cooperative during business hours. To become a member, a patient must provide a written statement from a treating physician assenting to marijuana therapy and must submit to a screening interview. If accepted as a member, the patient receives an identification card entitling him to obtain marijuana from the Cooperative.

In January 1998, the United States sued the Cooperative and its executive director, respondent Jeffrey Jones (together, the Cooperative), in the United States District Court for the Northern District of California. Seeking to enjoin the Cooperative from distributing and manufacturing marijuana, the United States argued that, whether or not the Cooperative's activities are legal under California law, they violate federal law. Specifically, the Government argued that the Cooperative violated the Controlled Substances Act's prohibitions on distributing, manufacturing, and possessing with the intent to distribute or manufacture a controlled substance. Concluding that the Government had established a probability of success on the merits, the District Court granted a preliminary injunction.

The Cooperative did not appeal the injunction but instead openly violated it by distributing marijuana to numerous persons. To terminate these violations, the Government initiated contempt proceedings. In defense, the Cooperative contended that any distributions were medically necessary. Marijuana is the only drug, according to the Cooperative, that can alleviate the severe pain and other debilitating symptoms of the Cooperative's patients. The District Court rejected this defense, however, after determining there was insufficient evidence that each recipient of marijuana was in actual danger of imminent harm without the drug. The District Court found the Cooperative in contempt and, at the Government's request, modified the preliminary injunction to empower the United States Marshal to seize the Cooperative's premises. Although recognizing that "human suffering" could result, the District Court reasoned that a court's "equitable powers [do] not permit it to ignore federal law." Three days later, the District Court summarily rejected a motion by the Cooperative to modify the injunction to permit distributions that are medically necessary.

The Cooperative appealed both the contempt order and the denial of the Cooperative's motion to modify. . . . According to the Court of Appeals, the medical necessity defense was a "legally cognizable defense" that likely would apply in the circumstances. 190 F.3d, at 1114. Moreover, the Court of Appeals reasoned, the District Court erroneously "believed that it had no discretion to issue an injunction that was more limited in scope than the Controlled Substances Act itself." *Id.*, at 1114–1115. Because, according to the Court of Appeals, district courts retain "broad equitable discretion" to fashion injunctive relief, the District Court could have, and should have, weighed the "public interest" and considered factors such as the serious harm in depriving patients of marijuana. Remanding the case, the Court of Appeals instructed the District Court to consider "the criteria for a medical necessity exemption, and, should it modify the injunction, to set forth those criteria in the modification order." *Id.*, at 1115. Following these instructions, the District Court granted the Cooperative's motion to modify the injunction to incorporate a medical necessity defense.

The United States petitioned for certiorari to review the Court of Appeals' decision that medical necessity is a legally cognizable defense to violations of the Controlled Substances Act. Because the decision raises significant questions as to the ability of the United States to enforce the Nation's drug laws, we granted certiorari.

II

The Controlled Substances Act provides that, "[e]xcept as authorized by this subchapter, it shall be unlawful for any person knowingly or intentionally . . . to manufacture, distribute, or dispense, or possess with intent to manufacture, distribute, or dispense, a controlled substance." 21 U.S.C. § 841(a)(1). The subchapter, in turn, establishes exceptions. For marijuana (and other drugs that have been classified as "schedule I" controlled substances), there is but one express exception, and it is available only for Government-approved research projects, § 823(f). Not conducting such a project, the Cooperative cannot, and indeed does not, claim this statutory exemption.

The Cooperative contends, however, that notwithstanding the apparently absolute language of § 841(a), the statute is subject to additional, implied exceptions, one of which is medical necessity. According to the Cooperative, because necessity was a defense at common law, medical necessity should be read into the Controlled Substances Act. We disagree. As an initial matter, we note that it is an open question whether federal courts ever have authority to recognize a necessity defense not provided by statute. A necessity defense "traditionally covered the situation where physical forces beyond the actor's control rendered illegal conduct the lesser of two evils." *United States v. Bailey*, 444 U.S. 394, 410 (1980). Even at common law, the defense of necessity was somewhat controversial. And under our constitutional system, in which federal crimes are defined by statute rather than by common law, it is especially so. As we have stated: "Whether, as a policy matter, an exemption should be created is a question for legislative judgment, not judicial inference." *United States v. Rutherford*, 442 U.S. 544, 559 (1979). Nonetheless, we recognize that this Court has discussed the possibility of a necessity defense without altogether rejecting it. We need not decide, however, whether necessity can ever be a defense when the federal statute does not expressly provide for it. In this case, to resolve the question presented, we need only recognize that a medical necessity exception for marijuana is at odds with the terms of the Controlled Substances Act. The statute, to be sure, does not explicitly abrogate the defense. But its provisions leave no doubt that the defense is unavailable.

Under any conception of legal necessity, one principle is clear: The defense cannot succeed when the legislature itself has made a "determination of values." 1 W. LaFave & A. Scott, *Substantive Criminal Law* § 5.4, p. 629 (1986). In the case of the Controlled Substances Act, the statute reflects a determination that marijuana has no medical benefits worthy of an exception (outside the confines of a Government-approved research project). Whereas some other drugs can be dispensed and prescribed for medical use, the same is not true for marijuana. Indeed, for purposes of the Controlled Substances Act, marijuana has "no currently accepted medical use" at all. § 812.

The structure of the Act supports this conclusion. The statute divides drugs into five schedules, depending in part on whether the particular drug has a currently accepted medical use. The Act then imposes restrictions on the manufacture and distribution of the substance according to the schedule in which it has been placed. Schedule I is the most restrictive schedule. The Attorney General can include a drug in schedule I only if the drug "has no currently accepted medical use in treatment in the United States," "has a high potential for abuse," and has "a lack of accepted safety for use . . . under medical supervision." §§ 812(b)(1)(A)–(C). Under the statute, the Attorney General could not put marijuana into schedule I if marijuana had any accepted medical use.

The Cooperative points out, however, that the Attorney General did not place marijuana into schedule I. Congress put it there, and Congress was not required to find that a drug lacks an accepted medical use before including the drug in schedule I. We are not persuaded that this distinction has any significance to our inquiry. Under the Cooperative's logic, drugs that Congress places in schedule I could be distributed when medically necessary whereas drugs that the Attorney General places in schedule I could not. Nothing in the statute, however, suggests that there are two tiers of schedule I narcotics, with drugs in one tier more readily available than drugs in the other. On the contrary, the statute consistently treats all schedule I drugs alike. Moreover, the Cooperative offers no convincing explanation for why drugs that Congress placed on schedule I should be subject to fewer controls than the drugs that the Attorney General placed on the schedule. Indeed, the Cooperative argues that, in placing marijuana and other drugs on schedule I, Congress "wishe[d] to assert the most restrictive level of controls created by the [Controlled Substances Act]." If marijuana should be subject to the most restrictive level of controls, it should not be treated any less restrictively than other schedule I drugs.

The Cooperative further argues that use of schedule I drugs generally—whether placed in schedule I by Congress or the Attorney General—can be medically necessary, notwithstanding that they have "no currently accepted medical use." According to the Cooperative, a drug may not yet have achieved general acceptance as a medical treatment but may nonetheless have medical benefits to a particular patient or class of patients. We decline to parse the statute in this manner. It is clear from the text of the Act that Congress has made a determination that marijuana has no medical benefits worthy of an exception. The statute expressly contemplates that many drugs "have a useful and legitimate medical purpose and are necessary to maintain the health and general welfare of the American people," § 801(1), but it includes no exception at all for any medical use of marijuana. Unwilling to view this omission as an accident, and unable in any event to override a legislative determination manifest in a statute, we reject the Cooperative's argument.

Finally, the Cooperative contends that we should construe the Controlled Substances Act to include a medical necessity defense in order to avoid what it considers to be difficult constitutional questions. In particular, the Cooperative asserts that, shorn of a medical necessity defense, the statute exceeds Congress' Commerce Clause powers, violates the substantive due process rights of patients, and offends the fundamental liberties of the people under the Fifth, Ninth, and Tenth Amendments. As the Cooperative acknowledges, however, the canon of constitutional avoidance has no application in the absence of statutory ambiguity. Because we have no doubt that the Controlled Substances Act cannot bear a medical necessity defense to distributions of marijuana, we do not find guidance in this avoidance principle. Nor do we consider the underlying constitutional issues today. Because the Court of Appeals did not address these claims, we decline to do so in the first instance.

For these reasons, we hold that medical necessity is not a defense to manufacturing and distributing marijuana.* * *

The judgment of the Court of Appeals is reversed, and the case is remanded for further proceedings consistent with this opinion.

It is so ordered.

STEVENS, J., concurring in the judgment.

Lest the Court's narrow holding be lost in its broad dicta, let me restate it here: "[W]e hold that medical necessity is not a defense to manufacturing and distributing marijuana." This confined holding is consistent with our grant of certiorari, which was limited to the question "[w]hether the Controlled Substances Act, 21 U.S.C. 801 et seq., forecloses a medical necessity defense to the Act's prohibition against manufacturing and distributing marijuana, a Schedule I controlled substance." And, at least with respect to distribution, this holding is consistent with how the issue was raised and litigated below. As stated by the District Court, the question before it was "whether [respondents'] admitted distribution of marijuana for use by seriously ill persons upon a physician's recommendation violates federal law," and if so, whether such distribution "should be enjoined pursuant to the injunctive relief provisions of the federal Controlled Substances Act." *United States v. Cannabis Cultivators Club*, 5 F.Supp.2d 1086, 1091 (N.D.Cal.1998). . . .

Apart from its limited holding, the Court takes two unwarranted and unfortunate excursions that prevent me from joining its opinion. First, the Court reaches beyond its holding, and beyond the facts of the case, by suggesting that the defense of necessity is unavailable for anyone under the Controlled Substances Act. Because necessity was raised in this case as a defense to distribution, the Court need not venture an opinion on whether the defense is available to anyone other than distributors. Most notably, whether the defense might be available to a seriously ill patient for whom there is no alternative means of avoiding starvation or extraordinary suffering is a difficult issue that is not presented here.

Second, the Court gratuitously casts doubt on "whether necessity can ever be a defense" to any federal statute that does not explicitly provide for it, calling such a defense into question by a misleading reference to its existence as an "open question." By contrast, our precedent has expressed no doubt about the viability of the common-law defense, even in the context of federal criminal statutes that do not provide for it in so many words.

Indeed, the Court's comment on the general availability of the necessity defense is completely unnecessary because the Government has made no such suggestion. Cf. Brief for United States 17–18 (narrowly arguing that necessity defense cannot succeed if legislature has already "canvassed the issue" and precluded it for a particular statute. The Court's opinion on this point is pure dictum.

The overbroad language of the Court's opinion is especially unfortunate given the importance of showing respect for the sovereign States that comprise our Federal Union. That respect imposes a duty on federal courts, whenever possible, to avoid or minimize conflict between federal and state law, particularly in situations in which the citizens of a State have chosen to "serve as a laboratory" in the trial of "novel social and economic experiments without risk to the rest of the country." *New State Ice Co. v. Liebmann*, 285 U.S. 262, 311 (1932). In my view, this is such a case. By passing Proposition 215, California voters have decided that seriously ill patients and their primary caregivers should be exempt from prosecution under state laws for cultivating and possessing marijuana if the patient's physician recommends using the drug for treatment. This case does not call upon the Court to deprive all such patients of the benefit of the necessity defense to federal prosecution, when the case itself does not involve any such patients.

I join the Court's judgment of reversal because I agree that a distributor of marijuana does not have a medical necessity defense under the Controlled Substances Act. I do not, however, join the dicta in the Court's opinion.

NOTES AND QUESTIONS

1. **The government's strategy.** Why do you think that the government sued the Cooperative, rather than individual patients? According to the majority opinion, would it matter if the defendant was a cooperative or other supplier of marijuana as opposed to a user of marijuana?

2. **The role of legislative intent.** Justice Thomas suggested that medical necessity might be available in other federal prosecutions, but not in

Controlled Substances Act cases. What kinds of cases might Justice Thomas have in mind? Why might the defense be available in such cases?

3. A possible new challenge. Justice Breyer recused himself because his brother Charles Breyer was the United States District Judge who granted the instruction. Given that Justice Breyer recused himself and that Justice Gorsuch has replaced Justice Scalia, should litigants consider raising medical necessity in a case in which the offender is a marijuana user, not supplier?

II. STATE LAW

State courts do not have to follow *United States v. Oakland Cannabis Buyers' Cooperative*, if a marijuana user seeks to raise the defense to a violation of state law. After all, Justice Thomas was interpreting the availability of the defense in the limited context of the CSA. Was his reasoning sufficiently compelling or would you predict that an offender might have a better chance at prevailing in a state court? The following case explores that question.

SOUTH DAKOTA V. DUCHENEAUX
South Dakota Supreme Court
671 N.W.2d 841 (S.D. 2003)

SABERS, J.

Matthew Ducheneaux was charged with possession of marijuana. The magistrate judge ruled that Ducheneaux was entitled to use the affirmative defense of necessity under SDCL 22–5–1. The State appealed the decision to the circuit court. The circuit court reversed and Ducheneaux attempted to appeal to this Court. After this Court dismissed his appeal, Ducheneaux was tried and convicted by a jury in magistrate court. The circuit court denied his appeal and Ducheneaux appeals. We affirm.

FACTS

On July 15, 2000, Officer Vinson Weber of the Minnehaha County Police Reserve Unit was patrolling the Yankton Trail Park in Sioux Falls during the city's annual "Jazz Fest." As Officer Weber rode his bicycle on the bike path, he noticed a cloud of smoke and an odor of marijuana. Officer Weber testified that he observed Ducheneaux passing a marijuana cigarette to another man while exhaling smoke. When questioned, Ducheneaux informed the officer that he had a prescription for the marijuana and handed Officer Weber a pill bottle labeled as a prescription for Ducheneaux for the drug Diazepam. The bottle contained pills and marijuana cigarettes. Ducheneaux was arrested and charged under SDCL 22–42–6 with possessing less than two ounces of marijuana.

Ducheneaux is 36 years old and was rendered quadriplegic by an automobile accident in 1985. His paralysis is nearly complete except that he has some movement in his hands. Ducheneaux suffers from a condition called spastic paralysis, which causes him to experience spastic tremors and pain throughout his body. His condition is a result of his quadriplegia and is therefore incurable. The only option for Ducheneaux is to treat the symptoms.

Ducheneaux testified that he has not had success with traditional drug therapies. The magistrate noted that other drugs have "created intolerable and possible fatal side-effects." Among the legal prescription drugs sometimes used for spastic paralysis is Marinol, a synthetic tetrahydrocannabinol (THC). THC is the essential active component in marijuana. Although Ducheneaux has a prescription for Marinol, he feels that it produces dangerous side effects without the benefits of natural marijuana.

Ducheneaux testified that he was authorized in 1993 to obtain natural marijuana from the federal government through the Investigational New Drug (IND) program. Through this mechanism, the federal government currently allows eight individuals nationwide to access marijuana for medical purposes. Ducheneaux testified that in order to obtain the marijuana, he needed to find a local pharmacy willing to fulfill the responsibility of storing, securing and dispensing the federally issued marijuana. He claims he was unable to find such a pharmacy, but does not specify his efforts in that respect. There is no evidence in the record other than Ducheneaux's testimony to verify his authorization through the IND. His claim is questionable given the fact that the IND program was suspended and ceased taking applications in 1992. Regardless, his alleged authorization through the IND compassionate use program is irrelevant because the marijuana in his possession was not issued to him through that program.

Based on his determination that all of his legal options were unacceptable, Ducheneaux decided to illegally purchase and use whole marijuana instead.

The magistrate ruled that the affirmative defense of necessity under SDCL 22–5–1 was available to Ducheneaux. The circuit judge reversed the magistrate and Ducheneaux petitioned this Court for an intermediate appeal, but the petition was not accepted. Thereafter, a jury trial was held in magistrate court and Ducheneaux was convicted of possession of two ounces or less of marijuana.

Ducheneaux appeals his conviction raising one issue:

Whether the affirmative defense of necessity under SDCL 22–5–1 encompasses a defense of medical necessity against a charge of possession of marijuana.

We affirm.

STANDARD OF REVIEW

Statutory construction is a question of law which we review de novo. "We determine the intent of a statute from the statute as a whole, from its language, and by giving it its plain, ordinary and popular meaning." *Christensen v. Carson*, 533 N.W.2d 712, 714 (S.D.1995). Application of a statute to particular facts is also a question of law which we review de novo.

WHETHER THE AFFIRMATIVE DEFENSE OF NECESSITY UNDER SDCL 22–5–1 ENCOMPASSES A DEFENSE OF MEDICAL NECESSITY AGAINST A CHARGE OF POSSESSION OF MARIJUANA.

SDCL 22–5–1 provides:

A person may not be convicted of a crime based upon conduct in which he engaged because of the use or threatened use of unlawful force upon him or upon another person, which force or threatened use thereof a reasonable person in his situation would have been lawfully unable to resist.

The defense of necessity is an affirmative defense and as such, "requires the defendant to present credible evidence in its support prior to submission to the trier of fact." *State v. Bowers*, 498 N.W.2d 202, 205–206 (S.D.1993); SDCL 22–1–2(3). We have established a standard for determining whether a necessity defense under SDCL 22–5–1 is submissible to a jury:

[T]he defense of necessity [is] properly raised when the offered evidence, if believed by the jury, would support a finding by them that the offense . . . was justified by a reasonable fear of death or bodily harm so imminent or emergent that, according to ordinary standards of intelligence and morality, the desirability of avoiding the injury outweighs the desirability of avoiding the public injury arising from the offense committed[.]

State v. Boettcher, 443 N.W.2d 1, 2 (S.D.1989). The analysis requires the court to "examine the circumstances surrounding the crime based on a reasonable person standard." *Miller*, 313 N.W.2d at 462. In order to submit the defense to the jury, the defendant must show that he had a "reasonable fear of death or bodily harm imminent or emergent" at the time he engaged in the unlawful act. *Boettcher*, 443 N.W.2d at 2 (S.D.1982).

Ducheneaux argues that he can predict when an attack or spasm is coming and that a jury could reasonably find that his fear of such an attack is reasonable. He contends that his concern over the health consequences of traditional treatments also amounts to "fear of imminent or emergent bodily harm." Based on these fears, Ducheneaux asserts that a jury could reasonably find that his possession of marijuana was justified under SDCL 22–5–1 because he had done everything in his power to control his condition and maintain his health and smoking marijuana was his only remaining option.

While Ducheneaux's arguments are somewhat compelling in light of our interpretive language, they fail when compared to the plain language of the statute. Regardless of how reasonable his actions may have been, it is still necessary that the actions fall within the scope of the statute. If his unlawful behavior is not encompassed by the statute, then the magistrate erred as a matter of law in ruling that the defense was available. The statute requires a showing that the defendant committed the crime "because of the use or threatened use of unlawful force upon him or upon another person," and that the he was "lawfully unable to resist." SDCL 22–5–1. The circumstances of this case do not meet these elements.

Ducheneaux cannot show that he engaged in the crime because of the "use or threatened use of unlawful force upon him." The only "force" threatened or used in this situation is that which his medical condition forces his muscles to exert. To find that his spastic paralysis constitutes "unlawful force" strains the language of the statute. The statutory language clearly implies force or threat of force by another actor and requires that the force or threat of force be unlawful. * * * Furthermore, even assuming he has shown the requisite force, Ducheneaux cannot show that any such force was "unlawful." Laws govern the actions or inactions of people, not medical conditions. It would be a strained interpretation of SDCL 22–5–1 to hold that its language supports the construction that a medical condition can exert unlawful force against a person.

Ducheneaux also fails to show that the "force" at issue was one which he was "lawfully unable to resist." Although he testified that traditional medications have unwanted and detrimental side effects, Ducheneaux had legal means to combat the pain and spasms accompanying his condition. As noted at his trial, his doctors prescribed several medications for his condition, including Marinol, the legal form of THC, and valium. His belief that his alternative treatments are inferior is insufficient justification for choosing an illegal remedy.

Clearly, this is not the typical possession of marijuana case. The Court is not unmoved by Matthew Ducheneaux's circumstances. However, the Court is bound to act within the realm of its authority. We cannot judicially graft language into SDCL 22–5–1 to permit it to be used in these circumstances. The question whether a defense of necessity applies against a possession of marijuana charge when the marijuana is alleged to be medically necessary is legislative. The Legislature has clearly spoken on the issue of marijuana possession in SDCL 22–42–6 which provides in part, "[n]o person may knowingly possess marijuana." The language is unequivocal and therefore, whether such a defense is allowed in South Dakota remains a question of policy best answered by the State Legislature. The Legislature has given no indication that it recognizes this defense under SDCL 22–5–1 and the Court cannot take it upon itself to judicially legislate the defense.

GILBERTSON, C.J., and KONENKAMP, J. ZINTER, J. and MEIERHENRY, J. concur.

NOTES AND QUESTIONS

1. **Choosing the litigant.** Would Ducheneaux have been a better litigant to raise the medical necessity defense than the *Oakland Cannabis Buyers' Cooperative* case? Although the federal government virtually never prosecutes individual users, someone like Ducheneaux might bring an action for an injunction or declaratory relief to get the case before a federal court.

2. **Sound policy.** Should the medical necessity defense be available? What would the risks be of allowing such a defense? Are those risks justified, and if so, how are they justified?

3. **Necessity in other states.** To date, most states agree with *Ducheneaux* and reject the medical necessity defense in medical marijuana cases. Five state courts have recognized at least the possibility of the defense. *See Jenks v. State,* 582 So. 2d 676 (Fl. Dist. Ct. App. 1991), *review denied,* 589 So. 2d 292 (1991); *State v. Bachman,* 595 P. 2d 287 (Haw. 1979); *State v. Hastings,* 801 So. 2d 563 (Idaho 1990); *State v. Christen,* 704 A. 2d 335 (Me. 1997); *State v. Kurtz,* 309 P. 3d 472 (Wash. 2013).

4. **NORML's exhortation.** Although the defense has had only limited success, the National Organization for the Reform of Marijuana Laws continues to encourage the defense, as is evident on its website: http://norml. org/marijuana/medical/item/medical-necessity-defense.

5. **A full state-by-state review of necessity.** In the early 2000s, NORML provided a state-by-state review of the medical necessity defense, available at the following website: http://norml.org/pdf_files/brief_bank/ NORML_Legal_Brief_Bank_Medical_Necessity_Defense_by_State.pdf.

6. **Added complexity.** The following excerpt from *State v. Kurtz,* 309 P. 3d 472 (Wash. 2013) demonstrates some of the complex issues that can arise when a state has a statute like the CSA, listing marijuana as a Schedule I drug but also has authorized medical marijuana:

> The common law medical necessity defense for marijuana was first articulated in *State v. Diana,* 24 Wash.App. 908, 916, 604 P.2d 1312 (1979), by Division Three of the Court of Appeals. In *Diana,* the defendant argued a defense of medical necessity when he was charged with possession of marijuana. * * *

> The Court of Appeals subsequently called the necessity defense into question in *State v. Williams,* 93 Wash.App. 340, 347, 968 P.2d 26 (1998), *review denied,* 138 Wash.2d 1002, 984 P.2d 1034 (1999). The *Williams* court determined that an accepted medical use was an implicit element of the medical necessity defense, that the legislature

was tasked with this determination, and that it had determined there was no accepted medical use for marijuana when it classified marijuana as a schedule I substance. *Id.* at 346–47, 968 P.2d 26 (citing *Seeley v. State,* 132 Wash.2d 776, 940 P.2d 604 (1997) (holding that the statute designating marijuana as a schedule I controlled substance does not violate the Washington Constitution)). Thus, *Williams* concluded there could be no common law medical necessity defense for schedule I substances, including marijuana, and interpreted *Seeley* as overruling *Diana* and *Cole* by implication. *Id.* at 347, 968 P.2d 26.

One month before the *Williams* opinion was published, the people passed Initiative 692, which was later codified in chapter 69.51.A RCW as the Act. The Act declared that the medical use of marijuana by qualifying patients is an affirmative defense to possession of marijuana. Former RCW 69.51A.040 (1999). The Act also stated that "[t]he people of Washington state find that some patients with terminal or debilitating illnesses, under their physician's care, may benefit from the medical use of marijuana." Former RCW 69.51A.005 (1999). * * *

We first address whether the Court of Appeals in *Williams* correctly concluded that *Seeley* implicitly abolished the common law medical necessity defense. In *Seeley,* we considered whether the legislature's classification of marijuana as a schedule I substance under the Uniform Controlled Substances Act (UCSA), chapter 69.50 RCW, violated the Washington Constitution. *Seeley,* 132 Wash.2d at 786, 940 P.2d 604. Although the UCSA authorizes the board of pharmacy to schedule or reschedule substances considering, among other factors, the effect of the substance under former RCW 69.50.201 (1998), the legislature made the initial classification of marijuana as a schedule I substance. *Seeley,* 132 Wash.2d at 784, 940 P.2d 604. With that in mind, we determined that there was substantial evidence to support the legislature's action. *Id.* at 813, 940 P.2d 604. While acknowledging the existence of a medical necessity defense, we did not comment on its validity or overrule *Diana. Id.* at 798, 940 P.2d 604. Rather, we simply stated, "The recognition of a potential medical necessity defense for criminal liability of marijuana possession is not relevant in this equal protection analysis." *Id.* Thus, we did not discuss the viability of the common law medical necessity defense as applied to marijuana.

In rejecting the medical necessity defense for marijuana, the *Williams* court stated that *Seeley* "makes it clear that the decision of whether there is an accepted medical use for particular dugs has been vested in the Legislature by the Washington Constitution." *Williams,* 93 Wash.App. at 347, 968 P.2d 26. This is incorrect. In fact, we stated that "the determination of whether new evidence regarding marijuana's potential medical use should result in the *reclassification* of marijuana is a matter for legislative or administrative, not judicial, judgment." *Seeley,* 132 Wash.2d at 805–06, 940 P.2d 604 (emphasis added). Nothing in *Seeley* suggests that by classifying marijuana as a schedule I controlled substance, the legislature also made a finding that marijuana has no accepted medical benefit for purposes of the common law medical necessity defense. *Cf. State v. Hanson,* 138 Wash.App. 322, 330–31, 157 P.3d 438 (2007) (determining that the Act only provided an affirmative defense to a drug crime and was not inconsistent with the scheduling statute). Indeed, the legislature defers to the state board of pharmacy for future additions, deletions, and rescheduling of substances which strongly suggests that the question of medical efficacy is subject to change. Former RCW 69.50.201(a). To conclude that a determination of medical use for scheduling purposes constitutes a legislative value determination of a substance for purposes of a necessity defense would yield the anomalous result that the necessity defense could be abrogated and reinstated whenever the board of pharmacy chooses to reclassify a controlled substance. We reject the contention that by scheduling a drug the legislature has also decided the efficacy of that substance for purposes of a medical necessity defense.

Our conclusion is bolstered by the passage of chapter 69.51A RCW, which evidences the legislature's belief that despite its classification of marijuana as a schedule I controlled substance there may be a beneficial medical use for marijuana. RCW 69.51A.005(1)(a) states, "The legislature finds that . . . [t]here is medical evidence that some patients with terminal or debilitating medical conditions may, under their health care professional's care, benefit from the medical use of cannabis." Accordingly, we agree with Kurtz that neither the legislature's classification of marijuana as a schedule I substance nor our decision in *Seeley* regarding legislative classification of marijuana abrogates the medical necessity defense.

Does the Washington Supreme Court analysis make sense?

PROBLEM 9-1

Assume that Defendant is severely impaired as a result of her military service in Iraq. She has confined to a wheelchair since she returned home from the war. Upon her return home, Veterans Administration doctors prescribed OxyContin, which led to her addiction to opioids. At the recommendation of a doctor in the VA, contrary to VA policy, she tried marijuana and has been able to segue off opioids. She has been able to grow several marijuana plants, yielding several ounces of useable marijuana that help her manage her pain and resist returning to opioids. After her arrest for possession of several ounces of marijuana, she has contacted you about representing her in her upcoming trial and asks for you to tell her whether she has a medical necessity defense. Defendant resides in a state that has not authorized marijuana for any purposes. Discuss fully.

B. EXEMPTIONS FOR INDIAN COUNTRY

Elsewhere, we cover tension between federal and state law and the doctrine of preemption. In addition, issues arise when one state makes marijuana lawful, but a neighboring state does not. The Supreme Court failed to resolve interstate conflicts when Colorado's neighboring states filed an action against it. This section covers a different inter-jurisdictional conflict between sovereigns.

Conflicts between Native American tribal law and federal policy offer one kind of conflicts that may arise. Another may arise when a reservation spans several states, some of which may allow access to recreational or medical marijuana, while others do not. The Navajo reservation, for example, is located in Arizona, Utah and New Mexico and shares a border with Colorado. Arizona and New Mexico have authorized the use of medical marijuana; Colorado has authorized medical and recreational marijuana. Utah allows neither.

A problem that has arisen in Washington, where recreational and medical marijuana is lawful, is that some tribes object to those laws. Washington agreed to exempt the Yakama nation from its marijuana laws. But that exemption did not extend to some of the land in Washington that was once Yakama nation ancestral land. Marijuana is available on that land. Other tribes recognized that, in effect, marijuana was there to stay. Those tribes entered agreements with Washington to allow those tribes to enter the marijuana business.

Legal issues are likely to arise in states, like South Dakota, where marijuana remains unlawful, but tribes within those states allow recreational marijuana on their reservations. In 2016, a South Dakota tribe that initially authorized recreational marijuana gave up its marijuana crop when South Dakota and federal officials threatened raids. No doubt, similar conflicts will arise in the future and no doubt will end up in the courts.

Finally, cases have arisen that have placed the federal government at odds with tribal nations. The following case develops some of the complex issues that can emerge in that context.

MENOMINEE INDIAN TRIBE OF WISCONSIN V. DRUG ENFORCEMENT ADMINISTRATION

United States District Court, E.D. Wisconsin
190 F.Supp.3d 843 (E.D. Wis. 2016)

GRIESBACH, C.J.

The Menominee Indian Tribe of Wisconsin filed this declaratory action against the United States Department of Justice and its Drug Enforcement Administration (hereinafter "the Government") after federal agents raided reservation lands and seized a crop of hemp grown pursuant to a 2015 tribal ordinance legalizing the cultivation of hemp. The Tribe seeks a judgment declaring that its cultivation of industrial hemp for agricultural or academic research purposes in connection with the College of Menominee Nation is lawful under a 2014 federal law, 7 U.S.C. § 5940, which created an exemption to the Controlled Substances Act for the cultivation of hemp in certain circumstances.

Before the Court are the Government's motion to dismiss and the Tribe's motion for summary judgment. For the reasons below, the Governments motion will be granted and the Tribe's motion will be denied.

BACKGROUND

Section 7606 of the Agricultural Act of 2014, entitled "Legitimacy of industrial hemp research," created the following provision:

> Notwithstanding the Controlled Substances Act (21 U.S.C. 801 et seq.), the Safe and Drug-Free Schools and Communities Act (20 U.S.C. 7101 et seq.), chapter 81 of Title 41, or any other Federal law, an institution of higher education (as defined in section 1001 of Title 20) or a State department of agriculture may grow or cultivate industrial hemp if—
>
> > (1) the industrial hemp is grown or cultivated for purposes of research conducted under an agricultural pilot program or other agricultural or academic research; and
> >
> > (2) the growing or cultivating of industrial hemp is allowed under the laws of the State in which such institution of higher education or State department of agriculture is located and such research occurs.

Pub. L. No. 113–79, § 7606, 128 Stat. 649, 912–13, codified at 7 U.S.C. § 5940(a).

In May 2015, the Menominee Indian Tribe of Wisconsin, a federally-recognized Indian tribe, passed a tribal ordinance legalizing the cultivation of industrial hemp on the Menominee Reservation by licensees of the Tribe. Hemp has known uses in textiles, foods, papers, body care products, detergents, plastics and building materials. According to the Tribe, hemp is one of the earliest-known domesticated plants, with a long history of cultivation and use around the world, including cultivation by Native American tribes before the arrival of European settlers. President George Washington is said to have heralded the plant, telling a gardener, "Make the most you can of the Indian Hemp seed and sow it everywhere." Thomas J. Ballanco, *The Colorado Hemp Production Act of 1995: Farms and Forests Without Marijuana*, 66 U. Colo. L. Rev. 1165, 1165 & n.1 (1995).

The Tribe's 2015 ordinance defines industrial hemp as all parts of the genera Cannabis that contain a THC concentration of 0.3 percent or less by weight, and the law creates a licensing procedure under which license applicants must demonstrate they are capable of growing industrial hemp and have adopted methods to ensure its safe production. The Tribe entered into an agreement with the College of the Menominee Nation to research the viability of industrial hemp. The Tribe thereafter issued a license to the College, which planted an industrial hemp crop on tribal lands for research purposes. According to the complaint, the Tribe cooperated with the DOJ and DEA to secure the testing of industrial hemp and ensure that THC levels did not exceed 0.3 percent, and agreed to destroy any industrial hemp that tested above this limit, as such hemp would be in violation of tribal law.

On October 23, 2015, federal agents entered the Menominee Reservation, and seized and destroyed the Tribe's industrial hemp crop. The complaint states that the raid was conducted despite no known THC test exceeding 0.3 percent.

On November 18, 2015, the Tribe filed this action for declaratory relief. The Tribe seeks a declaration from this Court that its cultivation of industrial hemp for agricultural or academic research purposes in conjunction with the College of Menominee Nation is lawful under 7 U.S.C. § 5940. Specifically, the complaint includes three "claims" for declaratory relief corresponding to the statutory requirements for the exception: (1) that in passing a tribal law legalizing the cultivation of industrial hemp on the Menominee Reservation, the Tribe acted as a "State," as required under § 5940; or alternatively (2) that the cannabis laws of the State of Wisconsin have no application to industrial hemp cultivation by the Tribe within the exterior boundaries of the Menominee Reservation, and that the cultivation of industrial hemp on the Menominee Reservation is therefore "allowed" under the laws of the State of Wisconsin, as required under § 5940; and (3) that the College of Menominee Nation is an "institution of higher education" under § 5940. As explained below, the Government responded to the complaint by filing a motion to dismiss on numerous grounds. The Tribe responded with a motion for summary judgment.

ANALYSIS

The Tribe's declaratory claims require the Court to interpret a federal statute. The Supreme Court has long held that "the standard principles of statutory construction do not have their usual force in cases involving Indian law." *Montana v. Blackfeet Tribe of Indians*, 471 U.S. 759, 766 (1985). Because of the unique trust relationship between the United States and Indians, statutes in cases involving Indian law are construed liberally in favor of Indians, and all ambiguities are resolved in their favor. Moreover, tribal sovereignty is preserved unless Congress's intent to the contrary is clear.

On the other hand, when a statute is not ambiguous, the foregoing canons do not come into play, and the statute must be given its plain meaning.

A. "State"

As noted above, the law at issue permits the growing or cultivation of industrial hemp by an institution of higher education if such growing/cultivation is conducted for research purposes and "allowed under the laws of the State" in which it occurs. 7 U.S.C. § 5940(a). The Tribe's first argument is that "State" includes Indian tribes, and that the Tribe thus acted as a "State" for purposes of the statute when it enacted a tribal law allowing hemp cultivation. The Tribe's position has some logical and grammatical support. The word "State" is commonly understood to mean peoples politically organized as sovereigns, and Indian tribes are considered sovereigns under federal law. Moreover, the Supreme Court made clear last term that the word "State" does not necessarily mean one of the 50 states, even when it is defined as such. See *King v. Burwell*, 135 S.Ct. 2480 (2015).

On the other hand, in the ordinary case it remains true that Congress's use of the word "State" in a federal law without further definition simply means one of the 50 states. Congress regularly defines "State" to include Indian tribes or otherwise specifies that Indian tribes are included in addition to states and other entities to which a statute applies.

The Tribe argues that the Agricultural Act of 2014 in which the hemp statute was included contains several definitions of "State" that encompass "any other territory or possession of the United States," 7 U.S.C. §§ 2132(d), 7202(14), 8751(8), language which courts have construed as broad enough to include Indian tribes. Drawing on these provisions, the Tribe argues that State, as used in the law, includes Indian tribes. The hemp statute, however, is a stand-alone provision specifically designated as "miscellaneous." Pub. L. No. 113–79, Subtitle F—Miscellaneous Provisions, § 7606, 128 Stat. at 655–56, codified at Title 7 of the United States Code, Chapter 88—Research, Subchapter VII—Miscellaneous Research Provisions. The hemp statute is not a part of any broader statutory scheme. Moreover, the hemp statute contains its own definitional subsection. Under these circumstances, it would be arbitrary to look to definitions in unrelated parts of the same title of the United States Code and apply such definitions to the statute at issue. For these reasons, the Court denies the Tribe's request for declaratory relief to the effect that "State" as used in the hemp statute includes Indian tribes, and rejects the Tribe's theory that it acted as a "State" when it enacted its own law allowing hemp cultivation.

B.   "Allowed"

At oral argument, the Tribe focused on its second, narrower, argument. The Tribe argues that the cannabis laws of the State of Wisconsin have no application to industrial hemp cultivation by the Tribe within the exterior boundaries of the Menominee Reservation, and that the cultivation of industrial hemp on the Menominee Reservation therefore is "allowed" under the laws of the State of Wisconsin.

The Government does not dispute the Tribe's contention that the cannabis laws of the State of Wisconsin have no application, by their own force, on the Reservation. By way of background, the Tribe was granted a reservation in Wisconsin by the Treaty of the Wolf River in 1854. In 1953, the Congress enacted Public Law 280, 67 Stat. 588, which, as amended, became 18 U.S.C. § 1162. Public Law 280 gave certain states, including Wisconsin, jurisdiction over crimes committed by or against Indians in Indian country within each state. The law excluded the Menominee Indian Reservation from the grant of jurisdiction to Wisconsin. On June 17, 1954, Congress enacted the Menominee Termination Act, Pub. L. No. 399, 68 Stat. 250, the purpose of which was "to provide for orderly termination of Federal supervision over the property and members of the Menominee Indian Tribe of Wisconsin." 68 Stat. at 250. Additionally, on August 24, 1954, Congress amended 18 U.S.C. § 1162 to strike the Menominee exception, thereby subjecting the Menominee Indian Reservation to the state's criminal jurisdiction as provided by 18 U.S.C. § 1162(a). As a result of these legislative actions, the Tribe became subject to the state's criminal and civil jurisdiction, and the area known as the Menominee Indian Reservation became Menominee County, Wisconsin's 72nd County.

On December 22, 1973, however, Congress repealed the Termination Act by enacting the Menominee Restoration Act. This legislation restored federal recognition status for the Tribe and returned tribal property to federal trusteeship. Effective March 1, 1976, the State of Wisconsin then "retroceded" state jurisdiction over the Menominee Indian Reservation by executive proclamation. Although Public Law 280 made no provision for states to retrocede or return jurisdiction to the United States, Congress amended Public Law 280 in 1968 in response to Indian dissatisfaction with state jurisdiction and states' unhappiness over the financial burdens of law enforcement in Indian country. The 1968 Amendments authorized the United States to accept any State's "retrocession" of "all or any measure of the criminal or civil jurisdiction, or both, acquired by such State pursuant to the provisions of" Public Law 280. Pub. L. No. 90-283, Title IV, § 403, 82 Stat 79. By proclamation issued on February 19, 1976, the Governor of Wisconsin did in fact offer to retrocede to the United States all civil and criminal jurisdiction acquired by the State of Wisconsin under the 1954 amendments to Public Law 280, and pursuant to the authority vested in him by the President, the United States Secretary of the Interior accepted the offer effective March 1, 1976.

As a result of this history, today the boundaries of Menominee County are generally coterminous with the boundaries of the Menominee Indian Reservation, and because the United States accepted Wisconsin's retrocession of jurisdiction over the Menominee Reservation, the Tribe is correct that it is not subject to the jurisdiction or laws of the State of Wisconsin, including those that prohibit cannabis cultivation. Based on this history, the Tribe contends that Wisconsin law "allows" it to grow hemp on its reservation.

But the exception to the Controlled Substances Act's prohibition of hemp cultivation applies only if the laws of the State in which the hemp is grown allow the growing and cultivation of hemp, not whether those laws are enforceable on the Tribe's reservation. Congress has chosen to condition the hemp exception to the Controlled Substances Act on the laws of the States in which the proposed growing operations would occur. Wisconsin's laws do not allow the growing and cultivation of hemp. It thus follows that the exception does not apply.

* * *

In enacting the Industrial Hemp Research Statute, Congress recognized the need to take into account that while some states prohibited the growing and cultivation of hemp, other states allowed it. It therefore conditioned the availability of the exception the statute created in the Controlled Substances Act on the law of the state in which the growing would occur. Wisconsin law does not allow the growing of hemp. While Wisconsin law is not enforceable on the Menominee Reservation, that does not change the fact that the growing or cultivating of industrial hemp is not allowed under the laws of the State of Wisconsin.

CONCLUSION

For all of these reasons, the Government's motion to dismiss is GRANTED, and the Tribe's motion for summary judgment is DENIED.

NOTES AND QUESTIONS

1. **Another state-tribe conflict.** Another case where tribal, state and federal laws have been at odds involves farmer Alex White Plume, a member of the Oglala Sioux tribe in South Dakota. Authorized to grow hemp by his tribal council, Plume faced off with federal authorities when they raided his farm and destroyed his crop. The DEA obtained a permanent injunction prohibiting White Plume from harvesting hemp without DEA registration. *United States v. White Plume*, 447 F.3d 1067 (8th Cir. 2006). After the change to § 7606 of the Agricultural Act of 2014 discussed in the lead case, White Plume moved the court to lift the injunction. The court lifted the injunction, but it noted that its order did not resolve the merits of whether federal law

authorizes cultivation of industrial hemp on the Pine Ridge Indian Reservation where White Plume farms. *United States v. White Plume*, No. 02-5071-JLV, 2016 U.S. Dist. LEXIS 40138 (D.S.D. Mar. 28, 2016). For a more detailed treatment of this issue, see Chapter 17, Hemp.

2. **Adding a level of complexity.** What kinds of problems exist if Native American tribes or their members are exempt from federal or state marijuana restrictions? Think back to lessons from your Contracts course. Assume that a Native American farmer is authorized to cultivate hemp and that he wants to enter into a contract with a non-Native American business owner that wants to produce hemp clothing. Assume further that the farmer and the business owner end up in a dispute over the quality of the product that the farmer sent the business owner. Will a federal or state court enforce the contract?

3. **The court's reasoning.** If statutes are to be construed liberally in favor of the Indians, as the court itself states, and the Wilkinson memo (see Chapter 17. Section B, pp. 563–564) indicates a certain correspondence between states and tribes for the purpose of enforcing marijuana laws, is the court correct to apply a literal definition of "state' in the statute? Further, in light of the principle of liberal construction, is the court correct to interpret "allowed' under § 7606 of the Agricultural Act of 2014 to bind the Menominee tribe by Wisconsin's prohibition against hemp growing, even though Wisconsin law does not apply to the Menominee Tribe Reservation?

4. **Overturned by Congress.** The holding of this case is ostensibly overturned by the Hemp Farming Act contained in the omnibus Agriculture Improvement Act of 2018 (the "Farm Bill"). The Hemp Farming Act authorizes tribal governments to implement hemp cultivation programs.

C. IMMUNITY

As states legalize medical or recreational marijuana, a host of issues arise. In Chapter 11 Criminal Issues Pertaining to Illegal Marijuana Possession and Distribution, we consider some areas of the law where traditional doctrine may have to evolve. For example, historically, an officer who smells marijuana has probable cause to arrest a suspect without more. But what if those events take place in a state where marijuana is authorized? That is only one example of the many evolving legal issues that can arise in a new and fast moving area of the law.

In this section, consider one specific problem. If a state legalizes medical marijuana, for example, how should a person who claims a right to use medical marijuana be able to raise that claim? Most often, a person who is charged with a crime may have a defense at trial on the charges. Thus, a state might make medical use of marijuana a defense to a criminal charge. Consider the inconvenience and risks involved in such a case. Going to trial may be expensive and a defendant may be tempted to accept a guilty plea to avoid the risk of an unfavorable verdict. Some states have created immunity from prosecution for medical marijuana users. The following case explores some of the issues that can arise in that context, including immunity and other possible defenses in a state that allows medical use of marijuana.

PEOPLE V. HARTWICK
Court of Appeals of Michigan
303 Mich. App. 247 (2013)

SAAD, J.

Defendant appeals the trial court's order that (1) held that he was not entitled to immunity under § 4 of the Michigan Medical Marihuana Act (MMMA) . . . . For the reasons set forth in this opinion, we affirm.

I. NATURE OF THE CASE

Defendant, who was arrested for illegally growing and possessing marijuana, holds a registry identification card under the MMMA, MCL 333.26421 *et seq.* He claims that mere possession of the card entitles him to (1) immunity from prosecution under § 4 of the MMMA and, in the alternative, (2) an affirmative defense under § 8 of the MMMA. The trial court rejected defendant's theory and instead held that defendant was not entitled to immunity under § 4 and that he had not presented the requisite evidence to make an affirmative defense under § 8.

We uphold the trial court and fully explore defendant's specific arguments that his possession of a registry identification card automatically immunizes him from prosecution under § 4 and grants him a complete defense under § 8. We reject these arguments because they ignore the primary purpose and plain language of the MMMA, which is to ensure that any marijuana production and use permitted by the statute is medical in nature and only for treating a patient's debilitating medical condition. To adopt defendant's argument would also put the MMMA at risk of abuse and undermine the act's stated aim of helping a select group of people with serious medical conditions that may be alleviated if treated in compliance with the MMMA. We therefore reject defendant's claim and hold that the trial court did not abuse its discretion when it (1) ruled that defendant was not entitled to immunity from criminal prosecution under § 4 and (2) denied defendant's request for dismissal under § 8 and held that he could not present the § 8 defense at trial.

II. FACTS AND PROCEDURAL HISTORY

Detective Mark Ferguson, a member of the Oakland County Sheriff's Office, received a tip that someone was distributing marijuana at a single-family home in Pontiac. On September 27, 2011, Detective Ferguson visited the house in question and met defendant outside. Detective Ferguson asked defendant if there was marijuana in the house. Defendant replied that there was and that he was growing marijuana in compliance with the

MMMA. Ferguson asked if he could see the marijuana, and defendant led him inside the house.

Defendant and Detective Ferguson went into a back bedroom that served as a grow room for the marijuana. The grow room door was unlocked and the room housed many marijuana plants. Detective Ferguson then asked if he could search the house; defendant agreed. Throughout the home, Detective Ferguson found additional marijuana plants, a shoebox of dried marijuana in the freezer, mason jars filled with marijuana in defendant's bedroom, and amounts of the drug that were not in containers near an entertainment stand in the living room.

Detective Ferguson then asked defendant if he sold marijuana. Defendant replied that he did not. He told Detective Ferguson that he acted as a caregiver for patients who used marijuana. The prosecuting attorney subsequently charged defendant with manufacturing marijuana and possessing it with the intent to deliver it. After the prosecutor presented his proofs at the preliminary examination, defendant moved to dismiss the charges under the MMMA's § 4 grant of immunity and the § 8 defense provision. In the alternative, defendant sought to assert a § 8 defense at trial.

THE EVIDENTIARY HEARING

Defendant was the only testifying witness at the evidentiary hearing. He claimed that (1) he was a medical marijuana patient and his own caregiver, and (2) he also served as a caregiver for five additional medical marijuana patients. Defendant possessed registry identification cards for himself and his five patients, and submitted the cards as evidence. The prosecution stipulated the validity of defendant's own registry identification card. Further, the cards demonstrate that defendant served as caregiver for the five additional patients in September 2011, when the police recovered marijuana from his home. Yet defendant was unfamiliar with the health background of his patients and could not identify the maladies or "debilitating conditions" suffered by two of his patients. He was not aware of how much marijuana any of his patients were supposed to use to treat their respective conditions or for how long his patients were supposed to use "medical marijuana." And he could not name each patient's certifying physician.

Defendant also testified that he had 71 plants in small Styrofoam cups. On cross-examination, the prosecutor asked defendant about this number, because Detective Ferguson's report had indicated that there were 77 plants. Defendant responded that the detective had included "six plants that I had just cut down and there was still the stalk there." The prosecutor pressed this point in closing arguments, noting that defendant was not entitled to dismissal under § 4 because he had more plants than permitted by that section.

But the prosecutor stressed that the number of plants was not the ultimate issue in the case. Instead, the prosecutor stated that he had rebutted defendant's § 4(d) presumption of immunity by showing defendant's failure to comply with the underlying purpose of the MMMA: the use and manufacture of marijuana for *medical* purposes. The prosecutor noted that "by [defendant's] own testimony he could not have been [providing marijuana to people diagnosed with a debilitating medical condition because] he doesn't know if anybody had a debilitating medical condition, what that is, what they require to use it. There's no way that it's possible for him to have been acting in accordance with the act."

The trial court agreed with the prosecutor's reasoning and held that defendant was not entitled to dismissal under § 4.

III. STANDARD OF REVIEW

A trial court's decision on a motion to dismiss is reviewed for an abuse of discretion. "A trial court's findings of fact may not be set aside unless they are clearly erroneous." *People v. Bylsma,* 493 Mich. 17, 26 (2012). A finding is "clearly erroneous 'if the reviewing court is left with a definite and firm conviction that the trial court made a mistake.' " *Id.* Questions of statutory interpretation, including interpretation of the MMMA, are reviewed de novo.

IV. ANALYSIS

A. THE MMMA

The MMMA originated as a citizen's initiative petition and was approved by the people of Michigan in November 2008. Its expressed purpose is to allow a "limited class of individuals the medical use of marijuana. . . ." *Kolanek,* 491 Mich. at 393. The statute emphatically "does *not* create a general right for individuals to use and possess marijuana in Michigan." *Id.* at 394. Nonmedical-related possession, manufacture, and delivery of the drug (and medical-related possession, manufacture, and delivery not in compliance with the MMMA) "remain punishable offenses under Michigan law." *Id.* The MMMA is best viewed as an "exception to the Public Health Code's prohibition on the use of controlled substances [that permits] the medical use of marijuana when carried out in accordance with the MMMA's provisions." *Bylsma,* 493 Mich. at 27. The statute's protections are "limited to individuals suffering from serious or debilitating medical conditions or symptoms, to the extent that the individuals' marijuana use 'is carried out in accordance with the provisions of [the MMMA].' " *Kolanek,* 491 Mich. at 394.

Accordingly, proper analysis of the MMMA must focus on its overriding medical purpose. The ballot initiative approved by the people specifically referred to "physician approved use of marijuana by registered patients with debilitating medical conditions including cancer, glaucoma, HIV, AIDS, hepatitis C, MS and other conditions as may be approved by the Department of Community Health." Michigan Proposal 08–1 (November 2008). The MMMA explicitly states in its title the law's medical intentions ("[a]n initiation of Legislation to allow under state law the medical use of marihuana. . . ."), and the MMMA makes explicit reference to its palliative, treatment-based goals throughout ("[m]odern medical research . . . has discovered beneficial uses for marihuana in treating or alleviating the pain, nausea, and other symptoms associated with a variety of debilitating medical conditions").

With these medical aims in mind, we turn to the specific requirements of the statute's immunity provisions (§ 4) and its § 8 defenses.

B. SECTION 4 IMMUNITY

Section 4 contains multiple parts, only some of which are relevant to this case. "Sections 4(a) and 4(b) contain parallel immunity provisions that apply, respectively, to registered qualifying patients and to registered primary caregivers." *Bylsma,* 493 Mich. at 28. With some conditions, § 4(a) provides "qualifying patient[s]" who hold "registry identification card[s]" immunity from criminal prosecution and other penalties. *Kolanek,* 491 Mich. at 394. In the relevant part, it states:

> A qualifying patient who has been issued and possesses a registry identification card shall not be subject to arrest, prosecution, or penalty in any manner, or denied any right or privilege, including but not limited to civil penalty or disciplinary action by a business or occupational or professional licensing board or bureau, for the medical use of marihuana in accordance with this act, provided that the qualifying patient possesses an amount of marihuana that does not exceed 2.5 ounces of usable marihuana, and, if the qualifying patient has not specified that a primary caregiver will be allowed under state law to cultivate marihuana for the qualifying patient, 12 marihuana plants kept in an enclosed, locked facility. Any incidental amount of seeds, stalks, and unusable roots shall also be allowed under state law and shall not be included in this amount. [MCL 333.26424(a).]

Section 4(b) provides similar rights to a "primary caregiver," who, among other things: (1) grows marijuana for patients "to whom he or she is connected through the department's registration process"; (2) has been "issued and possesses a registry identification card"; and (3) complies with certain volume and security requirements. MCL 333.26424(b)(1) to (3).

Section 4(d) creates a presumption that if the patient or primary caregiver (1) is "in possession of a registry identification card" and (2) "is in possession of an amount of marihuana that does not exceed the amount allowed under this act," he is engaged in the medical use of marijuana in accordance with the MMMA. MCL 333.26424(d)(1) and (2). The prosecution may rebut this presumption with "evidence that conduct related to marihuana was not for the purpose of alleviating the qualifying patient's debilitating medical condition or symptoms associated with the debilitating medical condition. . . ." MCL 333.26424(d)(2).

Here, defendant relies on § 4(b), but ignores § 4(d). Defendant asserts that the number of plants he allegedly possessed places his conduct within the number of marijuana plants permissible under § 4(b). He then claims that mere possession of a valid, state-issued registry identification card prevents the prosecution from rebutting the presumption that he was "engaged in the medical use of marihuana in accordance with this act" under § 4(d).

Neither argument is convincing. The first, related to the number of plants possessed by defendant, is moot. The trial court acts as the fact-finder to determine whether § 4 immunity applies. Here, the trial court clearly agreed with the prosecution's count of defendant's marijuana plants: 77, not the 71 claimed by defendant. Accordingly, defendant possessed 77 plants—five more than permitted to him by § 4(b)(2).

Yet, were we to accept defendant's numerical assessment, defendant would nonetheless not qualify for § 4 immunity. His interpretation of the MMMA ignores the underlying medical purposes of the statute, explicitly referred to in § 4(d). Mere possession of a state-issued card—even one backed by a state investigation—does not guarantee that the cardholder's *subsequent* use and production of marijuana was "for the purpose of alleviating the qualifying patient's debilitating medical condition or symptoms associated with the debilitating medical condition. . . ." MCL 333.26424(d)(2). Indeed, defendant's testimony provided ample evidence that he was not holding true to the medical purposes of the statute. He failed to introduce evidence of (1) some of his patients' medical conditions, (2) the amount of marijuana they reasonably required for treatment and how long the treatment should continue, and (3) the identity of their physicians.

Accordingly, we hold that defendant failed to produce sufficient evidence at the evidentiary hearing to qualify for the § 4(d) presumption of immunity and that he is not entitled to immunity under § 4 of the MMMA.

C.   SECTION 8(a) DEFENSE

The § 8(a) defense specifies three elements that an MMMA defendant must demonstrate before he can assert this defense. This burden is premised on the medical reasons that underlie the statute, and the specified elements are inclusive: § 8(a) requires evidence of every element for the defense to be presumed valid. MCL 333.26428(a).

* * *

Section 8 outlines the possible defenses a defendant can raise when charged with violating the act. In so doing, the section weaves together the obligations of each individual involved in the prescription, use, and production of marijuana for medical purposes. Under the act, doctors must have an ongoing relationship with their patients, where the doctor continuously reviews the patient's condition and revises his marijuana prescription accordingly. Further, patients must provide certain basic information regarding their marijuana use to their caregivers. And caregivers, to be protected under the MMMA, must ask for this basic information—specifically, information that details, as any pharmaceutical prescription would, how much marijuana the patient is supposed to use and how long that use is supposed to continue. Though patients and caregivers are ordinary citizens, not trained medical professionals, the MMMA's essential mandate is that marijuana be used for medical purposes. Accordingly, for their own protection from criminal prosecution, patients and caregivers must comply with this medical purpose—patients by supplying the necessary documentation to their caregivers, and caregivers by only supplying patients who provide the statutorily mandated information.

Possession of a registry identification card, without more, does nothing to address these § 8 medical requirements. It offers no proof of the existence of an ongoing relationship between patient and physician, as mandated by § 8(a)(1). Nor does it prove that the caregiver is aware of how much marijuana the patient is prescribed or for how long the patient is supposed to use the drug, as mandated by § 8(a)(2). And it does not ensure that the marijuana provided by the caregiver is actually being used by the patient for medical reasons, as mandated by § 8(a)(3). In sum: a registry identification card is necessary, but not sufficient, to comply with the MMMA but clearly does not satisfy the § 8 requirements for a total defense to a charge of violation of this act.

1.   SECTION 8(a)(1): THE BONA FIDE PHYSICIAN-PATIENT RELATIONSHIP

The first element of the affirmative defense of § 8(a) requires a defendant to present evidence that [a] physician has stated that, in the physician's professional opinion, after having completed a full assessment of the patient's medical history and current medical condition made in the course of a bona fide physician-patient relationship, the patient is likely to receive therapeutic or palliative benefit from the medical use of marihuana to treat or alleviate the patient's serious or debilitating medical condition or symptoms of the patient's serious or debilitating medical condition[.] [MCL 333.26428(a)(1).]

Here, the crux of defendant's § 8(a) defense lies within this first element. Again, defendant asserts, incorrectly, that his possession of state-issued medical marijuana patient and caregiver identification cards is enough to satisfy the physician's statement and "bona fide physician-patient relationship" required by the statute. Certainly, possession of a card does not demonstrate an ongoing relationship with a physician envisioned by the MMMA, where a doctor can prescribe a certain amount of marijuana for use over a specified period.

* * *

In light of these straightforward, common-sense definitions, defendant's argument becomes untenable. A registry identification card—even one verified by the state pursuant to the requirements of § 6—cannot demonstrate a "pre-existing" relationship between a physician and a patient, much less show "ongoing" contact between the two. Accordingly, mere possession of a patient's or caregiver's identification card does not satisfy the requirements of the first element of a § 8(a) defense. That the statute requires this outcome is in keeping with its medical purpose and protects the patients it is designed to serve. By requiring a bona fide physician-patient relationship for the § 8 defense, the MMMA prevents doctors who merely write prescriptions—such as the one featured in *Redden*—from seeing a patient once, issuing a medical marijuana prescription, and never checking on whether that prescription actually treated the patient or served as a palliative.

Here, defendant presented evidence of a bona fide physician-patient relationship between him and his doctor. But he presented no evidence that his patients have bona fide physician-patient relationships with their certifying physicians. None of his patients testified. Nor was defendant able to provide the names of his patients' certifying physicians. While it is true that the MMMA does not explicitly impose a duty on patients to provide such basic medical information to their primary caregivers, the plain language of § 8 obviously requires such information for a patient or caregiver to effectively assert the § 8 defense in a court of law.

Accordingly, we hold that mere possession of a patient's or caregiver's identification card does not satisfy the first element of § 8(a)'s affirmative defense. Therefore, the trial court was correct to rule that defendant did not present valid evidence with respect to the first element of the § 8 affirmative defense.

2. SECTION 8(a)(2): NO MORE MARIJUANA THAN "REASONABLY NECESSARY"

The second element of the § 8 affirmative defense requires a defendant to present evidence that [t]he patient and the patient's primary caregiver, if any, were collectively in possession of a quantity of marihuana that was not more than was reasonably necessary to ensure the uninterrupted availability of marihuana for the purpose of treating or alleviating the patient's serious or debilitating medical condition or symptoms of the patient's serious or debilitating medical condition[.] [MCL 333.26428(a)(2).]

This element thus involves two components: (1) possession, and (2) knowledge of what amount of marijuana is "reasonably necessary" for the patient's treatment.

Here, defendant argues that the volume limitations listed in § 4(b) should apply to § 8: namely, if a patient or caregiver possesses less than the amounts specified in § 4(b), that patient or caregiver possesses no more than a "reasonably necessary" amount of marijuana for medical treatment pursuant to § 8(a)(2).

This approach misstates the law and ignores the medical purposes of the MMMA. This Court has explicitly held that the amounts permitted under § 4 do not define what is "reasonably necessary" to establish the § 8 defense: "Indeed, if the intent of the statute were to have the amount in § 4 apply to § 8, the § 4 amount would have been reinserted into § 8(a)(2), instead of the language concerning an amount reasonably necessary to ensure . . . uninterrupted availability. . . ." *Redden,* 290 Mich.App. at 87. In addition, our Supreme Court recently stressed that § 4 and § 8 are separate sections, intended to address different situations with different standards. Further, importing § 4(b)'s volume limitations to § 8(a)(2) ignores the treatment-oriented nature of the act and § 8(a)'s specific medical requirements. Those requirements are intended for a patient or caregiver that is intimately aware of exactly how much marijuana is required to treat a patient's condition, which he learns from a doctor with whom the patient has an ongoing relationship.

Here, defendant lacks the requisite knowledge of how much marijuana is required to treat his patients' conditions—and even his own condition. He presented no evidence regarding how much marijuana he required to treat his pain and how often it should be treated. And he testified that he did not know how much marijuana his patients required to treat their conditions. Defendant thus failed to satisfy the second element of the § 8 affirmative defense. Accordingly, again the trial court properly held that defendant did not create a question of fact on this issue.

3. SECTION 8(a)(3): ACTUAL MEDICAL USE OF MARIJUANA

The third element of the § 8 affirmative defense requires a defendant to present evidence that [t]he patient and the patient's primary caregiver, if any, were engaged in the acquisition, possession, cultivation, manufacture, use, delivery, transfer, or transportation of marihuana or paraphernalia relating to the use of marihuana to treat or alleviate the patient's serious or debilitating medical condition or symptoms of the patient's serious or debilitating medical condition. [MCL 333.26428(a)(3).]

The trial court observed at the evidentiary hearing that defendant needed to satisfy § 8(a)(3), but did not make a finding regarding whether he did so. Therefore, we need not address whether defendant satisfied this element through his testimony.

V. CONCLUSION

Because (1) defendant possessed more marijuana than permitted under § 4(b), and (2) the prosecution presented evidence to rebut the medical-use presumption under § 4(d), defendant is not entitled to immunity from prosecution under § 4 of the MMMA. Further, because defendant did not present evidence demonstrating the first two elements of the § 8 defense, he was not entitled to have the case dismissed under that section, nor was he entitled to present the § 8 defense at trial. We therefore hold that the trial court did not abuse its discretion.

Affirmed.

NOTES AND QUESTIONS

1. **More about Michigan.** For more on *Hartwick* and Michigan law generally, see Mary Chartier, Navigating the Haze of Marijuana Law: An Overview of the Michigan Medical Marihuana Act, https://www.cndefenders.com/wp-content/uploads/sites/537/2017/07/2017-05-11-navigating-the-haze.pdf.

2. **California's approach.** Similar issues to those in *People v. Hartwick* have arisen in other states as well. For example, in *People v. Mower*, 49 P.3d 1067 (Cal. 2002), the California Supreme Court interpreted the Medical Use of Marijuana Act (Proposition 215) as "grant[ing] a defendant a limited immunity from prosecution, which not only allows a defendant to raise his or her status as a qualified patient or primary caregiver as a defense at trial, but also permits a defendant to raise such status by moving to set aside an indictment or information prior to trial on the ground of the absence of reasonable or probable cause to believe that he or she is guilty." However, Mower did not file such a motion before trial, and was therefore not entitled to partial immunity.

3. **More from California.** In *People v. Mentch*, 195 P.3d 1061 (Cal. 2008), the California Supreme Court held that in order to qualify for partial immunity as a primary caregiver, defendants must prove they "(1) consistently provided caregiving, (2) independent of any assistance in taking medical marijuana, (3) at or before the time he or she assumed responsibility for assisting with medical marijuana." Defendant Mentch was found not to meet the primary caregiver criteria because he could only establish a post-hoc relationship with the people to whom he sold marijuana, and "the provision of marijuana [was] itself the substance of the relationship."

4. **The view from Arizona.** The Arizona Medical Marijuana Act (Proposition 203) provides immunity from prosecution for licensed patients who possess and use the drug in accordance with the Act and for physicians who provide written certification that a patient would receive medical benefits from the use of marijuana. In *State v. Gear*, 372 P.3d 287 (Ariz. 2016), a

physician provided an undercover officer with a written recommendation, certifying that he had reviewed the patient's previous medical record, when indeed he had not. Dr. Gear was indicted for forgery and fraud, but the trial court dismissed the indictment, finding that the AMMA immunized him from prosecution. The court of appeals affirmed, finding that physicians are shielded from prosecution when stating their professional opinion. The Supreme Court of Arizona reversed, holding that the AMMA only immunized physicians from prosecution "based solely on their providing the statutorily authorized certifications or otherwise stating a professional opinion," and did not immunize them from fraudulent conduct.

5. **And from Massachusetts.** In *Commonwealth v. Vargas*, 55 N.E.3d 923 (Mass. 2016), the Supreme Judicial Court of Massachusetts found that Defendant was not entitled to patient immunity when he violated his probation by testing positive for marijuana use. Defendant's medical certificate did not immunize him because obtained it after he had already violated the terms of his probation and after he had already agreed to those terms.

6. **A final view from Montana.** In *State v. Stoner*, 285 P.3d 402 (Mont. 2012), the Supreme Court of Montana affirmed the trial court's denial of Defendant's motion to dismiss. The court refused to afford Stoner immunity from prosecution for several marijuana offenses because he did not obtain a medical marijuana registry identification card until two months after he committed the offenses.

7. **Conflicting policies.** How should the law deal with medical marijuana users in states that have authorized medical marijuana? What are the competing policies, as reflected in some of the cases described above?

PROBLEM 9-2

Defendant lives in a state that has authorized medical marijuana for qualified patients. Injured when he was a professional athlete, Defendant uses marijuana to control his pain. An officer received a tip from a reliable informant who told the officer that Defendant had a large amount of marijuana in his home. The informant told the officer that he had helped Defendant carry marijuana into Defendant's home because Defendant's physical disabilities limit Defendant's ability to carry heavy objects. Armed with a search warrant, officer went to Defendant's home to search for marijuana. Defendant showed officer his marijuana authorization card and told him that the only marijuana he possessed was for medical use. The officer insisted that he was entitled to enter Defendant's home and to search for marijuana to determine if this was true despite Defendant's assertion. Officer entered and found not only marijuana but also cocaine. Charged with possession of cocaine, Defendant has moved to suppress the evidence on the grounds that the original entry into his home was illegal. Discuss fully.

CHAPTER 10

RESCHEDULING MARIJUANA

∎ ∎ ∎

With the ferment over marijuana law since the enactment of the CSA, one fact has remained constant: its placement in Schedule I, which renders nearly every use of marijuana prohibited under federal law. Strictly speaking, there is no statute specifically criminalizing marijuana use as such, as there is for, let's say, burglary or arson. However, marijuana's placement in Schedule I makes its use illegal, except if done with DEA registration, which is only available for scientific research under very limited circumstances. Unregistered usage is subject to the sanctions listed in the CSA.

Hence there have been concerted efforts to reschedule marijuana from the time of its provisional control as a CSA Schedule I drug in 1970. In Chapter 3, we saw how marijuana was provisionally placed into Schedule I and early efforts to have it rescheduled, which came to naught. In this chapter we look at the most recent petitions to have marijuana rescheduled, and the response of the DEA and the courts, likewise unfavorable.

In Section A, we examine the most recent petition to reschedule marijuana, filed in 2011 and denied by DEA in 2016. This denial has not yet been reviewed by the courts. In Section B, we look at the most recent judicial opinion reviewing a petition for rescheduling, *Americans for Safe Access v. DEA* (D.C. Cir. 2013). In Section C, we survey FDA-approved synthetic and natural cannabinoid substances that have been transferred to a less restrictive schedule than Schedule I. Examined together, this material represents a microcosm of the administrative law of drug control.

A. THE RESCHEDULING PETITION

In this section, we focus on the process for petitioning to reschedule marijuana. First we look at the federal regulations governing the petition process and then the most recent petition for rescheduling. Although this high profile petition submitted by the governors of two states was denied by the DEA in 2016, it did result in certain changes and might point to how DEA may reschedule marijuana substances in the future.

Rescheduling marijuana can take place at both the federal and state levels. Several states have rescheduled marijuana to a less restrictive classification in their state versions of the Uniform Controlled Substances

Act. This is one of the methods that states have used to legalize or decriminalize marijuana.

However of more significance to the marijuana debate have been efforts to reschedule marijuana at the federal level. As to federal law, marijuana can be rescheduled in one of two ways, either by Congress amending the CSA or by administrative (DEA) action.

As to congressional action, although several bills have been introduced to reschedule marijuana, none have emerged out of committee for a vote on the floor—presumably because the issue is too politically charged. (The CARERS Act described in Chapter 3 perhaps came closest). With the Republican Party in control of the presidency and both houses of Congress as of summer 2018, congressional rescheduling in the near future seems a dim possibility.

The other avenue is administrative—the petitioning process through administrative agencies. In Chapter 3, we studied the controlling of marijuana in Schedule I and the first efforts to contest that scheduling. In that chapter we read two cases, *NORML v. Ingersoll*, 497 F.2d 654 (D.C. Cir. 1974) and *NORML v. DEA*, 559 F.2d 735 (D.C. Cir. 1977), adjudicating aspects of marijuana scheduling and reviewing the relevant 21 U.S.C. § 811 and § 812 rules and methods: most importantly, that marijuana is controlled in Schedule I because it was determined that 1) it has a high potential for abuse; 2) it has no currently accepted medical use in treatment in the United States; and 3) there is a lack of accepted safety for its use under medical supervision. This section continues the discussion of the rulemaking provisions of 21 U.S.C. §§ 811 and 812 (sections 201 and 202 of the CSA) as to the rescheduling process.

I.   RESCHEDULING PETITION RULES

INITIATION OF PROCEEDINGS FOR RULEMAKING
Drug Enforcement Administration
C.F.R. § 1308.43 (2018)

(a) Any interested person may submit a petition to initiate proceedings for the issuance, amendment, or repeal of any rule or regulation issuable pursuant to the provisions of section 201 of the Act.

(b) Petitions shall be submitted in quintuplicate to the Administrator. See the Table of DEA Mailing Addresses in Sec. 1321.01 of this chapter for the current mailing address. Petitions shall be in the following form:

_____ (Date)

Administrator, Drug Enforcement Administration _____ (Mailing Address)

Dear Sir: The undersigned _____ hereby petitions the Administrator to initiate proceedings for the issuance (amendment or repeal) of a rule or regulation pursuant to section 201 of the Controlled Substances Act.

Attached hereto and constituting a part of this petition are the following:

(A) The proposed rule in the form proposed by the petitioner. (If the petitioner seeks the amendment or repeal of an existing rule, the existing rule, together with a reference to the section in the Code of Federal Regulations where it appears, should be included.)

(B) A statement of the grounds which the petitioner relies for the issuance (amendment or repeal) of the rule. (Such grounds shall include a reasonably concise statement of the facts relied upon by the petitioner, including a summary of any relevant medical or scientific evidence known to the petitioner.)

(c) Within a reasonable period of time after the receipt of a petition, the Administrator shall notify the petitioner of his acceptance or nonacceptance of the petition, and if not accepted, the reason therefor. The Administrator need not accept a petition for filing if any of the requirements prescribed in paragraph (b) of this section is lacking or is not set forth so as to be readily understood. If the petitioner desires, he may amend the petition to meet the requirements of paragraph (b) of this section. If accepted for filing, a petition may be denied by the Administrator within a reasonable period of time thereafter if he finds the grounds upon which the petitioner relies are not sufficient to justify the initiation of proceedings.

(d) The Administrator shall, before initiating proceedings for the issuance, amendment, or repeal of any rule either to control a drug or other substance, or to transfer a drug or other substance from one schedule to another, or to remove a drug or other substance entirely from the schedules, and after gathering the necessary data, request from the Secretary a scientific and medical evaluation and the Secretary's recommendations as to whether such drug or other substance should be so controlled, transferred, or removed as a controlled substance. The recommendations of the Secretary to the Administrator shall be binding on the Administrator as to such scientific and medical matters, and if the Secretary recommends that a drug or other substance not be controlled, the Administrator shall not control that drug or other substance.

(e) If the Administrator determines that the scientific and medical evaluation and recommendations of the Secretary and all other relevant data constitute substantial evidence of potential for abuse such as to warrant control or additional control over the drug or other substance, or substantial evidence that the drug or other substances should be subjected to lesser control or removed entirely from the schedules, he shall initiate proceedings for control, transfer, or removal as the case may be.

(f)   If and when the Administrator determines to initiate proceedings, he shall publish in the Federal Register general notice of any proposed rule making to issue, amend, or repeal any rule pursuant to section 201 of the Act. Such published notice shall include a statement of the time, place, and nature of any hearings on the proposal in the event a hearing is requested pursuant to § 1308.44. Such hearings may not be commenced until after the expiration of at least 30 days from the date the general notice is published in the Federal Register. Such published notice shall also include a reference to the legal authority under which the rule is proposed, a statement of the proposed rule, and, in the discretion of the Administrator, a summary of the subjects and issues involved.

(g)   The Administrator may permit any interested persons to file written comments on or objections to the proposal and shall designate in the notice of proposed rule making the time during which such filings may be made.

II. MARIJUANA RESCHEDULING: THE GOVERNORS PETITION

PETITION TO RESCHEDULE MARIJUANA
Offices of the Governors
(November 30, 2011)

Chafee, Rhode Island Governor and Gregoire, Washington Governor.

Michele Leonhart, Administrator
Drug Enforcement Administration
Attn: Administrator
8701 Morrissette Drive
Springfield, VA 22152

>   **Subject: *Rulemaking petition to reclassify cannabis for medical use from a Schedule I controlled substance to a Schedule II controlled substance***

Dear Administrator Leonhart:

Pursuant to Section 1308.43 of Title 21 of the Code of Federal Regulations (CFR), we hereby petition to initiate proceedings for the issuance of an amendment of a rule or regulation pursuant to Section 201 of the Controlled Substances Act (CSA). Specifically, we petition for the reclassification of medical cannabis (also known as marijuana) from Schedule I to Schedule II of the CSA.

Attached hereto and constituting a part of this petition are the following as required by the CSA and the CFR:

Exhibit A—The proposed rule. We seek the amendment of an existing rule, so pursuant to 21 C.F.R. § 1308.43(6), we have included the existing rule together with a reference to the section in the CFR where it appears, along with our proposed amendment for your consideration.

Exhibit B—A statement of the grounds upon which we rely for the issuance of an amendment of the rule. As required, the grounds we rely on include a reasonably concise statement of the facts, including a summary of relevant medical or scientific evidence in the form of an eight factor analysis that the CSA specifies a petitioner must address (21 U.S.C. § 811(c)). The Secretary of the United States Department of Health and Human Services (HHS) through the Food and Drug Administration (FDA) will consider these factors in a report to you for purposes of informing your final decision. The factors include: (1) actual and potential for abuse; (2) pharmacology; (3) other current scientific knowledge; (4) history and current pattern of abuse; (5) scope, duration and significance of abuse; (6) public health risk; (7) psychic or physiological dependence liability; and (8) whether it is an immediate precursor of a controlled substance. The attached statement of grounds about the scientific and medical record, considering these eight factors, supports recognition of the accepted medical use of cannabis in the United States. Accordingly, we request you to open rulemaking to reschedule cannabis for medical purposes under the CSA from a Schedule I to a Schedule II controlled substance.

* * *

Sincerely

| Lincoln D. Chafee | Christine O. Gregoire |
| Governor of Rhode Island | Governor of Washington |

Enclosures:

Exhibit A—Proposed Rule

Exhibit B—Statement of Grounds

Submitted in quintuplicate pursuant to 21 C.F.R. § 1308.43

Exhibit A: Proposed Rule

We propose the following: that the rule placing "marihuana" in Schedule I [21 CFR 1308.11(d)(23) and 21 CFR 1308.11(d)(31)] is repealed and placed as a Schedule II drug. This is not a petition for the removal of marijuana from scheduling under the Controlled Substances Act (CSA), but a petition to have marijuana and related items removed from Schedule I and rescheduled as "medical cannabis" in Schedule II, and made on the basis of the scientific and medical evaluation required pursuant to the CSA, see Exhibit B, Statement of Grounds (21 USC 811(c)).

For the purposes of this petition, and in reference to the Drug Enforcement Administration (DEA) listing of Schedule I drugs, this will include all tetrahydrocannabinols (THC), which are naturally contained in a plant of the genus Cannabis (cannabis plant), as well as synthetic equivalents of the substances contained in the cannabis plant, or in the resinous extractives of such plant, and/or synthetic substances (not otherwise already classified as Schedule II or III), derivatives, and their isomers with similar chemical structure and pharmacological activity to those substances contained in the plant, such as the following:

—1 cis or trans tetrahydrocannabinol, and their optical isomers;

—6 cis or trans tetrahydrocannabinol, and their optical isomers; and

—3,4 cis or trans tetrahydrocannabinol, and its optical isomers.

Given that nomenclature of these substances is not internationally standardized, compounds of these structures, regardless of numerical designation of atomic positions covered are included.

The following is the proposed rule:

REMOVE: 21 CFR 1308.11(d) (23) and (31) and others sections that may relate to medical cannabis use:

"(d) Hallucinogenic substances. . . .:

. . .(23) Marihuana	7360
. . .(31) Tetrahydrocannabinols	7370

Meaning tetrahydrocannabinols naturally contained in a plant of the genus Cannabis (cannabis plant), as well as synthetic equivalents of the substances contained in the cannabis plant, or in the resinous extractives of such plant, and/or synthetic substances, derivatives, and their isomers with similar chemical structure and pharmacological activity to those substances contained in the plant, such as the following:
—1 cis or trans tetrahydrocannabinol, and their optical isomers
—6 cis or trans tetrahydrocannabinol, and their optical isomers
—3,4 cis or trans tetrahydrocannabinol, and its optical isomers
(Since nomenclature of these substances is not internationally standardized, compounds of these structures, regardless of numerical designation of atomic positions covered.)"

RESCHEDULED TO: 21 CFR 1308.12 Schedule II:

"(a) Schedule II shall consist of the drugs and other substances, by whatever official name, common or usual name, chemical name, or brand name designated, listed in this section. Each drug or substance has been assigned the Controlled Substances Code Number set forth opposite it.

. . .

(f)   Hallucinogenic substances.

---

(1) . . .

(2) Cannabis   (also   known   as   Marihuana,   including Tetrahydrocannabinols) for medicinal purposes only . . .

OTHER ISSUES FOR CONSIDERATION:

We would urge appropriate age and condition limitation.

[The petition is supported by several documents purporting to show how marijuana meets the criteria for Schedule II.]

NOTES AND QUESTIONS

1.   **Most recent petition accepted for filing.** This 106-page petition is the most recent and highest profile of the rescheduling petitions, as it was submitted by governors of two states in their official capacities. (Significantly DEA responded in its denial letter to the new governors of the states rather than personally to Christine Gregoire and Lincoln Chafee.) It was also endorsed by governors of other states, including Hawaii, Vermont and Colorado. This petition was denied on August 12, 2016. 81 Fed. Reg. 53,687.

2.   **Petitions for rescheduling.** Several petitions to reschedule marijuana have been accepted for filing by the DEA since passage of the CSA, all eventually denied. Although procedures of filing petitions may seem straight-forward, each petition went through a labyrinthine process between initial filing, DEA refusal, refiling, hearings, gathering necessary data, court orders and remands, and eventual denials, upheld on review. As a window into the administrative rulemaking process, it is worth reviewing this history, particularly as it relates to marijuana.

First Petition. Filed on May 18, 1972, by National Organization for the Reform of Marijuana Laws (NORML) and other organizations, requesting that marijuana be decontrolled, or transferred from Schedule I to Schedule V. On September 1, 1972, the Bureau for Dangerous Narcotics (predecessor to DEA) declined to accept the petition for filing in accord with 21 CFR Part 1308.43(c), on the grounds that the Single Convention on Narcotic Drugs precluded consideration of transferring marijuana to a less restrictive schedule or decontrolling it. 37 Fed. Reg. 18097 (1972). In *NORML v. Ingersoll*, 497 F.2d 654 (D.C. Cir. 1974), the court lambasted this refusal to accept the petition as there was "no procedural defect or failure to comply with a clear-cut requirement of law. . .It was not the kind of agency action that promoted the kind of interchange and refinement of views that is the lifeblood of a sound administrative process." The petition was remanded for an administrative hearing and a consideration on the merits. After a three-day hearing from January 28 to January 30, 1975, Administrative Law Judge (ALJ) Lewis Parker reported that certain marijuana components could be rescheduled consistent with the Treaty. However shortly thereafter, DEA's Acting Administrator, Henry Dogin, denied NORML's petition for rescheduling, as there was "currently no accepted medical use of marihuana in the United States." 40 Fed. Reg. 44164, 44168 (September 25, 1975).

On October 22, 1975 NORML filed for review. In *NORML v. DEA*, 559 F.2d 735 (D.C. Cir. 1977), the court ruled that before denial, DEA was first required by 21 U.S.C. § 811(a) and (b) to request scientific and medical evaluations from HEW (predecessor to HHS). In 1979, without holding additional hearings, DEA denied the petition. NORML filed a writ of mandamus to compel hearings. The court agreed and on October 16, 1980, ordered DEA to refer evaluations to HHS for scientific and medical findings and recommendations on scheduling. NORML v. DEA, No. 79-1660 (D.C. Cir. 1980). Hearings were held in 1987 and 1988; on January 20, 1987, NORML filed an amended petition requesting rescheduling to Schedule II (instead of Schedule V). Based on these hearings, on September, 6, 1988, DEA Administrative Law Judge Francis Young recommended that marijuana be rescheduled to Schedule II. *In re Matter of Marijuana Rescheduling Petition* (Docket No. 86-22 September, 6, 1988). However, a year later, DEA Administrator John Lawn again denied the petition as marijuana did not have "currently accepted medical use in treatment in the U.S." *Denial of Petition in In re Matter of Marijuana Rescheduling Petition*, 54 Fed. Reg. 53,767, 53,783 (Dec. 29, 1989).

On appeal, the court remanded this decision for reapplication of several factors which DEA failed to consider. *Alliance for Cannabis Therapeutics and NORML v. DEA*, 930 F.2d 936 (DC Cir.1991). DEA reapplied these factors and again denied the petition. *Denial of Petition in In re Matter of Marijuana Rescheduling Petition*, 57 Fed. Reg. 10,499 (March 21, 1992). This denial was affirmed in *Alliance for Cannabis Therapeutics v. DEA*, 15 F. 3d 1131, 1133 (DC Cir.1994). [This litigation is reviewed in Chapter 3.]

Second Petition. On September 6, 1992, Carl Olsen filed a petition to reschedule marijuana based on the 1986 rescheduling of Marinol. DEA declined to accept the petition, but was ordered to do so by the DC Court of Appeals. DEA denied the petition on May 16, 1994.

Third Petition. On July 10, 1995, Dr. Jon Gettman and High Times Magazine petitioned for rescheduling marijuana on the grounds that "there is no scientific evidence that [it has] sufficient abuse potential to warrant Schedule I or Schedule II status." The petition was denied on March 28, 2001. See *Drug Enforcement Administration Notice of Denial of Petition*, 66 Fed.Reg. 20037 (2001). The appeal of the petitioners was not considered on the merits as the court found that they lacked Article III standing to appeal, and the denial of petition was therefore affirmed. *Gettman v. DEA*, 290 F.3d 430 (D.C. Cir. 2002).

Fourth Petition. On October 9, 2002, Coalition to Reschedule Marijuana petitioned for rescheduling marijuana to Schedule III, IV, or V. On April 3, 2003, the DEA accepted the filing of that petition, but apparently took no action after that. On December 6, 2006, HHS delivered its evaluation, based on the five-part test, that there was no currently accepted medical use. On May 23, 2011, Petitioners filed for a writ of mandamus to compel the DEA to respond to the petition. Although the writ was granted, the petition was denied. See *Denial of Petition to Initiate Proceedings to Reschedule Marijuana*, 76 Fed. Reg. 40,552 (July 8, 2011). On review, the court found that one of the petitioners had standing as he could claim direct injury as a result of the scheduling of marijuana. Nonetheless the court affirmed the denial as within the discretion of DEA. *Americans for Safe Access v. DEA*, 706 F.3d 438 (D.C. Cir. 2013). [The relevant potion of this decision is laid out in Section B of this chapter.]

Fifth Petitions. On December 17, 2009, Bryan Krum, a psychiatric nurse practitioner and army veteran advocating for use of marijuana in treating post-traumatic stress disorder in veterans, filed a petition for rescheduling. On November 30, 2011 Governors Gregoire and Chafee filed the petition excerpted above. This petition was accepted for filing on January, 30, 2012. After receiving an evaluation from the FDA, DEA denied both petitions. 81 Fed. Reg. 53,687 (Aug 12, 2016). This denial is being appealed as of mid-2018.

   3.   **Rescheduling stages.** A rescheduling process proceeds in stages per 21 C.F.R. Part 1308.43, including the following possible actions: filing of the petition; acceptance or nonacceptance of the petition; denial of the petition for insufficient grounds to justify initiating proceedings; gathering necessary data; requesting from HHS (and the FDA and NIDA) a scientific and medical evaluation and recommendations as to whether such substance should be so controlled, transferred, or removed as a controlled substance; and initiating proceedings for control, transfer, or removal as the case may be, including publishing the recommendation in the Federal Register for a 30–60 day period for public comment. A point that has been in contention is what triggers the requirement to hold public hearings before DEA issues a final ruling?

   4.   **Reasonable time.** 21 C.F.R. Part 1308 mandates that submitted petitions should be resolved in a "reasonable time." The four accepted petitions took 22 years, 6 years, 13 years, and 7 years to resolve, respectively. Regardless of what one thinks the outcome should be, it would be hard to argue that this is a reasonable time to resolve these petitions, especially as they address similar and already adjudicated issues. Why the delays? Is it the fault of the procedures that themselves use vague terms, such as "reasonable time," "grounds. . .not sufficient to justify the initiation of proceedings," "gathering the necessary data," and the like? Or is it the fault of the parties? Several commentators have accused the DEA of dragging its feet on each petition. See e.g. John Hudak, *Marijuana: A Short History* (Brookings 2016), pp. 130–36.

Does this reflect a problem in the law which gives the same agency responsibility to interpret and apply the rules and criminally enforce its own regulations? The DEA has placed blame on the pro-marijuana parties for making "misleading accusations and communications" and on its own Administrative Law Judge, Francis Young, for his "erroneous," "incredible, and appalling" findings, leading to his conclusion that marijuana be rescheduled to Schedule II. See 54 Fed. Reg. 53,767, 53,783 (Dec. 29, 1989). Other commentators have placed blame on the nature of the marijuana plant itself, with the difficulty of scientifically and clinically assessing raw, botanical marijuana, given its various strains, its possible contamination, and the difficulty of administering it in precise, standardized, and reproducible doses. See e.g. Kevin A. Sabet, *Much Ado About Nothing: Why Rescheduling Won't Solve Advocates' Medical Marijuana Problem*, 58 Wayne L. Rev. 81, 87–88 (2012).

5.   **Currently accepted medical use.** Each court that has affirmed DEA denial of a petition has upheld the finding that marijuana is "without currently accepted medical use in treatment in the United States." Administrative Law Judge, Francis Young, among others, has asked: "Accepted by whom?" See *In re Matter of Marijuana Rescheduling Petition* (Docket No. 86-22, September, 6, 1988). Must marijuana be accepted for medical use throughout the entirety of the United States or only a sector? The entire medical and scientific community or only a portion? By the FDA exclusively? Does the fact that the majority of states have legalized and regulated medical marijuana mean, by itself, that there is currently accepted medical use of marijuana in the United States? In addition DEA has repeatedly argued that Schedule I "is the only schedule reserved for drugs without currently accepted medical use in treatment in the United States." In other words, even if a substance presents little danger of abuse and is safe for use under medical supervision—that is, it is relatively harmless—it must be controlled in Schedule 1, the most restrictive schedule, if it doesn't qualify under a rigorous standard of "currently accepted medical use of marijuana in the United States." See e.g. 66 Fed. Reg. 20038 (2001); 76 Fed. Reg. FR 40552 (2011). Does this reflect an inflexibility in the scheduling criteria that can lead to disadvantageous outcomes?

6.   **Concurrent constitutional challenges.** On October 10, 1973, near the beginning of its 22 year litigation of its first petition, NORML sought a declaratory judgment that the classification of marijuana as a controlled substance was unconstitutional, similar to allegations we examined in chapter 8. NORML alleged that controlling marijuana in Schedule I violated the right to privacy, the equal protection component of the due process clause, and was irrational in being both an under inclusive and over inclusive classification, and the penalties thereto constituted cruel and usual punishment—issues that in a way were the judicial equivalent of the administrative process it was litigating. After staying this proceeding while waiting for administrative resolution of the matter, the U.S. District Court for the District of Columbia held evidentiary hearings on the allegation. On February 11, 1980, in the

opinion we give in full in Chapter 2, the court rejected all of these challenges. *NORML v. Bell*, 488 F.Supp. 123 (D.D.C. 1980).

B. COURT REVIEW OF DEA DISCRETION

As we have seen, all four petitions accepted for filing have been denied by DEA after a long, laborious process. The most recent court review of a denial of a rescheduling petition follows.

AMERICANS FOR SAFE ACCESS V. DEA

United States Court of Appeals for the D.C. Circuit
706 F.3d 438 (D.C. Cir. 2013)

EDWARDS, J.

[As the court in the opinion outlines the 21 U.S.C. §§ 811, 812, procedures that we have already studied in Chapters 2 and 3, we summarize only excerpts of the first part of the opinion here. Petitioners appealed DEA's denial of their 2002 petition to initiate proceedings to reschedule marijuana as a Schedule III, IV, or V drug. The DEA had submitted Petitioners' rescheduling request to the Department of Health and Human Services (DHHS). *Denial of Petition,* 76 Fed. Reg. at 40,552. In its scientific and medical evaluation, DHHS concluded that "[t]here is no currently accepted medical use for marijuana in the United States. The DEA denied the petition on July 8, 2011, finding that "[t]he limited existing clinical evidence is not adequate to warrant rescheduling of marijuana under the CSA." On July 22, 2011, Petitioners filed for review of the DEA action. Unlike with previous cases, the court found that one of the named Petitioners had standing to challenge the agency's action. (The Petitioner was a disabled veteran who alleged injury from the Veteran Affairs Department's policy of refusing to provide referrals for state medical marijuana programs.) The court's consideration on the substance of Petitioner's claim follows.]

The DEA's Denial of the Petition to Initiate Proceedings to Reschedule Marijuana

On the merits, Petitioners claim that the DEA's final order denying their request to initiate proceedings to reschedule marijuana was arbitrary and capricious. Under the terms of the CSA, marijuana cannot be rescheduled to Schedules III, IV, or V without a "currently accepted medical use." 21 U.S.C. § 812(b)(3)–(5). To assess whether marijuana has such a medical use, the agency applies a five-part test: "(1) The drug's chemistry must be known and reproducible; (2) There must be adequate safety studies; (3) There must be adequate and well-controlled studies proving efficacy; (4) The drug must be accepted by qualified experts; and (5) The scientific evidence must be widely available." *Alliance for Cannabis Therapeutics*, 15 F. 3d 1131, 1135 (D.C. Cir.1994). Because the agency's factual findings in this case are supported by substantial evidence and because those factual findings reasonably support the agency's final decision not to reschedule marijuana, we must uphold the agency action.

Under the Administrative Procedure Act, a court may set aside an agency's final decision only if it is "arbitrary, capricious, an abuse of discretion, or otherwise not in accordance with law." 5 U.S.C. § 706(2)(A). Furthermore, the agency's interpretation of its own regulations "must be given controlling weight unless it is plainly erroneous or inconsistent with the regulation." *Thomas Jefferson Univ. v. Shalala*, 512 U.S. 504, 512 (1994). The CSA also directs this court to review the agency's findings of fact for substantial evidence. See 21 U.S.C. § 877. Under this standard, we must "ask whether a reasonable mind might accept a particular evidentiary record as adequate to support a conclusion." *Dickinson v. Zurko*, 527 U.S. 150, 162 (1999).

Petitioners do not seriously dispute the propriety of the five-part test approved in *Alliance for Cannabis Therapeutics*, 15 F. 3d at 1133. Thus, they are left with the difficult task of showing that the DEA has misapplied its own regulations. Petitioners challenge the agency's reasoning on each of the five factors. However, "[a] drug will be deemed to have a currently accepted medical use for CSA purposes only if all five of the foregoing elements are demonstrated." *Denial*, 76 Fed. Reg. at 40,579. In this case, we need only look at one factor, the existence of "adequate and well-controlled studies proving efficacy," to resolve Petitioners' claim. In its scientific and medical evaluation, DHHS concluded that "research on the medical use of marijuana ha[d] not progressed to the point that marijuana [could] be considered to have a 'currently accepted medical use' or a 'currently accepted medical use with severe restrictions.'" *Id.* at 40,560. As noted above, DHHS' recommendations are binding on the DEA insofar as they rest on scientific and medical determinations. 21 U.S.C. § 811(b). After an exhaustive examination of the issue, the DEA, adhering to DHHS' recommendation, reached the following conclusion:

> To establish accepted medical use, the effectiveness of a drug must be established in well-controlled, well-designed, well-conducted, and well-documented scientific studies, including studies performed in a large number of patients (57 FR 10499, 1992). To date, such studies have not been performed. The small clinical trial studies with limited patients and short duration are not sufficient to establish medical utility. Studies of longer duration are needed to fully characterize the drug's efficacy and safety profile. Scientific reliability must be established in multiple clinical studies. Furthermore, anecdotal reports and isolated case reports are not adequate evidence to support an accepted medical use of marijuana (57 FR 10499, 1992). The evidence from clinical

research and reviews of earlier clinical research does not meet this standard.

Denial, 76 Fed. Reg. at 40,579.

Petitioners contest these findings, arguing that their petition to reschedule marijuana cites more than two hundred peer-reviewed published studies demonstrating marijuana's efficacy for various medical uses, and that those studies were largely ignored by the agency. As we explain below, Petitioners' singular reliance on "peer-reviewed" studies misses the mark. It is also noteworthy that Petitioners' brief to this court fails to convincingly highlight any significant studies allegedly ignored by DHHS or the DEA. Petitioners' argument focuses at length on one study—the March 1999 report from the Institute of Medicine ("IOM")—that was clearly addressed by the DEA. The IOM report does indeed suggest that marijuana might have medical benefits. See, e.g., INST. OF MEDICINE, MARIJUANA AND MEDICINE: ASSESSING THE SCIENCE BASE 177 (Janet E. Joy et al. eds., 1999). However, the DEA fairly construed this report as calling for "more and better studies to determine potential medical applications of marijuana" and not as sufficient proof of medical efficacy itself. *Denial,* 76 Fed. Reg. at 40,580. In other words, "while the IOM report did support further research into therapeutic uses of cannabinoids, the IOM report did not 'recognize marijuana's accepted medical use' but rather the potential therapeutic utility of cannabinoids." *Id.*

At bottom, the parties' dispute in this case turns on the agency's interpretation of its own regulations. Petitioners construe "adequate and well-controlled studies" to mean peer-reviewed, published studies suggesting marijuana's medical efficacy. The DEA, in contrast, interprets that factor to require something more scientifically rigorous. In explaining its conclusion that there is a lack of clinical evidence establishing marijuana's "currently accepted medical use," the agency said the following:

> [A] limited number of Phase I investigations have been conducted as approved by the FDA. Clinical trials, however, generally proceed in three phases. See 21 C.F.R. 312.21 (2010). Phase I trials encompass initial testing in human subjects, generally involving 20 to 80 patients. Id. They are designed primarily to assess initial safety, tolerability, pharmacokinetics, pharmacodynamics, and preliminary studies of potential therapeutic benefit. (62 FR 66113, 1997). Phase II and Phase III studies involve successively larger groups of patients: usually no more than several hundred subjects in Phase II and usually from several hundred to several thousand in Phase III. 21 C.F.R. 312.21. These studies are designed primarily to explore (Phase II) and to demonstrate or confirm (Phase III) therapeutic efficacy and

benefit in patients. (62 FR 66113, 1997). No Phase II or Phase III studies of marijuana have been conducted. Even in 2001, DHHS acknowledged that there is "suggestive evidence that marijuana may have beneficial therapeutic effects in relieving spasticity associated with multiple sclerosis, as an analgesic, as an antiemetic, as an appetite stimulant and as a bronchodilator." (66 FR 20038, 2001). But there is still no data from adequate and well-controlled clinical trials that meets the requisite standard to warrant rescheduling.

Id. at 40,579–80. The DEA interprets "adequate and well-controlled studies" to mean studies similar to what the Food and Drug Administration ("FDA") requires for a New Drug Application ("NDA"). See *id*. at 40,562. DHHS found that "there have been no NDA-quality studies that have scientifically assessed the efficacy of marijuana for any medical condition." *Id*. It is well understood that, under FDA protocols, "adequate and well-controlled investigations" require "clinical investigations, by experts qualified by scientific training and experience to evaluate the effectiveness of the drug involved, on the basis of which it could fairly and responsibly be concluded by such experts that the drug will have the effect it purports or is represented to have under the conditions of use prescribed, recommended, or suggested in the labeling or proposed labeling thereof." 21 U.S.C. § 355(d). This is a rigorous standard.

Contrary to what Petitioners suggest, something more than "peer-reviewed" studies is required to satisfy DEA's standard, and for good reason. Petitioners may have cited some peer-reviewed articles in support of their position, but they have not pointed to "adequate and well-controlled studies" confirming the efficacy of marijuana for medicinal uses. If, as is the case here, "there is substantial evidence to support the [agency's] finding that the[ ] studies [offered by petitioner] are not helpful, then petitioner must fail." *Unimed, Inc. v. Richardson*, 458 F.2d 787, 789 (D.C. Cir. 1972). In making this assessment, we must "remind ourselves that our role in the Congressional scheme is not to give an independent judgment of our own, but rather to determine whether the expert agency entrusted with regulatory responsibility has taken an irrational or arbitrary view of the evidence assembled before it." *Id*.

The DEA's construction of its regulation is eminently reasonable. Therefore, we are obliged to defer to the agency's interpretation of "adequate and well-controlled studies. Judged against the DEA's standard, we find nothing in the record that could move us to conclude that the agency failed to prove by substantial evidence that such studies confirming marijuana's medical efficacy do not exist.

Finally, Petitioners suggested during oral argument that the Government had foreclosed the research that would be necessary to create sufficiently reliable clinical studies of marijuana's medical efficacy.

Because Petitioners did not properly raise this issue with the DEA and there is nothing in the record to support it, we do not consider it here. We note, however, that DHHS' recommendation explained that "[t]he opportunity for scientists to conduct clinical research with marijuana exists under the [D]HHS policy supporting clinical research with botanical marijuana." *Denial*, 76 Fed. Reg. at 40,562. Thus, it appears that adequate and well-controlled studies are wanting not because they have been foreclosed but because they have not been completed.

Conclusion. For the reasons discussed above, we hereby deny the petition for review.

[Dissent of HENDERSON, J., finding no standing, omitted.]

NOTES AND QUESTIONS

1. **Administrative discretion.** According to this case, what is the standard for judicial review of decisions of administrative agencies? The Administrative Procedure Act, 5 U.S.C. § 551 et seq governs rule-making by administrative agencies for administering congressional legislation. However these procedures can be overridden by procedures contained in the originating legislation. The CSA promulgates its own standard for judicial review of administrative decisions regarding drugs:

> All final determinations, findings, and conclusions of the Attorney General under this subchapter shall be final and conclusive decisions of the matters involved, except that any person aggrieved by a final decision of the Attorney General may obtain review of the decision in the United States Court of Appeals for the District of Columbia or for the circuit in which his principal place of business is located upon petition filed with the court and delivered to the Attorney General within thirty days after notice of the decision. Findings of fact by the Attorney General, if supported by substantial evidence, shall be conclusive.

CSA, section 877. This substantial "evidence standard" allows for wider judicial review than the "abuse of discretion standard" that the Administrative Procedure Act applies to other agency actions.

2. **Adequate studies.** The court also confirms the DEA's insistence on "adequate and well-controlled studies," interpreted as similar if not identical to FDA protocols. See 21 U.S.C. § 355; 21 C.F.R. part 312. These protocols include submitting non-clinical tests to determine toxicity; preliminary testing on animals; an IND (Investigating New Drug) application; and a rigorous three-phase clinical trial on humans. The essence of this three-phase trial can be summarized as large population, randomized, double-blind, placebo controlled, clinical trials. Does it make sense to demand that all scientific assessments in the scheduling process conform to this methodology? What should be the scientific weight given to the kind of peer review studies that DEA found inadequate in *American for Safe Access v. DEA*? What if these peer

review studies are "meta-analyses" that review several studies that meet the FDA protocol? Kevin A. Sabet, *Much Ado About Nothing: Why Rescheduling Won't Solve Advocates' Medical Marijuana Problem*, 58 Wayne L. Rev. 81 (2012) discusses the near impossibility of undertaking FDA protocol studies for a raw botanical drug like marijuana as an argument for the futility of rescheduling. But can it instead be seen as an argument for permitting different methodologies?

3.   New Drug Application. The court approves DEA interpretation that "adequate and well-controlled studies" are similar to what the Food and Drug Administration requires for a New Drug Application (NDA). Does it always make sense to apply criteria for a new drug scheduling to a rescheduling application for a drug long in use. In particular, does it make sense for a drug like marijuana which has been used for thousands of years, and intensively studied for a half century?

4.   Foreclosed research. The court rejects petitioners argument that the "government had foreclosed the research that would be necessary to create sufficiently reliable clinical studies of marijuana's medical efficacy," replying that "[t]he opportunity for scientists to conduct clinical research with marijuana exists under the DHHS policy supporting clinical research with botanical marijuana." However did the DEA in fact concede the point in its 2016 denial of the petition by the Rhode Island and Washington governors? While finding a lack of clinical evidence establishing marijuana's "currently accepted medical use," DEA announced changes to enhance high level research into marijuana. For example, it would register growers of research-grade marijuana, in addition to the previously exclusive NIDA-funded program at the University of Mississippi, and it would no longer require researchers to submit a proposed study of marijuana to the U.S. Public Health Service for review. See *Applications To Become Registered Under the Controlled Substances Act To Manufacture Marijuana To Supply Researchers in the United States.*81 Fed. Reg. 53486 (Aug. 12 2016).

5.   Further research. The court seems to devalue the comprehensive March 1999 report from the Institute of Medicine for calling for "more and better studies to determine potential medical applications of marijuana." Would the report be more authoritative if it advised against more and better studies?

PROBLEM 10-1

A new petition is filed with DEA requesting transfer for marijuana to Schedule II, based on the fact that the majority of states have found marijuana to be an effective medicine such that it is legalized for medical purposes. In addition many of these states have conducted studies, pre and post legalization, to justify their medical regulatory regime. Should this be sufficient to establish "currently accepted medical use in treatment in the United States"?

C. RESCHEDULED MARIJUANA SUBSTANCES

Although all petitions for rescheduling botanical marijuana have been denied, synthetic cannabinoids and a marijuana-derived extract have been scheduled to less restrictive schedules than Schedule I. The first such substance was Marinol, a synthetic cannabinoid, and other products which have the same formulation.

RULING TO RESCHEDULE MARINOL FROM SCHEDULE II TO SCHEDULE III

Drug Enforcement Administration
64 Fed. Reg. 35928 (July 2, 1999)

Marshall, Deputy Administrator.

[This is a final rule of the Deputy Administrator of the Drug Enforcement Administration (DEA) transferring the Marinol drug between schedules of the Controlled Substances Act (CSA) pursuant to 21 U.S.C. § 811. The DEA's summary and background portion of this Rule is omitted].

The Petition To Reschedule Marinol ®

On February 3, 1995, UNIMED Pharmaceuticals, Inc. petitioned the Administrator of DEA to transfer Marinol from schedule II to schedule III. In response to this petition, and in view of supplemental information that UNIMED provided to DEA on December 11, 1996, DEA had to determine whether this proposed rescheduling of Marinol would comport with United States obligations under the Convention on Psychotropic Substances, 1971 (Psychotropic Convention). See 21 U.S.C. 811(d). Under the Psychotropic Convention, dronabinol and all dronabinol-containing products, such as Marinol, are listed in schedule II. As a result, the United States is obligated under the Psychotropic Convention to impose certain restrictions on the export and import of Marinol. DEA has concluded that, in order for the United States to continue to meet its obligations under the Psychotropic Convention, DEA will continue to require import and export permits for international transactions involving Marinol, even though Marinol will be transferred to schedule III of the CSA.

After determining that Marinol could be transferred to schedule III while maintaining the controls required by the Psychotropic Convention, and after gathering the necessary data, on August 7, 1997, DEA requested from the Acting Assistant Secretary for Health, Department of Health and Human Services (DHHS), a scientific and medical evaluation, and recommendation, as to whether Marinol should be rescheduled, in accordance with 21 U.S.C. 811(b).

On September 11, 1998, the Acting Assistant Secretary for Health sent to DEA a letter recommending that Marinol be transferred from schedule II to schedule III of the CSA. Enclosed with the September 11, 1998, letter was a document prepared by the FDA entitled "Basis for the Recommendation for Rescheduling Marinol Capsules from schedule II to schedule III of the Controlled Substances Act (CSA)." In this document, the FDA defines the Marinol product as "an FDA-approved drug product containing synthetically produced dronabinol dissolved in sesame oil and encapsulated in soft gelatin capsules (2.5 mg, 5 mg, and 10 mg per dosage unit)." The document contained a review of the factors which the CSA requires the Secretary to consider, which are set forth in 21 U.S.C. 811(c).

The Proposed Rule

On November 7, 1998, the then-Acting Deputy Administrator of DEA published a notice of proposed rule making in the Federal Register (63 FR 59751), proposing to transfer Marinol from schedule II to schedule III of the CSA. The proposed rule was based on the DHHS scientific and medical evaluation and scheduling recommendation and DEA's independent evaluation. Also under the proposed rule, 21 CFR 1312.30 would be amended to include Marinol as a schedule III non-narcotic controlled substance specifically designated as requiring import and export permits pursuant to 21 U.S.C. 952(b)(2) and 953(e)(3). As discussed above, this proposed amendment to 21 CFR 1312.30 is necessary for the United States to continue to meet its obligations under the Psychotropic Convention. The notice of proposed rule provided an opportunity for all interested persons to submit their comments, objections, or requests for hearing in writing to DEA on or before December 7, 1998.

Comments From the Public

DEA received comments regarding the proposed rule from ten persons. Nine of the commenters supported the proposed rule. One commenter objected to the proposed rule and requested a hearing thereon. The comments are briefly summarized below.

The nine commenters who supported the proposed rule included organizations, physicians, and one individual. Eight of the nine commenters who supported the proposed rule expressed the opinion that Marinol is a safe and effective alternative to smoking marijuana for treatment of nausea and loss of appetite and has low abuse potential. One commenter who supported the proposed rule expressed the view that the rescheduling of Marinol should not serve as a substitute for making marijuana legally available for medical use. This commenter stated that it supported the use of marijuana for medical purposes and, therefore, wished to emphasize that the proposed rule affected the CSA status of Marinol— not that of marijuana, which remains a schedule I controlled substance.

The one commenter who objected to the proposed rule, and requested a hearing thereon, asserted that Marinol should not be transferred to schedule III unless and until marijuana and all other THC-containing drugs are simultaneously and likewise rescheduled. This commenter asserted that Marinol has the same potential for abuse as marijuana and all other THC-containing drugs. This commenter agreed with the proposed rule that Marinol's potential for abuse is less than the "high potential for abuse" commensurate with schedules I and II of the CSA. Accordingly, this commenter agreed that Marinol should be transferred to a less restrictive schedule than schedule II. However, this commenter disagreed with what would be the resultant status of Marinol vis-a-vis marijuana and THC if the NPRM [Notice of Proposed Rulemaking] becomes final: Marinol would be in schedule III while marijuana and THC would remain in schedule I. This commenter asserted that the CSA prohibited transferring Marinol to a less restrictive schedule unless marijuana and all THC-containing drugs are simultaneously transferred to the same schedule. DEA has determined that this commenter's objections are based on a misinterpretation of the CSA, which can be addressed, as a matter of law, without conducting a fact-finding hearing. Accordingly, as this commenter presented no material issues of fact, DEA denied this commenter's request for a hearing.

Findings

Relying on the scientific and medical evaluation and scheduling recommendations of the Assistant Secretary for Health, and based on DEA's independent review thereof, the Deputy Administrator of the DEA, pursuant to 21 U.S.C. 811(a) and 811(b), finds that:

Based on information now available, Marinol has a potential for abuse less than the drugs or other substances in schedules I and II.

Marinol is a FDA-approved drug product and has a currently accepted medical use in treatment in the United States; and

Abuse of Marinol may lead to moderate of low physical dependence or high psychological dependence.

Rescheduling Action

Based on the above findings, the Deputy Administrator of the DEA concludes that Marinol should be transferred from schedule II to schedule III.

[In the reminder of the Rule, DEA sets out the regulations for the newly-rescheduled Marinol as required by Title 21 of the Code of Federal Regulations including: Registration. Part 1301. Security. Secs. 1301.71, 1301.72(b), (c), and (d), 1301.73, 1301.74, 1301.75(b) and (c) and 1301.76. Labeling and Packaging. Secs. 1302.03–1302.07. Inventory. Secs. 1304.03, 1304.04 and 1304.11. Records. Secs. 1304.03, 1304.04 and 1304.21–1304.23. Prescriptions. Secs. 1306.03–1306.06 and 1306.21–1306.26. Importation and Exportation. 1312.30. Criminal Liability. Any unauthorized use of Marinol remains unlawful.]

NOTES AND QUESTIONS

1.   **Marinol.** Marinol is the trade name for a synthetic form of dronabinol, an isomer of THC, and thus is not a cannabis extract. It is the first synthetic cannabinoid approved by the FDA. Marinol contains synthetic dronabinol in sesame oil, encapsulated in gelatin capsules. Dronabinol is the United States Adopted Name (USAN) for the (-)-isomer of Delta-9-tetrahydrocannabinol [(-)-delta-9-THC]. This is the most common and active THC isomer in cannabis and is commonly known just as "THC." (An isomer is a chemical species with the same number and types of atoms as another chemical species, but possessing somewhat distinguished properties because the atoms are arranged in differing chemical structures.) Put simply, Marinol contains a laboratory-synthesized but chemically identical isomer of THC as its active ingredient.

As suggested in the Rule, Marinol has its own complicated history of scheduling. On May 31, 1985, FDA approved of Marinol for the treatment of nausea and vomiting associated with cancer chemotherapy. On May 13, 1986, following a recommendation from HHS, DEA transferred Marinol (and products of the same formulation) from Schedule I to Schedule II of the CSA in accord with 21 U.S.C. 811(a). 51 Fed.Reg. 17476 (May 13, 1986). THC in any other composition remains on Schedule I as having "no currently accepted medical use." 21 CFR Section 1308.11(d)(31). In 1992, Marinol was approved for use for AIDS patients. In 1999, Marinol became a Schedule III substance, as stated in the Rule and codified in 21 C.F.R. Section 1308.13(g)(1).

2.   **International drug conventions.** As with botanical marijuana rescheduling, DEA first takes into account whether rescheduling a drug is in accord with international treaties, in this case the 1971 Convention on Psychotropic Substances. Dronabinol was originally listed in Schedule I of the 1971 Convention on Psychotropic Substances. In 1991, upon the recommendation of the World Health Organization (WHO), the Commission on Narcotic Drugs (CND), the United Nations organization with mandated scheduling functions over the international treaties, transferred dronabinol from Schedule I to Schedule II of the Convention on Psychotropic Substances. Prompted in part by the rescheduling of dronabinol in the United States, WHO recommended in 2006 that dronabinol be further reassigned to Schedule III of the Convention on Psychotropic Substances. However the CND decided that no new evidence justified such rescheduling and has so far declined to do so.

3.   **Public hearings.** Rescheduling requires the administrative agency, among other procedures of 5 U.S.C. §§ 556 and 557, to issue a Notice of Proposed Rulemaking, to propose an interim rule, to hold public hearings on the interim rule, and finally to promulgate a final rule. As reported above, at the Marinol hearing several commentators objected to the proposed Rule, mostly as it relates to the scheduling of botanical marijuana. What was the precise nature of their objections? How would you evaluate the validity of these objections?

4. Other administrative requirements of rulemaking. It is relevant to assessing the likelihood of marijuana rescheduling to be aware of the many administrative requirements imposed for such actions, and the possible burdens administrative agencies may see in such procedures. For example, the DEA had to make the following certifications in accordance with the requirements of the CSA and administrative law in rescheduling Marinol: that these proceedings were exempt from review by the Office of Management and Budget pursuant to Executive Order (E.O.) 12866, section 3(d)(1); that the Deputy Administrator, in accordance with the Regulatory Flexibility Act (5 U.S.C. 605(b)), reviewed this final rule and by approving it certified that it will not have a significant economic impact on a substantial number of small entities; that the rule would not result in expenditure by State, local and tribal governments, or by the private sector, of $100,000,000 or more in any one year, and therefore, no actions were necessary under the Unfunded Mandates Reform Act of 1995; that the rule was not a major rule as defined by section 804 of the Small Business Regulatory Enforcement Fairness Act of 1996; that the rule would not result in a major increase in costs or prices; or significant adverse effects on competition, employment, investment, productivity, innovation, or on the ability of United States-based companies to compete with foreign-based companies in domestic and export markets; that the rule would not have substantial direct effects on the States, on the relationship between the national government and the States, or on the distribution of power and responsibilities among the various levels of government, and therefore, in accordance with Executive Order 12612, this rule, if finalized, would not have sufficient federalism implications to warrant the preparation of a Federalism Assessment.

5. Other FDA-approved marijuana–related substances. Syndros is synthetic dronabinol in an orally administered liquid solution. It was approved by the FDA in July 2016. 82 Fed. Reg. 14,815. Nabilone is another synthetic cannabinoid that is orally administered and mimics THC and is used as an antiemetic to treat nausea and vomiting caused by cancer chemotherapy. It is marketed as the capsule drug Cesamet and was approved by the FDA in 1987, 52 Fed. Reg. 11042 (April 7, 1987), although discontinued for several years (reintroduced to market in 2006). Both Syndros and Cesamet are Schedule II drugs. 21 C.F.R. Section 1308.12(f)(2). Nabiximols, sold overseas as Sativex, is an ethanol cannabis extract that is still under investigation by FDA.

Perhaps most significantly on June 25, 2018, the FDA gave its first approval to a drug, Epidiolex, containing a purified marijuana extract, as opposed to a synthetic cannabinoid. Epidiolex is an oral-based treatment for Lennox-Gastaut syndrome and Dravet syndrome, two rare forms of pediatric epilepsy. Its active ingredient is cannabidiol (CBD), a non-intoxicating marijuana cannabinoid. On September 28, 2018, DEA classified Epidiolex in schedule V, the first marijuana extract of the cannabis plant to be placed in a less stringent schedule than schedule I. 83 Fed. Reg. 48950 (September 28, 2018). However CBD, as a marijuana extract remains in Schedule I. See 21 C.F.R. 1308.11(d)(58). "Marihuana extract" is defined as "an extract containing one or more cannabinoids that has been derived from any plant of the genus

Cannabis, other than the separated resin (whether crude or purified) obtained from the plant." 81 Fed. Reg. 90194 (December 14, 2016).

6.   FDA role. As is evident from the materials in this chapter, the FDA plays a critical role in both assessing and approving drugs for rescheduling. By and large, if a drug is not approved by the FDA, it remains on Schedule I. If approved, it can be scheduled in Schedules II through V. Some commentators forecast a regime where marijuana is rescheduled and then FDA approval must be obtained. But this is an unlikely scenario, as this chapter indicates that the norm is that FDA approval precedes rescheduling. In other words, FDA approval is the crucial component to allow rescheduling. For an article on FDA regulation of cannabis if marijuana is descheduled see Sean. O'Connor & Erika Lietzan, *The Surprising Reach of FDA Regulation of Cannabis, Even After Descheduling (forthcoming Am. U. L. Rev.).* https://papers.ssrn.com/sol3/papers.cfm?abstract_id=3242870.

7.   FDA approval. Commentators have pointed out the many obstacles to FDA approval of whole plant marijuana. In Part A of this chapter, we pointed out Kevin Sabet's argument as to the obstacles in scientifically evaluating botanical marijuana, given its various strains, its possible contamination, and the difficulty of administering it in precise, standardized, and reproducible doses. Kevin A. Sabet, *Much Ado About Nothing: Why Rescheduling Won't Solve Advocates' Medical Marijuana Problem,* 58 Wayne L. Rev. 81, 87–88 (2012). From the FDA's perspective, a single molecule synthetic cannabinoid product with a single active ingredient is easier to measure and evaluate. Unlike a drug with one active ingredient, the marijuana plant contains hundreds of compounds, and it is difficult to ascertain the precise active and inactive ingredients in its therapeutic effects. Cannabis products from different strains will show different pharmacological and toxicological profiles. For consistent and reproducible results, the FDA might have to select one of the more than 700 identified strains of marijuana. Even within that strain, genetic differences could influence the potency, quality, and purity of the plant flowers and leaves. As to route of delivery, the FDA has not approved a drug that requires smoking or inhalation. Many commentators have predicted that under its current protocols[1] the FDA can never approve botanical marijuana. See Diane Hoffmann, Francis Palumbo, Y. Tony Yang, *Will The FDA's Approval Of Epidiolex Lead To Rescheduling Marijuana?,* Health Affairs Blog, July 12, 2018.DOI: 10.1377/hblog20180709.904289. If the marijuana plant is proved to be an effective and safe drug when taken under medical supervision, is there a way to overcome these hurdles to FDA approval? Should "currently accepted medical use" under the CSA be synonymous with FDA approval?

8.   Entourage effect. The "entourage" or "ensemble" effect refers to the possible advantage of whole plant medicine over isolated cannabinoids, in that plant compounds work together to maximize health effects and minimize

---

[1]   However, in December 2016, FDA loosened requirements to some degree for botanical data submissions. *See Guidance for Industry Botanical Drug Development.* 81 Fed. Reg. 96018 (December 29, 2016).

harmful side effects. See Ethan Russo, *Taming THC: potential cannabis synergy and phytocannabinoid-terpenoid entourage effects*. 163 Br J Pharmacol 1344 (Aug. 2011). If proven, what would this mean for FDA's history of approving single marijuana constituents—synthesized or extracted—but not the plant as a whole?

9. Any interested person. As stated in C.F.R. Part § 1308.43, "Any interested person" may submit a petition to initiate scheduling proceedings. DEA publications define interested party to include the manufacturer of a drug; a medical society or association; a pharmaceutical association; a public interest group concerned with drug abuse; a state or local government agency; or an individual citizen. Although this definition is quite broad, this chapter has demonstrated that the only successful scheduling petitions have been brought by pharmaceutical companies. This makes sense as only pharmaceutical companies have the resources and the profit incentive to conduct the extensive and expensive clinical trials required by FDA protocols. However if the only interested party that can succeed in petitioning is a pharmaceutical company, does this suggest a defect in the petitioning process, which, at least in theory, seems to encourage the participation of everyday citizens?

10. Administrative Law. This chapter has taken marijuana rescheduling as a case study of administrative law. You might want to use the concepts explored in this chapter to deepen your understanding of administrative regulations and procedures. Topics include the interaction of federal statutes (mostly codified in the United States Code), administrative regulations and rulings (codified in the Code of Federal Regulations), and the entire panoply of federal rulings, proposals, notices, orders, proclamations, etc. published in the Federal Register, the daily journal of the United States Government. In addition, marijuana rescheduling can be seen as a microcosm of the federal rule making process, with the complex and even controversial requirements we have seen in this chapter.

PROBLEM 10-2

In this chapter, you have read unsuccessful and successful efforts to reschedule marijuana substances. A client has hired you to petition the DEA to transfer botanical marijuana to Schedule II. You know that all previous petitions have washed up on the shoals of the three criteria for Schedule I:

- a high potential for abuse

- no currently accepted medical use in treatment in the United States

- lack of accepted safety for use under medical supervision

21 U.S.C. § 812.

What would be your strategy for overcoming these obstacles? What kind of studies would you present and what factors in the changed marijuana landscape would you rely on? What arguments would offer the greatest chance of success?

CHAPTER 11

CRIMINAL ISSUES PERTAINING TO ILLEGAL MARIJUANA POSSESSION AND DISTRIBUTION

■ ■ ■

This chapter and the next chapter focus on criminal law and procedure issues. One might ask why a book on marijuana law would cover issues that do not necessarily involve marijuana. For example, the state may rely on the doctrine of joint constructive possession in cases involving drugs other than marijuana. True, many of the issues in this chapter are a subset of issues that arise in cases involving drug crimes generally. But in that arena, marijuana is an especially large subset. Marijuana is the most widely used illegal substance. It is widely cultivated and readily available. Marijuana is often used among friends and sometimes left in the open. Unlike many illegal substances, marijuana has a distinctive odor, even if not burnt. As one scholar has argued, marijuana's wide use and distinctive odor make it the most likely cause for pretextual stops. Alex Kreit, *Marijuana Legalization and Pretextual Stops*, 50 U.C. Davis L. Rev. 741, 750–52 (2016). In a marijuana distribution gone awry, a relatively minor crime can lead to a stiff sentence, leading to appellate litigation. Not surprisingly, as you will see in this chapter, the lead cases all involve marijuana as the drug of arrest.

A. MARIJUANA POSSESSION

A police officer observes a person smoking marijuana, resulting in an arrest for possession of marijuana. The prosecution has no trouble proving possession. Or an officer stops a motorist and discovers marijuana in the driver's vehicle. Again, proving possession is a given. But many cases involve more difficult proof problems.

Think about the previous example, when an officer stops a vehicle and sees marijuana in the vehicle or smells marijuana in the vehicle. What if the driver was not the vehicle's owner? What if three individuals are in the vehicle, does each possess the marijuana? Or assume that police lawfully enter premises occupied by several people and find marijuana in a room where all of the occupants have access. Are they all guilty of possession of marijuana? These and similar issues arise frequently in cases around the country. The lead case explores several aspects of the issue and explains the elements of joint constructive possession.

ERVIN V. COMMONWEALTH

Court of Appeals of Virginia, Richmond
704 S.E.2d 135 (Va. Ct. App. 2011)

BEALES, J.

Samuel A. Ervin (appellant) was convicted of possession of marijuana with intent to distribute, in violation of Code § 18.2–248.1. Appellant argues on appeal that the evidence at trial was insufficient to prove beyond a reasonable doubt 1) that he constructively possessed the marijuana with knowledge of its nature and character and 2) that he possessed it with the requisite intent to distribute. A divided panel of this Court held that the evidence was insufficient to prove that appellant had guilty knowledge of the marijuana. We granted the Commonwealth's petition for rehearing *en banc* and stayed the mandate of the panel's decision. On rehearing *en banc,* we now lift the stay and affirm appellant's conviction for possession of marijuana with intent to distribute for the reasons stated below.

I.   BACKGROUND

On February 29, 2008, at 8:20 p.m., Portsmouth Officers O'Brien and Rad stopped a vehicle being driven by appellant after the officers observed a traffic violation. Appellant was the sole occupant of the vehicle. Neither officer observed him make any furtive movements during their observations of him. However, as the officers approached the vehicle, "a strong odor of marijuana" was discernible through the car's open windows.

The officers asked appellant for his driver's license and for the vehicle's registration. Appellant gave the officers his driver's license, which was suspended, but did not produce any registration. The record does not indicate that appellant ever attempted to look for the registration (or help the officers locate it), but instead he simply told the officers that the vehicle was not his.

After detecting the strong odor of marijuana coming from the vehicle and after determining that appellant's driver's license was suspended, the officers took appellant into custody and placed him in the police cruiser. The officers then searched the vehicle both for the source of the strong odor of marijuana and for the vehicle's registration. Using the key that was in the vehicle's ignition, Officer Rad unlocked the glove compartment. The officers immediately observed two Ziploc bags inside the glove compartment. One of the Ziploc bags held ten knotted plastic bag corners ("baggie corners") containing marijuana, and the other Ziploc bag held thirteen baggie corners containing marijuana. No smoking devices or drug paraphernalia were found inside the vehicle or in appellant's possession.

The vehicle belonged to Tiffany Killabrew, the mother of appellant's daughter. It was Killabrew's "secondary car," which she loaned to various people, including appellant, her brother, and her sister. Killabrew testified that appellant borrowed the vehicle sometime between 6:00 and 7:00 p.m. on February 29, 2008.

At trial, Officer Francisco Natal, an expert on the packaging and distribution of narcotics, testified that the marijuana found inside the glove compartment had a street value of over $200. Officer Natal explained that, in his expert opinion, the packaging of this quantity of marijuana was inconsistent with personal use. Furthermore, Officer Natal testified that he knew of no instance where someone possessed twenty-three individual baggie corners of marijuana for personal use.

Appellant testified in his own defense, denying ownership of the marijuana. When asked on cross-examination whether he was familiar with the smell of marijuana, appellant initially replied, "Maybe." When asked to clarify his answer, appellant then testified, "No, not really. Usually you can smell like—no, not really. I'm not even going to claim that. Not really."

The trial court denied appellant's motions to strike and found appellant guilty of possession with intent to distribute, noting that "either [appellant] had been smoking [the marijuana] or he had recently just had somebody in the car who was smoking it, or at least that's the conclusion that the Court can draw from this evidence."

The trial court also explained that the manner in which the marijuana was packaged proved that appellant possessed the marijuana with intent to distribute it.

II. ANALYSIS

A. Possession of the Marijuana

Appellant argues that the evidence at trial failed to establish beyond a reasonable doubt that he knowingly possessed the marijuana in the vehicle's glove compartment. When considering this issue, the parties agree that the principles of constructive possession are applicable here. Addressing these familiar principles, the Supreme Court of Virginia has held:

> In a prosecution for possession of a controlled substance, the Commonwealth must produce evidence sufficient to support a conclusion beyond a reasonable doubt that the defendant's possession of the drug was knowing and intentional. Actual or constructive possession alone is not sufficient. "The Commonwealth must also establish that the defendant intentionally and consciously possessed it *with knowledge of its nature and character.*"

Young v. Commonwealth, 275 Va. 587 at 591.

The trial court found that appellant's possession of the marijuana was knowing and intentional, proving that he constructively possessed the marijuana.

1.   Factors Indicative of Guilty Knowledge

This Court's holding in *Coward v. Commonwealth,* 48 Va.App. 653 (2006), although not controlling given the very different facts in this case, is a useful guide for determining whether circumstantial evidence is sufficient as a matter of law to prove that a vehicle occupant knowingly and intentionally possessed drugs found in the car. In *Coward,* the police stopped a Toyota, in which Coward was the passenger, in the middle of the night for an equipment violation. As the officer approached the Toyota, he directed the lights on his police car toward the Toyota, and he also used his flashlight to further illuminate the interior of the car. The officer was able to observe a clear plastic bag containing crack cocaine, sitting on the console between the driver's and passenger's seats. The driver told the officer that the Toyota belonged to his mother and that he had been driving it all evening. Coward made no statements to the officer. At Coward's trial, the trial court convicted Coward of possession of cocaine, basing its finding that Coward had guilty knowledge of the cocaine *solely* on his occupancy of the vehicle and his proximity to the cocaine.

On appeal, this Court reversed Coward's conviction, reiterating the familiar principle that mere occupancy and proximity, although factors to be considered among the totality of the circumstances, are insufficient *standing alone* to prove a defendant's guilty knowledge of illegal drugs. Therefore, although mindful of the deferential appellate standard of review in a sufficiency of the evidence case, this Court held that the evidence at Coward's trial was insufficient as a matter of law because it "did not establish *any other facts or circumstances* necessary to draw the legal conclusion that Coward was aware of the presence and character of the cocaine." *Id.* at 659.

Here, unlike in *Coward,* the evidence at trial *did* present other facts and circumstances permitting the trial court to draw the conclusion that appellant was aware of the presence and character of the marijuana in the glove compartment—and these facts and circumstances may be considered *in addition to* appellant's occupancy of the vehicle and proximity to the marijuana. Based on the combined force of these concurrent and related circumstances, the trial court's finding that appellant had guilty knowledge of the marijuana in the glove compartment was not plainly wrong or unsupported by the evidence.

a.   *The Strong Odor of Marijuana*

A defendant's knowledge of the presence and character of a drug may be shown by evidence of the acts, statements, or conduct of the accused, *Garland v. Commonwealth,* 225 Va. 182, 184 (1983), as well as by "other facts or circumstances" tending to demonstrate the accused's guilty knowledge of the drug, *Williams v. Commonwealth,* 42 Va.App. 723, 735 (2004). As the Supreme Court of Virginia recently explained in *Young,* a "drug's distinctive odor" can be circumstantial evidence to support a finding that a defendant knew of the nature and character of the substance in his possession. *Young,* 275 Va. at 591.

Here, appellant was driving a vehicle that smelled strongly of marijuana—the very same illegal drug discovered in the vehicle's glove compartment. This odor, which was readily discernible to both officers as marijuana when they approached appellant's vehicle, would certainly have been apparent to appellant as he sat in the vehicle. The strong and distinctive odor of the drug provided a significant indication to anyone inside (or even near) the vehicle that marijuana was located within the vehicle.

Based on the officers' testimony, the trial court found that the strong marijuana odor emanating from the vehicle was from marijuana that had been smoked. Making a distinction between the smell of burnt marijuana and "fresh" (i.e., not burnt) marijuana, appellant contends that the trial court erroneously inferred that he was aware of the marijuana in the glove compartment, which was fresh, based on the readily discernible smell of burnt marijuana.

However, . . . [t]he trial court not *only* found that the officers smelled *already* smoked marijuana, it *also* found that the marijuana had been *recently* smoked by appellant or someone in the car with him. The trial court's finding, which was certainly not unreasonable given the officers' testimony concerning the strength and obviousness of the marijuana odor as they approached the vehicle, is entitled to deference during appellate review for sufficiency of the evidence.

Furthermore, Killabrew's testimony established that appellant took possession of the vehicle between 6:00 and 7:00 p.m., approximately two hours before the traffic stop. Thus, the trial court's inference that the marijuana detected by the officers must have been smoked—either by appellant or by someone else in appellant's presence—while appellant was in possession of the vehicle was "reasonable and justified" based on the strength of the odor. *Sullivan,* 280 Va. at 676. Therefore, the officers' detection of the strong odor of recently burnt marijuana certainly does not undermine the trial court's conclusion that appellant was aware of the "fresh" marijuana in the glove compartment. *See Jackson,* 443 U.S. at 319 (stating that it is the province of the factfinder to draw reasonable inferences from basic facts to ultimate facts). Nothing in this record suggests any other means, in the approximately two hours that appellant had possessed the car, of creating such a strong odor of marijuana that people could readily identify the odor before actually reaching the vehicle.

Therefore, the presence of the strong odor of marijuana from within the vehicle is one factor to consider in this case because it tends "to show or allow the trial court to reasonably infer" that appellant was aware of the marijuana in the glove compartment. *Coward,* 48 Va.App. at 659. However, the strong odor of marijuana emanating from the vehicle, readily discernible by each of the officers, is not viewed in isolation of the other facts presented by this record on appeal. Instead, this factor must be viewed among the totality of the circumstances presented to the trial court. Several additional facts and circumstances in the record here further support the trial court's finding that appellant was aware of the presence and character of the marijuana discovered in the glove compartment.

b. *Appellant's Sole Possession of the Vehicle and His Possession of the Key to the Glove Compartment*

Appellant was in *sole* possession of the vehicle at the time the marijuana was found. Appellant also possessed the key to the vehicle and its glove compartment and, therefore, was the *sole* person at that time with means to access the glove compartment containing the marijuana. The trial court, acting as factfinder in this case, was permitted to consider these facts as circumstances further indicating appellant's guilty knowledge of the marijuana found in the glove compartment.

The Supreme Court's recent holding in *Cordon v. Commonwealth,* 280 Va. 691 (2010), is not controlling on the very different facts in this case. In *Cordon,* a police detective interviewed Cordon while investigating a burglary that occurred at a house on Finley Square in the City of Hampton. Cordon told the detective that his uncle, who was not present at that time, owned the house. Cordon said that he had been living in the Finley Square house while his uncle had been away and that one of its bedrooms was his, but Cordon also indicated in a handwritten statement regarding the burglary that an address in the City of Newport News was his residence. Two days later, the police executed a search warrant at the Finley Square house. Cordon's uncle was present, but Cordon was not. The police found a cooler containing cocaine in the bedroom that Cordon had identified as his own two days before during his interview with the detective.

Reversing Cordon's conviction for possession of the cocaine found in the cooler, the Supreme Court noted:

> *Cordon was not in the house or the bedroom when the cooler containing the cocaine was discovered.* There was no other physical evidence linking Cordon to the cooler or the contraband. The record showed that *two days had passed between the time Cordon was known to be at the Finley Square house and the seizure of the cooler containing cocaine.* While he referred to the bedroom as "his" and stated that he was staying there while his uncle was away at the time of the September burglary, Cordon listed his address as a location in Newport News. There was no evidence of

ownership of the cooler, a very portable item, and *no evidence placed Cordon at the house at any time between the day he received Baer's business card and the day the search warrant was executed.*

Id. at 696

Thus, as the Supreme Court emphasized, two days passed between when Cordon was known to occupy this bedroom of his uncle's house and when the cocaine actually was discovered in the cooler in the bedroom. This gap in the evidence against Cordon was consistent with his hypothesis of innocence that someone other than he had placed the cooler of cocaine in the bedroom of his uncle's house without Cordon's knowledge. The evidence here contrasts sharply with the evidence in *Cordon*. Appellant was present in the vehicle while the vehicle strongly smelled of marijuana and while its glove compartment held marijuana; appellant was the *sole* occupant of the vehicle at that time; and appellant had exclusive possession of the key that was capable of opening the glove compartment containing the baggies of cocaine—which were immediately observable upon opening the glove compartment. All of these circumstances, which simply did not exist in *Cordon,* render the Supreme Court's holding in *Cordon* inapplicable to the facts of this case.

Similarly, the facts in *Burchette v. Commonwealth,* 15 Va.App. 432, 438 (1992), upon which appellant relies, are distinguishable from the facts presented here. In *Burchette,* marijuana was found in one of two vehicles owned by Burchette. Burchette had personal items in this vehicle and had been observed near the vehicle, although not inside it, shortly before the marijuana was discovered. After reviewing this evidence, this Court reversed Burchette's conviction for possession of marijuana with intent to distribute, holding in pertinent part:

> The Commonwealth presented no evidence from which one reasonably could infer that *Burchette occupied the vehicle* or had exercised dominion over it while the marijuana was present in it. The evidence failed to show either *when Burchette may have used or occupied the vehicle* or when or for how long the drugs or paraphernalia had been in it. The evidence failed to show that Burchette was the exclusive or primary operator of the vehicle, or that he *possessed a set of keys* to the vehicle, or when or *by whom the vehicle had been most recently operated or occupied.* The circumstances were not such that one reasonably could infer, to the exclusion of other reasonable hypotheses, that Burchette, as the owner of the vehicle, knew of the presence, nature and character of the contraband that was found in it.

Id. at 435–36.

Unlike in *Burchette,* the Commonwealth here presented evidence establishing that appellant *was* in sole possession of the vehicle and *was* in possession of the key to the vehicle. The evidence also proved that appellant possessed the key to the glove compartment *while* the marijuana was in that glove compartment and *while* the vehicle smelled strongly of marijuana. The speculation required in *Burchette* was not required here, as these circumstances considered missing in *Burchette* are found here. Collectively, these circumstances support the factfinder's conclusion that appellant knew the nature and character of the leafy substance found in the glove compartment. However, additional circumstances in this record provide still further support for the court's finding of guilt.

c. *Appellant's Apparent Reluctance to Access the Glove Compartment*

The officers' testimony reflects that appellant did not attempt to retrieve the vehicle's registration from the glove compartment—where, of course, the officers eventually found the marijuana—despite the glove compartment's obvious utility as "a customary place" to find a vehicle's registration.

Despite being asked by the officers to produce both the registration and his driver's license, appellant readily provided the officers with only his driver's license, which was suspended. He did not even attempt to retrieve the vehicle's registration from the glove compartment. This evidence suggests that appellant was reluctant to access, in the officers' presence, the glove compartment where the drugs were located.

Based on this apparent reluctance to open the glove compartment, where the vehicle's registration would customarily be located, a rational factfinder could infer that appellant knew, if he opened the glove compartment, the officers would immediately observe the illegal substance. Again, considered in isolation this fact perhaps would not provide sufficient evidence on appeal to support the factfinder's determination that appellant was aware of the character and nature of the substance in the glove compartment. However, considered together with all the evidence presented at trial, this fact adds to the mounting collection of circumstances that support the trial court's finding of guilt.

d. *Appellant's Self-Serving Testimony*

The trial court obviously rejected appellant's testimony that the marijuana did not belong to him. The trial court also clearly rejected appellant's equivocal and ultimately self-serving testimony that he would not recognize the smell of marijuana.

This Court, following the precedent of the United States Supreme Court, has recognized a "general principle of evidence law that the factfinder is entitled to consider a party's dishonesty about a material fact as 'affirmative evidence of guilt.'" *Haskins,* 44 Va.App. at 11 n. 3. Here, given the strong odor of marijuana emanating from the vehicle and the circumstantial nature of this case, appellant's ability to recognize the smell of marijuana certainly concerned a relevant and material fact. The trial court, therefore, was permitted to assign appropriate weight to appellant's equivocal testimony that perhaps he could, and then that he could not, recognize the smell of marijuana. Again, this evidence is not an isolated factor in this case, but instead is further support for the trial court's determination that, based on the totality of the circumstances, appellant was aware of the presence of the marijuana in the glove compartment.

e.   *Abandonment of Valuable Contraband*

Although appellant asserts that the evidence failed to exclude the possibility that the marijuana baggies belonged to someone else and that he was simply unaware of the presence of drugs in the glove compartment, the Commonwealth "is not required to prove that there is no possibility that someone else may have planted, discarded, abandoned or placed the contraband where the contraband is discovered." *Kromer v. Commonwealth,* 45 Va.App. 812, 819 (2005). A factfinder is permitted to infer that "drugs are a commodity of significant value, unlikely to be abandoned or carelessly left in an area." *Ward v. Commonwealth,* 47 Va.App. 733, 753 n. 4 (2006).

Here, it is uncontested that the key to the vehicle's ignition also unlocked the glove compartment. The glove compartment's lock provided little security—given several people were known to use the vehicle. Thus, the person who put the marijuana in the glove compartment did so knowing that anyone who drove the vehicle would have the ability to open the locked glove compartment—for any reason—and would then see the marijuana, which was readily observable the moment the glove compartment was opened since it was then in plain view as it was not hidden by anything in the glove compartment. Any other driver of the vehicle, therefore, could easily take that marijuana from the glove compartment.

Under these circumstances, the trial court was entitled to find it highly unlikely that someone else simply left the marijuana—which had a street value of over $200—in the glove compartment of the car. This inference is another factor supporting the trial court's finding that appellant possessed the marijuana with knowledge of its nature and character.

III. CONCLUSION

Based on the totality of the circumstances found in this record, there was sufficient evidence for a rational factfinder to conclude beyond a reasonable doubt that appellant knowingly possessed the marijuana and to find that appellant intended to distribute the marijuana. Accordingly, we affirm appellant's conviction for possession of marijuana with intent to distribute.

Affirmed.

ALSTON, J., dissenting.

Although I respect the scholarly analysis of the majority, I find the Commonwealth failed to present sufficient evidence to establish appellant's possession of marijuana with knowledge of its nature and character. Accordingly, I would reverse appellant's conviction without reaching the merits of his second argument. Thus, I respectfully dissent from the majority opinion.

Virginia's jurisprudence is clear that the Commonwealth was required to prove *both* that appellant exercised dominion and control over the marijuana, as shown by his possession of the keys to the locked glove compartment, *and* that he was aware of the presence and character of the marijuana. It is the majority's conclusion as to the latter factor with which I cannot agree, as the result reached by the majority in this regard is irreconcilable with controlling precedent, both new and old.

As the majority notes, to sustain a conviction for possession of marijuana, "[t]he Commonwealth was required to prove that [appellant] 'intentionally and consciously possessed' the [marijuana], either actually or constructively, with knowledge of its nature and character." *Wilkins v. Commonwealth,* 18 Va.App. 293, 298 (1994). Here, the parties agree that our analysis is guided by principles of constructive possession. Constructive possession "can be shown by 'acts, statements, or conduct of the accused or other facts or circumstances which tend to show that the accused was aware of *both* the presence and character of the substance *and* that it was subject to his dominion and control.'" *Haskins v. Commonwealth,* 44 Va.App. 1, 6 (2004).

The majority concedes that "mere occupancy and proximity, although factors to be considered among the totality of the circumstances, are insufficient *standing alone* to prove a defendant's guilty knowledge of illegal drugs." (citing *Coward v. Commonwealth,* 48 Va.App. 653, 658 (2006)). Indeed,

> in order for ownership or occupancy of property or of a vehicle to be sufficient to support the inference that the owner or occupant also possessed contraband that was located on the property or in the vehicle, the owner or occupant must be shown to have exercised dominion and control over the premises *and to have known of the presence, nature, and character of the contraband at the time of such ownership or occupancy.*

Burchette v. Commonwealth, 15 Va.App. 432, 435, 425 (1992). Actual or constructive possession alone is not sufficient to prove that the drug possession was knowing and intentional.

> While "occupancy of a vehicle . . . where illicit drugs are found is a circumstance that may be considered together with other evidence tending to prove that the occupant . . . exercised

dominion and control over items in the vehicle[,]" it is "insufficient to prove knowing possession of drugs."

Coward, 48 Va.App. at 658.

In *Coward,* this Court reversed the defendant's conviction for possession of cocaine because the Commonwealth failed to present sufficient evidence that Coward was aware of the nature and character of the cocaine, located in the passenger console and immediately visible to the police officer who approached the vehicle in which Coward was a passenger. White, the driver of the car, told the officer that the car belonged to White's mother, but that he had been using the car "all evening" and no one else had driven or used the vehicle that night. Still, this Court held the Commonwealth did not establish any facts or circumstances, other than Coward's occupancy of the car and proximity to the cocaine, "necessary to draw the legal conclusion that Coward was aware of the presence and character of the cocaine," despite the fact that the cocaine was in plain sight upon the passenger console of the vehicle. This Court noted that "Coward did not attempt to hide the baggie containing the cocaine as the officer approached the car nor did he exhibit any other signs of guilty knowledge." *Id.* at 659–60. Thus, the Commonwealth did not meet its burden of proof beyond a reasonable doubt.

I suggest the facts of the instant case are analogous to those in *Coward* and therefore cannot accept the majority's conclusion. The majority concludes that *Coward* is distinguishable from the instant case, because the evidence at trial presented other indicia of appellant's knowledge of the presence and character of the marijuana in the glove compartment, in addition to appellant's occupancy of the vehicle and proximity to the marijuana. The five additional circumstances on which the majority opinion relies include: the odor of burnt marijuana; appellant's possession of the keys that unlocked the glove compartment; appellant's apparent reluctance to access the vehicle's glove compartment; the "abandonment" of the drugs in the vehicle; and appellant's "equivocation" in his statement regarding knowledge of the smell of marijuana. I respectfully disagree with the majority's portrayal of each of these facts and the legal significance the majority awards to them.

1. The Odor of Burnt Marijuana

First, the majority places great emphasis on the smell of marijuana emanating from the vehicle. The evidence established that when the officers approached the driver's side of the vehicle, they smelled a strong odor of marijuana coming from the car. As the majority notes, the trial judge interpreted the evidence as suggesting the odor was that of marijuana that had been smoked, *i.e.* burnt marijuana. The trial court stated, "Either [appellant] had been smoking [marijuana] or he had recently just had someone in the car who was smoking it." There was no evidence that the odor detected by the officers was coming from appellant's person, that appellant appeared intoxicated, that appellant showed any physical signs of having recently used marijuana, or that appellant possessed any drugs or drug paraphernalia on his person. Moreover, no matches, smoking devices, or remnants of previously smoked marijuana were apparently found in the car.

The record does not show that the odor was that of fresh marijuana, which might indicate that appellant had at least reason to suspect the vehicle contained fresh marijuana. The majority dismisses the importance of the distinction between the smell of fresh marijuana and the smell of burnt marijuana by noting simply that "viewing all the evidence in the light most favorable to the Commonwealth . . . the trial court's finding that appellant had guilty knowledge of the marijuana in the glove compartment is strengthened by the trial court's finding concerning the marijuana odor." However, the majority gives no reason why the trial court could reasonably infer, based on the smell of *burnt* marijuana, that appellant was aware of *fresh* marijuana in the glove compartment. Evidence of the smell of burnt marijuana simply does not provide a nexus from which the trial court could conclude appellant knew of the fresh marijuana in the glove compartment.

In support of its holding, the majority notes that in *Young,* the Supreme Court explained that a "drug's distinctive odor" may be circumstantial evidence that can support a finding that the defendant knew of the nature and character of the substance in his possession. 275 Va. at 591. In making this statement in *Young,* the Supreme Court referenced *Josephs,* 10 Va.App. 87, in which the defendant was convicted of possession of marijuana with intent to distribute, based in part on the strong odor of marijuana, readily apparent when the vehicle's trunk was opened. However, in *Josephs,* the evidence established that Josephs was in a rental car traveling from Florida to New York, Josephs' luggage was in the trunk next to 130 pounds of marijuana, and when questioned about the marijuana, Josephs "[s]aid she didn't know about the drugs. [First] time I've driven with that stuff." *Id.* at 100. Thus, while a drug's distinctive odor may be circumstantial evidence that can support a finding that the defendant knew of the nature and character of the substance in his possession, the Court in *Young* did not suggest this factor was dispositive. In fact, the *Young* Court explicitly stated,

> In *Josephs,* there was *ample* circumstantial evidence to support the trial court's conclusion that the defendant was aware of the nature and character of the drugs that she jointly possessed, and it was unnecessary for the Court of Appeals to rely on an inference of guilty knowledge based on possession alone. . . . *Countless scenarios can be envisioned in which controlled substances may be found in the possession of a person who is entirely unaware of their nature and character.*

Young, 275 Va. at 592.

Most significantly, in the *Josephs* case, the defendant by her own statement conceded that she was aware of the substance as she acknowledged that it was the first time she had "driven with that stuff." *Josephs,* 10 Va.App. at 100. I respectfully disagree with the majority's conclusion that *Josephs* supports the proposition that "[t]he strong and distinctive odor of the drug provided a significant indication to anyone inside (or even near) the vehicle that marijuana was located within the vehicle" in this case. In *Josephs,* the smell emanating from the trunk of the car was apparently that of fresh marijuana, the same form of marijuana found in the trunk. In contrast, in the case at bar, the smell of burnt marijuana in the vehicle provided no indication that fresh marijuana could also be found in the car.

The majority also relies upon the trial court's finding that the officers smelled marijuana that had been *recently* smoked by appellant or someone in the car with him and that appellant had taken possession of the vehicle approximately two hours before the traffic stop. Even if the trial court was entitled to conclude, based on the officers' testimony about the strength of the smell of the marijuana, that it had been "recently" smoked, this does not necessarily support the holding that appellant was aware of the character and nature of the marijuana in the glove compartment. Appellant took possession of the vehicle only two hours before the traffic stop. Marijuana could have been smoked in the car hours before appellant took possession of the vehicle and still resulted in a strong odor of marijuana suggesting it was "recently" smoked in the car.

The majority's emphasis on the odor of marijuana is counter to the language of *Young* suggesting that of the distinctive odor of a drug is not, by itself, sufficient circumstantial evidence to establish a defendant's knowledge of the character and presence of the drug. Although the majority cites additional factors that purportedly constitute circumstantial evidence of appellant's knowledge of the presence and character of the marijuana, their primary reliance on the odor of the drug in the car effectively affirms the conviction of appellant on the basis of possession of the *odor* of marijuana. Even more problematically, the smell of burnt marijuana is simply not indicative of the presence of fresh marijuana. Thus, the presence of the distinctive odor of burnt marijuana is not sufficient to establish appellant's knowledge of the fresh marijuana in the glove compartment.

2.   Appellant's Sole Possession of the Vehicle and His
Possession of the Key to the Glove Compartment

Next, the majority notes that appellant was the sole person with means to access the glove compartment containing the marijuana. While this establishes appellant's dominion and control over the vehicle and the items located therein, this fact does not prove appellant's knowledge about the nature and character of those items. In this case, the key that unlocked the glove compartment was the same key that was necessary to operate the vehicle. Put simply, the fact that appellant possessed that key does not logically lead to the inference, beyond a reasonable doubt, that appellant knew the glove compartment's contents.

3. Appellant's "Reluctance" to Access the Glove Compartment

Further, the majority notes that appellant did not attempt to produce the vehicle's registration and cites this failure as evidence that appellant was aware of the marijuana in the glove compartment. However, there is no evidence to suggest appellant refused to produce the registration or that he refused to look in the vehicle's glove compartment. Rather, appellant's testimony, corroborated by the arresting officers, was that when the officers approached the vehicle, appellant explained that he did not have the vehicle's registration because the car did not belong to him. Notably, the officers asked appellant for "*his* driver's license and registration," rather than simply "*the* registration" for the vehicle. Thus, appellant's statement that the vehicle did not belong to him was responsive to the officers' request; appellant was simply anticipating the officers' reason for requesting the registration and advising the officers that the registration would show he was not the owner of the vehicle.

Although appellant did not access the glove compartment here, there was no prevailing legal justification for the trial court to infer that he had knowledge of the glove compartment's contents. Where a fact "is equally susceptible of two interpretations one of which is consistent with the innocence of the accused, [the trier of fact] cannot arbitrarily adopt that interpretation which incriminates him." *Corbett v. Commonwealth,* 210 Va. 304, 307 (1969). In fact, the Commonwealth presented no evidence to suggest appellant made any motion toward the glove compartment as police stopped the vehicle, or that appellant engaged in any other behavior that would indicate he knew there were drugs in the locked glove compartment. There was no evidence that appellant appeared nervous, and in fact, the officers testified that appellant was entirely cooperative throughout the stop. I cannot reach the conclusion that these facts somehow support appellant's culpability in this instance.

4. "Abandonment" of Valuable Contraband

The majority also notes, " 'drugs are a commodity of significant value, unlikely to be abandoned or carelessly left in an area.' " However, in the instant case, there is no indication that the marijuana was "abandoned or carelessly left." On the contrary, the fact that the drugs were secured in a locked glove compartment could suggest the drugs' owner attempted to secure and hide the marijuana from the view of others. Thus, this factor does not support a finding that appellant knew the nature and character of the marijuana found in the car.

5.   Appellant's "Self-Serving" Testimony

Finally, the majority relies upon appellant's "equivocal" testimony that he would not recognize the smell of marijuana.

The majority characterizes these statements as "appellant's equivocal testimony that perhaps he could, and then that he could not, recognize the smell of marijuana" and states that the trial court was entitled to consider appellant's dishonesty as affirmative evidence of guilt.

However, appellant's initial statement that he may be familiar with the smell of marijuana followed by the statement "No, not really" does not amount to a change in statements, first suggesting that he is familiar with the smell of marijuana and then stating that he is not. "Maybe" is defined as both "perhaps" and "uncertainty." *Merriam-Webster's Collegiate Dictionary* 767 (Frederick C. Mish et al. eds., 11th ed. 2005). Thus, appellant's initial answer could have conveyed appellant's *uncertainty* about his own knowledge of the smell of marijuana, not a statement that "perhaps he could" recognize the smell of marijuana. Although appellant's testimony is capable of two interpretations, again, "where a fact is equally susceptible of two interpretations one of which is consistent with the innocence of the accused, [the trier of fact] cannot arbitrarily adopt that interpretation which incriminates him." *Corbett,* 210 Va. at 307.

Furthermore, even assuming the trial judge correctly determined appellant was familiar with the smell of marijuana based on appellant's equivocal testimony, there was no evidence presented by the Commonwealth suggesting appellant's familiarity with that smell proved that he had smoked marijuana in the vehicle, or knew the vehicle contained fresh marijuana *at the time he occupied the vehicle.*

For the foregoing reasons, I cannot join in the majority's conclusion, and I respectfully dissent from its holding.

NOTES AND QUESTIONS

1.   **Competing arguments.** The *Ervin* court was deeply divided over the key issues in the case. Does the majority or dissent have the better arguments? If you were on the jury, would you have voted to convict?

2.   **Constructive possession.** Judge Alston's dissent states the blackletter law governing constructive possession:

> Virginia's jurisprudence is clear that the Commonwealth was required to prove *both* that appellant exercised dominion and control over the marijuana, as shown by his possession of the keys to the locked glove compartment, *and* that he was aware of the presence and character of the marijuana.

704 S.E.2d at 149.

One critically important fact in the majority's view was the inference from the strong smell of marijuana. 704 S.E. 2d at 140–41. By comparison, the Virginia Supreme Court held in *Young v. Commonwealth*, 659 S.E. 2d 308, 310 (Va. 2008) that the evidence was insufficient to show that the defendant had constructive possession of an odorless, unlabeled bottle of pills.

3.   **Differing views of constructive possession.** Given the split in the *Ervin* court, one should not be surprised that some courts differ in their handling of constructive possession cases. For example, the Ninth Circuit concluded that evidence was insufficient to show which defendant possessed marijuana when marijuana was found in a bedroom that two defendants shared. All that the evidence showed, according to the court, was that one member of the couple possessed marijuana, but did not show which defendant possessed it. *Delgado v. United States,* 327 F. 2d 641 (9th Cir. 1984).

4.   **Mens rea issues.** One might conclude on the facts that the marijuana belonged to the defendant. But what if instead the evidence suggested that the marijuana belonged to someone else and that the defendant smelled the marijuana and considered that it might be marijuana. Instead of opening the glove compartment, the defendant decided just to ignore the smell. If those were the facts, would a finding of the mens rea be sufficient?

PROBLEM 11-1

A Customs agent stopped Defendant as he drove a vehicle in the U.S. from Tijuana, Mexico. The agent instructed Defendant to open the trunk of the vehicle and noticed that the trunk contained a petition, creating what the agent thought was a false compartment. Upon further investigation, agents found 110 pounds of marijuana in the vehicle. Confronted with the marijuana, Defendant explained that, when he and his companion were in Tijuana, a stranger identified as "Ray" offered to sell them marijuana and, when they declined, asked if they wanted to drive a car back to Los Angeles for $100. Defendant's companion "wanted no part of driving the vehicle." He testified, "It didn't sound right to me." Defendant accepted the offer. The Customs agent testified that Defendant stated "he thought there was probably something wrong and something illegal in the vehicle, but that he checked it over. He looked in the glove box and under the front seat and in the trunk, prior to driving it. He didn't find anything, and, therefore, he assumed that the people at the border wouldn't find anything either." The agent also asked Defendant whether he had seen the special compartment when he opened the trunk. He responded, "Well, you know, I saw a void there, but I didn't know what it was." He testified that he did not investigate further. Assume that the jury believes Defendant's testimony. Has the prosecution met its burden of proof to show that Defendant knowing possessed marijuana?

---

5.   **The actus reus of possession.** Often in cases like *Ervin,* the primary issue is whether the prosecution has satisfied the mens rea of the offense of possession. But often, closely related is whether the evidence is

sufficient to satisfy the actus reus of possession. Although in light of developments described in the next paragraph the issue arises less frequently today, the distinction between the actus reus and mens rea of possession is confusing.

When Congress enacted the Controlled Substance Act, the Nixon administration pressured the Uniform Law Commission members of follow suit. The commission did so and wrote the Uniform Controlled Substances Act. Prior to that time, many states made possession of marijuana a strict liability offense. That is, the mere possession of marijuana was (usually) a misdemeanor without regard to whether the offender was aware of the nature of the substance. Most states have now included a mens rea element, especially when they make possession of marijuana a felony. At the same time, even in a jurisdiction that makes possession of marijuana a strict liability offense, the prosecution must prove the actus reus of the offense. The following excerpt from *Commonwealth v. Sterling,* 361 A. 2d 799 (Pa. Super. 1976) provides a good example to explore the difference between actus reus and mens rea when the charge involves possession:

> The facts relating to appellant's arrest are not in dispute. On May 21, 1973, United States Customs officials in New York City, using a dog specifically trained to sniff out narcotics, became suspicious that a package addressed to Mrs. Donald Farr, c/o Mr. and Mrs. James Sterling, R.D. 1, Lehoy Forest Drive, Leola, Pennsylvania, contained contraband. The Customs officials opened the package and found a pewter antique pitcher, sealed with wax. A test boring through the paraffin revealed that the pitcher contained a large quantity of hashish.
>
> The Customs officials repackaged the pitcher and notified a Philadelphia Customs official, a Postal Inspector assigned to Philadelphia, and State Police located in Lancaster, that they were forwarding the pitcher. Before delivering the package, the State Police made another test boring to verify that the pitcher contained hashish and sprinkled the pitcher with fluorescent powder. The Postal Inspector then arranged with the rural postal carrier to attempt delivery of the package at appellant's home. At the same time, State Trooper Carl Harnish swore out a warrant authorizing a search of appellant's home.
>
> Police set up a surveillance of appellant's residence as soon as the package was delivered at 3:30 p.m., on June 7, 1973. Appellant and his wife arrived at about 6:45 p.m., retrieved the package and several letters from the mailbox, and went into their home. Trooper Harnish waited approximately forty-five minutes before executing the search warrant.
>
> Trooper Harnish found the package unopened in the kitchen. Appellant told the trooper that he had no knowledge of what was in the package. He did tell the trooper that he had recently received a

postcard from friends who were vacationing in Holland; the postcard stated: 'Hi y'all. Amsterdam hasn't changed a bit. Lots of young people here. Can't understand it. Keep your eye peeled for souvenirs, and we'll be seeing (you) in a couple of weeks.' After the trooper seized the package, he asked appellant whether he had any other contraband in the house. Appellant retrieved from one of the bedrooms a plastic bag containing approximately 90 grams of marijuana. The officer then explained that he was not authorized by the warrant to search further and requested that appellant consent to a search of the house and his automobile. Appellant signed a consent form and permitted the search. That search netted some marijuana seeds, pipes used for smoking marijuana, and some 'roaches,' (marijuana cigarette 'butts'). Concerning the package, appellant told the trooper that he suspected that it might contain drugs, but that he had no intention of opening it. Upon further investigation, the police estimated that the retail value of the hashish was about $90,000.00.

Assume that the relevant statute made possession of hashish a strict liability offense. Does the evidence above demonstrate that the defendant knew that he possessed hashish? What are the competing arguments?

The majority concluded that the evidence was insufficient. Importantly, it stated:

> The instant case raises a slightly different version of the same problem as presented in Fortune: there is no question that appellant and his wife were in possession of the hashish. One of them carried the package into their residence; the appellant directed the trooper to the package upon his request. There was no one else on the premises at the time of the search. The Commonwealth's evidence, however, did not prove that appellant had discovered the contents of the package and that he intended to exercise control over the hashish. The package was not addressed to the appellant, but only in care of appellant and his wife. He did not open the package to gain access to the secreted contraband.

361 A. 2d at 802.

Section 2.01(4) of the Model Penal Code defines the actus reus of possession as follows: "Possession is an act, within the meaning of this Section, if the possessor knowingly procured or received the thing possessed or was aware of his control thereof for a sufficient period to have been able to terminate his possession." The Comments provide an example to illustrate the kind of knowledge that one must have to meet the actus reus of possession:

> It should also be noted that the "thing possessed" refers to the physical object, not to its specific quality or properties. The extent to which the defendant must be aware of such specific qualities or properties is a matter of mens rea. Thus, if possession of a stolen automobile is the offense involved, the defendant has met the

requirement of Subsection (4) if he knowingly procured or received the car, or if he was aware of his control of it for a sufficient period of time to have been able to terminate his possession.

Model Penal Code, Comment to § 2.01 at 224.

PROBLEM 11-2

Defendant recently got a job working for a farmer who produced a variety of organic crops. The farmer asked Defendant to take a shift working at a local farmers' where the farmer usually sold his crops. Among the goods that the farmer had for sale was what Defendant believed to be organic oregano. In fact, he had a sold a large amount of the small bags of what was labeled oregano that morning. Later, when a police officer with a K-9 unit came through the market, the dog stopped at the farmer's area and signaled the presence of marijuana. Further investigation revealed that what Defendant believed to be oregano was in fact marijuana. Charged with possession of marijuana, Defendant wonders whether his belief that the marijuana was oregano is legally relevant. Discuss.

B. MARIJUANA DISTRIBUTION

The previous section focused on issues that arise in possession cases. This section focuses on a different issue: when does an offender cross the line between mere possession and possession with intent to deliver or to sell, typically a much more serious offense? That issue arises in a particularly interesting context in the case below.

KOHLER V. STATE
Court of Special Appeals of Maryland
36 A.3d 1013 (Md. App. 2012)

SALMON, J.

After using mostly fake money to purchase marijuana, Donald Kohler immediately fled from the seller, Warren Jerome Yates. Upon discovering the deception, Yates ran after Kohler and fired a shot that killed Shirley Worcester, an innocent bystander. Based on the State's theory that Kohler aided and abetted Yates's felony distribution of marijuana, a jury in the Circuit Court for Baltimore County convicted Kohler of second-degree felony murder and conspiracy to distribute marijuana. He was also convicted of possession of marijuana with intent to distribute. Kohler was sentenced to thirty years for the felony murder, five consecutive years for the conspiracy, and a concurrent five years on the possession charge. In this appeal Kohler does not take issue with his conviction of possession with intent to distribute marijuana but claims that the evidence was insufficient to sustain his conviction for either second-degree felony murder or conspiracy to distribute marijuana.

The question of whether the evidence was sufficient to support appellant's conviction for felony murder presents an issue of first impression. No reported Maryland appellate case addresses whether a buyer of a controlled dangerous substance ("CDS") may be convicted of distribution based on the theory that he or she "participated" in the sale as a second degree principal, i.e., as an aider or abettor of the distribution. * * *

For the reasons explained below, we conclude that the evidence presented by the State was insufficient to convict appellant of distributing marijuana, and therefore also insufficient to convict him of felony murder and conspiracy to distribute marijuana.

I.   FACTS

On the morning of January 7, 2009, Kohler met Christopher Jagd and Justin Wimbush at a house in Baltimore County where Johnny Moore lived. Kohler said to Jagd and Wimbush that he would like to steal some marijuana. Kohler inquired of Jagd and Wimbush if they knew anyone who might have "some pounds" of marijuana. Wimbush said that he needed to "make some calls" but believed "he could get it." Wimbush and Jagd then left. Later that day Wimbush, acting on Kohler's behalf, called Warren Yates and the two negotiated the sales price ($1,100.00 per pound) and the quantity of marijuana to be sold (four pounds). Wimbush and Yates then made arrangements concerning the time and place of the delivery. Ultimately it was agreed that the sale would occur at the townhouse on South Hawthorn Street where Johnny Moore lived.

On the evening of January 7, 2009, Yates, accompanied by Billy Griffin, arrived at the townhouse in Yates's car. Yates and Griffin entered the basement of Johnny Moore's house where they joined Jagd, Wimbush and others. Kohler stayed upstairs. He told Jagd that he wanted to see the marijuana before he bought it. Griffin gave Jagd a pound of marijuana, Jagd then gave the pound to Wimbush who went upstairs and showed it to Kohler. Kohler then asked to see all four pounds, but his request was denied by Yates. Finally, tired of waiting, Griffin and Yates announced they were leaving and went upstairs.

Just as Griffin and Yates were about to leave, Kohler said that he still wanted to buy the drugs. The marijuana was given to Jagd. Jagd handed the drugs to Wimbush, who gave the contraband to Kohler. Kohler, in turn, gave Wimbush a bag with money in it. The bag went to Jagd, who gave it to Yates.

Yates told everyone not to leave until he counted the money, but as soon as Jagd handed over the bag, Kohler grabbed the drugs and ran out the door. Yates immediately reported to Griffin that the money Kohler gave to him in exchange for the drugs was fake. Yates then chased after Kohler. During the chase Yates fired two shots, intending to hit Kohler. Kohler was not hit but one of the bullets went astray and killed Shirley Worcester, who happened to be standing nearby.

II. Discussion

A. Second Degree Felony Murder

Challenging the State's theory that appellant abetted Yates in his distribution of marijuana, appellant argues that his second degree felony murder conviction must be reversed because the evidence was insufficient to convict him of the predicate felony of distribution. In support, appellant points out that, at trial, the State's theory was not that appellant distributed the marijuana to others, but that appellant was "a participant" in the sale of marijuana by Yates because appellant was "the buyer" who "received it." In appellant's view, the State's "participant" argument "demonstrates its concession" that appellant did not distribute marijuana.

The State maintains that "[u]nder the unique facts of this case, . . . the evidence was sufficient to convict [appellant] of distribution of marijuana and of the felony murder." On appeal the State renews its trial argument that appellant "participated in the distribution . . . as a second degree principal" who aided and abetted the transaction by seeking "out Yates, inquir[ing] as to whether he could purchase four pounds of marijuana, set[ting] up the details of the exchange, and, ultimately, fraudulently entic[ing] Yates to relinquish possession of the marijuana." Of significance, the State argues, is the fact that appellant's "intent to defraud Yates and essentially trick him into transferring the drugs" was what ultimately led to the shooting of Ms. Worcester. As the trial court pointed out at sentencing, "but for Mr. Kohler's actions in seeking to have these drugs sold to him and all of the machinations about which we heard during the trial and his decision to effectuate the purchase in the way that he did[,]" "the victim in this case would not have been killed[.]" In these limited circumstances, the State posits, a buyer like appellant, who "takes an active role in soliciting the distributor and arranging the transaction," which "is occurring in the middle of the distribution chain, and not between the seller and user, . . . could be guilty of distribution."

"When reviewing the sufficiency of the evidence to sustain appellant's convictions, we must determine, after viewing the evidence in the light most favorable to the State, if any rational trier of fact could have found the essential elements of the crime beyond a reasonable doubt." *Yates v. State*, 202 Md.App. 700, 712 (2011). "To obtain a conviction for felony murder, the State is required to prove the underlying felony and that the death occurred during the perpetration of the felony." *Id.* at 227. Moreover, "the underlying felony must be sufficiently dangerous to life to justify application of the doctrine," so that the jury must be able to find beyond a reasonable doubt that "the felonious conduct, under all the circumstances, made death a foreseeable consequence[.]" *Id.* at 229. It is not necessary, however, for the State to separately charge the defendant with the predicate felony.

Maryland does not have an "aiding and abetting" statute. Nevertheless, under established case law, a person who did not actually commit the crime in question may nevertheless be guilty to the same degree as the person who did. *Handy v. State,* 23 Md.App. 239, 250, 251–52 (1974). Whereas principals in the first degree "commit the deed as perpetrating actors, either by their own hand or by the hand of an innocent agent," principals in the second degree are "present, actually or constructively, aiding and abetting the commission of the crime, but not themselves committing it[.]" *Id.* at 251. "An aider is one who assists, supports or supplements the efforts of another in the commission of a crime." "An abettor is one who instigates, advises or encourages the commission of a crime." *Id.*

Here, the State charged appellant with conspiring with Yates and Griffin to distribute marijuana in violation of the statutory prohibition against distributing marijuana and with possession of marijuana with the intent to distribute, which is a statutory felony.

Although appellant was not charged with distribution in violation of Crim. § 5–602(1), the State argued throughout trial that the second degree felony murder charges against both appellant and Yates were predicated on distribution, and that appellant was guilty of distribution as a second degree principal, based on his role in arranging the sale and receiving the marijuana from Yates. Defense counsel argued to the trial court, in support of his unsuccessful motions for acquittal, and to the jury in closing, that appellant could not be guilty of distribution or felony murder because a buyer cannot be convicted of distributing marijuana to himself.

The trial court instructed the jury that "the State must prove that the Defendant[,] or another participating in the crime with the Defendant[,] committed or attempted to commit the crime of distribution of marijuana, which is a felony." The court did not define "distribution" or further explain who might qualify as "another participating in the crime with the Defendant[.]"

In this Court, appellant points out that the Supreme Court unanimously rejected an analogous "drug buyer as facilitator" theory in *Abuelhawa v. United States,* 556 U.S. 816 (2009), and that courts in other states have similarly rejected the notion that a buyer can be convicted of CDS distribution as a second degree principal. We agree that these cases are instructive.

In *Abuelhawa,* the issue was whether a *buyer's* use of his cell phone to arrange drug purchases "facilitated" the seller's felony drug distribution, in violation of a federal statute criminalizing the use of communication devices in "facilitating the commission of . . . a felony[.]" A unanimous

Supreme Court held that the buyer, whose two separate purchases of one gram were misdemeanors, could not be convicted of the "facilitation" felony under that theory. *Abuelhawa,* 129 S.Ct. at 2104.

The *Abuelhawa* Court rejected the Fourth Circuit's holding that the buyer's use of his cell phone to purchase cocaine qualified as facilitation "because it 'undoubtedly made [the seller's] cocaine distribution easier; in fact, 'it made the sale possible.'" *Id.* Although "on the literal plane, the phone calls could be described as 'facilitating' drug distribution[,]" the Court concluded that "stopping there would ignore the rule that, because statutes are not read as a collection of isolated phrases, '[a] word in a statute may or may not extend to the outer limits of its definitional possibilities.'" *Id.* at 2105 In Abuelhawa's case, the Court explained,

> the Government's literal sweep of "facilitate" sits uncomfortably with common usage. Where a transaction like a sale necessarily presupposes two parties with specific roles, it would be odd to speak of one party as facilitating the conduct of the other. A buyer does not just make a sale easier; he makes the sale possible. No buyer, no sale; the buyer's part is already implied by the term "sale," and the word "facilitate" adds nothing. We would not say that the borrower facilitates the bank loan.

Id.

The Court also pointed out that "[t]he common usage that limits 'facilitate' to the efforts of someone other than a primary or necessary actor in the commission of a substantive crime has its parallel in" case law recognizing that "where a statute treats one side of a bilateral transaction more leniently, adding to the penalty of the party on that side for facilitating the action by the other would upend the calibration of punishment set by the legislature[.]" *Id.* at 2106. Explaining that Congress intended the meaning of the term "facilitate" to be "equivalent" to judicially interpreted "terms like 'aid,' 'abet,' and 'assist[,]'" *Id.* at 2106, the Court reasoned that the Government's "broader reading of 'facilitate' would for practical purposes skew the congressional calibration of respective buyer-seller penalties[,]" by ignoring that "Congress meant to treat purchasing drugs for personal use more leniently than the felony of distributing drugs, and to narrow the scope of the communications provision to cover only those who facilitate a drug felony." *Id.* at 2106–07.

Applying the lessons of *Abuelhawa* and other cases, we conclude that treating drug buyers as second-degree principals in the drug sellers' distribution stretches the concept of "participation" and "aiding and abetting" too far. The phrase "or dispense" 1) "means to deliver to the ultimate user or the human research subject by or in accordance with the lawful order of an authorized provider," 2) "dispense" indicates to prescribe, administer, package, label, or compound a substance for delivery. Crim. § 5–101(k). To "distribute" means, "with respect to a controlled dangerous substance, to deliver other than by dispensing." Crim. § 5–101(1). In turn, "deliver" means "to make an actual constructive, or attempted transfer or exchange from one person to another whether or not remuneration is paid[.]" Crim. § 5–101(h).

Because CDS "distribution" requires a delivery *to another person,* it is clear that the General Assembly intended the prohibition against distribution to encompass only those who deliver CDS, not those to whom CDS is delivered. The State's characterization of appellant as a participant in Yates's distribution would require us to ignore the "common usage" principles cogently articulated in *Abuelhawa.* We therefore agree with appellant that he may not be convicted of distribution based solely on his role as buyer and receiver of the marijuana.

The State's attempt to limit the scope of its "buyer as distributor" theory to certain types of buyers is not persuasive. In its brief, the State posits that

> as an aider and abettor to distribution is limited to those circumstances where, as here, the defendant's role in the transaction is more than simply an end-of-the-line, arm's length buyer purchasing for personal use. Where the buyer takes an active role in soliciting the distributor and arranging the transaction, and where it is clear that the transaction is occurring in the middle of the distribution chain, and not between the seller and user, the buyer could be guilty of distribution.

The "active role" component of the standard suggested by the State is untenably vague and overbroad. Allowing a jury to convict a drug buyer of distribution on an aiding and abetting theory that is circumscribed only by whether the buyer took an "active role in soliciting the distributor" could effectively eviscerate any distinction between possession and distribution, because any buyer who initiates a drug purchase arguably takes "an active role in soliciting the distributor."

Nor do we agree that a buyer who is in a "distribution chain" may be convicted as an aider and abettor of the seller's distribution. It is neither necessary nor consistent with the legislative scheme to treat a drug buyer who purchases with intent to distribute as a second-degree principal in the drug seller's distribution. There simply is no need to contort the language and meaning of Crim. § 5–602(1) to cover this scenario, because when a buyer purchases CDS with the intent to distribute it to others, that buyer may be convicted, as a first-degree principal, of possession with intent to distribute, which is a separate felony under Crim. § 5–602(2). And, if that same buyer actually takes steps toward distributing the CDS he has in his possession to another person, he may then be convicted, as a first-degree principal, of attempted distribution of marijuana, which, as the State concedes, is only a common law misdemeanor in Maryland. * * * Finally, if the buyer actually makes a delivery, then he or she is guilty of distribution, again as a first-degree principal.

For these reasons, although the State is correct that appellant's intent to distribute the marijuana differentiates his purchase from cases in which the buyer purchased CDS solely for personal use, we do not agree that this fact supports a conviction for distribution as a second degree principal. The appropriate charge in these circumstances—when the buyer solicits the sale and receives the CDS with the intent to later distribute it to others, but there is no evidence of any attempt at distribution—is possession with intent to distribute. A contrary conclusion would put the proverbial cart before the horse, by allowing the State to convict a CDS buyer like appellant, who purchases for re-distribution but has not yet acted upon his intent to distribute, of actually distributing the CDS.

In this case, the jury did convict appellant of felony possession with intent to distribute, in violation of Crim. § 5–602(2), and appellant does not challenge the sufficiency of the evidence supporting that conviction. Even though appellant might have been convicted of felony murder based on the alternative predicate felony of possession with intent to distribute, the prosecution did not argue that alternative, and the jury was not instructed about it.

To the extent that the State's position in this appeal may be understood as an assertion that there is no material difference between these two crimes, so that we may treat them as fungible felonies for purposes of affirming appellant's second degree felony murder conviction, we disagree. We acknowledge that possession with intent to distribute and distribution might fairly be viewed as two sides of the same coin because both crimes fall under Crim. § 5–602, and both crimes are punished as felonies under Crim. § 5–607(a). As this case demonstrates, however, there is a substantive difference between the two crimes when the State attempts to use them as the predicate for felony murder.

Here, the jury was permitted to convict appellant of felony murder based on the theory that he aided and abetted Yates in distributing the marijuana. Consequently, the jury, when determining whether the manner in which the marijuana was distributed created a substantial risk of death or bodily injury so as to warrant a felony murder conviction, naturally focused on the conduct of Yates, who came armed with a gun and later used it to shoot and kill an innocent bystander. In contrast, if the jury had been asked to convict appellant of felony murder based on the theory that he obtained possession of the marijuana with an intent to distribute it, its primary focus would not have been on the conduct of Yates, but on the conduct of appellant, who was unarmed during the purchase and obtained the marijuana through fraud and flight, rather than force. To be sure, it is also possible that the jury might have found beyond a reasonable doubt that the manner in which appellant committed that possession felony created a foreseeable risk of death, sufficient to convict him of second-degree felony murder. For purposes of this appeal, however, the material fact is that, depending on which of the two underlying felonies the jury was considering, it might have considered different evidence and/or weighed the evidence differently.

Because the evidence was insufficient to convict appellant of distribution as an aider and abettor, and the arguments and instructions pertaining to the felony murder charge allowed the jury to decide guilt based on the predicate felony of distribution, we are constrained to reverse appellant's second-degree felony murder conviction.

NOTES AND QUESTIONS

1.   **Analytical issues.** Is the court's analysis convincing? From a policy perspective, without reference to the victim's death and murder charge in this case, does it make sense to treat a buyer as an accomplice of the seller? If so, the buyer is equally guilty of the offense of distributing marijuana and typically subject to the same punishment. Equating buyers and sellers seemingly does not make sense.

2.   **Inferences of intent to sell.** Assume that Kohler purchased four pounds of marijuana and the police arrested him shortly after he left Moore's house. Would the evidence be sufficient to convict him of possession of marijuana with the intent to distribute or to sell marijuana? (I.e., that he really was a marijuana seller). That is the typical context in which the prosecution relies on an inference of an intent to distribute from the surrounding circumstances. *Williams v. State,* 625 S.E. 2d 509 (Ga. App. 2005) provides a more typical fact pattern:

> * * * [O]n June 19, 2003, Tony Corley was driving his sister's car, with Williams sitting in the front passenger seat and his friend Freddie Brown sitting in the back seat. A police officer stopped Corley because one of the car's brake lights did not work. During the stop, the officer discovered that Corley did not have a valid driver's license. The officer arrested Corley for driving without a valid license and impounded the vehicle since it did not belong to him or either passenger.
>
> Another officer, who had arrived to help with the stop, asked Williams to get out of the car so the officers could inventory the contents of the impounded vehicle. When Williams stepped out of the front passenger seat, the officer immediately saw a plastic bag containing suspected cocaine lying on the seat. Williams then began talking quickly and voluntarily told the officers that there was marijuana in the car, inside two baby shoes under the front seat. The officers looked under the front passenger seat and indeed found a pair of baby shoes stuffed full of a total of 20 small plastic bags of marijuana. One of the shoes contained a white leather pouch with twelve small marijuana bags in it, and the other shoe held eight small

bags of marijuana. According to one of the officers, such packaging of marijuana indicates an intent to sell it rather than keep it for personal use, and such small bags of marijuana are known as "dime bags" because they typically are sold for ten dollars apiece.

Corley testified that when he first encountered Williams on the night in question, Williams had approximately 20 small plastic bags of marijuana in a white leather pouch. Williams tried to sell the marijuana to him, but Corley did not have enough money to buy it. Shortly before the officer pulled him over, Corley saw Williams shoving the baby shoes, which belonged to Corley's niece, underneath the front passenger seat.

The state also introduced similar transaction evidence. According to that evidence, just a few months before the incident in Corley's car, Williams was found in possession of four small plastic bags of marijuana, and he was charged with possession of marijuana with intent to distribute.

625 S.E. 2d at 511–12.

Williams involved a number of issues. One contention was the evidence was insufficient to show that the appellant, not someone else in the vehicle, possessed the marijuana. A second contention was that the trial court erred in allowing introduction into evidence of the appellant's prior marijuana convictions for possession with intent to distribute. The court found that evidence admissible. For purposes of this discussion, however, focus on how the prosecution might contend that the evidence was sufficient to show an intent to distribute.

The prosecution must prove the intent to distribute beyond a reasonable doubt. Proof of intent in such cases is circumstantial. The jury draws the inference of intent from all of the surrounding circumstances. Thus, the fact that an offender has an amount of marijuana inconsistent with personal use may provide strong evidence of intent, especially if police find additional evidence, like scales for weighing marijuana, baggies for packaging marijuana and large amounts of cash, consistent with sales of marijuana. Some courts require that " '. . .circumstantial evidence must be so strong and convincing as to exclude every reasonable hypothesis except the defendants' guilt and must exclude any reasonable hypothesis of the defendants' innocence.' " *Alleyne v. State,* 42 So. 3d 948, 950 (Fl. App. 2010).

3.   The power of felony murder. In *Kohler,* the prosecution tried to use the appellant's participation in the purchase of marijuana as the vehicle to convict him of felony murder. Consider whether the prosecution could charge him with any form of homicide without reliance on felony murder. The victim's death was obviously unintentional. Was the appellant reckless or even criminally negligent in creating a risk of death by his conduct? Surely, without felony murder, the prosecution would have had a hard time convicting the appellant of homicide. That fact that the punishment for murder often seems out of proportion with the offender's underlying conduct often explains why courts and most commentators are critical of felony murder.

4.   **Limits on felony murder.** Assume that, in *Kohler,* the prosecution charged the appellant with felony murder based on theft. That is, a death did result during the commission of felony theft. Would that be sufficient to support a murder conviction based on a felony murder theory? The answer is almost universally, no. Do you see why, based on the discussion in *Kohler?*

5.   **More on felony murder.** What if in *Kohler,* the prosecution charged Yates with felony murder based on the fact that the victim's death took place during the commission of a felony sale of marijuana? Be clear: Yates might be found guilty of some form of homicide without reference to felony murder. But would the sale of marijuana satisfy the threshold question: is the sale of marijuana inherently dangerous to human life? Courts have differed on this question. Compare *People v. Patterson,* 778 P. 2d 549 (Ca. 1989) (remanding the case to the trial court to determine whether cocaine is inherently dangerous to human life) and *People v. Taylor,* 6 Cal. App. 4th 1084 (1992) (the inherent risk of selling PCP does not carry a sufficient inherent risk to meet the inherently dangerous to human life standard) with *Davis v. State,* 725 S.E. 2d 280 (Ga. 2012) (as committed, the sale of marijuana was dangerous to human life), *Ex parte Mitchell,* 936 So. 2d 1094 (Ala. App. 2006)(accord).

CHAPTER 12

MARIJUANA AND LAW OF SEARCH AND SEIZURE

▪ ▪ ▪

The War on Drugs has shaped the law governing searches and seizures. That has been especially true when one focuses on cases involving marijuana. Professor Mandiberg argues that courts used the significant number of marijuana-related search and seizure cases in the last few decades to restrict Fourth Amendment rights. Marijuana Prohibition and the Shrinking Fourth Amendment, Susan Mandiberg, 43 McGeorge L. Rev. 23. Because police detect illegal marijuana grow operations through overhead and technical surveillance, marijuana cases have been important in shaping search and seizure doctrine as to rights to privacy in the home, in curtilage, and in fields.

An increasingly important question arises today: while the smell of marijuana traditionally gave rise to probable cause for search and seizure, what is the impact of marijuana legalization in this area of law? (2012). Professor Alex Kreit has written that when states legalize marijuana, courts must determine whether traditional Fourth Amendment rules of search and seizure must change as well. Alex Kreit, *Marijuana Legalization and Pretextual Stops*, 50 U.C. Davis L. Rev. 741, 768 (2016).

In addition, as an empirical matter, marijuana is the drug discovered in most police car stops on our highways, as discovered by Samuel R. Gross and Katherine Y. Barnes. *See Road Work: Racial Profiling and Drug Interdiction on the Highway,* 101 Mich. L. Rev. 651, 658 (2002). Not surprisingly, as you will see in this chapter, the lead cases all involve marijuana as the drug of search.

A. SEARCH AND SEIZURE

Many commentators believe that the Fourth Amendment suffered collateral damage from the War on Drugs. Beginning in the 1970s, after President Nixon appointed four justices to the Court, the Court began to cabin some of the more defendant friendly cases decided by the Warren Court. The trend, narrowing Fourth Amendment protection, has continued, with occasional decisions reestablishing Fourth Amendment protections. Many of the Court's decisions have involved marijuana as the target of the police investigation.

The Fourth Amendment takes up a sizeable amount of space in Criminal Procedure casebooks. We do not pretend to cover all of that rich body of law. Instead, this section of the casebook highlights some of the special issues at the intersection of the Fourth Amendment and marijuana law.

The first set of cases involve the use of drug sniffing dogs. Often, police used drug-sniffing dogs to determine whether a person's luggage contained marijuana. For example, in *United States v. Chadwick,* 433 U.S. 1 (1977), police believed a footlocker contained a large quantity of marijuana. Before making an arrest or searching the footlocker, the police subjected the footlocker to a dog-sniff. Police seized the footlocker after the dog signaled the presence of marijuana. But consider those facts: was the dog-sniff a search? If so, wouldn't the police need probable cause to make an evidentiary search? *Chadwick* was argued on other grounds.

In an extensive dicta, the Court indicated that a dog-sniff is not a search. *See United States v. Place,* 462 U.S. 696 (1983), which is discussed below. The net result is that the Fourth Amendment provides a person no protection when the police expose luggage or another object to a dog-sniff. The cases below develop how far the police can go in using drug-sniffing dogs before running into the Fourth Amendment.

I.   CANINE FORENSICS

a.   Is a Dog Sniff a Search?

ILLINOIS V. CABALLES
United States Supreme Court
543 U.S. 405 (2005)

STEVENS, J.

Illinois State Trooper Daniel Gillette stopped respondent for speeding on an interstate highway. When Gillette radioed the police dispatcher to report the stop, a second trooper, Craig Graham, a member of the Illinois State Police Drug Interdiction Team, overheard the transmission and immediately headed for the scene with his narcotics-detection dog. When they arrived, respondent's car was on the shoulder of the road and respondent was in Gillette's vehicle. While Gillette was in the process of writing a warning ticket, Graham walked his dog around respondent's car. The dog alerted at the trunk. Based on that alert, the officers searched the trunk, found marijuana, and arrested respondent. The entire incident lasted less than 10 minutes.

Respondent was convicted of a narcotics offense and sentenced to 12 years' imprisonment and a $256,136 fine. The trial judge denied his motion to suppress the seized evidence and to quash his arrest. He held that the officers had not unnecessarily prolonged the stop and that the dog alert was sufficiently reliable to provide probable cause to conduct the search. Although the Appellate Court affirmed, the Illinois Supreme Court reversed, concluding that because the canine sniff was performed without any " 'specific and articulable facts' " to suggest drug activity, the use of the dog "unjustifiably enlarg[ed] the scope of a routine traffic stop into a drug investigation." 207 Ill.2d 504, 510.

The question on which we granted certiorari is narrow: "Whether the Fourth Amendment requires reasonable, articulable suspicion to justify using a drug-detection dog to sniff a vehicle during a legitimate traffic stop." Thus, we proceed on the assumption that the officer conducting the dog sniff had no information about respondent except that he had been stopped for speeding; accordingly, we have omitted any reference to facts about respondent that might have triggered a modicum of suspicion.

Here, the initial seizure of respondent when he was stopped on the highway was based on probable cause and was concededly lawful. It is nevertheless clear that a seizure that is lawful at its inception can violate the Fourth Amendment if its manner of execution unreasonably infringes interests protected by the Constitution. A seizure that is justified solely by the interest in issuing a warning ticket to the driver can become unlawful if it is prolonged beyond the time reasonably required to complete that mission. In an earlier case involving a dog sniff that occurred during an unreasonably prolonged traffic stop, the Illinois Supreme Court held that use of the dog and the subsequent discovery of contraband were the product of an unconstitutional seizure. We may assume that a similar result would be warranted in this case if the dog sniff had been conducted while respondent was being unlawfully detained.

In the state-court proceedings, however, the judges carefully reviewed the details of Officer Gillette's conversations with respondent and the precise timing of his radio transmissions to the dispatcher to determine whether he had improperly extended the duration of the stop to enable the dog sniff to occur. We have not recounted those details because we accept the state court's conclusion that the duration of the stop in this case was entirely justified by the traffic offense and the ordinary inquiries incident to such a stop.

Despite this conclusion, the Illinois Supreme Court held that the initially lawful traffic stop became an unlawful seizure solely as a result of the canine sniff that occurred outside respondent's stopped car. That is, the court characterized the dog sniff as the cause rather than the consequence of a constitutional violation. In its view, the use of the dog converted the citizen-police encounter from a lawful traffic stop into a drug investigation, and because the shift in purpose was not supported by any reasonable suspicion that respondent possessed narcotics, it was unlawful. In our view, conducting a dog sniff would not change the character of a traffic stop that is lawful at its inception and otherwise executed in a reasonable manner, unless the dog sniff itself infringed respondent's constitutionally protected interest in privacy. Our cases hold that it did not.

Official conduct that does not "compromise any legitimate interest in privacy" is not a search subject to the Fourth Amendment. *Jacobsen*, 466 U.S., at 123. We have held that any interest in possessing contraband cannot be deemed "legitimate," and thus, governmental conduct that *only* reveals the possession of contraband "compromises no legitimate privacy interest." *Ibid.* This is because the expectation "that certain facts will not come to the attention of the authorities" is not the same as an interest in "privacy that society is prepared to consider reasonable." *Id.*, at 122. In *United States v. Place*, 462 U.S. 696 (1983), we treated a canine sniff by a well-trained narcotics-detection dog as "*sui generis*" because it "discloses only the presence or absence of narcotics, a contraband item." *Id.*, at 707. Respondent likewise concedes that "drug sniffs are designed, and if properly conducted are generally likely, to reveal only the presence of contraband." Although respondent argues that the error rates, particularly the existence of false positives, call into question the premise that drug-detection dogs alert only to contraband, the record contains no evidence or findings that support his argument. Moreover, respondent does not suggest that an erroneous alert, in and of itself, reveals any legitimate private information, and, in this case, the trial judge found that the dog sniff was sufficiently reliable to establish probable cause to conduct a full-blown search of the trunk.

Accordingly, the use of a well-trained narcotics-detection dog—one that "does not expose noncontraband items that otherwise would remain hidden from public view," *Place*, 462 U.S., at 707—during a lawful traffic stop, generally does not implicate legitimate privacy interests. In this case, the dog sniff was performed on the exterior of respondent's car while he was lawfully seized for a traffic violation. Any intrusion on respondent's privacy expectations does not rise to the level of a constitutionally cognizable infringement.

This conclusion is entirely consistent with our recent decision that the use of a thermal-imaging device to detect the growth of marijuana in a home constituted an unlawful search. *Kyllo v. United States*, 533 U.S. 27 (2001). Critical to that decision was the fact that the device was capable of detecting lawful activity—in that case, intimate details in a home, such as "at what hour each night the lady of the house takes her daily sauna and bath." *Id.*, at 38. The legitimate expectation that information about perfectly lawful activity will remain private is categorically distinguishable from respondent's hopes or expectations concerning the nondetection of contraband in the trunk of his car. A dog sniff conducted during a concededly lawful traffic stop that reveals no information other than the location of a substance that no individual has any right to possess does not violate the Fourth Amendment.

The judgment of the Illinois Supreme Court is vacated, and the case is remanded for further proceedings not inconsistent with this opinion.

It is so ordered.

SOUTER, J., dissenting.

I would hold that using the dog for the purposes of determining the presence of marijuana in the car's trunk was a search unauthorized as an incident of the speeding stop and unjustified on any other ground. I would accordingly affirm the judgment of the Supreme Court of Illinois, and I respectfully dissent.

In *United States v. Place*, 462 U.S. 696 (1983), we categorized the sniff of the narcotics-seeking dog as *"sui generis"* under the Fourth Amendment and held it was not a search. *Id.*, at 707. The classification rests not only upon the limited nature of the intrusion, but on a further premise that experience has shown to be untenable, the assumption that trained sniffing dogs do not err. What we have learned about the fallibility of dogs in the years since *Place* was decided would itself be reason to call for reconsidering Place's decision against treating the intentional use of a trained dog as a search. The portent of this very case, however, adds insistence to the call, for an uncritical adherence to Place would render the Fourth Amendment indifferent to suspicionless and indiscriminate sweeps of cars in parking garages and pedestrians on sidewalks; if a sniff is not preceded by a seizure subject to Fourth Amendment notice, it escapes Fourth Amendment review entirely unless it is treated as a search. We should not wait for these developments to occur before rethinking Place's analysis, which invites such untoward consequences.

At the heart both of *Place* and the Court's opinion today is the proposition that sniffs by a trained dog are *sui generis* because a reaction by the dog in going alert is a response to nothing but the presence of contraband. Hence, the argument goes, because the sniff can only reveal the presence of items devoid of any legal use, the sniff "does not implicate legitimate privacy interests" and is not to be treated as a search.

The infallible dog, however, is a creature of legal fiction. Although the Supreme Court of Illinois did not get into the sniffing averages of drug dogs, their supposed infallibility is belied by judicial opinions describing well-trained animals sniffing and alerting with less than perfect accuracy, whether owing to errors by their handlers, the limitations of the dogs themselves, or even the pervasive contamination of currency by cocaine. * * * In practical terms, the evidence is clear that the dog that alerts hundreds of times will be wrong dozens of times.

Once the dog's fallibility is recognized, however, that ends the justification claimed in *Place* for treating the sniff as *sui generis* under the Fourth Amendment: the sniff alert does not necessarily signal hidden contraband, and opening the container or enclosed space whose emanations the dog has sensed will not necessarily reveal contraband or any other evidence of crime. This is not, of course, to deny that a dog's reaction may provide reasonable suspicion, or probable cause, to search the container or enclosure; the Fourth Amendment does not demand certainty of success to justify a search for evidence or contraband. The point is simply that the sniff and alert cannot claim the certainty that Place assumed, both in treating the deliberate use of sniffing dogs as *sui generis* and then taking that characterization as a reason to say they are not searches subject to Fourth Amendment scrutiny. And when that aura of uniqueness disappears, there is no basis in Place's reasoning, and no good reason otherwise, to ignore the actual function that dog sniffs perform. They are conducted to obtain information about the contents of private spaces beyond anything that human senses could perceive, even when conventionally enhanced. The information is not provided by independent third parties beyond the reach of constitutional limitations, but gathered by the government's own officers in order to justify searches of the traditional sort, which may or may not reveal evidence of crime but will disclose anything meant to be kept private in the area searched. Thus in practice the government's use of a trained narcotics dog functions as a limited search to reveal undisclosed facts about private enclosures, to be used to justify a further and complete search of the enclosed area. And given the fallibility of the dog, the sniff is the first step in a process that may disclose "intimate details" without revealing contraband, just as a thermal-imaging device might do, as described in *Kyllo v. United States*, 533 U.S. 27 (2001).

It makes sense, then, to treat a sniff as the search that it amounts to in practice, and to rely on the body of our Fourth Amendment cases, including Kyllo, in deciding whether such a search is reasonable. As a general proposition, using a dog to sniff for drugs is subject to the rule that the object of enforcing criminal laws does not, without more, justify suspicionless Fourth Amendment intrusions. Since the police claim to have had no particular suspicion that Caballes was violating any drug law, this sniff search must stand or fall on its being ancillary to the traffic stop that led up to it. It is true that the police had probable cause to stop the car for an offense committed in the officer's presence, which Caballes concedes could have justified his arrest. There is no occasion to consider authority incident to arrest, however, for the police did nothing more than detain Caballes long enough to check his record and write a ticket. As a consequence, the reasonableness of the search must be assessed in relation to the actual delay the police chose to impose, and as Justice GINSBURG points out in her opinion, the Fourth Amendment consequences of stopping for a traffic citation are settled law.

In *Berkemer v. McCarty*, 468 U.S. 420, 439–440 (1984), we held that the analogue of the common traffic stop was the limited detention for investigation authorized by *Terry v. Ohio*, 392 U.S. 1 (1968). While *Terry* authorized a restricted incidental search for weapons when reasonable suspicion warrants such a safety measure, the Court took care to keep a Terry stop from automatically becoming a foot in the door for all investigatory purposes; the permissible intrusion was bounded by the justification for the detention. Although facts disclosed by enquiry within this limit might give grounds to go further, the government could not otherwise take advantage of a suspect's immobility to search for evidence unrelated to the reason for the detention. That has to be the rule unless *Terry* is going to become an open sesame for general searches, and that rule requires holding that the police do not have reasonable grounds to conduct sniff searches for drugs simply because they have stopped someone to receive a ticket for a highway offense. Since the police had no indication of illegal activity beyond the speed of the car in this case, the sniff search should be held unreasonable under the Fourth Amendment and its fruits should be suppressed.

Nothing in the case relied upon by the Court, *United States v. Jacobsen*, 466 U.S. 109 (1984), unsettled the limit of reasonable enquiry adopted in Terry. In *Jacobsen*, the Court found that no Fourth Amendment search occurred when federal agents analyzed powder they had already lawfully obtained. The Court noted that because the test could only reveal whether the powder was cocaine, the owner had no legitimate privacy interest at stake. As already explained, however, the use of a sniffing dog in cases like this is significantly different and properly treated as a search that does indeed implicate Fourth Amendment protection.

In *Jacobsen*, once the powder was analyzed, that was effectively the end of the matter: either the powder was cocaine, a fact the owner had no legitimate interest in concealing, or it was not cocaine, in which case the test revealed nothing about the powder or anything else that was not already legitimately obvious to the police. But in the case of the dog sniff, the dog does not smell the disclosed contraband; it smells a closed container. An affirmative reaction therefore does not identify a substance the police already legitimately possess, but informs the police instead merely of a reasonable chance of finding contraband they have yet to put their hands on. The police will then open the container and discover whatever lies within, be it marijuana or the owner's private papers. Thus, while *Jacobsen* could rely on the assumption that the enquiry in question would either show with certainty that a known substance was contraband or would reveal nothing more, both the certainty and the limit on disclosure that may follow are missing when the dog sniffs the car.

The Court today does not go so far as to say explicitly that sniff searches by dogs trained to sense contraband always get a free pass under the Fourth Amendment, since it reserves judgment on the constitutional significance of sniffs assumed to be more intrusive than a dog's walk around a stopped car. For this reason, I do not take the Court's reliance on

Jacobsen as actually signaling recognition of a broad authority to conduct suspicionless sniffs for drugs in any parked car, about which Justice GINSBURG is rightly concerned, or on the person of any pedestrian minding his own business on a sidewalk. But the Court's stated reasoning provides no apparent stopping point short of such excesses. For the sake of providing a workable framework to analyze cases on facts like these, which are certain to come along, I would treat the dog sniff as the familiar search it is in fact, subject to scrutiny under the Fourth Amendment.

GINSBURG, J., dissenting.

* * * The Supreme Court of Illinois [in this case] held that the drug evidence should have been suppressed. Adhering to its decision in *People v. Cox*, 202 Ill.2d. 462 (2002), the court employed a two-part test taken from *Terry v. Ohio*, 392 U.S. 1 (1968) to determine the overall reasonableness of the stop. The court asked first "whether the officer's action was justified at its inception," and second "whether it was reasonably related in scope to the circumstances which justified the interference in the first place."

The court concluded that the State failed to offer sufficient justification for the canine sniff: "The police did not detect the odor of marijuana in the car or note any other evidence suggesting the presence of illegal drugs." *Ibid.* Lacking "specific and articulable facts" supporting the canine sniff, the court ruled, "the police impermissibly broadened the scope of the traffic stop in this case into a drug investigation." 207 Ill. 2d., at 509. I would affirm the Illinois Supreme Court's judgment and hold that the drug sniff violated the Fourth Amendment.

In *Terry,* the Court upheld the stop and subsequent frisk of an individual based on an officer's observation of suspicious behavior and his reasonable belief that the suspect was armed. In a *Terry*-type investigatory stop, "the officer's action [must be] justified at its inception, and . . . reasonably related in scope to the circumstances which justified the interference in the first place." *Id.*, at 20. In applying Terry, the Court has several times indicated that the limitation on "scope" is not confined to the duration of the seizure; it also encompasses the manner in which the seizure is conducted.

"A routine traffic stop," the Court has observed, "is a relatively brief encounter and 'is more analogous to a so-called *Terry* stop . . . than to a formal arrest.'" *Knowles v. Iowa*, 525 U.S. 113, 117 (1998). I would apply *Terry*'s reasonable-relation test, as the Illinois Supreme Court did, to determine whether the canine sniff impermissibly expanded the scope of the initially valid seizure of Caballes.

It is hardly dispositive that the dog sniff in this case may not have lengthened the duration of the stop. Terry, it merits repetition, instructs that any investigation must be "reasonably related in *scope* to the circumstances which justified the interference in the first place." 392 U.S., at 20. The unwarranted and nonconsensual expansion of the seizure here from a routine traffic stop to a drug investigation broadened the scope of the investigation in a manner that, in my judgment, runs afoul of the Fourth Amendment.

The Court rejects the Illinois Supreme Court's judgment and, implicitly, the application of *Terry* to a traffic stop converted, by calling in a dog, to a drug search. The Court so rules, holding that a dog sniff does not render a seizure that is reasonable in time unreasonable in scope. Dog sniffs that detect only the possession of contraband may be employed without offense to the Fourth Amendment, the Court reasons, because they reveal no lawful activity and hence disturb no legitimate expectation of privacy.

In my view, the Court diminishes the Fourth Amendment's force by abandoning the second *Terry* inquiry (was the police action "reasonably related in scope to the circumstances [justifying] the [initial] interference"). 392 U.S., at 20. A drug-detection dog is an intimidating animal. Injecting such an animal into a routine traffic stop changes the character of the encounter between the police and the motorist. The stop becomes broader, more adversarial, and (in at least some cases) longer. Caballes—who, as far as Troopers Gillette and Graham knew, was guilty solely of driving six miles per hour over the speed limit—was exposed to the embarrassment and intimidation of being investigated, on a public thoroughfare, for drugs. Even if the drug sniff is not characterized as a Fourth Amendment "search," the sniff surely broadened the scope of the traffic-violation-related seizure.

The Court has never removed police action from Fourth Amendment control on the ground that the action is well calculated to apprehend the guilty. Under today's decision, every traffic stop could become an occasion to call in the dogs, to the distress and embarrassment of the law-abiding population.

The Illinois Supreme Court, it seems to me, correctly apprehended the danger in allowing the police to search for contraband despite the absence of cause to suspect its presence. Today's decision, in contrast, clears the way for suspicionless, dog-accompanied drug sweeps of parked cars along sidewalks and in parking lots. Nor would motorists have constitutional grounds for complaint should police with dogs, stationed at long traffic lights, circle cars waiting for the red signal to turn green.

Today's decision also undermines this Court's situation-sensitive balancing of Fourth Amendment interests in other contexts. For example, in *Bond v. United States*, 529 U.S. 334, 338–339 (2000), the Court held that a bus passenger had an expectation of privacy in a bag placed in an overhead bin and that a police officer's physical manipulation of the bag constituted an illegal search. If canine drug sniffs are entirely exempt from Fourth Amendment inspection, a sniff could substitute for an officer's request to a bus passenger for permission to search his bag, with this significant difference: The passenger would not have the option to say "No."

* * *

This Court has distinguished between the general interest in crime control and more immediate threats to public safety. In *Michigan Dept. of State Police v. Sitz*, 496 U.S. 444 (1990), this Court upheld the use of a sobriety traffic checkpoint. Balancing the State's interest in preventing drunk driving, the extent to which that could be accomplished through the checkpoint program, and the degree of intrusion the stops involved, the Court determined that the State's checkpoint program was consistent with the Fourth Amendment. In *Indianapolis v. Edmond*, 531 U.S. 32 (2000), this Court held that a drug interdiction checkpoint violated the Fourth Amendment. Despite the illegal narcotics traffic that the Nation is struggling to stem, the Court explained, a "general interest in crime control" did not justify the stops. *Id.*, at 43–44. The Court distinguished the sobriety checkpoints in Sitz on the ground that those checkpoints were designed to eliminate an "immediate, vehicle-bound threat to life and limb." *Id.*, at 43. The use of bomb-detection dogs to check vehicles for explosives without doubt has a closer kinship to the sobriety checkpoints in *Sitz* than to the drug checkpoints in *Edmond*. As the Court observed in *Edmond*: "[T]he Fourth Amendment would almost certainly permit an appropriately tailored roadblock set up to thwart an imminent terrorist attack . . . ." 531 U.S., at 44. Even if the Court were to change course and characterize a dog sniff as an independent Fourth Amendment search, the immediate, present danger of explosives would likely justify a bomb sniff under the special needs doctrine.

* * *

For the reasons stated, I would hold that the police violated Caballes' Fourth Amendment rights when, without cause to suspect wrongdoing, they conducted a dog sniff of his vehicle. I would therefore affirm the judgment of the Illinois Supreme Court.

NOTES AND QUESTIONS

1. **The better argument.** Does the majority or dissent have the better argument in *Caballes*?

2. **Checkpoints.** Can the police set up a checkpoint on a street where police know that marijuana dealers congregate and stop every car to expose it to a drug-sniffing dog?

3. **Limits of dog sniffs.** Would it make any difference to the Court's analysis if, for example, the dog sniffed a person, rather than the vehicle or luggage? For a discussion of this issue, *see* Jacey Lara Gottlieb, *Who Let the Dogs Out—and While We're at It, Who Said They Could Sniff Me?: How the*

Unregulated Street Sniff Threatens Pedestrians' Privacy Rights, 82 Brooklyn L. Rev. 1377 (2017).

4. **Infallible Fido.** What do you make of Justice Souter's argument in dissent that dogs are quite fallible? The premise in *Place* was that a dog sniff revealed only contraband, something in which one cannot have a reasonable expectation of privacy. But if the dog has a poor track record, then the police may open luggage revealing personal possession without sufficient justification. That is, the underlying rationale for the rule that a dog sniff is not a search may be undercut.

5. **Proof of Fido's reliability.** Some courts have considered the burden that the state must meet to establish a dog's reliability, given the recognition of the fact that many dogs are, in fact, unreliable. For example, the Florida Supreme Court held that, "[T]he State must present . . . the dog's training and certification records, an explanation of the meaning of the particular training and certification, field performance records (including any unverified alerts), and evidence concerning the experience and training of the officer handling the dog, as well as any other objective evidence known to the officer about the dog's reliability." *Florida v. Harris,* 568 U.S. 237, 242–43 (2013). The Supreme Court rejected that approach and stated, "We think that demand inconsistent with the 'flexible, common-sense standard' of probable cause." 568 U.S. at 240.

PROBLEM 12-1

The local police department has created an anti-drug task force. To combat drugs, the task force has purchased several dogs trained to detect marijuana. The department has put in place a policy that requires officers who want to subject a vehicle to a drug sniffing dog to call in immediately for a K-9 unit to avoid unnecessary delays in getting the K-9 unit to the scene of the stop. On the date in question, Officer stopped Defendant's vehicle for a broken tail light. In truth, Officer wanted to determine if Defendant had contraband in his vehicle because Defendant was driving a "low rider," a vehicle often used by young drug dealers. When Officer called for the K-9 unit, he learned that it would be about 15 minutes before the unit could arrive. Officer took his time in writing up Defendant's traffic ticket because he expected a delay. The K-9 unit arrived twenty minutes after the initial stop. Several minutes later, the drug-sniffing dog signaled the presence of marijuana. The police then opened the trunk where the dog signaled that marijuana was present and found a large quantity of marijuana. Charged with possession of marijuana with intent to distribute, Defendant has moved to suppress the evidence. How should the court resolve that motion?

For a state case discussing the issues raised in Problem 12-1, *see People v. Campos-Barajas,* 2017 WL 2829167 (Cal. App. 2017)(unpublished).

b.   Are There Limits on Dog Searches?

FLORIDA V. JARDINES

United States Supreme Court
569 U.S. 1 (2013)

SCALIA, J.

We consider whether using a drug-sniffing dog on a homeowner's porch to investigate the contents of the home is a "search" within the meaning of the Fourth Amendment.

I

In 2006, Detective William Pedraja of the Miami-Dade Police Department received an unverified tip that marijuana was being grown in the home of respondent Joelis Jardines. One month later, the Department and the Drug Enforcement Administration sent a joint surveillance team to Jardines' home. Detective Pedraja was part of that team. He watched the home for fifteen minutes and saw no vehicles in the driveway or activity around the home, and could not see inside because the blinds were drawn. Detective Pedraja then approached Jardines' home accompanied by Detective Douglas Bartelt, a trained canine handler who had just arrived at the scene with his drug-sniffing dog. The dog was trained to detect the scent of marijuana, cocaine, heroin, and several other drugs, indicating the presence of any of these substances through particular behavioral changes recognizable by his handler.

Detective Bartelt had the dog on a six-foot leash, owing in part to the dog's "wild" nature and tendency to dart around erratically while searching. As the dog approached Jardines' front porch, he apparently sensed one of the odors he had been trained to detect, and began energetically exploring the area for the strongest point source of that odor. As Detective Bartelt explained, the dog "began tracking that airborne odor by . . . tracking back and forth," engaging in what is called "bracketing," "back and forth, back and forth." Detective Bartelt gave the dog "the full six feet of the leash plus whatever safe distance [he could] give him" to do this—he testified that he needed to give the dog "as much distance as I can." And Detective Pedraja stood back while this was occurring, so that he would not "get knocked over" when the dog was "spinning around trying to find" the source.

After sniffing the base of the front door, the dog sat, which is the trained behavior upon discovering the odor's strongest point. Detective Bartelt then pulled the dog away from the door and returned to his vehicle. He left the scene after informing Detective Pedraja that there had been a positive alert for narcotics.

On the basis of what he had learned at the home, Detective Pedraja applied for and received a warrant to search the residence. When the warrant was executed later that day, Jardines attempted to flee and was arrested; the search revealed marijuana plants, and he was charged with trafficking in cannabis.

At trial, Jardines moved to suppress the marijuana plants on the ground that the canine investigation was an unreasonable search. The trial court granted the motion, and the Florida Third District Court of Appeal reversed. On a petition for discretionary review, the Florida Supreme Court quashed the decision of the Third District Court of Appeal and approved the trial court's decision to suppress, holding (as relevant here) that the use of the trained narcotics dog to investigate Jardines' home was a Fourth Amendment search unsupported by probable cause, rendering invalid the warrant based upon information gathered in that search. 73 So.3d 34 (2011).

We granted certiorari, limited to the question of whether the officers' behavior was a search within the meaning of the Fourth Amendment.

II

The Fourth Amendment provides in relevant part that the "right of the people to be secure in their persons, houses, papers, and effects, against unreasonable searches and seizures, shall not be violated." The Amendment establishes a simple baseline, one that for much of our history formed the exclusive basis for its protections: When "the Government obtains information by physically intruding" on persons, houses, papers, or effects, "a 'search' within the original meaning of the Fourth Amendment" has "undoubtedly occurred." *United States v. Jones,* 565 U.S. 400 (2012). By reason of our decision in *Katz v. United States,* 389 U.S. 347 (1967), property rights "are not the sole measure of Fourth Amendment violations," *Soldal v. Cook County,* 506 U.S. 56, 64 (1992)—but though *Katz* may add to the baseline, it does not subtract anything from the Amendment's protections "when the Government *does* engage in [a] physical intrusion of a constitutionally protected area," *United States v. Knotts,* 460 U.S. 276, 286 (1983).

That principle renders this case a straightforward one. The officers were gathering information in an area belonging to Jardines and immediately surrounding his house—in the curtilage of the house, which we have held enjoys protection as part of the home itself. And they gathered that information by physically entering and occupying the area to engage in conduct not explicitly or implicitly permitted by the homeowner.

A

The Fourth Amendment "indicates with some precision the places and things encompassed by its protections": persons, houses, papers, and effects. *Oliver v. United States,* 466 U.S. 170, 176 (1984). The Fourth

Amendment does not, therefore, prevent all investigations conducted on private property; for example, an officer may (subject to *Katz*) gather information in what we have called "open fields"—even if those fields are privately owned—because such fields are not enumerated in the Amendment's text. *Hester v. United States,* 265 U.S. 57 (1924).

But when it comes to the Fourth Amendment, the home is first among equals. At the Amendment's "very core" stands "the right of a man to retreat into his own home and there be free from unreasonable governmental intrusion." *Silverman v. United States,* 365 U.S. 505, 511 (1961). This right would be of little practical value if the State's agents could stand in a home's porch or side garden and trawl for evidence with impunity; the right to retreat would be significantly diminished if the police could enter a man's property to observe his repose from just outside the front window.

We therefore regard the area "immediately surrounding and associated with the home"—what our cases call the curtilage—as "part of the home itself for Fourth Amendment purposes." *Oliver, supra,* at 180. That principle has ancient and durable roots. Just as the distinction between the home and the open fields is "as old as the common law," *Hester, supra,* at 59, so too is the identity of home and what Blackstone called the "curtilage or homestall," for the "house protects and privileges all its branches and appurtenants." 4 W. Blackstone, *Commentaries on the Laws of England* 223, 225 (1769). This area around the home is "intimately linked to the home, both physically and psychologically," and is where "privacy expectations are most heightened." *California v. Ciraolo,* 476 U.S. 207, 213 (1986).

While the boundaries of the curtilage are generally "clearly marked," the "conception defining the curtilage" is at any rate familiar enough that it is "easily understood from our daily experience." *Oliver,* 466 U.S., at 182, n. 12. Here there is no doubt that the officers entered it: The front porch is the classic exemplar of an area adjacent to the home and "to which the activity of home life extends." *Ibid.*

B

Since the officers' investigation took place in a constitutionally protected area, we turn to the question of whether it was accomplished through an unlicensed physical intrusion. While law enforcement officers need not "shield their eyes" when passing by the home "on public thoroughfares," *Ciraolo,* 476 U.S., at 213, an officer's leave to gather information is sharply circumscribed when he steps off those thoroughfares and enters the Fourth Amendment's protected areas. In permitting, for example, visual observation of the home from "public navigable airspace," we were careful to note that it was done "in a physically nonintrusive manner." *Ibid. Entick v. Carrington,* 2 Wils. K.B. 275, 95 Eng. Rep. 807 (K.B. 1765), a case "undoubtedly familiar" to "every American statesman" at the time of the Founding, *Boyd v. United States,* 116 U.S. 616, 626 (1886), states the general rule clearly: "[O]ur law holds the property of every man so sacred, that no man can set his foot upon his neighbour's close without his leave." 2 Wils. K.B., at 291, 95 Eng. Rep., at 817. As it is undisputed that the detectives had all four of their feet and all four of their companion's firmly planted on the constitutionally protected extension of Jardines' home, the only question is whether he had given his leave (even implicitly) for them to do so. He had not.

"A license may be implied from the habits of the country," notwithstanding the "strict rule of the English common law as to entry upon a close." *McKee v. Gratz,* 260 U.S. 127, 136 (1922) (Holmes, J.). We have accordingly recognized that "the knocker on the front door is treated as an invitation or license to attempt an entry, justifying ingress to the home by solicitors, hawkers and peddlers of all kinds." *Breard v. Alexandria,* 341 U.S. 622, 626 (1951). This implicit license typically permits the visitor to approach the home by the front path, knock promptly, wait briefly to be received, and then (absent invitation to linger longer) leave. Complying with the terms of that traditional invitation does not require fine-grained legal knowledge; it is generally managed without incident by the Nation's Girl Scouts and trick-or-treaters. Thus, a police officer not armed with a warrant may approach a home and knock, precisely because that is "no more than any private citizen might do." *Kentucky v. King,* 563 U.S. 452, 469 (2011).

But introducing a trained police dog to explore the area around the home in hopes of discovering incriminating evidence is something else. There is no customary invitation to do *that.* An invitation to engage in canine forensic investigation assuredly does not inhere in the very act of hanging a knocker. To find a visitor knocking on the door is routine (even if sometimes unwelcome); to spot that same visitor exploring the front path with a metal detector, or marching his bloodhound into the garden before saying hello and asking permission, would inspire most of us to—well, call the police. The scope of a license—express or implied—is limited not only to a particular area but also to a specific purpose. Consent at a traffic stop to an officer's checking out an anonymous tip that there is a body in the trunk does not permit the officer to rummage through the trunk for narcotics. Here, the background social norms that invite a visitor to the front door do not invite him there to conduct a search.

The State points to our decisions holding that the subjective intent of the officer is irrelevant. * * * But those cases merely hold that a stop or search *that is objectively reasonable* is not vitiated by the fact that the officer's real reason for making the stop or search has nothing to do with the validating reason. Thus, the defendant will not be heard to complain that although he was speeding the officer's real reason for the stop was racial harassment. Here, however, the question before the court is precisely *whether* the officer's conduct was an objectively reasonable search. As we have described, that depends upon whether the officers had an implied license to enter the porch, which in turn depends upon the purpose for which they entered. Here, their behavior objectively reveals a purpose to conduct a search, which is not what anyone would think he had license to do.

III

The State argues that investigation by a forensic narcotics dog by definition cannot implicate any legitimate privacy interest. The State cites for authority our decisions in *United States v. Place,* 462 U.S. 696 (1983), *United States v. Jacobsen,* 466 U.S. 109, and *Illinois v. Caballes,* 543 U.S. 405 (2005), which held, respectively, that canine inspection of luggage in an airport, chemical testing of a substance that had fallen from a parcel in transit, and canine inspection of an automobile during a lawful traffic stop, do not violate the "reasonable expectation of privacy" described in *Katz.*

Just last Term, we considered an argument much like this. *Jones* held that tracking an automobile's whereabouts using a physically-mounted GPS receiver is a Fourth Amendment search. The Government argued that the *Katz* standard "show[ed] that no search occurred," as the defendant had "no 'reasonable expectation of privacy' " in his whereabouts on the public roads, *Jones,* 565 U.S., at 406—a proposition with at least as much support in our case law as the one the State marshals here. But because the GPS receiver had been physically mounted on the defendant's automobile (thus intruding on his "effects"), we held that tracking the vehicle's movements was a search: a person's "Fourth Amendment rights do not rise or fall with the *Katz* formulation." *Jones, supra,* at 406. The *Katz* reasonable-expectations test "has been *added to,* not *substituted for,*" the traditional property-based understanding of the Fourth Amendment, and so is unnecessary to consider when the government gains evidence by physically intruding on constitutionally protected areas.

Thus, we need not decide whether the officers' investigation of Jardines' home violated his expectation of privacy under *Katz.* One virtue of the Fourth Amendment's property-rights baseline is that it keeps easy cases easy. That the officers learned what they learned only by physically intruding on Jardines' property to gather evidence is enough to establish that a search occurred.

For a related reason we find irrelevant the State's argument (echoed by the dissent) that forensic dogs have been commonly used by police for centuries. This argument is apparently directed to our holding in *Kyllo v. United States,* 533 U.S. 27 (2001), that surveillance of the home is a search where "the Government uses a device that is not in general public use" to "explore details of the home that would previously have been unknowable *without physical intrusion.*" *Id.,* at 40. But the implication of that statement (*inclusio unius est exclusio alterius*) is that when the government uses a physical intrusion to explore details of the home (including its curtilage), the antiquity of the tools that they bring along is irrelevant.

* * *

The government's use of trained police dogs to investigate the home and its immediate surroundings is a "search" within the meaning of the Fourth Amendment. The judgment of the Supreme Court of Florida is therefore affirmed.

It is so ordered.

KAGAN, J., concurring.

For me, a simple analogy clinches this case—and does so on privacy as well as property grounds. A stranger comes to the front door of your home carrying super-high-powered binoculars. He doesn't knock or say hello. Instead, he stands on the porch and uses the binoculars to peer through your windows, into your home's furthest corners. It doesn't take long (the binoculars are really very fine): In just a couple of minutes, his uncommon behavior allows him to learn details of your life you disclose to no one. Has your "visitor" trespassed on your property, exceeding the license you have granted to members of the public to, say, drop off the mail or distribute campaign flyers? Yes, he has. And has he also invaded your "reasonable expectation of privacy," by nosing into intimacies you sensibly thought protected from disclosure? *Katz v. United States,* 389 U.S. 347, 360 (1967). Yes, of course, he has done that too.

* * *

The Court today treats this case under a property rubric; I write separately to note that I could just as happily have decided it by looking to Jardines' privacy interests. A decision along those lines would have looked . . . well, much like this one. It would have talked about " 'the right of a man to retreat into his own home and there be free from unreasonable governmental intrusion.' " *Silverman v. United States,* 365 U.S. 505, 511 (1961). It would have insisted on maintaining the "practical value" of that right by preventing police officers from standing in an adjacent space and "trawl[ing] for evidence with impunity." *Ante,* at 1414. It would have explained that " 'privacy expectations are most heightened' " in the home and the surrounding area. *California v. Ciraolo,* 476 U.S. 207, 213 (1986). And it would have determined that police officers invade those shared expectations when they use trained canine assistants to reveal within the confines of a home what they could not otherwise have found there.

It is not surprising that in a case involving a search of a home, property concepts and privacy concepts should so align. The law of property "naturally enough influence[s]" our "shared social expectations" of what places should be free from governmental incursions. *Georgia v. Randolph,* 547 U.S. 103, 111 (2006). And so the sentiment "my home is my own," while originating in property law, now also denotes a common understanding—extending even beyond that law's formal protections—about an especially private sphere. Jardines' home was his property; it was also his most intimate and familiar space. The analysis proceeding from each of those facts, as today's decision reveals, runs mostly along the same path.

I can think of only one divergence: If we had decided this case on privacy grounds, we would have realized that *Kyllo v. United States,* 533 U.S. 27 (2001), already resolved it. The *Kyllo* Court held that police officers conducted a search when they used a thermal-imaging device to detect heat emanating from a private home, even though they committed no trespass. Highlighting our intention to draw both a "firm" and a "bright" line at "the entrance to the house," we announced the following rule:

> Where, as here, the Government uses a device that is not in general public use, to explore details of the home that would previously have been unknowable without physical intrusion, the surveillance is a 'search' and is presumptively unreasonable without a warrant.

That "firm" and "bright" rule governs this case: The police officers here conducted a search because they used a "device . . . not in general public use" (a trained drug-detection dog) to "explore details of the home" (the presence of certain substances) that they would not otherwise have discovered without entering the premises.

And again, the dissent's argument that the device is just a dog cannot change the equation. As *Kyllo* made clear, the "sense-enhancing" tool at issue may be "crude" or "sophisticated," may be old or new (drug-detection dogs actually go back not "12,000 years" or "centuries,", but only a few decades), may be either smaller or bigger than a breadbox; still, "at least where (as here)" the device is not "in general public use," training it on a home violates our "minimal expectation of privacy"—an expectation "that *exists,* and that is acknowledged to be *reasonable.*" 533 U.S., at 34, 36. That does not mean the device is off-limits, as the dissent implies, see *post,* at 1425–1426; it just means police officers cannot use it to examine a home without a warrant or exigent circumstance.

With these further thoughts, suggesting that a focus on Jardines' privacy interests would make an "easy cas[e] easy" twice over, *ante,* at 1417, I join the Court's opinion in full.

ALITO, J., dissenting.

The Court's decision in this important Fourth Amendment case is based on a putative rule of trespass law that is nowhere to be found in the annals of Anglo-American jurisprudence.

The law of trespass generally gives members of the public a license to use a walkway to approach the front door of a house and to remain there for a brief time. This license is not limited to persons who intend to speak to an occupant or who actually do so. (Mail carriers and persons delivering packages and flyers are examples of individuals who may lawfully approach a front door without intending to converse.) Nor is the license restricted to categories of visitors whom an occupant of the dwelling is likely to welcome; as the Court acknowledges, this license applies even to "solicitors, hawkers and peddlers of all kinds." And the license even extends to police officers who wish to gather evidence against an occupant (by asking potentially incriminating questions).

According to the Court, however, the police officer in this case, Detective Bartelt, committed a trespass because he was accompanied during his otherwise lawful visit to the front door of respondent's house by his dog, Franky. Where is the authority evidencing such a rule? Dogs have been domesticated for about 12,000 years; they were ubiquitous in both this country and Britain at the time of the adoption of the Fourth Amendment; and their acute sense of smell has been used in law enforcement for centuries. Yet the Court has been unable to find a single case—from the United States or any other common-law nation—that supports the rule on which its decision is based. Thus, trespass law provides no support for the Court's holding today.

The Court's decision is also inconsistent with the reasonable-expectations-of-privacy test that the Court adopted in *Katz v. United States,* 389 U.S. 347 (1967). A reasonable person understands that odors emanating from a house may be detected from locations that are open to the public, and a reasonable person will not count on the strength of those odors remaining within the range that, while detectible by a dog, cannot be smelled by a human.

For these reasons, I would hold that no search within the meaning of the Fourth Amendment took place in this case, and I would reverse the decision below.

NOTES AND QUESTIONS

1. **Privacy in, property out.** Prior to *Katz v. United States,* 389 U.S. 347 (1967), the Court relied heavily on property concepts in defining Fourth Amendment concepts. For example, the parties in *Katz* framed the issue as whether the police conduct in tapping Katz's phone call in a phone booth intruded into a constitutionally protected area. *Katz* rejected that formulation, ushering in a focus on reasonable expectation of privacy. Thus, in *Katz,* attaching a tap on the phone booth and listening to Katz's phone conversation was a search because Katz has a reasonable expectation of privacy.

2. **Property's comeback.** No long after his appointment to the Court, Justice Scalia made clear his disagreement with *Katz* and made clear that he would overrule *Katz* in favor of the original understanding of the Fourth Amendment (when property concepts largely controlled its interpretation). He

never won that battle. As Justice Scalia's *Jardines* opinion makes clear, Justice Scalia eventually made peace with *Katz.* Although few commentators accept his statement at face value, as he explained in *Jardines, Katz* added to Fourth Amendment protection and did not supplant property analysis.

3.   **Overlap between property and privacy.** Does it make a difference whether the Court interprets the Fourth Amendment in terms of privacy or property? Justice Kagan's concurring opinion makes clear that many cases will come out the same way under either analysis. *United States v. Jones,* 565 U.S. 400 (2012) demonstrates the kind of case where the analysis might differ: there, police placed a GPS device on Jones' car that allowed the police to follow his movements for 28 days. The Court was unanimous in finding that the police conduct was a search; but the majority avoided difficult questions about when the conduct amounted to a search under *Katz.* The physical attachment to collect information amounted to more than a technical trespass. The *Katz* analysis presented difficult questions: the Court had held that attaching a tracking device did not amount to a search when it was not attached to the defendant's property and when all that the device allowed the police to do was to learn what any member of the public could see. *United States v. Knotts,* 460 U.S. 276 (1983). At what point under the *Katz* analysis would a person have a reasonable expectation of privacy?

4.   **The new Fourth Amendment challenge.** *Carpenter v. United States,* 585 U.S. ___ (2018) demonstrates the imprecision of the *Katz* analysis in a similar area. There, the government collected large quantities of data about Carpenter's movements from the phone company, which provided cell tower data. A closely divided Court found that the police conduct was a search. Chief Justice Roberts emphasized the narrowness of the decision, in effect, signaling the difficulty of line-drawing in other cases. For a pre-*Carpenter* article analyzing the issues in such cases, *see* Michael Vitiello, *Katz v. United States: Back to the Future?* 52 U. Rich. L. Rev. 425 (2018).

5.   **Making sense out of Jardines.** In *Jardines,* does Justice Scalia or Justice Alito have the better argument? Is Justice Scalia's rendition of the facts accurate? If Justice Alito's rendition of the facts is more accurate, is the majority conclusion still defensible?

II. PROBABLE CAUSE

For most evidentiary searches, police need probable cause to believe that evidence will be found where the police want to search. To make a custodial arrest, the police need probable cause to believe that the person to be arrested has committed a crime. Courts have dealt with many issues relating to the meaning of probable cause and the need for warrants. Many of those cases cut across different areas of the criminal law.

This section deals specifically with cases where the legalization of marijuana creates unique problems for law enforcement agents and the courts. In states where marijuana is illegal, the odor of smoked or dry marijuana creates probable cause. As summarized by Professor Susan Mandiberg:

> At the Supreme Court level, marijuana has played a central role in cases where probable cause or reasonable suspicion was based at least in part on an officer's "plain smell." And lower-court cases show that officers continue to find it easy to detect the presence of marijuana while engaged in other lawful investigative enterprises. Police in search-and-seizure cases claim to have smelled burned or burning marijuana, unburned marijuana, and the odor of marijuana lingering on a subject's clothing. People evidently often smoke marijuana while driving, or have it in the car, or use it shortly before driving, and thus many cases involve police detecting the odor after stopping a vehicle for other reasons."

Susan F. Mandiberg, Marijuana Prohibition and the Shrinking Fourth Amendment, 43 McGeorge L. Rev. 23, 39–43 (2012).

But the issue gets more difficult in a state where marijuana possession does not violate state law. For example, does the smell of marijuana give an officer probable cause to search or to arrest? Issues like that have presented courts with interesting challenges.

PEOPLE V. STRASBURG

Court of Appeal, California
148 Cal. App. 4th 1052 (2007)

MARCHIANO, J.

Following the denial of his motion to suppress, defendant Gabriel Reed Strasburg pleaded no contest to misdemeanor possession of more than 28.5 grams of marijuana (Health & Saf.Code, § 11357, subd. (c)). He contends that the sheriff's deputy who seized the marijuana lacked probable cause to search his car because defendant was allowed to possess marijuana under the Compassionate Use Act of 1996 (Health & Saf.Code, § 11362.5). We disagree because the Compassionate Use Act provides a limited defense against prosecution, but does not provide a shield against reasonable investigations and searches. Accordingly, we affirm.

I.   FACTS

* * *

[Deputy Sheriff Mosely spotted defendant and another person sitting in a parked car at a gas station.] Mosely drove his patrol car into the parking lot and parked to the left and to the rear of defendant's vehicle. He was not blocking defendant's car from leaving and had not activated his lights or siren.

Mosely approached the driver's side of defendant's car. He did not have his gun drawn. As Mosely approached the car, defendant opened the driver's door. Mosely immediately smelled the odor of marijuana. Defendant admitted he had been smoking marijuana just before Mosely arrived. Defendant immediately told Mosely that he had "a medical marijuana card," but Mosely did not ask to see it. Mosely never saw a medical marijuana card because he never asked to see it. Mosely looked at defendant's driver's license and determined that it was valid.

Mosely asked defendant if he had marijuana on his person or in the car. Defendant said he did and retrieved a Ziploc bag which he gave to Mosely, claiming it contained about three-quarters of an ounce of marijuana.

At this point, Mosely asked defendant to get out of the car. The deputy saw another bag of marijuana in the car in plain sight, which defendant gave him. This second bag contained 2.2 grams of marijuana.

Mosely testified that after defendant got out of his car, defendant again told him that he had a medical marijuana card and asked Mosely to look at it. The deputy refused to look at the card and said "something along [the] lines" of "we don't buy that here in Napa County." Mosely was aware of the medical marijuana law, and knew that someone with a doctor's recommendation could legally possess up to eight ounces of marijuana—and he knew at that point in the encounter that defendant only possessed three-quarters of an ounce to an ounce. Mosely made his "we don't buy that" remark because he was under the mistaken impression that medical marijuana cards were not recognized in Napa County.

Mosely searched defendant while he was outside the car, and found nothing. Both parties characterize this search as a "pat-search," or frisk.

At this point Mosely considered defendant detained, but not under arrest. Defendant was not free to leave. Mosely walked defendant toward the back of his patrol vehicle. Defendant may or may not have been handcuffed. Before he placed defendant in the back of the patrol vehicle, Mosely asked defendant if there was more marijuana in the car. Defendant told Mosely there was, and that it was more than an ounce. Mosely searched the rest of defendant's car and found 23 ounces of marijuana and a scale. The scale was "not a mini-pocket scale," but "a full powered scale able to weigh that [the 23 ounces] all at once." Mosely arrested defendant after he found the 23 ounces and scale in defendant's car.

Defendant testified at the suppression hearing. He said he was getting out of his car as Mosely walked up to it, and did not realize Mosely was there until he turned after opening the car door. When Mosely asked him about the odor of marijuana, defendant told him he had a "medical marijuana card," which was actually a prescription for marijuana from his doctor. Defendant testified that Mosely looked at defendant's driver's license, but refused to look at the prescription, telling defendant that "We don't accept that in Napa County." (Defendant lived in Sonoma County, and that was indicated on his license.) Defendant told Mosely at least twice that Mosely had to accept the marijuana prescription.

The trial court denied the motion to suppress. The court stated: "I believe that once an officer smells marijuana coming from a car that officer can search the car for the marijuana, and I haven't been given any authority that possessing a medical marijuana card deprives the officer of the right to continue with that investigation."

After the motion was denied, defendant entered his no contest plea. The trial court sentenced defendant to two years' probation.

II. DISCUSSION

Defendant contends that once he produced a doctor's prescription for marijuana, Deputy Mosely had no basis to detain or frisk him, or to search his car. We disagree for the following reasons.

Issue

A.

[The court first discussed the kind of immunity from prosecution provided by Proposition 215. That is a subject covered in Chapter 5 State Regulatory Schemes.]

* * *

B.

Defendant contends that because he immediately produced a doctor's prescription for marijuana, thus identifying himself as a qualified patient under the Act, Deputy Mosely was made aware that defendant could possess up to eight ounces of marijuana—and thus had no grounds to detain him, frisk him, or search his car. But the issue is not that simple, in light of *Mower*'s guidance that the Act does not impair reasonable police investigations and searches. A physician's prescription or an identification card under Article 2.5, which defendant did not have, does not provide an automatic protective aegis against reasonable searches.

We agree with the trial court's approach to this case. The operative issue is whether Mosely had probable cause to search defendant's car at the moment he smelled the odor of marijuana, at the outset of his encounter with defendant who was with another person in a parked car in a public parking area. If Mosely did have probable cause to search from the outset, we need not review the grounds for detention, or decide when, or if, the detention ripened into an arrest.

* * *

Hornbook law states that the Fourth Amendment to the United States Constitution permits the warrantless search of an automobile with probable cause. The scope of such a warrantless search is defined by the nature of the items being sought: "If probable cause justifies the search of a lawfully stopped vehicle, it justifies the search of every part of the vehicle and its contents that may conceal the object of the search." (*Ross, supra,* at pp. 824–825.)

Under the facts and circumstances of this case, Deputy Mosely had probable cause to search defendant's car for marijuana after he smelled the odor of marijuana. (*People v. Dey* (2000) 84 Cal.App.4th 1318, 1320–1322 (*Dey*).) Defendant admitted smoking marijuana, and the deputy sheriff saw another bag of marijuana in the car after the defendant handed him one. Armed with the knowledge that there was marijuana in the car, "a person of ordinary caution would conscientiously entertain a strong suspicion that even if defendant makes only personal use of the marijuana found in [the passenger area], he might stash additional quantities for future use in other parts of the vehicle, including the trunk." (*Dey, supra,* at 1322.)

The fact that defendant had a medical marijuana prescription, and could lawfully possess an amount of marijuana greater than that Deputy Mosely initially found, does not detract from the officer's probable cause. As [*People v.*] *Mower* [28 Cal. 4th 457 (2002)] observes, the Act provides a limited immunity—not a shield from reasonable investigation. An officer with probable cause to search is not prevented from doing so by someone presenting a medical marijuana card or a marijuana prescription. Given the probable cause here, the officer is entitled to continue to search and investigate, and determine whether the subject of the investigation is in fact possessing the marijuana for personal medical needs, and is adhering to the eight-ounce limit on possession. Unlawful possession of marijuana remains a criminal offense under Health and Safety Code section 11350, subject to seriously ill persons using marijuana for medical purposes recommended by a physician (section 11362.5(b)(1)(A) not being subject to criminal liability (section 11362.765).

We note that defendant was not sitting at home nursing an illness with the medicinal effects of marijuana. He was smoking in a parked car in a public place, a gas station parking lot, with another person. Defendant initially produced a separate bag of marijuana, albeit under the eight-ounce limit. Deputy Mosely could reasonably suspect that defendant, who was in the driver's seat, was about to drive off after smoking marijuana. That point aside, the overall circumstances justified the deputy sheriff's search of the car to determine if more marijuana was present. Defendant's response led to a search that ultimately revealed defendant was in possession of 23 ounces of marijuana and a scale—a strong suggestion that he was using the Act as a façade to conceal illegal activity. A qualified patient is limited to eight ounces for personal medical use under sections 11362.765 and 11362.77.

Defendant relies on a number of cases for the proposition that an officer cannot "selectively ignore evidence that demonstrates a lack of . . .

probable cause." The cases are distinguishable because they involve situations in which no probable cause was initially present. Defendant's argument that his prescription showed a lack of probable cause is inaccurate. Probable cause was created by the odor and presence of marijuana in a parked car occupied by two persons. Had defendant possessed only eight ounces, he presumably could have invoked the Act as a defense to prosecution of the case. But Mosely did not have to stop searching in the face of the marijuana prescription and the circumstances of how the smoking occurred. Otherwise, every qualified patient would be free to violate the intent of the medical marijuana program expressed in section 11362.5 and deal marijuana from his car with complete freedom from any reasonable search.

[handwritten margin note: Reasoning for holding]

The trial court properly denied the motion to suppress.

III. DISPOSITION

The judgment and sentence are affirmed.

NOTES AND QUESTIONS

1. **Probable cause in light of state law.** Other state courts have come to a similar conclusion as did the *Strasburg* court. *See, e.g., People v. Zuniga,* 372 P.3d 1052 (CO 2016); *State v. Ellis,* 327 P. 3d 1247 (WA App. 2014). Massachusetts' Supreme Judicial Court has held otherwise. Thus, in *Commonwealth v. Cruz,* 945 N.E.2d 899 (MA 2011), the court held that the smell of burnt marijuana alone could not give an officer even reasonable suspicion of criminal activity after Massachusetts had decriminalized possession of up to one ounce of marijuana. Similarly, the court has held that finding a small amount of marijuana on an occupant of a vehicle does create probable cause to search the rest of the vehicle. *See, e.g., Commonwealth v. Pacheco,* 464 Mass. 768, 771–772, 985 N.E.2d 839 (2013) (presence of less than one ounce of marijuana in vehicle did not give rise to probable cause to search it for additional marijuana).

2. **Line drawing in light of state law.** What if a court, like the Massachusetts Supreme Judicial Court, has held that mere smell of burnt marijuana does not give an officer cause to believe that criminal activity is afoot and the officer smells the odor of unburnt marijuana? At some point, does that give the officer probable cause to believe that the suspect is violating the state's marijuana law? The Supreme Judicial Court faced that question in *Commonwealth v. Overmyer,* 11 N.E. 3d 1054 (MA 2014). The key facts there included the following:

> Both officers noticed a very strong odor of unburnt marijuana near the location of the Volvo, and Klink asked the defendant if any was present in his vehicle. Acknowledging that there was marijuana in the Volvo, the defendant gave Klink the keys to the glove compartment. Klink found what he described as a "fat bag" of marijuana, which was "rather large," inside the glove compartment.

After retrieving the bag from the glove compartment, the officers still perceived a strong smell of marijuana, and, based on their training and experience, believed that an unspecified amount of marijuana remained present in the Volvo. The officers did not observe anything else indicating the presence of marijuana.

11 N.E. 3d at 1056.

The lower court in *Overmyer* found that the officers did not have probable cause to search the rest of the vehicle based on the foregoing facts. The Supreme Judicial Court remanded the case to the trial court to determine whether the strong smell of marijuana amount to probable cause to believe that the vehicle contained a large quantity of marijuana, the possession of which would be a violation of the law. 11 N.E. 3d at 1060.

3. A scholar's view. For a thoughtful analysis of this issue, *see* Alex Kreit, *Marijuana Legalization and Pretextual Stops*, 50 U.C. Davis L. Rev. 741 (2016).

PROBLEM 12-2

Assume that you are an assistant prosecuting attorney representing Massachusetts on remand in the *Overmyer* case. You are going to prepare your witnesses, the two officers who arrested Overmyer. Your boss asks you to submit the questions that you want to explore with the officers to establish probable cause that, based on finding a quantity of marijuana in the glove compartment (which defense counsel has conceded was lawful), the officers had probable cause to search the rest of the vehicle. Discuss fully.

III. SURVEILLANCE

Section 1 (a) above discussed canine forensics. That discussion focused on the Supreme Court's test for determining when police conduct crossed into the Fourth Amendment in the context of dog sniffs. Framed differently, when does police conduct become a search within the meaning of the Fourth Amendment?

This section picks up with another area where courts have had to determine whether police surveillance crosses the line between mere investigation (and therefore, providing an offender no Fourth Amendment protection) and a search within the meaning of the Fourth Amendment. As discussed in *State v. Davis,* infra, the Supreme Court has addressed the question in two leading decisions.

STATE V. DAVIS
New Mexico Supreme Court
360 P.3d 1161 (2015)

BOSSON, J.

Defendant Norman Davis was convicted of possession of marijuana after New Mexico State Police officers consensually searched his greenhouse and seized 14 marijuana plants. That search was the result of "Operation Yerba Buena 2006," a comprehensive aerial surveillance of Davis' property and the surrounding area conducted by a coordinated law enforcement effort that allegedly discovered marijuana plants growing on Davis' property. We decide whether that aerial surveillance, and the manner in which it was conducted, amounted to a warrantless search of Davis' property contrary to rights secured to him under the Fourth Amendment to the U.S. Constitution. Concluding that his federal constitutional rights were violated in this instance, we reverse the opinion of the Court of Appeals to the contrary as well as Davis' conviction below.

BACKGROUND

Over a period of time during 2005 and 2006, the New Mexico State Police received several reports that residents were growing marijuana plants throughout rural areas of Taos County, New Mexico. The informants, however, were unable or unwilling to provide the police with specific locations where marijuana was growing due to the remoteness of the area and fear of retaliation. In investigating the reports, the New Mexico State Police, Region Three narcotic agents, and the New Mexico National Guard organized Operation Yerba Buena, described as "a collaborative effort in the identification of marijuana plantations in Taos County with the use of two Army National Guard OH 58 Jet Ranger helicopters."

During the operation, the helicopter observers were instructed to fly over the assigned portions of the search area to look for potential "marijuana plantations." Once an observer spotted marijuana plants, he was instructed to contact the corresponding ground team staged at a pre-identified area and guide the team to the location of the plants. The ground team would then approach and make contact with the particular house to confirm or deny the existence of marijuana. The helicopter was to remain in the vicinity to provide cover and safety to its ground team.

On August 23, 2006, at approximately 9:00 a.m., the helicopters departed the Taos Regional Airport. The total operation lasted approximately ten hours. During that time, the helicopter observers identified possible marijuana plantations at eight properties and directed the ground teams accordingly.

The Davis residence

Observer Travis Skinner, upon identifying a potential marijuana plantation, directed his ground team—five vehicles containing at least six armed law enforcement officers—to the Davis residence. Davis' property was enclosed from ground level view by fences that ran along the property line, several large trees and bushes, and a "shade screen." However, when looking down on Davis' property from the helicopter, Sergeant Skinner was able to see and relay to the ground team the presence of a greenhouse as well as what appeared to be marijuana plants located at the back of Davis' property near the house. Sergeant Skinner also informed the team that there were dogs on the property.

Davis stated he was "in bed and not feeling very well when [he] heard a helicopter hovering very low, right on top of [his] house." He stated that the helicopter was making "a considerable racket" and that when the sound did not go away, he went outside to see "what . . . was going on." He observed the helicopter hovering approximately 50 feet above his head "kicking up dust and debris that was swirling all around."

Sergeant Bill Merrell of the New Mexico State Police confronted Davis near Davis' front door. Other officers were present on either side of his driveway. Sergeant Merrell, as heard on the tape recording, approached Davis, identified himself, and said "it appears that the helicopter . . . [was] looking for marijuana plants and they believe they've located some at your residence." Sergeant Merrell asked Davis for permission to search the residence for the marijuana plants seen by the observer. The noise from the helicopter was audible in the background of Sergeant Merrell's recording.

In response to Sergeant Merrell's accusation, Davis admitted that he was growing marijuana in his greenhouse and allowed the officers to search his property. Davis signed a written consent authorizing a complete search of his greenhouse and residence. This Court previously upheld the validity of Davis' consent. The officers seized 14 marijuana plants from Davis' greenhouse. Neither the flyover of Davis' property nor the resulting search was accompanied by a search warrant.

Several nearby residents characterized the helicopter flyovers during Operation Yerba Buena as terrifying and highly disruptive. Kelly Rayburn watched a helicopter fly around his house about "half a dozen times." Rayburn said the helicopter flew so close to his roof that the downdraft lifted off a solar panel and scattered trash all over his property. Victoria Lindsay observed a helicopter sweeping back and forth over her property, sending debris and personal property all over the yard. Lindsay also observed the helicopter hovering very close to the ground at a neighbor's greenhouse. Merilee Lighty observed a helicopter flying over her property for about 15 minutes. She said it was so close that the downdraft affected her trees and her bushes.

Suppression hearing

A grand jury indicted Davis on possession of marijuana contrary to NMSA 1978, Section 30–31–23(A) and (B)(3) (2005), and possession of drug paraphernalia 4 contrary to NMSA 1978, Section 30–31–25(A) (2001), based on the items found during Operation Yerba Buena. Davis filed two suppression motions, arguing that 1) the helicopter surveillance violated his constitutional right to be free from unreasonable searches, and 2) his consent for the subsequent search of his property was involuntary.

The court analyzed the facts of this case under what it characterized as the Riley/Ciraolo rule, a list of factors used by the United States Supreme Court to assess the constitutionality of aerial surveillance.

According to the district court's findings, the helicopter circled over certain locations and then swooped in for closer looks. The court concluded that "[a] greater degree of intrusion is permissible if aerial surveillance is used to confirm facts, rather than flying around generally in an effort to spot greenhouses, then swooping in lower to see what could possibly be seen."

In totality, the court concluded as a matter of law that the helicopter surveillance "just barely" made it over the threshold of validity. The district court then found that Davis' subsequent consent to the search was valid and not given under duress or coercion. The court denied both of Davis' motions to suppress.

Following the hearing, Davis entered a conditional plea of guilty reserving his right to appeal the district court's pretrial denial of his motion to suppress. On Davis' first appeal, our Court of Appeals reversed the district court on the consent finding. We granted certiorari and reversed.

On remand, the Court of Appeals considered the validity of the aerial surveillance under both the U.S. and the New Mexico Constitutions. The Court of Appeals found the surveillance permissible under the Fourth Amendment to the U.S. Constitution, but impermissible under the New Mexico Constitution. Reversing the district court, the Court of Appeals suppressed all evidence obtained from the Davis search.

We again granted the State's petition for certiorari review, this time to determine 1) whether aerial surveillance is a violation of Article II, Section 10 of the New Mexico Constitution and, if so, 2) whether Davis' subsequent consent to search his property was sufficiently attenuated from the illegal search.

DISCUSSION

Under our interstitial analysis, we must first consider whether the claimed right is protected under the U.S. Constitution before considering whether the New Mexico Constitution offers broader protection

When interpreting independent provisions of our New Mexico Constitution for which there are analogous provisions in the U.S. Constitution, New Mexico utilizes the interstitial approach. In this case, therefore, we must first determine whether the aerial surveillance conducted during Operation Yerba Buena violated the Fourth Amendment. If so, we do not address Davis' state constitutional claim.

"The touchstone of Fourth Amendment analysis is whether a person has a constitutionally protected reasonable expectation of privacy [in the area searched]," in this case the curtilage of a private home. *Ciraolo,* 476 U.S. at 211. This inquiry normally embraces two discrete questions: "whether the individual, by his conduct, has exhibited an actual (subjective) expectation of privacy, . . . [and] whether the individual's subjective expectation of privacy is [objectively] one that society is prepared to recognize as reasonable." *Smith v. Maryland,* 442 U.S. 735, 740 (1979). The determination is based on the totality of circumstances in each particular case.

Whether Davis had a reasonable expectation of privacy from a helicopter conducting aerial observation over the curtilage of his home

The curtilage of a house is considered an extension of the home for Fourth Amendment purposes As such, the curtilage has "long been given protection as a place where the occupants have a reasonable and legitimate expectation of privacy that society is prepared to accept." *Dow Chem. Co. v. United States,* 476 U.S. 227, 235 (1986). * * *

Falling within the curtilage of a home, however, does not automatically warrant protection from all observation under the Fourth Amendment. The U.S. Supreme Court has consistently maintained that the Fourth Amendment offers no protection—even within the home or curtilage—if the observed area is knowingly exposed to public view. In order to claim protection under the Fourth Amendment, therefore, an individual must take affirmative steps to exhibit an expectation of privacy.

In this case, Davis did take affirmative steps to exhibit an expectation of privacy from ground level surveillance. He fully enclosed his property with ground level "fencing," using a combination of vegetation and artificial devices. But, exhibiting a reasonable expectation of privacy from ground level surveillance may not always be enough to protect from public or official observation from the air under the Fourth Amendment.

In two cases remarkably similar to the case at bar, the U.S. Supreme Court addressed the constitutionality of warrantless aerial observation of the curtilage of a home that, like Davis', was blocked from ground-level observation but left open to observation from the air. In the first case, *California v. Ciraolo,* the police attempted to observe the backyard of a private residence where marijuana was allegedly being grown. High double fences completely enclosed the yard, prohibiting all ground level observation, so officers secured a private plane and flew over the house. From the air, the officers identified marijuana plants and photographed the plants with a standard 35 mm camera.

The U.S. Supreme Court granted certiorari to determine whether officers violated the Fourth Amendment when they observed the fenced-in backyard within the curtilage of a home from a fixed-wing aircraft at an altitude of *1,000* feet. The Court determined there was no reasonable expectation of privacy when the observations "took place within public navigable airspace, in a physically nonintrusive manner." *Ciraolo,* 476 U.S. at 213.

In support of its holding, the Court stated "[t]he test of legitimacy is not whether the individual chooses to conceal assertedly 'private activity,' but instead whether the government's intrusion infringes upon the personal and societal values protected by the Fourth Amendment." *Id.* at 212.

Three years later in *Florida v. Riley,* the U.S. Supreme Court again addressed aerial observation under the Fourth Amendment. In that case, the officer utilized a helicopter to observe a targeted area. The Court granted certiorari to determine whether warrantless surveillance of a partially covered greenhouse in a residential backyard from a helicopter 400 feet above the greenhouse constituted a search under the Fourth Amendment.

The opinion in Riley was badly fractured, but a majority of the Court agreed that the observation was not a search under the Fourth Amendment. Justice White wrote an opinion for a plurality of four justices. Following the reasoning advanced in *Ciraolo,* the plurality reiterated that:

> [T]he home and its curtilage are not necessarily protected from inspection that involves no physical invasion. What a person knowingly exposes to the public, even in his own home or office, is not a subject of Fourth Amendment protection. As a general proposition, the police may see what may be seen from a public vantage point where they have a right to be. Thus the police, like the public, would have been free to inspect the backyard garden from the street if their view had been unobstructed. They were likewise free to inspect the yard from the vantage point of an aircraft flying in the navigable airspace. *Riley,* 488 U.S. at 449–50.

The plurality determined that the helicopter, like the airplane in *Ciraolo,* was hovering within the prescribed navigable airspace. In making that determination, the plurality relied on Federal Aviation Administration regulations that permit helicopters to operate at less than the minimum altitude for fixed-wing aircraft, as long as the "operation is conducted without hazard to persons or property on the surface." *Id.* at 451 n. 3.

Significantly for our case, the plurality emphasized that the helicopter was not violating the law, and there was no indication in the record that "the helicopter interfered with respondent's normal use of the greenhouse or of other parts of the curtilage," or caused undue noise, wind, dust, or threat of injury. *Id.* at 451–52. The plurality thus found that the police did no more than any member of the public could do flying in navigable airspace, and the Court held that the surveillance did not violate the Fourth Amendment. *Id.* at 451. Justice White cautioned, however, that not every inspection of the curtilage of a house from an aircraft will "pass muster under the Fourth Amendment simply because the plane is within the navigable airspace specified by law." *Id.*

Although we avoid the temptation to draw too much settled legal principle from either of these two opinions, we believe certain inferences are appropriate. First, it appears after *Ciraolo* and *Riley* that the Fourth Amendment affords citizens no reasonable expectation of privacy from aerial surveillance conducted in a disciplined manner—mere observation from navigable airspace of an area left open to public view with minimal impact on the ground. It also seems, however, that warrantless surveillance can go beyond benign observation in a number of different ways, one of those being when surveillance creates a "hazard"—a physical disturbance on the ground or unreasonable interference with a resident's use of his property. In that case, surveillance more closely resembles a physical invasion of privacy which has always been a violation of the Fourth Amendment. * * * For reasons that follow, this distinction, referenced in both *Ciraolo* and *Riley,* informs our constitutional analysis of what occurred on Davis' property.

We do not consider this question in a vacuum. Many state courts base their determination of whether a particular aerial surveillance violates the Fourth Amendment on the degree of physical intrusion on the ground below. In assessing intrusion, courts look at the legality of the flight, the altitude of the aircraft, the frequency and duration of the flight, and the nature of the area observed—factors similar to *Ciraolo* and *Riley* and factors employed by the district court in this very case.

Our review of these and other cases involving aerial observation of marijuana plants, both pre- and post-*Ciraolo* and *Riley,* leads us to certain conclusions. First, unobtrusive aerial observations of space open to the public are generally permitted under the Fourth Amendment. Even a minor degree of annoyance or irritation on the ground will not change that result. If that were all that occurred in the surveillance of the Davis property, this would likely not constitute an unreasonable search under the Fourth Amendment.

Our second conclusion, however, is that when low-flying aerial activity leads to more than just observation and actually causes an unreasonable intrusion on the ground—most commonly from an unreasonable amount of wind, dust, broken objects, noise, and sheer panic—then at some point courts are compelled to step in and require a warrant before law enforcement engages in such activity. The Fourth Amendment and its prohibition against unreasonable searches and seizures demands no less. Obviously, the line drawn between activity permitted with or without a warrant is fact-dependent; any further definition is elusive. For that reason, we must return to the evidentiary hearing conducted in this case and the resulting observations of the district court.

Although the district court concluded as a matter of law that Operation Yerba Buena did not amount to an unconstitutional search, many of its findings and much of the evidence suggest that the police went beyond mere observation as that term has been defined by Fourth Amendment jurisprudence. The district court's findings make multiple references to the degree of noise and disturbance on the ground and suggest that the helicopter swooped down low enough to cause panic among the residents.

Based on the evidence, therefore, we conclude that the official conduct in this case went beyond a brief flyover to gather information. The prolonged hovering close enough to the ground to cause interference with Davis' property transformed this surveillance from a lawful observation of an area left open to public view to an unconstitutional intrusion into Davis' expectation of privacy. We think what happened in this case to Davis and other persons on the ground is precisely what *did not* occur in either *Ciraolo* or *Riley* and what *did* occur in both *Oglialoro* and *Pollock*. Accordingly, we hold that the aerial surveillance over Davis' property was an unwarranted search in violation of the Fourth Amendment.

The New Mexico Constitution

Under our interstitial approach to the New Mexico Constitution as explained previously, because we find the asserted right to be protected under the Federal Constitution we do not reach the same claim under our New Mexico Constitution.

Davis' consent was not sufficiently attenuated from the unconstitutional search

We affirm the Court of Appeals' determination that Sergeant Merrell entered "[Davis'] property solely as a result of information obtained in the helicopter search," and there were no "intervening circumstances between the aerial search and [Davis'] consent." *Davis III,* 2014-NMCA-042, 31, 321 P.3d 955. As a result we hold that there was insufficient attenuation to purge Davis' consent of the taint resulting from the warrantless aerial search.

CONCLUSION

For the foregoing reasons we hold that this aerial surveillance amounted to an unconstitutional search under the Fourth Amendment and reverse the Court of Appeals' determination to the contrary. We affirm the ultimate determination of the Court of Appeals to suppress all evidence seized as a result and reverse the conviction in this case.

* * *

CHÁVEZ, J., concurring.

I concur in the result of the majority opinion which suppresses the evidence in this case, but I respectfully disagree with the analysis employed by the majority. In this case, law enforcement officers conducted an indiscriminate aerial surveillance over large areas in Taos County based on outdated, vague reports from anonymous sources whose reliability is unknown, that some undisclosed people were growing marijuana in unspecified locations. Utilizing helicopters for aerial surveillance, the law enforcement officers swooped down on house after house, including Defendant's house, as if the occupants did not have an expectation of privacy in and around their homes. The district court believed "that the police swooped in as if they were in a state of war, searching for weapons or terrorist activity," which "can be terrifying and intimidating to most normal persons." The majority concludes that people would not have a reasonable expectation of privacy in their homes and curtilage from aerial surveillance as long as during the surveillance law enforcement is disciplined enough not to be too noisy, kick up too much dust, cause too much wind, or otherwise unduly interfere with the owners' or occupants' use of the property. In this case the majority concludes that the law enforcement officers were not disciplined enough, and they therefore violated Defendant's Fourth Amendment rights, requiring suppression of the evidence.

Unlike the majority, I doubt that Defendant has a protected privacy interest under the Fourth Amendment of the United States Constitution, and I therefore would analyze this case under Article II, Section 10 of the New Mexico Constitution. I would hold that an individual's subjective expectation of privacy in his or her home from ground-level surveillance is coextensive with his or her subjective expectation of privacy from aerial surveillance. If an individual has taken steps to ward off inspection from the ground, the individual has also manifested an expectation to ward off inspection from the air.

NOTES AND QUESTIONS

1.   **Independent and adequate state law grounds.** Justice Chavez's concurring opinion raises an important point, often forgotten by lawyers. In some instances, a state's constitution may provide greater protection than does

the United States Constitution. Absent a conflict with federal law, the state law controls. Indeed, if a state court grounds a decision in its constitution, the U.S. Supreme Court lacks judicial power to review the state court's decision. When the state court opinion is ambiguous, the Court may take review. *See, e.g., Michigan v. Long,* 463 U.S. 1032 (1983).

2.   Counting the votes. The majority opinion in the lead case does a good job of developing the Supreme Court's case law, with one minor addition. It notes that the *Riley* Court was deeply divided and that Justice O'Connor joined the plurality to uphold the search. The *Davis* court did not explain the overlap between Justice O'Connor's opinion and the dissenters' position. Justice O'Connor agreed with the dissenters on the underlying standard for determining whether a defendant had a reasonable expectation of privacy. She and the dissenters focused on the frequency of overflight, not whether the flight was in lawful airspace. She differed with the dissent on the placement of the burden of proof. She voted with the plurality because she believed that the defendant carried the burden of proof to demonstrate the infrequency of overflight. The dissenters argued that, absent a warrant, the state must prove that police conduct was lawful.

3.   An open question. The *Davis* majority did not need to reach the dissenters' position because the helicopter flight violated the defendant's expectation of privacy even under the plurality's test.

4.   Knowing exposure to the public. Interestingly, in *Ciraolo*, the Court relied on the fact that a person in a commercial flight going over the defendant's property could view the defendant's backyard. Quite typical of many Supreme Court cases, the Court then reasoned that, when a defendant knowingly exposed something to the public, an offender did not have a reasonable expectation of privacy when law enforcement had access to the same view or information. Many of the Court's post-*Katz* cases relied on that argument to erode Fourth Amendment protection. For a fuller discussion, *see* Michael Vitiello, *Katz v. United States: Back to the Future?*, 52 U. Rich. L. Rev. 425 (2018). Recently, the Supreme Court has questioned whether that analysis still prevails. *See Carpenter v. United States,* 585 U.S. ___ (2018).

IV. SCOPE OF THE SEARCH

Any number of issues may arise when the police have probable cause to search. We have chosen the following case because it allows a discussion of a number of important issues relating to the scope of a search, the warrant requirement and the War on Drugs.

During the Warren Court years, especially between 1961 and 1969, the Court expanded protections under the Bill of Rights generally, and the Fourth Amendment specifically. The Court often stated a general principle, integrating the two clauses of the Fourth Amendment (protection against unreasonable searches and seizures, on the one hand, and the probable cause and warrant requirement, on the other). Under the Court's approach, the major premise was that the police needed probable cause and a warrant. That was subject to narrow exceptions. One scholar described that approach as the "principle of particular justification." James B. White, *The Fourth Amendment as a Way of Talking About People: A Study of Robinson and Matlock,* 1974 Sup. Ct. Rev. 165, 190, reprinted in James Boyd White, Justice as Translation: An Essay in Cultural and Legal Criticism, 176 (1990).

Although periodically, the Court has invoked that analysis since the end of the Warren Court, the Burger Court began eroding that principle almost immediately. Running on a Law and Order campaign, President Nixon was able to make four appointments to the Court within his first two years. Those justices, especially initially, tended to vote in favor of the government in criminal procedure cases. *United States v. Robinson*, 414 U.S. 218 (1973) demonstrates how the new Court's approach veered from the Warren Court approach. Instead of starting with the premise that exceptions to the probable cause-warrant requirement were few and should be narrowly construed, the Court started with a different question: was the police conduct reasonable? Further, in assessing reasonableness, the Court recognized the need for bright lines. Thus, a search might not be narrowly tailored to the underlying circumstance, but still be reasonable because it came within a bright line rule.

In reading the *Acevedo* opinions, see if you can see how these two different approaches are in evidence. That should help you see how following one approach might lead to a different result than following the other approach.

CALIFORNIA V. ACEVEDO
United States Supreme Court
500 U.S. 565 (1991)

BLACKMUN, J.

This case requires us once again to consider the so-called "automobile exception" to the warrant requirement of the Fourth Amendment and its application to the search of a closed container in the trunk of a car.

I

[Officer Coleman, located in Santa Ana, California was contacted by a federal drug enforcement agent in Hawaii. The agent explained that he seized a package of marijuana addressed to a J.R. Daza in Santa Ana. The agent sent the package to Coleman, who then brought the package to a Federal Express to await the person who claimed it. Two days later, a man named Jamie Daza picked up the package and returned to his apartment. Coleman, watching Daza from outside his apartment, left to obtain a search warrant after Daza took the contents of the package into his residence.

Twenty minutes after Coleman's departure, around 12:05 PM, additional officers outside of Daza's apartment observed Richard St. George leave the residence with a bag that was half-full. The officers pulled him over, searched the bag, and discovered 1.5 pounds of marijuana. Twenty-five minutes later, around 12:30, officers observed Respondent enter and subsequently leave the apartment with a paper bag that was roughly the size of the packages of marijuana observed in Daza's parcel. Respondent then placed the bag in his trunk and began to drive away when the officers, fearing loss of evidence, stopped him. They opened the bag in the trunk and discovered marijuana.]

Respondent was charged in state court with possession of marijuana for sale, in violation of Cal. Health & Safety Code Ann. § 11359. He moved to suppress the marijuana found in the car. The motion was denied. He then pleaded guilty but appealed the denial of the suppression motion.

The California Court of Appeal, Fourth District, concluded that the marijuana found in the paper bag in the car's trunk should have been suppressed. The court concluded that the officers had probable cause to believe that the paper bag contained drugs but lacked probable cause to suspect that Acevedo's car, itself, otherwise contained contraband. Because the officers' probable cause was directed specifically at the bag, the court held that the case was controlled by *United States v. Chadwick*, 433 U.S. 1 (1977), rather than by *United States v. Ross*, 456 U.S. 798 (1982). Although the court agreed that the officers could seize the paper bag, it held that, under *Chadwick,* they could not open the bag without first obtaining a warrant for that purpose. The court then recognized "the anomalous nature" of the dichotomy between the rule in *Chadwick* and the rule in *Ross.* 216 Cal.App.3d at 592. That dichotomy dictates that if there is probable cause to search a car, then the entire car-including any closed container found therein-may be searched without a warrant, but if there is probable cause only as to a container in the car, the container may be held but not searched until a warrant is obtained.

The Supreme Court of California denied the State's petition for review. On May 14, 1990, Justice O'CONNOR stayed enforcement of the Court of Appeal's judgment pending the disposition of the State's petition for certiorari, and, if that petition were granted, the issuance of the mandate of this Court.

We granted certiorari to reexamine the law applicable to a closed container in an automobile, a subject that has troubled courts and law enforcement officers since it was first considered in *Chadwick.*

II

The Fourth Amendment protects the "right of the people to be secure in their persons, houses, papers, and effects, against unreasonable searches and seizures." Contemporaneously with the adoption of the

Fourth Amendment, the First Congress, and, later, the Second and Fourth Congresses, distinguished between the need for a warrant to search for contraband concealed in "a dwelling house or similar place" and the need for a warrant to search for contraband concealed in a movable vessel. In *Carroll,* this Court established an exception to the warrant requirement for moving vehicles, for it recognized "a necessary difference between a search of a store, dwelling house or other structure in respect of which a proper official warrant readily may be obtained, and a search of a ship, motor boat, wagon or automobile, for contraband goods, where it is not practicable to secure a warrant because the vehicle can be quickly moved out of the locality or jurisdiction in which the warrant must be sought." 267 U.S., at 153.

It therefore held that a warrantless search of an automobile, based upon probable cause to believe that the vehicle contained evidence of crime in the light of an exigency arising out of the likely disappearance of the vehicle, did not contravene the Warrant Clause of the Fourth Amendment.

The Court refined the exigency requirement in *Chambers v. Maroney,* 399 U.S. 42 (1970), when it held that the existence of exigent circumstances was to be determined at the time the automobile is seized. The car search at issue in *Chambers* took place at the police station, where the vehicle was immobilized, some time after the driver had been arrested. Given probable cause and exigent circumstances at the time the vehicle was first stopped, the Court held that the later warrantless search at the station passed constitutional muster. The validity of the later search derived from the ruling in *Carroll* that an immediate search without a warrant at the moment of seizure would have been permissible. The Court reasoned in *Chambers* that the police could search later whenever they could have searched earlier, had they so chosen. Following *Chambers,* if the police have probable cause to justify a warrantless seizure of an automobile on a public roadway, they may conduct either an immediate or a delayed search of the vehicle.

In *United States v. Ross,* 456 U.S. 798, decided in 1982, we held that a warrantless search of an automobile under the *Carroll* doctrine could include a search of a container or package found inside the car when such a search was supported by probable cause. The warrantless search of Ross' car occurred after an informant told the police that he had seen Ross complete a drug transaction using drugs stored in the trunk of his car. The police stopped the car, searched it, and discovered in the trunk a brown paper bag containing drugs. We decided that the search of Ross' car was not unreasonable under the Fourth Amendment: "The scope of a warrantless search based on probable cause is no narrower—and no broader—than the scope of a search authorized by a warrant supported by probable cause." *Id.,* at 823. Thus, "[i]f probable cause justifies the search of a lawfully stopped vehicle, it justifies the search of every part of the vehicle and its contents that may conceal the object of the search." *Id.,* at 825. In *Ross,* therefore, we clarified the scope of the *Carroll* doctrine as properly including a "probing search" of compartments and containers within the automobile so long as the search is supported by probable cause. *Id.,* at 800.

In addition to this clarification, *Ross* distinguished the *Carroll* doctrine from the separate rule that governed the search of closed containers. The Court had announced this separate rule, unique to luggage and other closed packages, bags, and containers, in *Chadwick.* In *Chadwick,* federal narcotics agents had probable cause to believe that a 200-pound double-locked footlocker contained marijuana. The agents tracked the locker as the defendants removed it from a train and carried it through the station to a waiting car. As soon as the defendants lifted the locker into the trunk of the car, the agents arrested them, seized the locker, and searched it. In this Court, the United States did not contend that the locker's brief contact with the automobile's trunk sufficed to make the *Carroll* doctrine applicable. Rather, the United States urged that the search of movable luggage could be considered analogous to the search of an automobile.

The Court rejected this argument because, it reasoned, a person expects more privacy in his luggage and personal effects than he does in his automobile. Moreover, it concluded that as "may not be the case when automobiles are seized," secure storage facilities are usually available when the police seize luggage. *Id.,* at 13, n. 7.

In *Arkansas v. Sanders,* 442 U.S. 753 (1979), the Court extended *Chadwick*'s rule to apply to a suitcase actually being transported in the trunk of a car. In *Sanders,* the police had probable cause to believe a suitcase contained marijuana. They watched as the defendant placed the suitcase in the trunk of a taxi and was driven away. The police pursued the taxi for several blocks, stopped it, found the suitcase in the trunk, and searched it. Although the Court had applied the *Carroll* doctrine to searches of integral parts of the automobile itself, (indeed, in *Carroll,* contraband whiskey was in the upholstery of the seats), it did not extend the doctrine to the warrantless search of personal luggage "merely because it was located in an automobile lawfully stopped by the police." 442 U.S., at 765. Again, the *Sanders* majority stressed the heightened privacy expectation in personal luggage and concluded that the presence of luggage in an automobile did not diminish the owner's expectation of privacy in his personal items.

In *Ross,* the Court endeavored to distinguish between *Carroll,* which governed the *Ross* automobile search, and *Chadwick,* which governed the *Sanders* automobile search. It held that the *Carroll* doctrine covered searches of automobiles when the police had probable cause to search an entire vehicle, but that the *Chadwick* doctrine governed searches of luggage when the officers had probable cause to search only a container within the vehicle. Thus, in a *Ross* situation, the police could conduct a reasonable search under the Fourth Amendment without obtaining a warrant, whereas in a *Sanders* situation, the police had to obtain a warrant before they searched.

Justice STEVENS is correct, of course, that *Ross* involved the scope of an automobile search. *Ross* held that closed containers encountered by the police during a warrantless search of a car pursuant to the automobile exception could also be searched. Thus, this Court in *Ross* took the critical step of saying that closed containers in cars could be searched without a warrant because of their presence within the automobile. Despite the protection that *Sanders* purported to extend to closed containers, the privacy interest in those closed containers yielded to the broad scope of an automobile search.

III

The facts in this case closely resemble the facts in *Ross.* In *Ross,* the police had probable cause to believe that drugs were stored in the trunk of a particular car. Here, the California Court of Appeal concluded that the police had probable cause to believe that respondent was carrying marijuana in a bag in his car's trunk. Furthermore, for what it is worth, in *Ross,* as here, the drugs in the trunk were contained in a brown paper bag.

This Court in *Ross* rejected *Chadwick*'s distinction between containers and cars. It concluded that the expectation of privacy in one's vehicle is equal to one's expectation of privacy in the container, and noted that "the privacy interests in a car's trunk or glove compartment may be no less than those in a movable container." 456 U.S., at 823. It also recognized that it was arguable that the same exigent circumstances that permit a warrantless search of an automobile would justify the warrantless search of a movable container. In deference to the rule of *Chadwick* and *Sanders,* however, the Court put that question to one side. It concluded that the time and expense of the warrant process would be misdirected if the police could search every cubic inch of an automobile until they discovered a paper sack, at which point the Fourth Amendment required them to take the sack to a magistrate for permission to look inside. We now must decide the question deferred in *Ross*: whether the Fourth Amendment requires the police to obtain a warrant to open the sack in a movable vehicle simply because they lack probable cause to search the entire car. We conclude that it does not.

IV

Dissenters in *Ross* asked why the suitcase in *Sanders* was "more private, less difficult for police to seize and store, or in any other relevant respect more properly subject to the warrant requirement, than a container that police discover in a probable-cause search of an entire automobile?" *Id.,* 456 U.S., at 839–840. We now agree that a container found after a general search of the automobile and a container found in a car after a limited search for the container are equally easy for the police to store and for the suspect to hide or destroy. In fact, we see no principled distinction in terms of either the privacy expectation or the exigent circumstances between the paper bag found by the police in *Ross* and the paper bag found by the police here. Furthermore, by attempting to distinguish between a container for which the police are specifically searching and a container which they come across in a car, we have provided only minimal protection for privacy and have impeded effective law enforcement.

The line between probable cause to search a vehicle and probable cause to search a package in that vehicle is not always clear, and separate rules that govern the two objects to be searched may enable the police to broaden their power to make warrantless searches and disserve privacy interests. We noted this in *Ross* in the context of a search of an entire vehicle. Recognizing that under *Carroll,* the "entire vehicle itself . . . could be searched without a warrant," we concluded that "prohibiting police from opening immediately a container in which the object of the search is most likely to be found and instead forcing them first to comb the entire vehicle would actually exacerbate the intrusion on privacy interests." 456 U.S., at 821, n. 28. At the moment when officers stop an automobile, it may be less than clear whether they suspect with a high degree of certainty that the vehicle contains drugs in a bag or simply contains drugs. If the police know that they may open a bag only if they are actually searching the entire car, they may search more extensively than they otherwise would in order to establish the general probable cause required by *Ross.*

Such a situation is not farfetched. In *United States v. Johns*, 469 U.S. 478 (1985), Customs agents saw two trucks drive to a private airstrip and approach two small planes. The agents drew near the trucks, smelled marijuana, and then saw in the backs of the trucks packages wrapped in a manner that marijuana smugglers customarily employed. The agents took the trucks to headquarters and searched the packages without a warrant. Relying on *Chadwick,* the defendants argued that the search was unlawful. The defendants contended that *Ross* was inapplicable because the agents lacked probable cause to search anything but the packages themselves and supported this contention by noting that a search of the entire vehicle never occurred. We rejected that argument and found *Chadwick* and *Sanders* inapposite because the agents had probable cause to search the entire body of each truck, although they had chosen not to do so. We cannot see the benefit of a rule that requires law enforcement officers to conduct a more intrusive search in order to justify a less intrusive one.

To the extent that the *Chadwick-Sanders* rule protects privacy, its protection is minimal. Law enforcement officers may seize a container and hold it until they obtain a search warrant. "Since the police, by hypothesis, have probable cause to seize the property, we can assume that a warrant will be routinely forthcoming in the overwhelming majority of cases." *Sanders*, 442 U.S., at 770 (dissenting opinion). And the police often will be able to search containers without a warrant, despite the *Chadwick-Sanders* rule, as a search incident to a lawful arrest. In *New York v. Belton*, 453 U.S. 453 (1981), the Court said:

> "[W]e hold that when a policeman has made a lawful custodial arrest of the occupant of an automobile, he may, as a contemporaneous incident of that arrest, search the passenger compartment of that automobile.

> "It follows from this conclusion that the police may also examine the contents of any containers found within the passenger compartment."

Id., at 460.Under *Belton,* the same probable cause to believe that a container holds drugs will allow the police to arrest the person transporting the container and search it.

Finally, the search of a paper bag intrudes far less on individual privacy than does the incursion sanctioned long ago in *Carroll*. In that case, prohibition agents slashed the upholstery of the automobile. This Court nonetheless found their search to be reasonable under the Fourth Amendment. If destroying the interior of an automobile is not unreasonable, we cannot conclude that looking inside a closed container is. In light of the minimal protection to privacy afforded by the *Chadwick-Sanders* rule, and our serious doubt whether that rule substantially serves privacy interests, we now hold that the Fourth Amendment does not compel separate treatment for an automobile search that extends only to a container within the vehicle.

V

The *Chadwick-Sanders* rule not only has failed to protect privacy but also has confused courts and police officers and impeded effective law enforcement. The conflict between the *Carroll* doctrine cases and the *Chadwick-Sanders* line has been criticized in academic commentary. One leading authority on the Fourth Amendment, after comparing *Chadwick* and *Sanders* with *Carroll* and its progeny, observed: "These two lines of authority cannot be completely reconciled, and thus how one comes out in the container-in-the-car situation depends upon which line of authority is used as a point of departure." 3 W. LaFave, *Search and Seizure* 53 (2d ed. 1987).

The discrepancy between the two rules has led to confusion for law enforcement officers. For example, when an officer, who has developed probable cause to believe that a vehicle contains drugs, begins to search the vehicle and immediately discovers a closed container, which rule applies? The defendant will argue that the fact that the officer first chose to search the container indicates that his probable cause extended only to the container and that *Chadwick* and *Sanders* therefore require a warrant. On the other hand, the fact that the officer first chose to search in the most obvious location should not restrict the propriety of the search. The *Chadwick* rule, as applied in *Sanders,* has devolved into an anomaly such that the more likely the police are to discover drugs in a container, the less authority they have to search it. We have noted the virtue of providing " ' "clear and unequivocal" guidelines to the law enforcement profession.' " *Minnick v. Mississippi*, 498 U.S. 146, 151 (1990). The *Chadwick-Sanders* rule is the antithesis of a " 'clear and unequivocal' guideline."

Justice STEVENS argues that the decisions of this Court evince a lack of confusion about the automobile exception. The first case cited by the dissent, *United States v. Place*, 462 U.S. 696 (1983), however, did not involve an automobile at all. We considered in *Place* the temporary detention of luggage in an airport. Not only was no automobile involved, but the defendant, Place, was waiting at the airport to board his plane rather than preparing to leave the airport in a car. Any similarity to *Sanders,* in which the defendant was leaving the airport in a car, is remote at best. *Place* had nothing to do with the automobile exception and is inapposite.

Nor does Justice STEVENS' citation of *Oklahoma v. Castleberry*, 471 U.S. 146 (1985), support his contention. *Castleberry* presented the same question about the application of the automobile exception to the search of a closed container that we face here. In *Castleberry,* we affirmed by an equally divided court. That result illustrates this Court's continued struggle with the scope of the automobile exception rather than the absence of confusion in applying it.

Justice STEVENS also argues that law enforcement has not been impeded because the Court has decided 29 Fourth Amendment cases since *Ross* in favor of the government. In each of these cases, the government appeared as the petitioner. The dissent fails to explain how the loss of 29 cases below, not to mention the many others which this Court did not hear, did not interfere with law enforcement. The fact that the state courts and the Federal Courts of Appeals have been reversed in their Fourth Amendment holdings 29 times since 1982 further demonstrates the extent to which our Fourth Amendment jurisprudence has confused the courts.

Most important, with the exception of *United States v. Johns*, 469 U.S. 478 (1985), and *Texas v. Brown*, 460 U.S. 730 (1983), the Fourth Amendment cases cited by the dissent do not concern automobiles or the automobile exception. From *Carroll* through *Ross,* this Court has explained that automobile searches differ from other searches. The dissent fails to acknowledge this basic principle and so misconstrues and misapplies our Fourth Amendment case law.

The *Chadwick* dissenters predicted that the container rule would have "the perverse result of allowing fortuitous circumstances to control the outcome" of various searches. 433 U.S., at 22. The rule also was so confusing that within two years after *Chadwick,* this Court found it necessary to expound on the meaning of that decision and explain its application to luggage in general. Again, dissenters bemoaned the "inherent opaqueness" of the difference between the *Carroll* and *Chadwick* principles and noted "the confusion to be created for all concerned." *Id.,* at 771. Three years after *Sanders,* we returned in *Ross* to "this troubled area," 456 U.S., at 817, in order to assert that *Sanders* had not cut back on *Carroll.*

Although we have recognized firmly that the doctrine of *stare decisis* serves profoundly important purposes in our legal system, this Court has overruled a prior case on the comparatively rare occasion when it has bred confusion or been a derelict or led to anomalous results. *Sanders* was explicitly undermined in *Ross*, 456 U.S., at 824, and the existence of the dual regimes for automobile searches that uncover containers has proved as confusing as the *Chadwick* and *Sanders* dissenters predicted. We conclude that it is better to adopt one clear-cut rule to govern automobile searches and eliminate the warrant requirement for closed containers set forth in *Sanders.*

VI

The interpretation of the *Carroll* doctrine set forth in *Ross* now applies to all searches of containers found in an automobile. In other words, the police may search without a warrant if their search is supported by probable cause. The Court in *Ross* put it this way:

> "The scope of a warrantless search of an automobile . . . is not defined by the nature of the container in which the contraband is secreted. Rather, it is defined by the object of the search and the places in which there is probable cause to believe that it may be found." 456 U.S., at 824.

It went on to note: "Probable cause to believe that a container placed in the trunk of a taxi contains contraband or evidence does not justify a search of the entire cab." We reaffirm that principle. In the case before us, the police had probable cause to believe that the paper bag in the automobile's trunk contained marijuana. That probable cause now allows a warrantless search of the paper bag. The facts in the record reveal that the police did not have probable cause to believe that contraband was hidden in any other part of the automobile and a search of the entire vehicle would have been without probable cause and unreasonable under the Fourth Amendment.

Our holding today neither extends the *Carroll* doctrine nor broadens the scope of the permissible automobile search delineated in *Carroll, Chambers,* and *Ross.* It remains a "cardinal principle that 'searches conducted outside the judicial process, without prior approval by judge or magistrate, are *per se* unreasonable under the Fourth Amendment—subject only to a few specifically established and well-delineated exceptions.' " *Mincey v. Arizona,* 437 U.S. 385, 390 (1978). We held in *Ross:* "The exception recognized in *Carroll* is unquestionably one that is 'specifically established and well delineated.' " 456 U.S., at 825.

Until today, this Court has drawn a curious line between the search of an automobile that coincidentally turns up a container and the search of a container that coincidentally turns up in an automobile. The protections of the Fourth Amendment must not turn on such coincidences. We therefore interpret *Carroll* as providing one rule to govern all automobile searches. The police may search an automobile and the containers within it where they have probable cause to believe contraband or evidence is contained.

The judgment of the California Court of Appeal is reversed, and the case is remanded to that court for further proceedings not inconsistent with this opinion.

It is so ordered.

SCALIA, J. concurring.

I agree with the dissent that it is anomalous for a briefcase to be protected by the "general requirement" of a prior warrant when it is being carried along the street, but for that same briefcase to become unprotected as soon as it is carried into an automobile. On the other hand, I agree with the Court that it would be anomalous for a locked compartment in an automobile to be unprotected by the "general requirement" of a prior warrant, but for an unlocked briefcase within the automobile to be protected. I join in the judgment of the Court because I think its holding is more faithful to the text and tradition of the Fourth Amendment, and if these anomalies in our jurisprudence are ever to be eliminated that is the direction in which we should travel.

* * *

Although the Fourth Amendment does not explicitly impose the requirement of a warrant, it is of course textually possible to consider that implicit within the requirement of reasonableness. For some years after the (still continuing) explosion in Fourth Amendment litigation that followed our announcement of the exclusionary rule in *Weeks v. United States,* 232 U.S. 383 (1914), our jurisprudence lurched back and forth between imposing a categorical warrant requirement and looking to reasonableness alone. (The opinions preferring a warrant involved searches of structures.) * * * By the late 1960's, the preference for a warrant had won out, at least rhetorically.

The victory was illusory. Even before today's decision, the "warrant requirement" had become so riddled with exceptions that it was basically unrecognizable. In 1985, one commentator cataloged nearly 20 such exceptions, including "searches incident to arrest . . . automobile searches . . . border searches . . . administrative searches of regulated businesses . . . exigent circumstances . . . search[es] incident to nonarrest when there is probable cause to arrest . . . boat boarding for document checks . . . welfare searches . . . inventory searches . . . airport searches . . . school search[es]. . . ." *Bradley, Two Models of the Fourth Amendment*, 83 Mich. L. Rev. 1468, 1473–1474. Since then, we have added at least two more. *California v. Carney*, 471 U.S. 386 (1985) (searches of mobile homes); *O'Connor v. Ortega*, 480 U.S. 709 (1987) (searches of offices of government employees). Our intricate body of law regarding "reasonable expectation of privacy" has been developed largely as a means of creating these exceptions, enabling a search to be denominated not a Fourth Amendment "search" and therefore not subject to the general warrant requirement.

Unlike the dissent, therefore, I do not regard today's holding as some momentous departure, but rather as merely the continuation of an inconsistent jurisprudence that has been with us for years. Cases like *Chadwick* and *Sanders* have taken the "preference for a warrant" seriously, while cases like *Ross* and *Carroll* have not. There can be no clarity in this area unless we make up our minds, and unless the principles we express comport with the actions we take.

In my view, the path out of this confusion should be sought by returning to the first principle that the "reasonableness" requirement of the Fourth Amendment affords the protection that the common law afforded. I have no difficulty with the proposition that that includes the requirement of a warrant, where the common law required a warrant; and it may even be that changes in the surrounding legal rules * * * may make a warrant indispensable to reasonableness where it once was not. But the supposed "general rule" that a warrant is always required does not appear to have any basis in the common law and confuses rather than facilitates any attempt to develop rules of reasonableness in light of changed legal circumstances, as the anomaly eliminated and the anomaly created by today's holding both demonstrate.

And there are more anomalies still. Under our precedents (as at common law), a person may be arrested outside the home on the basis of probable cause, without an arrest warrant. Upon arrest, the person, as well as the area within his grasp, may be searched for evidence related to the crime. Under these principles, if a known drug dealer is carrying a briefcase reasonably believed to contain marijuana (the unauthorized possession of which is a crime), the police may arrest him and search his person on the basis of probable cause alone. And, under our precedents, upon arrival at the station house, the police may inventory his possessions, including the briefcase, even if there is no reason to suspect that they contain contraband. According to our current law, however, the police may not, on the basis of the same probable cause, take the less intrusive step of stopping the individual on the street and demanding to see the contents of his briefcase. That makes no sense *a priori,* and in the absence of any common-law tradition supporting such a distinction, I see no reason to continue it.

* * *

I would reverse the judgment in the present case, not because a closed container carried inside a car becomes subject to the "automobile" exception to the general warrant requirement, but because the search of a closed container, outside a privately owned building, with probable cause to believe that the container contains contraband, and when it in fact does contain contraband, is not one of those searches whose Fourth Amendment reasonableness depends upon a warrant. For that reason I concur in the judgment of the Court.

STEVENS, J., dissenting.

At the end of its opinion, the Court pays lipservice to the proposition that should provide the basis for a correct analysis of the legal question presented by this case: It is " 'a cardinal principle that "searches conducted outside the judicial process, without prior approval by judge or magistrate, are *per se* unreasonable under the Fourth Amendment-subject only to a few specifically established and well-delineated exceptions.' " *Mincey v. Arizona,* 437 U.S. 385, 390 (1978).

Relying on arguments that conservative judges have repeatedly rejected in past cases, the Court today—despite its disclaimer to the contrary—enlarges the scope of the automobile exception to this "cardinal principle," which undergirded our Fourth Amendment jurisprudence prior to the retirement of the author of the landmark opinion in *Chadwick.* As a preface to my response to the Court's arguments, it is appropriate to restate the basis for the warrant requirement, the significance of the *Chadwick* case, and the reasons why the limitations on the automobile exception that were articulated in Ross represent a fair accommodation between the basic rule requiring prior judicial approval of searches and the automobile exception.

I

* * * The [warrant] requirement * * * reflects the sound policy judgment that, absent exceptional circumstances, the decision to invade the privacy of an individual's personal effects should be made by a neutral magistrate rather than an agent of the Executive. In his opinion for the Court in *Johnson v. United States, i.d.,* at 13–14, Justice Jackson explained:

> "The point of the Fourth Amendment, which often is not grasped by zealous officers, is not that it denies law enforcement the support of the usual inferences which reasonable men draw from

evidence. Its protection consists in requiring that those inferences be drawn by a neutral and detached magistrate instead of being judged by the officer engaged in the often competitive enterprise of ferreting out crime."

Our decisions have always acknowledged that the warrant requirement imposes a burden on law enforcement. And our cases have not questioned that trained professionals normally make reliable assessments of the existence of probable cause to conduct a search. We have repeatedly held, however, that these factors are outweighed by the individual interest in privacy that is protected by advance judicial approval. The Fourth Amendment dictates that the privacy interest is paramount, no matter how marginal the risk of error might be if the legality of warrantless searches were judged only after the fact.

* * *

In *Chadwick,* the Department of Justice had mounted a frontal attack on the warrant requirement. The Government's principal contention was that "the Fourth Amendment Warrant Clause protects only interests traditionally identified with the home." *Id.,* at 6. We categorically rejected that contention, relying on the history and text of the Amendment, the policy underlying the warrant requirement, and a line of cases spanning over a century of our jurisprudence. We also rejected the Government's alternative argument that the rationale of our automobile search cases demonstrated the reasonableness of permitting warrantless searches of luggage.

We concluded that neither of the justifications for the automobile exception could support a similar exception for luggage. We first held that the privacy interest in luggage is "substantially greater than in an automobile." *Id.,* at 13. Unlike automobiles and their contents, we reasoned, "[l]uggage contents are not open to public view, except as a condition to a border entry or common carrier travel; nor is luggage subject to regular inspections and official scrutiny on a continuing basis." *Ibid.* Indeed, luggage is specifically intended to safeguard the privacy of personal effects, unlike an automobile, "whose primary function is transportation." *Ibid.*

We then held that the mobility of luggage did not justify creating an additional exception to the Warrant Clause. Unlike an automobile, luggage can easily be seized and detained pending judicial approval of a search. Once the police have luggage "under their exclusive control, there [i]s not the slightest danger that the [luggage] or its contents could [be] removed before a valid search warrant could be obtained. . . . With the [luggage] safely immobilized, it [i]s unreasonable to undertake the additional and greater intrusion of a search without a warrant" *Ibid.*

Two Terms after *Chadwick,* we decided a case in which the relevant facts were identical to those before the Court today. In *Sanders,* the police had probable cause to search a green suitcase that had been placed in the trunk of a taxicab at the Little Rock Airport. Several blocks from the airport, they stopped the cab, arrested the passengers, seized the suitcase and, without obtaining a warrant, opened and searched it.

The Arkansas Supreme Court held that the search was unconstitutional. Relying on *Chadwick,* the state court had no difficulty in concluding that there was "nothing in this set of circumstances that would lend credence to an assertion of impracticability in obtaining a search warrant." *Sanders v. State,* 262 Ark. 595, 600 (1977). Over the dissent of Justice BLACKMUN and then-Justice REHNQUIST, both of whom had also dissented in *Chadwick,* this Court affirmed. In his opinion for the Court, Justice Powell noted that the seizure of the green suitcase was entirely proper, but that the State nevertheless had the burden of justifying the warrantless search, and that it had "failed to carry its burden of demonstrating the need for warrantless searches of luggage properly taken from automobiles." 442 U.S., at 763.

Chief Justice Burger wrote separately to identify the distinction between cases in which police have probable cause to believe contraband is located somewhere in a vehicle—the typical automobile exception case— and cases like *Chadwick* and *Sanders* in which they had probable cause to search a particular container before it was placed in the car. He wrote:

"Because the police officers had probable cause to believe that respondent's green suitcase contained marihuana before it was placed in the trunk of the taxicab, their duty to obtain a search warrant before opening it is clear under [*Chadwick*]. The essence of our holding in *Chadwick* is that there is a legitimate expectation of privacy in the contents of a trunk or suitcase accompanying or being carried by a person; that expectation of privacy is not diminished simply because the owner's arrest occurs in a public place. Whether arrested in a hotel lobby, an airport, a railroad terminal, or on a public street, as here, the owner has the right to expect that the contents of his luggage will not, without his consent, be exposed on demand of the police. . . .

"The breadth of the Court's opinion and its repeated references to the 'automobile' from which respondent's suitcase was seized at the time of his arrest, however, might lead the reader to believe— as the dissenters apparently do—that this case involves the 'automobile' exception to the warrant requirement. * * * It does not. Here, as in *Chadwick,* it was the *luggage* being transported by respondent at the time of the arrest, not the automobile in which it was being carried, that was the suspected locus of the contraband." 442 U.S., at 766–767 (opinion concurring in judgment).

Chief Justice Burger thus carefully explained that *Sanders,* which the Court overrules today, "simply d[id] not present the question of whether a warrant is required before opening luggage when the police have probable cause to believe contraband is located *somewhere* in the vehicle, but when they do *not* know whether, for example, it is inside a piece of luggage in the trunk, in the glove compartment, or concealed in some part of the car's structure." *Id.,* at 767. We confronted that question in *Ross.*

We held in *Ross* that "the scope of the warrantless search authorized by [the automobile] exception is no broader and no narrower than a magistrate could legitimately authorize by warrant." See *Id.,* at 825. The inherent mobility of the vehicle justified the immediate search without a warrant, but did not affect the scope of the search. Thus, the search could encompass containers, which might or might not conceal the object of the search, as well as the remainder of the vehicle.

Our conclusion was supported not only by prior cases defining the proper scope of searches authorized by warrant, as well as cases involving the automobile exception, but also by practical considerations that apply to searches in which the police have only generalized probable cause to believe that contraband is somewhere in a vehicle. We explained that, in such instances, "prohibiting police from opening immediately a container in which the object of the search is most likely to be found and instead forcing them first to comb the entire vehicle would actually exacerbate the intrusion on privacy interests." *Id.,* at 821, n. 28. Indeed, because "the police could never be certain that the contraband was not secreted in a yet undiscovered portion of the vehicle," the most likely result would be that "the vehicle would need to be secured while a warrant was obtained." *Ibid.*

These concerns that justified our holding in *Ross* are not implicated in cases like *Chadwick* and *Sanders* in which the police have probable cause to search a *particular* container rather than the *entire* vehicle. Because the police can seize the container which is the object of their search, they have no need either to search or to seize the entire vehicle. Indeed, as even the Court today recognizes, they have no authority to do so.

In reaching our conclusion in *Ross,* we therefore did not retreat at all from the holding in either *Chadwick* or *Sanders.* Instead, we expressly endorsed the reasoning in Chief Justice Burger's separate opinion in *Sanders.* We explained repeatedly that *Ross* involved the *scope* of the warrantless search authorized by the automobile exception, and, unlike *Chadwick* and *Sanders,* did not involve the *applicability* of the exception to closed containers.

Thus, we recognized in *Ross* that *Chadwick* and *Sanders* had not created a special rule for container searches, but rather had merely applied the cardinal principle that warrantless searches are per se unreasonable unless justified by an exception to the general rule. *Ross* dealt with the scope of the automobile exception; *Chadwick* and *Sanders* were cases in which the exception simply did not apply.

II

In its opinion today, the Court recognizes that the police did not have probable cause to search respondent's vehicle and that a search of anything but the paper bag that respondent had carried from Daza's apartment and placed in the trunk of his car would have been unconstitutional. Moreover, as I read the opinion, the Court assumes that the police could not have made a warrantless inspection of the bag before it was placed in the car. Finally, the Court also does not question the fact that, under our prior cases, it would have been lawful for the police to seize the container and detain it (and respondent) until they obtained a search warrant. Thus, all of the relevant facts that governed our decisions in *Chadwick* and *Sanders* are present here whereas the relevant fact that justified the vehicle search in *Ross* is not present.

The Court does not attempt to identify any exigent circumstances that would justify its refusal to apply the general rule against warrantless searches. Instead, it advances these three arguments: First, the rules identified in the foregoing cases are confusing and anomalous. Second, the rules do not protect any significant interest in privacy. And, third, the rules impede effective law enforcement. None of these arguments withstands scrutiny.

The "Confusion"

In the nine years since *Ross* was decided, the Court has considered three cases in which the police had probable cause to search a particular container and one in which they had probable cause to search two vehicles. The decisions in all four of those cases were perfectly straightforward and provide no evidence of confusion in the state or lower federal courts.

In *United States v. Place*, 462 U.S. 696 (1983), we held that, although reasonable suspicion justifies the temporary detention of an airline passenger's luggage, the seizure in that particular case was unreasonable because of the prolonged delay in ascertaining the existence of probable cause. In the course of our opinion, we noted that the then-recent decision in *Ross* had not modified the holding in *Sanders*. We also relied on *Chadwick* for our conclusion that the temporary seizure of luggage is substantially less intrusive than a search of its contents.

In *Oklahoma v. Castleberry*, 471 U.S. 146 (1985), police officers had probable cause to believe the defendant carried narcotics in blue suitcases in the trunk of his car. After arresting him, they opened the trunk, seized the suitcases, and searched them without a warrant. The state court held that the search was invalid, explaining:

"If the officer has probable cause to believe there is contraband somewhere in the car, but he does not know exactly where, he may search the entire car as well as any containers found therein. If, on the other hand, the officer only has probable cause to believe there is contraband in a specific container in the car, he must detain the container and delay his search until a search warrant is obtained.

This Court affirmed by an equally divided Court.

In the case the Court decides today, the California Court of Appeal also had no difficulty applying the critical distinction. Relying on *Chadwick,* it explained that "the officers had probable cause to believe marijuana would be found only in a brown lunch bag and nowhere else in the car. We are compelled to hold they should have obtained a search warrant before opening it." 216 Cal.App.3d 586, 592 (1990).

In the case in which the police had probable cause to search two vehicles, *United States v. Johns,* 469 U.S. 478 (1985), we rejected the respondent's reliance on *Chadwick* with a straightforward explanation of why that case, unlike *Ross,* did not involve an exception to the warrant requirement. We first expressed our agreement with the Court of Appeals that the Customs officers who had conducted the search had probable cause to search the vehicles. We then explained:

"Under the circumstances of this case, respondents' reliance on *Chadwick* is misplaced. . . . *Chadwick* . . . did not involve the exception to the warrant requirement recognized in *Carroll* because the police had no probable cause to believe that the automobile, as contrasted to the footlocker, contained contraband. This point is underscored by our decision in *Ross,* which held that notwithstanding *Chadwick* police officers may conduct a warrantless search of containers discovered in the course of a lawful vehicle search. Given our conclusion that the Customs officers had probable cause to believe that the pickup trucks contained contraband, *Chadwick* is simply inapposite." 469 U.S., at 482–483.

The decided cases thus provide no support for the Court's concern about "confusion." The Court instead relies primarily on predictions that were made by Justice BLACKMUN in his dissenting opinions in *Chadwick* and *Sanders.* The Court, however, cites no evidence that these predictions have in fact materialized or that anyone else has been unable to understand the " 'inherent opaqueness,' " *ante,* at 1990, of this uncomplicated issue. The only support offered by the Court, other than the unsubstantiated allegations of prior dissents, is three law review comments and a sentence from Professor LaFave's treatise. None of the law review pieces criticize the holdings in *Chadwick* and *Sanders.* The sentence from Professor LaFave's treatise, at most, indicates that, as is often the case, there may be some factual situations at the margin of the relevant rules that are difficult to decide. Moreover, to the extent Professor LaFave criticizes our jurisprudence in this area, he is critical of *Ross* rather than *Chadwick* or *Sanders*. And he ultimately concludes that even *Ross* was correctly decided.

The Court summarizes the alleged "anomaly" created by the coexistence of *Ross, Chadwick,* and *Sanders* with the statement that "the more likely the police are to discover drugs in a container, the less authority they have to search it." *Ante,* at 1990. This juxtaposition is only anomalous, however, if one accepts the flawed premise that the degree to which the police are likely to discover contraband is correlated with their authority to search *without a warrant*. Yet, even proof beyond a reasonable doubt will not justify a warrantless search that is not supported by one of the exceptions to the warrant requirement. And, even when the police have a warrant or an exception applies, once the police possess probable cause, the extent to which they are more or less certain of the contents of a container has no bearing on their authority to search it.

To the extent there was any "anomaly" in our prior jurisprudence, the Court has "cured" it at the expense of creating a more serious paradox. For surely it is anomalous to prohibit a search of a briefcase while the owner is carrying it exposed on a public street yet to permit a search once the owner has placed the briefcase in the locked trunk of his car. One's privacy interest in one's luggage can certainly not be diminished by one's removing it from a public thoroughfare and placing it—out of sight—in a privately owned vehicle. Nor is the danger that evidence will escape increased if the luggage is in a car rather than on the street. In either location, if the police have probable cause, they are authorized to seize the luggage and to detain it until they obtain judicial approval for a search. Any line demarking an exception to the warrant requirement will appear blurred at the edges, but the Court has certainly erred if it believes that, by erasing one line and drawing another, it has drawn a clearer boundary.

The Privacy Argument

The Court's statement that *Chadwick* and *Sanders* provide only "minimal protection to privacy," *ante,* at 1989, is also unpersuasive. Every citizen clearly has an interest in the privacy of the contents of his or her luggage, briefcase, handbag or any other container that conceals private papers and effects from public scrutiny. That privacy interest has been recognized repeatedly in cases spanning more than a century.

Under the Court's holding today, the privacy interest that protects the contents of a suitcase or a briefcase from a warrantless search when it is in public view simply vanishes when its owner climbs into a taxicab. Unquestionably the rejection of the *Sanders* line of cases by today's decision will result in a significant loss of individual privacy.

To support its argument that today's holding works only a minimal intrusion on privacy, the Court suggests that "[i]f the police know that they may open a bag only if they are actually searching the entire car, they may search more extensively than they otherwise would in order to establish the general probable cause required by *Ross*." *Ante,* at 1988. As I have already noted, this fear is unexplained and inexplicable. Neither evidence uncovered in the course of a search nor the scope of the search conducted can be used to provide *post hoc* justification for a search unsupported by probable cause at its inception.

The Court also justifies its claim that its holding inflicts only minor damage by suggesting that, under *New York v. Belton*, 453 U.S. 454 (1981), the police could have arrested respondent and searched his bag if respondent had placed the bag in the passenger compartment of the automobile instead of in the trunk. In *Belton,* however, the justification for stopping the car and arresting the driver had nothing to do with the subsequent search, which was based on the potential danger to the arresting officer. The holding in *Belton* was supportable under a straightforward application of the automobile exception. I would not extend *Belton*'s holding to this case, in which the container—which was protected from a warrantless search before it was placed in the car—provided the only justification for the arrest. Even accepting *Belton*'s application to a case like this one, however, the Court's logic extends its holding to a container placed in the *trunk* of a vehicle, rather than in the passenger compartment. And the Court makes this extension without any justification whatsoever other than convenience to law enforcement.

The Burden on Law Enforcement

The Court's suggestion that *Chadwick* and *Sanders* have created a significant burden on effective law enforcement is unsupported, inaccurate, and, in any event, an insufficient reason for creating a new exception to the warrant requirement.

Despite repeated claims that *Chadwick* and *Sanders* have "impeded effective law enforcement," the Court cites no authority for its contentions. Moreover, all evidence that does exist points to the contrary conclusion. In the years since *Ross* was decided, the Court has heard argument in 30 Fourth Amendment cases involving narcotics. In all but one, the government was the petitioner. All save two involved a search or seizure without a warrant or with a defective warrant. And, in all except three, the Court upheld the constitutionality of the search or seizure.

In the meantime, the flow of narcotics cases through the courts has steadily and dramatically increased. No impartial observer could criticize this Court for hindering the progress of the war on drugs. On the contrary, decisions like the one the Court makes today will support the conclusion that this Court has become a loyal foot soldier in the Executive's fight against crime.

Even if the warrant requirement does inconvenience the police to some extent, that fact does not distinguish this constitutional requirement from any other procedural protection secured by the Bill of Rights. It is merely a part of the price that our society must pay in order to preserve its freedom. Thus, in a unanimous opinion that relied on both *Johnson* and *Chadwick,* Justice Stewart wrote:

> "Moreover, the mere fact that law enforcement may be made more efficient can never by itself justify disregard of the Fourth Amendment. *Cf. Coolidge v. New Hampshire*, supra, [403 U.S. 443, 481 (1981)]. The investigation of crime would always be simplified if warrants were unnecessary. But the Fourth Amendment reflects the view of those who wrote the Bill of Rights that the privacy of a person's home and property may not be totally sacrificed in the name of maximum simplicity in enforcement of the criminal law." *Mincey v. Arizona*, 437 U.S., at 393.

It is too early to know how much freedom America has lost today. The magnitude of the loss is, however, not nearly as significant as the Court's willingness to inflict it without even a colorable basis for its rejection of prior law.

I respectfully dissent.

NOTES AND QUESTIONS

1. **The evolving legal rule.** As discussed earlier in this chapter and in *Acevedo, United States v. Chadwick*, 433 U.S. 1 (1977) involved a dog sniff, resulting in the discovery that a footlocker contained marijuana. Police seized the footlocker after it was placed in a vehicle. The police seized the footlocker and moved it to a secure facility before officers opened it without procuring a warrant. Chief Justice Burger, no friend of the Warren Court's more-defendant-friendly Fourth Amendment case law, wrote the opinion for seven justices. In the courts below, the government argued that the warrantless search was justified based on alternative grounds: the footlocker was in an automobile and searches of automobiles come within an exception to the warrant requirement; or the search was justified as a search incident to a lawful arrest. In the Supreme Court, the government attempted a broader argument: the only place where the warrant requirement applied was when police sought to search a home. The Chief Justice described that view as an extreme one.

2. **Narrow and broad exceptions to the warrant requirement.** Justice Blackmun's majority opinion in *Acevedo* offers a detailed view of the post-*Chadwick* case law that began to erode the Warren Court's approach. Initially, for example, the Court took the view that when police developed probable cause that contraband was in a particular package, the police must

seize the package and secure a warrant before they could open the package. How is that consistent with the "principle of particular justification?"

3.   Probable cause as to a package or to a vehicle. Are the facts of *United States v. Ross* distinguishable from the facts of *Sanders* and *Chadwick*? If so, how are they different? Apply the "principle of particular justification" to the facts of *Ross*. Applying that principle, do you believe that the warrantless search violated the Fourth Amendment?

4.   The important distinction. How did the *Ross* majority distinguish *Sanders-Chadwick*? Can you understand that distinction? In *Acevedo,* what does Justice Blackmun say about that distinction?

5.   The distinction that lives on. As developed in Problem 12-5, that distinction continues to be important, even if not for understanding when police must get a warrant to search a package found in a vehicle.

PROBLEM 12-3

Police developed probable cause to believe that Defendant would be picking up a shipment of marijuana from his dealer's home. Officers set up surveillance of the dealer's home. They saw Defendant arrive at and then exit the dealer's home. Officers saw that Defendant was carrying a large envelope. They also saw Defendant open the trunk of his vehicle and place the envelope in the vehicle. At that point, Officers arrested Defendant and placed in him in the patrol car. One of the officers went back to the vehicle, opened the trunk, and found the envelope. She then opened the envelope and found only what looked like a student's law review comment in the envelope. She continued to look in the trunk and discovered, hidden in the spare time wheel well, a leather pouch. Opening the pouch, the officer discovered several ounces of marijuana. Charged with possession of marijuana with intent to distribute, Defendant has moved to suppress the evidence. Discuss how the court should rule on that motion.

PROBLEM 12-4

A state highway patrol trooper observed a car parked at a rest area in a state park during the early morning hours. When the trooper approached the driver's side window, Defendant lowered the window on that side, and the trooper smelled the strong odor of freshly burnt marijuana emanating from within the vehicle. He asked the driver to produce a license and registration and informed him that he was in the park after hours in violation of regulations. He asked Defendant if he had been smoking marijuana. He admitted that he had been smoking marijuana. Responding to the trooper's question whether there was still any marijuana in the vehicle, Defendant admitted that there was still a small amount inside.

The trooper ordered Defendant to turn off the engine. He then had him step out of the vehicle, so that he could conduct a search him "for weapons and contraband." He found neither. Defendant did tell the trooper that there was a bag of marijuana on the floor mat behind the front passenger seat. When the trooper illuminated the area with his flashlight, he could see a clear plastic bag containing what appeared to be marijuana. Upon closer inspection, the trooper concluded that the bag contained "a partial ounce" of the drug; he continued to search the interior of the vehicle for contraband but found nothing. The trooper then opened the trunk and found a black backpack, which he opened and searched. The trooper recovered a large amount of marijuana from inside the bag. Charged with possession of marijuana with intent to distribute, Defendant has moved to suppress the evidence. Discuss how the court should rule on that motion.

CHAPTER 13

CRIMINAL PENALTIES FOR ILLEGAL MARIJUANA POSSESSION AND DISTRIBUTION

■ ■ ■

In earlier chapters, you have learned about shifting attitudes towards cannabis. Hence, earlier in our history, cannabis founds its way into the Pharmacopeia for various ailments. Farmers produced hemp for many purposes, including cloth and rope. As one commentator observed, at the end of the Civil War, tea was subject to far more regulation than was cannabis. That would change by the first third of the last century when it became the "demon weed." Through the Twentieth Century, attitudes continued to shift, often dramatically. Congress flirted with decriminalizing marijuana in 1970, only to include it in the Controlled Substance Act as a Schedule I drug. Again, during Jimmy Carter's presidency, policy makers considered a softer approach towards marijuana. That trend was short-lived. During the Reagan presidency, the War on Drugs ratcheted up. Not only did Congress increase penalties for marijuana offenses, but also, Congress began to imbed other collateral consequences in thousands of federal laws.

States have not been immune from the same kinds of shifts in attitude towards marijuana. Many states increased penalties for marijuana offenses, often tracking federal law. Often, state and federal officials have cooperated in joint operations in a shared war on drugs. That is changing in some states, as increasing numbers of states have reduced penalties for marijuana offenses, legalized marijuana for medical purposes or legalized marijuana for recreational purposes. As a result, generalizing about criminal sentences for marijuana offenses is difficult because sentences vary so dramatically around the country.

Despite popular support for legalizing marijuana, some states and the federal government continue to punish marijuana offenses with very long sentences. This chapter first addresses some of those extreme punishments. The second section of this chapter explores the extent to which an offender can claim that an extremely long prison sentence violates the prohibition against cruel and unusual punishment. As indicated, Congress and other legislatures have also added any number of collateral consequences (far too numerous to cover in a casebook). Finally, the chapter turns to one other possible criminal sanction for members of the cannabis industry: tax penalties. Chapter 14, Civil Penalties for Illegal Marijuana Possession and Distribution explores collateral consequences and civil forfeiture.

A. PENALTIES AND SENTENCING

As indicated above, sentencing schemes vary considerably around the country, especially since many states began legalizing marijuana for medical and then recreational use. While sentencing varies widely, the following description gives a broad summary of criminal sentences available for marijuana offenses in the federal and state court systems.

The Controlled Substances Act imposes minimum and maximum sentences of imprisonment for a federal conviction. Federal sentencing guidelines include a detailed set of guidelines for imposing these sentences for federal marijuana offenses. The sentence levels are determined by the identity and quantity of the controlled substance, with the quantity measured by the weight of the mixture rather than that of the pure controlled substance. An offender's sentence may be enhanced depending on various factors, such as joint criminal activity resulting in death or serious bodily injury, use of a dangerous weapon, bribery, pollution, trafficking in prison, misuse of a licensed professional, and cultivation on state, federal, or tribal land.

More specifically, the Controlled Substances Act, as amended at various times, including most notably during the Reagan administration, provides specific sentencing ranges. For example, under 21 U.S.C. § 844, simple possession is a misdemeanor, punishable by up to one-year in prison and a minimum fine of $1,000. A second offense is subject to a term of imprisonment of 15 days to two years and a minimum fine of $2,500. Subsequent convictions lead to a minimum sentence of 90 days to three years in prison and a minimum fine of $5,000.

Trafficking in marijuana is a felony. As defined in 21 U.S.C. § 841, trafficking includes manufacture, cultivation, distribution, dispensation, or possession with intent to commit such an offense. Often an offender is not parole-eligible. The punishment for a second offense is basically double the term for the first offense. Sentencing depends on the amount of marijuana involved.

Here is a list of the punishments available for a violation of § 841:

Trafficking of less than 50 kilograms of marijuana is punishable by up to 5 years' imprisonment and a maximum $250,000 fine. Trafficking of 50 to 99 kilograms (or 50 to 99 plants) is punishable by up to 20 years' imprisonment and a maximum $1 million fine. Trafficking of 100 to 999 kilograms (or 100–999 plants) is punishable by a mandatory minimum of 10 years to a life sentence of imprisonment, with a maximum fine of $10 million.

Notice that some terms of imprisonment depend on the weight of the marijuana possessed by the offender. At one point, federal law enforcement officials would weigh marijuana when it was wet, a practice that was authorized until 1995. In 1995, the federal sentencing guidelines made clear that the controlling weight was dry weight.

Congress has added various enhancements for marijuana and other drug offenses. For example, trafficking of more than 5 grams to a minor or within 1000 feet of a school or various other facilities doubles the amount of sentence. *See* 21 U.S.C. §§ 859–60. Federal law allows for the death penalty for "drug kingpins," i.e., in instances where the amount of drugs or gross receipts exceed certain limits. *See* 18 U.S.C. § 3591(b).

Many states followed the federal lead in the 1970s when Congress enacted the Controlled Substances Act. President Nixon urged the Uniform Law Commission to draft a provision tracking federal law. By the end of the 1970s, the overwhelming majority of states had adopted the Uniform Controlled Substances Act, as drafted by the Uniform Law. Even in earlier years, states have been less draconian in their sentencing of marijuana offenders. As summarized by Osbeck and Bromberg, the Uniform Controlled Substances Act "provides more flexibility for states to set penalties for violations of drug laws. Nevertheless, most states enacted penalties similar to those set out in the CSA. Since 1996, many states have amended their state controlled substances act so as to account for their legalization of medicinal and recreational marijuana." *Id.* at 86–87.

Apart from violations of state drug laws, some states impose extremely long sentences on offenders under those states' habitual offender statutes. Louisiana has made headlines in a number of cases where offenders have been given long terms of imprisonment when the offender's most recent crime has involved possession of a small amount of marijuana. *See,* for example, *State v. Howard*, https://www.courthousenews.com/wp-content/uploads/2017/05/marijuana.pdf.

NOTES AND QUESTIONS

1. **Sentencing provisions and weight.** Notice that some terms of imprisonment depend on the weight of the marijuana possessed by the offender. At one point, federal law enforcement officials would weigh marijuana when it was wet, a practice that was authorized until 1995. In 1995, the federal sentencing guidelines made clear that the controlling weight was dry weight. The difference in sentencing may be substantial. Remember that under the CSA, weight of the marijuana determines the minimum and maximum sentence. In *United States v. Carter,* 110 F. 3d 759 (11th Cir. 1997), the offender was guilty of a count of a conspiracy to possess marijuana with intent to distribute. He was responsible for 950 kilograms of marijuana. Based on the CSA and the sentencing guidelines, Carter faced a term of imprisonment from 121 to 151 months. On appeal, he contended that his sentence was based

on the weight of wet marijuana. "[H]e further claimed that the dried marijuana 'didn't probably weigh half of what it weighed in its wet-down form.' " 110 F. 3d at 760. The Eleventh Circuit remanded the case for reconsideration of Carter's sentence, reflective of the fact that the length of the offender's sentence might be significantly less based on the much lower amount of dry marijuana.

    2. Defining a "plant." As discussed above, some provisions of the Controlled Substances Act refer to weight or number of plants possessed. Thus, § 841 defines one level of the offense alternatively in terms of number of plants or weight of the marijuana possessed. What is a "plant" within the meaning of marijuana statutes? Federal courts have given the term "plant" its ordinary dictionary meaning, not a scientific definition. *See, e.g., United States v. Robinson,* 35 F. 3d 442 (9th Cir. 1994).

    3. Extracts. Another issue that a well-crafted guideline system should resolve is how to treat extracts of cannabis. What, for example, about hash oil? Compare the weight of, say, marijuana buds with that of hash oil: the hash oil's concentration of THC is far greater than is the concentration of THC in the plant buds. Congress has provided equivalencies in some instances. For example, § 841 equates 50 kilograms of marijuana with 10 kilograms of hashish, or 1 kilogram of hashish oil.

    The next section takes up the question whether extremely long prison sentences violate the Eighth Amendment's prohibition against cruel and unusual punishment.

B. CRUEL AND UNUSUAL PUNISHMENT

    The Eighth Amendment to the Constitution provides that "Excessive bail shall not be required, nor excessive fines imposed, nor cruel and unusual punishments inflicted." In numerous decisions, the Supreme Court has held that the death penalty may be cruel and unusual because the punishment is excessive to the underlying crime. The Court's case law dealing with terms of imprisonment is less vigorous. Despite that limited precedent, many litigants face extremely long prison sentences for violating both federal and state marijuana laws. Can an extremely long prison term violate the Eighth Amendment when the sentence is imposed on an individual who has violated those laws? Does it matter that a majority of Americans support legalization of marijuana?

UNITED STATES V. ANGELOS
United States Court of Appeals for the Tenth Circuit
433 F.3d 738 (2011)

BRISCOE, J.

    Defendant Weldon Angelos was convicted of multiple drug, firearms, and money laundering offenses and sentenced to a term of imprisonment of fifty-five years and one day. Angelos now appeals his convictions and sentence. We exercise jurisdiction pursuant to 28 U.S.C. § 1291 and affirm.

I.

In May and June of 2002, the government, with the assistance of a confidential informant (CI), conducted three controlled purchases of marijuana from Angelos. On each of the three occasions, the CI purchased eight ounces of marijuana from Angelos in exchange for cash. On two of the three occasions, the CI observed Angelos in possession of a 10 millimeter Glock pistol.

Angelos's involvement in the three controlled purchases led to his indictment by a federal grand jury on November 13, 2002. The indictment charged Angelos with three counts of marijuana distribution in violation of 21 U.S.C. § 841(a)(1), one count of carrying or possessing a firearm during or in relation to a drug trafficking crime in violation of 18 U.S.C. § 924(c), and one count of possessing a firearm with an obliterated serial number in violation of 18 U.S.C. § 922(k).

Angelos was subsequently arrested on November 15, 2002. A consensual search of Angelos's apartment produced three pounds of marijuana, three firearms, a large amount of cash, and two opiate suckers. A subsequent search at a house leased by Angelos produced, among other things, additional marijuana and several large duffle bags that contained marijuana residue.

On June 18, 2003, the government obtained a superseding indictment charging Angelos with seventeen criminal counts, including additional marijuana distribution counts and additional § 924(c) counts. On October 1, 2003, following the completion of a criminal investigation by the Internal Revenue Service, the government obtained a second superseding indictment charging Angelos with twenty criminal counts, including: six counts of distributing marijuana in violation of 21 U.S.C. § 841(a)(1); five counts of possessing a firearm during and in relation to a drug trafficking crime in violation of 18 U.S.C. § 924(c)(1); two counts of possessing a stolen firearm in violation of 18 U.S.C. § 922(j); one count of possessing a firearm which had the importer's and manufacturer's serial number removed, obliterated and altered, in violation of 18 U.S.C. § 922(k); three counts of possessing a firearm while being an unlawful user of controlled substances in violation of 18 U.S.C. § 922(g)(3); one count of engaging in and attempting to engage in a monetary transaction through or to a financial institution in criminally derived property in violation of 18 U.S.C. § 1957; and two counts of conducting and attempting to conduct financial transactions which involved the proceeds of marijuana distribution in violation of 18 U.S.C. § 1956(a)(1)(A)(i).

The case proceeded to trial in December 2003, where a jury found Angelos guilty of sixteen counts, including three § 924(c) counts. Following trial, a presentence investigation report (PSR) was prepared which recommended that Angelos, who had no prior adult criminal history, be sentenced to a term of imprisonment of sixty-one and a half (61.5) years, including six and a half (6.5) years for the drug and money laundering convictions and fifty-five (55) years for the three § 924(c) convictions. After receiving the PSR, the district court expressed concern about imposing what it characterized as "an extraordinarily long prison term," and thus directed the parties to file briefs addressing a number of sentencing-related issues, including whether the mandatory minimum sentences required under § 924(c) were consistent with the Eighth Amendment's prohibition against cruel and unusual punishment. . . . Angelos argued in response that the fifty-five year sentence required to be imposed under § 924(c) violated the Eighth Amendment's prohibition against cruel and unusual punishment.

On November 16, 2004, the district court sentenced Angelos to a term of imprisonment of fifty-five years and one day. In doing so, the district court rejected Angelos's Eighth Amendment . . . challenges to his sentence.

* * *

Eighth Amendment challenge to Angelos's sentences

Angelos, joined in an amicus brief filed by a group of individuals, including former federal judges, United States Attorneys General, and high-ranking United States Department of Justice officials, contends the district court erred in concluding that the fifty-five year sentence mandated in his case by § 924(c) did not violate the Eighth Amendment's prohibition against cruel and unusual punishment. We review de novo the question of whether a criminal sentence violates the Eighth Amendment.

"The Eighth Amendment . . . contains a 'narrow proportionality principle' that 'applies to noncapital sentences.'" *Ewing v. California,* 538 U.S. 11, 20 (2003). Under this narrow proportionality principle, the Eighth Amendment "does not require strict proportionality between crime and sentence." *Id.* at 23. "Rather, it forbids only extreme sentences that are 'grossly disproportionate' to the crime." *Id.*

Although the Supreme Court has reviewed Eighth Amendment challenges to a number of state and federal sentences, it has struck down only two of them over the past century. In *Weems v. United States,* 217 U.S. 349, 367 (1910), the Court invalidated under the Eighth Amendment a sentence of fifteen years in chains and at hard labor, plus permanent surveillance and civil disabilities, for the crime of falsifying a public document. Seventy-three years later, in *Solem v. Helm,* 463 U.S. 277 (1983), the Court invalidated under the Eighth Amendment a sentence of life imprisonment without the possibility of parole imposed under South Dakota law against a nonviolent recidivist whose final crime was writing a "no account" check with the intent to defraud.

In contrast to these two cases, the Supreme Court has rejected Eighth Amendment challenges to the following sentences:

- A life sentence, with the possibility of parole, under a Texas recidivist statute for successive convictions of (1) fraudulent use of a credit card to obtain $80 worth of goods or services, (2) passing a forged check in the amount of $28.36, and (3) obtaining $120.75 by false pretenses. *Rummel v. Estelle,* 445 U.S. 263, 285 (1980).

- A forty-year sentence for possession and distribution of 9 ounces of marijuana. *Hutto v. Davis,* 454 U.S. 370, 375 (1982).

- A life sentence, without the possibility of parole, for possession of more than 650 grams of cocaine. *Harmelin,* 501 U.S. at 1005.

- A twenty-five year to life sentence imposed under a California recidivist statute for the offense of felony grand theft (i.e., stealing three golf clubs worth approximately $1,200). *Ewing,* 538 U.S. at 30–31.

- Two consecutive twenty-five-year to life sentences under a California recidivist statute for two counts of petty theft. *Lockyer v. Andrade,* 538 U.S. 63, 77 (2003).

Considered together, these cases clearly support the Supreme Court's recent statement in *Andrade* that "[t]he gross disproportionality principle reserves a constitutional violation for only the extraordinary case." 538 U.S. at 76.

Applying these principles to the case at hand, we conclude that this is not an "extraordinary" case in which the sentences at issue are "grossly disproportionate" to the crimes for which they were imposed. The Supreme Court has noted that the "basic purpose" of § 924(c) is "to combat the 'dangerous combination' of 'drugs and guns.'" *Muscarello v. United States,* 524 U.S. 125, 126 (1998). The Court has also noted that "the provision's chief legislative sponsor . . . said that the provision seeks 'to persuade the man who is tempted to commit a Federal felony to leave his gun at home.'" *Id.* In addition, the Court has concluded that it was entirely rational for Congress to penalize the mere presence of a firearm during a drug transaction: "Whether guns are used as the medium of exchange for drugs sold illegally or as a means to protect the transaction or dealers, their introduction into the scene of drug transactions dramatically heightens the danger to society." *Smith,* 508 U.S. at 239. In this same vein, the Third Circuit has held that "[i]t is likely that Congress," in enacting § 924(c), "meant . . . to protect our communities from violent criminals who repeatedly demonstrate a willingness to employ deadly weapons by punishing them more harshly." *United States v. Couch,* 291 F.3d 251, 255 (3d Cir.2002). In sum, the lengthy sentences mandated by § 924(c) were intended by Congress to (a) protect society by incapacitating those criminals who demonstrate a willingness to repeatedly engage in serious felonies while in possession of firearms, and (b) to deter criminals from possessing firearms during the course of certain felonies. Notably, both of these penological theories have been held by the Supreme Court to be valid and subject to deference by the courts.

Although Angelos attempts to downplay the nature of his crimes, the record on appeal clearly supports the jury's findings that Angelos possessed a handgun during the course of the first two controlled purchases, and likewise possessed firearms at his apartment in conjunction with drug-trafficking materials. All of these firearms appear to have facilitated his drug trafficking by, if nothing else, providing protection from purchasers and others. Although Angelos emphasizes that he never used any of the firearms, his possession of the firearms clearly heightened the threat of danger to society. In particular, it undoubtedly increased the likelihood of violence occurring to neighbors in and around the residences where the firearms were maintained, as well as to others that happened to be in the vicinity of wherever he chose to conduct his drug transactions.

It is also important to note that Angelos's possession of firearms facilitated his possession and distribution of illegal drugs. In *Harmelin,* the Supreme Court emphasized the seriousness of drug trafficking crimes, noting that the "[p]ossession, use, and distribution of illegal drugs represent 'one of the greatest problems affecting the health and welfare of our population.' " 501 U.S. at 1002. In particular, "drugs relate to crime in at least three ways: (1) A drug user may commit crime because of drug-induced changes in physiological functions, cognitive ability, and mood; (2) A drug user may commit crime in order to obtain money to buy drugs; and (3) A violent crime may occur as part of the drug business or culture." *Id.* at 1002. Thus, as in *Harmelin,* Angelos's "suggestion that his crime was nonviolent . . . is false to the point of absurdity." *Id.* at 1002. "To the contrary," his "crime[s] threatened to cause grave harm to society." *Id.*

Thus, Congress "could with reason conclude that the threat posed to the individual and society" by possessing firearms in connection with serious felonies, in particular drug-trafficking crimes, was "momentous enough to warrant the deterrence and retribution" of lengthy consecutive sentences, such as those imposed on Angelos in this case. *Id.* at 1003. In turn, that is enough to conclude that the sentences imposed on Angelos are not grossly disproportionate to his crimes. *Id.* at 1004 ("The severity of petitioner's crimes brings his [life sentence without parole] within the constitutional boundaries established by our prior decisions.").

The district court reached this same conclusion, but took a somewhat different route. The district court initially concluded that it was required to examine three "factors" first mentioned in Justice Powell's dissenting opinion in *Davis,* and subsequently discussed in *Solem* and *Harmelin:* "(1)

the nature of the crime and its relation to the punishment imposed, (2) the punishment for other offenses in this jurisdiction, and (3) the punishment for similar offenses in other jurisdictions." Applying these factors, the district court concluded that "the 55-year enhancement" it was required to impose pursuant to § 924(c) was grossly disproportionate to the crimes committed by Angelos. In support of this conclusion, the district court stated that Angelos "did not engage in force or violence, or threats of force or violence. . . ." Further, the district court noted that, under the Sentencing Guidelines, the penalty for Angelos's "firearms conduct" would be "about 24 months. . . ." With respect to the second "factor," the district court concluded that § 924(c) effectively treated Angelos "in the same manner as, or more severely than, criminals who have committed far more serious crimes." With respect to the third factor, the district court concluded that Angelos's sentence under § 924(c) was "longer than he would receive in any of the fifty states." *Id.* In sum, the district court concluded that analysis of these three factors led "to the conclusion that . . . Angelos' sentence violate[d] the Eighth Amendment." However, the district court concluded that the Supreme Court's decision in *Davis* prevented it from declaring Angelos's sentence violative of the Eighth Amendment. More specifically, the district court noted that "if 40 years in prison for possessing nine ounces of marijuana d[id] not violate the Eighth Amendment, it [wa]s hard to see how 61 years [the sentence urged by the government in this case] for distributing sixteen ounces (or more) would do so."

Angelos argues that the district court erred in concluding that the Supreme Court's decision in *Davis* remains good law and in turn concluding that the decision in *Davis* required the district court to reject Angelos's Eighth Amendment challenge to his sentence. The flaw in Angelos's argument is his assertion that *Davis* is no longer good law. Although the Court in *Davis* rejected application of the three-factor test later discussed in *Solem* and *Harmelin,* it is the ultimate holding in that case (i.e., that a forty-year sentence for a marijuana trafficking crime does not violate the Eighth Amendment) that remains important. Further, the Supreme Court has continued to recognize and discuss *Davis* anytime it has been faced with an Eighth Amendment challenge to a sentence— thereby clearly indicating that the holding in *Davis* remains "good law."

The amici "suggest that once [*Harmelin's*] three factor test has been satisfied, the analysis ends, and a finding that a sentence is unconstitutional under *Harmelin* is not inconsistent with *Davis*." This suggestion, however, is only partially correct. As noted in *Hawkins v. Hargett,* 200 F.3d 1279, 1282 (10th Cir.1999), "Justice Kennedy's opinion in *Harmelin* . . . sets forth the applicable Eighth Amendment proportionality test." Under that test, a court first examines whether the sentence at issue is grossly disproportionate to the crime for which it was imposed. If there is no gross disproportionality, that is the end of the analysis; only if gross disproportionality is found must a court "proceed to the comparative analyses" of the second and third factors.

Importantly, however, that does not change the outcome here because, for the reasons discussed in detail above, it is clear that the first, and controlling, "factor" in *Harmelin,* i.e., whether the sentence at issue is grossly disproportionate to the crime, has not been satisfied. Although the district court concluded that Angelos's sentence was disproportionate to his crimes, we disagree. In our view, the district court failed to accord proper deference to Congress's decision to severely punish criminals who repeatedly possess firearms in connection with drug-trafficking crimes, and erroneously downplayed the seriousness of Angelos's crimes. Although it is true that Angelos had no significant adult criminal history, that appears to have been the result of good fortune rather than Angelos's lack of involvement in criminal activity. The evidence presented by the government at trial clearly established that Angelos was a known gang member who had long used and sold illicit drugs. Further, the government's evidence established that, at the time of his arrest, Angelos was a mid-to-high drug dealer who purchased and in turn sold large quantities of marijuana. In addition, the government's evidence established that Angelos possessed and used a number of firearms, some stolen, to facilitate his drug-dealing activities. Lastly, the evidence established that although Angelos had some involvement in the music industry, he failed to financially profit from that involvement and indeed never reported any positive earnings to the Internal Revenue Service. Thus, the only reasonable inference that could be drawn was that Angelos's sole source of income was his drug-trafficking operations.

In sum, we conclude there is no merit to Angelos's Eighth Amendment challenge to his sentence under § 924(c).

AFFIRMED.

NOTES AND QUESTIONS

1.   **The rest of the story.** In 2016, after a widespread campaign on Angelos' behalf, a federal judge reduced Angelos' sentence from 55 to 13 years, leading to his release and reunion with his family. Here is one story about his reunion with his family: http://www.dailymail.co.uk/news/article-3625397/ Music-producer-long-sentence-drew-outcry-free-early.html Utah Law School Professor Paul Cassell was Angelos' sentencing judge when Professor Cassell served as a federal district court judge in Utah. He made clear his disagreement with Angelos' long sentence, as indicated in: https://abcnews.go. com/US/federal-judge-regrets-55-year-marijuana-sentence/story?id=288694 67.

2.   **The Supreme Court's case law.** The court discusses the relevant case law, including *Solem v. Helm*, 463 U.S. 277 (1983). There, the Court found that a true-life sentence imposed on a repeat offender whose most recent crime

(issuance of a no-account check) was a minor offense violated the Eighth Amendment's prohibition against cruel and unusual punishment. In light of Angelos' crimes, does the court's conclusion surprise you?

3.   **The Supreme Court's case law and marijuana.** Can you imagine a case in which the Supreme Court might find that a long term of imprisonment imposed on a person who violated marijuana laws was excessive under the Court's Eighth Amendment test? Would you be able to distinguish the case that you have imagined from the facts of *Hutto v. Davis*, 454 U.S. 370 (1982), discussed in the lead case?

4.   **Better luck in state courts?** Occasionally, state courts have found that punishment imposed on offenders for marijuana offenses have been excessive. *See, e.g., Commonwealth v. Eby*, 784 A.2d 204 (Pa. Super. 2001) (based on an abuse of discretion in applying state sentencing guideline provisions); *People v. Lorentzen*, 194 N.W.2d 827 (Mich. 1972) (20-year minimum sentence violated both the Eighth Amendment's cruel and unusual punishment clause and the state's parallel constitutional provision). On the other hand, some state courts have rejected claims that very long punishments violate the law. *See, e.g., Brooker v. State*, 219 So.3d 695 (Ala. Crim. App. 2015) (a life sentence without the possibility of parole imposed on a 76-year-old habitual offender whose current crime involved possession of less than three pounds of marijuana was lawful.) The Supreme Court denied the writ of certiorari. *See Brooker v. Alabama*, ___ U.S. ___, 136 S.Ct. 1659 (2016).

5.   **Another view from a state court.** In *Conner v. State*, 626 N.E. 2d 803 (Ind. 1993), the Indiana Supreme Court held that an eight-year sentence for selling *fake* marijuana was excessive under the state constitution, which contains a protection broader than the Eighth Amendment's protection against cruel and unusual punishment. Not only was the sentence extreme, but the sentence was longer than would have been the sentence had the offender sold real marijuana.

6.   **The death penalty for drug kingpins.** In March, 2018, Attorney General Sessions announced that federal prosecutors can seek the death penalty for drug kingpins under 18 U.S.C. § 3591(b). Would such a sentence violate the Eighth Amendment? In *Coker v. Georgia,* 433 U.S. 584 (1977), the Court held that the death penalty imposed on the defendant for the crime of rape of an adult woman was excessive in violation of the Eighth Amendment. In *Kennedy v. Louisiana,* 554 U.S. 407 (2008), the Court extended its holding in *Coker.* The Court found that the imposition of the death penalty on a defendant who raped but did not kill his 8 year old stepdaughter violated the Eighth Amendment. In light of those cases, most commentators believe that imposing the death penalty on a drug kingpin, absent a death, would be unconstitutional.

7.   **Drugs and/or guns.** If the sentence in *Angelos* seems excessive to you, does the fault lie in harsh penalties for marijuana possession or for the mandatory firearms-related enhancements that are added to drug offenses?

8.   **Rethinking Hutto v. Davis?** Review the Supreme Court's test for assessing whether a term of imprisonment violates the Eighth Amendment. Of what relevance is it that many states have decriminalized marijuana possession or reduced it from a felony to a misdemeanor or to an offense?

PROBLEM 13-1

A member of the police department arrested Defendant, when the officer saw Defendant smoking marijuana near a public school, giving the state the option of charging the misdemeanor possession offense as a felony. When Prosecutor learned that Defendant had a prior felony conviction, she charged him as a habitual offender and sought a term of imprisonment of 25 years-to-life. To avoid the chance of that sentence, Defendant agreed to a minimum term of 18 years in prison, but reserved the right to challenge the legality of that sentence as excessive. On appeal, Defendant has challenged the sentence as in violation of the Eighth Amendment's prohibition against cruel and unusual punishment. Discuss how the court should resolve that question consistent with existing precedent.

C. TAX PENALTIES

DEPARTMENT OF REVENUE OF MONTANA V. KURTH RANCH

United States Supreme Court
511 U.S. 767 (1994)

STEVENS, J.

This case presents the question whether a tax on the possession of illegal drugs assessed after the State has imposed a criminal penalty for the same conduct may violate the constitutional prohibition against successive punishments for the same offense.

I

Montana's Dangerous Drug Tax Act took effect on October 1, 1987. The Act imposes a tax "on the possession and storage of dangerous drugs," Mont. Code Ann. § 15–25–111 (1987), and expressly provides that the tax is to be "collected only after any state or federal fines or forfeitures have been satisfied." § 15–25–111(3). The tax is either 10 percent of the assessed market value of the drugs as determined by the Montana Department of Revenue (DOR) or a specified amount depending on the drug ($100 per ounce for marijuana, for example, and $250 per ounce for hashish), whichever is greater. § 15–25–111(2). The Act directs the state treasurer to allocate the tax proceeds to special funds to support "youth evaluation" and "chemical abuse" programs and "to enforce the drug laws." §§ 15–25–121, 15–25–122.

In addition to imposing reporting responsibilities on law enforcement agencies, the Act also authorizes the DOR to adopt rules to administer and enforce the tax. Under those rules, taxpayers must file a return within 72 hours of their arrest. Mont.Admin.Rule 42.34.102(1) (1988). The Rule also provides that "[a]t the time of arrest law enforcement personnel shall complete the dangerous drug information report as required by the department and afford the taxpayer an opportunity to sign it." Rule 42.34.102(3). If the taxpayer refuses to do so, the law enforcement officer is required to file the form within 72 hours of the arrest. *Ibid*. The "associated criminal nature of assessments under this act" justifies the expedited collection procedures. See Rule 42.34.103(3). The taxpayer has no obligation to file a return or to pay any tax unless and until he is arrested.

II

The six respondents, all members of the extended Kurth family, have for years operated a mixed grain and livestock farm in central Montana. In 1986 they began to cultivate and sell marijuana. About two weeks after the new Dangerous Drug Tax Act went into effect, Montana law enforcement officers raided the farm, arrested the Kurths, and confiscated all the marijuana plants, materials, and paraphernalia they found. The raid put an end to the marijuana business and gave rise to four separate legal proceedings.

In one of those proceedings, the State filed criminal charges against all six respondents in the Montana District Court, charging each with conspiracy to possess drugs with the intent to sell, Mont.Code Ann. § 45–4–102 (1987), or, in the alternative, possession of drugs with the intent to sell, § 45–9–103. Each respondent initially pleaded not guilty, but subsequently entered into a plea agreement. On July 18, 1988, the court sentenced Richard Kurth and Judith Kurth to prison and imposed suspended or deferred sentences on the other four family members.

The county attorney also filed a civil forfeiture action seeking recovery of cash and equipment used in the marijuana operation. The confiscated drugs were not involved in that action, presumably because law enforcement agents had destroyed them after an inventory. Respondents settled the forfeiture action with an agreement to forfeit $18,016.83 in cash and various items of equipment.

The third proceeding involved the assessment of the new tax on dangerous drugs. Despite difficulties the DOR had in applying the Act for the first time, it ultimately attempted to collect almost $900,000 in taxes on marijuana plants, harvested marijuana, hash tar and hash oil, interest, and penalties. The Kurths contested the assessments in administrative proceedings. Those proceedings were automatically stayed in September 1988, however, when the Kurths initiated the fourth legal proceeding triggered by the raid on their farm: a petition for bankruptcy under Chapter 11 of the Bankruptcy Code.

In the bankruptcy proceedings, the Kurths objected to the DOR's proof of claim for unpaid drug taxes and challenged the constitutionality of the Montana tax. After a trial, the Bankruptcy Court held most of the assessment invalid as a matter of state law, but concluded that an assessment of $181,000 on 1,811 ounces of harvested marijuana was authorized by the Act. It held that assessment invalid under the Federal Constitution.

Relying primarily on *United States v. Halper,* 490 U.S. 435 (1989), the Bankruptcy Court decided that the assessment constituted a form of double jeopardy. The court rejected the State's argument that the tax was not a penalty because it was designed to recover law enforcement costs; as the court noted, the DOR "failed to introduce one scintilla of evidence as to cost of the above government programs or costs of law enforcement incurred to combat illegal drug activity." After noting that a portion of the assessment resulted in a tax eight times the product's market value, the court explained that the punitive character of the tax was evident

> "because drug tax laws have historically been regarded as penal in nature, the Montana Act promotes the traditional aims of punishment—retribution and deterrence, the tax applies to behavior which is already a crime, the tax allows for sanctions by restraint of Debtors' property, the tax requires a finding of illegal possession of dangerous drugs and therefore a finding of *scienter,* the tax will promote elimination of illegal drug possession, and the tax appears excessive in relation to the alternate purpose assigned, especially in the absence of any record developed by the State as to societal costs. Finally, the tax follows arrest for possession of illegal drugs and the tax report is made by law enforcement officers, not the taxpayer, who may or may not sign the report." *Id.,* at 75–76.

These aspects led the court to the "inescapable conclusion" that the drug tax statute's purpose was deterrence and punishment. *Id.,* at 76.

The District Court affirmed. Agreeing with the Bankruptcy Court's findings and reasoning, it concluded that the Montana Dangerous Drug Tax Act "simply punishes the Kurths a second time for the same criminal conduct." *In re Kurth Ranch,* CV-90-084-GF, 1991 WL 365065 (D.Mont., Apr. 23, 1991). That and the DOR's failure to provide an accounting of its actual damages or costs convinced the Bankruptcy Court that the tax assessments violated the Fifth Amendment's Double Jeopardy Clause.

The Court of Appeals for the Ninth Circuit also affirmed, but based its conclusion largely on the State's refusal to offer evidence justifying the tax, and accordingly refused to hold the tax unconstitutional on its face. The court first determined that under *Halper,* a disproportionately large civil penalty can be punitive for double jeopardy purposes. That the assessment is called a tax, as opposed to some kind of penalty, is not controlling. The central inquiry under *Halper,* the court determined, is whether the sanction imposed is rationally related to the damages the government suffered. That inquiry only applies to cases in which there has been a separate criminal conviction, however. The court concluded that the Kurths were entitled to an accounting to determine if the sanction constitutes an impermissible second punishment, and because the State refused to offer any such evidence, it held the tax unconstitutional as applied to the Kurths.

While this case was pending on appeal, the Montana Supreme Court reversed two lower state-court decisions that had held that the Dangerous Drug Tax Act was a form of double jeopardy. Over the dissent of two justices, the State Supreme Court found that the legislature had intended to establish a civil, not a criminal, penalty and that the tax had a remedial purpose other than promoting retribution and deterrence. The court found that *Halper* was not controlling, both because it expressly announced " 'a rule for the rare case' " and because the case involved a civil penalty, not a tax. 254 Mont., at 67, 836 P.2d, at 32–33. The *Sorensen* court concluded that the drug tax was not excessive and that a tax, unlike the civil sanction at issue in *Halper,* requires no proof of the State's remedial costs on the part of the State.

The Montana Supreme Court's decision is directly at odds with the conclusion reached in the federal proceedings involving the Kurths. We therefore granted certiorari to review the decision of the Court of Appeals. We now affirm its judgment.

III

In *Halper* we considered "whether and under what circumstances a civil penalty may constitute 'punishment' for the purposes of double jeopardy analysis." 490 U.S., at 436. Our answer to that question does not decide the different question whether Montana's tax should be characterized as punishment.

Halper was convicted of 65 separate violations of the criminal false claims statute, 18 U.S.C. § 287, each involving a demand for $12 in reimbursement for medical services worth only $3. After Halper was sentenced to two years in prison and fined $5,000, the Government filed a separate action to recover a $2,000 civil penalty for each of the 65 violations. The District Court found that the $130,000 recovery the statute authorized "bore no 'rational relation' to the sum of the Government's $585 actual loss plus its costs in investigating and prosecuting Halper's false claims." 490 U.S., at 439. In the court's view, a civil penalty "more than 220 times greater than the Government's measurable los [s] qualified as punishment" that was barred by the Double Jeopardy Clause. *Ibid.*

On direct appeal to this Court, we rejected the Government's submission that the Double Jeopardy Clause only applied to punishment imposed in criminal proceedings, reasoning that its violation "can be identified only by assessing the character of the actual sanctions imposed on the individual by the machinery of the state." *Id.,* at 447. In making such an assessment, "the labels 'criminal' and 'civil' are not of paramount importance." Accepting the District Court's findings, we held that "a defendant who already has been punished in a criminal prosecution may not be subjected to an additional civil sanction to the extent that the second sanction may not fairly be characterized as remedial, but only as a deterrent or retribution." *Id.,* at 448–449.

Halper thus decided that the legislature's description of a statute as civil does not foreclose the possibility that it has a punitive character. We also recognized in *Halper* that a so-called civil "penalty" may be remedial in character if it merely reimburses the government for its actual costs arising from the defendant's criminal conduct. *Id.,* at 449–450. We therefore remanded the case to the District Court to determine what portion of the statutory penalty could be sustained as compensation for the Government's actual damages.

Halper did not, however, consider whether a tax may similarly be characterized as punitive.

IV

Criminal fines, civil penalties, civil forfeitures, and taxes all share certain features: They generate government revenues, impose fiscal burdens on individuals, and deter certain behavior. All of these sanctions are subject to constitutional constraints. A government may not impose criminal fines without first establishing guilt by proof beyond a reasonable doubt. A defendant convicted and punished for an offense may not have a nonremedial civil penalty imposed against him for the same offense in a separate proceeding. *United States v. Halper,* 490 U.S. 435 (1989). A civil forfeiture may violate the Eighth Amendment's proscription against excessive fines. And a statute imposing a tax on unlawful conduct may be invalid because its reporting requirements compel taxpayers to incriminate themselves.

As a general matter, the unlawfulness of an activity does not prevent its taxation. Montana no doubt could collect its tax on the possession of marijuana, for example, if it had not previously punished the taxpayer for the same offense, or, indeed, if it had assessed the tax in the same proceeding that resulted in his conviction. Here, we ask only whether the tax has punitive characteristics that subject it to the constraints of the Double Jeopardy Clause.

Although we have never held that a tax violated the Double Jeopardy Clause, we have assumed that one might. In the context of other constitutional requirements, we have repeatedly examined taxes for constitutional validity. We have cautioned against invalidating a tax simply because its enforcement might be oppressive or because the legislature's motive was somehow suspect. Yet we have also recognized that "there comes a time in the extension of the penalizing features of the so-called tax when it loses its character as such and becomes a mere penalty with the characteristics of regulation and punishment." *Child Labor Tax Case,* 259 U.S. 20, 38 (1922). That comment, together with *Halper*'s unequivocal statement that labels do not control in a double jeopardy inquiry, indicates that a tax is not immune from double jeopardy scrutiny simply because it is a tax.

Halper recognized that "[t]his constitutional protection is intrinsically personal," and that only "the character of the actual sanctions" can substantiate a possible double jeopardy violation. 490 U.S., at 447. Whereas fines, penalties, and forfeitures are readily characterized as sanctions, taxes are typically different because they are usually motivated by revenue-raising, rather than punitive, purposes. Yet at some point, an exaction labeled as a tax approaches punishment, and our task is to determine whether Montana's drug tax crosses that line.

We begin by noting that neither a high rate of taxation nor an obvious deterrent purpose automatically marks this tax as a form of punishment. In this case, although those factors are not dispositive, they are at least consistent with a punitive character. A significant part of the assessment was more than eight times the drug's market value—a remarkably high tax. That the Montana Legislature intended the tax to deter people from possessing marijuana is beyond question. The DOR reminds us, however, that many taxes that are presumed valid, such as taxes on cigarettes and alcohol, are also both high and motivated to some extent by an interest in deterrence. Indeed, although no double jeopardy challenge was at issue, this Court sustained the steep $100-per-ounce federal tax on marijuana in *United States v. Sanchez,* 340 U.S. 42 (1950). Thus, while a high tax rate and deterrent purpose lend support to the characterization of the drug tax as punishment, these features, in and of themselves, do not necessarily render the tax punitive.

Other unusual features, however, set the Montana statute apart from most taxes. First, this so-called tax is conditioned on the commission of a crime. That condition is "significant of penal and prohibitory intent rather than the gathering of revenue." Moreover, the Court has relied on the absence of such a condition to support its conclusion that a particular federal tax was a civil, rather than a criminal, sanction. In this case, the tax assessment not only hinges on the commission of a crime, it also is exacted only after the taxpayer has been arrested for the precise conduct that gives rise to the tax obligation in the first place. Persons who have been arrested for possessing marijuana constitute the entire class of taxpayers subject to the Montana tax.

Taxes imposed upon illegal activities are fundamentally different from taxes with a pure revenue-raising purpose that are imposed *despite* their adverse effect on the taxed activity. But they differ as well from mixed-motive taxes that governments impose both to deter a disfavored activity and to raise money. By imposing cigarette taxes, for example, a government wants to discourage smoking. But because the product's benefits—such as creating employment, satisfying consumer demand, and providing tax revenues—are regarded as outweighing the harm, that government will allow the manufacture, sale, and use of cigarettes as long as the manufacturers, sellers, and smokers pay high taxes that reduce consumption and increase government revenue. These justifications vanish when the taxed activity is completely forbidden, for the legitimate revenue-raising purpose that might support such a tax could be equally well served by increasing the fine imposed upon conviction.

The Montana tax is exceptional for an additional reason. Although it purports to be a species of property tax—that is, a "tax on the possession and storage of dangerous drugs," Mont.Code Ann. § 15–25–111 (1987)—it is levied on goods that the taxpayer neither owns nor possesses when the tax is imposed. Indeed, the State presumably *destroyed* the contraband goods in this case before the tax on them was assessed. If a statute that amounts to a confiscation of property is unconstitutional, a tax on previously confiscated goods is at least questionable. A tax on "possession" of goods that no longer exist and that the taxpayer never lawfully possessed has an unmistakable punitive character. This tax, imposed on criminals and no others, departs so far from normal revenue laws as to become a form of punishment.

Taken as a whole, this drug tax is a concoction of anomalies, too far-removed in crucial respects from a standard tax assessment to escape characterization as punishment for the purpose of double jeopardy analysis.

V

Because Montana's tax is fairly characterized as punishment, the judgment of the Court of Appeals must be affirmed. In *Halper,* we recognized that a civil penalty may be imposed as a remedy for actual costs to the State that are attributable to the defendant's conduct. 490 U.S., at 452. Yet as The Chief Justice points out, tax statutes serve a purpose quite different from civil penalties, and *Halper*'s method of determining whether the exaction was remedial or punitive "simply does not work in the case of a tax statute." Subjecting Montana's drug tax to *Halper*'s test for civil penalties is therefore inappropriate. Even if it were proper to permit such a showing, Montana has not claimed that its assessment in this case even remotely approximates the cost of investigating, apprehending, and prosecuting the Kurths, or that it roughly relates to any actual damages that they caused the State. And in any event, the formula by which

Montana computed the tax assessment would have been the same regardless of the amount of the State's damages and, indeed, regardless of whether it suffered any harm at all.

This drug tax is not the kind of remedial sanction that may follow the first punishment of a criminal offense. Instead, it is a second punishment within the contemplation of a constitutional protection that has "deep roots in our history and jurisprudence," *Halper,* 490 U.S., at 440, and therefore must be imposed during the first prosecution or not at all. The proceeding Montana initiated to collect a tax on the possession of drugs was the functional equivalent of a successive criminal prosecution that placed the Kurths in jeopardy a second time "for the same offence."

The judgment of the Court of Appeals is affirmed.

It is so ordered.

REHNQUIST, C.J., dissenting.

Without giving any indication that it is doing so, the Court's opinion drastically alters existing law. We have never previously subjected a tax statute to double jeopardy analysis, but under today's decision a state tax statute is struck down because its application violates double jeopardy. The Court starts off on the right foot. It correctly recognizes that our opinion in *United States v. Halper,* 490 U.S. 435 (1989), says nothing about the possible double jeopardy concerns of a tax, as opposed to a civil fine like the one confronted in *Halper.* I agree with the Court's rejection of the *Halper* mode of analysis, which, with its effort to determine whether a penalty statute is remedial or punitive, simply does not fit in the case of a tax statute. But the Court then goes astray and the end result of its decision is a hodgepodge of criteria—many of which have been squarely rejected by our previous decisions—to be used in deciding whether a tax statute qualifies as "punishment."

* * *

The proper question to be asked is whether the Montana drug tax constitutes a second punishment under the Double Jeopardy Clause for conduct already punished criminally. The Court asks the right question, but reaches the wrong conclusion.

Taxes are customarily enacted to raise revenue to support the costs of government. It is also firmly established that taxes may be enacted to deter or even suppress the taxed activity. Constitutional attacks on such laws have been regularly turned aside in our previous decisions. In *A. Magnano Co. v. Hamilton,* 292 U.S. 40 (1934), for example, the Court upheld against a due process challenge a steep excise tax imposed by the State of Washington on processors of oleomargarine during the depths of the depression. In *Sonzinsky v. United States,* the Court upheld an annual federal firearms tax as a valid exercise of the taxing power of Congress.

The Court there said "it has long been established that an Act of Congress which on its face purports to be an exercise of the taxing power is not any the less so because the tax is burdensome or tends to restrict or suppress the thing taxed." In *United States v. Sanchez,* 340 U.S. 42 (1950), the Court upheld the former federal tax on marijuana at the rate of $100 per ounce against a challenge that the tax was a penalty, rather than a true tax. In so doing, the Court noted that "[i]t is beyond serious question that a tax does not cease to be valid merely because it regulates, discourages, or even definitely deters the activity taxed." *Id.,* at 44. And, as the Court concedes, it is well settled that the unlawfulness of an activity does not prevent its taxation.

The Court's opinion today gives a passing nod to these cases, but proceeds to hold that a high tax rate and a deterrent purpose "lend support to the characterization of the drug tax as punishment." The Court then discusses "[o]ther unusual features" of the Montana tax which, it concludes, brands this tax as a criminal penalty.

The Court first points to its conclusion that the so-called tax is conditioned on the commission of a crime a conclusion that the State disputes, and for good reason. The relevant provision of the rule, Mont.Admin.Rule 42.34.102(1) (1988), which provides that the tax return "shall be filed within 72 hours of . . . arrest," merely acknowledges the practical realities involved in taxing an illegal activity. Then, quite contrary to the teachings of *Marchetti, Constantine,* and *James v. United States,* 366 U.S. 213 (1961), the Court states that the justifications for mixed-motive taxes—imposed both to deter and to raise revenue—vanish "when the taxed activity is completely forbidden."

A second "unusual feature" identified by the Court is that the tax is levied on drugs that the taxpayer neither owns or [sic] possesses at the time of taxation. But here, the Court exalts form over substance. Surely the Court is not suggesting that the State must permit the Kurths to keep the contraband in order to tax its possession. And although Montana's "Dangerous Drug Tax" is described as a tax on storage and possession, it is clear from the structure and purpose of the Act that it was passed for the legitimate purpose of raising revenue from the profitable underground drug business.

I do not dispute the Court's conclusion that an assessment which is labeled a "tax" could, under some conceivable circumstances, constitute "punishment" for purposes of the Double Jeopardy Clause. The Court made a similar finding in *United States v. Constantine, supra,* although in the context of a different sort of challenge. At issue in that case was the validity of a special $1,000 excise tax levied against all persons dealing in the liquor business contrary to local law. In striking down the tax as an unlawful penalty rather than a tax, the Court noted that the assessment was conditioned on the imposition of a crime, and that it was "highly exorbitant." *Id.,* at 295.

But the *Constantine* factors are not persuasive in the present context. As discussed above, I do not find the conditioning of the tax on criminal conduct and arrest to be fatal to this tax's validity; this characteristic simply reflects the reality of taxing an illegal enterprise. Furthermore, the rate of taxation clearly supports petitioner here. In *Constantine,* the special $1,000 excise tax on the sale of alcohol was 40 times as great when compared to the otherwise applicable $25 fee for retail liquor dealers such as respondent. When compared to the Montana tax, two points are noteworthy. First, unlike the situation in *Constantine,* no tax or fee is otherwise collected from individuals engaged in the illicit drug business. Thus, an entire business goes without taxation. Second, the Montana tax is not as disproportionate as the additional excise tax in *Constantine.* The Court makes much of the fact that the bulk of the assessment—that imposed on the low-grade "shake"—was more than eight times the market value of the drug. But the Court glosses over the fact that the tax imposed on the higher quality "bud" amounted to only 80% of that product's market value.

After averaging the effective tax rates on the two marijuana products, the Court concludes that Montana's tax rate of four times the market value appears to be "unrivaled." That may be so. But the proper inquiry is not whether the tax rate is "unrivaled," but whether it is so high that it can only be explained as serving a punitive purpose. When compared to similar types of "sin" taxes on items such as alcohol and cigarettes, these figures are not so high as to be deemed arbitrary or shocking. This is especially so given both the traditional deference accorded to state authorities regarding matters of taxation, and the fact that a substantial amount of the illegal drug business will escape taxation altogether.

In short, I think the Court's conclusion that the tax here is a punishment is very much at odds with the purpose and effect of the Montana statute, as well as our previous decisions. After reviewing the structure and language of the tax provision and comparing the rate of taxation with similar types of sin taxes imposed on lawful products, I would reach the contrary conclusion—that the Montana tax has a nonpenal purpose of raising revenue, as well as the legitimate purpose of deterring conduct, such that it should be regarded as a genuine tax for double jeopardy purposes.

O'CONNOR, J., dissenting.

* * *

The government may, of course, tax illegal activity. In fact, we have upheld, as within Congress' taxing authority, a $100 per ounce tax on marijuana. But the power to tax illegal activity carries with it the danger that the legislature will use the tax to punish the participants for engaging in that activity. This is particularly true of taxes assessed on the possession of illegal drugs: Because most drug offenses involve the manufacture, possession, transportation, or distribution of controlled substances, the State might use a tax on possession to punish a participant in a drug crime twice for the same conduct. We would certainly examine a $100 per ounce *fine* levied against a person who had previously been convicted and sentenced for marijuana possession for consistency with the Double Jeopardy Clause. Because in my view there is no constitutional distinction between such a fine and the tax at issue in this case, a tax imposed on the possession of illegal drugs is subject to double jeopardy analysis.

To hold, however, that Montana's drug tax is not *exempt* from scrutiny under the Double Jeopardy Clause says nothing about whether imposition of the tax is unconstitutional. "Congress may impose both a criminal and a civil sanction in respect to the same act or omission; for the double jeopardy clause prohibits merely *punishing* twice, or attempting a second time to punish criminally, for the same offense." *Helvering v. Mitchell,* 303 U.S. 391, 399 (1938). The Fifth Amendment says "nor shall any person be subject for the same offense to be twice put in jeopardy," and a civil proceeding following a criminal prosecution simply is not a second "jeopardy." But we have recognized that the Constitution constrains the States' ability to denominate proceedings as "civil" and so dispense with the criminal procedure protections embodied in the Bill of Rights. Some governmental exactions are so punitive that they may only be imposed in a criminal proceeding. And because the Double Jeopardy Clause prohibits successive criminal proceedings for the same offense, the government may not sanction a defendant for conduct for which he has already been punished *insofar as the subsequent sanction is punitive,* because to do so would necessitate a criminal proceeding prohibited by the Constitution.

The question, then, is whether Montana's drug tax is punitive. Our double jeopardy cases make clear that a civil sanction will be considered punishment to the extent that it serves only the purposes of retribution and deterrence, as opposed to furthering any nonpunitive objective. This will obtain when, as in *Halper,* the amount of the sanction is "overwhelmingly disproportionate" to the damages caused by the wrongful conduct and thus "is not rationally related to the goal of making the Government whole." 490 U.S., at 449, 451.

The State and Federal Governments spend vast sums on drug control activities. The Kurths are directly responsible for some of these expenditures—the costs of detecting, investigating, and raiding their operation, the price of prosecuting them and incarcerating those who received prison sentences, and part of the money spent on drug abuse education, deterrence, and treatment. The State of Montana has a legitimate nonpunitive interest in defraying the costs of such activities.

[citations omitted]. For example, readily available statistics indicate that apprehension, prosecution, and incarceration of the Kurths will cost the State of Montana at least $120,000.

But measuring the costs actually imposed by every participant in the illegal drug trade would be, to the extent it is even possible, so complex as to make the game not worth the candle. Thus, the government must resort to approximation—in effect, it exacts liquidated damages. The Montana Legislature has determined that $100 per ounce of marijuana is an appropriate estimate of its costs of drug control, and at least 22 other States have made a similar determination and tax marijuana at approximately the same rate.

The Court of Appeals recognized that imposition of the drug tax on the Kurths' possession of marijuana would not be punishment if the sanction bore some rational relationship to "the staggering costs associated with fighting drug abuse in this country." *In re Kurth Ranch,* 986 F.2d 1308, 1312 (CA9 1993). But the court held that "allowing the state to impose this tax, *without any showing of some rough approximation of its actual damages and costs,* would be sanctioning a penalty which *Halper* prohibits." *Ibid.* As evidenced by the highlighted phrase, the Court of Appeals skipped a step in the double jeopardy analysis. In *Halper,* we held that determining whether an exaction is punitive entails a two-part inquiry:

> "Where a defendant previously has sustained a criminal penalty and the civil penalty sought in the subsequent proceeding bears no rational relation to the goal of compensating the Government for its loss, but rather appears to qualify as 'punishment' in the plain meaning of the word, *then* the defendant is entitled to an accounting of the Government's damages and costs to determine if the penalty sought *in fact* constitutes a second punishment." 490 U.S., at 449–450.

In other words, the defendant must first show the absence of a rational relationship between the amount of the sanction and the government's nonpunitive objectives; the burden then shifts to the government to justify the sanction with reference to the particular case. This bifurcated approach to the double jeopardy question makes good sense. The presumption of constitutionality to which every state statute is entitled means in this context that a sanction denominated as civil must be presumed to be nonpunitive. This presumption would be rendered nugatory if the government were required to prove that the sanction is in fact nonpunitive before imposing it in a particular case. Rather, the defendant must show that the sanction may be punitive as applied to him before the government can be required to justify its imposition. As we emphasized in *Halper,* it will be the "rare case" in which a litigant will succeed in satisfying the first prong of the constitutional analysis. We do not know whether this is such a case because the courts below improperly faulted the State for failing to prove its actual damages even though the Kurths have not shown that the amount of the tax is not rationally related to the government's legitimate nonpunitive objectives.

The Court avoids this problem by asserting that "[s]ubjecting Montana's drug tax to *Halper's* test for civil penalties is . . . inappropriate." To reach this conclusion, the Court holds that imposition of the drug tax is *always* punitive, regardless of the nature of the offense or the offender. The consequences of this decision are astounding. The State of Montana—along with about half of the other States—is now precluded from *ever* imposing the drug tax on a person who has been punished for a possessory drug offense. A defendant who is arrested, tried, and convicted for possession of one ounce of marijuana cannot be taxed $100 therefor, even though the State's law enforcement costs in such a case average more than $4,000. See Montana Criminal Justice Expenditures 24. Moreover, presumably the State cannot tax *anyone* for possession of illegal drugs without providing the full panoply of criminal procedure protections found in the Fifth and Sixth Amendments, given the Court's holding that "[t]he proceeding Montana initiated to collect a tax on the possession of drugs was the functional equivalent of a successive criminal prosecution."

Today's decision is entirely unnecessary to preserve individual liberty, because the Excessive Fines Clause is available to protect criminals from governmental overreaching. On the other hand, today's decision will be felt acutely by law-abiding taxpayers, because it will seriously undermine the ability of the State and Federal Governments to collect recompense for the immense costs criminals impose on our society. I therefore respectfully dissent from the Court's unwarranted expansion of our double jeopardy jurisprudence. I would simply vacate the judgment below and remand the case for further proceedings consistent with this opinion and *Halper*.

[JUSTICE SCALIA and THOMAS' dissent is omitted]

NOTES AND QUESTIONS

1. **More on marijuana-related businesses and taxation.** Chapter 15, Issues Pertaining to Marijuana-Related Businesses takes up in more detail the federal government's approach to taxing marijuana related businesses. In brief summary, § 280E of the Internal Revenue Code prevents businesses from deducting what would otherwise be ordinary business expenses from gross income associated with trafficking of a Schedule I substance. That, obviously, includes marijuana, which remains a Schedule I substance. As developed in Chapter 15, participants in the industry have attempted various arguments to challenge the application of § 280E to marijuana businesses in states where they are legal. To date, those challenges have almost universally been unsuccessful. *See, e.g., Olive v. Commissioner,* 792 F. 3d 1146 (9th Cir. 2015). Can you see a perverse effect of applying such a provision to marijuana

businesses in states that have legalized medical or recreational marijuana? What is the remedy?

2.   *Kurth Ranch* and the Court. Who has the best argument in *Kurth Ranch*?

3.   Scholarly reactions to *Kurth Ranch*. The reactions to *Kurth Ranch* were generally unfavorable. As one student author observed,

> [T]he Supreme Court inappropriately expanded the scope of the Double Jeopardy Clause by ignoring the distinction between multiple punishments and prosecutions to compensate for some of the Clause's limitations. This Note then concludes that the Supreme Court did not need to expand double jeopardy protection, because other areas of the Constitution already adequately compensate for these limitations. The Court could have achieved more satisfying and practical results by first acknowledging the limits of Double Jeopardy protection, and then turning to the Excessive Fines Clause for additional protection.

John Hildy, *Fifth Amendment—Double Jeopardy and the Dangerous Drug Tax,* 85 J. Crim. L. & Criminology 936, 936–37 (1995).

Another writer concluded that the Court's technical analysis might lead "to a victory that might enable a drug dealer to get back on the street" if participants in the system are not aware of its complexities. Travis Dayhuff, *McMullin's Double Jeopardy Protection May be a Casualty of South Carolina's War on Drugs,* 48 S.C.L. Rev. 405, 413 (1997). Yet another commenter suggested that the Court unwisely swept aside fifty years of precedent that was deferential and narrow to allow taxing of dangerous drugs. James M. Curley, *Expanding Double Jeopardy: Department of Revenue v. Kurth Ranch,* 75 B. U. L. Rev. 505 (1995).

PROBLEM 13-2

Police arrested Defendant for possession of a large amount of marijuana, a second degree felony under state law. Subsequent to his arrest and indictment, but before jeopardy attached in the criminal prosecution, the state comptroller assessed Defendant with a tax of $50,000, based on the amount of marijuana that Defendant possessed, consistent with the state's Controlled Substances Act. Notice of the assessment told Defendant not only that he owed the tax on the marijuana but also that the amount assessed included a late penalty. It also informed him that additional penalties and interest would be assessed if he did not pay in a timely manner. Defendant submitted a check for $100 towards payment of the total tax liability. Defendant has filed a motion for the writ of habeas corpus with the trial court where his criminal case was pending. The basis of his claim was that the criminal prosecution violated his right to be free from double jeopardy. Discuss how the court should rule on his motion.

CHAPTER 14

CIVIL PENALTIES FOR ILLEGAL MARIJUANA POSSESSION AND DISTRIBUTION

■ ■ ■

The previous chapter covered Criminal Penalties for Illegal Marijuana Possession and Distribution. This chapter focuses on civil penalties. Indeed, as you work your way through this material, you will see that those penalties may be substantial, often as detrimental as criminal sanctions. Congress has created hundreds of collateral consequences for marijuana users or offenders.

The first section of this chapter turns to some of the collateral consequences created by Congress. Beyond prison sentences and collateral consequences, marijuana offenders may face additional punishment in the form of asset forfeiture. The second section explores some of the legal issues that may arise in asset forfeiture cases.

A. COLLATERAL CONSEQUENCES

I. PUBLIC HOUSING

FOREST CITY RESIDENTIAL MANAGEMENT, INC. v. BEASLEY

United States District Court, Eastern District of Michigan
71 F.Supp.3d 715 (E.D. Michigan 2014)

COX, J.

This is a declaratory judgment action. Plaintiff Forest City Residential Management, Inc. ("Plaintiff" or "Forest City") filed a Complaint for Declaratory Judgment on October 31, 2013, seeking to have this Court declare that, among other things, Defendants Lashawn Beasley ("Beasley") and Eugene Kenyon ("Kenyon") are not entitled to a reasonable accommodation under the Fair Housing Act and/or Rehabilitation Act to use medical marijuana in their rental units at Plaintiff's Section 8 federally assisted housing facilities.

This matter is before the Court on Defendant Beasley's Motion to Dismiss Pursuant to Federal Rules of Civil Procedure 12(b)(1) and (6) and Plaintiff's Motion for Summary Judgment. The motions have been fully briefed by the parties and the Court heard oral argument on November 13,

2014. For the reasons set forth below, the Court shall DENY Defendant Beasley's Motion to Dismiss and GRANT IN PART and DENY IN PART Plaintiff's Motion for Summary Judgment.

BACKGROUND

A. Procedural Background

Forest City filed this action against Defendants Beasley and Kenyon on October 31, 2013. Beasley, who is represented by counsel, filed an Answer to the Complaint on January 16, 2014. Forest City filed a First Amended Complaint for Declaratory Judgment and Injunctive Relief on February 4, 2014.

Defendant Kenyon has not answered or appeared in this action. On December 11, 2013, Forest City obtained a Clerk's Entry of Default as to Kenyon. Forest City has not yet sought entry of a default judgment as to Kenyon.

* * *

On March 24, 2014, Forest City filed the instant Motion for Summary Judgment. That motion was fully briefed by the parties and oral arguments were scheduled to be heard on October 9, 2014. However, on October 6, 2014, Defendant filed a Motion to Dismiss Pursuant to Fed.R.Civ.P. 12(b)(1) and (6), challenging Plaintiff's standing to maintain this suit, arguing that the Court should decline to intervene in what she characterizes as a landlord-tenant issue, and arguing that Plaintiff has failed to state a claim upon which relief may be granted. The motion cut-off date in this case was March 24, 2014. Nonetheless, because standing is an issue touching upon subject matter jurisdiction and can be raised at any time, the Court found it appropriate to consider Defendant's motion on the merits.

B. Factual Background

The underlying facts of this case are largely undisputed.

Beasley was diagnosed with Multiple Sclerosis in April of 2009. (Her income is Supplemental Security Income ("SSI") based on her disability of Multiple Sclerosis.)

Beasley's physician prescribed medicinal marijuana to help with her symptoms of Multiple Sclerosis. Beasley obtained a Medical Marijuana card issued by the State of Michigan pursuant to the Michigan Medical Marihuana Act.

Forest City is a management company that manages apartment complexes. Beasley entered into a Lease Agreement with Forest City on February 6, 2013 to occupy a townhome apartment at Plymouth Square Village in the City of Detroit.

Plymouth Square is a project-based, Section 8, federally assisted housing complex. Plymouth Square receives a portion of Beasley's monthly rent in the form of a subsidy from the United States Department of Housing and Urban Development ("HUD") via the Michigan State Housing and Development Authority.

The Lease Agreement and Lease Addendum are regulated by HUD. The Lease Agreement provides that the landlord, Forest City, "may" terminate the agreement for various reasons, including:

> (4) Drug-related criminal activity engaged in on or near the premises by any Resident, household member, or guest, or any such activity engaged in on the premises by any other person under the Resident's control;
>
> . . . .
>
> (9) If the landlord determines that the Resident, any member of the Resident's household, a guest or another person under the Resident's control has engaged in the criminal activity, regardless of whether the Resident, any member of the Resident's household, a guest or another person under the Resident's control has been arrested or convicted for such activity.

The Lease further states that

> [f]or tenancy terminations involving criminal activity, including drug-related criminal activity, below are regulatory definitions in 24 Code of Federal Regulations Part 5, Subpart I:
>
> **Drug** means a controlled substances [sic] as defined in section 102 of the Controlled Substances Act
>
> **Drug-related criminal activity** means the illegal manufacture, sale, distribution, or use of a drug, or the possession of a drug with intent to manufacture, sell, distribute or use the drug (including commercial drug crimes).

On the same day that Beasley executed her lease, she also signed a "Tenancy Termination Addendum For HUD Housing Programs," which stated that the landlord "may" terminate the lease agreement for various reasons, including the following reasons that Beasley acknowledged by placing her initials next to them:

> 4. *Drug-related criminal activity engaged in or near the premises by any tenant,* household member, or guest, or any such activity engaged in on the premises by any other person under the tenant's control, pursuant to 24 CFR Section 5.858; or
>
> 5. *A household member is illegally using a drug* or it is determined that a pattern of illegal use of a drug interferes with

the health, safety, or right to peaceful enjoyment of the premises by other residents, pursuant to 24 CFR Section 5.858

In July of 2013, Forest City filed a Complaint in the 36th District Court, Wayne County, Michigan, seeking to terminate Beasley's tenancy. In responding to the Complaint, Beasley stated that she has Multiple Sclerosis, and that her physician had prescribed medical marijuana to help with her symptoms. Beasley requested, in connection with that proceeding, that Forest City grant her a reasonable accommodation under the Fair Housing Act and allow her to use medical marijuana in her own rental unit.

Thereafter, Forest City dismissed the state court action and filed this declaratory action in this court. Plaintiff Forest City now seeks Summary Judgment in its favor. Defendant Beasley has filed a response in opposition to Plaintiff's motion, and Plaintiff has replied.

Defendant has also moved for dismissal of this action on the following bases: 1) that Plaintiff lacks standing because it has suffered no injury in fact; 2) that this Court should decline to exercise jurisdiction to avoid involvement in a state-law landlord-tenant dispute; and 3) Plaintiff has failed to state a claim upon which relief may be granted. Plaintiff filed a response to Defendant's motion and Defendant has replied.

ANALYSIS

I. Should This Court Grant Defendant's Motion to Dismiss?

A. Standing

[The court rejected the defendant's motion to dismiss on standing grounds. It found that the complaint alleged sufficient facts to demonstrate standing.]

II. Should This Court Grant Plaintiff's Motion for Summary Judgment?

* * *

A. Does The Federal Controlled Substances Act Preempt The Michigan Medical Marihuana Act?

Plaintiff requests in its First Amended Complaint that this Court declare that the federal Controlled Substances Act preempts the Michigan Medical Marihuana Act.

[The court found that the CSA did not preempt state law. For more on preemption, see Chapter 7, Federal Preemption.]

B. Is Allowing Beasley To Use Medical Marijuana In Her Rental Unit A Reasonable Accommodation Under The FHA Or Section 504 of the Rehabilitation Act?

1. FHA

Section 3604 of the FHA prohibits discrimination in sale or rental of public housing on the basis of disability. It provides, in pertinent part:

As made applicable by section 3603 of this title and except as exempted by sections 3603(b) and 3607 of this title, it shall be unlawful—

(f)(1) To discriminate in the sale or rental, or to otherwise make unavailable or deny, a dwelling to any buyer or renter because of a handicap of—

(A) that buyer or renter,

(B) a person residing in or intending to reside in that dwelling after it is so sold, rented, or made available; or

(C) any person associated with that buyer or renter.

42 U.S.C. § 3604. The FHA further defines discrimination:

(3) For purposes of this subsection, discrimination includes—

(B) a refusal to make reasonable accommodations in rules, policies, practices, or services, when such accommodations may be necessary to afford such person equal opportunity to use and enjoy a dwelling . . . .

42 U.S.C. § 3604(f)(3)(B).

An FHA reasonable-accommodation plaintiff must establish that the proposed modification is both reasonable and necessary. "[T]he crux of a reasonable-accommodation . . . claim typically will be the question of reasonableness." *Hollis v. Chestnut Bend Homeowners Ass'n,* 760 F.3d 531, 541 (6th Cir. 2014). An accommodation is reasonable when it imposes "no fundamental alteration in the nature of a program" or "undue financial and administrative burdens." *Smith & Lee Assocs., Inc. v. City of Taylor,* 102 F.3d 781, 795 (6th Cir. 1996). An accommodation is necessary if, "but for the requested accommodation, [the plaintiff] 'likely will be denied an equal opportunity to enjoy the housing of [his or her] choice.' " *Hollis,* 760 F.3d at 541.

In addition to establishing reasonableness and necessity, the plaintiff must also prove "that she suffers from a disability, that she requested an accommodation . . ., that the defendant housing provider refused to make the accommodation . . . and that the defendant knew or should have known of the disability at the time of the refusal." *Hollis,* 760 F.3d at 540.

Beasley argues that her request for permission to use medical marijuana in her apartment is reasonable under the FHA because it poses no undue burden on Plaintiff. Beasley also argues that her request does not require a fundamental alteration to Plaintiff's existing policies, practices, or procedures.

Plaintiff maintains that Beasley's request is unreasonable because it would amount to a fundamental alteration in the nature of its operations. In support of its position, Plaintiff has submitted a HUD memorandum that was drafted by HUD's general counsel. Plaintiff argues that this Court must give the HUD memorandum substantial deference under *Chevron, U.S.A., Inc. v. Natural Res. Def. Council, Inc.*, 467 U.S. 837 (1984).

* * *

Congress has not addressed the exact issue in this case. However, because the HUD memorandum is not a statute, regulation, or formal judicial interpretation, the Court finds that it does not have the force of law. Accordingly, *Chevron* deference is inapplicable. The issue then becomes whether the HUD memorandum is persuasive, and therefore worthy of *Skidmore* deference.

The Court shall, per *Skidmore*, give weight to HUD's conclusion that a medical marijuana accommodation is not reasonable under the Fair Housing Act because it would constitute a fundamental alteration in the nature of a PHA or owner's operations. HUD General Counsel's memorandum thoroughly discusses the legal implications of state-sanctioned medical marijuana use under the FHA, the ADA, and section 504 of the Rehabilitation Act. The HUD memorandum contains citations to both statutes and case law, and the writer's reasoning is logically and legally sound. Even though the HUD memorandum does not have the force of law, HUD does have congressionally delegated authority to issue regulations implementing and interpreting the FHA. Based on the foregoing, the Court shall give weight to HUD's opinion regarding medical marijuana and the FHA.

ii. Would Requiring Reasonable Accommodation of Medical Marijuana Use In Federally Assisted Housing Fundamentally Alter The Nature Of The Program?

Plaintiff manages Plymouth Square Village, a project-based Section 8 federally subsidized housing community, where Beasley currently rents a townhome. "The purpose of the Section 8 program is to provide low-income families with decent, safe and sanitary rental housing through the use of a system of housing assistance payments." 24 C.F.R. § 880.101. Congress has further clarified that "the Federal Government has a duty to provide public and other federally assisted low-income housing that is decent, safe, and *free from illegal drugs* . . . ." 42 U.S.C. § 11901(1).

In furtherance of this policy statement, Congress mandates that the owner of federally assisted housing must prohibit admission of a household if it is determined that any household member is currently engaging in illegal use of a drug. A household must also be denied admission to federally assisted housing if the owner has reasonable cause to believe that a household's illegal use of drugs "may interfere with the health, safety, or right to peaceful enjoyment of the premises by other residents." 24 C.F.R. § 5.854(b)(2).

Under federal law, marijuana is a Schedule I controlled substance with "no currently accepted medical use in treatment in the United States." 21 U.S.C. § 812(b)(1). As previously discussed in section I, the federal Controlled Substances Act impliedly preempts the MMMA. Accordingly, to require Plaintiff to grant Defendant a reasonable accommodation to use marijuana would be to require Plaintiff to violate federal law. Such a requirement would fundamentally alter the nature of Plaintiff's operation by thwarting Congress's mission to provide drug-free federally assisted housing.

Considering Congress's clear policy initiative behind its Section 8 federally assisted housing program, and giving due *Skidmore* deference to HUD's interpretation of the FHA, the Court shall GRANT IN PART Plaintiff's Motion for Summary Judgment because the Court finds that Defendant is not entitled to a reasonable accommodation for medical marijuana use under the FHA.

2.   Section 504 of the Rehabilitation Act of 1973

Initially, the Court notes that Plaintiff, in its First Amended Complaint, does not request a declaration regarding whether Defendant is entitled to a reasonable accommodation under section 504 of the Rehabilitation Act. Nor has Defendant requested accommodation under the Rehabilitation Act in her Answer. Therefore, it is unclear whether this issue is properly before the Court for consideration.

Nevertheless, Plaintiff raised the issue in its Motion and the Court shall address it for that reason. Plaintiff argues that Defendant is not entitled to a reasonable accommodation under section 504 of the Rehabilitation Act because "illegal drug users are prohibited from the definition" of a disabled individual.

Beasley appears to agree with Forest City that she is not entitled, as a reasonable accommodation under the Rehabilitation Act, to use medical marijuana in her apartment.

Furthermore, Plaintiff's analysis is correct. Under the Rehabilitation Act of 1973, "[n]o otherwise qualified individual with a disability in the United States, as defined in section 705(20) of this title shall, solely by reason of her or his disability, be excluded from participation in, be denied the benefits of, or be subject to discrimination under any program or activity received Federal financial assistance . . . ." 29 U.S.C. § 794(a). It appears undisputed that Plaintiff is a recipient of federal funds and, thus, subject to the Rehabilitation Act's requirements.

For purposes of the Rehabilitation Act, "the term 'disability' means, with respect to an individual, a physical or mental impairment that substantially limits one or more major life activities of such individual . . . ." 29 U.S.C. § 705(20)(B); 42 U.S.C. § 12102(1)(A). However, "for purposes of [section 794], the term 'individual with a disability' does not include an individual who is currently engaging in the illegal use of drugs, when a covered entity acts on the basis of such use." 29 U.S.C. § 705(20)(C)(i).

Therefore, the Court finds, and Defendant appears to agree, that Defendant is not a qualified individual with a disability under section 504 of the Rehabilitation Act because she uses an illegal drug (according to federal law) and Plaintiff is, or is attempting to, discriminate against her on the basis of such drug use.

Therefore, the Court finds that Defendant is not entitled to a reasonable accommodation to use medical marijuana under section 504 of the Rehabilitation Act.

C.   May Plaintiff Evict Defendant For Her Use Of Medical Marijuana?

Plaintiff, in its First Amended Complaint, requests that this Court declare that "the use, possession, manufacture, sale or distribution of marijuana in violation of the Controlled Substances Act is cause for Plaintiff to evict the tenants in violation thereof and such conduct is not exempted by the Michigan Medical Marijuana Act."

The Court shall decline to issue such a declaration. To do so would, in this Court's view, go beyond what is necessary to resolve the core dispute in this case—the core dispute being whether the Fair Housing Act requires Plaintiff to reasonably accommodate Defendant's use of state-sanctioned medical marijuana. The state courts have jurisdiction to determine whether, and under what circumstances, a landlord may evict a tenant for violation of lease provisions. This Court finds it prudent to leave eviction determinations to the sound discretion of those state courts. Therefore, the Court shall decline to exercise its jurisdiction over this portion of Plaintiff's First Amended Complaint and DISMISS Plaintiff's First Amended Complaint to the extent that it seeks a declaration regarding its ability to evict Defendant.

D.   Should The Court Permanently Enjoin Defendant From Smoking Marijuana On Plaintiff's Premises?

Plaintiff requests that this Court issue a permanent injunction enjoining Defendant from using marijuana on its property. To establish its entitlement to a permanent injunction, Plaintiff must show "(1) that it has suffered an irreparable injury; (2) that remedies available at law, such as monetary damages, are inadequate to compensate for that injury; (3) that, considering the balance of hardships between the plaintiff and defendant, a remedy in equity is warranted; and (4) that the public interest would not be disserved by a permanent injunction." *eBay Inc. v. MercExchange, L.L.C.*, 547 U.S. 388, 391 (2006). Plaintiff asserts, in a conclusory fashion, that all four factors are met.

The Court finds that Plaintiff has failed to establish all four elements necessary for the Court to issue a permanent injunction in this case. Therefore, the Court shall DENY Plaintiff's Motion for Summary Judgment to the extent that Plaintiff seeks a permanent injunction prohibiting Defendant from smoking marijuana on its premises.

CONCLUSION

Based on the foregoing, the Court shall:

1) DENY Defendant's Motion To Dismiss,

2) GRANT IN PART Plaintiff's Motion for Summary Judgment, to the extent that the Court hereby DECLARES that

    A) The Controlled Substances Act, 21 U.S.C. § 801 *et seq.*, preempts the Michigan Medical Marihuana Act, *M.C.L. § 333.26421 et seq.*, and

    B) The Fair Housing Act does not require Plaintiff to grant Defendant a reasonable accommodation to use medical marijuana in its federally-assisted housing complexes;

3) DENY Plaintiff's Motion for Summary Judgment in all other respects; and

4) DECLINE TO EXERCISE JURISDICTION and DISMISS Plaintiff's First Amended Complaint to the extent that Plaintiff seeks a declaration "[t]hat the use, possession, manufacture, sale or distribution of marihuana in violation of the controlled Substances Act is cause for Plaintiff to evict the tenants in violation thereof."

IT IS SO ORDERED.

NOTES AND QUESTIONS

1. **More on landlord-tenant issues.** Chapter 15, Issues Pertaining to Marijuana-Related Businesses, deals in more depth with issues relating to landlord-tenant issues. Conflicts between individuals who are complying with state law and property owners have proliferated in states where marijuana is lawful for medical and recreational use. Here, the focus is on governmental power to impose collateral consequences on marijuana offenders.

2.   Equities and the letter of the law. Are the facts in the lead case sympathetic? Increased interest in medical marijuana has brought to national attention many sympathetic patients who claim significant benefit from using marijuana medicinally. For example, CNN did a three part series on "Weed," including a powerful segment about young children whose seizures could be controlled effectively only through the use of a cannabis based product. See, WEED, https://www.youtube.com/watch?v=PRLYV0_6zY8. In light of cases like those portrayed in WEED, is the court's opinion in the lead case in error?

3.   Winners and losers in *Forest City*. Who won in *Forest City*? The plaintiff won on some of the key legal issues. But, of course, the court also refused to issue a declaration that a violation of federal marijuana law was a cause for plaintiff to evict tenants and to rule whether it would be a violation of state law.

4.   Public housing and drug laws. The Supreme Court decided a related question in *Dep't of Housing v. Rucker,* 535 U.S. 125 (2002). There, as described below, the issue was whether a person in public housing could be evicted absent a showing that the tenant knew or should have known that members of the household were involved in drug activity. More precisely, the Court framed the issue as follows:

> With drug dealers "increasingly imposing a reign of terror on public and other federally assisted low-income housing tenants," Congress passed the Anti-Drug Abuse Act of 1988. § 5122, 102 Stat. 4301, 42 U.S.C. § 11901(3) (1994 ed.). The Act, as later amended, provides that each "public housing agency shall utilize leases which . . . provide that any criminal activity that threatens the health, safety, or right to peaceful enjoyment of the premises by other tenants or any drug-related criminal activity on or off such premises, engaged in by a public housing tenant, any member of the tenant's household, or any guest or other person under the tenant's control, shall be cause for termination of tenancy." 42 U.S.C. § 1437d(*l*)(6) (1994 ed., Supp. V). Petitioners say that this statute requires lease terms that allow a local public housing authority to evict a tenant when a member of the tenant's household or a guest engages in drug-related criminal activity, regardless of whether the tenant knew, or had reason to know, of that activity. Respondents say it does not.

Petitioners proceeded in state court against the respondents, leaseholders in public housing. The petitioners sought orders of eviction because members of their households were found to have been involved in drug activity, including, in one instance, smoking marijuana in the parking lot of the housing unit. The Supreme Court rejected the Ninth Circuit's *en banc* decision, which found for petitioners and held that the government had to make some kind of showing of scienter. The Supreme Court disagreed, based on statutory language and its view that due process required only notice of the regulation and an opportunity to dispute whether the lease terms were violated. 535 U.S. at 135–36.

5. **Felons.** Congress and state legislatures have historically imposed various disabilities on offenders convicted of felonies. Those include the denial of the right to vote, to hold public office, to serve on a jury, to serve in the military, and to receive a variety of federal benefits. But, especially during the height of the War on Drugs, Congress has singled out drug convictions for special onerous treatment. Congress has embedded such consequences in thousands of federal statutes. "These include denial of federal benefits such as grants, contracts, and licenses." Mark K. Osbeck and Howard Bromberg, Marijuana Law in a Nutshell (West Academic Pub. 2017) at 109. Why are such collateral consequences justified? In light of changing views on cannabis, are those policy justifications still valid? What would move Congress to reform the many laws creating such disabilities?

II. IMMIGRATION

MONCRIEFFE V. HOLDER

United States Supreme Court
569 U.S. 184 (2013)

SOTOMAYOR, J.

The Immigration and Nationality Act (INA), 66 Stat. 163, 8 U.S.C. § 1101 *et seq.,* provides that a noncitizen who has been convicted of an "aggravated felony" may be deported from this country. The INA also prohibits the Attorney General from granting discretionary relief from removal to an aggravated felon, no matter how compelling his case. Among the crimes that are classified as aggravated felonies, and thus lead to these harsh consequences, are illicit drug trafficking offenses. We must decide whether this category includes a state criminal statute that extends to the social sharing of a small amount of marijuana. We hold it does not.

I

A

The INA allows the Government to deport various classes of noncitizens, such as those who overstay their visas, and those who are convicted of certain crimes while in the United States, including drug offenses. Ordinarily, when a noncitizen is found to be deportable on one of these grounds, he may ask the Attorney General for certain forms of discretionary relief from removal, like asylum (if he has a well-founded fear of persecution in his home country) and cancellation of removal (if, among other things, he has been lawfully present in the United States for a number of years). But if a noncitizen has been convicted of one of a narrower set of crimes classified as "aggravated felonies," then he is not only deportable, § 1227(a)(2)(A)(iii), but also ineligible for these discretionary forms of relief. See §§ 1158(b)(2)(A)(ii), (B)(i); §§ 1229b(a)(3), (b)(1)(C).

The INA defines "aggravated felony" to include a host of offenses. § 1101(a)(43). Among them is "illicit trafficking in a controlled substance." § 1101(a)(43)(B). This general term is not defined, but the INA states that it "includ[es] a drug trafficking crime (as defined in section 924(c) of title 18)." *Ibid.* In turn, 18 U.S.C. § 924(c)(2) defines "drug trafficking crime" to mean "any felony punishable under the Controlled Substances Act," or two other statutes not relevant here. The chain of definitions ends with § 3559(a)(5), which provides that a "felony" is an offense for which the "maximum term of imprisonment authorized" is "more than one year." The upshot is that a noncitizen's conviction of an offense that the Controlled Substances Act (CSA) makes punishable by more than one year's imprisonment will be counted as an "aggravated felony" for immigration purposes. A conviction under either state or federal law may qualify, but a "state offense constitutes a 'felony punishable under the Controlled Substances Act' only if it proscribes conduct punishable as a felony under that federal law." *Lopez v. Gonzales,* 549 U.S. 47, 60, 127 S.Ct. 625 (2006).

B

Petitioner Adrian Moncrieffe is a Jamaican citizen who came to the United States legally in 1984, when he was three. During a 2007 traffic stop, police found 1.3 grams of marijuana in his car. This is the equivalent of about two or three marijuana cigarettes. Moncrieffe pleaded guilty to possession of marijuana with intent to distribute, a violation of Ga.Code Ann. § 16–13–30(j)(1) (2007). Under a Georgia statute providing more lenient treatment to first-time offenders, § 42–8–60(a) (1997), the trial court withheld entering a judgment of conviction or imposing any term of imprisonment, and instead required that Moncrieffe complete five years of probation, after which his charge will be expunged altogether.

Alleging that this Georgia conviction constituted an aggravated felony, the Federal Government sought to deport Moncrieffe. The Government reasoned that possession of marijuana with intent to distribute is an offense under the CSA, 21 U.S.C. § 841(a), punishable by up to five years' imprisonment, § 841(b)(1)(D), and thus an aggravated felony. An Immigration Judge agreed and ordered Moncrieffe removed. The Board of Immigration Appeals (BIA) affirmed that conclusion on appeal.

The Court of Appeals denied Moncrieffe's petition for review. The court rejected Moncrieffe's reliance upon § 841(b)(4), a provision that, in effect, makes marijuana distribution punishable only as a misdemeanor if the offense involves a small amount of marijuana for no remuneration. It held that in a federal criminal prosecution, "the default sentencing range for a marijuana distribution offense is the CSA's felony provision, § 841(b)(1)(D), rather than the misdemeanor provision." 662 F.3d 387, 392 (C.A.5 2011). Because Moncrieffe's Georgia offense penalized possession of marijuana with intent to distribute, the court concluded that it was "equivalent to a federal felony." *Ibid.*

We granted certiorari, to resolve a conflict among the Courts of Appeals with respect to whether a conviction under a statute that criminalizes conduct described by both § 841's felony provision and its misdemeanor provision, such as a statute that punishes all marijuana distribution without regard to the amount or remuneration, is a conviction for an offense that "proscribes conduct punishable as a felony under" the CSA. *Lopez,* 549 U.S., at 60. We now reverse.

II

A

When the Government alleges that a state conviction qualifies as an "aggravated felony" under the INA, we generally employ a "categorical approach" to determine whether the state offense is comparable to an offense listed in the INA. See, *e.g., Nijhawan v. Holder,* 557 U.S. 29, 33–38 (2009); *Gonzales v. Duenas-Alvarez,* 549 U.S. 183, 185–187 (2007). Under this approach we look "not to the facts of the particular prior case," but instead to whether "the state statute defining the crime of conviction" categorically fits within the "generic" federal definition of a corresponding aggravated felony. *Id.,* at 186. By "generic," we mean the offenses must be viewed in the abstract, to see whether the state statute shares the nature of the federal offense that serves as a point of comparison. Accordingly, a state offense is a categorical match with a generic federal offense only if a conviction of the state offense " 'necessarily' involved . . . facts equating to [the] generic [federal offense]." *Shepard v. United States,* 544 U.S. 13, 24 (2005) (plurality opinion). Whether the noncitizen's actual conduct involved such facts "is quite irrelevant." *United States ex rel. Guarino v. Uhl,* 107 F.2d 399, 400 (C.A.2 1939) (L. Hand, J.).

Because we examine what the state conviction necessarily involved, not the facts underlying the case, we must presume that the conviction "rested upon [nothing] more than the least of th[e] acts" criminalized, and then determine whether even those acts are encompassed by the generic federal offense. *Johnson v. United States,* 559 U.S. 133, 137 (2010). But this rule is not without qualification. First, our cases have addressed state statutes that contain several different crimes, each described separately, and we have held that a court may determine which particular offense the noncitizen was convicted of by examining the charging document and jury instructions, or in the case of a guilty plea, the plea agreement, plea colloquy, or " 'some comparable judicial record' of the factual basis for the plea." *Nijhawan,* 557 U.S., at 35. Second, our focus on the minimum conduct criminalized by the state statute is not an invitation to apply "legal imagination" to the state offense; there must be "a realistic probability, not a theoretical possibility, that the State would apply its statute to conduct that falls outside the generic definition of a crime." *Duenas-Alvarez,* 549 U.S., at 193.

* * *

B

The aggravated felony at issue here, "illicit trafficking in a controlled substance," is a "generic crim[e]." *Nijhawan,* 557 U.S., at 37. So the categorical approach applies. As we have explained, this aggravated felony encompasses all state offenses that "proscrib[e] conduct punishable as a felony under [the CSA]." *Lopez,* 549 U.S., at 60. In other words, to satisfy the categorical approach, a state drug offense must meet two conditions: It must "necessarily" proscribe conduct that is an offense under the CSA, and the CSA must "necessarily" prescribe felony punishment for that conduct.

Moncrieffe was convicted under a Georgia statute that makes it a crime to "possess, have under [one's] control, manufacture, deliver, distribute, dispense, administer, purchase, sell, or possess with intent to distribute marijuana." Ga.Code Ann. § 16–13–30(j)(1). We know from his plea agreement that Moncrieffe was convicted of the last of these offenses. We therefore must determine whether possession of marijuana with intent to distribute is "necessarily" conduct punishable as a felony under the CSA.

We begin with the relevant conduct criminalized by the CSA. There is no question that it is a federal crime to "possess with intent to . . . distribute . . . a controlled substance," 21 U.S.C. § 841(a)(1), one of which is marijuana, § 812(c). So far, the state and federal provisions correspond. But this is not enough, because the generically defined federal crime is "any felony punishable under the Controlled Substances Act," 18 U.S.C. § 924(c)(2), not just any "offense under the CSA." Thus we must look to what punishment the CSA imposes for this offense.

Section 841 is divided into two subsections that are relevant here: (a), titled "Unlawful acts," which includes the offense just described, and (b), titled "Penalties." Subsection (b) tells us how "any person who violates subsection (a)" shall be punished, depending on the circumstances of his crime (*e.g.,* the type and quantity of controlled substance involved, whether it is a repeat offense). Subsection (b)(1)(D) provides that if a person commits a violation of subsection (a) involving "less than 50 kilograms of marihuana," then "such person shall, except as provided in paragraphs (4) and (5) of this subsection, be sentenced to a term of imprisonment of not more than 5 years," *i.e.,* as a felon. But one of the exceptions is important here. Paragraph (4) provides, "Notwithstanding paragraph (1)(D) of this subsection, any person who violates subsection (a) of this section by distributing a small amount of marihuana for no remuneration shall be treated as" a simple drug possessor, 21 U.S.C. § 844, which for our purposes means as a misdemeanant. These dovetailing provisions create two mutually exclusive categories of punishment for CSA marijuana distribution offenses: one a felony, and one not. The only way to know whether a marijuana distribution offense is "punishable as a felony" under the CSA, *Lopez,* 549 U.S., at 60, is to know whether the conditions described in paragraph (4) are present or absent.

A conviction under the same Georgia statute for "sell[ing]" marijuana, for example, would seem to establish remuneration. The presence of remuneration would mean that paragraph (4) is not implicated, and thus that the conviction is necessarily for conduct punishable as a felony under the CSA (under paragraph (1)(D)). In contrast, the fact of a conviction for possession with intent to distribute marijuana, standing alone, does not reveal whether either remuneration or more than a small amount of marijuana was involved. It is possible neither was; we know that Georgia prosecutes this offense when a defendant possesses only a small amount of marijuana. So Moncrieffe's conviction could correspond to either the CSA felony or the CSA misdemeanor. Ambiguity on this point means that the conviction did not "necessarily" involve facts that correspond to an offense punishable as a felony under the CSA. Under the categorical approach, then, Moncrieffe was not convicted of an aggravated felony.

III

A

The Government advances a different approach that leads to a different result. In its view, § 841(b)(4)'s misdemeanor provision is irrelevant to the categorical analysis because paragraph (4) is merely a "mitigating exception," to the CSA offense, not one of the "elements" of the offense. And because possession with intent to distribute marijuana is "presumptive[ly]" a felony under the CSA, the Government asserts, any state offense with the same elements is presumptively an aggravated felony. *Id.,* at 37. These two contentions are related, and we reject both of them.

First, the Government reads our cases to hold that the categorical approach is concerned only with the "elements" of an offense, so § 841(b)(4) "is not relevant" to the categorical analysis. *Id.,* at 20. It is enough to satisfy the categorical inquiry, the Government suggests, that the "elements" of Moncrieffe's Georgia offense are the same as those of the CSA offense: (1) possession (2) of marijuana (a controlled substance), (3) with intent to distribute it. But that understanding is inconsistent with *Carachuri-Rosendo,* our only decision to address both "elements" and "sentencing factors." There we recognized that when Congress has chosen to define the generic federal offense by reference to punishment, it may be necessary to take account of federal sentencing factors too. In that case the relevant CSA offense was simple possession, which "becomes a 'felony punishable under the [CSA]' only because the sentencing factor of recidivism authorizes additional punishment beyond one year, the criterion for a felony." We therefore called the generic federal offense "recidivist simple possession," even though such a crime is not actually "a separate offense" under the CSA, but rather an " 'amalgam' " of offense elements and sentencing factors.

In other words, not only must the state offense of conviction meet the "elements" of the generic federal offense defined by the INA, but the CSA must punish that offense as a felony. Here, the facts giving rise to the CSA offense establish a crime that may be either a felony or a misdemeanor, depending upon the presence or absence of certain factors that are not themselves elements of the crime. And so to qualify as an aggravated felony, a conviction for the predicate offense must necessarily establish those factors as well.

The Government attempts to distinguish *Carachuri-Rosendo* on the ground that the sentencing factor there was a "narrow" aggravating exception that turned a misdemeanor into a felony, whereas here § 841(b)(4) is a narrow mitigation exception that turns a felony into a misdemeanor. This argument hinges upon the Government's second assertion: that any marijuana distribution conviction is "presumptively" a felony. But that is simply incorrect, and the Government's argument collapses as a result. Marijuana distribution is neither a felony nor a misdemeanor until we know whether the conditions in paragraph (4) attach: Section 841(b)(1)(D) makes the crime punishable by five years' imprisonment "*except* as provided" in paragraph (4), and § 841(b)(4) makes it punishable as a misdemeanor "*[n]otwithstanding* paragraph (1)(D)" when only "a small amount of marihuana for no remuneration" is involved. The CSA's text makes neither provision the default. Rather, each is drafted to be exclusive of the other.

Like the BIA and the Fifth Circuit, the Government believes the felony provision to be the default because, in practice, that is how federal criminal prosecutions for marijuana distribution operate. It is true that every Court of Appeals to have considered the question has held that a defendant is eligible for a 5-year sentence under § 841(b)(1)(D) if the Government proves he possessed marijuana with the intent to distribute it, and that the Government need not negate the § 841(b)(4) factors in each case. Instead, the burden is on the defendant to show that he qualifies for the lesser sentence under § 841(b) (4).

We cannot discount § 841's text, however, which creates no default punishment, in favor of the procedural overlay or burdens of proof that would apply in a hypothetical federal criminal prosecution. In *Carachuri-Rosendo,* we rejected the Fifth Circuit's " 'hypothetical approach,' " which examined whether conduct " 'could have been punished as a felony' 'had [it] been prosecuted in federal court.' " The outcome in a hypothetical prosecution is not the relevant inquiry. Rather, our "more focused, categorical inquiry" is whether the record of conviction of the predicate offense necessarily establishes conduct that the CSA, on its own terms, makes punishable as a felony.

The analogy to a federal prosecution is misplaced for another reason. The Court of Appeals cases the Government cites distinguished between elements and sentencing factors to determine which facts must be proved to a jury, in light of the Sixth Amendment concerns addressed in *Apprendi v. New Jersey,* 530 U.S. 466 (2000). The courts considered which "provision . . . states a complete crime upon the fewest *facts,*" which was significant after *Apprendi* to identify what a jury had to find before a defendant could receive § 841(b)(1)(D)'s maximum 5-year sentence. But those concerns do not apply in this context. Here we consider a "generic" federal offense in the abstract, not an actual federal offense being prosecuted before a jury. Our concern is only which facts the CSA relies upon to distinguish between felonies and misdemeanors, not which facts must be found by a jury as opposed to a judge, nor who has the burden of proving which facts in a federal prosecution.

Because of these differences, we made clear in *Carachuri-Rosendo* that, for purposes of the INA, a generic federal offense may be defined by reference to both " 'elements' in the traditional sense" and sentencing factors. Indeed, the distinction between "elements" and "sentencing factors" did not exist when Congress added illicit drug trafficking to the list of aggravated felonies, Anti-Drug Abuse Act of 1988, 102 Stat. 4469–4470, and most courts at the time understood both § 841(b)(1)(D) and § 841(b)(4) to contain sentencing factors that draw the line between a felony and a misdemeanor. *Carachuri-Rosendo* controls here.

Finally, there is a more fundamental flaw in the Government's approach: It would render even an undisputed misdemeanor an aggravated felony. This is "just what the English language tells us not to expect," and that leaves us "very wary of the Government's position." *Lopez,* 549 U.S., at 54. Consider a conviction under a New York statute that provides, "A person is guilty of criminal sale of marihuana in the fifth degree when he knowingly and unlawfully sells, *without consideration,* [marihuana] of an aggregate weight of *two grams or less*; or one cigarette containing marihuana." N.Y. Penal Law Ann. § 221.35 (West 2008). This statute criminalizes only the distribution of a small amount of marijuana for no remuneration, and so all convictions under the statute would fit within the CSA misdemeanor provision, § 841(b)(4). But the Government would categorically deem a conviction under this statute to be an aggravated felony, because the statute contains the corresponding "elements" of (1) distributing (2) marijuana, and the Government believes all marijuana distribution offenses are punishable as felonies.

The same anomaly would result in the case of a noncitizen convicted of a misdemeanor in federal court under § 841(a) and (b)(4) directly. Even in that case, under the Government's logic, we would need to treat the federal misdemeanor conviction as an aggravated felony, because the conviction establishes elements of an offense that is presumptively a felony. This cannot be. "We cannot imagine that Congress took the trouble to incorporate its own statutory scheme of felonies and misdemeanors," only to have courts presume felony treatment and ignore the very factors that distinguish felonies from misdemeanors. *Lopez,* 549 U.S., at 58.

B

Recognizing that its approach leads to consequences Congress could not have intended, the Government hedges its argument by proposing a remedy: Noncitizens should be given an opportunity during immigration proceedings to demonstrate that their predicate marijuana distribution convictions involved only a small amount of marijuana and no remuneration, just as a federal criminal defendant could do at sentencing. This is the procedure adopted by the BIA in *Matter of Castro Rodriguez,* 25 I. & N. Dec. 698, 702 (2012), and endorsed by Justice ALITO's dissent, *post,* at 1701–1702.

This solution is entirely inconsistent with both the INA's text and the categorical approach. As noted, the relevant INA provisions ask what the noncitizen was "convicted of," not what he did, and the inquiry in immigration proceedings is limited accordingly. 8 U.S.C. §§ 1227(a)(2)(A)(iii), 1229b(a)(3); see *Carachuri-Rosendo,* 560 U.S., at ___. The Government cites no statutory authority for such case-specific factfinding in immigration court, and none is apparent in the INA. Indeed, the Government's main categorical argument would seem to preclude this inquiry: If the Government were correct that "the fact of a marijuana-distribution conviction *alone* constitutes a CSA felony," then all marijuana distribution convictions would categorically be convictions of the drug trafficking aggravated felony, mandatory deportation would follow under the statute, and there would be no room for the Government's follow-on factfinding procedure. The Government cannot have it both ways.

Moreover, the procedure the Government envisions would require precisely the sort of *post hoc* investigation into the facts of predicate offenses that we have long deemed undesirable. The categorical approach serves "practical" purposes: It promotes judicial and administrative efficiency by precluding the relitigation of past convictions in minitrials conducted long after the fact. Yet the Government's approach would have our Nation's overburdened immigration courts entertain and weigh testimony from, for example, the friend of a noncitizen who may have shared a marijuana cigarette with him at a party, or the local police officer who recalls to the contrary that cash traded hands. And, as a result, two noncitizens, each "convicted of" the same offense, might obtain different aggravated felony determinations depending on what evidence remains available or how it is perceived by an individual immigration judge. The categorical approach was designed to avoid this "potential unfairness." *Taylor,* 495 U.S., at 601.

Furthermore, the minitrials the Government proposes would be possible only if the noncitizen could locate witnesses years after the fact, notwithstanding that during removal proceedings noncitizens are not guaranteed legal representation and are often subject to mandatory detention, § 1226(c)(1)(B), where they have little ability to collect evidence. A noncitizen in removal proceedings is not at all similarly situated to a defendant in a federal criminal prosecution. The Government's suggestion that the CSA's procedures could readily be replicated in immigration proceedings is therefore misplaced.

The Government defends its proposed immigration court proceedings as "a subsequent step *outside the categorical approach* in light of Section 841(b)(4)'s 'circumstance-specific' nature." This argument rests upon *Nijhawan,* in which we considered another aggravated felony, "an offense that . . . involves fraud or deceit in which the loss to the victim or victims exceeds $10,000." 8 U.S.C. § 1101(a)(43)(M) (i). We held that the $10,000 threshold was not to be applied categorically as a required component of a generic offense, but instead called for a "circumstance-specific approach" that allows for an examination, in immigration court, of the "particular circumstances in which an offender committed the crime on a particular occasion." The Government suggests the § 841(b)(4) factors are like the monetary threshold, and thus similarly amenable to a circumstance-specific inquiry.

We explained in *Nijhawan,* however, that unlike the provision there, "illicit trafficking in a controlled substance" is a "generic crim[e]" to which the categorical approach applies, not a circumstance-specific provision. That distinction is evident in the structure of the INA. The monetary threshold is a limitation, written into the INA itself, on the scope of the aggravated felony for fraud. And the monetary threshold is set off by the words "in which," which calls for a circumstance-specific examination of "the conduct involved 'in' the commission of the offense of conviction." *Nijhawan,* 557 U.S., at 39. Locating this exception in the INA proper suggests an intent to have the relevant facts found in immigration proceedings. But where, as here, the INA incorporates other criminal statutes wholesale, we have held it "must refer to generic crimes," to which the categorical approach applies. *Id.,* at 37.

Finally, the Government suggests that the immigration court's task would not be so daunting in some cases, such as those in which a noncitizen was convicted under the New York statute previously discussed or convicted directly under § 841(b)(4). True, in those cases, the record of conviction might reveal on its face that the predicate offense was punishable only as a misdemeanor. But most States do not have stand-alone offenses for the social sharing of marijuana, so minitrials concerning convictions from the other States, such as Georgia, would be inevitable. The Government suggests that even in these other States, the record of conviction may often address the § 841(b)(4) factors, because noncitizens "will be advised of the immigration consequences of a conviction," as defense counsel is required to do under *Padilla v. Kentucky,* 559 U.S. 356

(2010), and as a result counsel can build an appropriate record when the facts are fresh. Even assuming defense counsel "will" do something simply because it is required of effective counsel (an assumption experience does not always bear out), this argument is unavailing because there is no reason to believe that state courts will regularly or uniformly admit evidence going to facts, such as remuneration, that are irrelevant to the offense charged.

In short, to avoid the absurd consequences that would flow from the Government's narrow understanding of the categorical approach, the Government proposes a solution that largely undermines the categorical approach. That the only cure is worse than the disease suggests the Government is simply wrong.

C

The Government fears the consequences of our decision, but its concerns are exaggerated. The Government observes that, like Georgia, about half the States criminalize marijuana distribution through statutes that do not require remuneration or any minimum quantity of marijuana. As a result, the Government contends, noncitizens convicted of marijuana distribution offenses in those States will avoid "aggravated felony" determinations, purely because their convictions do not resolve whether their offenses involved federal felony conduct or misdemeanor conduct, even though many (if not most) prosecutions involve either remuneration or larger amounts of marijuana (or both).

Escaping aggravated felony treatment does not mean escaping deportation, though. It means only avoiding mandatory removal. Any marijuana distribution offense, even a misdemeanor, will still render a noncitizen deportable as a controlled substances offender. At that point, having been found not to be an aggravated felon, the noncitizen may seek relief from removal such as asylum or cancellation of removal, assuming he satisfies the other eligibility criteria. But those forms of relief are discretionary. The Attorney General may, in his discretion, deny relief if he finds that the noncitizen is actually a member of one "of the world's most dangerous drug cartels," just as he may deny relief if he concludes the negative equities outweigh the positive equities of the noncitizen's case for other reasons. As a result, "to the extent that our rejection of the Government's broad understanding of the scope of 'aggravated felony' may have any practical effect on policing our Nation's borders, it is a limited one."

In any event, serious drug traffickers may be adjudicated aggravated felons regardless, because they will likely be convicted under greater "trafficking" offenses that necessarily establish that more than a small amount of marijuana was involved. Of course, some offenders' conduct will fall between § 841(b)(4) conduct and the more serious conduct required to trigger a "trafficking" statute. Those offenders may avoid aggravated felony status by operation of the categorical approach. But the Government's objection to that underinclusive result is little more than an attack on the categorical approach itself. We prefer this degree of imperfection to the heavy burden of relitigating old prosecutions. And we err on the side of underinclusiveness because ambiguity in criminal statutes referenced by the INA must be construed in the noncitizen's favor.

* * *

This is the third time in seven years that we have considered whether the Government has properly characterized a low-level drug offense as "illicit trafficking in a controlled substance," and thus an "aggravated felony." Once again we hold that the Government's approach defies "the 'commonsense conception' " of these terms. *Carachuri-Rosendo,* 560 U.S., at ___. Sharing a small amount of marijuana for no remuneration, let alone possession with intent to do so, "does not fit easily into the 'everyday understanding' " of "trafficking," which " 'ordinarily . . . means some sort of commercial dealing.' " *Carachuri-Rosendo,* 560 U.S., at ___. Nor is it sensible that a state statute that criminalizes conduct that the CSA treats as a misdemeanor should be designated an "aggravated felony." We hold that it may not be. If a noncitizen's conviction for a marijuana distribution offense fails to establish that the offense involved either remuneration or more than a small amount of marijuana, the conviction is not for an aggravated felony under the INA. The contrary judgment of the Court of Appeals is reversed, and the case is remanded for further proceedings consistent with this opinion.

It is so ordered.

[THOMAS, J. and ALITO, J. filed dissenting opinions.]

* * *

NOTES AND QUESTIONS

1. **Marijuana and deportation.** In 2015, according to a Human Rights Watch report, the United States deported over 50,000 people for marijuana offenses between 2007 and 2012. The increased attention on immigration and deportation is likely to increase those numbers.

2. *Carachuri-Rosendo.* In *Moncrieffe,* the Court discussed its earlier decision in *Carachuri-Rosendo* extensively. The facts there are quite compelling:

> Petitioner, a lawful permanent resident of the United States, faced deportation after committing two misdemeanor drug offenses in Texas. For the first, possession of a small amount of marijuana, he received 20 days in jail. For the second, possession without a prescription of one antianxiety tablet, he received 10 days. Texas law, like federal law, authorized a sentencing enhancement if the State proved that petitioner had been previously convicted of a similar

offense, but Texas did not seek such an enhancement here. After the second conviction, the Federal Government initiated removal proceedings. Petitioner conceded that he was removable, but claimed that he was eligible for discretionary cancellation of removal under the Immigration and Nationality Act (INA) because he had not been convicted of any "aggravated felony," 8 U.S.C. § 1229b(a)(3). Section 1101(a)(43)(B) defines that term to include, *inter alia,* "illicit trafficking in a controlled substance . . . including a drug trafficking crime" as defined in 18 U.S.C. § 924(c), which, in turn, defines a "drug trafficking crime" as a "felony punishable under," *inter alia,* "the Controlled Substances Act (21 U.S.C. 801 et seq.)." A felony is a crime for which the "maximum term of imprisonment authorized" is "more than one year." § 3559(a). Simple possession offenses are ordinarily misdemeanors punishable with shorter sentences, but a conviction "after a prior conviction under this subchapter [or] the law of any State . . . has become final," 21 U.S.C. § 844(a)—a "recidivist" simple possession offense—is "punishable" as a "felony" under § 924(c)(2) and subject to a 2-year sentence. Only this "recidivist" simple possession category might be an "aggravated felony" under 8 U.S.C. § 1101(a)(43). A prosecutor must charge the existence of the prior conviction. See 21 U.S.C. § 851(a)(1). Notice and an opportunity to challenge its validity, §§ 851(b)–(c), are mandatory prerequisites to obtaining a punishment based on the fact of the prior conviction and necessary prerequisites to "authorize" a felony punishment, 18 U.S.C. § 3559(a), for the simple possession offense at issue.

3.   A single possession offense and INS. Perhaps not surprisingly, the INS has created an exception to its rules governing deportability for a "single offense involving possession of one's own use of 30 grams or less of marijuana." 8 U.S.C. § 1227(a)(2)(B)(i). Can you figure out the policy supporting such an exception?

4.   Guilty pleas and knowledge of collateral consequences. When a defendant pleads guilty to a criminal charge, the court typically must determine if the defendant is aware of the consequences of the guilty plea. For example, the defendant must know that she is giving up the right to a trial. Historically, a defendant did not have to know of collateral consequences. In *Padilla v. Kentucky,* 559 U.S. 356 (2010), the Supreme Court dealt with a related question: is a defense attorney incompetent if she fails to inform her client that his guilty plea will lead to his deportation from the United States? The Court held as follows: "We agree with Padilla that constitutionally competent counsel would have advised him that his conviction for drug distribution made him subject to automatic deportation. Whether he is entitled to relief depends on whether he has been prejudiced, a matter that we do not address." 559 U.S. at 360.

5.   Deportation and Double Jeopardy. Historically, the Court has held that deportation is civil in nature; therefore, it does not implicate Double Jeopardy. Aaron S. Haas, an immigration lawyer, has argued:

The traditional notion that deportation is separate from criminal punishment may have made sense in the late 1800s, but is increasingly untenable in light of the many changes to the law since that time. The dramatic expansion of removable offenses, the elimination of most judicial discretion, and the increasing use of deportation in response to criminal behavior have all made deportation look and feel like punishment for criminal behavior. This intuition that removal of criminal aliens is punitive is supported by modern case law discounting statutory labels and focusing on the actual relation of the penalty to the conduct. Regardless of the stated and actual purpose, a penalty that functions like a punishment will be treated as a punishment by the courts. Under this paradigm, deportation is not only a punishment, but a severe punishment that often exceeds the crime committed. The Supreme Court recognized these changes last term in *Padilla v. Kentucky,* signaling their acknowledgement of the inseparable relationship between criminal and deportation law.

With this new understanding in mind, the harshness of deportation for minor criminal conduct can no longer be justified through legal fictions and outdated categories. It is important to start thinking of a new foundation for deportation law that will be sturdier than the present one. While I have provided suggestions such as incorporating the deportation decision into the criminal sentencing process and restoring discretion to immigration judges, the most important first step is to acknowledge the increasingly tenuous state of the current system. The false dichotomy between punishment and deportation seems continually harder to justify, yet is used to support more and greater injustice. Once the wall between criminal and deportation law is removed, we can begin to imagine a better, fairer system for all.

Deportation and Double Jeopardy after Padilla, 26 Geo. Immigr. L. J. 121, 160 (2011).

6. **A slowly emerging standard?** In a provocative article, Professor Kari Hong argues that collateral consequences "impose an additional penalty for a crime in a separate context that is not willing or able to distinguish the degrees of harm swept up by criminal law... [C]ollateral consequences, inherent to their nature, have no gradations or nuance, rendering them arbitrary and often disproportionate to the original crime." *The Absurdity of Crime-Based Deportation,* 50 Davis L. Rev. 2067, 2075–76 (2017). She contends further that a trilogy of Supreme Court cases demonstrate the Court's quiet move towards rejecting the relevance of the mere commission of a crime in deportation cases and that Congress should follow suit, requiring courts to base deportation decisions on the actual seriousness of an offender's conduct, rather than relying on the mere commission of a crime.

PROBLEM 14-1

Assume that you are on the legislative staff for a member of Congress. She is concerned whether the Supreme Court's decisions in *Moncrieffe* and *Carachuri-Rosendo* make sense as a matter of policy. (She recognizes that the Court was interpreting a federal statute and, thus, Congress can overrule the Court.). She asks you to prepare a memo discussing whether those cases reflect sound immigration policy. Discuss fully.

PROBLEM 14-2

Assume that you are on the legislative staff for a member of Congress from a state that has legalized medical and recreational marijuana. He fears that immigrants living in his state may fail to understand that their involvement in marijuana transactions violates federal law and may lead to their deportation. He would like you to revise the statutory language discussed in *Moncrieffe* and *Carachuri-Rosendo* to provide protection for such immigrants. Prepare draft statutory language and a memo explaining your proposed changes to the law.

B. ASSET FORFEITURE

Civil forfeiture has deep roots in American law. Civil forfeiture's origins date back to the founding of the United States. Civil forfeiture is an action against the property, i.e., "in rem." Typically, the government must prove only by a preponderance of the evidence that "the property . . . was used during the commission of a crime or the property constituted proceeds from a crime." Arthur W. Leach & John G. Malcom, *Solutions to the Debate,* 10 Ga. St. U. L. Rev. 241, 246 (1994). See also 18 U.S.C. § 983(c).

Criminal forfeiture is a more recent addition to American law. It provides prosecutors an additional and often powerful tool. Federal statutes like RICO, 18 U.S.C. § 1963, and the Continuing Criminal Enterprise statute, 21 U.S.C. §§ 848, 853, are modern examples where Congress has authorized criminal forfeiture. Typically, the government brings criminal forfeiture as part of its criminal case against an offender and must prove that the offender committed the underlying criminal offense. As a result, the government must prove its case beyond a reasonable doubt.

The Controlled Substances Act mandates both criminal forfeiture, 21 U.S.C. § 853, and civil forfeiture, 21 U.S.C. § 881, 18 U.S.C. § 981(b), of assets related to illegal drug activity. Most states have similar laws in place.

Asset forfeiture provides governments with an extraordinarily powerful tool. Imagine in the context of drug activity how law enforcement agents are able to use forfeiture. Not only can agents target property used by marijuana growers or sellers, but they can also seize cash.

Demonstrating that cash was used during the commission of a crime is not difficult if agents can detect the odor of marijuana detected on the currency. Law enforcement agencies have seized cash, cars, real estate, airplanes and yachts when the police have been able to establish that the property was used to commit the offense.

At various times, law enforcement's use of forfeiture has been controversial. Police contend that forfeiture cripples criminal actors. Critics suggest that allowing law enforcement agencies to retain the property for police use creates an improper incentive to seek forfeiture. Infamously, police in California raided a reclusive rancher's property with a search warrant for marijuana. Police ended up shooting the rancher when he emerged from his bedroom with a weapon. Police found no marijuana. An investigation suggested that the primary motivation for the raid was to seize the rancher's assets. See *Bradbury v. Superior Court,* 57 Cal. Rptr. 2d 207 (1997).

Litigants subject to forfeiture have raised a variety of challenges to asset forfeiture. The following case explores the extent to which forfeiture is a form of punishment.

UNITED STATES V. URSERY

United States Supreme Court
518 U.S. 267 (1996)

REHNQUIST, C.J.

In separate cases, the United States Court of Appeals for the Sixth Circuit and the United States Court of Appeals for the Ninth Circuit held that the Double Jeopardy Clause prohibits the Government from both punishing a defendant for a criminal offense and forfeiting his property for that same offense in a separate civil proceeding. We consolidated those cases for our review, and now reverse. These civil forfeitures (and civil forfeitures generally), we hold, do not constitute "punishment" for purposes of the Double Jeopardy Clause.

I

No. 95-345: Michigan Police found marijuana growing adjacent to respondent Guy Ursery's house, and discovered marijuana seeds, stems, stalks, and a grow light within the house. The United States instituted civil forfeiture proceedings against the house, alleging that the property was subject to forfeiture under 84 Stat. 1276, as amended, 21 U.S.C. § 881(a)(7), because it had been used for several years to facilitate the unlawful processing and distribution of a controlled substance. Ursery ultimately paid the United States $13,250 to settle the forfeiture claim in full. Shortly before the settlement was consummated, Ursery was indicted for manufacturing marijuana, in violation of § 841(a)(1). A jury found him guilty, and he was sentenced to 63 months in prison.

The Court of Appeals for the Sixth Circuit by a divided vote reversed Ursery's criminal conviction, holding that the conviction violated the Double Jeopardy Clause of the Fifth Amendment of the United States Constitution. The court based its conclusion in part upon its belief that our decisions in *United States v. Halper*, 490 U.S. 435 (1989), and *Austin v. United States*, 509 U.S. 602 (1993), meant that any civil forfeiture under § 881(a)(7) constitutes punishment for purposes of the Double Jeopardy Clause. Ursery, in the court's view, had therefore been "punished" in the forfeiture proceeding against his property, and could not be subsequently criminally tried for violation of 21 U.S.C. § 841(a)(1).

No. 95-346: Following a jury trial, Charles Wesley Arlt and James Wren were convicted of: conspiracy to aid and abet the manufacture of methamphetamine, in violation of 21 U.S.C. § 846; conspiracy to launder monetary instruments, in violation of 18 U.S.C. § 371; and numerous counts of money laundering, in violation of § 1956. The District Court sentenced Arlt to life in prison and a 10-year term of supervised release, and imposed a fine of $250,000. Wren was sentenced to life imprisonment and a 5-year term of supervised release.

Before the criminal trial had started, the United States had filed a civil *in rem* complaint against various property seized from, or titled to, Arlt and Wren, or Payback Mines, a corporation controlled by Arlt. The complaint alleged that each piece of property was subject to forfeiture both under 18 U.S.C. § 981(a)(1)(A), which provides that "[a]ny property . . . involved in a transaction or attempted transaction in violation of" § 1956 (the money-laundering statute) "is subject to forfeiture to the United States"; and under 21 U.S.C. § 881(a)(6), which provides for the forfeiture of (i) "[a]ll . . . things of value furnished or intended to be furnished by any person in exchange for" illegal drugs, (ii) "all proceeds traceable to such an exchange," and (iii) "all moneys, negotiable instruments, and securities used or intended to be used to facilitate" a federal drug felony. The parties agreed to defer litigation of the forfeiture action during the criminal prosecution. More than a year after the conclusion of the criminal trial, the District Court granted the Government's motion for summary judgment in the civil forfeiture proceeding.

Arlt and Wren appealed the decision in the forfeiture action, and the Court of Appeals for the Ninth Circuit reversed, holding that the forfeiture violated the Double Jeopardy Clause. The court's decision was based in part upon the same view as that expressed by the Court of Appeals for the Sixth Circuit in Ursery's case-that our decisions in *Halper, supra,* and *Austin, supra,* meant that, as a categorical matter, forfeitures under §§ 981(a)(1)(A) and 881(a)(6) always constitute "punishment."

We granted the Government's petition for certiorari in each of the two cases, and we now reverse.

II

The Double Jeopardy Clause provides: "[N]or shall any person be subject for the same offence to be twice put in jeopardy of life or limb." U.S. Const., Amdt. 5. The Clause serves the function of preventing both "successive punishments and . . . successive prosecutions." *United States v. Dixon,* 509 U.S. 688, 696 (1993). The protection against multiple punishments prohibits the Government from " 'punishing twice, or attempting a second time to punish criminally for the same offense.' " *Witte v. United States,* 515 U.S. 389, 396 (1995).

In the decisions that we review, the Courts of Appeals held that the civil forfeitures constituted "punishment," making them subject to the prohibitions of the Double Jeopardy Clause. The Government challenges that characterization of the forfeitures, arguing that the courts were wrong to conclude that civil forfeitures are punitive for double jeopardy purposes.

A

* * *

One of the first cases to consider the relationship between the Double Jeopardy Clause and civil forfeiture was *Various Items of Personal Property v. United States,* 282 U.S. 577 (1931). In *Various Items,* the Waterloo Distilling Corporation had been ordered to forfeit a distillery, warehouse, and denaturing plant, on the ground that the corporation had conducted its distilling business in violation of federal law. The Government conceded that the corporation had been convicted of criminal violations prior to the initiation of the forfeiture proceeding, and admitted that the criminal conviction had been based upon "the transactions set forth . . . as a basis for the forfeiture." *Id.,* at 579. Considering the corporation's argument that the forfeiture action violated the Double Jeopardy Clause, this Court unanimously held that the Clause was inapplicable to civil forfeiture actions:

> "[This] forfeiture proceeding . . . is *in rem*. It is the property which is proceeded against, and, by resort to a legal fiction, held guilty and condemned as though it were conscious instead of inanimate and insentient. In a criminal prosecution it is the wrongdoer in person who is proceeded against, convicted, and punished. *The forfeiture is no part of the punishment for the criminal offense. The provision of the Fifth Amendment to the Constitution in respect of double jeopardy does not apply.*" *Id.,* at 581, 51 S.Ct., at 284 (citations omitted; emphasis added).

In reaching its conclusion, the Court drew a sharp distinction between *in rem* civil *forfeitures* and *in personam* civil *penalties* such as fines: Though the latter could, in some circumstances, be punitive, the former could not. *Ibid.* Referring to a case that was decided the same day as *Various Items,* the Court made its point absolutely clear:

"In *United States v. La Franca,* [282 U.S.] 568 (1931)], we hold that, under § 5 of the Willis-Campbell Act, a civil action to recover taxes, which in fact are penalties, is punitive in character and barred by a prior conviction of the defendant for a criminal offense involving the same transactions. This, however, is not that case, but a proceeding *in rem* to forfeit property used in committing an offense." *Id.,* at 580.

Had the Court in *Various Items* found that a civil forfeiture could constitute a "punishment" under the Fifth Amendment, its holding would have been quite remarkable. As that Court recognized, "[a]t common law, in many cases, the right of forfeiture did not attach until the offending person had been convicted and the record of conviction produced." *Ibid.* In other words, at common law, not only was it the case that a criminal conviction did not *bar* a civil forfeiture, but, in fact, the civil forfeiture could not be *instituted* unless a criminal conviction had already been obtained. Though this Court had held that common-law rule inapplicable where the right of forfeiture was "created by statute, *in rem,* cognizable on the revenue side of the exchequer," *The Palmyra, supra,* at 14, it never had suggested that the Constitution *prohibited* for statutory civil forfeiture what was *required* for common-law civil forfeiture. For the *Various Items* Court to have held that the forfeiture was prohibited by the prior criminal proceeding would have been directly contrary to the common-law rule, and would have called into question the constitutionality of forfeiture statutes thought constitutional for over a century.

Following its decision in *Various Items,* the Court did not consider another double jeopardy case involving a civil forfeiture for 40 years. Then, in *One Lot Emerald Cut Stones v. United States,* 409 U.S. 232 (1972) the Court's brief opinion reaffirmed the rule of *Various Items.* In *Emerald Cut Stones,* after having been acquitted of smuggling jewels into the United States, the owner of the jewels intervened in a proceeding to forfeit them as contraband. We rejected the owner's double jeopardy challenge to the forfeiture, holding that "[i]f for no other reason, the forfeiture is not barred by the Double Jeopardy Clause of the Fifth Amendment because it involves neither two criminal trials nor two criminal punishments." 409 U.S., at 235. Noting that the forfeiture provisions had been codified separately from parallel criminal provisions, the Court determined that the forfeiture clearly was "a civil sanction." *Id.,* at 236. The forfeitures were not criminal punishments because they did not impose a second *in personam* penalty for the criminal defendant's wrongdoing.

In our most recent decision considering whether a civil forfeiture constitutes punishment under the Double Jeopardy Clause, we again affirmed the rule of *Various Items.* In *United States v. One Assortment of*

89 Firearms, 465 U.S. 354 (1984), the owner of the defendant weapons was acquitted of charges of dealing firearms without a license. The Government then brought a forfeiture action against the firearms under 18 U.S.C. § 924(d), alleging that they were used or were intended to be used in violation of federal law.

In another unanimous decision, we held that the forfeiture was not barred by the prior criminal proceeding. We began our analysis by stating the rule for our decision:

> "Unless the forfeiture sanction was intended as punishment, so that the proceeding is essentially criminal in character, the Double Jeopardy Clause is not applicable. The question, then, is whether a § 924(d) forfeiture proceeding is intended to be, or by its nature necessarily is, criminal and punitive, or civil and remedial." 89 *Firearms, supra,* at 362.

Our inquiry proceeded in two stages. In the first stage, we looked to Congress' intent, and concluded that "Congress designed forfeiture under § 924(d) as a remedial civil sanction." 465 U.S., at 363. This conclusion was based upon several findings. First, noting that the forfeiture proceeding was *in rem,* we found it significant that "[a]ctions *in rem* have traditionally been viewed as civil proceedings, with jurisdiction dependent upon seizure of a physical object." *Ibid.* Second, we found that the forfeiture provision, because it reached both weapons used in violation of federal law and those "intended to be used" in such a manner, reached a broader range of conduct than its criminal analog. Third, we concluded that the civil forfeiture "further[ed] broad remedial aims," including both "discouraging unregulated commerce in firearms" and "removing from circulation firearms that have been used or intended for use outside regulated channels of commerce." *89 Firearms, supra,* at 364.

In the second stage of our analysis, we looked to " 'whether the statutory scheme was so punitive either in purpose or effect as to negate' Congress' intention to establish a civil remedial mechanism," 465 U.S., at 365. Considering several factors that we had used previously in order to determine whether a civil proceeding was so punitive as to require application of the full panoply of constitutional protections required in a criminal trial, see *id.,* at 248, we found only one of those factors to be present in the § 924(d) forfeiture. By itself, however, the fact that the behavior proscribed by the forfeiture was already a crime proved insufficient to turn the forfeiture into a punishment subject to the Double Jeopardy Clause. Hence, we found that the gun owner had "failed to establish by the 'clearest proof' that Congress has provided a sanction so punitive as to 'transfor[m] what was clearly intended as a civil remedy into a criminal penalty.' " *89 Firearms, supra,* at 366. We concluded our decision by restating that civil forfeiture is "not an additional penalty for the commission of a criminal act, but rather is a separate civil sanction, remedial in nature." *89 Firearms, supra,* at 366.

B

Our cases reviewing civil forfeitures under the Double Jeopardy Clause adhere to a remarkably consistent theme. Though the two-part analytical construct employed in *89 Firearms* was more refined, perhaps, than that we had used over 50 years earlier in *Various Items,* the conclusion was the same in each case: *In rem* civil forfeiture is a remedial civil sanction, distinct from potentially punitive *in personam* civil penalties such as fines, and does not constitute a punishment under the Double Jeopardy Clause.

In the cases that we currently review, the Court of Appeals for the Ninth Circuit recognized as much, concluding that after *89 Firearms,* "the law was clear that civil forfeitures did not constitute 'punishment' for double jeopardy purposes." 33 F.3d, at 1218. Nevertheless, that court read three of our decisions to have "abandoned" *89 Firearms* and the oft-affirmed rule of *Various Items.* According to the Court of Appeals for the Ninth Circuit, through our decisions in *United States v. Halper,* 490 U.S. 435 (1989), *Austin v. United States,* 509 U.S. 602 (1993), and *Department of Revenue of Mont. v. Kurth Ranch,* 511 U.S. 767 (1994), we "changed [our] collective mind," and "adopted a new test for determining whether a nominally civil sanction constitutes 'punishment' for double jeopardy purposes." 33 F.3d, at 1218–1219. The Court of Appeals for the Sixth Circuit shared the view of the Ninth Circuit, though it did not directly rely upon *Kurth Ranch.* We turn now to consider whether *Halper, Austin,* and *Kurth Ranch* accomplished the radical jurisprudential shift perceived by the Courts of Appeals.

In *Halper,* we considered "whether and under what circumstances a civil penalty may constitute 'punishment' for the purposes of double jeopardy analysis." *Halper, supra,* at 436. Based upon his submission of 65 inflated Medicare claims, each of which overcharged the Government by $9, Halper was criminally convicted of 65 counts of violating the false-claims statute, 18 U.S.C. § 287 (1982 ed.), as well as of 16 counts of mail fraud, and was sentenced to two years in prison and fined $5,000. Following that criminal conviction, the Government successfully brought a civil action against Halper under 31 U.S.C. § 3729 (1982 ed. and Supp. II). The District Court hearing the civil action determined that Halper was liable to the Government for over $130,000 under § 3729, which then provided for liability in the amount of $2,000 per violation, double the Government's actual damages, and court costs. The court concluded that imposing the full civil penalty would constitute a second punishment for Halper's already-punished criminal offense, however, and therefore reduced Halper's liability to double the actual damages suffered by the Government and the costs of the civil action. The Government directly appealed that decision to this Court.

This Court agreed with the District Court's analysis. We determined that our precedent had established no absolute and irrebuttable rule that a civil fine cannot be "punishment" under the Double Jeopardy Clause. Though it was well established that "a civil remedy does not rise to the level of 'punishment' merely because Congress provided for civil recovery in excess of the Government's actual damages," we found that our case law did "not foreclose the possibility that in a particular case a civil penalty . . . may be so extreme and so divorced from the Government's damages and expenses as to constitute punishment." 490 U.S., at 442. Emphasizing the case-specific nature of our inquiry, we compared the size of the fine imposed on Halper, $130,000, to the damages actually suffered by the Government as a result of Halper's actions, estimated by the District Court at $585. Noting that the fine was more than 220 times greater than the Government's damages, we agreed with the District Court that "Halper's $130,000 liability is sufficiently disproportionate that the sanction constitutes a second punishment in violation of double jeopardy." *Id.,* at 452. We remanded to the District Court so that it could hear evidence regarding the Government's actual damages, and could then reduce Halper's liability to a nonpunitive level. *Ibid.*

In *Austin,* we considered whether a civil forfeiture could violate the Excessive Fines Clause of the Eighth Amendment to the Constitution, which provides that "[e]xcessive bail shall not be required, nor excessive fines imposed. . . ." Aware that Austin had sold two grams of cocaine the previous day, police searched his mobile home and body shop. Their search revealed small amounts of marijuana and cocaine, a handgun, drug paraphernalia, and almost $5,000 in cash. Austin was charged with one count of possessing cocaine with intent to distribute, to which he pleaded guilty. The Government then initiated a civil forfeiture proceeding against Austin's mobile home and auto shop, contending that they had been "used" or were "intended for use" in the commission of a drug offense. See 21 U.S.C. §§ 881(a)(4) and (a)(7). Austin contested the forfeiture on the ground of the Excessive Fines Clause, but the District Court and the Court of Appeals held the forfeiture constitutional.

We limited our review to the question "whether the Excessive Fines Clause of the Eighth Amendment applies to forfeitures of property under 21 U.S.C. §§ 881(a)(4) and (a)(7)." *Austin, supra,* at 604. We began our analysis by rejecting the argument that the Excessive Fines Clause was limited solely to criminal proceedings: The relevant question was not whether a particular proceeding was criminal or civil, we determined, but rather was whether forfeiture under §§ 881(a)(4) and (a)(7) constituted "punishment" for the purposes of the Eighth Amendment. *Austin, supra,* at 610. In an effort to answer that question, we briefly reviewed the history of civil forfeiture both in this country and in England, taking a categorical approach that contrasted sharply with *Halper*'s case-specific approach to determining whether a civil penalty constitutes punishment. Ultimately, we concluded that "forfeiture under [§§ 881(a)(4) and (a)(7)] constitutes 'payment to a sovereign as punishment for some offense,' and, as such, is subject to the limitations of the Eighth Amendment's Excessive Fines Clause." 509 U.S., at 622.

In *Department of Revenue of Mont. v. Kurth Ranch, supra,* we considered whether a state tax imposed on marijuana was invalid under the Double Jeopardy Clause when the taxpayer had already been criminally convicted of owning the marijuana that was taxed. We first established that the fact that Montana had labeled the civil sanction a "tax" did not end our analysis. We then turned to consider whether the tax was so punitive as to constitute a punishment subject to the Double Jeopardy Clause. Several differences between the marijuana tax imposed by Montana and the typical revenue-raising tax were readily apparent. The Montana tax was unique in that it was conditioned on the commission of a crime and was imposed only after the taxpayer had been arrested: Thus, only a person charged with a criminal offense was subject to the tax. We also noted that the taxpayer did not own or possess the taxed marijuana at the time that the tax was imposed. From these differences, we determined that the tax was motivated by a " 'penal and prohibitory intent rather than the gathering of revenue.' " *Id.,* at 781. Concluding that the Montana tax proceeding "was the functional equivalent of a successive criminal prosecution," we affirmed the Court of Appeals' judgment barring the tax. *Id.,* at 784.

We think that the Court of Appeals for the Sixth Circuit and the Court of Appeals for the Ninth Circuit misread *Halper, Austin,* and *Kurth Ranch.* None of those decisions purported to overrule the well-established teaching of *Various Items, Emerald Cut Stones,* and *89 Firearms. Halper* involved not a civil *forfeiture,* but a civil *penalty.* That its rule was limited to the latter context is clear from the decision itself, from the historical distinction that we have drawn between civil forfeiture and civil penalties, and from the practical difficulty of applying *Halper* to a civil forfeiture.

In *Halper,* we emphasized that our decision was limited to the context of civil penalties:

> "What we announce now is a rule for the rare case, the case such as the one before us, where *a fixed-penalty provision* subjects a prolific but small-gauge offender to a sanction overwhelmingly disproportionate to the damages he has caused. The rule is one of reason: Where a defendant previously has sustained a criminal penalty and the *civil penalty* sought in the subsequent proceeding bears no rational relation to the goal of compensating the Government for its loss, but rather appears to qualify as

'punishment' in the plain meaning of the word, then the defendant is entitled to an accounting of the Government's damages and costs to determine if the penalty sought in fact constitutes a second punishment." 490 U.S., at 449–450.

The narrow focus of *Halper* followed from the distinction that we have drawn historically between civil forfeiture and civil penalties. Since at least *Various Items,* we have distinguished civil penalties such as fines from civil forfeiture proceedings that are *in rem.* While a "civil action to recover . . . penaltie[s], is punitive in character," and much like a criminal prosecution in that "[i]t is the wrongdoer in person who is proceeded against . . . and punished," in an *in rem* forfeiture proceeding, "it is the property which is proceeded against, and by resort to a legal fiction, held guilty and condemned." *Various Items,* 282 U.S., at 580–581. Thus, though for double jeopardy purposes we have never balanced the value of property forfeited in a particular case against the harm suffered by the Government in that case, we have balanced the size of a particular civil penalty against the Government's harm. Indeed, the rule set forth in *Halper* developed from the teaching of *Rex Trailer* and *Hess.*

It is difficult to see how the rule of *Halper* could be applied to a civil forfeiture. Civil penalties are designed as a rough form of "liquidated damages" for the harms suffered by the Government as a result of a defendant's conduct. See *Rex Trailer, supra,* at 153–154. The civil penalty involved in *Halper,* for example, provided for a fixed monetary penalty for each false claim count on which the defendant was convicted in the criminal proceeding. Whether a "fixed-penalty provision" that seeks to compensate the Government for harm it has suffered is "so extreme" and "so divorced" from the penalty's nonpunitive purpose of compensating the Government as to be a punishment may be determined by balancing the Government's harm against the size of the penalty. Civil forfeitures, in contrast to civil penalties, are designed to do more than simply compensate the Government. Forfeitures serve a variety of purposes, but are designed primarily to confiscate property used in violation of the law, and to require disgorgement of the fruits of illegal conduct. Though it may be possible to quantify the value of the property forfeited, it is virtually impossible to quantify, even approximately, the nonpunitive purposes served by a particular civil forfeiture. Hence, it is practically difficult to determine whether a particular forfeiture bears no rational relationship to the nonpunitive purposes of that forfeiture. Quite simply, the case-by-case balancing test set forth in *Halper,* in which a court must compare the harm suffered by the Government against the size of the penalty imposed, is inapplicable to civil forfeiture.

We recognized as much in *Kurth Ranch.* In that case, the Court expressly disclaimed reliance upon *Halper,* finding that its case-specific approach was impossible to apply outside the context of a fixed civil-penalty provision. Reviewing the Montana marijuana tax, we held that because "tax statutes serve a purpose quite different from civil penalties, . . . *Halper*'s method of determining whether the exaction was remedial or punitive simply does not work in the case of a tax statute." *Kurth Ranch,* 511 U.S., at 784. This is not to say that there is no occasion for analysis of the Government's harm. *89 Firearms* makes clear the relevance of an evaluation of the harms alleged. The point is simply that *Halper*'s case-specific approach is inapplicable to civil forfeitures.

In the cases that we review, the Courts of Appeals did not find *Halper* difficult to apply to civil forfeiture because they concluded that its case-by-case balancing approach had been supplanted in *Austin* by a categorical approach that found a civil sanction to be punitive if it could not "fairly be said solely to serve a remedial purpose." See *Austin,* 509 U.S., at 610, 113 S.Ct., at 2806. But *Austin,* it must be remembered, did not involve the Double Jeopardy Clause at all. *Austin* was decided solely under the Excessive Fines Clause of the Eighth Amendment, a constitutional provision which we never have understood as parallel to, or even related to, the Double Jeopardy Clause of the Fifth Amendment. The only discussion of the Double Jeopardy Clause contained in *Austin* appears in a footnote that acknowledges our decisions holding that "[t]he Double Jeopardy Clause has been held not to apply in civil forfeiture proceedings . . . where the forfeiture could properly be characterized as remedial." *Austin, supra,* at 608, n. 4, 113 S.Ct., at 2805, n. 4. And in *Austin* we expressly recognized and approved our decisions in *One Lot Emerald Cut Stones v. United States,* 409 U.S. 232 (1972), and *United States v. One Assortment of 89 Firearms,* 465 U.S. 354 (1984).

We acknowledged in *Austin* that our categorical approach under the Excessive Fines Clause was wholly distinct from the case-by-case approach of *Halper,* and we explained that the difference in approach was based in a significant difference between the purposes of our analysis under each constitutional provision. It is unnecessary in a case under the Excessive Fines Clause to inquire at a preliminary stage whether the civil sanction imposed in that particular case is totally inconsistent with any remedial goal. Because the second stage of inquiry under the Excessive Fines Clause asks whether the particular sanction in question is so large as to be "excessive," see *Austin,* 509 U.S., at 622–623. A preliminary-stage inquiry that focused on the disproportionality of a particular sanction would be duplicative of the excessiveness analysis that would follow. Forfeitures effected under 21 U.S.C. §§ 881(a)(4) and (a)(7) are subject to review for excessiveness under the Eighth Amendment after *Austin;* this does not mean, however, that those forfeitures are so punitive as to constitute punishment for the purposes of double jeopardy. The holding of *Austin* was limited to the Excessive Fines Clause of the Eighth Amendment, and we decline to import the analysis of *Austin* into our double jeopardy jurisprudence.

In sum, nothing in *Halper, Kurth Ranch,* or *Austin* purported to replace our traditional understanding that civil forfeiture does not constitute punishment for the purpose of the Double Jeopardy Clause. Congress long has authorized the Government to bring parallel criminal proceedings and civil forfeiture proceedings, and this Court consistently has found civil forfeitures not to constitute punishment under the Double Jeopardy Clause. It would have been quite remarkable for this Court both to have held unconstitutional a well-established practice, and to have overruled a long line of precedent, without having even suggested that it was doing so. *Halper* dealt with *in personam* civil penalties under the Double Jeopardy Clause; *Kurth Ranch* with a tax proceeding under the Double Jeopardy Clause; and *Austin* with civil forfeitures under the Excessive Fines Clause. None of those cases dealt with the subject of these cases: *in rem* civil forfeitures for purposes of the Double Jeopardy Clause.

C

We turn now to consider the forfeitures in these cases under the teaching of *Various Items, Emerald Cut Stones,* and *89 Firearms.* Because it provides a useful analytical tool, we conduct our inquiry within the framework of the two-part test used in *89 Firearms.* First, we ask whether Congress intended proceedings under 21 U.S.C. § 881 and 18 U.S.C. § 981 to be criminal or civil. Second, we turn to consider whether the proceedings are so punitive in fact as to "persuade us that the forfeiture proceeding[s] may not legitimately be viewed as civil in nature," despite Congress' intent. 465 U.S., at 366.

There is little doubt that Congress intended these forfeitures to be civil proceedings. As was the case in *89 Firearms,* "Congress' intent in this regard is most clearly demonstrated by the procedural mechanisms it established for enforcing forfeitures under the statute[s]." *Id.,* at 363. Both 21 U.S.C. § 881 and 18 U.S.C. § 981, which is entitled "Civil forfeiture," provide that the laws "relating to the seizure, summary and judicial forfeiture, and condemnation of property for violation of the customs laws . . . shall apply to seizures and forfeitures incurred" under §§ 881 and 981. See 21 U.S.C. § 881(d); 18 U.S.C. § 981(d). Because forfeiture proceedings under the customs laws are *in rem,* it is clear that Congress intended that a forfeiture under § 881 or § 981, like the forfeiture reviewed in *89 Firearms,* would be a proceeding *in rem.* Congress specifically structured these forfeitures to be impersonal by targeting the property itself. "In contrast to the *in personam* nature of criminal actions, actions *in rem* have traditionally been viewed as civil proceedings, with jurisdiction dependent upon seizure of a physical object." *89 Firearms, supra,* at 363.

Other procedural mechanisms governing forfeitures under §§ 881 and 981 also indicate that Congress intended such proceedings to be civil. Forfeitures under either statute are governed by 19 U.S.C. § 1607, which provides that actual notice of the impending forfeiture is unnecessary when the Government cannot identify any party with an interest in the seized article, and by § 1609, which provides that seized property is subject to forfeiture through a summary administrative procedure if no party files a claim to the property. And 19 U.S.C. § 1615, which governs the burden of proof in forfeiture proceedings under §§ 881 and 981, provides that once the Government has shown probable cause that the property is subject to forfeiture, then "the burden of proof shall lie upon [the] claimant." In sum, "[b]y creating such distinctly civil procedures for forfeitures under [§§ 881 and 981], Congress has 'indicate[d] clearly that it intended a civil, not a criminal sanction.'" *89 Firearms, supra,* at 363.

Moving to the second stage of our analysis, we find that there is little evidence, much less the "'clearest proof'" that we require, see *89 Firearms, supra,* at 365, suggesting that forfeiture proceedings under 21 U.S.C. §§ 881(a)(6) and (a)(7), and 18 U.S.C. § 981(a)(1)(A), are so punitive in form and effect as to render them criminal despite Congress' intent to the contrary. The statutes involved in these cases are, in most significant respects, indistinguishable from those reviewed, and held not to be punitive, in *Various Items, Emerald Cut Stones,* and *89 Firearms.*

Most significant is that § 981(a)(1)(A) and §§ 881(a)(6) and (a)(7), while perhaps having certain punitive aspects, serve important nonpunitive goals. Title 21 U.S.C. § 881(a)(7), under which Ursery's property was forfeited, provides for the forfeiture of "all real property . . . which is used or intended to be used, in any manner or part, to commit, or to facilitate the commission of" a federal drug felony. Requiring the forfeiture of property used to commit federal narcotics violations encourages property owners to take care in managing their property and ensures that they will not permit that property to be used for illegal purposes. *Bennis v. Michigan,* 516 U.S. 442, 452 (1996). In many circumstances, the forfeiture may abate a nuisance.

The forfeiture of the property claimed by Arlt and Wren took place pursuant to 18 U.S.C. § 981(a)(1)(A) and 21 U.S.C. § 881(a)(6). Section 981(a)(1)(A) provides for the forfeiture of "[a]ny property" involved in illegal money-laundering transactions. Section 881(a)(6) provides for the forfeiture of "[a]ll . . . things of value furnished or intended to be furnished by any person in exchange for" illegal drugs; "all proceeds traceable to such an exchange"; and "all moneys, negotiable instruments, and securities used or intended to be used to facilitate" a federal drug felony. The same remedial purposes served by § 881(a)(7) are served by §§ 881(a)(6) and 981(a)(1)(A). Only one point merits separate discussion. To the extent that § 881(a)(6) applies to "proceeds" of illegal drug activity, it serves the additional nonpunitive goal of ensuring that persons do not profit from their illegal acts.

Other considerations that we have found relevant to the question whether a proceeding is criminal also tend to support a conclusion that

§ 981(a)(1)(A) and §§ 881(a)(6) and (a)(7) are civil proceedings. First, in light of our decisions in *Various Items, Emerald Cut Stones,* and *89 Firearms,* and the long tradition of federal statutes providing for a forfeiture proceeding following a criminal prosecution, it is absolutely clear that *in rem* civil forfeiture has not historically been regarded as punishment, as we have understood that term under the Double Jeopardy Clause. Second, there is no requirement in the statutes that we currently review that the Government demonstrate scienter in order to establish that the property is subject to forfeiture; indeed, the property may be subject to forfeiture even if no party files a claim to it and the Government never shows any connection between the property and a particular person. See 19 U.S.C. § 1609. Though both §§ 881(a) and 981(a) contain an "innocent owner" exception, we do not think that such a provision, without more indication of an intent to punish, is relevant to the question whether a statute is punitive under the Double Jeopardy Clause. Third, though both statutes may fairly be said to serve the purpose of deterrence, we long have held that this purpose may serve civil as well as criminal goals. We recently reaffirmed this conclusion in *Bennis v. Michigan, supra,* at 452, where we held that "forfeiture . . . serves a deterrent purpose distinct from any punitive purpose." Finally, though both statutes are tied to criminal activity, as was the case in *89 Firearms,* this fact is insufficient to render the statutes punitive. It is well settled that "Congress may impose both a criminal and a civil sanction in respect to the same act or omission," *Helvering,* 303 U.S., at 399. By itself, the fact that a forfeiture statute has some connection to a criminal violation is far from the "clearest proof" necessary to show that a proceeding is criminal.

We hold that these *in rem* civil forfeitures are neither "punishment" nor criminal for purposes of the Double Jeopardy Clause. The judgments of the Court of Appeals for the Sixth Circuit, in No. 95-345, and of the Court of Appeals for the Ninth Circuit, in No. 95-346, are, accordingly, reversed.

It is so ordered.

* * *

[KENNEDY, J. Concurrence and SCALIA, J. and THOMAS, J. Concurrence Omitted]

STEVENS, J., concurring in the judgment in part and dissenting in part.

The question the Court poses is whether civil forfeitures constitute "punishment" for purposes of the Double Jeopardy Clause. Because the numerous federal statutes authorizing forfeitures cover such a wide variety of situations, it is quite wrong to assume that there is only one answer to that question. For purposes of analysis it is useful to identify three different categories of property that are subject to seizure: proceeds, contraband, and property that has played a part in the commission of a crime. The facts of these two cases illustrate the point.

In No. 95-346 the Government has forfeited $405,089.23 in currency. Those funds are the proceeds of unlawful activity. They are not property that respondents have any right to retain. The forfeiture of such proceeds, like the confiscation of money stolen from a bank, does not punish respondents because it exacts no price in liberty or lawfully derived property from them. I agree that the forfeiture of such proceeds is not punitive and therefore I concur in the Court's disposition of No. 95-346.

None of the property seized in No. 95-345 constituted proceeds of illegal activity. Indeed, the facts of that case reveal a dramatically different situation. Respondent Ursery cultivated marijuana in a heavily wooded area not far from his home in Shiawassee County, Michigan. The illegal substance was consumed by members of his family, but there is no evidence, and no contention by the Government, that he sold any of it to third parties. Acting on the basis of the incorrect assumption that the marijuana plants were on respondent's property, Michigan police officers executed a warrant to search the premises. In his house they found marijuana seeds, stems, stalks, and a grow light. I presume those items were seized, and I have no difficulty concluding that such a seizure does not constitute punishment because respondent had no right to possess contraband. Accordingly, I agree with the Court's opinion insofar as it explains why the forfeiture of contraband does not constitute punishment for double jeopardy purposes.

The critical question presented in No. 95-345 arose, not out of the seizure of contraband by the Michigan police, but rather out of the decision by the United States attorney to take respondent's home. There is no evidence that the house had been purchased with the proceeds of unlawful activity and the house itself was surely not contraband. Nonetheless, 21 U.S.C. § 881(a)(7) authorized the Government to seek forfeiture of respondent's residence because it had been used to facilitate the manufacture and distribution of marijuana. Respondent was then himself prosecuted for and convicted of manufacturing marijuana. In my opinion none of the reasons supporting the forfeiture of proceeds or contraband provides a sufficient basis for concluding that the confiscation of respondent's home was not punitive.

* * *

The recurrent theme of the Court's opinion is that there is some mystical difference between *in rem* and *in personam* proceedings, such that only the latter can give rise to double jeopardy concerns. The Court claims that "[s]ince at least *Various Items*," we have drawn this distinction for purposes of applying relevant constitutional provisions. *Ante,* at 2144. That statement, however, is incorrect. We have repeatedly rejected the idea that the nature of the court's jurisdiction has any bearing on the constitutional protections that apply at a proceeding before it. "From the relevant constitutional standpoint, there is no difference between a man who 'forfeits' $8,674 because he has used the money in illegal gambling activities and a man who pays a 'criminal fine' of $8,674 as a result of the same course of conduct." *Coin & Currency,* 401 U.S., at 718. Most recently, in our application of *Halper*'s definition of punishment, we stated that "[w]e do not understand the Government to rely separately on the technical distinction between proceedings *in rem* and proceedings *in personam,* but we note that any such reliance would be misplaced." *Austin,* 509 U.S., at 615.

The notion that the label attached to the proceeding is dispositive runs contrary to the trend of our recent cases. In *Halper* we stated that "the labels 'criminal' and 'civil' are not of paramount importance" in determining whether a proceeding punishes an individual. 490 U.S., at 447. In *Kurth Ranch* we held that the Double Jeopardy Clause applies to punitive proceedings even if they are labeled a tax. Indeed, in reaching that conclusion, we followed a 1931 decision that noted that a tax statute might be considered punitive for double jeopardy purposes. It is thus far too late in the day to contend that the label placed on a punitive proceeding determines whether it is covered by the Double Jeopardy Clause.

The pedantic distinction between *in rem* and *in personam* actions is ultimately only a cover for the real basis for the Court's decision: the idea that the property, not the owner, is being "punished" for offenses of which it is "guilty." Although the Court prefers not to rely on this notorious fiction too blatantly, its repeated citations to *Various Items* make clear that the Court believes respondent's home was "guilty" of the drug offenses with which he was charged. See *ante,* at 2144–2145. On that rationale, of course, the case is easy. The *owner* of the property is not being punished when the Government confiscates it, just the *property.* The same sleight-of-hand would have worked in *Austin,* too: The owner of the property is not being excessively fined, just the property itself. Despite the Government's heavy reliance on that fiction in *Austin,* we did not allow it to stand in the way of our holding that the seizure of property may punish the owner.

Even if the point had not been settled by prior decisions, common sense would dictate the result in this case. There is simply no rational basis for characterizing the seizure of this respondent's home as anything other than punishment for his crime. The house was neither proceeds nor contraband and its value had no relation to the Government's authority to seize it. Under the controlling statute an essential predicate for the forfeiture was proof that respondent had used the property in connection with the commission of a crime. The forfeiture of this property was unquestionably "a penalty that had absolutely no correlation to any damages sustained by society or to the cost of enforcing the law." *United States v. Ward,* 448 U.S., at 254. As we unanimously recognized in *Halper,* formalistic distinctions that obscure the obvious practical consequences of governmental action disserve the " 'humane interests' " protected by the Double Jeopardy

Clause. 490 U.S., at 447. Fidelity to both reason and precedent dictates the conclusion that *this forfeiture* was "punishment" for purposes of the Double Jeopardy Clause.

* * *

One final example may illustrate the depth of my concern that the Court's treatment of our cases has cut deeply into a guarantee deemed fundamental by the Founders. The Court relies heavily on a few early decisions that involved the forfeiture of vessels whose entire mission was unlawful and on the Prohibition-era precedent sustaining the forfeiture of a distillery-a property that served no purpose other than the manufacture of illegal spirits. Notably none of those early cases involved the forfeiture of a home as a form of punishment for misconduct that occurred therein. Consider how drastic the remedy would have been if Congress in 1931 had authorized the forfeiture of every home in which alcoholic beverages were consumed. Under the Court's reasoning, I fear that the label "civil," or perhaps *"in rem,"* would have been sufficient to avoid characterizing such forfeitures as "punitive" for purposes of the Double Jeopardy Clause. Our recent decisions in *Halper, Austin,* and *Kurth Ranch* dictate a far different conclusion. I remain persuaded that those cases were correctly decided and should be followed today.

Accordingly, I respectfully dissent from the judgment in No. 95-345.

NOTES AND QUESTIONS

1. **Convincing arguments?** Is the majority opinion convincing? From the perspective of the person whose property is seized, does asset forfeiture look like a fine?

2. ***Pennoyer v. Neff* and all that jazz.** Think back to your Civil Procedure course. You first encountered the distinction between "in rem" and "in personam" jurisdiction when you read *Pennoyer v. Neff,* 95 U.S. 714 (1878). The distinction was highly formalistic, but the kind of notice, for example, that a person was entitled to under due process turned on whether an action was in rem or in personam. In *Shaffer v. Heitner,* 433 U.S. 186 (1978), the Court abandoned the distinction because it was so highly formalistic. As explained by Justice Marshall:

> The case for applying to jurisdiction in rem the same test of "fair play and substantial justice" as governs assertions of jurisdiction in personam is simple and straightforward. It is premised on recognition that "(t)he phrase, 'judicial jurisdiction over a thing', is a customary elliptical way of referring to jurisdiction over the interests of persons in a thing." Restatement (Second) of Conflict of Laws s 56, Introductory Note (1971) (hereafter Restatement). This recognition leads to the conclusion that in order to justify an exercise of jurisdiction in rem, the basis for jurisdiction must be sufficient to justify exercising "jurisdiction over the interests of persons in a

thing." The standard for determining whether an exercise of jurisdiction over the interests of persons is consistent with the Due Process Clause is the minimum-contacts standard elucidated in International Shoe.

433 U.S. at 206. Does that same argument against the Court's reasoning in *Ursery* apply? If so, why; if not, why not?

3. An originalist's view. Professor Caleb Nelson, an originalist, discussed possible constitutional challenges to civil forfeiture proceedings and concluded that they do not violate the Due Process Clause:

> These conclusions give me no pleasure. I am skeptical that current forfeiture laws are good policy. But laws can be unwise and even unfair without being unconstitutional. In my view, the basic characteristics of civil and administrative forfeiture considered in this Feature are consistent with the original meaning of the Constitution as liquidated over time. Reform efforts should continue to focus on the political branches, not the courts.

The Constitutionality of Civil Forfeiture, 125 Yale L. J. 2446, 2456 (2016).

4. The odor of money. The courts have had to resolve a number of other issues relating to forfeiture. For example, is the smell of marijuana on U.S. currency probative of whether the person in possession of the currency is involved in the drug trade? At least according to media reports, a great deal of currency in circulation has been exposed to illegal drugs in the United States. How should courts resolve the issue of whether the smell of marijuana on currency establishes a sufficient link to drug activity to allow forfeiture? See, e.g., *United States v. $63,530.00 in U.S. Currency,* 781 F. 3d 949 (8th Cir. 2015).

PROBLEM 14-3

Mr. Cash entered an Amtrak train station. He was carrying a garment bag, a shoulder bag, and a briefcase. As Cash was about to board a departing train, a DEA agent approached him and identified himself as a police officer working interdiction activities at the train station. The agent then asked Cash if he could talk with him and see his train ticket. Cash complied. Also with Cash's permission, the agent searched Cash's luggage and found a large amount of case, wrapped in a large envelope. Cash explained that he had recently made a cash withdrawal from his bank. The agent noticed that some of the currency emitted a smell of marijuana. The agent told Cash that he was turning over the currency to the Seizure/Forfeiture Unit of the DEA. Several hours later, the agent was able to expose the currency to a drug-sniffing dog, which signaled the presence of marijuana residue on the currency. The total amount of currency was approximately $150,000.

The agent referred the matter to the FBI. Agents for the FBI learned that Cash had not made any large withdrawals from his bank in recent months. Armed with this information and fully aware that the government lacked sufficient evidence to prove that Cash was involved in drug trafficking, the U.S.

Attorney's Office proceeded in rem against the currency. After presenting the foregoing to the magistrate, the magistrate concluded that the government had probable cause to believe that Cash's currency was subject to seizure. Thereafter, Cash filed a claim for the currency and a motion to strike the government's claim against the cash found in his luggage. Discuss how the court should resolve Cash's claims that the government's action is insufficient.

CHAPTER 15

ISSUES CONFRONTING MARIJUANA-RELATED BUSINESSES

■ ■ ■

Marijuana-related businesses that operate in states that have legalized medical and/or adult recreational use of marijuana face a number of unique hurdles that make operating such businesses a challenge. Due to the conflict between federal and state laws that exists in legalization states concerning marijuana possession and distribution, marijuana-related businesses face challenges concerning everything from real estate issues to insurance issues to federal bankruptcy protection. And to complicate matters further, the laws are often evolving, so that marijuana-related businesses cannot easily have confidence that way they are operating today will be acceptable tomorrow.

This chapter looks at five potential areas of concern for marijuana-related businesses operating in legalization states. Section A examines certain employment issues that marijuana-related businesses face, such as whether employers can lawfully terminate employees who test positive for marijuana use, even though they have valid state-issued medical-use licenses. Section B explores the difficulty many marijuana-related businesses have had in trying to obtain banking services to operate their businesses efficiently. Section C concerns the inability of marijuana-related businesses to obtain relief under the federal bankruptcy laws. Section D looks at the taxation of marijuana-related businesses, focusing specifically on the inability of these businesses to deduct ordinary business expenses of their federal tax returns. And Section E discusses problems marijuana-related businesses have had in finding adequate insurance coverage.

A. EMPLOYMENT ISSUES

One important issue facing the courts and legislatures in legalization states is how to strike the correct balance between an employee's latitude under state law to use marijuana products, versus the employer's right to keep the workplace drug free, particularly in light of marijuana's illegal status under federal law. While nearly everyone would agree that employers should be free to discipline and/or terminate employees who use marijuana while working or are impaired on the job, the more difficult issues are posed by employees who use legal marijuana—whether medical or recreational—on their own time and are not impaired while working, but nevertheless test positive for marijuana use in random drug tests.

The following California Supreme Court case, *Ross v. RagingWire Telecommunications*, addresses this question. It does so by considering whether the California Fair Employment and Housing Act (FEHA), which is California's state-law version of the federal Americans with Disabilities Act (ADA), protects the rights of employees to use medical marijuana, in the same way that the FEHA protects the rights of employees to use prescription drugs, e.g., opioids, to treat disabilities. The court holds that it does not, finding no indication that the voters intended to provide such protections to employees when they enacted the state's medical marijuana act.

ROSS V. RAGINGWIRE TELECOMMUNICATIONS

Supreme Court of California
174 P.3d 200 (Cal. 2008)

WERDEGAR, J.

The Compassionate Use Act of 1996 (Health & Saf. Code, § 11362.5, added by initiative, Prop. 215, as approved by voters, Gen. Elec. (Nov. 5, 1996)) gives a person who uses marijuana for medical purposes on a physician's recommendation a defense to certain state criminal charges involving the drug, including possession. Federal law, however, continues to prohibit the drug's possession, even by medical users. *See Gonzales v. Raich* (2005) 545 U.S. 1, 26–29; *United States v. Oakland Cannabis Buyers' Cooperative* (2001) 532 U.S. 483, 491–495.

Plaintiff, whose physician recommended he use marijuana to treat chronic pain, was fired when a pre-employment drug test required of new employees revealed his marijuana use. The lower courts held plaintiff could not on that basis state a cause of action against his employer for disability-based discrimination under the California Fair Employment and Housing Act (hereafter the FEHA) or for wrongful termination in violation of public policy. We conclude the lower courts were correct: Nothing in the text or history of the Compassionate Use Act suggests the voters intended the measure to address the respective rights and duties of employers and employees. Under California law, an employer may require pre-employment drug tests and take illegal drug use into consideration in making employment decisions. We thus affirm.

I.   FACTS

This case comes to us on review of a judgment entered after the superior court sustained a demurrer to plaintiff's complaint without leave to amend. In this procedural posture, the only question before us is whether plaintiff can state a cause of action. In reviewing the complaint to answer that question, we treat the demurrer as admitting the complaint's well-pleaded allegations of material fact, but not its contentions, deductions or conclusions of law. The complaint's allegations may be summarized for this purpose as follows:

Plaintiff Gary Ross suffers from strain and muscle spasms in his back as a result of injuries he sustained while serving in the United States Air Force. Because of his condition, plaintiff is a qualified individual with a disability under the FEHA and receives governmental disability benefits. In September 1999, after failing to obtain relief from pain through other medications, plaintiff began to use marijuana on his physician's recommendation pursuant to the Compassionate Use Act.

On September 10, 2001, defendant RagingWire Telecommunications, Inc., offered plaintiff a job as lead systems administrator. Defendant required plaintiff to take a drug test. Before taking the test, plaintiff gave the clinic that would administer the test a copy of his physician's recommendation for marijuana. Plaintiff took the test on September 14 and began work on September 17. Later that week, the clinic informed plaintiff by telephone that he had tested positive for tetrahydrocannabinol (THC), a chemical found in marijuana. On September 20, defendant informed plaintiff he was being suspended as a result of the drug test. Plaintiff gave defendant a copy of his physician's recommendation for marijuana and explained to defendant's human resources director that he used marijuana for medical purposes to relieve his chronic back pain. Defendant's representative told plaintiff that defendant would call his physician, verify the recommendation, and advise him of defendant's decision regarding his employment. On September 21, defendant's board of directors met to discuss the matter and, on September 25, defendant's chief executive officer informed plaintiff that he was being fired because of his marijuana use.

Plaintiff's disability and use of marijuana to treat pain, he alleges, do not affect his ability to do the essential functions of the job for which defendant hired him. Plaintiff has worked in the same field since he began to use marijuana and has performed satisfactorily, without complaints about his job performance.

Based on these allegations, plaintiff alleges defendant violated the FEHA by discharging him because of, and by failing to make reasonable accommodation for, his disability. Plaintiff also alleges defendant terminated his employment wrongfully, in violation of public policy. The superior court sustained defendant's demurrer without leave to amend and entered judgment for defendant. The Court of Appeal affirmed. We granted plaintiff's petition for review.

II. DISCUSSION

A. The FEHA

The FEHA declares and implements the state's public policy against discrimination in employment. The particular section of the FEHA under which plaintiff attempts to state a claim, Government Code section 12940, provides that "[i]t shall be an unlawful employment practice . . . [¶] (a) For an employer, because of the . . . physical disability [or] medical condition . . . of any person, to refuse to hire or employ the person . . . or to bar or to discharge the person from employment. . . ." An employer may discharge or refuse to hire a person who, because of a disability or medical condition, "is unable to perform his or her essential duties even with reasonable accommodations." The FEHA thus inferentially requires employers in their hiring decisions to take into account the feasibility of making reasonable accommodations.

Plaintiff, seeking to bring himself within the FEHA, alleges he has a physical disability in that he "suffers from a lower back strain and muscle spasms in his back. . . ." He uses marijuana to treat the resulting pain. Marijuana use, however, brings plaintiff into conflict with defendant's employment policies, which apparently deny employment to persons who test positive for illegal drugs. By denying him employment and failing to make reasonable accommodation, plaintiff alleges, defendant has violated the FEHA. Plaintiff does not in his complaint identify the precise accommodation defendant would need to make in order to enable him to perform the essential duties of his job. One may fairly infer from plaintiff's allegations, however, that he is asking defendant to accommodate his use of marijuana at home by waiving its policy requiring a negative drug test of new employees. "Just as it would violate the FEHA to fire an employee who uses insulin or Zoloft," plaintiff argues, "it violates [the] statute to terminate an employee who uses a medicine deemed legal by the California electorate upon the recommendation of his physician." In this way, plaintiff reasons, "the [FEHA] works together with the Compassionate Use Act . . . to provide a remedy to [him]."

Plaintiff's position might have merit if the Compassionate Use Act gave marijuana the same status as any legal prescription drug. But the act's effect is not so broad. No state law could completely legalize marijuana for medical purposes because the drug remains illegal under federal law, even for medical users. Instead of attempting the impossible, as we shall explain, California's voters merely exempted medical users and their primary caregivers from criminal liability under two specifically designated state statutes. Nothing in the text or history of the Compassionate Use Act suggests the voters intended the measure to address the respective rights and obligations of employers and employees.

The FEHA does not require employers to accommodate the use of illegal drugs. The point is perhaps too obvious to have generated appellate litigation, but we recognized it implicitly in *Loder v. City of Glendale*, supra, 14 Cal.4th 846 (*Loder*). Among the questions before us in *Loder* was whether an employer could require prospective employees to undergo testing for illegal drugs and alcohol, and whether the employer could have access to the test results, without violating California's Confidentiality of Medical Information Act. We determined that an employer could lawfully do both. In reaching this conclusion, we relied on a regulation adopted under the authority of the FEHA that permits an employer to condition an offer of employment on the results of a medical examination. We held that such an examination may include drug testing and, in so holding, necessarily recognized that employers may deny employment to persons who test positive for illegal drugs. The employer, we explained, was "seeking information that [was] relevant to its hiring decision and that it legitimately may ascertain." We determined the employer's interest was legitimate "[i]n light of the well-documented problems that are associated with the abuse of drugs and alcohol by employees—increased absenteeism, diminished productivity, greater health costs, increased safety problems and potential liability to third parties, and more frequent turnover. . . ." We also noted that the plaintiff in that case had "cite[d] no authority indicating that an employer may not reject a job applicant if it lawfully discovers that the applicant currently is using illegal drugs or engaging in excessive consumption of alcohol." The employer's legitimate concern about the use of illegal drugs also led us in *Loder* to reject the claim that pre-employment drug testing violated job applicants' state constitutional right to privacy. In so holding we relied in part on *Wilkinson v. Times Mirror Corp.* (1989) 215 Cal.App.3d 1034, 1046–1053, in which the Court of Appeal had earlier reached the same conclusion.

> The Compassionate Use Act does not eliminate marijuana's potential for abuse or the employer's legitimate interest in whether an employee uses the drug. Marijuana, as noted, remains illegal under federal law because of its "high potential for abuse," its lack of any "currently accepted medical use in treatment in the United States," and its "lack of accepted safety for use . . . under medical supervision." (21 U.S.C. § 812(b)(1)). Although California's voters had no power to change federal law, certainly they were free to disagree with Congress's assessment of marijuana, and they also were free to view the possibility of beneficial medical use as a sufficient basis for exempting from criminal liability under state law patients whose physicians recommend the drug. The logic of this position, however, did not compel the voters to take the additional step of requiring employers to accommodate marijuana use by their employees. The voters were entitled to change the criminal law without also speaking to employment law.

* * *

The proponents of the Compassionate Use Act consistently described the proposed measure to the voters as motivated by the desire to create a narrow exception to the criminal law. The proponents spoke, for example, of their desire to "protect patients from criminal penalties for marijuana," and not to "send cancer patients to jail for using marijuana." Although the measure's *opponents* argued the act would "make it legal for people to smoke marijuana in the workplace . . . or in public places . . . next to your children," the argument was obviously disingenuous because the measure did not purport to change the laws affecting public intoxication with controlled substances or the laws addressing controlled substances in such places as schools and parks, and the act expressly provided that it did "not supersede legislation prohibiting persons from engaging in conduct that endangers others" Proponents reasonably countered the argument by observing that, under the measure, "[p]olice officers can still arrest anyone for marijuana offenses. Proposition 215 simply gives those arrested a defense in court, *if they can prove they used marijuana with a doctor's approval*."

In conclusion, given the Compassionate Use Act's modest objectives and the manner in which it was presented to the voters for adoption, we have no reason to conclude the voters intended to speak so broadly, and in a context so far removed from the criminal law, as to require employers to accommodate marijuana use. As another court has observed, "the proponents' ballot arguments reveal a delicate tightrope walk designed to induce voter approval, which we would upset were we to stretch the proposition's limited immunity to cover that which its language does not.

* * *

NOTES AND QUESTIONS

1. **Reconciling state medical marijuana acts and other statutory protections.** *Ross v. RagingWire Telecommunications, Inc.* discussed the interpretation of California's medical marijuana act in light of the state's version of the ADA. In *Coats v. Dish Network, LLC*, 350 P.3d 849 (Colo. 2015), by contrast, the Colorado Supreme Court interpreted Colorado's medical marijuana act in light of a Colorado statute (C.R.S. § 24–34–402.5) that prohibited employers from discharging employees who engage in "lawful activities" outside of work during nonworking hours. The plaintiff in that case argued that medical marijuana use was a lawful activity within the meaning of the statute because he had a valid license to use medical marijuana. However, the court rejected the plaintiff's claim, holding that an activity must be lawful under both state law and federal law to come within the protection of the state statute. Since the plaintiff's medical marijuana use was unlawful under federal law, it did not count as a "lawful activity" within the meaning of the statute. Do you think the result would have been different if the medical marijuana act specifically provided that employers could not terminate or discipline employees for marijuana use that was in conformance with the act?

2. State statutes that specifically protect employees using medical marijuana. *Ross v. RagingWire Telecommunications* is representative of a number of state cases that have upheld the rights of employers to terminate employees who test positive for marijuana use at the workplace, even if the employees have valid medical marijuana licenses, use marijuana only at home, and are not impaired at work. Certain states, however, have passed legislation that specifically prohibits employers from terminating medical marijuana users who use marijuana at home and are not impaired at work. For example, the Minnesota legislature passed Minn. Stat. Ann. § 152.32(3)(c) (2015), which provides:

> (c) Unless a failure to do so would violate federal law or regulations or cause an employer to lose a monetary or licensing-related benefit under federal law or regulations, an employer may not discriminate against a person in hiring, termination, or any term or condition of employment, or otherwise penalize a person, if the discrimination is based upon either of the following:

> (1) the person's status as a patient enrolled in the registry program under sections 152.22 to 152.37; or

> (2) a patient's positive drug test for cannabis components or metabolites, unless the patient used, possessed, or was impaired by medical cannabis on the premises of the place of employment or during the hours of employment.

By enacting the statute, the Minnesota legislature provided direct protection to employees who use medical marijuana off the premises and are not impaired at work, rather than leaving it to the courts to determine whether more general protective statutes apply to medical marijuana users. But look at the exception in the first sentence: what types of employees does it exempt from the statute's requirements?

3. Counseling employers. The uncertainty around an employee's right to use medical marijuana in legalization states often makes it challenging for employers to formulate law-compliant company drug policies. Here is the advice of one employment lawyer who practices in Idaho:

> While the Americans with Disabilities Act prohibits discrimination based on disability, it expressly permits an employer to prohibit the illegal use of drugs at the workplace and also permits an employer to hold an employee who engages in illegal drug use to the same standards as other employees, even if the unsatisfactory performance is related to drug use for treatment of a disability. Even in those states which have legalized medical marijuana and/or "lawful activities" statutes, because marijuana remains illegal under federal law, courts will likely continue to consider both recreational and medical marijuana use "illegal" in the employment context. However, for those employers in any of the 11 states with a job protection statute (AK, AZ, CT, DE, IL, ME, MN, NY, NV, PA and RI), best practice would be that such employers have a policy that

provides certain accommodations for those legally using medical marijuana. . . . [T]he issue of marijuana in the workplace is nuanced, primarily around the use of medical marijuana outside of the work place. However, even for those 11 states with a job protection statute, employers must implement a robust drug policy. For the remaining states, employers may elect to promulgate a policy that insists upon zero tolerance. Unless and until the federal government legalizes cannabis use, an unlikely event under the current administration, in Idaho, zero-tolerance policies remain the most conservative, and likely, best practice.

Jennifer Schrack Dempsey, *The Impact of Legal Marijuana Use on the Workplace: Should Employers Hire Marijuana Users*, 60 Advocate 27 (2017).

PROBLEM 15-1

State X has legalized medical marijuana, but the state's medical marijuana act does not address employee/employer rights. Employee E works for company C, which has instituted a zero-tolerance drug policy for its employees. Employee E tested negative for all illegal drugs, but one week later, a fellow employee reported to the HR department that she saw employee E smoking marijuana on his front porch when she walked by his house on a weekend. Can the employer legally terminate employee E pursuant to its zero-tolerance drug policy, based upon this report?

B. BANKING ISSUES

Perhaps the greatest challenge marijuana dispensaries and other marijuana-related businesses have faced in operating their businesses is the difficulty in obtaining banking services. The banking system in the United States is highly regulated by federal law, and under federal law, banks generally cannot do business with illegal business entities. Since marijuana is illegal under federal law, banks are accordingly prohibited from dealing with marijuana-related businesses.

This creates a serious problem for marijuana-related businesses. For the most part, they have had to run cash-only businesses because they cannot open checking accounts or savings accounts, or even take credit cards, since those transactions are also subject to federal law. As a result, marijuana-related businesses have had to pay vendors and employees in non-conventional ways, which can create a significant private and public safety issue, given the potential for theft. To pay employees, for example, the companies have often had to either arrange secret locations where they can meet employees and pay them in cash—putting everyone present in danger—or assume the risk of transporting large amounts of cash to entities that will issue money orders that they can then pay to the order of vendors and employees. These difficulties have created concern on the part of the owners of marijuana-related businesses that has led to calls for changes to federal law to enable such businesses to have better access to traditional banking services.

The following case, *Fourth Corner Credit Union v. Federal Reserve Board of Kansas City,* deals with this issue. Specifically, it addressed whether the regional Federal Reserve Bank properly denied plaintiff credit union a master account that would have enabled the credit union to access the Federal Reserve System's services, including its electronic payments system. The credit union was set up for the purpose of providing banking services to marijuana-related businesses. The court of appeals ultimately vacated the district court's order denying the credit union's claim, and it remanded the case back to the district court to allow the credit union to re-file if it chose to do so. However, the three members of the court of appeals were deeply divided as to the substantive issue, and each opinion offers a different rationale for deciding the matter.

FOURTH CORNER CREDIT UNION V. FEDERAL RESERVE BOARD OF KANSAS CITY

U.S. Court of Appeals for the Tenth Circuit
861 F.3d 1052 (10th Cir. 2017)

PER CURIAM.

In this appeal, we vacate the district court's order and remand with instructions to dismiss the amended complaint without prejudice. This disposition is addressed in three opinions—one by each member of the panel. Judge Moritz would affirm the dismissal with prejudice. Judge Matheson would vacate and remand with instructions to dismiss the amended complaint without prejudice on prudential-ripeness grounds. Judge Bacharach would reverse the dismissal of the amended complaint. By remanding with instructions to dismiss the amended complaint without prejudice, our disposition effectuates the judgment of the two panel members who would allow the Fourth Corner Credit Union to proceed with its claims.

Finally, we deny the Federal Reserve Bank of Kansas City's motion to strike the Fourth Corner Credit Union's reply-brief addenda.

MORITZ, J.

The Fourth Corner Credit Union applied for a master account from the Federal Reserve Bank of Kansas City. The Reserve Bank denied the application, effectively crippling the Credit Union's business operations. The Credit Union sought an injunction requiring the Reserve Bank to issue it a master account. The district court dismissed the action, ruling that the Credit Union's raison d'être—to provide banking services to marijuana-related businesses—would violate the Controlled Substances Act (CSA). Because the district court correctly declined to lend its equitable power to illegal activity, I would affirm the dismissal with prejudice.

BACKGROUND

In 2012, Colorado amended its constitution to legalize a wide array of recreational marijuana activity. An industry of marijuana growers and retailers sprang up to supply this new market, but they face a significant obstacle: traditional banks are wary of serving marijuana-related businesses (MRBs). Many MRBs thus operate solely in cash, a restriction that "raise[s] significant public safety concerns for customers and employees" and "make[s] it more difficult for the state and federal government to regulate and audit [MRBs]." App. 215.

The Credit Union aims to fill this banking void. Its purpose, according to its amended complaint, is to "provide much needed banking services to compliant, licensed cannabis and hemp businesses" and to marijuana-legalization supporters. But there are many hurdles for a would-be depository institution to clear. The relevant hurdle here is obtaining a master account. A master account is, put simply, a bank account for banks. It gives depository institutions access to the Federal Reserve System's services, including its electronic payments system. In the Credit Union's words, "Without such access, a depository institution is nothing more than a vault."

The Credit Union applied to the Federal Reserve Bank of Kansas City for a master account. The Reserve Bank denied the application by letter, citing a host of concerns. In general, the Reserve Bank determined that the Credit Union simply posed too great a risk to the Federal Reserve System— in large part because of its "focus on serving [MRBs]."

In response, the Credit Union filed this suit. It sought a declaratory judgment that the Credit Union is entitled to a master account and an injunction requiring the Reserve Bank to issue it one. The Credit Union asserted that the Reserve Bank is required by statute to issue a master account to every applicant, citing 12 U.S.C. § 248a. The Reserve Bank moved to dismiss the complaint, arguing that (1) the Reserve Bank retains statutory discretion to deny master-account applications; (2) the district court couldn't use its equitable power to facilitate illegal activity—namely, violations of the CSA; and (3) the Credit Union's Colorado charter is preempted and void under the Supremacy Clause because it conflicts with the CSA. In apparent response to the Reserve Bank's illegality argument, the Credit Union amended its complaint. In its amended complaint, the Credit Union repeatedly alleges that it will serve MRBs only if it's authorized to do so by law. The Credit Union then moved for summary judgment on its claim, and the Reserve Bank renewed its motion to dismiss.

The district court granted the Reserve Bank's motion to dismiss and denied the Credit Union's motion for summary judgment. The district court didn't accept the Credit Union's allegations that it would follow the law. And based on the principle that "courts cannot use equitable powers to issue an order that would facilitate criminal activity," The district court concluded that it couldn't grant the Credit Union its requested injunction. The district court declined to reach the Reserve Bank's preemption and statutory discretion arguments.

The Credit Union filed a motion for reconsideration requesting, in part, that the court decide the preemption and statutory discretion issues. The district court denied that motion. The Credit Union appeals.

DISCUSSION

The Credit Union argues that the district court erred in dismissing its claim based on the Reserve Bank's illegality defense. This court reviews de novo the district court's grant of the Reserve Bank's motion to dismiss, applying the same standard as the district court. Specifically, we accept the well-pleaded allegations of the complaint as true and construe them in the light most favorable to the Credit Union.

The Reserve Bank's illegality defense is straightforward. It begins with the principle—which the Credit Union doesn't dispute—that a court won't use its equitable power to facilitate illegal conduct. By its own allegations, the Credit Union would use the court's equitable relief to facilitate illegal activity. If given a master account, the Credit Union "intends to provide banking services to compliant state licensed cannabis and hemp businesses." But even if these businesses are "compliant" with Colorado law, their conduct plainly violates the CSA. By providing banking services to these businesses, the Credit Union would—by its own admission—facilitate their illegal activity by giving them bank access that they currently lack. And, critically, the Credit Union concedes that it won't be able to serve MRBs without the court's equitable relief. A court-ordered master account would thus serve as the linchpin for the Credit Union's facilitation of illegal conduct.

In response to the Reserve Bank's illegality defense, the Credit Union argues that the MRBs it proposes to serve aren't violating federal law. Specifically, it asserts that "[c]onduct in full compliance with a presumptively valid state medical or recreational marijuana law is legal under state and federal law until the state law is formally invalidated." But the Credit Union seemed to abandon this position at oral argument, and for good reason: the CSA, by virtue of the Supremacy Clause, is the law of the land. Conduct prohibited by federal law is illegal, regardless of what Colorado law may permit. For the same reason, I would decline the Credit Union's request to decide whether the CSA preempts Colorado law. Regardless of how we might resolve that issue, the MRBs' conduct would remain federally illegal.

The Credit Union also argues that it may legally serve MRBs pursuant to certain Executive Branch guidance documents. In 2014, then-Deputy Attorney General James Cole issued a DOJ memorandum outlining that agency's marijuana-banking enforcement priorities. But while the Cole Memorandum suggested that the DOJ may decline to prosecute banks that meet certain criteria, the Memorandum also made clear that its guidance didn't create a legal defense for violations of the CSA or certain money-laundering statutes. *See* App. 488 (explaining that "[t]his memorandum does not alter in any way the [DOJ's] authority to enforce federal law, including federal laws relating to marijuana, regardless of state law" and doesn't "provide[ ] a legal defense to a violation of federal law, including . . . violation of the CSA, the money laundering and unlicensed money transmitter statutes, or the [Bank Secrecy Act]").

Likewise, the Treasury Department's Financial Crimes Enforcement Network ("FinCEN"), which is responsible for enforcing certain money-laundering statutes, issued its own marijuana-related guidance concurrently with the Cole Memorandum. The FinCEN Guidance purported to "clarif[y] how financial institutions can provide services to marijuana-related businesses consistent with their [anti-money laundering] obligations." But this guidance, like the Cole Memorandum, didn't nullify the CSA or federal money-laundering statutes. And the Credit Union doesn't explain how Executive Branch enforcement decisions could undermine substantive law.

Perhaps recognizing the gossamer-thin nature of its interpretation of federal law, the Credit Union alternatively argues that it won't serve MRBs unless doing so is legal. Specifically, it argues that its amended complaint plausibly alleges that the Credit Union intends to abide by federal law and that the district court erred in declining to presume these allegations are true. I agree with the district court: the Credit Union's equivocations don't allay my concern that the equitable relief it seeks will facilitate illegal activity.

* * *

The Credit Union asserts that its promises to follow the law are plausible. And this court presumes that the amended complaint's well-pleaded factual allegations are true and construes them in the light most favorable to the Credit Union. That principle might benefit the Credit Union if it unequivocally alleged that it won't serve MRBs. But it never does. Instead, the amended complaint's allegations are all conditional: *if* serving MRBs is illegal, *then* the Credit Union won't serve them. We don't owe the presumption of truth to illusory allegations The Credit Union will either serve MRBs or it won't—its allegations can't depend on the answer to a legal question. As one court explained, "There is a significant difference between pleading alternative theories of law based upon given facts and pleading alternative statements of fact to support a given principle of law."

The Credit Union's promise to follow the law is particularly unworthy of credence because the amended complaint both asserts that the Credit Union plans to serve MRBs "in strict accordance with state and federal laws, regulations and guidance," while at the same time carefully avoiding any concessions regarding what the law actually is ("Whatever the law is, [the Credit Union] will obey.").

After setting aside the Credit Union's non-committal, conclusory allegations, the amended complaint tells a clear story. The Credit Union "intends to provide banking services to compliant state licensed cannabis and hemp businesses, their employees, [and] industry vendors." *Id.* at 204. The district court correctly declined to facilitate this illegality.

Accordingly, I would affirm the district court's dismissal of the amended complaint with prejudice.

MATHESON, J., dissenting.

We should dismiss this case on ripeness grounds.

A. The Credit Union's New Claim

The Credit Union was formed primarily to serve MRBs. It requested a master account from the Reserve Bank to do so. The Reserve Bank denied the Credit Union's application for a master account, citing the Credit Union's "focus on serving marijuana-related businesses." The Credit Union sued. The Reserve Bank again expressed its misgiving about the Credit Union's plan to serve MRBs in a motion to dismiss the original complaint.

The Credit Union did not re-apply for a master account to alleviate the Reserve Bank's concern about MRBs, but instead just amended its complaint to allege it will serve MRBs only if doing so is legal.

Assuming this allegation is true, as we must, it raises ripeness concerns because this case has become divorced from the factual backdrop that gave rise to the original dispute. As the Reserve Bank points out, the new Credit Union—the Credit Union that excludes MRBs from its membership until serving them becomes legal—is a "fundamentally different[ ] entity" than the one the Reserve Bank turned down.

B. Ripeness

* * *

In assessing prudential ripeness, this court has taken guidance from *Abbott Laboratories v. Gardner*, 387 U.S. 136 (1967), which "instructs courts to assess 'both the fitness of the issues for judicial decision and the hardship to the parties of withholding court consideration.' "

1. *Fitness*

"First, on fitness, we focus on whether determination of the merits turns upon strictly legal issues or requires facts that may not yet be sufficiently developed." The Credit Union's amended complaint reveals this case is no longer based on sufficiently developed facts. In particular, the amended complaint does not and cannot tell us whether the Reserve Bank would grant a master account on the condition that the Credit Union will not serve MRBs unless doing so is legal. It cannot do so because, as the Credit Union explained to the district court, it has never approached the Reserve Bank about obtaining a master account on the terms now alleged.

* * *

The Credit Union's plan to serve MRBs was a key reason why the Reserve Bank denied the master account application. With that justification gone, we do not know what would happen under the Credit Union's revised stance. The Reserve Bank's letter to the Credit Union explained it was denying a master account based on the Credit Union's planned MRB service and "[o]ther factors" "[t]aken together." The other factors included: (1) "the nature of [the Credit Union's] proposed business model"; (2) lack of capital; (3) failure to obtain insurance; and (4) its status as a "de novo depository institution."

These other factors do not mitigate the ripeness concern that the amended complaint has spawned. First, the Reserve Bank based its master account denial on these "[o]ther factors" "[t]aken together" with the MRB concern, suggesting its reasons collectively formed the basis for the denial. *Id.* In other words, the denial letter did not say whether any reason, standing alone, would have been enough to deny the master account. Second, the Reserve Bank identified some of these other concerns as intertwined with the Credit Union's planned service of MRBs. For example, the denial letter tied the "de novo" justification to the MRBs. Third, although the Reserve Bank's lawyer told the district court he "seriously doubt[ed]" a promise from the Credit Union not to serve MRBs would make a difference, *id.* at 656, this was an inconclusive prediction. As discussed below, the Reserve Bank identifies many unanswered questions in its supplemental brief about an MRB-free Credit Union, suggesting the possibility of a different outcome.

Despite its new position that it will serve MRBs only if legal, the Credit Union argues that submitting another master account application would be futile. This ignores why the Reserve Bank denied the first application. The Credit Union's business plan was not part of its master account application, but the Credit Union's planned service of MRBs was part of the reasoning for the Reserve Bank's denial. The Credit Union has not sought a master account on the new condition that it will not serve MRBs unless legal, and its revised litigation position does not substitute for a new application to the Reserve Bank. The Credit Union has filed two complaints contemplating two very different financial entities, but it has submitted only one master account application. As the Reserve Bank points out, an MRB-free "application would raise numerous questions that have yet to be asked, much less answered." Given the change in circumstances, submitting another application would hardly be an empty gesture. And even if the result is another denial, it would at least make the factual scenario created by the amended complaint real rather than hypothetical.

In short, we do not know what would happen if the Credit Union were to seek a master account based on the new plan alleged in its amended complaint. As the Reserve Bank discerns, the Credit Union is attempting "to retroactively alter the nature of the dispute." The issues the Credit Union raises are not yet fit for judicial decision.

2. *Hardship*

In the second part of our ripeness analysis, we assess the potential "hardship from withholding judicial review" by asking "whether the challenged action creates a direct and immediate dilemma for the parties.". The Reserve Bank faces no hardship. As for the Credit Union, the challenged action is the Reserve Bank's denial of a master account, which the Credit Union argues should have issued within days of its initial request. Without a master account, the Credit Union contends, it cannot conduct its affairs. The Credit Union's supplemental briefing also alludes to an unspecified "irremediable adverse consequence that would flow from requiring a later challenge," but it provides no particulars on how a dismissal on ripeness grounds would alter the status quo.

* * *

C. Conclusion

As the Reserve Bank observes, the Credit Union "is apparently seeking court review of a decision that [the Reserve Bank] has never made and that the district court never considered." I would dismiss this appeal as premature and remand to the district court to vacate the judgment and dismiss without prejudice.

BACHARACH, J.

This case involves the denial of a request for a master account. A master account is required to purchase services that are indispensable for all financial institutions. Without a master account, a financial institution must obtain these services through another institution serving as a "middleman." To avoid the middleman, a financial institution must obtain a master account from one of the regional Federal Reserve Banks.

The plaintiff, The Fourth Corner Credit Union, is a credit union that requested a master account from one of the regional Federal Reserve Banks (the Federal Reserve Bank of Kansas City). This request would ordinarily be considered routine for the Federal Reserve Bank of Kansas City. But the Federal Reserve Bank of Kansas City learned from a third party that Fourth Corner wanted to service marijuana-related businesses in a state that had legalized these businesses. The Federal Reserve Bank of Kansas City refused to grant the master account, prompting Fourth Corner to sue for a declaratory judgment and an injunction.

The Federal Reserve Bank of Kansas City moved to dismiss, arguing in part that Fourth Corner would use the master account to violate federal drug laws. The district court agreed and dismissed the amended complaint.

In my view, this ruling was erroneous for two reasons. First, the district court should have presumed that Fourth Corner would follow the law as determined by the court. Second, in the amended complaint, Fourth Corner promised to obey the law. By seeking a declaratory judgment, Fourth Corner acknowledged that the court was the sole arbiter of the law. Thus, the amended complaint indicates that Fourth Corner would obey a ruling that servicing marijuana-related businesses is illegal.

* * *

I.   Standard of Review

In the amended complaint, Fourth Corner stated that it would service marijuana-related businesses only if authorized by federal law. Fourth Corner argued that servicing these businesses had been legalized by recent guidance from federal agencies. But in the amended complaint, Fourth Corner promised that "[w]hatever the law is, [Fourth Corner] will obey." Elsewhere in the amended complaint, Fourth Corner committed to obey the law, stating:

[Fourth Corner's charter] states [that Fourth Corner] is "authorized to conduct business pursuant to all of the powers conferred upon it by law, until this charter is suspended, revoked or otherwise surrendered in the manner directed by statute." [Fourth Corner] takes this grant of authority to mean it must comply with both state and federal law, and it intends to do so.

* * *

Fourth Corner also explained that if servicing marijuana-related businesses is illegal, Fourth Corner would confine its business to servicing members of social groups supporting the legalization of marijuana. This part of Fourth Corner's business plan was legal, and no one has suggested otherwise. But servicing marijuana-related businesses is different, and the district court properly concluded that this part of Fourth Corner's plan would have violated federal drug laws.

Upon drawing this conclusion, the district court interpreted Fourth Corner's promise to obey the law. In the district court's view, Fourth Corner was promising to follow its own understanding of the law, not to obey the district court's pronouncement of the law. Interpreted this way, the promise gave the district court little confidence that Fourth Corner would obey federal drug laws, for Fourth Corner had argued that servicing marijuana-related businesses was legal. Suspicious that Fourth Corner would follow its own understanding of the law rather than the court's, the district court granted the motion to dismiss.

This ruling was erroneous in two ways.

First, the district court improperly discounted Fourth Corner's stated intent to obey federal law. This allegation of intent constituted a factual allegation. And like any other factual allegation, this one should have been interpreted favorably to Fourth Corner (as the non-movant).

At a bench trial, the district court could freely decide whether Fourth Corner actually intended to obey federal law. But here the district court evaluated the validity of Fourth Corner's assertion at the motion-to-dismiss stage. At this stage, the district court must accept as true all of Fourth Corner's well-pleaded factual allegations and view them in the light most favorable to Fourth Corner. *See* Part I, above. The district court was not free to scuttle these requirements.

Second, the district court should have presumed that Fourth Corner would obey the ruling that servicing marijuana-related businesses is illegal. This presumption is especially fitting here, where Fourth Corner acknowledged the court's role as arbiter of the law by the very act of asking for a declaratory judgment. But even without this acknowledgment, the district court should have presumed that Fourth Corner would abide by the ruling.

Nothing in the amended complaint overcame this presumption. Indeed, as explained above, the amended complaint indicated that Fourth Corner intended to obey the law. And by acknowledging the court's role as arbiter of the law, Fourth Corner's promise to obey the law meant that Fourth Corner would obey the court's eventual pronouncement of the law.

Nonetheless, the district court interpreted Fourth Corner's promise to obey the law in a way that conflicted with the amended complaint as a whole and Fourth Corner's acknowledgment of the court as arbiter of the law. As stated above, Fourth Corner effectively asserted that it intended to obey the district court. Given this assertion, it makes little sense to interpret Fourth Corner's promise merely as a pledge to obey what Fourth Corner already thought the law was. At this stage of the proceedings, the only reasonable interpretation is that Fourth Corner promised to acquiesce in the district court's pronouncement of the law.

The district court's contrary interpretation was erroneous because it rested on misapplication of the standard on a motion to dismiss and abandonment of the presumption that Fourth Corner would follow the law.

* * *

NOTES AND QUESTIONS

1. **Plurality opinion.** The opinion in *Fourth Corner Credit Union* is a pure plurality opinion, in that each of the three judges writes a separate opinion, and each reaches a different result. The district court had dismissed

the Credit Union's complaint with prejudice, holding that it had no authority to issue an order that would facilitate criminal activity. Judge Moritz agreed with the district court, and voted to affirm the dismissal. Judge Bacharach, by contrast, voted to reverse the district court's decision, on the ground that the complaint on its face alleged no illegality. And Judge Matheson voted to dismiss the complaint without prejudice, on the basis of the judicial ripeness doctrine. Accordingly, the net result of the court of appeals' ruling was to remand the case to the district court with instructions to dismiss the complaint without prejudice. But other than that, the district court received little guidance as to how it should proceed.

In light of the disparate holdings of the three judges on the Court of Appeals, what do you think would happen if the credit union refiled its complaint? And what guidance can lawyers and courts in future cases glean from the court of appeals' decision in this case with respect to the law, or with respect to what they should expect from courts in the future?

2.   **Treasury Department guidance.** As discussed in other chapters of this book, the Obama administration assumed an essentially hands-off approach to the enforcement of federal marijuana laws, to the extent federal law conflicted with state laws legalizing marijuana for medical and/or adult use. Accordingly, the administration issued several directives to federal agencies, indicating that they should refrain from interfering in state legalization schemes so long as the states followed certain requirements. In 2013, the Department of Justice issued the so-called Cole Memo, which indicated that the federal government would not interfere with state legalization schemes, so long as certain enumerated enforcement priorities were observed, such as preventing the distribution of marijuana to minors, preventing drugged driving, etc. Similarly, in 2014, the Treasury Department's Financial Crimes Enforcement Network issued a "Guidance" indicating that banks and other financial institutions would not be prosecuted for doing business with marijuana-related businesses, so long as the banks undertook certain due diligence requirements to ensure that the Cole Memo enforcement priorities were observed, and that the banks also filed appropriate Suspicious Activity Reports with the Department.

3.   **The Trump Administration.** In early 2018, the Department of Justice (now under the direction of the Trump administration) reversed course in part, rescinding the Cole Memo. Attorney General Sessions issued a new memorandum, informing the nation's United States Attorneys that the Justice Department would no longer follow the Obama administration's "hands-off" approach toward state legalization, and that the U.S. Attorneys now had the discretion to prioritize enforcement the CSA as they deemed appropriate, considering the illegal nature of cannabis possession and distribution under federal law. The Attorney General's action has caused some consternation on the part of industry actors in legalization states. To date, however, the various United States Attorneys have not taken an aggressive approach toward state legalization schemes. And thus far the Treasury Department has not rescinded

its Guidance with respect to banking operations involving marijuana-related business.

4. Current status. If you were in charge of a financial institution and wanted to offer banking services to marijuana-related businesses, would you feel comfortable doing so, the light of the Justice Department's action in withdrawing the Cole Memo?

C. BANKRUPTCY ISSUES

The United States Bankruptcy Code provides important protections to struggling businesses that face possible dissolution due to the claims of creditors. Another difficult challenge facing marijuana-related businesses is their apparent inability to obtain relief from creditor claims in United States Bankruptcy Court. While the number of reported decisions on this issue is somewhat limited, it appears that the federal bankruptcy courts are in accord in refusing to allow relief to marijuana-related businesses. The legal grounds courts have relied are primarily (1) the equitable doctrine of unclean hands, and (2) the bankruptcy code's requirement of good faith.

The following bankruptcy-court decision from the District of Colorado, *Rent-Rite Super Kegs West, Ltd.*, explores these issues in the context of a Chapter 11 bankruptcy petition, which seeks reorganization of the debtor's business. There the U.S. Bankruptcy Court for the District of Colorado refused to sustain the debtor's Chapter 11 bankruptcy petition because 25% of the debtor's revenues from came leasing warehouse space to tenants who were engaged in the business of growing marijuana, in violation of federal law. Since the debtor was engaged in criminal activity under federal law, it held, the court was precluded from granting the relief the debtor sought.

IN RE RENT-RITE SUPER KEGS WEST, LTD

United States Bankruptcy Court, D. Colorado
484 B.R. 799 (2012)

ORDER ON MOTION TO DISMISS

TALLMAN, C.J.

This case comes before the Court on *Secured Creditor VFC Partners 14 LLC's Motion to Dismiss* (docket # 31) (the "Motion").

The Debtor's business involves a continuing violation of the federal Controlled Substances Act. *See.* Debtor candidly acknowledges that it derives roughly 25% of its revenues from leasing warehouse space to tenants who are engaged in the business of growing marijuana. This activity—arguably legal under Colorado law—forms the basis for the instant Motion filed by VFC Partners 14 LLC ("VFC"). VFC seeks dismissal of this case under the "clean hands doctrine" and argues that Debtor's activities, which the Court finds to be illegal under federal law, make it unworthy of the equitable protection of the bankruptcy court. In addition, VFC argues that Debtors' case was filed in bad faith and should be dismissed on that basis.

At the preliminary hearing on November 27, 2012, the parties confined their arguments to the legal issue of whether the case must be dismissed under the clean hands doctrine.

I.   FACTUAL BACKGROUND

1.   This case was filed on October 18, 2012.

2.   The Debtor owns a warehouse building located at 3850 to 3900 E. 48th Avenue, Denver, Colorado (the "Warehouse"). Debtor values the property at $2.3 million.

3.   On July 22, 2005, Debtor executed a promissory note to Commercial Federal Bank, FSB, in the face amount of $1.8 million (the "Note"). That obligation is secured by a Deed of Trust, Assignment of Rents and Security Agreement dated April 6, 2001, and modified on July 22, 2005, granting Commercial Federal a lien on the Debtor's Warehouse including rents and personal property (the "Deed of Trust").

4.   On December 21, 2011, the Note and Deed of Trust were assigned to VFC.

5.   Approximately 25% of the Debtor's income is produced from leasing space in the Debtor's Warehouse to tenants who use that space for the cultivation of marijuana.

II.   DISCUSSION

A.   Debtor's Business Operations Violate the Controlled Substances Act

For the reasons that follow, the Court concludes that the Debtor engages in conduct that, while legal under Colorado law, violates the federal Controlled Substances Act ("CSA").

The CSA has been described by the United States Supreme Court as "a lengthy and detailed statute creating a comprehensive framework for regulating the production, distribution, and possession of five classes of 'controlled substances.' Under the CSA, marijuana is classified as a Schedule I controlled substance. When a substance is placed on Schedule I, that represents a legislative judgment that "[t]he drug or other substance has a high potential for abuse; . . . [t]he drug or other substance has no currently accepted medical use in treatment in the United States; [and] . . . [t]here is a lack of accepted safety for use of the drug or other substance under medical supervision.". Under the CSA, any person who seeks to manufacture, distribute, or possess a Schedule I controlled substance must apply for and obtain a certificate of registration from the Drug Enforcement

Agency (DEA). At hearing, the Debtor did not argue that any of its tenants, whose operations are at issue here, are operating under DEA approval.

Under § 856 of the CSA, it is a federal crime to

> manage or control any place, . . . as an owner, . . . and knowingly and intentionally rent, lease, profit from, or make available for use, with or without compensation, the place for the purpose of unlawfully manufacturing, storing, distributing, or using a controlled substance.

Debtor freely admits that it leases Warehouse space to tenants who use the space for the cultivation of marijuana. The Court, therefore, finds that the Debtor is engaged in an ongoing criminal violation of the federal Controlled Substances Act.

The Debtor argues the law is in flux. Under state law in Colorado, it is legal to cultivate and distribute marijuana for medical purposes. Voters recently took marijuana legalization a step further and passed, by referendum, Amendment 64 to the Colorado Constitution, which legalizes the recreational production and sale of marijuana and possession of up to one ounce of marijuana.

That there is a sharp difference between state and federal law where the growing of marijuana is concerned does not make the controlling law unsettled or ambiguous. The Debtor cannot reasonably argue that legalization of marijuana cultivation on the state level nullifies the provisions of the CSA.

        * * *

In light of Colorado's laws and constitutional amendment legalizing marijuana, federal prosecutors may well choose to exercise their prosecutorial discretion and decline to seek indictments under the CSA where the activity that is illegal on the federal level is legal under Colorado state law. Be that as it may, even if the Debtor is never charged or prosecuted under the CSA, it is conducting operations in the normal course of its business that violate federal criminal law. Unless and until Congress changes that law, the Debtor's operations constitute a continuing criminal violation of the CSA and a federal court cannot be asked to enforce the protections of the Bankruptcy Code in aid of a Debtor whose activities constitute a continuing federal crime.

B.   VFC's Collateral is at Risk

Due to the Debtor's ongoing criminal activity under the CSA, VFC's collateral is placed at risk of forfeiture. The criminal penalty applicable to a violation of subsection (a) of 21 U.S.C. § 856 is "a term of imprisonment of not more than 20 years or a fine of not more than $500,000, or both, or a fine of $2,000,000 for a person other than an individual." Because the Debtor is committing an ongoing criminal violation that is punishable by a prison sentence of more than one year, the forfeiture statute comes into play. "All real property . . . which is used, or intended to be used, in any manner or part, to commit, or to facilitate the commission of, a violation of [the Controlled Substances Act] punishable by more than one year's imprisonment" is subject to forfeiture. Thus, VFC's collateral is at risk. Moreover, under 11 U.S.C. § 362(b)(b)(4), the automatic stay does not enjoin governmental entities against actions that constitute an exercise of governmental police powers.

The Debtor might argue that any such risk is highly theoretical, speculative and remote. As a practical matter, the Court suspects that is true. Yet, the Court cannot use the adjudicative authority granted to it by Congress to force VFC to bear even a highly improbable risk of total loss of its collateral in support of the Debtor's ongoing violation of federal criminal law.

C. The "Clean Hands Doctrine" is Applicable to Bankruptcy Proceedings

The simple act of filing a voluntary bankruptcy petition invokes protections under the Bankruptcy Code including the automatic stay. The protections invoked by a debtor by filing a bankruptcy petition are enforced by the bankruptcy courts.

Traditionally, bankruptcy courts are regarded as courts of equity. Nonetheless, a bankruptcy court's equitable powers "must and can only be exercised within the confines of the Bankruptcy Code." *Norwest Rank Worthington v. Ahlers,* 485 U.S. 197, 206 (1988).

The Debtor seeks to reorganize its financial affairs under the shelter of the Bankruptcy Code. A reorganization under chapter 11 affords a debtor the protection of the automatic stay in order for the debtor to use that breathing spell to formulate its reorganization plan. The Court's power to adjust the debtor-creditor relationship in the process of confirming a plan of reorganization goes to the essence of the Court's equitable jurisdiction and requires the Court to look to equitable factors to determine the propriety of the Debtor's filing.

In the case of *Marrama v. Citizens Bank,* 549 U.S. 365 (2007), the Supreme Court held that the bankruptcy court's equitable powers, as set out in 11 U.S.C. § 105(a), were sufficient authority to deny a debtor's request to convert his case from chapter 7 to chapter 13. The debtor in that case had fraudulently under-reported his assets in his schedules and he sought the conversion after the chapter 7 trustee determined that the debtor owned assets that could be administered in the chapter 7 case. Despite the fact that 11 U.S.C. § 706 contains no qualification of the right to convert to chapter 13, except that the debtor must be eligible to be a debtor under that chapter, the Supreme Court deemed the debtor's bad faith to be sufficient to invoke the bankruptcy court's equitable powers and to disallow the conversion.

　　　　"[T]he equitable maxim that 'he who comes into equity must come with clean hands' . . . closes the doors of a court of equity to one tainted with inequitableness or bad faith relative to the matter in which he seeks relief. . . . That doctrine is rooted in the historical concept of court of equity as a vehicle for affirmatively enforcing the requirements of conscience and good faith. . . . '[E]quity does not demand that its suitors shall have led blameless lives,' as to other matters, it does require that they shall have acted fairly and without fraud or deceit as to the controversy in issue."

Precision Instrument Mfg. Co. v. Automotive Maintenance Machinery Co., 324 U.S. 806, 814–15. Thus, as a court that utilizes equitable principles, this Court, like the bankruptcy court in *Marrama,* recognizes that a debtor's bad faith—in this case, the Debtor's criminal violation—in suitable cases will result in a denial or a limitation of the relief a debtor may hope to be granted.

　　　The Court finds that the Debtor's misconduct is of such a nature to justify the application of the clean hands doctrine. "[O]ne's misconduct need not necessarily have been of such a nature as to be punishable as a crime or as to justify legal proceedings of any character. Any willful act concerning the cause of action which rightfully can be said to transgress equitable standards of conduct is sufficient cause for the invocation of the [clean hands] maxim by the chancellor." The Debtor freely admits that it leases space to those who are engaged in the cultivation of marijuana. Even if the Debtor's holds a good faith—albeit misguided—belief that Colorado state law would prevail over the federal law or that the federal law is unlikely to be enforced, that is quite beside the point. The Debtor has knowingly and intentionally engaged in conduct that constitutes a violation of federal criminal law and it has done so with respect to its sole income producing asset. Worse yet, every day that the Debtor continues under the Court's protection is another day that VFC's collateral remains at risk.

　　　* * *

　　　The statute sets out a two step process. First, the Court must determine if "cause" exists for dismissal or conversion of the chapter 11 case. Next, the Court must determine whether dismissal or conversion of the case is in the best interests of creditors and the estate.

　　　A finding of "cause" in any context is, at bottom, an equitable determination. Congress specifically understood, in drafting § 1112(b)'s list of factors that a court may consider in its determination of "cause" for dismissal or conversion, that it was not restricting a court's ability to consider other factors that are not enumerated there. The legislative history to § 1112 states that:

Subsection (b) gives wide discretion to the court to make an appropriate disposition of the case when a party in interest requests. . . . The list [appearing in § 1112(b)] is not exhaustive. The court will be able to consider other factors as they arise, and to use its equitable powers to reach an appropriate result in individual cases.

It is, therefore, appropriate for the Court to give consideration, in addition to the enumerated factors in § 1112(b), to VFC's equitable clean hands argument.

1)   11 U.S.C. § 1112(b)(4)(B)

Where a court finds "gross mismanagement of the estate" by a debtor, that finding compels a conclusion that "cause" exists for dismissal or conversion of the chapter 11 case. In this case, the Court finds gross mismanagement. The Debtor has freely acknowledged that it engages in conduct that exposes the Debtor to criminal liability and that exposes its primary asset to forfeiture. It acknowledges that its criminal behavior has continued post-petition. The fact that it engaged in this conduct and entered into the leases with its tenants pre-petition does not constitute mismanagement of the estate because the estate is a post-petition entity. However, the Debtor entered its bankruptcy case with the offending leases in place and has maintained those leases during the pendency of its chapter 11 bankruptcy case. It is that post-petition presence of activity on the Debtor's property—pursuant to leases that it knowingly entered into—that violates the CSA; exposes the Debtor to criminal liability; and exposes both the Debtor and its mortgage creditor to forfeiture of the Warehouse that constitutes gross mismanagement of the estate and requires the Court to either convert this case to a case under chapter 7 or to dismiss it.

2)   Debtor's Lack of Clean Hands

Whether it is characterized, strictly speaking, as an application of the clean hands doctrine or simply as part of the Court's totality of the circumstances "cause" analysis, the Debtor's continued criminal activity satisfies the requirement of "cause" under § 1112(b) and requires dismissal or conversion of this chapter 11 bankruptcy case. As detailed above, the Court finds that the Debtor is engaged in an ongoing criminal violation of the CSA.

Title 11 U.S.C. § 1129(a)(3) provides that a plan may only be confirmed if it is "proposed in good faith and not by any means forbidden by law." Because a significant portion of the Debtor's income is derived from an illegal activity, § 1129(a)(3) forecloses any possibility of this Debtor obtaining confirmation of a plan that relies in any part on income derived from a criminal activity. This Debtor has no reasonable prospect of getting its plan confirmed. Even if § 1129 contained no such good faith requirement, under no circumstance can the Court place itself in the position of condoning the Debtor's criminal activity by allowing it to utilize the shelter of the Bankruptcy Code while continuing its unlawful practice of leasing space to those who are engaged in the business of cultivating a Schedule I controlled substance.

* * *

NOTES AND QUESTIONS

1. **Bankruptcy court protection.** The court's holding in Rent-Rite ultimately turned on its refusal to allow the debtor to "utilize the shelter of the Bankruptcy Code while continuing its unlawful practice of leasing space to those who are engaged in the business of cultivating a Schedule 1 controlled substance." Other courts that have considered this issue are largely in accord. *See, e.g., In re Arenas*, 535 B.R. 845, B.A.P. (10th Cir., Aug. 21, 2015) (engaging in conduct that constituted criminal activity under federal law provided good cause to deny bankruptcy relief to petitioner); *In re Johnson*, 532 B.R. 53 (Bankr. W.D. Mich. 2015) ("In the court's view, the Debtor cannot conduct an enterprise that admittedly violates federal criminal law while enjoying the federal benefits the Bankruptcy Code affords him."). How does that rationale bear on the protections provided by the federal bankruptcy laws to other individuals who violate the Controlled Substances Act? Should the federal bankruptcy courts deny bankruptcy protection to licensed medical marijuana users on the basis of the Clean Hands Doctrine, if their debt is partly due to medical marijuana purchases? And what about the federal courts more generally? Should, for example, federal courts refuse to allow civil actions (e.g., for breach of contract actions) between marijuana-related businesses on the grounds that the courts do not want to aid activity that is illegal under federal law?

2. **Protection for intellectual property.** As with bankruptcy protection, marijuana-related businesses receive little protection for their intellectual property. They cannot obtain federal patents or trademarks for their cannabis products because the products are not deemed to be lawful products under the CSA. *See* Sam Kamin & Vivian Moffat, *Trademark Laundering, Useless Patents, and Other IP Challenges for the Marijuana Industry*, 73 Wash. & Lee L. Rev. 217 (2016).

PROBLEM 15-2

In state Y, which has legalized both medical and recreational marijuana, company C produces and sells fertilizer. Approximately 25% of its sales are to marijuana cultivation facilities in state Y. Company C is now insolvent and wants to seek protection from its creditors in federal bankruptcy court. Will the unclean hands doctrine prevent it from doing so? Would your answer be different if the percentage of company C's sales to marijuana cultivators made up only 2% of its overall sales?

D. TAX ISSUES

Marijuana-related businesses also receive harsher treatment under the United States' Internal Revenue Code, in that they are not allowed to deduct the types of ordinary business expenses that other businesses can deduct. Thus, unlike most businesses, marijuana-related businesses cannot take deductions on their federal tax returns for such expenses as office rent, internet and phone, other administrative expenses, business-related travel and entertainment, automobile expenses, or employee benefits. This makes the cost of operating marijuana-related businesses relatively high, and it puts them at a significant competitive disadvantage versus other businesses.

Specifically, under § 162(a) of the Internal Revenue Code, businesses of all types are typically allowed to deduct the necessary and ordinary expenses associated with running the business, as well as losses incurred in operating the business. However, under § 280E of the Internal Revenue Code, Congress specifically exempts from the scope of § 162(a) all business expenses—whether legal or illegal—of businesses trafficking in controlled substances that are listed under Schedules I and II of the Controlled Substances Act. And since marijuana is a Schedule I controlled substance, even businesses that operate legally (under state law) in legalization states cannot deduct their ordinary business expenses.

The following case from the United States Court of Appeals for the 9th Circuit, *Olive v. Commissioner*, examines the applicability of I.R.C. § 280E to the operation of a medical marijuana dispensary. There the court upheld the tax court's decision precluding the dispensary from deducting business expenses, on the ground that the operation of the dispensary consisted of trafficking in a controlled substance within the meaning of § 280E.

OLIVE V. COMMISSIONER

United States Court of Appeals, Ninth Circuit
792 F.3d 1146 (2015)

GRABER, C.J.

Petitioner Martin Olive appeals the Tax Court's decision assessing deficiencies and penalties for tax years 2004 and 2005, which arise from Petitioner's operation of the Vapor Room Herbal Center ("Vapor Room"), a medical marijuana dispensary in San Francisco. The Tax Court held, among other things, that 26 U.S.C. (I.R.C.) § 280E precluded Petitioner from deducting any amount of ordinary or necessary business expenses associated with operation of the Vapor Room because the Vapor Room is a "trade or business . . . consist [ing] of trafficking in controlled substances . . . prohibited by Federal law." Reviewing that legal conclusion de novo, we agree and, therefore, affirm the Tax Court's decision.

Established in 2004, the Vapor Room provides its patrons a place where they can socialize, purchase medical marijuana, and consume it using the Vapor Room's vaporizers. The Vapor Room sells medical marijuana in three forms: dried marijuana leaves, edibles, and a concentrated version of THC. Customers who purchase marijuana at the Vapor Room pay varying costs, depending on the quantity and quality of the product and on the individual customer's ability to pay.

The Vapor Room is set up much like a community center, with couches, chairs, and tables located throughout the establishment. Games, books, and art supplies are available for patrons' general use. The Vapor Room also offers services such as yoga, movies, and massage therapy. Customers can drink complimentary tea or water during their visits, or they can eat complimentary snacks, including pizza and sandwiches. The Vapor Room offers these activities and amenities for free.

Each of the Vapor Room's staff members is permitted under California law to receive and consume medical marijuana. Petitioner purchases, for cash, the Vapor Room's inventory from licensed medical marijuana suppliers. Patrons who visit the Vapor Room can buy marijuana and use the vaporizers at no charge, or they can use the vaporizers (again, at no charge) with marijuana that they bought elsewhere. Sometimes, staff members or patrons sample Vapor Room inventory for free. When staff members interact with customers, occasionally one-on-one, they discuss illnesses; provide counseling on various personal, legal, or political matters related to medical marijuana; and educate patrons on how to use the vaporizers and consume medical marijuana responsibly. All these services are provided to patrons at no charge.

Petitioner filed business income tax returns for tax years 2004 and 2005, which reported the Vapor Room's net income during those years as $64,670 and $33,778, respectively. Although Petitioner reported $236,502 and $417,569 in Vapor Room business expenses for 2004 and 2005, the Tax Court concluded that § 280E of the Internal Revenue Code precluded Petitioner from deducting any of those expenses. Petitioner timely appeals.

The Internal Revenue Code provides that, for the purpose of computing taxable income, an individual's or a business's "gross income" includes "all income from whatever source derived," including "income derived from business. The Code further allows a business to deduct from its gross income "all the ordinary and necessary expenses paid or incurred during the taxable year in carrying on [the] trade or business." *Id.* § 162(a). But there are exceptions to § 162(a). *See, e.g., id.* §§ 261–280H (listing "Items Not Deductible"). One such exception applies when the "amount paid or incurred during the taxable year" is for the purpose of "carrying on any trade or business. . .consist[ing] of trafficking in controlled substances." Although the use and sale of medical marijuana are legal under California state law, the use and sale of marijuana remain prohibited under federal law.

We turn first to the text of I.R.C. § 280E. To determine whether Petitioner may deduct the expenses associated with the Vapor Room, then, we must decide whether the Vapor Room is a "trade or business [that] consists of trafficking in controlled substances . . . prohibited by Federal law." We start with the phrase "trade or business."

The test for determining whether an activity constitutes a "trade or business" is "whether the activity 'was entered into with the dominant hope and intent of realizing a profit.'. The parties agree, and the Tax Court found, that the *only* income-generating activity in which the Vapor Room engaged was its sale of medical marijuana. The other services that the Vapor Room offered—including, among other things, the provision of vaporizers, food and drink, yoga, games, movies, and counseling—were offered to its patrons at no cost to them. The only activity, then, that the Vapor Room "entered into with the dominant hope and intent of realizing a profit," *Am. Bar Endowment,* 477 U.S. at 110 n. 1, was the sale of medical marijuana. Accordingly, Petitioner's "trade or business," for § 162(a) purposes, was limited to medical marijuana sales.

Given the limited scope of Petitioner's "trade or business," we conclude that the business "consist[ed] of trafficking in controlled substances . . . prohibited by Federal law." The income-generating activities in which the Vapor Room engaged consisted *solely* of trafficking in medical marijuana which, as noted, is prohibited under federal law. Under § 280E, then, the expenses that Petitioner incurred in the course of operating the Vapor Room cannot be deducted for federal tax purposes.

Petitioner's argument relies primarily on the phrase "consists of," rather than on the phrase "trade or business." According to Petitioner, the use of the words "consists of" is most appropriate "when a listing is meant to be exhaustive"; the word "consisting," he argues, is not synonymous with the word "including." Relying on that proposition, Petitioner contends that, for § 280E purposes, a business "consists of" a service only when that service is the *sole* service that the business provides. Because the Vapor Room provides caregiving services *and* sells medical marijuana, Petitioner concludes that his business does not "consist of" either one alone and therefore does not fall within the ambit of § 280E.

To support that line of reasoning, Petitioner cites the Tax Court's decision in *Californians Helping to Alleviate Medical Problems, Inc. v. Commissioner (CHAMP),* 128 T.C. 173 (2007). His reliance on *CHAMP* is misplaced. In *CHAMP,* the petitioner's income-generating business included the provision not only of medical marijuana, but also of "extensive" counseling and caregiving services. The Tax Court noted that the business's "primary purpose was to provide caregiving services to its members" and that its "secondary purpose was to provide its members with medical marijuana." The court found, after considering the "degree of economic interrelationship between the two undertakings," that the petitioner was involved in "more than one trade or business." That is not the case here. Petitioner does not provide counseling, caregiving, snacks, and so forth for a separate fee; the only "business" in which he engages is selling medical marijuana.

An analogy may help to illustrate the difference between the Vapor Room and the business at issue in *CHAMP*. Bookstore A sells books. It also provides some complimentary amenities: Patrons can sit in comfortable seating areas while considering whether to buy a book; they can drink coffee or tea and eat cookies, all of which the bookstore offers at no charge; they can obtain advice from the staff about new authors, book clubs, community events, and the like; they can bring their children to a weekend story time or an after-school reading circle. The "trade or business" of Bookstore A "consists of" selling books. Its many amenities do not alter that conclusion; presumably, the owner hopes to attract buyers of books by creating an alluring atmosphere. By contrast, Bookstore B sells books but also sells coffee and pastries, which customers can consume in a cafe-like seating area. Bookstore B has two "trade[s] or business[es]," one of which "consists of" selling books and the other of which "consists of" selling food and beverages.

Petitioner's arguments related to congressional intent and public policy are similarly unavailing. He contends that I.R.C. § 280E should not be construed to apply to medical marijuana dispensaries because those dispensaries did not exist when Congress enacted § 280E. Congress added that provision, he maintains, to prevent street dealers from taking a deduction. According to Petitioner, Congress could not have intended for medical marijuana dispensaries, now legal in many states, to fall within the ambit of "items not deductible" under the Internal Revenue Code. We are not persuaded.

That Congress might not have imagined what some states would do in future years has no bearing on our analysis. It is common for statutes to apply to new situations. And here, application of the statute is clear. Application of the statute does not depend on the illegality of marijuana sales under state law; the only question Congress allows us to ask is whether marijuana is a controlled substance "prohibited by Federal law." If Congress now thinks that the policy embodied in § 280E is unwise as applied to medical marijuana sold in conformance with state law, it can change the statute. We may not.

* * *

In summary, the Tax Court properly concluded that I.R.C. § 280E precludes Petitioner from deducting, pursuant to I.R.C. § 162(a), the ordinary and necessary business expenses associated with his operation of the Vapor Room. We therefore affirm the Tax Court's decision.

AFFIRMED

NOTES AND QUESTIONS

1. **Statutory interpretation.** The court's holding in *Olive* turned on its interpretation of the statutory requirement in § 280E that the taxpayer be a "trade or business that consists of trafficking in controlled substances." The Vapor Room had argued that a business consists of trafficking in controlled substances only when that service is the sole service that the business provides. Conversely, the Vapor Room argued, it provided other services to customers in addition to selling marijuana. The court rejected that argument, however, on the ground that marijuana sales were the only income-generating service the company provided. Does it follow from this that the Vapor Room could have avoided the application of § 280E (and therefore deducted its business expenses) if it had charged for the ancillary services it provided, such as food and beverages, games, and counseling services?

2. **Earlier internal revenue code provisions.** Section 280E of the Internal Revenue Code is not the only exception to I.R.C. § 162(a) (which allows companies to deduct ordinary business expenses) that may affect marijuana-related businesses. In addition, a common-law doctrine known as the "frustration doctrine" has sometimes been used in the past to disallow business expenses and losses incurred by marijuana-related businesses. For example, in *Holt v. Commissioner*, 69 T.C. 75 (1975), a taxpayer who was engaged in the business of selling marijuana was arrested, and certain assets connected with the business were seized. The taxpayer was assessed taxes on his marijuana-related income, but he was not allowed to deduct his expenses or losses, because the court held that doing so would frustrate a sharply defined policy against marijuana use. *But see Edmonson v. Commissioner*, 42 T.C.M. (CCH) 1533 (1981) (holding that a trafficker in marijuana and other illegal drugs could deduct the expenses of his rent, packaging, company automobile, etc., incurred in connection with his illegal business). However, with respect to deductions of business *expenses*, it appears that the frustration doctrine is no longer applicable, having been preempted statutorily by the enactment of I.R.C. §§ 162(c) and (f), which disallow deductions for illegal business expenses, such as bribes, kickbacks, and criminal fines. With respect to business *losses* under I.R.C. § 165, however, such as forfeitures, it appears that the frustration doctrine is still applicable. *See, e.g., Holmes Enterprises, Inc. v. Commissioner*, 69 T.C. 114 (1977).

3. **Other Illegal Businesses.** Another glaring disparity that § 280E creates concerns other types of illegal businesses. Ironically, in the states that have legalized licensed marijuana-related businesses, § 280E imposes harsher federal tax treatment on those businesses than the federal tax code imposes on businesses that are illegal under both state and federal law. This is because the legal expenses of illegal businesses are now usually deductible under § 162(a). For example, an illegal gambling operation can deduct the cost of its

rent and utilities under the federal tax code, since there is nothing illegal about rent and utility fees. But a marijuana-related business cannot do the same because of the specific prohibition in § 280E on businesses that traffic in controlled substances. To postulate another, more extreme example, a business engaged in assassination for hire could arguably deduct the cost of its bullets; in contrast, a lawful marijuana business cannot deduct the cost of its employee salaries, or its internet and phone expenses. *See* Douglas A. Kahn & Howard J. Bromberg, *Tax Treatment of a Marijuana Business,* 8 Colum. J. Tax L. 23 (2017).

E. INSURANCE ISSUES

One other area where marijuana-related businesses have encountered difficulty is in the area of insurance law. Because of the conflict between state law and federal law in legalization states, many insurers are reluctant to provide insurance to marijuana-related businesses, fearing that they will be adjudged complicit in the violation of federal criminal laws if they provide such insurance. Thus, it can be difficult for marijuana-related businesses to obtain adequate insurance products. In addition, marijuana-related businesses have sometimes had their claims denied because insurers have taken the position that their contractual obligations under the contracts are void as a matter of public policy under the contract doctrine of "illegality," due to the illegal nature of the contracts under federal law.

The following case from the United States District Court for the District of Hawaii, *Tracy v. USAA Insurance Co.,* examines this latter issue. There the insured, an individual, submitted a claim under a homeowner's insurance policy, seeking recovery for the value of 12 marijuana plants that were stolen from the property. The insurer argued that it was not obligated to pay the claim because, among other things, it would be contrary to public policy to give effect to the homeowner's insurance agreement, given that marijuana was illegal under federal law. The court agreed with the insurer and granted summary judgment in its favor.

TRACY v. USAA INSURANCE CO.

United States District Court, District of Hawaii
2012 WL 928186 (2012) (unreported)

ORDER GRANTING DEFENDANT'S MOTION
FOR SUMMARY JUDGMENT

KOBAYASHI, J.

Before the Court is Defendant USAA Casualty Insurance Company's ("Defendant") Motion for Summary Judgment ("Motion"), filed on October 20, 2011. Plaintiff Barbara Tracy ("Plaintiff") filed her memorandum in opposition on January 10, 2012, and Defendant filed its reply on January 13, 2012. This matter came on for hearing on January 30, 2012. After careful consideration of the Motion, supporting and opposing documents, and the arguments of counsel, Defendant's Motion is HEREBY GRANTED because the cultivation of marijuana, even for the State-authorized medical use, violates federal law and the enforcement of an insurance policy under the particular circumstances of this case is contrary to public policy, as set forth more fully below.

BACKGROUND

Plaintiff filed the instant action in the Circuit Court of the Third Circuit, State of Hawai'i, on July 11, 2011. Defendant removed the action on August 10, 2011, based on diversity jurisdiction.

Plaintiff's Complaint alleges that Defendant breached the parties' insurance coverage contract by failing to pay Plaintiff's insurance claims for stolen property. Plaintiff, who owns and resides at a property in the Puna District of the State and County of Hawaii, purchased a homeowners insurance policy from Defendant ("the Policy") on May 18, 2010. On or about July 30, 2010, twelve plants were stolen from Plaintiff's property. Nine of the twelve plants were fully matured cannabis sativa, commonly known as marijuana plants. The remaining three plants were less mature plants. Plaintiff states that she "lawfully possessed, grew, nurtured and cultivated the plants consistent with the laws of the State of Hawaii . . . permitt[ing] individuals to possess and grow marijuana for medical purposes[.]"

Plaintiff asserts that she is entitled to coverage under the Policy for the loss of these plants because the Policy includes coverage for loss to " 'trees, shrubs, and other plants.' " Plaintiff alleges that she notified Defendant of the loss of the twelve plants, presenting a claim of $4,000 for each mature plant and $3,200 for each of the less mature plants, for a total of $45,600. Defendant initially agreed to pay Plaintiff's claim and issued a payment to Plaintiff for the loss, but Plaintiff claimed that the amount was insufficient.

Plaintiff alleges that, on or about May 27, 2011, Defendant notified Plaintiff that it would not make any further payment for the loss because Plaintiff did not have an insurable interest in the plants, which could not be lawfully replaced. Plaintiff argues that Defendant could have inspected Plaintiff's property at any time during the Policy period, and Defendant had notice that Hawai'i law permits individuals such as Plaintiff to lawfully grow marijuana for medical purposes. Plaintiff alleges that the Policy specifically allows for coverage of irreplaceable "plants", without excluding any particular type of plant, with payment in the form of actual cash value. She alleges that insurers regularly pay for such claims.

Although not clearly enumerated in the Complaint, Plaintiff's claims appears to be as follows: breached the insurance contract; unreasonable/bad faith denial of her insurance claim; and a violation of Haw. Rev. Stat. Chap. 480. Plaintiff seeks: the fair and reasonable value of the stolen plants; contract and Chapter 480 damages; reasonable attorneys' fees and court costs; and interest.

* * *

Marijuana and Federal Law

Defendant next argues that, even if Plaintiff has an insurable interest in her marijuana plants under Hawai'i law, Defendant is precluded from providing coverage for the plants because it would be contrary to federal law and federal public policy.

As noted, *supra,* under Hawai'i law, a court may refuse to enforce a contract that is illegal or in violation of public policy. *Inland Boatmen's Union,* 77 Hawai'i at 194. Defendant's position is that, even if a layperson would have reasonably expected that Plaintiff's Policy included coverage for the loss of medical marijuana plants, this Court should not enforce that interpretation of the Policy because it would be contrary to federal public policy. Defendant argues that *Gonzales v. Raich,* 545 U.S. 1 (2005), held that the federal Controlled Substances Act ("CSA"), 21 U.S.C. § 801 *et seq.,* prevails over any state law permitting the medical use of marijuana. In *Gonzales,* the respondents were California residents who used marijuana for medical purposes under California's Compassionate Use Act and pursuant to the recommendation of their licensed, board-certified, family practitioners. The respondents sued the Attorney General of the United States and the head of the Drug Enforcement Administration, seeking injunctive and declaratory relief prohibiting the enforcement of the CSA to the extent that it prevented them from possessing, obtaining, or manufacturing marijuana for their personal medical use. *Id.* at 6–7. The Supreme Court vacated the Ninth Circuit's opinion reversing the denial of a preliminary injunction and ordering the district court to enter the injunction. *Id.* at 8, 33. The Supreme Court held that the intrastate, non-commercial cultivation, possession, and use of marijuana was still subject to the CSA. *Id.* at 32–33. In so holding, the Supreme Court stated that:

> The CSA designates marijuana as contraband for *any* purpose; in fact, by characterizing marijuana as a Schedule I drug, Congress expressly found that the drug has no acceptable medical uses. Moreover, the CSA is a comprehensive regulatory regime specifically designed to regulate which controlled substances can be utilized for medicinal purposes, and in what manner. . . . Thus, even if respondents are correct that marijuana does have accepted medical uses and thus should be re-designated as a lesser schedule drug, the CSA would still impose controls beyond what is required by California law. . . [T]he mere fact that marijuana—

like virtually every other controlled substance regulated by the CSA—is used for medicinal purposes cannot possibly serve to distinguish it from the core activities regulated by the CSA.

. . . [L]imiting the activity to marijuana possession and cultivation "in accordance with state law" cannot serve to place respondents' activities beyond congressional reach. The Supremacy Clause unambiguously provides that if there is any conflict between federal and state law, federal law shall prevail. . . .

Id. at 27–29 (emphasis in original).

Other federal courts have repeatedly recognized that *Gonzales* establishes that the possession and cultivation of marijuana for medical use is illegal under federal law, even when it is permitted under state law. For example, in *United States v. Stacy,* the United States District Court for the Southern District of California stated:

Under California's Compassionate Use Act), a patient who possesses or cultivates marijuana for the personal medical purposes of the patient upon the written or oral recommendation or approval of a physician, cannot be prosecuted under Cal. Health & Safety Code § 11357, relating to the possession of marijuana, or Cal. Health & Safety Code § 11358, relating to the cultivation of marijuana. However, California law does not purport to render the use of medical marijuana lawful under federal law. In fact, the use of medical marijuana remains unlawful under federal law. *See Gonzales v. Raich,* 545 U.S. 1, 27 (2005) (explaining that even if marijuana is used "for personal medical purposes on the advice of a physician," it is still considered contraband under the CSA, which designates marijuana as contraband "for *any* purpose").

In *United States v. Hicks,* the United States District Court for the Eastern District of Michigan stated:

It is indisputable that state medical-marijuana laws do not, and cannot, supersede federal laws that criminalize the possession of marijuana. *See Gonzales*, 545 U.S. at 29. Further, when it enacted Hawaii's medical marijuana laws, the State Legislature expressly recognized that the use of marijuana was prohibited under federal law. 2000 Haw. Sess. Laws Act 228, § 1 at 595.

The rule under Hawai'i law that courts may decline to enforce a contract that is illegal or contrary to public policy applies where the enforcement of the contract would violate federal law. The employer in *Inland Boatmen's Union* argued that the court should decline to enforce one aspect of the arbitrator's interpretation of the collective bargaining agreement because its implementation would cause the employer to violate 46 U.S.C. § 8104 (1988). The Hawai'i Supreme Court, however, ultimately held that the employer had not established that the arbitrator's finding conflicted with § 8104.

Insofar as Defendant seeks summary judgment, this Court must view the evidence in the light most favorable to Plaintiff. The Court therefore assumes, for purposes of the instant Motion, that the "Trees, Shrubs and Other Plants" provision of the Policy covered the loss of Plaintiff's medical marijuana plants. Even in light of that assumption, this Court cannot enforce the provision because Plaintiff's possession and cultivation of marijuana, even for State-authorized medical use, clearly violates federal law. To require Defendant to pay insurance proceeds for the replacement of medical marijuana plants would be contrary to federal law and public policy, as reflected in the CSA, *Gonzales,* and its progeny. The Court therefore CONCLUDES that, as a matter of law, Defendant's refusal to pay for Plaintiff's claim for the loss of her medical marijuana plants did not constitute a breach the parties' insurance contract. The Court GRANTS Defendant's Motion as to Plaintiff's breach of contract claim.

Plaintiff's Remaining Claims

Insofar as this Court has concluded that it cannot enforce the provision of the Policy which purportedly covers the loss of medical marijuana plants, this Court also CONCLUDES that, as a matter of law, Defendant's denial of Plaintiff's claim did not constitute either a violation of Haw.Rev.Stat. Chapter 480 or the tort of unreasonableness/bad faith. The Court therefore GRANTS Defendant's Motion as to Plaintiff's Chapter 480 claim and Plaintiff's unreasonableness/bad faith claim.

CONCLUSION

On the basis of the foregoing, Defendant's Motion for Summary Judgment, filed October 20, 2011, is HEREBY GRANTED. The Court directs the Clerk's Office to enter judgment in favor Defendant and to close the case.

IT IS SO ORDERED.

NOTES AND QUESTIONS

1. **Contrary authority.** In a later federal case from Colorado, *GreenEarth Wellness Center, LLC v. Atain Specialty Insurance Co.,* 163 F.Supp.3d 821, 833–835 (D. Colo. 2016), the court expressly declined to follow *Tracy.* It granted the claim of a marijuana cultivation facility that had suffered a loss of marijuana plants due to smoke from a nearby wildfire. The court held that the Obama administration's "hands-off" policy with respect to enforcement of federal marijuana laws created an ambiguity in the agreement with respect to its enforceability. In addition, the court held, because the insurer had knowingly and willingly entered into the policy to cover insurance marijuana crops, it was precluded from now denying coverage. Thus, the court held for the insured on the applicability of the illegality doctrine.

2.   Distinguishing the contrary authorities. One commentator has attempted to reconcile *Tracy* and *Green Earth* by arguing that they are distinguishable, based on their facts:

> First, with respect to the factors favoring enforcement of the insurance policy, *Green Earth* adjudicated a policy specifically underwritten to provide protection to a state-legal marijuana business, whereas *Tracy* involved a general homeowner's policy under which marijuana plants were not specifically contemplated. As the *Green Earth* court concluded, "Atain chose to insure Green Earth's inventory, apparently without taking any apparent precautions to carefully delineate what types of inventory would and would not be covered. Atain's newfound concerns that writing such a Policy might somehow be unlawful thus ring particularly hollow and its request for an advisory opinion appears to be somewhat disingenuous." In short, Atain assumed this risk "of its own will, knowingly and intelligently." It is certainly the case that Green Earth had justified expectations of coverage in light of the insurer's express assumption of the risk of losses suffered by a state-legal insurance business. In contrast, Tracy did not expressly bargain for coverage of her plants as part of the general homeowner's coverage. Additionally, Green Earth paid insurance premiums specifically for its marijuana business, and so would have suffered a forfeiture if the policy was not enforced, subject only to the willingness of the court to return all premiums in restitution. In contrast, Tracy arguably received the full benefit of the homeowner's policy because coverage was afforded for numerous risks. Finally, Colorado has expressed a special public interest favoring the marijuana industry in a statute that provides that it "is the public policy of the state of Colorado that a contract is not void or voidable as against public policy if it pertains to lawful activities" under Colorado law. In contrast, the medical marijuana scheme in *Tracy* simply exempted persons from state criminal prosecution.

Francis J. Mootz III, *E/Insuring the Marijuana Industry*, 49 U. Pac. L. Rev. 43, 61–62 (2017). Do you agree with Professor Mootz that the two cases can be distinguished in such a principled manner? Does it matter that the Obama administration's "hands-off" policy has been disclaimed by the Trump administration?

3.   State courts vs. federal courts. Both *Tracy* and *Green Earth* arise from federal district court decisions. Do you think state courts in legalization states might be more inclined than the federal courts to enforce insurance agreements involving marijuana-related businesses? Consider also the effect of state legislation. The Oregon Legislature enacted a statute in 2016 that provides that: "A contract is not unenforceable on the basis that manufacturing, distributing, dispensing, possessing or using marijuana is prohibited by federal law." Or. Rev. Stat. Ann. § 475B.535, Contracts. Is a federal court likely to give deference to such a statute?

CHAPTER 16

PROFESSIONAL RESPONSIBILITY ISSUES FOR LAWYERS

▪ ▪ ▪

Whereas most of the other chapters in this book concern the way various laws affect marijuana-related businesses, and individuals who possess or distribute marijuana, this chapter focuses on the ethical obligations lawyers are bound to follow under state rules of professional responsibility. The conflict between state and federal marijuana law in legalization states has raised several unique issues with respect to the professional responsibility duties of lawyers in these states, and the state bar associations and courts are still working their way through these issues.

With the exception of a few states, rules of professional responsibility that the various states have enacted track quite closely the American Bar Association's Model Rules of Professional Conduct. But these rules are subject to interpretation, and the individual states do not always interpret them the same way. Within each state, the state's highest court is generally charged with promulgating and interpreting that state's rules of professional conduct. In addition, the bar associations within the various states generally have committees that issue interpretive advisory opinions of these rules, subject to the authority of each state's supreme court to follow or not follow these opinions, and to either amend the state's rules, or add interpretive comments to them. In the area of marijuana law, the states that have published opinions regarding the ethical issues arising from state marijuana legalization have not always taken similar positions on their lawyers' duties of professional responsibility.

Three main issues have arisen with respect to lawyers' professional responsibility duties as regards marijuana law. Central to all three issues, as is the case with marijuana law generally, is the conflict between federal law and state law in legalization states.

The most widely discussed issue that has concerned the state bars is whether lawyers in legalization states can ethically assist marijuana-related businesses in transactional matters, such as drafting contracts and negotiating leases, in light of marijuana's illegal status under federal law. The second issue that has been discussed, though somewhat less frequently, is whether lawyers themselves may personally own or invest in marijuana-related businesses. And the third issue is whether lawyers may themselves partake of marijuana in legalization states.

The following sections in this chapter consider each of these issues in turn, focusing on advisory opinions that have been issued by various state-bar ethics committees. As you'll see, a fair amount of divergence exists between the various state bar associations that have considered these issues, particularly with regard to the latter two issues, and in many cases the state supreme courts have yet to issue definitive guidelines. As you read this chapter, consider how these issues might impact your career if you decide to practice in a legalization state and represent marijuana-related businesses.

A. REPRESENTING MARIJUANA-RELATED BUSINESSES

The most pressing ethical issue that has confronted lawyers in legalization states (medical or recreational) is whether lawyers may ethically represent marijuana-related businesses in those states, notwithstanding the illegal status of marijuana under federal law. Such representation arguably implicates ABA Model Rule 1.2, which provides, in relevant part:

> *Rule 1.2: Scope of Representation & Allocation of Authority Between Client & Lawyer*
>
> * * *
>
> *(d) A lawyer shall not counsel a client to engage, or assist a client, in conduct that the lawyer knows is criminal or fraudulent, but a lawyer may discuss the legal consequences of any proposed course of conduct with a client and may counsel or assist a client to make a good-faith effort to determine the validity, scope, meaning or application of the law.*

Model Rules of Prof'l Conduct R. 1.2 (Am. Bar Ass'n 2016).

The issue with respect to Rule 1.2 is not whether lawyers may represent marijuana clients *per se*. They certainly can. Lawyers represent criminal defendants all the time, and Rule 1.2 specifically excludes from its scope client counseling in an attempt to determine the requirements of the law, as well as advising clients with respect to the possible consequences they may face if they pursues a particular course of action. But what a lawyer cannot do under Rule 1.2 is *assist* the client in carrying out illegal activities. So while lawyers can clearly advise marijuana-related businesses and the individuals involved in them as to the law and the possible legal consequences of their actions under state and federal law, it is not so clear that lawyers can *assist* such clients in drafting transactional documents, such as contracts, leases, and articles of incorporation, or that lawyers can negotiate deals on behalf of such clients, or that they can provide advice to such clients as the best ways to structure and operate their businesses. Given that possession and distribution of marijuana are criminal activities under federal law, such assistance arguably violates Rule 1.2, even if the activities are legally permissible under state law.

The following opinion from the Supreme Court of Ohio's Board of Professional Conduct addresses this issue. In it, the Board, which is an advisory body to the Ohio Supreme Court, concluded that a lawyer may not ethically provide legal services necessary for a client to establish and operate a medical marijuana enterprise, or to transact business with a person or entity engaged in a medical marijuana enterprise. Do you agree with the Board's interpretation of Rule 1.2 as it pertains to marijuana related businesses?

THE SUPREME COURT OF OHIO BOARD OF PROFESSIONAL CONDUCT

Issued August 5, 2016

Ethical Implications for Lawyers under Ohio's Medical Marijuana Law

SYLLABUS: A lawyer may not advise a client to engage in conduct that violates federal law, or assist in such conduct, even if the conduct is authorized by state law. A lawyer cannot provide legal services necessary for a client to establish and operate a medical marijuana enterprise or to transact business with a person or entity engaged in a medical marijuana enterprise. A lawyer may provide advice as to the legality and consequences of a client's proposed conduct under state and federal law and explain the validity, scope, meaning, and application of the law.

A lawyer's personal use of medical marijuana pursuant to a state regulated prescription, ownership in, or employment by a medical marijuana enterprise, subjects the lawyer to possible federal prosecution, and may adversely reflect on a lawyer's honesty, trustworthiness, and overall fitness to practice law.

QUESTIONS: Several lawyers seek guidance concerning Ohio Sub. H.B. 523, effective September 8, 2016, that permits the cultivation, processing, sale, and use of medical marijuana under a state licensing and regulatory framework. This opinion addresses three questions:

(1) Whether an Ohio lawyer may ethically counsel, advise, provide legal services to, and represent state regulated medical marijuana cultivators, processors, and dispensaries, as well as business clients seeking to transact with regulated entities; (2) Whether an Ohio lawyer may operate, hold employment or an ownership interest in, a licensed medical marijuana enterprise; and (3) Whether an Ohio lawyer may ethically use medical marijuana with a prescription.

APPLICABLE RULES: Prof.Cond.R. 1.2(d), 8.4(b), 8.4(h).

OPINION: Ohio Sub. H.B. 523 permits a patient, upon the recommendation of a physician, to use medical marijuana to treat a qualifying medical condition. Three state regulatory agencies are permitted to issue licenses to persons and entities for the purposes of cultivating, processing, testing, dispensing, and prescribing medical marijuana. The law provides that a registered patient or caregiver is not subject to arrest or criminal prosecution for using, obtaining, possessing, or administering marijuana and establishes an affirmative defense to a criminal charge to the possession of marijuana. The law immunizes professional license holders, including lawyers, from any professional disciplinary action for engaging in professional or occupational activities related to medical marijuana. Notwithstanding this provision, this advisory opinion analyzes the questions presented in light of rules promulgated by the Supreme Court pursuant to Ohio Const. Art. IV, Section 2(B)(1)(g).

On and after September 8, 2016, a direct conflict will exist between Ohio law and federal law. The federal Controlled Substances Act ("CSA") currently designates marijuana as a Schedule I controlled substance, which makes its use for any purpose, including medical applications, a crime. 21 USC §§ 812(b)(1), 841(a)(1). Additionally, under the CSA, it is illegal to manufacture, distribute, or dispense a controlled substance, including marijuana (21 USC § 841(a)(1)), or conspire to do so (21 USC § 846). Consequently, any Ohio citizen engaged in cultivating, processing, prescribing, or use of medical marijuana is in violation of federal law.

In 2013, the U.S. Department of Justice ("USDOJ") issued a memorandum stating its general policy not to interfere with the medical use of marijuana pursuant to state laws, provided the state tightly regulates and controls the medical marijuana market. Memorandum from James M. Cole, Deputy Attorney General, to All United States Attorneys, Guidance Regarding Marijuana Enforcement (August 29, 2013) ("Cole Memorandum"). The Cole Memorandum does not override federal law enacted by Congress or grant immunity to individuals or businesses from federal prosecution.

The conflict between the Ohio and federal marijuana laws complicates the application of the Rules of Professional Conduct for Ohio lawyers. While Ohio law permits certain conduct by its citizens and grants immunity from prosecution for certain state crimes for the cultivation, processing, sale, and use of medical marijuana, the same conduct constitutes a federal crime, despite instructions to U.S. attorneys from the current administration to not vigorously enforce the law, and therefore implicates Prof.Cond.R. 1.2 for lawyers with clients seeking to engage in activities permissible under state law.

ANALYSIS:

Advice and Legal Services Provided to Clients Engaged in Conduct as a State Regulated Marijuana Enterprise

A lawyer cannot assist a client who engages or seeks to engage in conduct the lawyer knows to be illegal. Prof.Cond.R. 1.2(d). Nor can a lawyer recommend to a client the means by which an illegal act may be committed. Prof.Cond.R. 1.2(d), cmt. [9]. Prof.Cond.R. 1.2(d) embodies a lawyer's important role in promoting compliance with the law by providing legal advice and assistance in structuring clients' conduct in accordance with the law. The rule underscores an essential role of lawyers in preventing clients from engaging in conduct that is criminal in nature or when the legality of the proposed conduct is unclear. N.Y. Op. 1024 (2014). http://www.justice.gov/iso/opa/resources/3052013829132756857467.pdf. Federal laws ordinarily preempt inconsistent state laws under the federal Supremacy Clause. In *Gonzales v. Raich*, 545 U.S. 1 (2005), the Court rejected a claim that Congress exceeded its authority under the Commerce Clause insofar as the marijuana prohibition applied to personal use of marijuana for medical purposes. Additionally, the federal government always may enforce its own criminal statutes. "Marijuana remains illegal under federal law, even in those states in which medical marijuana has been legalized." *United States v. Canori*, 737 F.3d 181, 184 (2d Cir. 2013). Op. 2016-6 4.

Prof.Cond.R. 1.2(d) does not distinguish between illegal client conduct that will, or will not, be enforced by the federal government. The first inquiry of a lawyer is whether the legal services to be provided can be construed as assisting the client in conduct that is a violation of either state or federal law. If the answer is in the affirmative under either law, Prof.Cond.R. 1.2(d) precludes the lawyer from providing those legal services to the client.

Under Prof.Cond.R. 1.2(d), a lawyer cannot deliver legal services to assist a client in the establishment and operation of a state regulated marijuana enterprise that is illegal under federal law. The types of legal services that cannot be provided under the rule include, but are not limited to, the completion and filing of marijuana license applications, negotiations with regulated individuals and businesses, representation of clients before state regulatory boards responsible for the regulation of medical marijuana, the drafting and negotiating of contracts with vendors for resources or supplies, the drafting of lease agreements for property to be used in the cultivation, processing, or sale of medical marijuana, commercial paper, tax, zoning, corporate entity formation, and statutory agent services. See also, Colo. Op. 125 (2013). Similarly, a lawyer cannot represent a property owner, lessor, supplier or business in transactions with a marijuana regulated entity, if the lawyer knows the transferred property, facilities, goods or supplies will be used to engage in conduct that is illegal under federal law. Even though the completion of any of these services or transactions may be permissible under Ohio law, and a lawyer's assistance can facilitate their completion, the lawyer ultimately would be assisting the client in engaging in conduct that the lawyer knows to be illegal under federal law.

However, Prof.Cond.R. 1.2(d) does not foreclose certain advice and counsel to a client seeking to participate in the Ohio medical marijuana industry. Prof.Cond.R. 1.2(d) also provides: "A lawyer may discuss the legal consequences of any proposed course of conduct with a client and may counsel or assist a client in making a good faith effort to determine the validity, scope, meaning, or application of the law." Jurisdictions in accord with this view include Connecticut (Conn. Op. 2013-02); Hawaii (Haw. Op. 49 (2015)); Maine (Me. Op. 199 (2010)); and Colorado (Colo. Op. 125 (2014)). Op. 2016-6 5 This portion of the rule permits a lawyer to explain to the client the conflict that currently exists between state and federal law, the consequences of engaging in conduct that is permissible under Ohio law but contrary to federal law, and the likelihood of federal enforcement given the policies of the current administration. A lawyer may counsel and advise a client regarding the scope and general requirements of the Ohio medical marijuana law, the meaning of its provisions, and how the law would be applied to a client's proposed conduct. A lawyer also can advise a client concerning good faith arguments regarding the validity of the federal or state law and its application to the client's proposed conduct.

In addition to the permissible range of advice permitted under Prof.Cond.R. 1.2(d), the rule does not preclude a lawyer from representing a client charged with violating the state medical marijuana law, representing a professional license holder before state licensing boards, representing an employee in a wrongful discharge action due to medical marijuana use, or aiding a government client in the implementation and administration of the state's regulated licensing program. With regard to the latter, lawyers assisting a government client at the state or local level in the establishment, operation, or implementation of the state medical marijuana regulatory system are not advising or assisting the client in conduct that directly violates federal law. The state or a local government is not directly involved in the sale, processing, or dispensing of medical marijuana prohibited by federal law, even though it is arguably enabling the conduct through the issuance of licenses and the maintenance of its regulatory system.

For these reasons, the Board concludes that a lawyer violates Prof.Cond.R. 1.2(d) when he or she transitions from advising a client regarding the consequences of conduct under federal and state law to counseling or assisting the client to engage in conduct the lawyer knows is prohibited under federal law. Colo. Op. 125 (2013). Unless and until federal law is amended to authorize the use, production, and distribution of medical marijuana, a lawyer only may advise a client as to the legality of conduct either permitted under state law or prohibited under federal law and explain the scope and application of state and federal law to the client's proposed conduct. However, the lawyer cannot provide the types of legal services necessary for a client to establish and operate a medical marijuana enterprise or to transact with medical marijuana businesses. To document compliance with his or her ethical obligations, a lawyer approached by a prospective client seeking to engage in activities permitted by Ohio Sub. H.B. 523 should enter into a written fee agreement with the client that encompasses a mutual understanding about Op. 2016-6 6 the exact scope of services the lawyer is ethically and lawfully able to provide under Prof.Cond.R. 1.2(d).

The Board is mindful that the current state of the law creates a unique conflict for Ohio lawyers and deprives certain clients of the ability to obtain a full range of legal services in furtherance of activities deemed lawful by the General Assembly. The Supreme Court may amend the Rules of Professional Conduct to address this conflict. Several jurisdictions have reached similar conclusions to those contained in this opinion and have amended, or are considering amending Rule 1.2 or the comments to that rule. These states include Illinois, Alaska, Colorado, Nevada, Oregon, Washington, and Hawaii.

* * *

CONCLUSION: Federal law currently prohibits the sale, cultivation, processing, or use of marijuana, for any purpose. Prof.Cond.R. 1.2 prohibits a lawyer from counseling or assisting a client to engage in conduct the lawyer knows is illegal under any law. The rule does not contain an exception if the federally prohibited conduct is legal under state law. However, a lawyer may advise a client as to the legality of conduct either permitted under state law or prohibited under federal law, explain the scope and application of the law to the client's conduct, but a lawyer cannot provide the legal services necessary to establish and operate a medical marijuana enterprise or transact with a medical marijuana business.

* * *

Advisory Opinions of the Board of Professional Conduct are informal, nonbinding opinions in response to prospective or hypothetical questions regarding the application of the Supreme Court Rules for the Government of the Bar of Ohio, the Op. 2016-6 8 Supreme Court Rules for the Government of the Judiciary, the Rules of Professional Conduct, the Code of Judicial Conduct, and the Attorney's Oath of Office.

NOTES AND QUESTIONS

1. **The Board's decision and the majority view among other states.** The Board's decision in Opinion 2016-6 was based upon marijuana's status under federal law. The Board noted that Rule 1.2 does not distinguish between state and federal law, and likewise it does not distinguish between illegal conduct that will, or will not, be enforced by the federal government. (Therefore, the Board deemed the Cole Memo to be irrelevant to the interpretation of Rule 1.2.) However, the Board did note that it was mindful that the current state of the law creates a conflict for lawyers that may deprive marijuana clients of the ability to obtain a full range of legal services in furtherance of activities deemed lawful by the state. Accordingly, the Board anticipated that the Ohio Supreme Court may need to amend the rules of professional conduct to address that conflict. In fact, not long afterward, the Ohio Supreme Court did precisely that, adopting an amendment to Rule 1.2 in October 2016. This amendment made it clear that Ohio lawyers are allowed to assist marijuana-related businesses in accordance with Ohio's medical marijuana statute, provided they also advise the clients regarding the conflict with federal law. In so doing, the Ohio Supreme Court brought Ohio in line with the majority of states that have considered this issue. *See, e.g.,* Colorado Rules of Professional Conduct, Rule Change 2014(05) (adding Comment [14] that expressly authorizes lawyers to assist clients in conduct that is permitted under state law); New York State Bar Ethics Opinion 1024 (2014); Maryland Ethics Docket Opinion 2016-10 (2016); Illinois State Bar Ethics Opinion 14-07 (2014); Maine Professional Ethics Commission 215 (2017); Rhode Island Supreme Court Ethics Advisory Panel Op. 2017-01 (2017). As the Arizona Bar Association's ethics committee framed the issue: prohibiting lawyers from assisting marijuana-related businesses and the individuals involved in them would amount to "depriving clients of the very legal advice and assistance that is needed to engage in the conduct of the state law expressly permits. The maintenance of an independent legal profession, and of its right to advocate for the interests of clients, is a bulwark of our system of government." *See* State Bar of Arizona Ethics Opinion 11-01 (2011).

2. **State legislation.** While most of the interpretations of Rule 1.2 have been issued either by state bar ethics committees, or by state supreme courts, the legislature decided the issue in Minnesota via a state statute that immunizes attorneys in Minnesota from disciplinary action if they provide legal assistance to marijuana-related businesses. Specifically, the state legislature adopted Minn. Stat. § 152.32(2)(i), which provides as follows:

> An attorney may not be subject to disciplinary action by the Minnesota Supreme Court or a professional responsibility board for providing legal assistance to prospective or registered manufacturers or others related to activity is no longer subject to criminal penalties under state law pursuant to sections 152.22 to 152.37.

In enacting this statute, the Minnesota legislature took the unusual step of codifying an aspect of the professional duties of Minnesota lawyers, rather than leaving it to the state supreme court to interpret Rule 1.2.

3. Possible conflicts between state and federal courts. While a significant majority of state bar associations and state supreme courts in legalization states have taken the position that lawyers may assist and advise marijuana-related businesses in transactional and other matters, it is not clear that the federal courts in such states will follow suit with respect to their own disciplinary rules. The experience in Colorado, in particular, raises significant questions in this regard. As noted above, the Colorado Supreme Court in 2014 amended its Rule 1.2 to add an interpretive comment, which made it clear that lawyers may assist marijuana-related businesses and similar clients in conduct that the lawyers reasonably believe to be permitted under state law, so long as they also advise the clients regarding related federal law. *See* Colorado Rules of Professional Conduct, Rule Change 2014(05). But subsequently the Colorado federal courts specifically excluded this interpretation from their standards of professional responsibility. *See* D.C. Colo. L. Atty. R. 2(b)(2). Thus, it appears that, in Colorado at least, lawyers practicing in federal courts may be subject to different ethical duties with respect to representing marijuana clients than they are subject to in state courts. If so, a lawyer in Colorado presumably could not represent a marijuana-related business seeking to have a contract enforced in a federal court, if that contract involved an illegal distribution of marijuana under federal law. But could a Colorado lawyer nevertheless *draft* such a contract for the marijuana related business, given that drafting contracts is practicing law, but does not involve practicing before any particular court?

PROBLEM 16-1

In State X, a state that has legalized medical marijuana, lawyer L represents company C, a marijuana dispensary, in a transactional matter. This representation is consistent with the state's ethical guidelines. Later, company C is sued in state court for breach of contract by a marijuana cultivation company for failure to pay for a shipment of marijuana. Is it ethical for lawyer L to represent company C in the state court litigation matter? What if the action is brought in federal court instead?

B. LAWYERS INVESTING IN MARIJUANA-RELATED BUSINESSES

Another important ethical issue that the states have been grappling with involves lawyers' personally investing in marijuana-related businesses. As is the case with lawyers' *representing* marijuana-related businesses, the issue arises because of the conflict between state and federal law in legalization states. In such states, marijuana-related businesses, such as dispensaries and growers, remain illegal enterprises under federal law, even though their activities are now permissible under state law. The question, then, is whether lawyers engage in criminal conduct when they obtain ownership interests in such marijuana-related businesses, since these businesses are involved in the distribution of a Schedule I drug.

The Model Rules of Professional Conduct that are arguably implicated by lawyers' investing in marijuana-related businesses are Rules 1.2 and 8.4. As noted in the previous section, Rule 1.2 prohibits lawyers from "assisting a client in conduct that the lawyer knows is criminal or fraudulent. . ." By investing in a marijuana related business, a lawyer arguably assists the client in conduct that is criminal under federal law. Model Rule 8.4(b) provides, in relevant part:

> *Rule 8.4: Misconduct*
>
> *It is professional misconduct for a lawyer to:*
>
> *(b) commit a criminal act that reflects adversely on the lawyer's honesty, trustworthiness or fitness as a lawyer in other respects;*
> * * *

Model Rules of Prof'l Conduct R. 8.4 (Am. Bar Ass'n 2016).

Given that possession and distribution of marijuana are clearly "criminal acts" under federal law, ownership of a marijuana-related business appears to meet that part of Rule 8.4(b). The remaining question is whether it is the type of criminal act that "reflects adversely on the lawyer's honesty, trustworthiness or fitness as a lawyer in other respects."

In the following ethics opinion, the Maryland State Bar Association's Committee on Ethics considers, among other things, whether these rules prohibit Maryland attorneys for having ownership interests in medical-marijuana businesses (Maryland at the time of the opinion did not permit recreational marijuana use). The Committee concludes that they do not, though the Committee also explicitly notes that its position is subject to certain status-quo conditions, including the federal government's maintaining its hands-off policy with respect to state legalization, as set out in the Cole Memo.

MARYLAND STATE BAR ASSOCIATION, INC. COMMITTEE ON ETHICS
Ethics Docket No. 2016-10

Do the Maryland Rules of Professional conduct prohibit attorneys from advising clients seeking to engage in conduct pursuant to Maryland's Medical Marijuana Laws? Similarly, do the Rules prohibit Maryland attorneys from having an ownership interest in medical marijuana businesses?

Questions Presented:

Do the Maryland Rules of Professional conduct prohibit attorneys from advising clients seeking to engage in conduct pursuant to Maryland's

Medical Marijuana Laws? Similarly, do the Rules prohibit Maryland attorneys from having an ownership interest in medical marijuana businesses?

Summary Conclusion:

(1) Maryland attorneys are not prohibited under the Maryland Rules of Professional Conduct from advising clients as to medical marijuana business related activities in Maryland, or providing legal services such as contracting or negotiating to advance such projects; and (2) Maryland attorneys are not prohibited by the Rules of Professional Conduct from owning a business interest in such a venture. However, the Committee emphasizes that this opinion is subject to several limitations, which are included at the conclusion of this opinion.

Opinion:

The extraordinary landscape surrounding medical marijuana laws and policy coupled with federal acquiescence in state authorization of marijuana use has left an attorney's related ethical obligations unclear. A number of State ethics opinions predating this opinion offer good background as to lawyers' ethical conduct at the point where state authorized medical marijuana or recreational marijuana use—and the legal services associated with those uses—intersect. We now offer our interpretation of this legal landscape under the Maryland Rules of Professional Conduct ("MRPC").

Since 2013, Maryland's legislature has taken steps to legalize marijuana production, sale, and use for medical purposes, including enacting the Maryland Medical Cannabis Law, Md. Code Ann. Health General § 13–3301, et seq. ("Maryland Medical Marijuana Law" or "the Law"). This statutory scheme contemplates permissible marijuana-related activities defined and regulated by statute, including the licensing of growers who will "operate in the State to provide cannabis to: [similarly licensed] (i) Processors. . .; Dispensaries. . . .; Qualifying patients and caregivers; and Independent testing laboratories. . . ." See § 13–3301 to 13–3311. The statute contemplates that individuals and organizations who engage in marijuana-related processing, dispensing, use, and testing in accordance with the statute are "[e]xempt[ed] from arrest, prosecution, or any civil or administrative penalty; penalty for distributing, possessing, manufacturing, or using cannabis diverted from [an] approved program." See § 13–3313. The statute further expressly prohibits a number of activities, including smoking cannabis in a public place or operating motor vehicles and other vehicles under the influence of cannabis. See § 13–3314. The Act contemplates the fragile foundation upon which the Act stands given possible federal prosecution, stating that "[t]he Governor may suspend implementation of this subtitle on making a determination that there is a reasonable chance of federal prosecution of State employees for involvement with implementation of this subtitle. Under § 13–3316, additional Code of Maryland Regulations (COMAR) regulations governing this law were adopted in 2014.

While Maryland law now permits certain cannabis related activities, the federal Controlled Substances Act, 21 USC §§ 801–904 ("CSA"), however, continues to criminalize the production, distribution, and use of marijuana. Noteworthy to the Committee is the fact that the CSA—with its attendant provisions criminalizing such conduct—existed when the Maryland legislature enacted the Maryland Medical Marijuana Law. It is clear from the provisions of the Law that the legislature intended and expected that individuals and businesses would seek licenses and take other action necessary to operate businesses to accomplish the purposes of the Maryland Medical Marijuana Law.

To further complicate the landscape, while the federal government has not repealed the federal law criminalizing medical marijuana, it has repeatedly stated that it does not wish to impede retails sales of medical marijuana permitted under state law. See, e.g., Memorandum from David W. Ogden, Deputy Attorney General, to Selected United States Attorneys, re Investigations and Prosecutions in States Authorizing the Medical Use of Marijuana (Oct. 19, 2009), available at http://www.justice.gov/sites/default/files/opa/legacy/2009/10/19/medical-marijuana.pdf (underlining in original); Memorandum from James M. Cole, Deputy Attorney General, to United States Attorneys, re Guidance Regarding the Ogden Memo in Jurisdictions Seeking to Authorize Marijuana for Medical Use (June 29, 2011) (underlining in original), available at http://www.justice.gov/oip/docs/dag-guidance-2011-for-medical-marijuana-use.pdf; Memorandum from James M. Cole, Deputy Attorney General, to All United States Attorneys, re Guidance Regarding Marijuana Enforcement (Aug. 29, 2013). Additionally, Congress in 2014 appears to have financially prevented the Department of Justice from enforcing the CSA insofar as state medical marijuana schemes are concerned. See the Consolidated and Further Continuing Appropriations Act, 2015, H.R. 83, 113th Cong. § 538 (2014). This summary is cursory and should not be relied upon as exhaustive or authoritative. Instead, it is illustrative of the factual background the Committee assumes for the assessment of these ethical questions: State law has legalized medical marijuana, its production, distribution and use (and created a statutory and regulatory scheme for businesses to create this industry), while federal law still criminalizes marijuana use, production and distribution, although the expressed federal policy is not to enforce its criminal laws in this context.

* * *

Attorneys holding interest in medical marijuana businesses

In general, the MRPC do not limit attorneys from engaging in business activities available to other members of their communities. For the reasons stated above, the Committee feels that an attorney is not prohibited from holding an ownership interest in a medical marijuana business that conforms to Maryland's Medical Cannabis Laws. MRPC rules applicable to any business transactions with clients can still affect the appropriateness of business activities under specific circumstances and must be applied. For instance, under Rule 1.8, an attorney cannot obtain a business interests in a client's business absent the client seeking and receiving independent advice.

Caveats

This Committee points out that this opinion is limited by many factors, and attorneys employing it must understand the limitations of this opinion as well as unresolved legal and ethical issues, including, but not limited to:

1. This opinion is offered under unique circumstances where this State has enacted a law that directly runs in contradiction with federal law, but where the United States has expressly acquiesced to the state action by stating it will not interfere with activities complying with the state law. Whether the Committee would reach the same conclusion in other situations should not be predicted, and this opinion should not be extrapolated to any other context. And, as always, ultimately what is deemed ethical under the MRPC is up to the Court of Appeals, for whom this Committee cannot speak.

2. The medical marijuana landscape is unique. Nothing in this opinion implies that lawyers are free in any other circumstance to disregard established law, conflicts in law, or to attempt to circumvent ethical obligations by applying a "rule of reason approach" to other ethical duty or ethical question before them.

3. The Committee's position is largely predicated upon the DOJ's stated position it will leave appropriately state regulated medical marijuana activities unmolested. Should the DOJ alter its stance, the proposed conduct may no longer be appropriate.

4. This opinion, like all ethics opinions, is not intended as legal advice, and it does not immunize any lawyer from disciplinary action or prosecution by authorities with such powers. This Committee does not specialize in the shifting and complicated legal landscape of medical marijuana laws or of the DOJ approaches to enforcement or non-enforcement. The questions posed by the party soliciting this opinion required an overview of the legal landscape, but this Committee's overview should not be relied upon as legal research, and it is by no means exhaustive. For further

guidance on the legal posture, one could request an opinion of the Attorney General's Office.

5. The Local Rules of the U.S. District Court for the District of Maryland contain rules contemplating potential attorney discipline before the federal bar for violations of ethical obligations. This fact is applicable to any potential interpretation of the Rules of Professional Conduct. However, we raise it in this context given the competing federal law that runs contrary to the state scheme raises the possibility that a federal arbiter of an attorney's ethical obligations may hold opinions contrary to this Committee's position and take action against attorneys admitted to practice before the federal court system for activities under Maryland's Medical Marijuana Law.

6. The Committee's opinion is limited to application of the MRPC to activities that the DOJ has acquiesced to under Maryland's Medical Marijuana Law. There always remains the possibility that certain acts of counsel or clients could be deemed by the DOJ as outside of the scope of conduct permitted by state law. Concern was particularly raised in the Committee's discussion of the questions presented whether medical marijuana activities involving interstate rather than intrastate activities might be deemed to fall outside of the DOJ's stance as to what Medical Marijuana activities it will not prosecute. Such potential activities are potentially innumerable, and this Committee cannot speak for the DOJ or its views, preventing any meaningful analysis of those circumstances. However, a prudent attorney engaging in a medical marijuana business or related legal services should constantly gauge whether proposed conduct or legal assistance might be deemed appropriate by the DOJ, and that where such conduct is deemed to be outside of the protections offered by the DOJ's acquiescence, it may similarly be deemed unethical under the MRPC.

In conclusion, this Committee feels that the MRPC do not prohibit attorneys from advising and assisting medical marijuana businesses by providing legal services to advance the business's interests and to ensure compliance with Maryland's statutory regulation scheme, nor do they prohibit ownership of such ventures by attorneys. This position is subject to the limitations enumerated above, including principally the federal government maintaining its acquiescence of allowing states to authorize the intrastate production, distribution and use of marijuana for medicinal purposes without interference.

The Committee is further of the opinion that it would be beneficial for the Court of Appeals, assuming it is in agreement with this opinion, to amend the Maryland Rules of Professional Conduct to reflect the ethical nature of assisting in or conducting business activities under Maryland's Medical Malpractice Law. The Committee hereby offers whatever assistance the Court desires to accomplish that task.

NOTES AND QUESTIONS

1. **Basis for the committee's decision.** The Maryland Committee's decision in this matter is explicitly premised upon the Department of Justice's "hands off" policy with respect to enforcement of federal marijuana laws in legalization states, as set out in the Cole memo and related policy statements. Specifically, the Committee notes that its decision depends upon "the federal government maintaining its acquiescence in allowing states to authorized intrastate production, distribution and use of marijuana for medicinal purposes without interference." In January 2018, however, Attorney General Sessions announced that the Justice Department was retracting the Cole memo, leaving open the possibility of prosecuting marijuana possession and distribution, even if they are in compliance with state law. In light of this shift in policy by the Trump administration's Justice Department, can a Maryland lawyer feel confident about investing in a marijuana-related business in that state? Does it make a difference that every year since 2014, Congress has prohibited the Department of Justice from using federal funds to prosecute state-compliant medical marijuana businesses?

2. **Conflicting authority.** So far, the state bars and state supreme courts (or in this case, the Maryland Court of Appeals) have not addressed the issue of lawyer investments in marijuana-related businesses nearly as often as they have addressed the issue of lawyers' representing marijuana-related businesses in transactional matters. As a result, there is limited authority to guide lawyers on this issue, and what authority there is has not been consistent. For example, the Washington State Bar's Committee on Professional Ethics issued an opinion in 2015 that concluded that lawyer investment in marijuana-related businesses was not in violation of Rule 8.4:

> A lawyer going into a business with a client that complies with [state marijuana laws] would not, without more, constitute either a "criminal act that reflects adversely on the lawyer's honesty, trustworthiness or fitness as a lawyer in other respects," RPC 8.4(b), or an "act involving moral turpitude, or corruption, or any unjustified act of assault or other act which reflects disregard for the rule of law." RPC 8.4(i).

Washington State Bar Association, Advisory Opinion 201501 (2015). But in Nevada, in 2017 the Nevada Supreme Court added a Comment to Rule 8.4(b), advising lawyers that engaging in conduct that involves the distribution of marijuana in any form may trigger disciplinary proceedings, which seems to suggest that lawyers investing in marijuana-related businesses is prohibited.

The situation in the few other states that have considered the issue is less clear. In August 2016, for example, the Board of Professional Conduct of the Supreme Court of Ohio opined that a lawyer's investment in a marijuana-related business, or even working as an employee in such a business, may implicate Rule 8.4. *See* Opinion 2016-1. However, as noted in the previous section, the Supreme Court of Ohio effectively overruled Opinion 2016-1 with respect to lawyers' representing marijuana-related businesses when it subsequently amended the state's version of Rule 1.2. The court did not address the issue of investment under Rule 8.4, though, so it remains unclear whether the Board's opinion with respect to lawyers' investing in marijuana related businesses is still valid. Likewise, the Colorado Supreme Court has so far refrained from addressing the issue, even though a sub-committee of the court's Standing Rules Committee had recommended adding a new rule that would have allowed such investment. Thus, it appears that the state bars and state supreme courts are far from reaching a consensus on the propriety of lawyers investing in marijuana-related businesses in legalization states.

3. Other professions. Law is not the only profession wrestling with the question whether its practitioners who invest in foreign marijuana-related businesses violate the rules of professional conduct in their professions. *See, e.g.,* Rick L. Crosser, *Ownership of a Legal Marijuana Business: Certified Management Accountant Obligations*, 10 J. Critical Incidents 62 (2017) (discusses whether accountant who owns a majority share of a marijuana-related business in Colorado violates ethical principles of the accounting profession in light of marijuana's illegal status under federal law).

4. Foreign investment. To date, the state bars and the state supreme courts have also not addressed the issue of foreign investment in marijuana-related businesses. Canada, for example has now legalized adult-use marijuana. Suppose an American lawyer wanted to invest in a Canadian marijuana-related business that was publicly traded on the Canadian exchange. Would that investment violate Rule 8.4, given marijuana's illegal status under United States law?

PROBLEM 16-2

Lawyer L practices in state Y, a state that has legalized both medical and recreational marijuana. Lawyer L wishes to invest in a marijuana-related business in state Y. Is it ethical for lawyer L to do so? Why or why not? Is it ethical for lawyer M, who lives and practices in an adjoining state that does not have legalized marijuana, to invest in the same business?

C. LAWYERS' PERSONAL USE OF MARIJUANA IN LEGALIZATION STATES

The third ethical issue that the state bar associations and state supreme courts have been grappling with is whether lawyers can ethically purchase and use marijuana products themselves, if such use is legal under state law. And once again, the issue arises because of the conflict between state and federal law in legalization states. In such states, the possession of marijuana (medical or full recreational, depending on the state) is legally permissible, but under federal law, it constitutes a crime.

As is the case with lawyers' investing in marijuana-related businesses, a lawyer's personal use of marijuana arguably violates Model Rule 8.4. As noted in the previous section, Rule 8.4(b) prohibits lawyers from committing criminal acts that reflects adversely on the lawyer's honesty, trustworthiness or fitness as a lawyer in other respects. Specifically, Rule 8.4(b) provides:

> *Rule 8.4: Misconduct*
>
> *It is professional misconduct for a lawyer to:*
>
> *(b) commit a criminal act that reflects adversely on the lawyer's honesty, trustworthiness or fitness as a lawyer in other respects;*
>
> * * *

Model Rules of Prof'l Conduct R. 8.4 (Am. Bar Ass'n 2016).

Possession and use of marijuana are clearly "criminal acts" under federal law, so once again the operative question is whether marijuana use and possession are the types of criminal acts that "reflect adversely on the lawyer's honesty, trustworthiness or fitness as a lawyer in other respects."

In the following ethics opinion, the State Bar Association of the North Dakota Ethics Committee takes up this question. North Dakota is not itself a legalization state. Nevertheless, the issue arose there because an attorney who lived in North Dakota sought to use medical marijuana to treat a medical condition in Minnesota, while continuing to maintain a license to practice law in North Dakota. (Thus, the conduct that the lawyer sought to engage in, use of marijuana, was illegal not only under federal law, but also under the law of the state in which the lawyer practiced, i.e., North Dakota.) The Committee concluded that the attorney's repeated use of medical marijuana as part of his treatment program in the state of Minnesota would constitute the "pattern of repeated offenses" and constituted a violation of N.D.R.'s version of Rule 8.4.

STATE BAR ASSOCIATION OF NORTH DAKOTA ETHICS COMMITTEE

Opinion No. 14-02

THIS OPINION IS ADVISORY ONLY

QUESTION PRESENTED

The Ethics Committee has been asked to render its opinion on whether Attorney may live and use medical marijuana prescribed by a physician in Minnesota and be licensed to practice law in North Dakota.

OPINION

Based on the facts presented below, Attorney would not be able to live and use medical marijuana prescribed by a physician in Minnesota while being licensed to practice law in North Dakota. The conduct would be a violation of N.D.R. Prof. Conduct 8.4(b).

APPLICABLE NORTH DAKOTA RULES
OF PROFESSIONAL CONDUCT

Rule 8.4, N.D.R. Prof. Conduct: Misconduct

FACTS PRESENTED

Attorney, who currently lives in North Dakota, has a nonterminal medical condition qualifying the attorney for medical marijuana treatment under Minnesota law. Attorney has tried other treatments, which have been unsuccessful in maintaining Attorney's desired quality of life. Attorney wishes to move to Minnesota to participate in a medical marijuana treatment program while continuing to have a license to practice law in North Dakota.

DISCUSSION

Attorney recognizes that N.D.R. Prof. Conduct 8.4(b) is the governing authority on whether the conduct would be a per se ethical violation. Attorney suggests that use of medical marijuana is not within the scope of N.D.R. Prof. Conduct 8.4(b).

The rule provides that "[i]t is professional misconduct for a lawyer to . . . commit a criminal act that reflects adversely on the lawyer's honesty, trustworthiness, or fitness as a lawyer in other respects[.]" N.D.R. Prof. Conduct 8.4(b). The comment to the rule notes the distinction between criminal acts that are ethical violations and criminal acts that are not: "Although a lawyer is personally answerable to the entire criminal law, a lawyer should be professionally answerable only for offenses that indicate lack of those characteristics relevant to law practice." N.D.R. Prof. Conduct 8.4(b) cmt. Beyond that distinction, the comment points out that recurring criminal acts may also be an ethical violation: "A pattern of repeated offenses, even ones of minor significance when considered separately, can indicate indifference to legal obligations."

The comment's explanation about a pattern of repeated offenses shows why Attorney's conduct would be an ethical violation. As Attorney acknowledges, federal law designates the use of marijuana for any purpose, even a medical one, as a crime. See 21 U.S.C. § 841(a)(1). As a schedule I controlled substance under federal law, marijuana has been determined to have a high potential for abuse and to have no accepted medical use for treatment and lack accepted safety for use under medical supervision. See 21 U.S.C. § 812(b)(1). Thus physicians, practitioners, and pharmacists are prohibited under federal law from prescribing or dispensing marijuana. See

United States v. Oakland Cannabis Buyers' Co-op., 532 U.S. 483, 491 (2001) (Controlled Substances Act has no medical necessity exception for marijuana).

Further, it is unquestionable that the federal government has authority to prohibit marijuana for all purposes despite valid state laws authorizing the medical use of marijuana. See *Gonzales v. Raich*, 545 U.S. 1 (2005). So if Attorney purchased, possessed or ingested marijuana in Minnesota, the attorney would be violating federal law each and every time Attorney did so. In other words, Attorney would be engaging in a "pattern of repeated offenses" that indicates indifference to legal obligations and constitute a violation of N.D.R. Prof. Conduct 8.4(b). N.D.R. Prof. Conduct 8.4(b) cmt.

North Dakota law bolsters the conclusion that Attorney's conduct would constitute a violation. Indeed, North Dakota law on controlled substances—and marijuana in particular—aligns with federal law. As under federal law, the manufacture, possession, and use of marijuana for any purpose, even a medical one, is a crime under North Dakota law. See N.D.C.C. § 19–03.1–23. As under federal law, marijuana is classified as a schedule I controlled substance and thus has been determined to (1) have high potential for abuse and (2) have no accepted medical use in treatment in the United States or lack accepted safety for use in treatment under medical supervision. See N.D.C.C. § 19–03.1–05(5)(h); N.D.C.C. § 19–03.1–04. North Dakota even criminalizes marijuana ingestion and provides for prosecution either where the offender takes marijuana into the body or where marijuana is merely detected in the offender's body. See N.D.C.C. § 19–03.1–22.3.

Further, our supreme court has recently recognized North Dakota's policy against marijuana and adhering to the supremacy of federal law. *State v. Kuruc*, 2014 ND 95, 846 N.W.2d 314. Earlier this year, the court in Kuruc considered criminal defendants' claim that their Washington prescriptions for marijuana provided a defense to controlled substance crimes. Recognizing that marijuana was a schedule I controlled substance, the court explained that "it does not logically follow that there could be a valid prescription for a substance that has no medical use or lacks accepted safety." Rejecting the defendants' claim, the court reasoned that the legislature did not enact controlled substance laws "to put North Dakota in the perplexing position where it must recognize out-of-state marijuana prescriptions even though the same exact prescription cannot be made legal for its own citizens." The court also emphasized that medical marijuana is still illegal under federal law and thus under the Supremacy Clause, "a state law that conflicts with federal law is without effect." (Citing U.S. Const. art. VI and State ex rei. *Stenehjem v. FreeEats.com, Inc.* 2006 ND 84, ~ 19, 712 N.W.2d 828).

In short, federal law and North Dakota law and policy show that Attorney's conduct would be unlawful and unethical. Attorney's conduct (participating in a medical marijuana treatment program) would constitute a "pattern of repeated offenses" that indicates indifference to legal obligations and constitutes a violation of N.D.R. Prof. Conduct 8.4(b).

CONCLUSION

Attorney's conduct would frequently violate federal law and North Dakota policy. The conduct thus would constitute a pattern of repeated offenses in violation of N.D.R. Prof. Conduct 8.4(b).

This opinion was drafted by Cheri Clark and was approved by the Ethics Committee 4–2 on the 12th day of August, 2014.

This opinion is provided under Rule 1.2(b), North Dakota Rules for Lawyer Discipline, which states:

A lawyer who acts with good faith and reasonable reliance on a written opinion or advisory letter of the ethics committee of the association is not subject to sanction for violation of the North Dakota Rules of Professional Conduct as to the conduct that is the subject of the opinion or advisory letter.

NOTES AND QUESTIONS

1. **Basis for the committee's decision.** The Committee's decision in Opinion No. 14-02 appears to be based not only on marijuana's illegal status under federal law, but also on its illegal status under North Dakota law. As the Committee states in its conclusion: "In short, federal law and North Dakota law and policy show that Attorneys conduct would be unlawful and unethical." But is the status of marijuana under North Dakota law really necessary to the Committee's decision? Is it unethical, under the Committee's rationale, for an attorney to do something that is illegal under North Dakota law, even if it is performed in a state where it is legally permissible? If so, does that make it unethical for a North Dakota lawyer to gamble in Las Vegas, if gambling is illegal under North Dakota law?

2. **Lawyer impairment.** Rule 8.4 is not the only ethical rule that bears on a lawyer's personal use of marijuana. Rule 1.1 provides that "A lawyer shall provide competent representation to a client." Competence has generally been interpreted to include a lack of cognitive impairment on the part of lawyers, so that a lawyer who was "high" in court due to the lawyer's personal use of medical marijuana would likely violate Rule 1.1, even if the lawyer's conduct did not violate Rule 8.4, in the same way that the lawyer's drunkenness in court would likely violate Rule 1.1. Thus, an interpretation of Rule 8.4 that allows the personal use of marijuana by lawyers in legalization states does not shield lawyers from ethical sanctions if such use causes impairment that interferes with their ability to provide competent counsel to their clients.

3.   Other states' positions with respect to personal use. Thus far, there is not a lot of authority on the question whether lawyers can legally partake of marijuana for personal use in legalization states, assuming such use complies with state law. The states that have considered the issue have issued mixed results. On the one hand, the Washington state bar issued an opinion in 2015 stating that lawyers "may purchase and consume marijuana consistently with [state law] to the same extent that non-lawyers may generally do so." Washington State Bar Association, Advisory Opinion 201501 (2015). In Nevada, on the other hand, the state supreme court issued an order in February 2017 amending Rule 8.4 to add the following interpretive Comment:

> Because use, possession, and distribution of marijuana at any form still violates federal law, attorneys are advised that engaging in such conduct may result in federal prosecution and trigger discipline proceedings under SCR 111.

Comment [1] to Nevada Rule of Professional Conduct 8.4(b). Thus, the Nevada Supreme Court's interpretation of Rule 8.4 appears to prohibit personal use by attorneys in the state. And in Colorado, the situation remains unclear. In 2014, the Colorado Standing Committee on the Rules of Professional Conduct proposed a change to Rule 8.4 that would have made it clear that a lawyer's personal use of marijuana was permissible, so long as such use complied with state law, and the lawyer was not materially impaired in the lawyer's ability to represent the lawyer's clients. But the Colorado Supreme Court declined to modify Rule 8.4 accordingly, even though at the same time it modified Rule 1.2 so as to allow lawyers to ethically represent and assist marijuana-related businesses. Therefore, the court appeared to leave the propriety of personal use an open question. Nevertheless, the Colorado State Bar ethics committee has indicated that it will not pursue disciplinary action against lawyers based solely on their using marijuana, so long as such use complies with state law and does not result in impairment affecting the lawyer's ability to represent clients.

4.   Disparate treatment. In states such as Nevada and North Dakota that apparently do not condone the personal use of marijuana on the part of their attorneys, a lawyer suffering from seizure disorder or chronic pain would be unable to treat these conditions with medical marijuana without violating the lawyer's ethical duties, even though other citizens of the state can legally use medical marijuana to treat these conditions. Do you think it is fair to deny lawyers the same privileges that other citizens in a state enjoy when it comes to fundamental issues, such as medical care?

CHAPTER 17

HEMP

. . .

Hemp is a versatile agricultural product manufactured from varieties of the cannabis plant, cultivated for industrial purposes. As hemp contains minimal tetrahydrocannabinol (THC) content, it is not intoxicating. Nevertheless, the marijuana plant, whether psychoactive or not, is controlled under schedule I of the CSA. As a result, farming hemp, and to a lesser extent its commercial use, has for the most part been illegal in the United States. Recent exceptions to this prohibition are explored in the second part of this chapter. In particular, the Hemp Farming Act, enacted in December 2018, has removed many of the restrictions on hemp cultivation, in excluding it from the CSA definition of marijuana.

North Dakota and South Dakota have been the locus of significant litigation concerning hemp cultivation and are the focus of the major cases in this chapter, including *Monson v. DEA* (2009), *Hemp Indus. Ass'n. v. DEA I* (2003), *Hemp Indus. Ass'n. v. DEA II* (2004), *United States v. White Plume I* (2008), and *United States v. White Plume II* (2016). These cases have shaped interpretation of the treatment of hemp under the CSA, under recent federal legislation, and under American Indian law.

A. CULTIVATING HEMP

North Dakota legalized the cultivation and manufacture of hemp in 1999, thereby becoming the hotbed for disputes between North Dakota hemp farmers and the DEA.

MONSON V. DRUG ENFORCEMENT ADMINISTRATION (DEA)

United States Court of Appeals, Eighth Circuit
589 F.3d 952 (8th Cir. 2009)

BOWMAN, J.

David Monson and Wayne Hauge appeal from an order of the District Court dismissing their action for a declaration that the Controlled Substances Act (CSA or Act), 21 U.S.C. §§ 801–971, does not apply to their planned cultivation of Cannabis sativa L. (cannabis) pursuant to licenses they obtained from the State of North Dakota. Monson and Hauge argue that the District Court erred by failing to accept as true the factual allegations in their complaint, by finding that cannabis cultivated for industrial use under state law is subject to regulation under the CSA, and by determining that Congress has authority under the Commerce Clause to regulate their cultivation of cannabis. The Drug Enforcement Administration (DEA) and the Department of Justice (DOJ) argue that although the District Court properly dismissed the complaint, the court should have dismissed on jurisdictional grounds. We affirm the judgment of the District Court in all respects.

Monson and Hauge are North Dakota farmers who wish to grow cannabis pursuant to state law legalizing and regulating the cultivation of "industrial hemp." N.D. Cent.Code § 4–41–01. They intend to sell parts of the harvested cannabis for industrial use. Both industrial hemp and the drug commonly known as marijuana derive from the plant designated Cannabis sativa L. In general, drug-use cannabis is produced from the flowers and leaves of certain strains of the plant, while industrial-use cannabis is typically produced from the stalks and seeds of other strains of the plant. All cannabis plants contain tetrahydrocannabinol (THC), the substance that gives marijuana its psychoactive properties, but strains of the plant grown for drug use contain a higher THC concentration than those typically grown for industrial use. Monson and Hauge acknowledge that the plants they seek to grow are of the species Cannabis sativa L. They contend, however, that cannabis grown for industrial purposes, i.e., industrial hemp as defined by the North Dakota statute, is not marijuana within the meaning of the CSA and thus is not subject to federal regulation. Monson and Hauge filed this lawsuit in the District Court seeking a declaration that their "cultivation of industrial hemp pursuant to and in accordance with the licenses issued by the North Dakota Agriculture Commissioner does not and will not violate the" CSA. They assert that the CSA could not be applied to their cultivation of industrial hemp under state law without violating the Commerce Clause. The DEA and the DOJ filed a motion to dismiss for lack of jurisdiction or, in the alternative, for failure to state a claim upon which relief could be granted.

The District Court granted the DEA and DOJ's motion to dismiss. The court declined to dismiss on jurisdictional grounds and, proceeding to the merits, held that the cannabis plants Monson and Hauge proposed to cultivate fell within the CSA's definition of marijuana and thus that their planned cultivation of industrial hemp under state law was subject to regulation under the CSA. The court also concluded that Congress has authority under the Commerce Clause to regulate the manufacture of all cannabis plants, regardless of the THC concentration or ultimate use of those plants. Monson and Hauge appeal the dismissal of their complaint, and the DEA and the DOJ appeal the District Court's jurisdictional rulings. We first discuss the federal and state statutes before turning to the specific issues raised on appeal.

The CSA establishes a comprehensive federal system to regulate the manufacture and distribution of controlled substances, making it unlawful to "manufacture, distribute, or dispense" any controlled substance "[e]xcept as authorized by" the Act. 21 U.S.C. § 841(a)(1). The CSA defines "manufacture" to include "production," and it in turn defines "production" to include the "planting, cultivation, growing, or harvesting of a controlled substance." *Id.* § 802(22).

The CSA categorizes controlled substances into five separate schedules, depending on the characteristics of a particular substance. Marijuana is listed in Schedule I, the most restrictive schedule, because, like the other substances listed, it "has a high potential for abuse," "no currently accepted medical use in treatment in the United States," and "a lack of accepted safety for use under medical supervision." *Id.* § 812(b)(1)(A)–(C). Marijuana is defined in the CSA to include "all parts of the plant Cannabis sativa L." and anything made therefrom except, in general, mature stalks, fiber produced from those stalks, sterilized seeds, and oil from the seeds. *Id.* § 802(16). Under the CSA, any person seeking to manufacture a Schedule I controlled substance must obtain a registration from the DEA. Before issuing a registration, the DEA considers several factors, including the applicant's "maintenance of effective controls against diversion," "compliance with applicable State and local law," "prior conviction record," and "past experience in the manufacture of controlled substances." *Id.* § 823(a).

In 1999, the North Dakota Legislative Assembly legalized the growth, possession, and sale of "industrial hemp." N.D. Cent.Code § 4–41–01. The state statute defines industrial hemp as "(cannabis sativa l.), having no more than three-tenths of one percent" THC. Unlike the CSA, the North Dakota statute distinguishes among cannabis plants based on THC concentration. The state requires licensing for persons wishing to cultivate industrial hemp, imposes strict THC limits in an effort to prevent the cultivation of cannabis plants for drug use, and attempts to ensure that only those parts of the industrial hemp plant that are excluded from the CSA's definition of marijuana will leave a farmer's property and enter interstate commerce. Recognizing that industrial hemp as defined by the state is regulated under the CSA as marijuana, the state statute originally provided that any person seeking to grow industrial hemp in North Dakota was required to comply not only with the state's licensing requirements but also with the CSA's registration requirements.

Shortly after the state statute was enacted, the North Dakota Commissioner of Agriculture (Commissioner) requested that the DEA waive the CSA's registration requirement for all North Dakota farmers seeking to grow industrial hemp as defined and regulated by state law. In February 2007, the DEA denied the Commissioner's request, noting that "Congress expressly commanded the [DOJ] to take the lead in controlling licit and illicit drug activity through enforcement of the CSA [F]or [the] DEA to simply turn over to any state the agency's authority and responsibility to enforce the CSA would be directly at odds with the Act." The DEA also cautioned that registration pursuant to the CSA was necessary for the cultivation of industrial hemp because, unlike the North Dakota statute, the CSA includes all Cannabis sativa L. plants in its definition of marijuana, regardless of THC concentration.

Thereafter, the Commissioner submitted to the DEA applications for registration on behalf of Monson and Hauge for their proposed industrial hemp cultivation. In March 2007, less than one month after submitting those applications, the Commissioner sent the DEA a letter demanding action on the applications by April 1, 2007. The DEA responded that the Commissioner's proposed deadline was unrealistic given the agency's obligations to comply with notice and comment requirements, conduct background investigations, and complete onsite inspections of Monson and Hauge's manufacturing facilities. The North Dakota Legislative Assembly then amended the state statute by eliminating the DEA-registration requirement. In light of the DEA's pronouncements, however, Monson and Hauge did not immediately begin cultivating industrial hemp under their state licenses. Instead, they filed a lawsuit in the District Court seeking a declaration that the CSA does not apply to persons seeking to cultivate industrial hemp pursuant to North Dakota law.

[The Court first affirmed the ruling of the district court that Plaintiffs-Appellants Monson and Hauge were targets of DEA action and thus had actual injury sufficient to confer standing to pursue their claims. In addition, the Court held that their claims were ripe for review, and that the district court had subject matter jurisdiction to consider the claims for declaratory relief raised by Monson and Hauge. The Court then reviewed the substance of their claims.]

We now turn to Monson and Hauge's contention that the District Court erred in dismissing their complaint on the merits. Monson and Hauge first argue that in granting the DEA's motion to dismiss, the District Court erred by failing to "accept as true the allegations that the industrial hemp plant itself is useless as drug marijuana and that there is no way industrial hemp could be diverted to use" as drug marijuana. This argument is without merit. The "facts" that Monson and Hauge claim were improperly rejected by the District Court amount to nothing more than "sweeping legal conclusions" and "unwarranted inferences" that the court was not required to consider in ruling on the motion to dismiss.

Under the CSA, marijuana is defined to include all Cannabis sativa L. plants, regardless of THC concentration. See 21 U.S.C. § 802(16). The CSA likewise makes no distinction between cannabis grown for drug use and that grown for industrial use. In *United States v. White Plume*, 447 F.3d 1067, 1069 (8th Cir.2006), we held that "industrial hemp," defined by tribal ordinance as "[a]ll parts and varieties of the plant Cannabis sativa" that "contain a [THC] concentration of one percent or less by weight," was subject to regulation as a Schedule I controlled substance under the CSA because as a species of Cannabis sativa L., it fell squarely within the definition of marijuana set forth in the CSA. We also noted that "[t]he language of the CSA unambiguously bans the growing of marijuana, regardless of its use," and we concluded that "[b]ecause the CSA does not distinguish between marijuana and hemp in its regulation, and because farming hemp requires growing the entire marijuana plant which at some point contains psychoactive levels of THC, the CSA regulates the farming of hemp." Considering the legislative history of the CSA, we found "no evidence that Congress intended otherwise" than to ban the growth of all varieties of the Cannabis sativa L. plant absent compliance with the registration requirements of the CSA. *Id.* at 1072; *see also N.H. Hemp Council*, 203 F.3d at 6–8 (concluding that cannabis cultivated for industrial use and possessing a low THC concentration is nevertheless marijuana under the CSA and is subject to regulation by the DEA); cf. *United States v. Curtis*, 965 F.2d 610, 616 (8th Cir.1992) (observing that male marijuana plants, which may have lower THC concentrations than female plants, are still marijuana plants for sentencing purposes).

In ruling on the DEA's motion to dismiss, the District Court was not required to accept as true Monson and Hauge's alleged facts that were nothing more than "unsupported conclusions, unwarranted inferences and sweeping legal conclusions" directly at odds with the CSA and Circuit precedent. In sum, the District Court properly construed and dismissed the complaint; the court did not err in rejecting Monson and Hauge's alleged facts, and it properly concluded that industrial hemp as defined by the North Dakota statute is marijuana for purposes of the CSA.

Monson and Hauge next argue that the District Court erred by concluding "that the CSA can constitutionally be extended to reach the proposed intrastate cultivation of industrial hemp under North Dakota law." According to Monson and Hauge, because the only portion of the industrial hemp plant that would leave their North Dakota farms and enter interstate commerce is the *unregulated* portions of the plant-the mature stalk, fiber, non-viable seed and oil-Congress has no authority to regulate their state-sanctioned cultivation of cannabis. It is well established, and Monson and Hauge do not dispute, that enactment of the CSA was within Congress's authority under the Commerce Clause. What Monson and Hauge do dispute, however, is Congress's authority under the Commerce Clause to regulate what they describe as purely intrastate activity. Like the District Court, we find this argument unavailing.* * *

The Supreme Court's decision in *Gonzales v. Raich*, 545 U.S. 1 (2005), disposes of Monson and Hauge's argument that the CSA cannot be interpreted to reach their intrastate cultivation and processing of cannabis without violating the Commerce Clause. In *Raich*, users and growers of medical marijuana under a California statute sought a declaration that the

CSA was unconstitutional as applied to their intrastate activities. The Supreme Court held that Congress has authority under the Commerce Clause to regulate marijuana that is grown and consumed intrastate for non-commercial, personal medical reasons. The Court explained that "Congress has the power to regulate activities that substantially affect interstate commerce," and that as part of this well-established power, Congress is permitted to "regulate purely local activities that are part of an economic 'class of activities' that have a substantial effect on interstate commerce." *Id.* at 17. The Court held that it was not necessary to determine whether the activities in question, "taken in the aggregate, substantially affect interstate commerce in fact, but only whether a 'rational basis' exists for so concluding." *Id.* at 22. Because of "the enforcement difficulties that attend distinguishing between marijuana cultivated locally and marijuana grown elsewhere and concerns about diversion into illicit channels," the Court had "no difficulty concluding that Congress had a rational basis for believing that failure to regulate the intrastate manufacture and possession of marijuana would leave a gaping hole in the CSA." *Id.* The fact that the CSA was likely to impact some purely intrastate activities was of no concern to the Court.

Here, Monson and Hauge's proposed cultivation of cannabis falls more squarely within the scope of Congress's Commerce Clause authority than did the *Raich* plaintiffs' proposed cultivation of marijuana. Unlike the *Raich* plaintiffs, who sought to grow marijuana plants on a small scale for their personal medical use, Monson and Hauge seek to grow cannabis on a large scale for the undeniably commercial purpose of generating products for sale in interstate commerce.

Monson and Hauge's attempts to distinguish *Raich* are unpersuasive. They contend that because Congress chose to exclude certain components of the Cannabis sativa L. plant from the CSA's definition of marijuana, Congress "cannot constitutionally regulate intrastate state-regulated and licensed activity that results only in putting" those unregulated components into interstate commerce. This argument misses the mark. The question is not whether Congress could have decided to regulate a narrower class of economic activity than it chose to regulate. Rather, the question is whether Congress had any rational basis to conclude that the economic activity it chose to regulate—the manufacture of all marijuana plants, regardless of THC content and intended use—substantially affects interstate commerce.

Congress's decision to regulate the manufacture of all marijuana plants—whatever their ultimate use—was a rational means of achieving one of Congress's primary objectives: "to control the supply and demand of controlled substances in both lawful and unlawful drug markets." *Id.* at 19. As we observed in *White Plume*, " 'problems of detection and enforcement easily justify a ban [on Cannabis sativa L.] broader than the psychoactive variety of the plant.'" 447 F.3d at 1073. It is likewise no answer to Congress's concern about enforcement problems to assert that "North Dakota law requires that no plant and no part of the plant regulated by the CSA may ever leave the farmer's property." The Supreme Court rejected a similar argument in *Raich*, observing that state restrictions on marijuana possession and cultivation "cannot serve to place [the challenged] activities beyond congressional reach." 545 U.S. at 29.

The CSA defines marijuana to include all Cannabis sativa L. plants, regardless of THC concentration or intended use. Congress had a rational basis for concluding that it was necessary to regulate the cultivation of all Cannabis sativa L. plants in order to maintain the CSA's highly regulated system of drug distribution and its controls against unlawful diversion of controlled substances. By regulating all Cannabis sativa L. plants, Congress, through the CSA, vested the DEA with the authority to determine whether a particular proposal for its growth is sufficiently controlled so as not to undermine the objectives of the Act. And any attempt by Monson and Hauge to draw distinctions between Cannabis sativa L. varieties for purposes of Commerce Clause analysis ignores the indisputable fact that they seek to engage in a commercial enterprise that will result in the introduction of goods into interstate commerce. Regardless of Congress's purpose, because cultivation of Cannabis sativa L. substantially affects the interstate market for commodities such as the fiber, seed, and oil of the plant, Congress may regulate that cultivation. The District Court properly rejected Monson and Hauge's Commerce Clause challenge.

We affirm the judgment of the District Court in all respects.

NOTES AND QUESTIONS

1. **Industrial hemp.** Hemp is a variety of the Cannabis sativa L. plant bred as a source of valuable agricultural and industrial products, estimated at 25,000 uses. Hemp is a sturdy, durable, quick-growing and versatile crop. Hemp stalk and fibers (bast) are high in tensile strength and are largely pest-resistant. The fibers have traditionally been used to manufacture clothing, paper, canvas, carpet, twine, and sails. Hemp seeds and oilcake have concentrated nutritional value and are used in healthy foodstuffs and dietary products. Hemp oil is used for cosmetics, body care products, and synthetic biofuel. Hemp pulp and hurds (woody core of the stalk) are used for plastics, boards, mulch, animal bedding, insulation, and furniture. Hempcrete is a construction material akin to concrete. The production of hemp is explicitly allowed for in Article 28(3) of the 1961 United Nations Single Convention on Narcotic Drugs and hence in international law. Over 30 nations grow significant amounts of hemp for manufacturing purposes. China is the largest producer, at about 44,000 metric tons annually; China and Canada are the largest hemp exporters to the United States. The United States is the only industrial country in the world that banned the cultivation of hemp. Thus to

the extent that hemp products have been allowed in the U.S., they are mostly derived from imported hemp. An informative summary of the commercial, legal, and legislative status of hemp is Renée Johnson, *Hemp as an Agricultural Commodity*, Congressional Research Service Report RL32725 (June 22, 2018).

2.   Industrial hemp in the U.S. The ban on hemp in the United States began with the CSA in 1970, which defined any cannabis plant as marijuana, of any variety, regardless of TCH content. Before that, hemp was a major American crop, especially in the 18th and 19th centuries. Its utility declined with greater use of cotton and the invention of synthetic materials. The Marihuana Tax Act of 1937 included the definition of marijuana that would be adopted under the CSA, thus including hemp plants, but largely exempted hemp from taxation. In World War II, due to loss of imported fibers, hemp reached a peak production in the United States of more than 150 million pounds annually.

3.   Hemp is not intoxicating. Hemp and psychoactive marijuana are the same genus of cannabis, and hence were classified together under the CSA under the term "marihuana" with no legal distinction, but are different cultivars (varieties) of the genus, with distinct genetic and chemical properties. Psychoactive cannabis contains a concentration of about 3% to 25% THC, mostly in the flowering tops of the female plant. It is estimated that cannabis requires a concentration of at least 1% to begin to have an intoxicating effect. Hemp is cultivated for the sturdiness of fibers with reduced THC. Thus hemp is commonly defined in state law as having a concentration of less than 0.3 % of THC and is non-intoxicating.

4.   Hemp is banned. Hemp is not a term used in the CSA. For the purposes of the CSA, all varieties of the cannabis plant were subsumed under the term marihuana, without correlating to botanical definitions and concentrations of THC. Although hemp products may be derived from parts of the cannabis plant that are not included in the CSA definition, from the stalks of the marijuana plant, or from the male plant which has no flowers, they can only be produced from a marijuana plant, and thus hemp could not be grown in the United States, without federal registration, which was rarely given. DEA has opposed hemp farming as a necessary component of the war against marijuana. Some of the rationales given by DEA include:

- Hemp farmers would have the greatest opportunity to divert marijuana from legitimate purposes to illegal drug traffic.

- Marijuana plants with varying psychotropic properties are visually indistinguishable. DEA surveillance of illegal marijuana cultivation is largely visual and aerial, which would be impeded by the necessity of distinguishing hemp from psychoactive marijuana in a field.

- Enforcement of the CSA is facilitated by detecting marijuana as a genus and not by its constituent elements like concentration levels of THC, which require laboratory testing.

- Public support for a ban on marijuana would be weakened if cultivation of a variety of the cannabis plant was permitted.

- Although varieties of cannabis may contain such low levels of THC that they would be impractical to use as a drug, the necessity of eliminating the dangers of marijuana justifies a prohibition broader than the psychcactive variety of the plant.

5. Importing hemp. Although cultivating hemp was illegal in the United States, its commercial use was permitted if derived from parts of the cannabis plant not defined under the CSA as marijuana, and imported under strict controls. Hemp can be imported as a component of a finished product or as a raw ingredient to be processed in manufacturing.

6. State legalization. States began legalizing hemp in 1999. North Dakota was the first state to do so, creating a highly regulated licensing scheme. Agriculture is the largest industry in North Dakota, worth $4 billion, and employing 20% of the workforce. In addition, American Indian tribes of North and South Dakota have traditionally cultivated hemp. As of December 2018, over 40 states have enacted some form of state legalization of hemp.

7. Hemp manufacturers sue. In response to state legalization, in 2001 DEA promulgated a new regulation, prohibiting hemp products if containing traces of THC, and in particular hemp seed and hemp oil for human consumption, regardless of the source in the cannabis plant. 66 Fed. Reg. 51,530 (October 9, 2001). However, in two cases brought by the association of hemp manufacturers, *Hemp Industries Association v. Drug Enforcement Administration*, 333 F.2d 1082 (9th Circuit 2004) ("Hemp I") and *Hemp Industries Association v. Drug Enforcement Administration*, 357 F.2d 1012 (9th Circuit 2004) ("Hemp II"), the Ninth Circuit enjoined enforcement of the DEA's rule. The court held that the CSA prohibits only naturally-occurring THC contained within the parts of the cannabis plant defined as marijuana, and synthetic THC. Products made from the excluded parts of the plant under the CSA definition—such as mature stalks, and oil and cake made from the seeds, which contain only naturally-occurring trace THC—fall outside the CSA and can be manufactured as component parts of hemp products. The Ninth Circuit's rationale was that if the definition of THC under the CSA included naturally-occurring THC, the scheduling of marijuana would be redundant, as all parts of the cannabis plant contain at least traces of THC.

8. Gonzales v. Raich. In Chapters 3 and 8, we discussed the seminal case of *Gonzales v. Raich*, 545 U.S. 1 as to the extent of federal authority to proscribe marijuana consumption. On what basis do the Plaintiffs in *Monson v. DEA* distinguish *Gonzales v. Raich* and how does the Court answer their arguments?

9. DEA registration. As noted in the case, after being rebuffed by the DEA, the North Dakota legislature amended its state licensing laws to eliminate the requirement of DEA registration. According to what you have learned about preemption and federal law, what impact would this amendment have in "legalizing" hemp cultivation in North Dakota.

10. Factual allegations. The Eighth Circuit states that the district court below did not err in declining to "accept as true the allegations that the industrial hemp plant itself is useless as drug marijuana and that there is no way industrial hemp could be diverted to use" as drug marijuana. As the non-intoxicating content of hemp is a scientific question over which there is no disagreement, how are these allegations "sweeping legal conclusions" and "unwarranted inferences" and not facts?

11. Intent of Congress. Hemp proponents argue that given the favorable treatment of hemp under the Marihuana Tax Act of 1937, and the legislative hearings leading to passage of the CSA, Congress did not mean to prohibit hemp in the CSA, or at least did not pay sufficient attention to how hemp would be treated under the complicated provisions of that Act. Assuming that this is true and can be established, would it make a difference in how the law of hemp is applied, given the actual language of the CSA?

B. ALLOWING HEMP USE

The decade-long litigation odyssey of White Plume, a farmer and member of the Oglala Sioux tribe of South Dakota, reflects the complicated interaction of federal, state, and Indian law as to hemp. This litigation, most recently conducted in 2016, throws light on important changes that have been made in the law of hemp in recent years, explains exemptions to the hemp ban recently introduced, and points to fuller legalization in the near future.

UNITED STATES V. WHITE PLUME

United States District Court, South Dakota, Western Division
2016 WL 1228585 (2016)

VIKEN, C.J.

INTRODUCTION

Defendant Alexander "Alex" White Plume ("defendant") filed a motion and supporting brief pursuant to Fed. R. Civ. P. 60(b) seeking relief from the permanent injunction entered on December 30, 2004. The United States resists the motion. For the reasons stated below, the defendant's motion is granted.

ANALYSIS

To properly analyze defendant's motion it is necessary to review the history of the relationship between the United States and Mr. White Plume. On August 9, 2002, the United States filed a complaint against Mr. White Plume and his brother, Percy White Plume, seeking a declaratory judgment and injunctive relief. The government alleged the defendants were "manufacturing and distributing marijuana, in violation of 21 U.S.C. § 856(a)(1)." The specific claim of the government was that the defendants Alexander White Plume and Percy White Plume as "enrolled members of the Oglala Sioux Tribe . . . in concert with others, have manufactured, planted, cultivated and grown marijuana on three successive crop years beginning with the 2000 crop year . . . . [and] have utilized federal trust lands for the manufacture, distribution and possession with the intent to distribute . . . marijuana." The United States sought a permanent injunction enjoining the defendants from violating 21 U.S.C. §§ 841(a)(1) and 856(a)(1).

The defendants denied the government's allegations and filed a counterclaim. In their answer the defendants asserted, among other defenses, they were "cultivat[ing] industrial hemp exclusively for industrial or horticultural purposes" and were "exempt from [the] application of the Controlled Substances Act . . . ." They alleged "industrial hemp . . . cannot be properly classified as a Schedule I substance under 21 U.S.C. [§] 812, since it contains no or insufficient THC to create a hallucinogenic 'high' and therefore cannot have a high or any substantive potential for abuse." The defendants sought declaratory and injunctive relief to prevent the government from seizing and destroying their industrial hemp crop. * * *

[T]he court found that "[h]emp is a variety of Cannabis sativa L." and is subject to the CSA. "[S]ince the hemp form and the drug form of marijuana are both Cannabis sativa L., and differentiate only chemically, it is not irrational that hemp would be included with marijuana as a Schedule I drug." The court found "that it is in the public's best interest, and that it is their desire, to tightly regulate the cultivation of cannabis."

On December 30, 2004, the court filed an amended judgment permanently enjoining Alexander White Plume and other defendants "from cultivating Cannabis sativa L., otherwise known as marijuana or hemp, without a valid Drug Enforcement Administration registration." On May 17, 2006, the Eighth Circuit affirmed the decision of the district court. *United States v. White Plume*, 447 F.3d 1067 (8th Cir. 2006).

On July 30, 2015, Alexander White Plume filed a motion pursuant to Rule 60(b) seeking to vacate the permanent injunction. Federal Rule of Civil Procedure 60 provides grounds for relief from a final judgment or order. * * *

Mr. White Plume argues that "[i]n the decade since this decision, state and federal action has significantly altered the legal landscape surrounding Cannabis."

To date, twenty-two states have legalized non-drug industrial hemp. Moved, in part, by this sea change, the Department of Justice has issued policy guidance memoranda introducing an eight-factor assessment for federal prosecutors that adds discretion to their enforcement of the Controlled Substances Act ("CSA"). Further, in the 2014 Farm Bill, Congress recognized a distinction between marijuana and industrial hemp, creating for the first time an exception to the CSA allowing for the growth, cultivation, and study of industrial hemp in certain circumstances. Because industrial hemp stalks and seeds are often used to make textiles, foods, papers, body care products, detergents, plastics, biofuels, and building materials, the crop has significant economic and environmental value. Under the new Farm Bill paradigm, individual farmers, universities, and state agriculture departments are now able to explore this potential industrial hemp farming bounty.

Mr. White Plume asserts that "[g]iven these changes, the injunction . . . is outdated at best. . . . Now, it is time for this Court to recognize these changes and lift the injunction put in place . . . more than ten years ago."

The United States resists Mr. White Plume's motion. It claims "White Plume has not met his burden of proving exceptional circumstances exist that justify the dissolution of the permanent injunction. Rather, White Plume essentially seeks license, through this motion, to violate the CSA." The government argues "the legal conclusion that the CSA prohibits the cultivation of hemp or industrial hemp on the Pine Ridge Indian Reservation is not properly challenged under Rule 60(b)(5). Moreover, White Plume does not fall within the narrow exceptions created in 7 U.S.C. § 5940 [of the Agricultural Act of 2014]."

Whether and where Mr. White Plume can legally cultivate industrial hemp if the injunction is lifted is not currently a question before this Court. And to be clear, Mr. White Plume's request for Rule 60(b) relief does not ask this Court for a declaratory judgment that Mr. White Plume is permitted to grow industrial hemp on the Pine Ridge Indian Reservation. Nor does the Court need to reach the broader issue of whether cultivation of industrial hemp on the Pine Ridge Indian Reservation is legal as a general matter.

Mr. White Plume contends "[t]he only question properly before the Court is whether a decade-old injunction targeting Mr. White Plume—the only one of its kind in history—can properly stand given the recent legislative and executive action that have altered the conditions under which the injunction was issued." Mr. White Plume and the Oglala Sioux Tribe ("OST"), in its amicus curiae brief, alternatively urge the court to rule they are entitled to the same rights as the States and the citizens of those States to engage in industrial hemp production under the Agricultural Act of 2014.

A motion for relief from a judgment must be brought "within a reasonable time." Fed. R. Civ. P. 60(c)(1). "What constitutes a reasonable time is dependent on the particular facts of the case in question and is reviewed for abuse of discretion." *Watkins v. Lundell*, 169 F.3d 540, 544 (8th Cir. 1999). The court looks to a number of factors to resolve the timeliness issue. First, the Attorney General of the United States issued two critically relevant memoranda in 2013 and 2014. Those are the memorandum from Deputy Attorney General James M. Cole directed to all United States Attorneys and providing "Guidance Regarding Marijuana Enforcement," August 29, 2013 ("Cole Memorandum") and the memorandum from Monty Wilkinson, Director of the Executive Office for United States Attorneys, directed to all United States Attorneys, First Assistant United States Attorneys, Criminal Chiefs, Appellate Chiefs, OCDETF Coordinators and Tribal Liaisons entitled "Policy Statement Regarding Marijuana Issues in Indian Country," October 28, 2014 ("Wilkinson Memorandum").

Following legalization of marijuana in Colorado and Washington, the Cole Memorandum outlined eight priorities for Department of Justice enforcement of the CSA against conduct associated with the substance.

- Preventing the distribution of marijuana to minors;

- Preventing revenue from the sale of marijuana from going to criminal enterprises, gangs, and cartels;

- Preventing the diversion of marijuana from states where it is legal under state law in some form to other states;

- Preventing state-authorized marijuana activity from being used as a cover or pretext for the trafficking of other illegal drugs or other illegal activity;

- Preventing violence and the use of firearms in the cultivation and distribution of marijuana;

- Preventing drugged driving and the exacerbation of other adverse public health consequences associated with marijuana use;

- Preventing the growing of marijuana on public lands and the attendant public safety and environmental dangers posed by marijuana production on public lands; and

- Preventing marijuana possession or use on federal property.

The Cole Memorandum acknowledged that "[i]n jurisdictions that have enacted laws legalizing marijuana in some form and that have also implemented strong and effective regulatory and enforcement systems to control the cultivation, distribution, sale, and possession of marijuana, conduct in compliance with those laws and regulations is less likely to threaten the federal priorities set forth above."

The Wilkinson Memorandum specifically addressed drug enforcement in Indian country. "With a number of states legalizing marijuana for use and production, some tribes have requested guidance on the enforcement of the Controlled Substances Act . . . on tribal lands by the United States

Attorneys' offices." After discussing the Cole Memorandum priorities, the Wilkinson Memorandum stated:

> Indian Country includes numerous reservations and tribal lands with diverse sovereign governments, many of which traverse state borders and federal districts. Given this, the United States Attorneys recognize that effective federal law enforcement in Indian Country, including marijuana enforcement, requires consultation with our tribal partners in the districts and flexibility to confront the particular, yet sometimes divergent, public safety issues that can exist on any single reservation. . . . The eight priorities in the Cole Memorandum will guide United States Attorneys' marijuana enforcement efforts in Indian Country, including in the event that sovereign Indian Nations seek to legalize the cultivation or use of marijuana in Indian Country. Consistent with the Attorney General's 2010 Indian Country Initiative, in evaluating marijuana enforcement activities in Indian Country, each United States Attorney should consult with the affected tribes on a government-to-government basis.

The second major factor considered in judging the timeliness of Mr. White Plume's motion was the enactment of the Agricultural Act of 2014. Section 5940 of the Act is subtitled "Legitimacy of industrial hemp research." 7 U.S.C. § 5940. That section permits the cultivation of industrial hemp under certain conditions:

> Notwithstanding the Controlled Substances Act (21 U.S.C. 801 et seq.), the Safe and Drug-Free Schools and Communities Act (20 U.S.C. 7101 et seq.), chapter 81 of Title 41, or any other Federal law, an institution of higher education (as defined in section 1001 of Title 20) or a State department of agriculture may grow or cultivate industrial hemp if—
>
> (1) the industrial hemp is grown or cultivated for purposes of research conducted under an agricultural pilot program or other agricultural or academic research; and
>
> (2) the growing or cultivating of industrial hemp is allowed under the laws of the State in which such institution of higher education or State department of agriculture is located and such research occurs.

Id. § 5940(a). The Act defines "industrial hemp" as "the plant Cannabis sativa L. and any part of such plant, whether growing or not, with a delta-9 tetrahydrocannabinol concentration of not more than 0.3 percent on a dry weight basis." *Id.* § 5940(b)(2).

The third major factor concerning the timeliness issue is the May 7, 2015, letter from OST President John Yellow Bird Steele to the Acting

United States Attorney for the District of South Dakota. President Yellow Bird Steele sought the assistance of the Acting United States Attorney to permit Mr. White Plume and the other members of the Oglala Sioux Tribe on the Pine Ridge Indian Reservation to cultivate industrial hemp in accordance with OST Ordinance No. 98-27. The letter pointed out "that the State of Oregon has issued commercial hemp licenses to at least one of its citizens and, if the White Plume Hemp Injunction is not promptly lifted, the Oglala Sioux Tribe will require a formal response from [the] United States Department of Justice explaining why our members of the Oglala Sioux Tribe are not being treated favorably [sic] than a citizen of the State of Oregon who is similarly situated." President Yellow Bird Steele sought a response by the end of May to his call for assistance. According to the OST amicus brief, it does not appear the Acting United States Attorney responded to the letter.

The fourth major factor on the timeliness issue is the fact that Mr. White Plume filed his Rule 60(b) motion on July 30, 2015. This was only sixty days after the response deadline of the letter from the OST President to the Acting United States Attorney for the District of South Dakota.

The court finds these factors support a finding that the motion was brought "within a reasonable time" following the culmination of these major events. * * * The court finds there has been a significant shift in the legal landscape since 2004 which makes "continued enforcement" of the permanent injunction "detrimental to the public interest." In making this declaration, the court declines the parties' invitation to re-litigate the initial soundness of the permanent injunction. Whether the Fort Laramie Treaty of 1868 should have protected Mr. White Plume from the injunction originally or whether the Oglala Sioux Tribe should be considered on equal footing with the States under the Agricultural Act of 2014 need not be resolved in the present motion.

What is material to the court's analysis is the shifting national focus on industrial hemp as a viable agricultural crop and the decision of the Attorney General of the United States to engage in a dialogue with the various tribes on the relationship between the CSA and the Agricultural Act of 2014. The government did not challenge Mr. White Plume's assertion that "[w]ith the Agricultural Act of 2014, the Federal government joined the twenty-two states that have enacted legislation on industrial hemp."). Nor did the government challenge the representation that seven states have ventured into the area of agricultural or academic research of industrial hemp. Under these laws, researchers and commercial farmers are already growing industrial hemp. Several universities in Kentucky, including the University of Kentucky, are growing hemp to research the viability of certain types of hemp seed in Kentucky soil, cultivation for medical research, applications for cleaning tainted soil, and agricultural issues such as production cost. These 2014 pilot projects were extremely successful, yielding substantial data about farming techniques and alternative uses for industrial hemp. Hundreds of applicants sought permits for the 2015 programs in Kentucky. Oregon has also issued its first hemp farming permit. In both states, the DEA and the U.S. Attorney's Offices have neither disallowed hemp farming nor moved to confiscate or destroy the hemp crop.

The shifting legal landscape is also illustrated by the action of the 2016 South Dakota Legislature. During this past legislative session, it considered House Bill No. 1054, a bill to authorize the production and sale of industrial hemp. A review of the proposed legislation suggests the Legislature was seeking to comply with the requirements of 7 U.S.C. § 5940 of the Agricultural Act of 2014. House Bill No. 1054 was approved by the House of Representatives on a 57–11 vote but then was deferred to the 41st legislative day by the Senate Agriculture and Natural Resources Committee, effectively killing the bill for this year.

All of these factors constitute "changed circumstances—changes in the nature of the underlying problem, changes in governing law or its interpretation by the courts, and new policy insights—that warrant reexamination of the original judgment." The shift in this country in permitting marijuana and industrial hemp production are of paramount interest to the public. These factual and legal changes "make[ ] continued enforcement inequitable." Mr. White Plume carried his burden under Rule 60(b)(5) of "establishing that changed circumstances warrant relief." The court would abuse its discretion if "it refuse[d] to modify [the permanent] injunction . . . in light of [these] changes."

ORDER

Based on the above analysis, it is

ORDERED that Mr. White Plume's motion is granted.

IT IS FURTHER ORDERED that the permanent injunction set out in the amended judgment of December 30, 2004 is vacated as it relates to Alexander "Alex" White Plume.

IT IS FURTHER ORDERED that Mr. White Plume's motion for alternative relief is denied without prejudice.

IT IS FURTHER ORDERED that this order does *not* authorize Mr. White Plume to cultivate industrial hemp or violate the Controlled Substances Act.

IT IS FURTHER ORDERED that this order does *not* resolve whether cultivation of industrial hemp on the Pine Ridge Indian Reservation is legal.

IT IS FURTHER ORDERED that this order does *not* resolve whether the Agricultural Act of 2014 authorizes cultivation of industrial hemp on the Pine Ridge Indian Reservation.

NOTES AND QUESTIONS

1.   **Injunctive relief.** The procedural posture of this case is whether the permanent injunction against Plaintiff White Plume to farm hemp should be dissolved. Rules for enforcing and dissolving injunctions are complex but for the purposes of this case it is enough to focus on "a substantial likelihood of plaintiffs prevailing on the merits." Why does the Court find that the permanent injunction applied against White Plume in 2004, and affirmed by the Eighth Circuit in 2006, should be vacated in 2016? What is the impact of the Court's findings as to hemp law on the list of orders it issues at the conclusion of its opinion?

2.   **Changed circumstances.** The Court holds that White Plume is entitled to relief from the DEA injunction because of "changed circumstances— changes in the nature of the underlying problem, changes in governing law or its interpretation by the courts, and new policy insights" in the law of hemp. Among the changed circumstances the Court discusses are the Cole Memorandum; the Wilkinson Memorandum; that non-Indians have been granted commercial hemp licenses while Indians like White Plume have been enjoined; and the Agricultural Act of 2014, allowing state pilot projects to license universities to grow hemp for research purposes. How do these factors indicate changed circumstances? Would any of these changed circumstances provide an actual basis for White Plume to engage in hemp farming under current law? If not, are these factors actually relevant to the question of whether to dissolve the injunction? While the court is agnostic on the final disposition of several of these issues, do they point to maintaining the injunction rather than dissolving it?

3.   **Congressional reform of hemp law.** Congress enacted the most significant reforms to the federal law of hemp in its two most recent "Farm Bills." Farm bills are the common name for the omnibus, mutibillion dollar, agricultural law, enacted every four or so years to implement farm and food policy in the United States.

> *Agricultural Act of 2014.* This rendition of the farm bill promulgated the Hemp Pilot Program (P.L. 113-79, § 7606), summarized in the *White Plume* opinion. This law allows states to run pilot programs cultivating hemp in conjunction with state departments of agriculture and universities. To constitute hemp under the bill, Cannabis plants can contain no more than 0.3% of THC on a dry weight basis. As of 2018, 41 states have launched pilot hemp growing programs under the farm bill or legalized hemp. In addition, Congress's annual appropriation bills since passage of the 2014 farm bill prohibit law enforcement agencies from interfering with these pilot programs. It should be noted, however, that the Hemp Pilot Program, § 7606 of the Farm Bill, authorizes cultivation of hemp only for research purposes, including marketing research, but not for general commercial activity. In addition both the Farm Bill and the appropriations amendment must be reauthorized by Congress.

Agriculture Improvement Act of 2018. This rendition of the farm bill, enacted as this casebook was going to press, includes the Hemp Farming Act, the most far-reaching reform of hemp law, since passage of the CSA in 1970. It excludes cannabis plants and their compounds with less than 0.3% THC from the CSA definition of marijuana, thus removing most of the restrictions to the cultivation, processing, manufacture, and commercial use of hemp. In addition, the Agriculture Improvement Act of 2018 treats hemp as an agricultural commodity, allowing hemp farmers to access Federal Crop Insurance. States and tribal goverments are authorized to regulate and implement hemp cultivation within their borders. Nevertheless, hemp will remain a highly regulated industry. State plans must track and inspect hemp production, enforce hemp restrictions, and share information on hemp growers with federal officials. Hemp farmers must be licensed. Important federal restrictions on hemp remain, for example, mandating agency oversight, requiring background checks and excluding drug felons from participating in hemp programs, and leaving FDA authority for hemp food products.

4.   Hemp and American Indian Law. White Plume is apparently the only person to have been permanently enjoined from growing hemp. On the one hand, this can be seen as preemptive action against a person and demographic group who have traditionally cultivated hemp and announced plans to do so again. On the other hand, as suggested by the letter from the OST President to the Acting United States Attorney for the District of South Dakota, this may reflect a historic bias against Native Americans. The Court in White Plume does not address whether Indian tribes should be considered on an equal footing with the states under the Agricultural Act of 2014. For this issue see the discussion in Chapter 9 of *Menominee Indian Tribe of Wisconsin vs. DEA and U.S. Department of Justice* (2016). For an argument that Oglala Sioux Tribe (OST) is entitled to grow hemp on their reservation by long-standing treaty right, see Lori Murphy, *Enough Rope: Why United States v. White Plume was Wrong on Hemp and Treaty Rights, and What it Could Cost the Federal Government*, 35 Am. Indian L. Rev. 767 (2011).

C. IMPLEMENTING RULES FOR IMPORTING HEMP

It is the task of the federal agency authorized by law to administer the CSA—the Drug Enforcement Administration—to enact regulations and rules implementing the congressional legislation and judicial decisions as to importing hemp. The U.S. Customs and Border Protection Agency enforces these rules at the border. Although these rules are entitled to deference by the courts, they are not immune from judicial review, such as the painstaking review of 21 C.F.R. § 1308.35 regulations in *Hemp Indus. Ass'n. v. DEA I* (2003) and *Hemp Indus. Ass'n. v. DEA II* (2004). DEA acceded to the Ninth's Circuit's ruling in those cases, in the following 2018 directive.

INTERNAL DIRECTIVE REGARDING THE PRESENCE OF CANNABINOIDS IN PRODUCTS AND MATERIALS MADE FROM THE CANNABIS PLANT
Drug Enforcement Administration
https://www.deadiversion.usdoj.gov/schedules/marijuana/dea_internal_
directive_cannabinoids_05222018.html (May 22, 2018)

In 2004, the U.S. Court of Appeals for the Ninth Circuit enjoined DEA from enforcing certain regulations with respect to tetrahydrocannabinols (THC). *See Hemp Industries Ass'n v. DEA*, 357 F.3d 1012 (9th Cir. 2004). The government did not seek Supreme Court review of that decision. In response to various inquiries, DEA hereby issues to DEA personnel the following internal directive on how to carry out their duties in light of the Ninth Circuit's decision. The Ninth Circuit enjoined enforcement of what is now 21 C.F.R. § 1308.11(d)(31) (drug code 7370) with respect to products that are excluded from the definition of marijuana in the Controlled Substances Act (CSA). DEA thus does not enforce that provision as to such products. Consistent with the Ninth Circuit's decision, DEA does not enforce 21 C.F.R. § 1308.35.

Products and materials that are made from the cannabis plant and which fall outside the CSA definition of marijuana (such as sterilized seeds, oil or cake made from the seeds, and mature stalks) are not controlled under the CSA. Such products may accordingly be sold and otherwise distributed throughout the United States without restriction under the CSA or its implementing regulations. The mere presence of cannabinoids is not itself dispositive as to whether a substance is within the scope of the CSA; the dispositive question is whether the substance falls within the CSA definition of marijuana.

The Controlled Substances Import and Export Act incorporates the schedules of the CSA. *See generally* 21 U.S.C. §§ 951–971. Accordingly, any product that the U.S. Customs and Border Protection determines to be made from the cannabis plant but which falls outside the CSA definition of marijuana may be imported into the United States without restriction under the Controlled Substances Import and Export Act. The same considerations apply to exports of such products from the United States, provided further that it is lawful to import such products under the laws of the country of destination.

The United States Department of Homeland Security: United States Customs and Border Protection controls import of cannabis-derived products. The Department posted the following instructions on its website.

IMPORTING HEMP PRODUCTS INTO THE U.S.

United States Customs and Border Protection
(As of December, 2018)
https://help.cbp.gov/app/answers/detail/a_id/17
51/~/importing-hemp-products-into-the-u.s.

* * * Federal law prohibits human consumption and possession of schedule I controlled substances. Products containing tetrahydrocannabinols (THC), the hallucinogenic substance in marijuana are illegal to import. Products that do not cause THC to enter the human body are therefore legal products. The following hemp products such as clothing, hats, shirts, shoes, cosmetics, lotion, paper, rope, twine, yarn, shampoo, and soap (containing sterilized cannabis seeds or oils extracted from the seeds), etc. may be imported into the U.S. * * *

NOTES AND QUESTIONS

1. **C.F.R. § 1308.35 not enforced.** C.F.R. § 1308.35 purports to prohibit products made from parts of the cannabis plant containing any amount of THC, even those excluded from the CSA definition of marijuana, if intended for human consumption. Given the difficulty in capturing scientific properties of the cannabis plant in legal language, the varying judicial decisions, the congressional amendments that overwrite the CSA in piecemeal fashion, and the DEA's own aggressive interpretation of the law, reflecting its role as enforcer of the regulations as well as administrator—it is not surprising that the parameters of importing hemp to the United States may be confusing. Are the above rules for importing hemp products, published by the U.S. Customs and Border Protection on its website as of December 2018, consistent with DEA's directive not to enforce C.F.R. § 1308.35?

2. **CBD.** The regulations of the DEA and the Customs and Border Protections Agency as to importing hemp are difficult of exact interpretation, especially as agents deal with complex cannabis-related ingredients and products at the border. This is particularly the case with Cannabidiol[1] (CBD), a non-intoxicating cannabinoid that is derived from the cannabis plant and that many people believe has important therapeutic and medical value. Of the over one hundred cannabinoids in the cannabis plant, THC and CBD predominate. THC is intoxicating; CBD is not. Thus advocates have argued the legality of CBD as a derivative of hemp. However, DEA considers CBD as a Schedule I substance. It is a constituent ("derivative," "extract," or "resin") of the cannabis plant and is produced from parts of the cannabis plant—flowering tops, resin, leaves—that are included in the CSA definition of marijuana. Although CBD may be found on the parts of the plant that are excluded from the CSA definition of marijuana—stalks and seeds—its presence is a result of contact with the resin produced by the parts of the plant explicitly included in the CSA definition. In the past, DEA also asserted as a reason that all CBD extracts contain at least small amounts of other cannabinoids, including THC.

---

[1]   2-[1R-3-methyl-6R-(1-methylethenyl)-2-cyclohexen-1-yl]-5-pentyl-1,3-benzenediol.

Establishment of a New Drug Code for Marihuana Extract. 81 Fed. Reg. 90196, FN 1 (December 14, 2016). In June 2018, the Food and Drug Administration (FDA) approved the oral solution Epidiolex, with purified CBD as the operative agent, for two forms of childhood epilepsy. Epidiolex is the first FDA-approved drug that contains a substance derived from marijuana and is scheduled under Schedule V. Other CBD products remain in Schedule I.

3.   Marihuana Extracts. Adding to the confusion, in January 2017 the DEA amended 21 C.F.R. 1308.11(d), which defines marijuana, to include a new subparagraph (58) which creates a new code number in Schedule I as follows:

> "(58) Marihuana Extract—7350
>
> "Meaning an extract containing one or more cannabinoids that has been derived from any plant of the genus Cannabis, other than the separated resin (whether crude or purified) obtained from the plant."

81 Fed. Reg. 90194, 90196 (Dec. 14, 2016). Alarm was raised by hemp manufacturers that this amendment meant that CBD as well as other non-psychoactive cannabis extracts would now be confiscated. The Hemp Association sued. In May, 2018, the Ninth Circuit affirmed the DEA rule, although it stated that CBD can be extracted from hemp cultivated per Section 7606 of the 2014 Farm Act. *Hemp Industries Association, et al. v. U.S. Drug Enforcement Administration* (Case No. 17-70162) LEXIS 11005 (9th Circuit 2018).

4.   DEA clarification. The DEA issued a clarification which purported to explain that the new coding was an internal, administrative matter, not a substantive change. However DEA also argued that cannabinoids, such as CBD are "found in the parts of the cannabis plant that fall within the CSA definition of marijuana, such as the flowering tops, resin, and leaves." They are "not found in the parts of the cannabis plant that are excluded from the CSA definition of marijuana, except for trace amounts. . . ."

> Thus, based on the scientific literature, it is not practical to produce extracts that contain more than trace amounts of cannabinoids using only the parts of the cannabis plant that are excluded from the CSA definition of marijuana, such as oil from the seeds.

Clarification of the New Drug Code (7350) for Marijuana Extract (March 14, 2017).

PROBLEM 17-1

A Member of Congress believes that marijuana should remain a prohibited drug under both federal and state law. She is known as a pro-growth advocate who won election to her primarily agricultural state on a job-creation platform. Her state has legalized hemp and participates in the Hemp Pilot Program, Section 7606 of the Agricultural Act of 2014. However the state imports most of the hemp commercially used in the state. She recently gave a speech to an agricultural association in which she spoke of the difficulties in making fine distinctions between the varieties of the cannabis plant for the purposes of creating rational hemp regulations. She mentioned that even her own congressional staff had difficulty sorting out the law as applied to hemp products, and was still assessing the highly technical rules regarding marihuana extracts and the equally technical, difficult, and perhaps confusing "clarification" issued by the DEA. To resolve the confusion generated by the conflux of CSA definitions, various court rulings, DEA regulations, and the like, she has introduced a bill to Congress that would amend the CSA with the language of the United Nations 1961 Single Convention on Narcotics, Article 28(3), to the effect that "The CSA, like the Single Convention, shall not apply to the cultivation of the cannabis plant exclusively for industrial purposes (fibre and seed) or horticultural purposes." Her bill defines industrial cannabis as any cannabis plant or part, derivative, or extract thereof that contains a concentration of no more than 0.3% of THC on a dry weight basis. If these requirements are met, the plant is not a controlled substance, and no special licensing or registration is required for cultivation, sale, interstate commerce, or use as a foodstuff; only that medicines using such extracts would need to be approved by the FDA, like any other drug.

Considering hemp law in its entirety, how do you assess this bill?

CHAPTER 18

HEALTH EFFECTS OF MARIJUANA: THE MEDICAL EVIDENCE

■ ■ ■

The debate over the health effects of marijuana looms over marijuana law. The three criteria for placing a controlled substance in Schedule I are medical. Marijuana is controlled on Schedule I of the CSA because the federal government has determined as a scientific matter that marijuana 1) has a high potential for abuse; 2) no currently accepted medical use in treatment in the United States; and 3) there is a lack of accepted safety for use of marijuana under medical supervision. 21 U.S.C. § 812(c). If science shows otherwise, federal law provides a mechanism for rescheduling marijuana or even decontrolling it entirely.

Who decides the scientific criteria in assessing marijuana? We have seen that this role is played largely by the Drug Enforcement Administration (DEA), in addition to its primary role as the agency that enforces U.S. drug laws. Although required by the CSA to collate scientific data from other administrative agencies such as the FDA and the NIDA, the DEA makes the ultimate conclusions that determine scheduling, absent action by Congress. In this way the controlling of marijuana is as much a legal decision as a scientific one.

What role is played by the courts? They certainly have a role in monitoring the actions of the DEA to ensure compliance with CSA procedures for scheduling drugs. But as we have also seen in earlier chapters, the courts defer to the DEA in accord with the norms of administrative law and 21 U.S.C. § 877. When should courts independently examine the health effects of marijuana?

In this chapter, we consider the evidence for the health effects of marijuana. In Section A, we look at a recent court decision which examined the medical effects of marijuana under constitutional standards of evidence, apart from the rescheduling mechanism. In Section B, we review the conclusions of the 2017 Report, *The Health Effects of Cannabis and Cannabinoids: The Current State of Evidence and Recommendations for Research*, conducted by the National Academies of Sciences, Engineering, and Medicine. This exhaustive study of the health effects of marijuana has a good claim for being the gold standard for assessing the medical evidence.

A. MEDICAL EVIDENCE IN COURT

Courts have consistently deferred to the DEA as to its decision to leave marijuana in Schedule I. The following case presents a more fundamental challenge: whether classification of marijuana as a Schedule I substance under the Controlled Substances Act (CSA) is unconstitutional as lacking a rational basis in the medical evidence.

UNITED STATES V. PICKARD
United States District Court, E.D. California
100 F. Supp. 3d 981 (2015)

MUELLER, J.

It has been forty-five years since Congress passed the Controlled Substances Act, including marijuana in Schedule I. Defendants say the law as passed can no longer stand. The government says that is not for this court to decide. To say the landscape with respect to marijuana has changed significantly since 1970, in many ways, is an understatement. While the court is not blind to the practical context in which it operates, its duty as a resident of the third branch of our republican form of government is to resolve the legal questions presented by the parties, fairly and evenly, not as a maker of public policy. The court fulfills this duty without respect to who is arguing what position, or what the newspapers, blogs and commentators say; it does so while putting aside preconceptions and dispositions, likes and dislikes, bias and prejudice. Because defendants' motion challenges a decision made by Congress, which is the first, representative branch of government, the court treads lightly as it is required to do. In performing its duty the court takes the factual record as the parties have developed it through the introduction of documentary evidence and, in this case, an evidentiary hearing. Having approached defendants' constitutional challenges to marijuana's Schedule I status with an open mind, the court had to be prepared to grant their motion to dismiss if the law and facts supported that decision. At some point in time, in some court, the record may support granting such a motion. But having carefully considered the facts and the law as relevant to this case, the court concludes that on the record in this case, this is not the court and this is not the time.

BACKGROUND

The motion before the court was brought originally by defendant Brian Justin Pickard; he moves to dismiss the government's indictment. The remaining defendants join in the motion. Defendants argue the indictment must be dismissed because the classification of marijuana as a Schedule I substance under the Controlled Substances Act (CSA) is unconstitutional. For the reasons set forth below, the court DENIES the motion.

On October 20, 2011, sixteen individuals were indicted for conspiracy to manufacture at least 1,000 marijuana plants, in violation of 21 U.S.C. §§ 846, 841(a)(1). On November 20, 2013, Mr. Pickard moved to dismiss the indictment, arguing that the classification of marijuana as a Schedule I substance under the CSA, 21 U.S.C. § 801 et seq., violates his Fifth Amendment equal protection rights and that the government's allegedly disparate enforcement of the federal marijuana laws violates the doctrine of equal sovereignty of the states under the Tenth Amendment. In the same motion, defendant requested that this court hold an evidentiary hearing to take testimony on defendant's constitutional challenges. The other defendants joined in the motion. The government opposed defendants' motion, and defendants replied.

On March 25, 2014, the court granted defendants' request for an evidentiary hearing. The evidentiary hearing occupied five days between October 24, 2014 and October 30, 2014. During the evidentiary hearing, the court heard testimony from Gregory T. Carter, M.D., Carl L. Hart, Ph.D., Philip A. Denney, M.D., Christopher Conrad, and Bertha K. Madras, Ph.D. After the evidentiary hearing, the court set a post-evidentiary hearing briefing schedule and a date for closing arguments. The government filed its post-evidentiary hearing brief on December 31, 2014, and defendants filed theirs on January 5, 2015. The parties replied on January 21, 2015. The parties presented their closing arguments on February 11, 2015, after which the court submitted the motion.

In addition, on February 6, 2015, defendants filed a request for judicial notice, asking that the court take notice of (1) certain statements made by the United States Surgeon General on February 4, 2015, and (2) the introduction of H.R. 5762, the Veterans Equal Access Act of 2014, in the House of Representatives on November 20, 2014. [H.R. 5762 would authorize VA health care providers to recommend participation in their state's marijuana programs.] The court takes judicial notice of the fact that the U.S. Surgeon General, during a televised interview on "CBS This Morning" on February 4, 2015, made a statement about marijuana's efficacy for some medical conditions and symptoms. However, the court declines to take judicial notice of H.R. 5762, as it does not have the force of law.

Defendant also asked the court to consider a new piece of evidence identified as exhibit AAA, a study published on January 28, 2015, which defendant argues "directly refutes the methods and findings" of government exhibit 209. The court grants that request under the rule of completeness. Government exhibit 209 is a study published in the Journal of Neuroscience in April 2014. That study, titled "Cannabis Use is Quantitatively Associated with Nucleus Accumbens and Amygdala Abnormalities in Young Adult Recreational Users," concludes that marijuana exposure is associated with brain changes. Exhibit AAA is also a study published in the Journal of Neuroscience, in January 2015. The study, titled "Daily Marijuana Use is not associated with Brain Morphometric Measures in Adolescents or Adults," concludes otherwise. The latter study cites the former study and argues it was erroneous. It is fair to allow exhibit AAA into evidence, for what it is worth.* * *

JURISDICTIONAL CONSIDERATIONS

Standing

The government contends defendants lack standing to argue that "the continued inclusion of marijuana as a Schedule I controlled substance in Title 21 of the federal statutes passes constitutional muster," because "neither their criminal liability nor their eventual criminal sentence depend on marijuana's status as a Schedule I substance." The government points out that defendants are charged with violating 21 U.S.C. § 841(a), which applies to any controlled substance; thus, it says "their charges are not dependent upon marijuana's status as a Schedule I substance." The government argues that the sentences provided for in the statute "apply regardless of whether marijuana is on Schedule I" as long as "marijuana is treated as a controlled substance at all." "Put plainly, a decision holding that it is unconstitutional for marijuana to be treated as a Schedule I substance will have no impact on whether [d]efendants go to jail or for how long."

Defendants counter that they are "not petitioning this [c]ourt to reschedule marijuana, but rather [are] contesting the constitutionality of [21 U.S.C. § 812(c)(10), (17)], the Congressional Act which classifies marijuana as a Schedule I [c]ontrolled [s]ubstance. Should the defense prevail, these statutory provisions are deemed invalid, and thus marijuana and THC would be removed from the CSA, not simply replaced within the Schedule. In effect, no controlled substance could be identified to support a prosecution under 21 U.S.C. [§] 841(a)."

Here, defendants have established Article III standing. Defendants are charged with conspiracy, 21 U.S.C. § 846, to manufacture marijuana, a controlled substance, *id.* § 841(a)(1). The indictment specifies defendants allegedly conspired to manufacture at least 1,000 marijuana plants on private property. Section 846 punishes "[a]ny person who . . . conspires to commit any offense defined in this subchapter" with "the same penalties as those prescribed for the offense, the commission of which was the object of the . . . conspiracy." 21 U.S.C. § 846. Section 841 makes it unlawful "to manufacture . . . a controlled substance." Id. § 841(a)(1). In turn, § 812(c) lists "Marihuana" and "Tetrahydrocannabinols" as Schedule I controlled substances. 21 U.S.C. § 812(c)(10), (17). If defendants are convicted, their sentences will be calculated based on marijuana's Schedule I status.

Defendants have shown concrete and imminent injury: incarceration as a result of their charged violations of the CSA, if they are convicted.

Defendants have also shown that inclusion of marijuana as a Schedule I controlled substance is the cause of their injury. If this court were to find that Congress acted unconstitutionally in placing marijuana on Schedule I, marijuana would no longer be considered a controlled substance because it is classified as a controlled substance only under Schedule I and not under any other schedule.

Stated simply, if marijuana were absent from that schedule, defendants could not be charged with violation of sections 841(a), and 846 and the sentences provided for in sections 841 and 844 would not apply. * * *

Jurisdiction

In its February 13, 2014 opposition to defendants' motion to dismiss the indictment, the government argued this court had no jurisdiction to hear defendants' arguments, in light of the provisions of 21 U.S.C. section 877. Defendants reply section 877 "by its terms applies to judicial review of administrative action, not Congressional Acts." During a hearing in March 2014, the court heard argument on the question of subject matter jurisdiction and ruled it had jurisdiction, noting it would remain alert to that question as the case proceeded, in the event its initial determination required reconsideration. At hearing, defendants stated their position as follows:

> We're not asking for reclassification. We're asking that the statute be struck because it is unconstitutional at this particular day and this particular time in the history of the evolution of the evidence with regard to the effects of marijuana.

Defendants have not wavered from this position.

Later in March 2014, the government sought reconsideration of the court's order granting an evidentiary hearing, stating that it "initially opposed the defendants' motion to dismiss the indictment on the grounds that the [c]ourt lacks jurisdiction to consider any challenge to the scheduling of marijuana" but it now accepts the court's determination "that jurisdiction is proper." The government sought reconsideration of the grant of a hearing, arguing in part that "there is no occasion for an evidentiary hearing or a fresh examination of the equal protection challenge, as the Ninth Circuit has already decided the issue" (citing *United States v. Miroyan,* 577 F.2d 489, 495 (9th Cir.1978)).

During the April 2014 hearing on the government's motion for reconsideration, the court confirmed the government conceded jurisdiction. The court explained it did not "think the [g]overnment has satisfied its burden of showing the [c]ourt should reconsider" its prior decision; it further explained the grant of a hearing because it "believe[s] there is a question raised about the statutory listing of marijuana as a Schedule I drug in light of the three factors [under 21 U.S.C. § 812(b)(1)(A)–(C)], applicable to maintaining that substance on the list."

In May 2014, the government renewed its section 877 argument. The government explained that while it previously accepted the court's jurisdiction to consider any challenge to the statute's constitutionality, the court's clarification that it is considering a challenge to maintaining marijuana as a Schedule I controlled substance provided a basis for a new argument. The government argued 21 U.S.C. section 877 deprives the court of jurisdiction to entertain "whether the continued inclusion of marijuana as a Schedule I controlled substance . . . passes constitutional muster," because "the agencies assigned by Congress to make such scheduling determinations have decided not to re-schedule or deschedule it." The government argues "[b]ecause Congress provided that the exclusive forum for making such a challenge is in the Circuit Courts after the administrative process, this [c]ourt lacks subject matter jurisdiction to consider or decide the question in this criminal prosecution."

The CSA, enacted in 1970, organizes substances into five schedules based on certain factors. *See* 21 U.S.C. § 812(b). The criteria concern current medical uses, potential for abuse, and possible physical or psychological dependency effects. Schedule I is at the high end and lists substances including heroin, morphine, peyote, and marijuana. *Id.* Sch. I(b)(10), (14)–(16); (c)(10), (12). Schedule V is at the low end, and includes any compound containing not more than 200 milligrams of codeine per 400 grams, among others. *Id.* § 812(b)(5). "Unlike Schedule I drugs, federal law permits individuals to obtain Schedule II, III, IV, or V drugs for personal medical use with a valid prescription." *Americans for Safe Access v. Drug Enforcement Admin.,* 706 F.3d 438, 441 (D.C.Cir.2013).

The specific statutory findings required for Schedule I listing are as follows:

A.   The drug or other substance has a high potential for abuse.

B.   The drug or other substance has no currently accepted medical use in treatment in the United States.

C.   There is a lack of accepted safety for use of the drug or other substance under medical supervision.

Id. § 812(b)(1). As noted, when the CSA was enacted, Congress classified marijuana as a Schedule I controlled substance. It did so based, in part, on the recommendation of the Secretary of Health, Education, and Welfare. *See Gonzales v. Raich,* 545 U.S. 1, 14 n. 22 (2005); *Nat'l Org. for Reform of Marijuana Laws (NORML) v. Bell,* 488 F.Supp. 123, 135 n. 32 (D.D.C.1980) (noting "[t]his recommendation came in a letter. . . ."). The CSA provides that the Attorney General may add, remove, or transfer a substance to, from, or between schedules. *See id.* § 811(a). The law lists various factors for the Attorney General to consider when making that determination. *See id.* § 811(b)–(c). The CSA provides for a process by which parties aggrieved by a final decision of the Attorney General may appeal the decision. Under the CSA:

> All final determinations, findings, and conclusions of the Attorney General under this subchapter shall be final and conclusive decisions of the matters involved, except that any person aggrieved by a final decision of the Attorney General may obtain review of the decision in the United States Court of Appeals for the District of Columbia or for the circuit in which his principal place of business is located upon petition filed with the court and delivered to the Attorney General within thirty days after notice of the decision. Findings of fact by the Attorney General, if supported by substantial evidence, shall be conclusive.

Id. § 877. "Despite considerable efforts to reschedule marijuana" through the administrative process, "it remains a Schedule I drug." *Gonzales v. Raich,* 545 U.S. 1, 15 n. 23 (2005).

The essence of the government's argument against jurisdiction is that section 877 bars the court from considering defendants' constitutional challenge to marijuana's scheduling. "Federal courts are courts of limited jurisdiction," possessing "only that power authorized by Constitution and statute." *Gunn v. Minton* 568 U.S. 251 (2013). This court has a duty to address the question of jurisdiction before it can proceed to the merits. Here, the court finds it has jurisdiction to hear defendants' arguments. Defendants are not seeking reclassification of marijuana, nor have they filed an administrative petition with the Attorney General for such reclassification with a decision pending. Rather, defendants argue 21 U.S.C. section 812 violates the equal protection clause of the Fifth Amendment because marijuana's classification as a Schedule I substance is arbitrary. A constitutional challenge to the classification of a substance by Congress in a statute is not beyond the jurisdiction of this court. *See, e.g., United States v. Rodriquez-Camacho,* 468 F.2d 1220, 1222 (9th Cir.1972) (addressing a constitutional challenge to the regulation of marijuana and holding "[i]t is sufficient that Congress had a rational basis for making its findings"); *Miroyan,* 577 F.2d at 495 (rejecting the argument that "[m]arijuana . . . cannot rationally be deemed to meet the criteria required for a Schedule I controlled substance [under the CSA]"). And while the Ninth Circuit has held that "substantive collateral attacks on permanent scheduling orders are impermissible in criminal cases . . .," *United States v. Forrester,* 616 F.3d 929, 937 (9th Cir.2010), this is not an action where a party is attacking a permanent scheduling order established by the Attorney General. Instead, the court is faced with a constitutional challenge to the statute that forms the basis for the charges in the indictment. The court has jurisdiction to hear that challenge.

A provision conferring jurisdiction to entertain such a challenge is not required to be included in the CSA itself, nor is the statute insulated from constitutional review by Congressional delegation of authority to an agency to consider an administrative petition. The government has not pointed to any "clear and convincing" evidence that Congress intended to preclude review of constitutional claims regarding the CSA.

In performing the constitutional review requested here, this court is exercising one of its essential duties. *See Marbury v. Madison,* 5 U.S. 137, 177–80 (1803). A court has that power even if, as here, it does not exercise it. The court has jurisdiction to consider defendants' motion.* * *

EVIDENTIARY HEARING RECORD

At the evidentiary hearing, the court heard live testimony from defense witnesses Gregory T. Carter, M.D. Carl L. Hart, Ph.D., Philip A. Denney, M.D., and marijuana cultivator and processor Christopher Conrad. The government's witness was Bertha K. Madras, Ph.D. While the hearing transcript and documentary record speaks for itself, the court summarizes portions of testimony most relevant here.

1.   Defense Experts

Dr. Carter is a medical doctor of almost thirty years, is board certified by several medical associations, and is the co-author of a report regarding the cannabis plant's therapeutic value, among other things. He, along with two other authors, prepared the latter report at the request of the former Washington State Governor Christine Gregoire, who "wanted to petition . . . to have cannabis rescheduled[ ]"). Dr. Carter testified that "polls would show . . . the majority of physicians. . . feel . . . cannabis has medical benefit." He conceded that other qualified individuals, including Dr. Madras, disagree with his opinion that marijuana has a currently accepted use. Dr. Carter agreed that the position of the American Medical Association, the National Institute on Drug Abuse, and the Institute of Medicine on the medical benefits of marijuana is that it "might have efficacy," but not that it certainly has. Dr. Carter conceded that marijuana can change the brain "physically and functionally." In addition, he testified that the Diagnostic and Statistical Manual of Mental Disorders (DSM)-V and DSM-IV, authoritative references on mental disorders, recognize cannabis use disorder.

Dr. Carter has advocated for reclassifying marijuana as a Schedule II substance. The latter part of Dr. Carter's testimony is important because the first criterion under both Schedule I and II is the same: "[t]he drug or other substance has a high potential for abuse." 21 U.S.C. § 812(b)(1)(A), (b)(2)(A). When asked on redirect whether marijuana had a high potential for abuse, he responded, "moderate." Dr. Carter was adamant in his opinion, based on research with human subjects, "that marijuana has a tremendous potential" in treating patients suffering from Amyotrophic

Lateral Sclerosis ("ALS"). Dr. Carter acknowledged that the chemistry of "whole plant" marijuana is "complex," with a hundred components classified as cannabinoids, and another two to three hundred components that are "mostly terpenoids." He opined that there is a "fairly good understanding" of cannabinoids, with "more to be known" about the other components.

According to Dr. Carter, there exists a "Catch-22" that prevents the development of medical information demonstrating conclusively marijuana's medical value: "[It is] very difficult to do research in this area" because researchers cannot get funding and they cannot get funding because marijuana is a Schedule I substance.

Dr. Carl Hart is an associate professor in the psychiatry department at Columbia University, with a Ph.D in psychology and neuroscience, among other credentials. His laboratory at Columbia is authorized by the Drug Enforcement Agency (DEA) to administer controlled substances to human subjects for scientific studies, with the result that Dr. Hart has been able to study marijuana's effects "utilizing the scientific methodology which best predicts causation, rather than association, in human subjects." Along with others, Dr. Hart has received grants for more than $10 million from private and public entities which have funded research projects "focused on substance abuse or the effects of specified controlled substances in a controlled setting, including but not limited to drug effects in the workplace, and the effect of THC and Marijuana on HIV-positive persons."

Dr. Hart has a unique first-hand perspective informed by the fact that his laboratory is "one of the few laboratories in the Nation to have federal permission to conduct clinical trials . . . and[,] therefore, [he] [has] personally observed human subjects under the influence of illegal substances for lawful research purposes." Dr. Hart testified that he was "in the majority" of qualified people who have concluded marijuana has medical use. "He testified specifically that a number of studies on clinical populations show marijuana has a benefit for HIV-positive patients: [S]moking marijuana increases food intake in HIV-positive people to the same extent as . . . Marinol." In addition, Dr. Hart opined there is "growing evidence that marijuana might be useful in post-traumatic stress syndrome." To counter the harmful effects of smoking marijuana, patients can use vaporizers. As to the potential negative effects of smoking marijuana, Dr. Hart agreed "that any psychoactive drug has potential negative effects, as well as potential positive effects." But one "must weigh the risk-benefit ratio to determine whether or not . . . that drug should be used [as medicine]." "[W]ith marijuana," "the potential benefits outweigh the potential risk." To illustrate the latter conclusion, Dr. Hart provided an example of someone suffering from multiple sclerosis who experiences symptom relief from using marijuana, and reasoned that because "the benefits of . . . symptom relief from multiple sclerosis outweigh [the] negatives[,]" that person should be able to use marijuana as medicine. In response to the government's question whether he agreed "heavy marijuana use resulted in a decrease in IQ when tracked from youth to midlife," Dr. Hart noted the users' IQs "remained within the normal range of functioning."

Dr. Hart confirmed, as suggested by Dr. Carter, that research into the medical benefits of marijuana is somewhat limited by the need to obtain the approvals that he has received, and that there is only one approved supplier of marijuana for research purposes, the University of Mississippi.

Dr. Denney, a California licensed physician of approximately forty years, has been involved "in the emerging field of cannabis medicine since 1999. . . ." During his private practice, he operated clinics in several locations throughout California. In the Redding office, Dr. Denney saw between twenty and twenty-five patients a day, "seeking medical marijuana recommendations." Towards the end of his practice, which he closed in 2010, Dr. Denney had made approximately 12,000 marijuana recommendations. His testimony was consistent with that of Drs. Hart and Carter, that there is a minority view holding marijuana had no medical use. While Dr. Denney personally "disagree[d] with the material in DSM-[V] related to marijuana," he agreed that "there is lots of room for dispute . . . and divergence of opinions."

Christopher Conrad, experienced in the legal cultivation and processing of marijuana, has "qualified as an expert witness on marijuana related issues such as cultivation, consumption, genetics, cloning, crop yields, medical use, recreational use, commercial sales, and medical distribution" in several counties, states, and countries. The essence of his testimony is that the marijuana plant's chemistry is "known and reproducible." Mr. Conrad testified the marijuana plant "is the most studied plant in the history of the world[.]" That the marijuana plant's chemistry is reproducible is important, he says, because among other things it will allow the determination of whether there are any contaminants in the plant. That, in turn, is important for controlling the marijuana plant's quality.

2.   Government Expert

The government's witness, Dr. Madras, is a professor of psychobiology at Harvard Medical School. In addition to her substantial academic and professional work, Dr. Madras has served as Deputy Director for Demand Reduction for the White House Office of National Drug Control Policy, where she served from 2005 to 2008. Dr. Madras has provided testimony to legislative bodies on proposed medical marijuana bills and has made presentations for government agencies internationally. She has not conducted studies with marijuana on human subjects. She opined "that the science strongly supports a conclusion that marijuana has a high potential for abuse, has no currently accepted medical use in the United States, and that sufficient assurances of safety for use of marijuana under medical supervision are lacking." She further stated that "[a] substantial majority—perhaps the vast majority—of scientists familiar with the literature and research agree that, at this time, marijuana does not have medical application." Dr. Madras testified that any clinical trials involving smoking as the method of administration will never be accepted as a basis for finding medical benefit.

At the same time, Dr. Madras agreed that the components of marijuana, known as cannabinoids, "should be evaluated because there is tantalizing evidence in the literature that they may have therapeutic benefit." She further agreed that "[t]here is tantalizing good evidence that they do have a medical benefit."

On the question of risk-benefit analysis, Dr. Madras disagreed with the defense witnesses; she testified "the risks involved in the cannabis plant outweigh the benefits for the medical use[.]" Furthermore, as to IQ changes in early marijuana users, unlike Dr. Hart, Dr. Madras testified that she believes the documented drop in IQs is significant because it takes adolescents from average to below average. Finally, as to the Schedule I criteria—whether marijuana has currently—accepted medical use, whether it has a high potential for abuse, and whether it can be administered safely under a physician's care—Dr. Madras concluded that while "reasonable people could make the opposite conclusion" that all those three factors are met, "there would have to be a denial of some evidence" to reach that conclusion.

3. Percipient Witnesses

The court also received evidence in documentary form, including declarations by Sergeant Ryan D. Begin and Jennie Stormes. The court accepted "their declaration testimony as percipient witnesses about their use of marijuana for medicinal purposes." Sgt. Begin served in the U.S. Marine Corps from 2001 to 2007. During his second deployment to Iraq in 2004, he was severely injured, resulting in having over thirty-five surgeries on his right elbow. He is unable to bend his right arm and suffers constant pain. Sgt. Begin has been diagnosed with posttraumatic stress syndrome (PTSD). Sgt. Begin started using medical cannabis in 2009 and noticed that cannabis made him "feel more emotionally stable and also helped [him] to appropriately manage the pain in his elbow. . . ." Eventually, "with the brutal pain in [his] right arm, [he] began consuming a greater quantity of cannabis. . . ." As a result, he "started feeling noticeably more mentally and emotionally healthy than [he] had since before [his] deployments[ ]" and "[t]he pain in [his] elbow became manageable. . . ."

Jennie Stormes is a nurse and mother of two, one of whom, her fifteen year old son, suffers from Dravet Syndrome. Dravet Syndrome is a rare form of epilepsy. Stormes' observations of her son's symptoms include, among other things, cognitive delays, language speech delays, inability to recognize danger, and frequent seizures. During his entire life, he has been given approximately twenty different medications in approximately fifty different combinations and has had several surgeries. In 2012, he began using medical cannabis and, "[a]lmost immediately[,] he came out of fog[;] . . . was more open and alert[;] and began to show signs of cognitive improvements, lessened seizure intensity and quicker recovery from seizure events." Furthermore, he "is less hyperactive[ ] and exhibits fewer self destructive [sic] tendencies."

EQUAL PROTECTION: CLASSIFICATION OF MARIJUANA

In determining whether a regulation violates the equal protection clause of the Fifth Amendment, courts first determine the level of scrutiny to apply. Laws alleged to violate the Equal Protection Clause are subject to one of three levels of scrutiny: (1) strict scrutiny, (2) intermediate scrutiny, or (3) rational basis review. Strict scrutiny applies when a classification is made on suspect grounds, such as race or ancestry, or if the classification infringes on a fundamental right, such as privacy, marriage, voting, travel, or freedom to associate. Intermediate scrutiny applies, on the other hand, when a law discriminates based on a quasi-suspect classification. Classifications based on sex and legitimacy, as well as children of undocumented aliens denied public education, have been reviewed under intermediate scrutiny. When no suspect or quasi-suspect class is involved and no fundamental right is burdened, courts apply a rational basis test to determine the legitimacy of the classification.

a.   Fundamental Right

Defendants argue that strict scrutiny is warranted because their fundamental right to liberty is at stake. The government agrees "[d]efendants enjoy a fundamental right to liberty," but argues the statute at issue "does not encroach on that liberty interest." *Washington v. Glucksberg,* 521 U.S. 702, 721 (1997) teaches that courts must adopt a narrow definition of the interest at stake. Hence, the right asserted in this case cannot be the broad fundamental liberty interest defendants claim. The court is unpersuaded by defendants' argument that a fundamental right is implicated by the CSA's scheduling of marijuana.

b.   Suspect Classification

Because the CSA is neutral on its face, to trigger strict scrutiny defendants must prove the following two elements of a prima facie case: (1) the law has a disparate impact on a particular group, and (2) the impact on this group is intentional in the sense that it results from a discriminatory purpose or design. To show a disparate impact, defendants must show that the law's practical effect is to burden one group of persons more heavily than others. To show discriminatory purpose, defendants must show that discriminatory purpose was a motivating factor in the decision to enact the particular law. That is, the law must have been adopted "at least in part 'because of,' not merely 'in spite of,' its adverse effects upon an identifiable group." The discriminatory purpose element can be proven in a number of ways, among other things, by (1) legislative history; (2) the manner of adoption; (3) inferring intent from application; or (4) other circumstantial evidence.

Defendants argue they have established discriminatory purpose on Congress's part based on certain offensive statements allegedly made at some point by Harry Anslinger, former Commissioner of the Federal Bureau of Narcotics. Mr. Anslinger's statements, made to Congress in 1937 at the time the Marijuana Tax Act was passed, painted a picture of marijuana users as mainly racial minorities. Defendants do not assert that Congress relied on those statements when it enacted the CSA thirty-three years later, or that Anslinger was part of any body whose decisions lay the groundwork for the CSA's enactment. Anslinger's statements cannot form the basis for a discriminatory purpose claim. Because defendants ask the court to "ascribe a discriminatory intent to Congress based on rather sketchy and unpersuasive bits of information," *United States v. Johnson*, 40 F.3d 436, 440 (D.C.Cir.1994), the court cannot find Congress acted with a discriminatory purpose in designating marijuana as a Schedule I substance under the CSA. Defendants are not entitled to strict scrutiny on the basis of a suspect class.

c. Rational Basis

If a law does not involve a suspect or quasi-suspect classification and does not discriminate with respect to a fundamental right, courts apply a rational basis test to decide whether the law violates the equal protection clause. This is a very deferential standard and precludes judges from second-guessing Congress's "wisdom, fairness, or logic of legislative choices." *Heller v. Doe*, 509 U.S. 312, 319 (1993). Rather, courts must uphold a classification against an equal protection challenge so long as any reasonably conceivable facts might provide a rational basis for the classification. Courts must accept Congress's generalizations even when means and ends do not fit perfectly together. A classification will not fail rational-basis review even if "it is not made with mathematical nicety or because in practice it results in some inequality." However, "even the standard of rationality . . . must find some footing in the realities of the subject addressed by the legislation." *Id.*

Here, defendants have not submitted any evidence that Congress classified marijuana as a Schedule I controlled substance because of animus or some discriminatory legislative purpose. Nor is there any evidence that defendants are members of a politically unpopular group targeted by the CSA. There is no justification for applying a more rigorous version of rational basis review in this case.

Under the deferential standard of rational basis review, then, as long as there is some conceivable reason for the challenged classification of marijuana, the CSA should be upheld. Such a classification comes before the court "bearing a strong presumption of validity," and the challenger must "negative every conceivable basis which might support it. . . ." *F.C.C. v. Beach Commc'ns, Inc.,* 508 U.S. 307, 314–15 (1993). The asserted rationale may rest on "rational speculation unsupported by evidence or empirical data." The law may be overinclusive, underinclusive, illogical, and unscientific and yet pass constitutional muster. In addition, under rational basis review, the government "has no obligation to produce evidence to sustain the rationality of a statutory classification." *Heller,* 509 U.S. at 320.

Courts that have considered the constitutional question at issue in this case have consistently applied rational basis review. *See, e.g., Miroyan,* 577 F.2d at 495; *United States v. Oakland Cannabis Buyers' Co-op.,* 259 Fed.Appx. 936, 938 (9th Cir. 2007) (unpublished) ("The district court properly concluded that the placement of marijuana in Schedule I of the Controlled Substances Act satisfies rational basis review."); *United States v. White Plume,* 447 F.3d 1067, 1076 (8th Cir.2006) ("[C]ategorizing marijuana . . . as a Schedule I substance passes muster under the rational basis test . . ."); *United States v. Washington,* 887 F.Supp.2d 1077, 1102 (D.Mont. 2012) (applying rational basis review); *United States v. McFarland,* No. 12-40082-02, 2012 WL 5864008, at *1 (D.S.D. Nov. 19, 2012) (same); *United States v. Zhuta,* No. 09-357, 2010 WL 5636212, at *4 (W.D.N.Y. Oct. 29, 2010) ("[E]ven assuming, arguendo, that marijuana has some currently accepted medical uses, the Schedule I classification may nevertheless be rational in view of countervailing factors such as the current pattern, scope, and significance of marijuana abuse and the risk it poses to public health." Given the circumstances of this case, this court follows suit.

ANALYSIS

In light of the foregoing, the question before the court is a narrow one: whether Congress acted rationally in classifying marijuana as a Schedule I substance in light of the record created before this court. To ask that question in this case, under rational basis review, is to answer it. This court cannot say that Congress could not reasonably have decided that marijuana belongs and continues to belong on Schedule I of the CSA. As explained below, the record here does not demonstrate there is only one supportable point of view about marijuana's safe, medical value or abuse potential.

As noted above, the statutory section in the CSA entitled "Placement on schedules; findings required," provides as follows, in relevant part:

> [A] drug or other substance may not be placed in any schedule unless the findings required for such schedule are made with respect to such drug or other substance. The findings required for [Schedule I] are as follows:(1) Schedule I-(A) The drug or other

substance has a high potential for abuse.(B) The drug or other substance has no currently accepted medical use in treatment in the United States.(C) There is a lack of accepted safety for use of the drug or other substance under medical supervision.

21 U.S.C. § 812(b). Defendants claim that the weight of current medical knowledge shows marijuana does not satisfy these three criteria. The Supreme Court has observed that "the constitutionality of a statute predicated upon the existence of a particular state of facts may be challenged by showing to the court that those facts have ceased to exist." *United States v. Carolene Products Co.*, 304 U.S. 144, 153. Here, the facts relating to the three criteria as applied to marijuana, on which Congress initially relied in 1970, have not been rendered obsolete however much they may be changed and changing. Selected facts relevant to each criterion illustrate this point, as reviewed below.

a. High Potential for Abuse

As shown from the evidence in the record, there are conflicts in testimony and material disagreements as to whether marijuana has a high potential for abuse. For example, Dr. Carter testified that he advocated for reclassifying marijuana as a Schedule II substance. That testimony is important because the first criterion under both Schedule I and II is the same: "[t]he drug or other substance has a high potential for abuse." 21 U.S.C. § 812(b)(1)(A), (b)(2)(A). On redirect, however, he testified marijuana's potential for abuse was "moderate." Dr. Madras, on the other hand, was adamant in her opinion that marijuana has a high potential for abuse: "[T]here is no question that extensive data and practical experience support the conclusion that marijuana has a high potential for abuse, and is actually abused." Congress could rationally find marijuana has a high potential for abuse.

b. No Currently Accepted Medical Use

Similarly, the evidence shows that disagreements among well-informed experts as to marijuana's medical use persist. Dr. Carter testified that although he believes the majority of physicians believe marijuana has medical benefit, other qualified professionals, including Dr. Madras, disagree with his opinion. Dr. Hart's testimony was consistent with Dr. Carter's observation that he was "in the majority" of qualified people who think marijuana has medical use. And Dr. Denney's testimony corroborated Drs. Hart's and Carter's testimony that there is a recognized minority view holding marijuana had no medical use.

Dr. Madras, on the other hand, stated that "[a] substantial majority—perhaps the vast majority—of scientists familiar with the literature and research" attest that, at this time, marijuana has no confirmed medical application. She conceded at most that cannabinoids, the components of marijuana, should be evaluated because there is scientific evidence that they may have medical benefit. Dr. Madras opined that while reasonable experts could find a way to conclude otherwise, that whole plant marijuana is known to have medical value, they would be ignoring some of the evidence to reach that conclusion.

The Surgeon General's statements to a media outlet about marijuana's efficacy for certain medical conditions and symptoms, of which the court has taken judicial notice, do not eliminate the principled disagreements of the experts here.

Congress could rationally conclude that marijuana, the undifferentiated plant that appears on Schedule I, has no established medical value.

c.   Lack of Accepted Safety for Use of Marijuana under Medical Supervision

Finally, the evidence is conflicting as to whether there is accepted safety for marijuana's use under medical supervision. Dr. Hart, who has personally administered "thousands of doses of marijuana" to human subjects, testified that marijuana's safe administration under medical supervision is established. Dr. Denney, who has recommended marijuana to approximately 12,000 patients in California during his career, testified more generally that none of his patients ever reported major issues.

On the other hand, Dr. Madras reasoned marijuana cannot be used safely because, among other things, there is no adequate understanding of its composition. ("There are simply too many variables to assure safety to potential patients at this time, and to assure that drug-drug interactions will be harmless."). In addition, "in view of marijuana's negative side-effects, one simply cannot be assured that marijuana can be safely used, even under medical supervision, for long term open-ended use." Dr. Madras was not aware, despite her thorough review of the literature, of any "recent study with a large cohort of marijuana-naive subjects that would compel the conclusion that there is an acceptable level of safety for use of marijuana under medical supervision." Dr. Madras concluded that "adequate safety assurances for the use of marijuana, even under medical supervision, are lacking."

Congress could rationally conclude there is a lack of accepted safety for use of marijuana under medical supervision.

3.   Conclusion

In sum, the evidence of record shows there are serious, principled differences between and among prominent, well-informed, equivalently credible experts. There are some positive anecdotal reports from persons who have found relief from marijuana used for medical purposes; those reports do not overcome the expert disputes. Consistent with the conclusions other courts have reached, this court finds "[t]he continuing questions about marijuana and its effects make the classification rational." *NORML,* 488 F.Supp. at 136.

As another district court has observed,

> [e]ven assuming, arguendo, that marijuana does not fall within a literal reading of Schedule I, the classification still is rational. Placing marijuana in Schedule I furthered the regulatory purposes of Congress. The statutory criteria of section 812(b)(1) are guides in determining the schedule to which a drug belongs, but they are not dispositive. Indeed, the classifications at times cannot be followed consistently, and some conflict exists as to the main factor in classifying a drug potential for abuse or possible medical use.

Id. at 140.

One is tempted to say, with apologies to Yogi Berra, it's "déjà vu all over again." As the Second Circuit observed in 1973: "It is apparently true that there is little or no basis for concluding that marihuana is as dangerous a substance as some of the other drugs included in Schedule I." *United States v. Kiffer,* 477 F.2d 349, 356 (2d Cir. 1973). With the research that has been conducted since passage of the CSA, the observation is just as true if not more so today. But relative dangerousness is not the test the court applies in resolving the constitutional question before it.

Defendants, here, have not met their "heavy burden of proving the irrationality of the Schedule I classification of marijuana," *United States v. Fogarty,* 692 F.2d 542, 547 (8th Cir. 1982), because they have not negated "every conceivable basis which might support it," *F.C.C.,* 508 U.S. at 315. Even though the medical landscape related to marijuana clearly has changed and is changing, "[w]hen Congress undertakes to act in areas fraught with medical and scientific uncertainties, legislative options must be especially broad and courts should be cautious not to rewrite legislation, even assuming, arguendo, that judges with more direct exposure to the problem might make wiser choices." *See Marshall v. United States,* 414 U.S. 417, 427 (1974). In view of the principled disagreements among reputable scientists and practitioners regarding the potential benefits and detrimental effects of marijuana, this court cannot say that its placement on Schedule I is so arbitrary or unreasonable as to render it unconstitutional. Congress still could rationally choose one side of the debate over the other.

After careful consideration, the court joins the chorus of other courts considering the same question, and concludes as have they that—assuming the record created here is reflective of the best information currently available regarding marijuana—the issues raised by the defense are policy issues for Congress to revisit if it chooses.

[The Court's analysis and ruling as to discriminatory application of the CSA by prosecutors as to certain individuals and the disparate impact of the CSA on states are omitted as not addressing the health effects of marijuana.]

For the foregoing reasons, the court DENIES defendants' motion.

IT IS SO ORDERED.

NOTES AND QUESTIONS

1. **Challenge to the CSA.** This case presents a different kind of challenge to the marijuana prohibition in the CSA than we have examined in earlier chapters. Those challenges were based on the DEA scheduling of marijuana as a matter of administrative agency discretion or were based on a specific constitutional provision such as freedom of speech or cruel and unusual punishment. What is the specific constitutional basis of this challenge? Even more unusual is the procedural posture of this case. It does not represent a direct attack on the CSA but is collateral to a criminal prosecution of marijuana manufacturers (cultivators) who challenged the medical evidence as providing insufficient constitutional basis for the criminal charges against them. Does the evidentiary hearing granted to the defendants in this case mean that every defendant who is prosecuted under the CSA is entitled to a collateral evidentiary hearing as to the medical evidence underlying the statute?

2. **Changed landscape.** In its introduction, the Court states that "the landscape with respect to marijuana has changed significantly since 1970." In what way has the landscape changed to necessitate the Court taking up the constitutional challenge presented by the Defendants in the midst of a criminal trial? If the landscape is ripe for such a challenge, why does the Court conclude that it must join the "chorus of other courts" in finding that the scheduling of marijuana in Schedule I should be retained?

3. **Rational basis.** What are the different legal standards to apply when defendants present a constitutional challenge to the CSA classification of marijuana, as opposed to a petition to reschedule marijuana? The Court must address which standard of evidence to apply in assessing the health effects of marijuana and whether its classification under Scheduling I criteria violates the Equal Protection Clause of the Fifth Amendment. (Although the Fifth Amendment does not contain an explicit Equal Protection Clause, U.S. Supreme Court jurisprudence indicates that the Due Process Clause of the Fifth Amendment includes equal protection rights equivalent to the Equal Protection Clause of the Fourteenth Amendment.) What are defendants' arguments as to why their equal protection claim should be reviewed under a strict scrutiny standard and why does the court resolve the claim on a rational basis standard?

4. **Jurisdiction.** What are the arguments for and against this federal district court having jurisdiction and why does the Court decide as it does in this matter? Likewise, why do Defendants have Article III standing?

5. Expert witnesses. The Court addresses the rational basis of the marijuana classification by calling expert witnesses on the medical effects of marijuana. Calling such witnesses is common when courts consider cases involving social issues. Nevertheless, the hearing of witnesses on broad scientific topics is more common in the legislative arena than in court, especially when ancillary to a criminal prosecution. The Court in this case states that it is engaged in a judicial function "not as a maker of public policy." Is this true? Why do the particular witnesses called in this case have a larger say than other scientists, scientific reports, and comprehensive studies, such as The National Academies of Sciences, Engineering, and Medicine Report we examine in Section B? If the weight of evidence of these particular witnesses were that marijuana has safe and effective uses as a medical drug, could the Court have found the classification of marijuana in Schedule I to be unconstitutional?

6. Dravet Syndrome. One of the witnesses discusses the therapeutic use of marijuana in treating Dravet Syndrome, a rare, childhood form of epilepsy. As mentioned in Chapter 10, in June 2018, the FDA approved Epidiolex, a cannabidiol (CBD) oral solution, for the treatment of seizures associated with Dravet syndrome in patients two years of age and older. In September 2018, Epidiolex was placed in Schedule V.

PROBLEM 18-1

Defendant is federally indicted for manufacturing (cultivating) marijuana in violation of the Controlled Substances Act (CSA). Defendant moves to dismiss the government's indictment in federal district court on the grounds that the classification of marijuana as a Schedule I substance under the CSA is unconstitutional as denying her the equal protection of the laws under the Fifth Amendment to the U.S. Constitution. In the same motion, Defendant requests the court hold an evidentiary hearing to take testimony on defendant's constitutional challenges as to the rational basis for classifying marijuana in Schedule I. The government replies that such a collateral hearing is unnecessary, if for no other reason that this question was disposed of by *United States v. Pickard*. Defendant counters that while she accepts that *United States v. Pickard* established that as a matter of law she is entitled only to rational basis, not strict scrutiny, review of her claim, she also asserts that as a factual matter, she is entitled to present her evidence that the Schedule I classification is not rational. She asserts not only that she has different evidence for this proposition than was presented in *United States v. Pickard*, but that the expert testimony she will present is more persuasive. As her particular "case or controversy" raises new factual questions, Defendant asserts that she is entitled to an evidentiary hearing. How should the federal district judge rule on the question of whether Defendant is entitled to the same kind of collateral, evidentiary hearing granted to the *Pickard* Defendants?

B. SCIENTIFIC REPORT ON
THE MEDICAL EVIDENCE

In 2017, National Academies of Sciences, Engineering, and Medicine (NAS) published a comprehensive, 395-page study titled, *The Health Effects of Cannabis and Cannabinoids: The Current State of Evidence and Recommendations for Research* (Washington, DC: The National Academies Press, 2017) (hereafter *NAS Current Evidence*). Available at https://www.nap.edu/catalog/24625/the-health-effects-of-cannabis-and-cannabinoids-the-current-state. *NAS Current Evidence* studied over 10,000 scientific papers to reach almost 100 conclusions as to the health effects of marijuana (referred to as cannabis and cannabinoids in *NAS Current Evidence*). The scientific studies were performed by both U.S. and international researchers, and consisted of both clinical studies and systematic reviews of research.

NAS Current Evidence was written by 16 health care experts and scientists associated with major universities and hospitals. It was then reviewed by a second panel of leading medical experts and scientists. It divides its conclusions into conclusive or substantial evidence, moderate evidence, limited evidence, and insufficient evidence. Both positive and negative health effects are systematically presented. The most important conclusions of the study are summarized below.

I. CONCLUSIVE OR SUBSTANTIAL EVIDENCE

The most significant conclusions of the *NAS Current Evidence* concern those that have conclusive or substantial support. By *conclusive evidence* is meant strong evidence from randomized controlled trials and good quality studies with no credible opposing findings. By *substantial evidence* is meant strong evidence from good quality studies to support or refute a statistical association with few or no credible opposing findings.

The *NAS Current Evidence* found conclusive or substantial evidence that cannabis or cannabinoids are effective

- for treating chronic pain in adults, resulting in a significant reduction in pain symptoms;

- as antiemetics (effective in controlling nausea and vomiting) caused by chemotherapy;

- in treating spasticity symptoms for patients with multiple scleroses, as reported by patients.

As to health risks, the *NAS Current Evidence* found substantial evidence of a statistical association between

- long-term smoking of cannabis and worsening respiratory symptoms (such as chronic cough and phlegm production)

and more frequent bronchitis episodes (symptoms improve upon cessation of smoking);

• maternal cannabis smoking and lower birth rate of offspring;

• development of schizophrenia or other psychoses among the most frequent cannabis users.

II. MODERATE EVIDENCE

By *moderate evidence* is meant some evidence from good to fair-quality studies with few or no credible opposing findings.

The *NAS Current Evidence* found moderate evidence that marijuana is

• effective for improving short-term sleep outcomes in individuals with sleep disturbance associated with obstructive sleep apnea syndrome, fibromyalgia, chronic pain, and multiple sclerosis;

• associated with better cognitive performance among individuals with psychotic disorders.

As to health risks, *NAS Current Evidence* found moderate evidence of a statistical association between cannabis use and

• impairment in the cognitive domains of learning, memory, and attention after immediate (24 hours) use;

• increased incidence of suicide thoughts and completion and social anxiety disorder, especially among heaviest users;

• the development of substance dependence and/or a substance abuse disorder for substances, including alcohol, tobacco, and other illicit drugs;

• possible links to an anti-motivational syndrome, especially when cannabis use is initiated at an early age;

• increased risk of overdose injuries among pediatric populations in legalized states.

But *NAS Current Evidence* found moderate evidence indicating no statistical association between smoking cannabis and

• incidence of lung cancer;

• incidence of head and neck cancer.

III. LIMITED EVIDENCE

By *limited evidence* is meant weak evidence from fair-quality studies or mixed findings. This limited evidence indicates that cannabis may be effective for

- increasing appetite and decreasing weight loss associated with HIV/AIDS;

- improving clinician-measured multiple sclerosis spasticity symptoms;

- improving symptoms of Tourette syndrome;

- improving anxiety symptoms, as assessed by a public speaking test, in individuals with social anxiety disorders;

- improving symptoms of posttraumatic stress disorder and a statistically better outcome in terms of mortality and disability after a traumatic brain injury or intracranial hemorrhage;

- anti-inflammatory activity from regular exposure to cannabis smoke.

However, limited evidence indicates that cannabis is ineffective for

- improving symptoms associated with dementia;

- improving intraocular pressure associated with glaucoma;

- reducing depressive symptoms in individuals with chronic pain or multiple sclerosis.

As to health risks, the Report found limited evidence of

- impairment in the cognitive domains of learning, memory, and attention that may continue after cessation of cannabis use;

- a statistical association between cannabis use and impaired academic achievement and educational outcomes;

- a statistical association between cannabis use and increased symptoms of anxiety;

- an association of cannabis use with one sub-type of testicular cancer;

- cannabis smoking is associated with risks of acute heart attack and stroke;

- maternal cannabis smoking and pregnancy complications for the mother;

- increased symptoms of bipolar disorder from daily cannabis use by those who have bipolar disorder

Significantly, *NAS Current Evidence* found no or insufficient evidence to support or refute the conclusions that cannabis or cannabinoids are an effective treatment for

- cancers

- epilepsy

- symptoms of Irritable Bowel syndrome

- motor system symptoms of Parkinson's disease

- dystonia

but cannabis does not have adverse effects on immune status in individuals with HIV.

IV. METHODOLOGICAL POINTS

NAS Current Evidence includes in its assessment of health effects both marijuana and synthesized cannabinoids drugs that have been approved by FDA. Likewise *NAS Current Evidence* differentiated among the various delivery methods of consuming cannabis and cannabinoids.

The intoxicating effects of cannabis include a "pleasurable" rush but can also include decreased, short-term memory, dry mouth, and impaired perception and motor skills. High blood levels of THC may result in panic attacks, paranoid thoughts, and hallucinations.

As to the addictive qualities of cannabis, *NAS Current Evidence* found that both greater frequency of cannabis use and initiating cannabis use at a younger age, increase the likelihood of developing problem cannabis use. (A 1996 report by the Institute of Medicine, as the medical division of NAS was called at the time, found that cannabis withdrawal symptoms are short-lived and mild, characterized by irritability, insomnia, nausea, and cramping.)

Finally *NAS Current Evidence* concluded that the following barriers inhibit research into the medical effects of cannabis:

- its classification as a Schedule I substance;

- difficulty in gaining access to the quantity, quality, and type of cannabis necessary for specific research questions;

- need to obtain a diverse network of funders needed to support research.

NOTES AND QUESTIONS

1. **The National Academies of Sciences, Engineering, and Medicine.** The National Academies of Sciences, Engineering, and Medicine (NAS) are private, nonprofit scientific institutions founded in 1863 by Act of Congress (signed by President Abraham Lincoln), operating under federal charter (36 U.S.C. §§ 150301–150304). NAS is widely reputed for independent, expert advice on scientific, engineering, and medical issues. NAS is charged with "providing independent, objective advice to the nation on matters related to science and technology. . . . to provide scientific advice to the government

'whenever called upon' by any government department. NAS receives no compensation from the government for its services." *NAS Current Evidence* was sponsored by numerous governmental and non-governmental agencies, including those tasked under the CSA with undertaking research into controlled substances, such as the Food and Drug Administration, the Centers for Disease Control and Prevention, and the National Institute on Drug Abuse.

NAS Current Evidence has a good claim to be the most comprehensive, objective, and influential report on the medical evidence as to marijuana. Significantly, this is not a single study but a rigorous comparison and review of thousands of studies published since 1999. (In 1999, the medical division of the NAS, then called the Institute of Medicine, published a comprehensive analysis titled *Marijuana and Medicine: Assessing the Science Base*. Washington, DC: The National Academies Press. https://doi.org/10.17226/63 76.)

2.   Status of *NAS Current Evidence*. In *United States v. Pickard*, the court is careful to take judicial notice of certain facts and items with the force of law. Given the quasi-official status of the NAS and the comprehensiveness of *NAS Current Evidence*, what evidentiary value should it be accorded by courts and the DEA? For example, when considering rescheduling, the DEA obtains a length report on the health effects of marijuana from the FDA. Should the law explicitly allow DEA to rely also on third-party meta-analysis such as *NAS Current Evidence*? If the Court in *United States v. Pickard* had the *NAS Current Evidence* Report available as evidence, what effect, if any, should it have on the Court's decision?

3.   Conflicting views. A fair summary of *NAS Current Evidence* would seem to be that marijuana has both therapeutic value and health care risks. Not surprisingly the report has been embraced by both marijuana legalization opponents and proponents. For example, Kevin Sabet of the anti-legalization group Smart Approaches to Marijuana stated that "This report completely vindicates the scientific community that has been saying for years marijuana is a serious health issue." On the other hand, the Drug Policy Alliance, a pro-legalization group, stated that "To have such a thorough review of the evidence conclude that there are benefits to medical marijuana should boost the case for federal reform." https://www.washingtonpost.com/news/wonk/wp/2017/01/13/ the-definitive-guide-to-what-experts-know-about-the-effects-of-marijuana-use/?utm_term=.76e30c30c03a.

4.   Limits of *NAS Current Evidence*. The scientists who wrote *NAS Current Evidence* acknowledge limitations of the report. Because of limited clinical studies, the report was unable to draw conclusions about the effectiveness of cannabis for certain medical conditions that may yet be proved by further study. For example, studies of Epidiolex were not yet available, limiting conclusions that could be drawn about cannabis and epilepsy. Likewise statistical evidence of association does not necessarily prove causation but could reflect elements that travel together due to common factors. For example, the statistical association between cannabis and schizophrenia may reflect a common vulnerability factor. See Daniele Piomelli,

A Guide to the National Academy of Science Report on Cannabis: An Exclusive Discussion with Panel Members, 2(1) Cannabis Cannabinoid Res. 155–159 (2017).

5.   Science and Schedule I. Do the conclusions contained in the *NAS Current Evidence* mandate a change in the assessment of marijuana as to Schedule I criteria that cannabis has: 1) high potential for abuse; 2) no currently accepted medical use in treatment in the United States; 3) lack of accepted safety for use of the drug or other substance under medical supervision?

PROBLEM 18-2

A debate on the health effects of cannabis and cannabinoids has been organized at the local university. To keep the debate manageable and focused, you have been asked to outline the most significant health benefits and risks for cannabis and cannabinoids. What evidence will you select?

PROBLEM 18–3

Same scenario as the previous problem. For reasons of time and credibility, you will allow only topics to be presented that are "substantial" in demonstrating health benefits or risks. The pro-legalization side proposes as a topic the "euphoria" that many marijuana users experience, with enhanced feelings of relaxation and well-being. They claim that these are therapeutic benefits that qualify for inclusion in the debate. In contrast, the anti-legalization side points out that some users, especially inexperienced ones, report adverse emotional effects, such as dysphoria and short-lived anxiety. They object to including the marijuana "high" as a benefit, but insist that the side effects of intoxication, which distort sensory perception and motor skills, are a negative health effect.

What do you decide?

CHAPTER 19

COMPARING MARIJUANA TO OTHER PSYCHOACTIVE SUBSTANCES: POLICY ISSUES

■ ■ ■

Many important issues in marijuana law flow directly from the conflict between federal laws that prohibit marijuana and state/local laws that allow its use for medical and/or recreational purposes. Without this conflict, many of the issues discussed in this book would cease to be relevant. For example, the difficulties marijuana related businesses have had in obtaining banking services, or in obtaining relief in federal bankruptcy courts, only exist because marijuana distribution is strictly prohibited under federal law.

Under the federal Controlled Substances Act, marijuana is among the most strictly controlled substances. As a Schedule I drug under the CSA, its possession is prohibited in almost all contexts, on par with the other Schedule I drugs, such as heroin, LSD, ecstasy, and mescaline. Were marijuana to be re-scheduled to a lower schedule, it could potentially be made available as a prescription drug. And if it were removed from the CSA altogether, it could be legalized for recreational use nationwide, and perhaps be regulated in the same way that alcohol and tobacco are regulated.

Given the conflict between federal law and state/local laws, and the numerous difficulties that flow from this conflict, it appears that a reassessment of marijuana's legal status from a public policy perspective is long overdue. And one important aspect of any such an assessment would be to consider how other psychoactive substances are treated under the law, and whether marijuana is relevantly different or similar to those substances. Accordingly, this chapter undertakes an assessment of marijuana status by looking analytically at three groups of substances that could arguably serve as precedents for the appropriate legal treatment of marijuana. Section A compares marijuana to other commonly used (illegal) recreational drugs. Section B compares marijuana to psychoactive substances that can be legally prescribed as medications. And Section C compares marijuana to alcohol and tobacco.

A. MARIJUANA VS. ILLEGAL RECREATIONAL DRUGS

The Controlled Substances Act lists the various controlled substances in five "schedules' (Schedule I–Schedule V). The most tightly controlled are in Schedule I; the least controlled are in Schedule V. Those substances in Schedule I are essentially prohibited for all purposes, with some very minor exceptions for scientific research. The following is a summary of the various schedules, along with some of the substances that are included on them, that comes from the website of the DEA's Diversion Control Division:

Schedule I   Controlled Substances

Substances in this schedule have no currently accepted medical use in the United States, a lack of accepted safety for use under medical supervision, and a high potential for abuse.

Some examples of substances listed in Schedule I are: heroin, lysergic acid diethylamide (LSD), marijuana (cannabis), peyote, methaqualone, and 3,4-methylenedioxymethamphetamine ("Ecstasy").

Schedule II/IIN   Controlled Substances (2/2N)

Substances in this schedule have a high potential for abuse which may lead to severe psychological or physical dependence.

Examples of Schedule II narcotics include: hydromorphone (Dilaudid®), methadone (Dolophine®), meperidine (Demerol®), oxycodone (OxyContin®, Percocet®), and fentanyl (Sublimaze®, Duragesic®). Other Schedule II narcotics include: morphine, opium, codeine, and hydrocodone.

Examples of Schedule II stimulants include: amphetamine (Dexedrine®, Adderall®), methamphetamine (Desoxyn®), and methylphenidate (Ritalin®).

Other Schedule II substances include: amobarbital, glutethimide, and pentobarbital.

Schedule III/IIIN   Controlled Substances (3/3N)

Substances in this schedule have a potential for abuse less than substances in Schedules I or II and abuse may lead to moderate or low physical dependence or high psychological dependence.

Examples of Schedule III narcotics include: products containing not more than 90 milligrams of codeine per dosage unit (Tylenol with Codeine®), and buprenorphine (Suboxone®).

Examples of Schedule IIIN non-narcotics include: benzphetamine (Didrex®), phendimetrazine, ketamine, and anabolic steroids such as Depo®-Testosterone.

Schedule IV   Controlled Substances

Substances in this schedule have a low potential for abuse relative to substances in Schedule III.

Examples of Schedule IV substances include: alprazolam (Xanax®), carisoprodol (Soma®), clonazepam (Klonopin®), clorazepate (Tranxene®), diazepam (Valium®), lorazepam (Ativan®), midazolam (Versed®), temazepam (Restoril®), and triazolam (Halcion®).

Schedule V   Controlled Substances

Substances in this schedule have a low potential for abuse relative to substances listed in Schedule IV and consist primarily of preparations containing limited quantities of certain narcotics.

Examples of Schedule V substances include: cough preparations containing not more than 200 milligrams of codeine per 100 milliliters or per 100 grams (Robitussin AC®, Phenergan with Codeine®), and ezogabine.

As you can see from the DEA's summary, marijuana is included on Schedule I of the CSA, along with a number of other so-called "recreational" drugs that Congress has deemed to be unsafe, highly subject to abuse, and lacking any accepted medical use. These include drugs such as LSD, mescaline, Ecstasy (MDMA), and heroin. Other drugs commonly used for recreational purposes are on lower schedules. These include most prescription opioids (Schedule II), cocaine (Schedule II), amphetamines and barbiturates (Schedule II), and the benzodiazepines, such as Valium and Xanax (Schedule IV).

In the following case, *People v. McCabe,* the Illinois Supreme Court considered a constitutional challenge to an Illinois criminal statute that treated marijuana possession in the same or even harsher fashion these other drugs. The court struck down the statute, holding that the statute's classification of marijuana was arbitrary and lacked a reasonable basis, and therefore deprived the defendant of his equal protection rights.

PEOPLE V. MCCABE

Supreme Court of Illinois
49 Ill.2d 338 (1971)

PER CURIUM.

Following a jury trial in the circuit court of Kane County the defendant, Thomas McCabe, was found guilty of the unlawful sale of marijuana in violation of the Criminal Code of Illinois. (Ill.Rev.Stat.1969, ch. 38, par. 22–3). Pursuant to the provisions for mandatory minimum penalties for the unlawful sale of a narcotic drug (Ill.Rev.Stat.1969, ch. 38, par. 22–40) the defendant, who had no prior convictions, was sentenced to the penitentiary for a period of ten years to ten years and a day. On this appeal he raises these grounds for reversal: (1) the classification of marijuana in the Narcotic Drug Act (Ill.Rev.Stat.1969, ch. 38, par. 22–1 et seq.), with mandatory minimum statutory penalties for a first conviction, deprived the defendant of due process and equal protection of the law in violation of the constitution of the United States.

* * *

To begin it will be helpful to exclude some of the potential questions the defendant does not raise regarding the classification of marijuana. It is not denied, for example, that the State has authority under its general police power to prohibit the sale, use, or possession of marijuana. Nor does the defendant contend that the State must limit its exercise of that power to the regulation, as opposed to the prohibition, of the drug. Finally, the defendant does not claim that the State, having chosen to proscribe the use, possession, and sale of marijuana, must similarly act in the cases of substances such as alcohol, tobacco and caffeine, whose use may be harmful.

The equal-protection argument that is raised is narrow and limited. It simply is that the present placing or classifying of marijuana under the Narcotic Drug Act rather than classifying it under the Drug Abuse Control Act (Ill.Rev.Stat.1969, ch. 111 ½, par. 801 et seq.) with the 'stimulant or depressant' drugs is constitutionally invalid as an improper classification, considering the present state of knowledge concerning the comparative natures and effects of the drugs named in the two statutes. Unlike the Narcotic Drug Act, which provides for a mandatory ten-year minimum sentence upon a first conviction for the sale of marijuana, the Drug Abuse Control Act provides, upon a first conviction for the sale of drugs named in it, a maximum jail term of but one year and probation is not prohibited. The defendant says that there is no rational basis for distinguishing a first sale of marijuana from the first sale of a stimulant or depressant drug under the Drug Abuse Control Act and that the gross disparity between the penalties violates his rights under the equal-protection clause.

In determining whether a statutory classification violates the equal-protection clause, we must begin with the presumption that the classification is valid and must impose the burden of showing invalidity on the party challenging the classification. The equal-protection clause does not deny the States the power to classify in the exercise of their police power and it recognizes the existence of a broad latitude and discretion in classifying. If any state of facts may reasonably be conceived which would justify the classification, it must be upheld if clause is thus limited. As this court put it in *Thillens, Inc. v. Morey*, 11 Ill.2d 579, 593 'whether the enactment is wise or unwise; whether it is based on sound economic theory; whether it is the best means to achieve the desired results, and whether the legislative discretion within its prescribed limits should be exercised in a particular manner are matters for the judgment of the legislature, and the honest conflict of serious opinion does not suffice to bring them within the range of judicial cognizance.' But it is required that there be a reasonable basis for distinguishing the class to which the law is applicable from the class to which it is not. Appropriate respect should be given to the fact of a legislative classification, but there is a judicial obligation to insure that the power to classify has not been exercised arbitrarily and, if it has been, the legislation cannot be justified under the label of 'classification.' It was observed recently: '[A] state may not, under the guise of classification, arbitrarily discriminate against one and in favor of another similarly situated.' *Lake Shore Auto Parts Co. v. Korzen,* 49 Ill.2d 137, 148.

Measuring by these criteria we must determine whether any rational basis exists to justify the substantially greater penalties imposed for a first conviction for the sale of marijuana than for a first conviction for the sale of a drug named in the Drug Abuse Control Act. This consideration will require an assessment of the relevant scientific, medical and social data found, including the voluminous materials assembled by the parties here, which are pertinent to support and to defeat the classification. We are aware that any compilation and examination of materials cannot comprehend all studies that have been made. We know, too, that knowledge in this whole area is not nearly complete. We proceed not to determine scientific questions, but to judge whether the data presently available provides a reasonable basis for the described classification of marijuana. The consideration of this data, of course, will not extend to the wisdom or unwisdom of the legislative classification. We confine our examination to the question whether the challenged classification can be supported on any rational basis.

Knowledge of the characteristics and effects of the drug commonly called marijuana, which is obtained from the leaves of the female hemp plant, cannabis sativa, has developed rapidly in the last decade. Studies by Presidential commissions, whose memberships have included psychiatrists, pharmacologists, sociologists and law enforcement officials as well as intensified research in the medical and scientific communities have contributed to this advancement. The consensus is that although marijuana has been commonly associated with the opioids, such as morphine and heroin, there are important differences between the so-called abuse characteristics of the two. Heroin and morphine are true narcotic analgesics in the sense that their use produces a marked indifference to pain. In addition, when injected intravenously a warm flushing of the skin and intense pleasurable sensations in the lower abdomen will result. Repeated usage of these drugs in a comparatively short time will result in the development of a tolerance, that is, a state which requires a gradually increasing dosage to permit the drug to attain the effect desired. Both a psychological and compelling physical dependence result from the use of 'hard narcotics.' The physical dependence develops in intensity with continued use and requires the continued administration of the drug to avoid withdrawal symptoms. It appears that the subjective action of the morphine-type drugs also involve changes in mood, an inability to concentrate and the development of apathy. Physical degeneration occurs, arising from drug preoccupation, personal neglect, malnutrition and susceptibility to infections. Overdosage can cause death through excessive respiratory depression.

Early withdrawal symptoms include lacrimation, nasal discharge, yawning and perspiration. Later, dilated pupils, loss of appetite, gooseflesh, (thus, the expression 'cold turkey') restlessness and increased irritability and tremor will appear. At its peak intensity, the syndrome includes high irritability, insomnia, violent yawning, severe sneezing and lacrimation. Nausea and vomiting are common, as are intestinal spasms and diarrhea. Increased heart beat and elevated blood pressure, as well as muscular spasms, abdominal cramps and pains in the bones and muscles of the back are common. Death due to cardiovascular collapse can result from withdrawal. The symptoms are caused by the drug-induced alterations at the cellular level, most prominently in the central nervous system. Most authorities consider that the drug addict's frequent involvement in criminal activity results from his acute need for the drug rather than because of the action of the drug itself. The term addiction refers to the physical, rather than a psychological dependence on the drug.

Cocaine, which is placed with marijuana and the opioids in the Narcotic Drug Act, is a powerful stimulant, whereas the morphine-type drugs have a depressing action. Too, cocaine is further unlike the opioids in that it does not have effects of tolerance or physical dependence and abstention does not cause acute withdrawal symptoms. However, because of its potent nature, it induces intense physical and mental excitation and a marked reduction in normal inhibitions which often results in aggressive and even violent behavior. Intense hallucinations and paranoid delusions are common and, because of this, cocaine users frequently attempt to dilute the experience with a depressant such as heroin or morphine.

The properties and consequences of the use of marijuana differ from those attending the use of opioids or cocaine. The acute physical symptoms of marijuana use typically induced are an increase in pulse rate, a slight elevation in blood pressure, conjunctival vascular congestion, a rise in blood sugar, urinary frequency, dryness of the mouth and throat. Nausea, vomiting and occasional diarrhea have been observed, as has the inability to coordinate voluntary muscular movements. There is usually a marked increase in appetite. Deaths due to overdose apparently have not been reported.

The mental or subjective effects of the administration of this drug are variable and depend on the interaction of several factors including the physical and pharmacological properties of the particular marijuana used, the amount of dosage, and more importantly, what has been called the character structure of the user, (including his experience with the drug, his attitude and expectations) and the social setting or environment in which the drug is used. The most common reaction is the development of a euphoric state of altered consciousness in which ideas seem disconnected, uncontrollable and freely flowing. Time perception is distorted with minutes seeming like hours. Spatial conception may also be disturbed. Vivid hallucinations, usually, but not always, pleasant, can occur with increased dosage. There may be marked alterations of mood, usually manifested by an extreme feeling of well being which is often accompanied by uncontrollable laughter. Later a more somber or depressed mood will appear. The drug's influence can cause anxiety, confusion or disorientation, and with larger doses temporary psychotic episodes have been observed in predisposed individuals. Inhibitions are reduced but violent or otherwise aggressive behavior seem to be rare.

Almost all authorities agree that marijuana is not a narcotic or addictive in the sense that the terms are precisely used. Unlike the opiate drugs, it does not produce a physical dependence, and upon abstention there are no withdrawal symptoms. A tolerance to the drug does not develop. Marijuana use does, however, lead to a mild psychological dependence. The short-hand descriptive phrase most often applied to the drug is 'mild hallucinogen,' although this refers to only one of its many effects.

The depressant and stimulant drugs within the Drug Abuse Control Act include the barbiturates (depressants,), the amphetamines (stimulants), and the hallucinogens. The drugs psilocybin, peyote, mescaline and what is commonly called LSD are examples of the hallucinogens. Frequent use of the barbiturates at high dosage levels leads invariably to the development of physical dependence, tolerance and severe withdrawal symptoms, similar to those associated with heroin use. The effects of barbiturate intoxication resemble those of alcoholic intoxication. There is a general sluggishness, difficulty in concentrating and thinking, speech impairment, memory lapse, faulty judgment and exaggeration of basic personality traits. Irritability and quarrelsomeness are common. Hostile and paranoid ideas as well as suicidal tendencies can occur. Barbiturates are said to be the most frequently used chemical in suicides in the United States. Accidental death from an overdose also can occur. There is a clear association between barbituric intoxication and accidents and traffic fatalities. The drug can depress a wide range of functions, including the nerves, skeletal muscles and the cardiac muscle. Barbiturates are frequently used by heroin addicts to boost the effect of weak heroin.

The consensus of the amphetimines (stimulants) is that, unlike the barbiturates, their abuse does not lead to a physical dependence, but the development of a high tolerance and a strong psychological dependence are common. Occasional dosage under medical supervision causes only an elevation in mood and a state of wellbeing. Long term dependence, however, leads to serious mental and physical problems. Malnutrition and debilitation due to self-neglect will appear. A well known complication of amphetamine abuse is paranoid schizophrenia. The user may react violently to his persecutive delusions. Visual and auditory hallucinations occur and can persist long after use is discontinued. Although true withdrawal symptoms do not occur, the latter stages of excitement and mental disarrangement are difficult to endure. To take the edge off this tense euphoria, the user will sometimes turn to barbiturates or the opioids.

Special mention should be made of one particular amphetamine, methamphetamine, commonly called 'speed.' Its effects are generally the same as other amphetamines, only markedly intensified. There is evidence that large doses result in permanent brain damage. The drug's lethal qualities are well documented. The potential for violence, paranoia and physical depletion are substantially more severe.

Also placed under the Drug Abuse Control Act are the hallucinogens or the 'psychedelics.' LSD is the best known and one of the highly potent forms of these drugs. Less potent hallucinogens include psilocybin, peyote, and mescaline and hashish (another derivative of the plant from which marijuana comes). As with marijuana usage, a true physical addiction does not occur with LSD, in that withdrawal effects do not follow abstinence. Frequent use of LSD will lead rapidly, however, to the development of a high tolerance. Psychological dependence develops as it does with exposure to almost any substance which alters the state of consciousness. During LSD-intoxication severe panic and paranoid reactions are encountered. Attempts at suicide as well as uncontrolled aggression are among the dangers to the intoxicant. Hallucinations are common, accompanied by feelings of grandiosity and omnipotence. Recurrences of the LSD experience weeks or months after the last drug intake are well known. Various emotional disorders have been observed following exposure to LSD. A chronic anxiety state is the most common. Prolonged psychotic reactions also have been identified with LSD. Too, there is also growing evidence that LSD can cause chromosomal damage.

Against this background of comparison one would conclude that neither the chemical properties of the drugs nor their effects on the behavior of the users provides any justifiable or reasonable basis for the sharply disparate penalties which are imposed for a first sale of marijuana and for a first sale of a drug under the Drug Abuse Control Act. Too, the consequences of abusive use of marijuana certainly appear not to be comparable to the demonstrated and profound ill-effects of opiate or cocaine addiction. Marijuana, in terms of abuse characteristics, shares much more in common with the barbiturates, amphetamines and, particularly, the hallucinogens than it does with the 'hard drugs' classified in the Narcotic Drug Act. Marijuana does differ from the barbiturates and amphetamines in that it has no established medical use, but neither do LSD, peyote, or mescaline. Thus, one cannot reasonably distinguish marijuana from the substances under the Drug Abuse Control Act on this basis.

Nor is there any reasonable basis for placing marijuana under the Narcotic Drug Act and not under the Drug Abuse Control Act because of any compulsion to abuse. The compulsion associated with marijuana has been described as moderate or mild. The same is true of the amphetamines. The opioids and cocaine, on the other hand, have a maximal compulsive quality in this regard. Barbiturates, too, have this quality. Thus, in this respect, marijuana is dissimilar from the other drugs in the Narcotic Drug Act. Indeed, from this limited standard of comparison it is the barbiturates under the Drug Abuse Control Act, and not marijuana, which approximate the characteristics of the true narcotics.

Another factor which has been frequently advanced to provide a justifiable basis for classifying marijuana under the Narcotic Drug Act rather than under the Drug Abuse Control Act is that the use of marijuana progresses to heroin use and addiction. This thesis, once broadly entertained, has recently encountered serious challenge. Today it is reported that the vast majority of marijuana users do not graduate to the use of heroin. In 1969, Dr. Stanley F. Yolles, then Director of the National Institute of Mental Health, testified before the Congress that there is nothing in the properties of marijuana which predisposes the use of heroin. He also estimated that only a small percentage of chronic users of marijuana go on to use heroin. This is not to deny any association between marijuana and heroin. The most commonly accepted thesis today is that a drug sequence or movement from one drug to another results from the cumulative effect of several factors, including: the pharmacological properties and effects of the drugs, the personality structure of the user, and the pressures of the so-called host environment. Thus, the chronic use of any drug presents a danger of graduation to other and more dangerous drugs. Observed, for example, has been a clear association between barbiturate abuse and heroin addiction. The barbiturate-heroin connection in also true with respect to the criminal trafficking in these drugs. Whatever can be said of marijuana use leading to the use of other and so-called harder drugs can be applied, and to a probably greater extent, to barbiturates, methamphetamine and LSD.

The extensive criminal involvement of persons addicted to heroin is well known. The intense craving for the drug, and the dread of symptoms following its withdrawal lead addicts to engage in criminal activities to finance their habit. It has been said that marijuana use also causes violence, crime and antisocial acts. However, since tolerance, physical dependence, or withdrawal symptoms do not attend its use, this thesis has been criticized. Some say that since the effect of marijuana is to induce a passivity in the user, the drug has a negative relation to criminality and aggressive behavior. But as marijuana is generally a disinhibitor, it must be recognized that antisocial conduct can occur in a predisposed individual. But this is, of course, equally true regarding the stimulant or depressant drugs and the hallucinogens. And, violent and aggressive conduct is a more common reaction to these latter drugs because of the paranoiac psychosis which they can produce in the user. Thus, it can be concluded that the thesis that marijuana use, as does the use of the opioids and cocaine, leads to criminal activity cannot provide a basis for distinguishing marijuana from the depressant and stimulant drugs or the hallucinogens.

Observations to be drawn on marijuana are that it is not a narcotic and it is not truly addictive. Its use does not involve tolerance, physical dependence or the withdrawal syndrome. Physical ill effects from its use are, so far as is known, relatively moderate. Its abuse does not have the profound and ill consequences observed in the use of some of the other drugs considered. Its use does not singularly or extraordinarily lead to opiate addiction or to aggressive behavior or criminal activity.

Against the entire background of the drugs considered we judge that the classification of marijuana under the Narcotics Drug Act rather than under the Drug Abuse Control Act has been arbitrary. A comparison of the drugs leads to a conclusion that marijuana more closely resembles drugs placed in the Drug Abuse Control Act. It is, comparatively speaking, dissimilar from drugs under the Narcotic Drugs Act. We do not find a rational basis for the classification, a consequence of which is that one first convicted of the sale of marijuana must without qualification receive a sentence ten times greater than one permitted to be imposed on one convicted for the first time of a sale of drugs under the Drug Abuse Act. The absence of a rational basis for distinguishing first convictions for sales of marijuana from first convictions for sales of drugs placed in the Drug Abuse Control Act compels the conclusion that the present classification of marijuana offends the equal-protection clause of the United States constitution and our new constitution of Illinois and was in violation of section 22 of article IV of the former constitution of this State.

We would observe that the legislature has recently removed marijuana, from the Narcotic Drug Act and reclassified it under the Cannabis Control Act, H.B. 788, P.A. 77-758, approved August 16, 1971. Henceforth, a first sale of a small quantity of marijuana to an adult, as was the case here, will result in only minor criminal penalties. This reclassification is not inconsistent with what we have said here.

It is appropriate to note that we are not unmindful of the prior Federal and State decisions which had rejected constitutional attacks on Federal and State statutes classifying marijuana with the 'hard drugs.' We would point out that the constitutional ground raised by the defendant here was not presented in any of the cited cases.

The State contends that the constitutional argument which the defendant has presented here was waived and not preserved for review because it was not raised in his written motion for a new trial. The record shows that the defendant plainly raised the constitutional question in his pretrial motion to quash the indictment, argued it, and secured the court's ruling on the question. It was not the character of claimed error to be raised on a motion for a new trial. He referred to the constitutional point orally in his post-trial motion and we regard that as an oral motion for arrest of judgment. We consider that the defendant preserved the constitutional question for review. We hold that the present classification of marijuana is arbitrary and deprives the defendant of equal protection of the law. The remainder of the Narcotic Drug Act is not affected by this holding, as we judge it is severable from that portion of the statute which concerns marijuana.

It will not be necessary to consider the other contentions advanced by the defendant. For the reasons given, the judgment of the circuit court of Kane County is reversed.

Judgment reversed.

* * *

RYAN, J.

I join in the dissent of Chief Justice Underwood and add thereto the following:

The majority opinion does not focus on what I consider to be the critical aspect of the question of classification. The majority is concerned with the characteristics of the various drugs discussed and their effects on the human body and behavior pointing out similarities and differences. I do not consider these comparisons important. Instead we must be concerned with the purpose of the classification and the problems the legislature was attempting to alleviate thereby. In *Billings v. Illinois*, 188 U.S. 97, 102, 23 S.Ct. 272, 273, 47 L.Ed. 400, the court stated: 'Things may have very diverse qualities, and yet be united in a class. They may have very similar qualities, and yet be cast in different classes. * * * All classification must primarily depend upon purpose-the problem presented'.

In 1931 marijuana, opium and cocoa leaves were classified together in the Narcotic Drug Control Law and penalties were provided for the illegal sale and possession thereof. In 1957 Illinois adopted the Uniform Narcotic Drug Act.). The list of drugs brought within the Act had increased to eleven in number and by 1967 the number of drugs included in the classification had grown to fifteen. A reading of these various Acts makes it clear that the legislature was not attempting to classify drugs of similar characteristics and effects but was attempting to classify these drugs for the purpose of combating the social evil found in the illegal sale, possession and use of the same.

In 1967 the legislature enacted the Drug Abuse Control Act, (Ill.Rev.Stat.1967, Ch. 111 ½, par. 801 et seq.) In this Act, as the Uniform Narcotic Drug Act, drugs of diverse characteristics and effects are grouped together for the purpose of controlling the illegal traffic in the various members of the class. The majority opinion concludes that marijuana more closely resembles the new list of drugs classified under the Drug Abuse Act, thus rendering the present classification of marijuana violative of the equal-protection clause.

The conclusion of the majority ignores the fact that traffic in marijuana had been a social problem of sufficient magnitude to warrant legislative action for many years. Material submitted with the briefs indicates that although a relatively small percentage of marijuana users become addicted to the so-called 'hard drugs' a high percentage of 'hard drug' addicts first became acquainted with the use of drugs through the use of marijuana. Also, certain studies indicate that marijuana is the most widely used drug among the young drug users. These are facts which the legislature may well have considered as justification for retaining marijuana under the Uniform Narcotic Drug Act and for not classifying it with the drugs listed in the Drug Abuse Control Act. The presumption of the reasonableness of the classification is with the State and the same will not be set aside as a denial of equal protection if any facts reasonably may be conceived to justify it.

The defendant's brief has also focused on the characteristics and effects of the various drugs and has ignored the problem-to-be-solved approach. The burden is on the defendant to present evidence which shows that the apparently reasonable basis for this classification does not exist. The defendant has failed to produce any evidence concerning the nature of the traffic in the various drugs or the need to control the same. The presumption of the validity of the classification must therefore prevail.

   * * *

There is a great diversity of opinion as to the effects of marijuana. As the majority opinion states, knowledge in this area is not nearly complete. This court cannot therefore, take judicial notice thereof. The defendant having offered no evidence thereon, this court cannot make findings and comparisons of marijuana with the other drugs. With the record in this state, the defendant has not sustained the burden of proving the classification invalid.

NOTES AND QUESTIONS

1. **Reliance on ordinary language.** The court's decision in *McCabe* was based upon marijuana's inclusion in Illinois' Narcotic Drug Act, along with drugs such as cocaine and heroin, rather than in the state's Drug Control Act, which apply to drug such as barbiturates, amphetamines, and the hallucinogens (e.g., LSD). The court found that there was no reasonable basis for punishing marijuana possession the same as possession of narcotics. Thus it found that the Narcotic Drug Act violated the defendant's constitutional rights. The federal Controlled substances Act, however, classifies these various drugs somewhat differently. As set out in the chart at the beginning of this section, Schedule I includes the hallucinogens, but excludes cocaine and many opioids, which are listed in the less restrictive Schedule II. In light of these differences in classification, does the *McCabe* court's holding with respect to marijuana's inclusion in the Illinois Narcotic Drug Act reasonably bear on the federal Controlled Substances Act's inclusion of marijuana within Schedule I?

2. **Constitutional challenges to drug statutes.** The Illinois Supreme Court was not the only state Supreme Court to strike down a state drug-control statute on constitutional grounds. As discussed in Chapter 1 of this book, the Michigan Supreme Court made a similar ruling in the case *People v. Sinclair*, 194 N.W.2d 878 (1972). In that case, the defendant, John Sinclair, received a prison term of 9.5–10 years for possession of two marijuana joints. The Michigan Supreme Court unanimously reversed the conviction in a plurality opinion. Five of the seven justices found that the sentence and/or the conviction violated Sinclair's constitutional rights, and the other two justices found that the defendant was improperly entrapped. As the *McCabe* court points out in its opinion, however, a majority of courts that have considered constitutional challenges to state and federal drug laws have sided with the government. For example (as discussed above in Chapter 2), in *National Organization for the Reform of Marijuana Laws (NORML) v. Bell,* 488 F.Supp. 123 (D.D.C. 1980), the United States District Court for the District of Columbia rejected a constitutional challenge to the CSA's classification of marijuana under Schedule I. The court held that "the legislative branch, and not the judicial, is the proper battleground for the fight to decriminalize the possession of marijuana. The people, and not the courts, must decide whether the battle will be won or lost." *Id.* at 143.

3. **Medical use of hallucinogenic drugs.** Marijuana is not the only Schedule I drug that shows promise for medical use. In the following excerpt from a medical journal, a research psychiatrist, Henry Nasrallah discusses the potential medical uses in the field of psychiatry for drugs such as LSD and Ecstasy. He concludes:

> [P]sychiatry is finally recognizing the therapeutic value inherent in traditionally 'evil' street drugs that we euphemistically refer to as 'recreational drugs.' Even methamphetamine, the universally condemned and clearly harmful drug, was recently reported to be neuroprotective at low dosages! Could our field have suffered from a blind eye to the benefits of these hallucinogens and ignored the

possibility that some persons with addiction who use these 'recreational drugs' may have been self-medicating to alleviate their un-diagnosed psychiatric disorder? We need to re-conceptualize the pejorative term 'mind-altering drug' because of its implicitly negative connotation. After all, alteration may indicate a favorable, not just a deleterious, outcome.

Henry Nasrallah, *Maddening Therapies: How Hallucinogens Morphed Into Novel Treatments*, 16 Current Psychiatry 19 (2017).

B. MARIJUANA VS. PSYCHOACTIVE PRESCRIPTION DRUGS

A majority of states now authorize medical marijuana use for persons who obtain a physician's recommendation. But because marijuana is in Schedule I of the Controlled Substances Act, doctors cannot prescribe it legally, as they can most of the drugs on the lower CSA schedules (Note, however the drug must still undergo extensive testing and FDA approval before it can be prescribed as a medication.) Furthermore, some of the drugs that can be prescribed legally are potentially quite dangerous and have a widespread history of abuse, such as prescription opioids, barbiturates, amphetamines, and benzodiazepines (e.g., Xanex, Valium). Given that marijuana appears to be safer and less prone to abuse than at least some of these other drugs, and given that it is used quite extensively in a majority of states for medical purposes, many people question why it cannot be prescribed by physicians.

In the following case, *United States v. Garrison*, the United States Court of Appeals for the Ninth Circuit considered an appeal from a conviction for conspiracy to distribute a controlled substance, in this case, OxyContin, which is a prescription opioid. The court affirmed the conviction based on the evidence. The case illustrates well the serious social consequences of the current opioid crisis, which is due in large part to prescription medications such as OxyContin. Consider as you read this case whether it makes sense from a public policy perspective to prohibit the use of marijuana as a prescription drug, while at the same time allowing many of the opioids to be prescribed.

UNITED STATES V. GARRISON
United States Court of Appeals, 9th Circuit
2018 WL 1938523 (9th Cir. 2018)

GOLD, J.

After a jury trial, David James Garrison was convicted of conspiracy to distribute controlled substances in violation of 21 U.S.C. § 846. During trial, the government offered evidence that Garrison and his co-conspirators had abused their positions as healthcare providers by intentionally prescribing OxyContin, a powerful opioid pain reliever, for no legitimate medical purpose as part of a scheme to sell the drug on the street. Garrison appeals his conviction, arguing (1) that there was insufficient evidence to support his conviction, and (2) that the district court should have dismissed the charges against him, acquitted him, or granted him a mistrial because the government did not timely disclose certain information. We affirm.

I

There is now an epic crisis of deadly opioid abuse and overuse. In 2016, roughly 11.5 million people in the United States misused prescription opioids. U.S. Dep't of Health and Human Services, *About the U.S. Opioid Epidemic*. That same year, 116 people on average died every day from opioid-related drug overdoses. And in 2017, the Acting Secretary of Health and Human Services declared the national opioid abuse epidemic a public health emergency. U.S. Dep't of Health and Human Services, *HHS Acting Secretary Declares Public Health Emergency to Address National Opioid Crisis* (2017).

In the midst of this crisis, we trust doctors and healthcare professionals to be conscientious gatekeepers to these dangerous and potentially fatal drugs. But unfortunately some medical professionals betray their duty to do no harm as healthcare providers and abuse their prescription pads. This is exactly what happened at the Lake Medical Group clinic (the "Clinic"), where Garrison worked as a licensed physician's assistant from summer 2009 until the Clinic was closed in February 2010.

The Clinic was what is often described as a "pill mill," and the activities of people working there led to the illicit street-sale of more than a million maximum-strength OxyContin tablets. From August 2008 to September 2010, the Clinic generated 13,207 prescriptions for OxyContin—all but six of which were for the drug's maximum dosage. The Clinic employed "patient recruiters" who induced people living in homeless shelters and rescue missions to visit the Clinic. These of course were not true "patients" in the ordinary sense of that word. The Clinic would then use the names and Medicare or Medi-Cal cards of the recruited patients to generate fraudulent OxyContin prescriptions. The recruited patients did not retain the OxyContin that they were prescribed. Instead, people working for the Clinic retrieved the drug from participating pharmacists or from the recruited patients, and the Clinic operators then had the pills sold illegally. The government learned of the Clinic's operations and took steps to shut the Clinic down and prosecute those it believed responsible for the scheme.

A

On September 28, 2011, Garrison and eleven other codefendants were indicted. Garrison was indicted for conspiracy to distribute controlled substances in violation of 21 U.S.C. § 846, based on his alleged role in the conspiracy to distribute OxyContin for no legitimate medical purpose. A second superseding indictment was filed, and the case proceeded to trial. Garrison was tried with four alleged co-conspirators: Elza Budagova, who acted as a medical assistant at the Clinic, and pharmacists Theodore Yoon, Phic Lim, and Perry Tan Nguyen.

An expert testified that there were indications from the Clinic's medical files that the prescriptions from the Clinic were not for a proper medical purpose. Many files had minimal patient histories and in other files the patient histories were virtually identical, indicating that they had been forged. Further, there was expert testimony that immediately prescribing maximum strength OxyContin, as was done at the Clinic, was not a proper medical practice.

At trial, the government offered documentary and testimonial evidence against Garrison. Garrison stipulated that he wrote and signed hundreds of prescriptions for OxyContin with similar diagnoses on the prescription pads of other medical professionals. Garrison also agreed that it was his handwriting on numerous prescriptions for OxyContin that appeared to have been pre-signed by other persons working at the Clinic. He also signed and left blank prescription forms in his own name, apparently for the use of others in making prescriptions to the phony patients.

Recruited patients testified at trial that they had never been examined by anyone at the Clinic, yet their medical files reflected that they had been given an OxyContin prescription in Garrison's handwriting, though on other physicians' prescription pads. There was also video evidence of Garrison prescribing OxyContin to a person posing as a recruited patient after a six minute interaction. A medical expert testified that there was no medical need for that OxyContin prescription.

Garrison also lied to an investigator about the extent of the physician oversight he received at the Clinic—claiming that almost all of his patient examinations were signed off on by a physician, whereas the investigator found that the vast majority of Garrison's examinations were not cosigned by a licensed physician.

Two cooperating witnesses testified against Garrison: Eleanor Santiago and Julie Shishalovsky. Santiago, a former licensed physician, had pled guilty to health care fraud after falsifying Medi-Cal claims while she was working at the Clinic. Santiago testified that the Clinic was a pain management clinic with a focus on people suffering from chronic pain, which meant that many of the patients had already tried to use less intense pain medications.

She testified that Garrison saw patients without her oversight and that Garrison had prescribed OxyContin on a prescription slip that

Santiago had pre-signed. Santiago also testified that Garrison would sometimes give her medical charts to cosign, and that she had noticed that he had prescribed all his patients OxyContin. She told Garrison that some of the patients did not need that drug, but he continued prescribing OxyContin for them anyway.

Shishalovsky worked as a receptionist at the Clinic and testified that the Clinic's operators directed that all of the Clinic's patients should be prescribed the highest strength OxyContin, even when there was no need for OxyContin. She also testified that Garrison completed pre-signed prescriptions "very often," and also pre-signed his own prescriptions.

Garrison made extensive efforts to impeach the credibility of both of these witnesses, stressing that they both had criminal records and had engaged in fraudulent conduct in the past. Garrison did not call any witnesses of his own in his defense. Garrison's main line of defensive argument was that he was not aware of the conspiracy and that he did not knowingly participate in the conspiracy.

* * *

II

When faced with a sufficiency of the evidence challenge, we "must consider the evidence presented at trial in the light most favorable to the prosecution" and then must determine whether the evidence is sufficient to allow "any rational trier of fact to find the essential elements of the crime beyond a reasonable doubt." *United States* v. Nevils, 598 F.3d 1158, 1164 (9th Cir. 2010) (en banc). *Nevils* applied the well-known standard developed by the Supreme Court in *Jackson v. Virginia,* 443 U.S. 307 (1979), which vests in the jury a great deal of leeway in reaching its verdict, and promises that a jury verdict will be sustained when a rational trier of fact, viewing the evidence in the light most favorable to the government, could find all elements of the crime proved beyond a reasonable doubt. Our decision on sufficiency of the evidence is made *de novo*. By contrast, we review for abuse of discretion a district court's decision about what sanction to impose for the untimely disclosure of *Brady* and *Giglio* material.

III

Garrison was charged with conspiracy to distribute OxyContin in violation of 21 U.S.C. § 846 on the grounds that he had distributed OxyContin outside the course of usual medical practice and for no legitimate medical purpose in violation of 21 U.S.C. § 841. "To establish a drug conspiracy, the government must prove (1) an agreement to accomplish an illegal objective; and (2) the intent to commit the underlying offense." Further, to demonstrate the underlying violation of § 841 the government must prove three elements:

(1) that the practitioner distributed controlled substances, (2) that the distribution of those controlled substances was outside the usual course of professional practice and without a legitimate medical purpose, and (3) that the practitioner acted with intent to distribute the drugs and *with intent to distribute them outside the course of professional practice.* United States *v. Feingold*, 454 F.3d 1001, 1008 (9th Cir. 2006). Here, Garrison is not challenging that there was a conspiracy to run a pill mill out of the Clinic; rather, he contends that there was inadequate evidence at trial to demonstrate that he was aware of the conspiracy or knowingly participated in the conspiracy.

We do not consider this to be a close case on sufficiency of evidence. As to the underlying violation, there was expert testimony that Garrison acted outside the scope of usual medical practice and that he participated in distributing OxyContin in an alarmingly high volume and strength for no legitimate medical purpose. Further, Garrison pre-signed prescriptions, filled out pre-signed prescriptions, and wrote OxyContin prescriptions for people neither he nor anyone else at the clinic had ever examined. He also lied to an investigator about his standard practices. Inconsistencies or lying can lead a jury to infer intent. This evidence was sufficient to allow a reasonable jury to draw the inference that Garrison was prescribing OxyContin with the intent to do so for no legitimate medical purpose.

Even though there was no direct evidence that Garrison had entered into an agreement to participate in a drug conspiracy, it is well-established that "a jury may infer the existence of an agreement from circumstantial evidence, such as the defendant's conduct." *United States v. Reed*, 575 F.3d 900, 924 (9th Cir. 2009). There is no dispute here that there was a conspiracy to improperly distribute OxyContin. "[O]nce a conspiracy is established only a slight connection to the conspiracy is necessary to support a conviction," meaning "that a defendant need not have known all the conspirators, participated in the conspiracy from its beginning, participated in all its enterprises, or known all its details." *United States v. Herrera-Gonzalez*, 263 F.3d 1092, 1095 (9th Cir. 2001).

Here, Garrison had much more than a slight connection with the conspiracy. He was a major actor in it. He filled out prescriptions for OxyContin that had been pre-signed by other medical professionals—often repeating similar diagnoses to support those prescriptions—and he pre-signed his own prescription pad, apparently so others could draw prescriptions from it. Coordination like this is "strong circumstantial proof of agreement" in a conspiracy case. Garrison need not have been aware of or participated in the full scope of the scheme—so long as he had agreed to further a portion of its illicit operations by colluding in writing fraudulent prescriptions, he could be convicted. There was sufficient evidence to lead a reasonable jury to conclude that Garrison had agreed to further the scheme run out of the Clinic to illicitly distribute OxyContin.

* * *

We conclude that there was sufficient evidence to sustain Garrison's conviction. We also conclude that there is no error here in the remedies the trial court crafted for the government's late disclosures or in the jury instructions the court gave regarding the abrupt departure of Yoon and Lim, and the dismissal of some charges against Nguyen.

AFFIRMED.

NOTES AND QUESTIONS

1. **Marijuana and the 3-pronged Schedule I test.** Recall that the test for a substance's inclusion under Schedule I of the CSA is three-pronged: (1) the substance must have a high potential for abuse; (2) there must be no medically accepted use for the substance; and (3) the substance must be unsafe even under medical supervision. As noted above, a number of seemingly more dangerous and potentially abusive substances—most notably the prescription opioids—are included under Schedule II of the CSA, and therefore not barred from medical use. Indeed, the country is currently in the grips of an opioid crisis, and yet the opioids (with the notable exception of heroin) are available by prescription and widely used, while marijuana remains strictly prohibited. As one court stated with respect to the opioid crisis:

> The heroin and opioid epidemic is one of the great public health problems of our time. The CDC found that opioids, primarily prescription pain relievers and heroin, are the chief drugs associated with overdose deaths. 2015, the most recent year for which data is available, opioids were involved in 33,091 deaths, more than 63% of all drug overdose deaths. On average, 91 Americans die from opioid overdose every day. Preliminary numbers for 2016 suggested overdose deaths are growing at a rate comparable to the rate of HIV-related deaths at the height of the HIV epidemic. In a November 2016 report, the DEA referred to opioid prescription drugs, heroin, and fentanyl as the most significant drug-related threats to the United States. Indeed opioid overdoses of quadrupled nationally since 1999. According to the CDC, the significant increase in overdose deaths is attributable to synthetic opioids such as heroin and fentanyl.

United States v. Walker, 2017 WL 4225039 (S.D.W.V. 2017). Given the devastating effects of the opioid crisis, many people legitimately wonder how the Justice Department can continue to justify marijuana's inclusion on Schedule I, when it appears to be significantly less dangerous and less addictive than the prescription opioids.

2. **Medical use of marijuana.** Perhaps the strongest argument for keeping marijuana on Schedule I is the second prong of the three-part test referenced above: that marijuana has no currently accepted medical use. However, the reality is that marijuana is currently being used for medical purposes in the majority of states, and in order to use it legally, medical

marijuana patients must obtain the recommendation of a physician. However, opponents of legalization argue that, even if marijuana has *some* medical use, e.g., as a pain reliever, there are better alternatives available, and so marijuana is not needed as a prescription drug. Again, though, this argument seems rather suspect, given that there are numerous prescription drugs available for many different types of ailments (e.g., there are many different types of blood pressure medications), and so it would seem that a similar argument could be made with respect to many drugs currently made available by prescription. Furthermore, even if marijuana is not as efficacious for some uses (e.g., pain relief) as some currently available drugs (e.g., the prescription opioids), its use as an adjunct therapy may still make it quite useful. A 2016 study by researchers at the University of Michigan, for example, concluded that patients who treated chronic pain with marijuana in addition to prescription opioids were able to reduce their use of opioids by 64%. *See* Kevin F. Boehnke, et al., *Medical Cannabis Use Is Associated With Decreased Opiate Medication Use in a Retrospective Cross-Sectional Survey of Patients with Chronic Pain,* 17 J. of Pain 739 (2016).

   3.   **THC Available by Prescription.** Many people are unaware that, while marijuana itself is strictly prohibited as a Schedule I substance, the chief psychoactive component of marijuana, THC, has long been available legally as a prescription drug (e.g., Marinol). In *Seeley v. State of Washington,* 940 P.2d 604 (Wash. 1997), the Washington Supreme Court rejected a state constitutional challenge to this disparate treatment. The court held that the state's Uniform Controlled Substances Act, which tracked the federal CSA and included marijuana within Schedule I, passed the rational-basis test under the Washington Constitution because the respondent had failed to show that the state legislature's decision regarding classification of marijuana was so unrelated to the achievement of legitimate purposes as to render it arbitrary or obsolete. The court found that marijuana, unlike prescription THC, contained over 400 different chemicals and was not amenable to a standardized dosing system, the way prescription THC was. Accordingly, it held, the legislature could reasonably distinguish marijuana from prescription THC. Some proponents of marijuana legalization tend to view decisions such as the one in *Seeley* as little more than pretexts for throwing a bone to the pharmaceutical companies. What do you think?

C. MARIJUANA VS. ALCOHOL AND TOBACCO

   Two legally available substances, alcohol and tobacco, provide a further obvious point of comparison for marijuana. With the exception of the prohibition era in the 1920s, during which time alcohol was illegal to sell, both of these substances have always been legal in the United States, though subject to some significant regulation, as well as to heavy taxation. Currently, both fall within the jurisdiction of the Bureau of Alcohol, Tobacco, and Firearms (ATF), which investigates and prosecutes noncompliant sales of the substances (e.g., bootlegging). In effect, alcohol and tobacco are America's officially sanctioned recreational drugs. For that reason, they arguably provide a fair precedent for legalizing marijuana for recreational use. Advocates of legalization for adult recreational use of marijuana frequently argue that marijuana is a safer substance than either tobacco or alcohol, and that it should receive similar treatment under federal law.

In the following case, *United States v Fry*, the United States Court of Appeals for the 4th Circuit considered an appeal from a conviction for growing and distributing marijuana in violation of the Controlled Substances Act. In doing so, the court rejected the defendant's argument that the equal protection clause of the United States Constitution requires marijuana to be treated the same as alcohol and tobacco under federal law.

UNITED STATES V. FRY

United States Court of Appeals, 4th Circuit
787 F.2d 903 (4th Cir. 1986)

HAYNESWORTH, J.

This is an appeal from Fry's conviction for growing and conspiring to grow and distribute marijuana in violation of 21 U.S.C.A. §§ 841(a) and 846. He contends that the imposition of criminal sanctions upon the production of marijuana is so unreasonable and arbitrary as to be unconstitutional. He also challenges the sufficiency of the evidence that the plants he grew were marijuana plants.

We find no merit in either argument, though, at the defendant's request, we withheld decision to permit him to file a long supplemental brief in further support of the constitutional claims. We have carefully considered that brief, as well as the briefs filed by counsel and oral argument.

I.

After an aerial survey of Monroe County, West Virginia, State Trooper Coburn seized and destroyed 36 suspected marijuana plants on Fry's land and 3600 suspected marijuana plants on land owned by Ernie Aguilar. None of the plants were subjected to chemical analysis before their destruction.

In Fry's indictment, Aguilar and Tom Curran were named as unindicted co-conspirators. Aguilar was charged with growing marijuana, and was sentenced to three years imprisonment upon his plea of guilty. After Curran had been granted use immunity, he and Aguilar testified against Fry at Fry's trial. Fry was found guilty on both the conspiracy and the production counts and sentenced to five years in prison.

II.

Fry contends that the imposition of criminal penalties for the production and distribution of marijuana is so irrational and arbitrary that it violates the due process and equal protection clauses of the Fifth Amendment and his Ninth Amendment "liberty" right to be free of "gross arbitrary control" in his pursuit of happiness.

Fry claims that the Ninth Amendment guarantees him freedom to "recreate" through altering his consciousness. It is a fundamental right, he says, the exercise of which can be restricted or denied only upon a compelling governmental interest.

Of course, there are limitations upon governmental regulation of private lives and upon activity in the privacy of one's home, but Fry does not stand convicted of "private" activity. He stands convicted of participation in a conspiracy to manufacture and distribute a large quantity of marijuana and not for simple possession or use of a small quantity of the drug. *See* 21 U.S.C.A. § 844(a). Fry was convicted of commercial activity. There is no fundamental right to produce or distribute marijuana commercially.

The congressional decision to impose criminal penalties upon these activities must be upheld unless it bears no rational relation to a legitimate governmental purpose.

Fry and the government have produced masses of conflicting medical and scientific data bearing upon the harmfulness of marijuana. We, however, do not sit as a "superlegislature to judge the wisdom or desirability of legislative policy determinations." *New Orleans v. Dukes,* 427 U.S. 297, 303 (1976). Congress made such a legislative determination when it imposed criminal sanctions upon the commercial production and distribution of marijuana. We must defer to that determination. Upon the conflicting evidence, we cannot agree that the congressional decision to prohibit marijuana production and distribution was so irrational as to deprive Fry of due process.

It is also contended that since alcohol and tobacco are legal substances, the prohibition of the production and distribution of marijuana is so arbitrary as to amount to a deprivation of equal protection. Whatever the harmful effects of alcohol and tobacco, however, Congress is not required to attempt to eradicate all similar evils. *See Williamson v. Lee Optical Co.,* 348 U.S. 483, 489 (1955). It is for Congress to weigh the conflicting considerations and determine the necessity and appropriateness of prohibiting trafficking in a dangerous substance, and it may conclude that prohibition of the trafficking in one such substance is appropriate though trafficking in another is left untouched. In holding that the challenged statutes are constitutional, we join those other courts of appeals which uniformly have rejected constitutional challenges to them.

* * *

IV

We find no infirmity in the conviction.

AFFIRMED.

NOTES AND QUESTIONS

1.   **Public policy considerations.** The court in *Fry* rejected the defendant's equal protection challenge, holding that he was not disadvantaged vis a vis alcohol and tobacco users: "[w]hatever harmful effects of alcohol tobacco, however, Congress is not required to attempt to eradicate all similar evils." The court further held that it was within Congress's discretion to allow trafficking in one dangerous substance while leaving trafficking in another dangerous substance untouched. The court did not, however, offer a detailed equal protection analysis; instead, it merely cited to a number of other federal authorities. Constitutional analysis aside, do you think as a matter of public policy that it makes sense to allow alcohol and tobacco to be used legally, while strictly prohibiting marijuana use?

2.   **Regulating marijuana similar to alcohol and tobacco.** If marijuana were to be treated similarly to alcohol and tobacco, what do you think regulation at the federal level would look like? Would marijuana be subject to the jurisdiction of the ATF, the way the other two substances are? Would it be restricted to adult-use only, the way the other two substances are? Would public use be allowed, as it is for alcohol and tobacco, subject to age and other limitations? How else should marijuana be regulated if Congress removes it from the CSA?

3.   **The relative dangers of marijuana vs. alcohol and tobacco.** Many proponents of legalization argue that marijuana is less dangerous than alcohol or tobacco, and therefore, should not be treated in a harsher manner. Considering the significant detrimental health consequences of alcohol and tobacco, that is not an unreasonable position. In terms of health consequences, marijuana, while not benign, does appear to be a somewhat less dangerous drug than either tobacco or alcohol, considering the huge burden tobacco and alcohol impose on public health. As for tobacco, its deleterious health effects are well-documented. Ever since the United States Surgeon General's Office issued its first health advisory for tobacco smoking in 1964, the evidence of tobacco's damaging effects has become increasingly clear. According to the Center for Disease Control, cigarette smoking affects nearly every organ of the body and causes many diseases. It accounts for almost 20% of all deaths each year in the United States. On average, smokers die 10 years earlier than non-smokers. Smoking causes approximately one third of all cancers, including lung cancer and cancers of the digestive tract, among others. In addition, smoking causes heart disease, stroke, and COPD, and contributes to a variety of other health problems, such as diabetes. For every person who dies from smoking, moreover, another 30 people live with serious smoking-related illnesses. Furthermore, the health consequences of smoking are not limited to the smoker; secondhand smoke inflicts a number of these health problems on

non-smokers as well. Thus, tobacco use is considered the leading preventable cause of death in the United States. As for alcohol, it too is responsible for a number of serious health problems. According to the Center for Disease Control, alcohol causes approximately one in 10 deaths in the United States among adults between the ages of 20 and 64, and it shortens the lives of those people by an average of 30 years. Excessive alcohol consumption causes liver disease, heart disease and strokes, certain cancers, memory problems and dementia, and mental health problems, and contributes to a variety of other health problems. Alcohol is also highly addictive, and therefore alcohol dependence is also a significant health problem.

PROBLEM 19-1

Which of the following drugs are on Schedule I of the CSA, and therefore deemed to have no accepted medical use in the United States?

- Cocaine
- Ecstasy (MDMA)
- Peyote
- Anabolic steroids
- Methamphetamine

Check your results by looking at the DEA's list in section A above. Are you surprised by the government's classifications as to any of these substances?

PROBLEM 19-2

If a substance is not listed on Schedule I, is it necessarily the case that a licensed medical doctor can legally prescribe it to a patient? If not, why not?

CHAPTER 20

SOCIAL ISSUES PERTAINING
TO MARIJUANA LAW

■ ■ ■

Marijuana law intersects with social and public policy issues in a number of ways. In this chapter we explore several of the most important ones. Section A looks at the ways marijuana legalization may affect family law determinations. Section B explores the public policy issues associated with impaired driving due to marijuana consumption. Section C focuses on how enforcement of marijuana laws has had a disparate racial impact. Section D examines the social problem of addiction and abuse in light of marijuana use in a marital context. And Section E looks at how legalization of marijuana for adult use might create the unintended consequence of adolescent use.

A. FAMILY LAW ISSUES

Marijuana law's impact on family law is somewhat tangential, since marijuana use *per se* by a parent or spouse is rarely a decisive factor in family law determinations. Nevertheless, courts do take marijuana use into account in making child custody and marital fault determinations, where such use is extreme, or where it is shown to affect the well-being of the child. In the following case, for example, the Michigan Court of Appeals of Michigan considered whether the trial court properly terminated the father's parental rights, based in part upon his use of medical marijuana pursuant to Michigan's Medical Marijuana Act. The court interpreted an important provision in the Act in holding that the trial court abused its discretion in terminating the father's parental rights.

IN RE T.L. FOWLER, MINOR
Court of Appeals of Michigan
2016 WL 6106486 (Mich. App. 2016)

MURRAY, CAVANAGH, and WILDER, JJ.

PER CURIAM.

Respondent father appeals as of right an order terminating his parental rights to the minor child, TLF, under MCL 712A.19b(3)(c)(*i*)(conditions that led to adjudication continue to exist), (g) (failure to provide proper care or custody), and (j) (reasonable likelihood, based on conduct or capacity of custodian, that child will be harmed if returned home). For the reasons stated below, we reverse the trial court's order terminating respondent's parental rights and remand for further proceedings consistent with this opinion.

* * *

Next, respondent argues that the trial court erred in finding that sufficient evidence established statutory grounds for termination. We agree.

"This Court reviews for clear error the trial court's factual findings and ultimate determinations on the statutory grounds for termination." *In re White*, 303 Mich.App 701, 709 (2014). A trial court's findings of fact are clearly erroneous if "we are definitely and firmly convinced that it made a mistake." *Id.* at 709–710.

Natural parents have a fundamental liberty interest in the "care, custody, and control of their children." *In re Beck*, 488 Mich. 6, 11 (2010). If termination of parental rights is pursued, the petitioner bears the burden of showing that the allegations establish a statutory basis for termination by clear and convincing evidence. *In re Hudson*, 294 Mich.App 261, 264; 817 NW2d 115 (2011). "Evidence is clear and convincing when it 'produce[s] in the mind of the trier of fact a firm belief or conviction as to the truth of the allegations sought to be established, evidence so clear, direct and weighty and convincing as to enable [the factfinder] to come to a clear conviction, without hesitancy, of the truth of the precise facts in issue.' " *In re Martin*, 450 Mich. 204, 227 (1995). "Only one statutory ground for termination need be established." *In re Olive/Metts*, 297 Mich.App 35, 41 (2012). If the court finds that there are grounds for termination, and that termination is in the child's best interests, the court must order termination of parental rights. *In re Beck*, 488 Mich. at 11, quoting MCL 712A.19b(5).

Respondent's parental rights were terminated pursuant to MCL 712A.19b(3)(c)(*i*), (g), and (j). Under MCL 712A.19b(3)(c)(*i*), a court may terminate a respondent's parental rights if "182 or more days have elapsed since the issuance of an initial dispositional order," and there is clear and convincing evidence that "[t]he conditions that led to the adjudication continue to exist and there is no reasonable likelihood that the conditions will be rectified within a reasonable time considering the child's age." A reasonable time to correct such conditions is determined by considering both the period needed for the parent to rectify the conditions and the period the child can wait. This Court has held that termination was proper under MCL 712A.19b(3)(c)(*i*) where "the totality of the evidence amply support[ed] that [the respondent] had not accomplished any meaningful change in the conditions" that led to adjudication. *In re Williams*, 286 Mich.App 253, 272; 779 NW2d 286 (2009). In this case, clear and convincing evidence did not support the termination of respondent's parental rights under MCL 712A.19b(3)(c)(*i*) because the conditions that led to adjudication, and that could justify termination, did not continue to exist at the time of termination. * * *

The last condition that led to adjudication was respondent's marijuana use, which indisputably continued to exist at the time of termination. However, Michigan's Medical Marihuana Act (MMMA), *MCL 333.26371 et seq.,* addresses parental rights when the parent holds a valid medical marijuana card, and provides, in relevant part:

> A person shall not be denied custody or visitation of a minor for acting in accordance with this act, unless the person's behavior is such that it creates an unreasonable danger to the minor that can be clearly articulated and substantiated. [MCL 333.26424(c).]

Respondent had a medical marijuana card at the time of termination, which means that his use of marijuana, in accordance with the MMMA, could not be grounds for termination unless his marijuana use created a clearly articulated and substantiated unreasonable danger to TLF. See MCL 333.26424(c).

Martin [the Child Protective Services worker] claimed that respondent's marijuana use presented a risk of harm to TLF "[b]ecause you don't know how marijuana will affect the body and it is a [sic] illegal substance and not knowing how it affects the brain." Petitioner asserted that respondent's marijuana use presented a risk of danger to TLF because "you never know what's gonna [sic] happen when you have a parent who's using illegal substances around the child . . . and when you're using illegal substances usually that's a criminal act in itself, of course, . . . [and] the people that you're associating yourself with when you have to purchase those illegal substances . . . that presents another—another risk of harm . . . [and] [t]here's just unsavory people who are involved in the drug dealing business." Similarly, the guardian ad litem asserted that respondent's marijuana use presented a risk of danger to TLF because "if you're hanging with those, playing games who are using drugs . . . that puts this child at risk." However, these general allegations did not rise to the level of "clearly articulated and substantiated unreasonable danger." Further, the trial court did not even make a specific finding related to the unreasonable danger respondent's marijuana use may have presented to TLF. Thus, while this condition that led to adjudication continued to exist at the time of termination, respondent was legally permitted to use medical marijuana, and the trial court failed to make the particularized finding necessary to justify termination of respondent's parental rights on that basis.

Accordingly, the inadequate housing and income conditions that led to adjudication did not continue to exist at the time of termination, and the record did not support a finding that clear and convincing evidence established that there was no reasonable likelihood that those conditions would be rectified within a reasonable time considering TLF's age. Further, because respondent obtained a medical marijuana license, and because the trial court failed to make a specific finding demonstrating that respondent's marijuana use created a clearly articulated and substantiated unreasonable danger to TLF, the trial court erred in finding termination was proper under MCL 712A.19b(3)(c)(*i*).

Termination of parental rights is proper under MCL 712A.19b(3)(g) where "[t]he parent, without regard to intent, fails to provide proper care or custody for the child and there is no reasonable expectation that the parent will be able to provide proper care and custody within a reasonable time considering the child's age." A parent's failure to obtain and maintain suitable housing can be grounds for termination under MCL 712A.19b(3)(g). Clear and convincing evidence also did not support the termination of respondent's parental rights under MCL 712A.19b(3)(g). The trial court found termination was proper under this subsection "based on the fact that [respondent] [is] still using substances that presents a substantial risk of harm to [ ] the child and . . . [t]here's no expectation that that's going to be taken care of in a reasonable time" as respondent had not demonstrated "any sobriety." However, as discussed above, respondent's medical marijuana use could not justify termination without the required particularized finding that his marijuana use created a clearly articulated and substantiated unreasonable danger to TLF.

* * *

In sum, the trial court clearly erred by finding that termination was proper under MCL 712A.19b(3)(c)(*i*), because respondent obtained employment and adequate housing and because respondent's marijuana use could not justify termination absent a specific finding by the trial court that his marijuana use created a clearly articulated and substantiated unreasonable danger to TLF. The trial court also clearly erred by finding termination was proper under MCL 712A.19b(3)(g), as respondent obtained employment, obtained appropriate housing, complied with his parent-agency agreement, and there was no independent basis for the trial court to conclude that respondent would be unable to provide proper care and custody to TLF within a reasonable time. Last, because the record does not provide any basis from which to conclude that TLF would be harmed if she was returned to respondent, the trial court erred when it determined that termination was proper under MCL 712A.19b(3)(j).

Finally, respondent argues that the trial court erred in finding by a preponderance of the evidence that termination of his parental rights was in the best interests of the child. Because the trial court erred by concluding that any of the statutory bases for termination were proved, we need not review the court's best interests determination.

Reversed and remanded for further proceedings consistent with this opinion. We do not retain jurisdiction.

NOTES AND QUESTIONS

1. Statutory requirement in Michigan. The court in *Fowler* based its decision on the trial court's failure to make a specific evidentiary finding that the father's medical marijuana use "created a clearly articulated and substantiated unreasonable danger" to the child. Why did the court deem such a finding necessary, rather than just weighing the father's medical marijuana use as one factor to consider in determining the best interests of the child?

2. Statutory protections generally. At least one commentator has argued that statutory protections for medical marijuana patients of the kind found in the Michigan Medical Marijuana Act (which requires a showing of "unreasonable danger" due to a parent's marijuana use) are important to prevent discrimination against medical marijuana patients. *See,* Alice Kwak, *Medical Marijuana and Child Custody: The Need to Protect Patients and Their Families from Discrimination*, 28 Hastings Women's L. Rev. 119, 137 (2017) ("Such anti-custody discrimination provisions are important to include in all medical marijuana statutes because the result of a child custody case involving medical marijuana largely depends on whether the people involved, Child Protective Services ["CPS"], judges, and attorneys have biases against parents who use marijuana, even for medical purposes.").

3. States without statutory protections. But even in states whose medical marijuana acts are silent with respect to the effect of marijuana use on parental rights, courts have generally adopted rules similar to the statutory rule that *Fowler* applies. Thus, they tend to take a parent's marijuana use into account for purposes of child custody only if such use demonstrably affects the well-being of the child. For example, in *Barton v. Hirshberg*, 767 A.2d 874 (Md. Ct. Spec. App. 2001), the Maryland Court of Special Appeals upheld the trial court's award of joint legal custody, finding that the father's illegal marijuana use did not automatically disqualify him as a fit parent. On the other hand, if the evidence establishes that a parent's marijuana use *does* affect the best interests of the child, the courts will take it into account. *See, e.g., Co v. Matson*, 313 P.3d 521 (Alaska 2013) (upholding an award of sole custody to the mother based in part on the court's evidentiary finding that the father's marijuana use negatively affected the emotional well-being of the children).

4. Divorce. In the majority of states, marijuana use does not per se affect a married person's right to get divorced, since most states allow only no-fault divorces. In the minority of states that still allow a spouse to file for a divorce based upon the other spouse's fault (which may affect considerations such as alimony), marijuana use, and illegal drug use generally, may enter into the fault determination. For example, in *Carambat v. Carambat,* 72 So.3d 505 (Miss. 2011) (which is set out and discussed in Section D below), the Mississippi Supreme Court upheld a divorce decree for fault based on the husband's marijuana use. The court found that the evidence supported a finding that the husband's long-time marijuana use was grounds for the divorce under a statutory factor set out in Mississippi Code § 93–5–1 (Rev.2004), which lists "habitual and excessive use of opium, morphine, or other like drug" as a statutory ground for divorce. The court held that marijuana counted as "other like drug" within the meaning of the statute.

PROBLEM 20-1

Husband and Wife live in State X, a medical marijuana state. They are involved in a child custody battle in family court. State X's medical marijuana act does not address child custody. Wife claims that she should receive full legal and physical custody because exposing the children to Husband's medical marijuana use is not in their best interests. Husband has a valid medical marijuana license in state X. He smokes marijuana twice per day to treat chronic pain. He does not smoke in the house, but only in their unattached garage. He does not smoke in the presence of the children. He also keeps his supply of marijuana locked in a drawer that is inaccessible to the children. Nevertheless, Wife claims that Husband's consumption of marijuana is harmful to the children because it causes him to be emotionally detached and interferes with his ability to care properly for the children's needs. Will Wife prevail in her effort to acquire full custody?

B. PREVENTING IMPAIRED DRIVING

Every state that has legalized medical or recreational marijuana has had to grapple with important question of how to prevent impaired driving resulting from marijuana consumption. For one thing, preventing impaired driving was one of the eight priorities set out in the Obama administration's Cole Memo, which set the conditions states had to comply with to prevent federal interference with their legalization schemes. Different states have taken different approaches in their attempts to prevent impaired driving due to marijuana and other drugs. Some states have adopted a "zero tolerance" approach, according to which, impairment is presumed if the driver has any amount of a controlled substance in the driver's body at the time of arrest. Arizona is one such state.

In the following case, *Dobson v. McClennen*, the Arizona Supreme Court considered the interpretation of Arizona's impaired driving statute in light of the Arizona Medical Marijuana Act. And while it upheld the defendant's conviction for impaired driving, it also found that there is an affirmative defense to the statute for those medical marijuana patients who can show, by a preponderance of the evidence, that the concentration of marijuana or its impairing metabolite in their bodies was insufficient to cause impairment.

DOBSON V. MCCLENNEN

Supreme Court of Arizona
238 Ariz. 389 (2015)

BALES, C.J.

The Arizona Medical Marijuana Act ("AMMA"), passed by voters in 2010 and codified as A.R.S. §§ 36–2801–2819, allows a person who has been diagnosed by a physician as having a debilitating medical condition to apply for a card identifying the holder as a registered qualifying patient. Such patients may possess and use limited amounts of marijuana for medical reasons. The AMMA broadly immunizes them from prosecution for using medical marijuana consistent with the Act.

Arizona's laws generally make it a crime for a person to drive with any amount of certain drugs, including marijuana or its impairing metabolite, in the person's body. A.R.S. § 28–1381(A)(3). We today hold that the AMMA does not immunize a medical marijuana cardholder from prosecution under § 28–1381(A)(3), but instead affords an affirmative defense if the cardholder shows that the marijuana or its metabolite was in a concentration insufficient to cause impairment.

I.

Kristina Dobson and Marvelle Anderson ("Petitioners") were each charged with two counts of driving under the influence ("DUI"). Count one alleged a violation of A.R.S. § 28–1381(A)(1), which prohibits a person from driving a vehicle in Arizona "[w]hile under the influence of . . . any drug . . . if the person is impaired to the slightest degree." Count two alleged a violation of § 28–1381(A)(3), which prohibits driving a vehicle "[w]hile there is any drug defined in § 13–3401 or its metabolite in the person's body." Cannabis (marijuana) is a drug defined in A.R.S. § 13–3401(4). Blood tests showed that each Petitioner had marijuana and its impairing metabolite in his or her body.

The municipal court denied Dobson's motion to present evidence at trial that she held an Oregon-issued medical marijuana card and granted the State's motion in limine to preclude evidence that Anderson held an Arizona-issued medical marijuana card. Neither Petitioner sought to introduce any evidence other than their respective medical marijuana cards. The State dismissed the (A)(1) charges and Petitioners, after submitting the issue of guilt to the court based on a stipulated record, were each convicted of the (A)(3) charge.

Petitioners timely appealed to the Maricopa County Superior Court, which affirmed their convictions. They then sought special action review in the court of appeals, which accepted jurisdiction but denied relief. The court of appeals held that "neither A.R.S. § 36–2811(B) nor § 36–2802(D) provides immunity for defendants facing charges for driving with an impermissible drug or impairing metabolite in their bodies under A.R.S. § 28–1381(A)(3)."

We granted review because whether the AMMA immunizes a medical marijuana cardholder from DUI prosecution under § 28–1381(A)(3) presents a recurring issue of statewide importance. We have jurisdiction under Article 6, Section 5(3) of the Arizona Constitution and A.R.S. § 12–120.24.

II.

We review questions of statutory interpretation de novo. A reviewing court's "primary objective in construing statutes adopted by initiative is to give effect to the intent of the electorate." *State v. Gomez,* 212 Ariz. 55, 57 (2006). "When two statutes conflict, we adopt a construction that reconciles them whenever possible, giving force and meaning to each." *State v. Jones,* 235 Ariz. 501, 502 (2014).

A.

The AMMA broadly immunizes registered qualifying patients for their medical use of marijuana, providing:

> A registered qualifying patient . . . is not subject to arrest, prosecution or penalty in any manner, or denial of any right or privilege, including any civil penalty or disciplinary action by a court or occupational or professional licensing board or bureau: (1) For the registered qualifying patient's medical use of marijuana pursuant to this chapter, if the registered qualifying patient does not possess more than the allowable amount of marijuana.

A.R.S. § 36–2811(B)(1).

This grant of immunity is not absolute. For instance, the AMMA does not prohibit prosecution for "[o]perating, navigating or being in actual physical control of any motor vehicle, aircraft or motorboat while under the influence of marijuana." A.R.S. § 36–2802(D). However, "a registered qualifying patient shall not be considered to be under the influence of marijuana solely because of the presence of metabolites or components of marijuana that appear in insufficient concentration to cause impairment." *Id.*

Arizona's DUI laws identify separate offenses for driving while a person is under the influence of marijuana and "impaired to the slightest degree," A.R.S. § 28–1381(A)(1), and driving while there is marijuana or its metabolite "in the person's body." § 28–1381(A)(3). An (A)(3) violation, unlike an (A)(1) violation, does not require the state to prove that the defendant was in fact impaired while driving or in control of a vehicle. Instead, marijuana users "violate (A)(3) if they are discovered with any amount of THC or an impairing metabolite in their body." *Id.*

The (A)(1) and (A)(3) offenses also differ with respect to possible defenses. When the state charges a person with driving while impaired by drugs in violation of (A)(1), "[i]t is not a defense . . . that the person is or has been entitled to use drugs under the laws of this state." § 28–1381(B). In contrast, a person cannot be convicted under (A)(3) for using a drug as prescribed by a licensed medical practitioner. A.R.S. § 28–1381(D). Subsection (D) thus provides an affirmative defense to an (A)(3) charge.

In *Harris,* we held that "[d]rivers cannot be convicted of the (A)(3) offense based merely on the presence of a non-impairing metabolite that may reflect the prior usage of marijuana." 322 P.3d at 164. Although we observed that "a driver who tests positive for any amount of an impairing drug is legally and irrefutably presumed to be under the influence," 322 P.3d at 164, in *Harris* we did not consider the scope of the subsection (D) affirmative defense. Nor did that case involve a driver who was a qualified registered patient.

Here, we must resolve how the AMMA affects (A)(3) prosecutions. The State argues that the AMMA, which provides that a registered card holder cannot be considered to be under the influence of marijuana if it is present in an "insufficient concentration to cause impairment," § 36–2802(D), does not affect (A)(3) prosecutions at all because the State is not required to prove a defendant's impairment to establish an (A)(3) violation. Dobson and Anderson counter that the AMMA immunizes them from an (A)(3) prosecution because they cannot be considered to be under the influence based solely on the mere presence of marijuana or its metabolite in their bodies. They also contend that the affirmative defense afforded by § 28–1381(D) applies to them.

Neither position urged by the parties represents the best reading of the statutory provisions. The State's view effectively renders superfluous the "shall not be considered to be under the influence" clause in A.R.S. § 36–2802(D). This language would be unnecessary if it only prohibited prosecution under statutes, such as § 28–1381(A)(1), that require the state to prove that the defendant is in fact impaired as a result of the presence of marijuana or its metabolite. Section 36–2802(D) is more plausibly interpreted as applying to statutes like § 28–1381(A)(3), which, as we noted in *Harris,* presume that a defendant is impaired based on the mere presence of any amount of marijuana or its potentially impairing metabolites in a person's body.

Petitioners, however, are also not convincing in arguing that § 36–2802(D) immunizes registered qualifying patients from *any* prosecution under § 28–1381(A)(3). Section 36–2802(D) does not say that registered qualifying patients cannot be prosecuted for (A)(3) violations. Instead, it provides that such patients, who use marijuana "as authorized" by the AMMA, *id.* § 36–2802(E), cannot "be considered to be under the influence of marijuana *solely* because of the presence of metabolites or components of marijuana that appear in insufficient concentration to cause impairment." *Id.* § 36–2802(D) (emphasis added).

Violations of § 28–1381(A)(3) include, but are not limited to, situations in which drivers have a non-impairing amount of certain drugs in their bodies. This reflects that the legislature, in seeking to combat the serious problem of impaired driving, recognized that for certain drugs it may be difficult to identify concentrations that definitively establish whether a defendant is impaired. *Harris,* 234 Ariz. at 347; *cf.* A.R.S. § 28–1381(A)(2) (proscribing driving with an alcohol concentration of .08 or more irrespective of proof of actual impairment). Thus, the (A)(3) offense does not require the state to prove that the defendant is in fact impaired "to the slightest degree," § 28–1381(A)(1), but instead requires the state to prove that the defendant has been driving or in control of a vehicle while any amount of the proscribed drugs or their impairing metabolites are present "in the person's body." *Id.* 28–1381(A)(3).

Section (A)(3) thus casts a net that embraces drivers who have proscribed drugs or their impairing metabolites in their bodies but who may or may not be impaired. By its terms, § 36–2802(D) does not shield registered qualifying patients from prosecution under (A)(3), but instead says they cannot be considered to be "under the influence" based solely on concentrations of marijuana or its metabolites that are insufficient to cause impairment. When read together, the statutory provisions suggest that the AMMA gives qualifying patients a limited defense rather than a general immunity in (A)(3) prosecutions.

We reject, however, Petitioners' argument that qualifying patients can rely on the defense afforded by § 28–1381(D) for the use of prescribed drugs. Medical marijuana used pursuant to "written certifications" under the AMMA is not "prescribed," and the § 28–1381(D) defense applies to drugs prescribed by a different class of licensed "medical providers" than those who may issue medical marijuana certifications.

Section 36–2802(D), rather than § 28–1381(D), defines the affirmative defense available to a registered qualifying patient to an (A)(3) charge. If their use of marijuana is authorized by § 36–2802(D), such patients cannot be deemed to be under the influence—and thus cannot be convicted under (A)(3)—based solely on concentrations of marijuana or its metabolite insufficient to cause impairment. Possession of a registry card creates a presumption that a qualifying patient is engaged in the use of marijuana pursuant to the AMMA, so long as the patient does not possess more than the permitted quantity of marijuana. That presumption is subject to rebuttal as provided under § 36–2811(A)(2).

A qualifying patient may be convicted of an (A)(3) violation if the state proves beyond a reasonable doubt that the patient, while driving or in control of a vehicle, had marijuana or its impairing metabolite in the patient's body. The patient may establish an affirmative defense to such a charge by showing that his or her use was authorized by the AMMA—which is subject to the rebuttable presumption under § 36–2811(A)(2)—and that the marijuana or its metabolite was in a concentration insufficient to cause impairment. The patient bears the burden of proof on the latter point by a preponderance of the evidence, as with other affirmative defenses.

Petitioners contend that it is inappropriate to assign to qualifying patients the burden of showing that they did not have marijuana concentrations sufficient to cause impairment because there is no commonly accepted threshold for identifying such concentrations. This contention, however, argues in favor of assigning the burden to patients to prove, by a preponderance, that the marijuana concentration in their bodies while they were driving was not sufficient to cause impairment. The risk of uncertainty in this regard should fall on the patients, who generally know or should know if they are impaired and can control when they drive, rather than on the members of the public whom they encounter on our streets.

B.

Petitioners made no effort to show that the marijuana in their bodies was in an insufficient concentration to cause impairment. Instead, they argued that the AMMA categorically barred the (A)(3) charge, and they offered only their respective registry identification cards into evidence. Although evidence of possession of a registry card would generally be admissible in an (A)(3) prosecution to invoke the presumption that the patient was using marijuana pursuant to the AMMA, it does not suffice to establish the § 36–2802(D)affirmative defense. Any error by the trial court in excluding evidence of the registry cards was harmless in light of the stipulations by Petitioners that they had marijuana in their bodies while driving (blood tests revealed both THC and its impairing metabolite hydroxy-THC) and their failure to offer any evidence that the concentrations were insufficient to cause impairment.

III.

Rather than shielding registered qualifying patients from any prosecution under A.R.S. § 28–1381(A)(3), the AMMA affords an affirmative defense for those patients who can show, by a preponderance of the evidence, that the concentration of marijuana or its impairing metabolite in their bodies was insufficient to cause impairment. We vacate the opinion of the court of appeals and affirm the Petitioners' convictions.

NOTES AND QUESTIONS

1.   **Affirmative defense.** The court in *Dobson* holds that there is an affirmative defense to A.R.S. § 28–1381, Arizona's impaired driving statute, which applies to licensed medical marijuana patients who can show that the

concentration of marijuana in their bodies was insufficient to cause impairment. Contrast this with § D of statute, which exempts prescription drug users from the zero-tolerance prong of the statute, meaning that prescription drug users violate § 28–1381 only if they demonstrate actual impairment, though such impairment need only be slight. Why do you suppose the court did not just take this approach with licensed medical marijuana users, bringing them within the scope of § D? Are the two approaches substantively different?

2.   **Different state approaches.** While every state statute dealing with impaired driving due to marijuana and other illegal drugs is a little different, there are three main approaches that the states have followed. The traditional approach relies on observational evidence about whether the driver is impaired, employing various physical and cognitive tests (for example, whether the driver had slurred speech, could recite the alphabet, etc.) to make the determination. A second approach, as discussed above in *Dobson,* is a zero tolerance policy, whereby the drivers are presumed to be impaired if any amount of a controlled substance is detected in the driver's body, regardless of whether the driver was actually impaired while driving the vehicle. The third main approach relies on *per se* limits with regard to prohibited substances such as marijuana. This approach is similar to the approach most states use to test for drunk driving. It establishes low-level percentages for impairing substances, above which a drivers is presumed to be impaired. For example, Washington and Colorado both impose limits of 5 ng/ml of THC in the blood, although they differ in their enforcement of this limit. In Washington, the law presumes a driver is impaired if operating at or above this limit; in Colorado, by contrast, the jury is merely allowed to draw an inference of impairment. There are advantages and disadvantages to each of these approaches, and a number of states, such as Arizona, employ more than one approach. Unfortunately, however, testing for impairment due to drugs is more challenging than testing for impairment due to alcohol for several reasons, one of which is that particular blood-alcohol levels track impairment in drivers who have consumed alcohol much more accurately than they do in drivers who have consumed marijuana or other drugs.

3.   **Future possibilities.** To date, the states have not come up with very satisfactory solutions to the problem of impaired driving due to marijuana and other drugs. Meanwhile, researchers are trying to develop more accurate tests, looking for specific chemical markers that can more precisely identify impairment. The ideal for detecting impairment would be a noninvasive roadside test that could be easily administered on the road by police officers, in the same way breathalyzers are employed to detect drunk driving. Challenges remain, however, particularly in light of the numerous different ways THC can be consumed, from smoking to edibles to pills.

C. RACIAL DISPARITY

Marijuana prohibition has long been tied to racism in the United States. For example, when western states in the first decades of the twentieth century passed the first laws prohibiting marijuana, several legislatures framed the debate in explicitly anti-Mexican terms. In the 1930s and 1940s, marijuana gained additional opprobrium from its supposed link to African American jazz musicians. And in recent decades, attention has focused on racial disparities arising in the context of law enforcement. Several studies have shed light on racial disparities in marijuana law and their effect on prosecutorial discretion. A summary of these studies is set out below.

1) *The War* on *Marijuana in Black and White: Billions of Dollars Wasted on Racially Biased Arrests.* (ACLU Foundation 2013). Available at https://www.aclu.org/report/report-war-marijuana-black-and-white.

This comprehensive and much publicized report from the American Civil Liberties Union (ACLU) purports to demonstrate the racial disparities that run throughout marijuana law. The report analyzed marijuana arrests throughout the United States between 2001 and 2010. Its chief finding was that in the most recent year analyzed, black individuals were 3.73 times more likely to be arrested than white individuals for marijuana possession, despite comparable use rates of whites and blacks, reflecting racial disparity in enforcement of marijuana prohibitions.

This 185-page report analyzed marijuana possession arrest rates from 2001 to 2010 for all 50 states and the District of Columbia, gathered from the Uniform Crime Reports (UCR) official data, published by the Federal Bureau of Investigation (FBI), and from the U.S. Census Bureau annual county population estimates. Of the 8,244,943 marijuana arrests in the United States between 2001 and 2010, 88% (7,295,880) were for possession. In the entire decade, arrests were heavily skewed against minority populations. For example, in 2010, the arrest rate of blacks for marijuana possession was 716 per 100,000 compared to an arrest rate of whites of 192 per 100,000, an arrest rate 3.73 times higher. This disparity exists despite roughly equal rates of marijuana use and non-use as demonstrated in statistics (figures 21–23, pp. 66–67), drawn from the National Survey on Drug Use and Health, 2001–2010. The Report concludes that this differential, largely uniform throughout the United States, reflects enforcement of marijuana laws "selectively against Black people and communities" and thus the government's "War on Marijuana has largely been a war on people of color" (p. 9).

2) Steven Bender, *The Colors of Cannabis: Race and Marijuana*, 50 U.C. Davis L. Rev. 689 (2016).

In this article, the author argues that "marijuana use by youth of color has been the focal point of the War on Drugs from its inception." The author traces the linkage of marijuana enforcement to race, from the anti-Mexican campaigns of the early 1900s, through the state decriminalization campaigns of the late 1960s and early 1970s, which lessened sentences as white, middle class youth discovered marijuana, to the continuing racial inequity in marijuana arrests of African American and Latino youth. According to the author, marijuana law, both in prohibition states and legalized states, reflects pervasive discrimination against people of color. For example, the collateral consequences of marijuana convictions, such as deportation, falls more heavily on Latino communities. Other consequences of marijuana convictions that have a disproportionate impact on racial minorities include student loan ineligibility, NCAA drug testing suspensions, denials of federally subsidized housing and state financial subsidies. The author points out that even under legalization, disparities remain. For example, the typical regulatory requirements that marijuana retailers boast a clean criminal record can exclude a disproportionate number of minority entrepreneurs from booming marijuana commerce.

3) *Marijuana, Fairness and Public Safety: A Report on the Legalization of Recreational Marijuana in the United States* (Office of Manhattan District Attorney, May 2018) available at https://www.manhattanda.org/wp-content/uploads/2018/05/DANY-Report-on-the-Legalization-of-Recreational-Marijuana-Final.pdf.

In this report, the Office of the Manhattan District Attorney, one of the nation's most influential prosecutor's office, concluded on the basis of arrest records, that "black and Hispanic individuals in low-income neighborhoods of color continue to be arrested for marijuana offenses at much higher rates than their similarly situated counterparts in predominantly white communities." For example, "in 2017, 16,925 people in New York City were arrested on the charge of Criminal Possession of Marihuana in the Fifth Degree. Of that total, 86 percent were people of color: 48 percent were black, 38 percent were Hispanic, and 9 percent were white." Largely as a result of these statistics, the Manhattan District Attorney announced that as of August 1, 2018, his office would no longer prosecute people arrested for smoking or possessing small amounts of marijuana.

NOTES AND QUESTIONS

1.   **Neutral laws?** All marijuana laws are written racially-neutral on their face, that is, they contain no language in racial or ethnic terms, and purport to apply to all racial demographics equally. Given the empirical evidence, can criminal marijuana laws be rewritten to eliminate racial disparity? Should the language be retained, but efforts made with police departments to change arrest patterns? In his Report, the Manhattan District Attorney stated that efforts to change disparity through police behavior have failed. Is the only solution then prosecutorial discretion?

2.   **Poverty.** Multiple studies conclude that there is racial disparity in marijuana arrests. Are there legitimate interpretations of the disparity in marijuana arrests other than racial discrimination? Could the impact of the

disparities be explained, at least in part, by differences in poverty and crime rates associated with different populations?

3. Collateral consequences and race. One of the most important consequences of convictions for marijuana arrests are the collateral consequences. In ending prosecutions for marijuana possession, the Manhattan District Attorney stated that "such arrests, of course, can have significant impacts on arrestees' jobs, schooling, families, and futures." One of the collateral consequences that may have national impact is the disproportionate number of young black males who are disqualified from voting in states that prohibit voting by convicts or those with criminal records. If the majority of such states are those with a history of voter suppression of minorities, and evidence is found that some legislators had partisan motives in enacting disenfranchisement of felons, what implications would that have for marijuana criminal law?

PROBLEM 20-2

To address its disparity in arrests of white and minority populations for marijuana consumption, a legislator in State X introduces a bill that, unless arrests bear a near correlation to marijuana usage by these populations over a sample time period, the state and municipal police will be prohibited from making arrests for simple possession of marijuana. Assuming that state legislators want to retain their state prohibition for simple possession of marijuana, but also want to address problems of racial inequality and create a more equal justice system, what arguments can they make for and against such a legislative proposal?

D. ADDICTION AND ABUSE

In the first part of this chapter, we explored the role of marijuana law in family law. These questions of family relations also inevitably raise the issues of drug abuse and addiction. But if marijuana is not a drug that is prone to abuse or addiction, should it be a fundamental or dispositive issue in the law of domestic relations? In the following case, *Carambat v. Carambat*, the Mississippi Supreme Court addressed the issue of abuse and addiction in marital relations.

CARAMBAT V. CARAMBAT
Supreme Court of Mississippi
72 So. 3d 505 (Miss. 2011)

KING, for the court en banc.

The Hancock County Chancery Court granted Stacy Ruth Carambat a divorce from James Edward Carambat on the ground of habitual and excessive drug use. Aggrieved, James appeals, arguing that the chancellor erred by granting the divorce, because his marijuana use did not affect the marriage, was not excessive, and was not akin to using opium, morphine, or other, like drugs. We find no error and affirm the chancery court's judgment.

FACTS AND PROCEDURAL HISTORY

James and Stacy married on March 20, 1993, in Metairie, Louisiana. They eventually moved to Mississippi, where they resided throughout the marriage, finally settling in Diamondhead, Mississippi, in 2004. The couple had twin boys—James Eugene Carambat and Tyler William Carambat—who were born on January 9, 1999. James and Stacy separated in August 2008, and Stacy filed for divorce on September 17, 2008.

Stacy alleged three grounds for divorce: irreconcilable differences, habitual cruel and inhuman treatment, and habitual and excessive drug use. She requested custody of the twins, child support, equitable distribution of the assets, alimony, and attorney's fees. James answered Stacy's complaint for divorce on July 20, 2009. In his answer, James denied Stacy's grounds for divorce, her claim that they had not cohabited since the separation, and her claim that she should have custody of the twins.

James's Drug Use

During the trial, Stacy, James, and Barbara Ruth (Stacy's mother) testified about the couple's marriage. Before the couple married, Stacy knew that James regularly smoked marijuana, and James admitted that he had been smoking marijuana since he was fourteen years old. James continued smoking marijuana throughout the marriage.

Although the couple had conversations about James's need to cease his marijuana use, James stated Stacy never asked him to quit. Stacy thought James would stop his drug use once the twins were born. According to Barbara, James called her after the twins were born, acknowledged his drug use as a problem, and told her he intended to quit. Because of James's marijuana use, Stacy was afraid that he would get into legal trouble, especially since he often picked her up from work with marijuana in the car. Several times during the marriage, James managed to go weeks without using marijuana. He said the longest period of time was one month. But he would always start using again.

Stacy testified that James had used other drugs. He once smoked cocaine at the beginning of their marriage, and he used Xanax, which was not prescribed to him, to cope with sleep deprivation. James stated that the cocaine incident had happened one time in 1995 or 1996. He said he took Xanax for two years, but that was several years ago. James testified that he had not used marijuana since January 2009, and he was willing to take a drug test.

James was questioned about the frequency of his marijuana use. James testified that he would purchase one quarter-ounce bag of marijuana per month, which cost between thirty-five and fifty dollars.

James could make six to seven cigarettes with this amount. Stacy said James smoked marijuana multiple times a day, starting in the morning before work. Both parties stated that the children were never exposed to James's drug use because James smoked the marijuana in the garage.

James's Interaction with the Family

According to Stacy, James's drug use affected his interactions with the family, causing him to develop a routine:

> [H]e would leave for work and smoke, and then go to work [sic] and then come home, and he would get undressed, go out to the garage and smoke again, and then he would come home, sit on the couch and wait for dinner to be fixed. And then eat dinner and then return back to the couch or to the computer room. He almost isolated himself from us totally.

Stacy often went to bed alone, and James would stay awake to use the computer or to watch television. Stacy stated that this took a toll on their marriage. Stacy also testified that, after the twins were born, she withdrew from James on an intimate level. James agreed and stated that Stacy's disinterest caused him to withdraw as well.

Stacy also testified that it was a chore to get James to participate in family activities. Most times, James would stay home instead of coming to family functions. Barbara echoed Stacy's sentiments, stating that James had become disinterested in attending family functions three years ago. James said that his marijuana use was casual, and that he was not dependent on it. According to James, marijuana had a calming effect on him. He explained that marijuana did not keep him from family functions; he just did not care to be around Stacy's family. James also stated that he was actively involved with the twins and their extracurricular activities— fishing, "bb" guns, and sports. James said he also helped the twins with their homework. Stacy agreed, but she said that James had come to only a few of the twins' school activities—such as parent-teacher conferences.

Financial Trouble

Stacy testified that James's marijuana use affected his work productivity. While employed with a printing company in Biloxi, Mississippi, James botched a printing job that cost several thousand dollars to reprint. He was demoted as a result. The demotion caused James to lose his bonus pay. According to Stacy, James told her that his drug use probably played a part in the incident. Stacy said that, afterwards, James tried to stop smoking marijuana. On cross examination, James's trial counsel impeached Stacy with her deposition testimony. In her deposition, Stacy was asked whether James's work incident was a mistake or a result of his drug use. Stacy responded that it was a mistake. She also agreed with trial counsel's statement that no one at James's job had linked the error to his marijuana use.

James denied telling Stacy that marijuana had caused his work error. He said he did not smoke marijuana before work, and his marijuana use never affected his job performance. James said the printing industry was stressful, and he smoked marijuana after work to relax. James also stated that he had never been fired from a job, but he had been laid off by at least two previous employers.

Stacy testified that James's drug use and mistake on the job affected the family's financial stability. James blamed their financial issues on Stacy's credit-card use. Stacy said they had borrowed $3,000 to $5,000 from her parents because they could not pay their bills, and James had continued to purchase marijuana during their financial troubles. Barbara testified that she and her husband had loaned Stacy and James up to $7,000. In addition, James said that he had borrowed at least $25,000 from his brother after he was laid off. James said he had used the money to pay for a dental surgery, credit-card debt, and the family's living expenses after Hurricane Katrina. * * *

According to James, in 2008, he and Stacy attended a party at the home of Royce Wilkinson, one of Stacy's male friends. James felt uncomfortable at the party because other men were flirting with Stacy. James stated that, later that year, he had called Stacy and questioned her about her whereabouts. Stacy had informed James that she was at Wilkinson's home taking care of his dog, and she and the twins had taken a ride in Wilkinson's golf cart. James said he was upset because, if anyone had seen his wife and children in Wilkinson's golf cart, they might have gotten the wrong idea. An argument ensued, during which Stacy told James that she was no longer happy and wanted a divorce. When Stacy filed for divorce, James thought that they could work it out. According to James, Stacy complained only that they were no longer a family and that he was not helping out at home. James said Stacy never mentioned his marijuana use, and Stacy testified that she did not give James an ultimatum concerning his marijuana use. James had suggested that they seek counseling, but he stated that Stacy was not interested. They did seek counseling individually but not as a couple. James did not believe that his marijuana use contributed to the demise of the marriage. Instead, he believed that their arguments caused the separation.

The Chancellors Ruling

The chancellor entered the "Judgment of Divorce" on September 24, 2009. The chancellor found James's own admission that he had regularly smoked marijuana from fourteen years of age to fifty-five years of age was evidence that his use was habitual and frequent. The chancellor found that James's drug use was excessive and uncontrollable because James smoked daily, he could not quit, and his drug use affected his work productivity and finances. Last, the chancellor found James's marijuana use met the definition of "other like drug" and caused his marriage to be repugnant to his spouse. Although not the same chemical make-up as opium and morphine, the chancellor determined that marijuana had the same effect, impairing James's ability to perform his job and to support his family.

For those reasons, the chancellor granted Stacy's divorce on the ground of habitual and excessive use of drugs. The chancellor awarded Stacy custody of the twins, the marital home, and attorney's fees. The chancellor granted James visitation and ordered him to pay child support and obtain medical insurance for the twins.

James filed several post-trial motions regarding his visitation and child-support obligation. The chancellor denied James's requested relief. On April 7, 2010, James filed a motion to reopen the time for appeal. The chancellor granted James's request on July 20, 2010. On July 26, 2010, James timely filed his notice of appeal.

ANALYSIS

In a divorce proceeding, the chancellor is the finder of fact, and the assessment of witness credibility lies within his sole province. Thus, we will not disturb a chancellor's findings when supported by substantial evidence unless the chancellor's judgment was manifestly wrong, clearly erroneous or an erroneous legal standard was applied.

Whether the chancellor erred by granting Stacy a divorce on the ground of habitual and excessive use of opium, morphine, or other like drug.

James argues that the chancellor erred by granting Stacy a divorce because she did not prove that his drug use was excessive and an "other like drug" as required by the statute. James also maintains that Stacy condoned his marijuana use and that his marijuana use did not cause any family, marital, or work issues. Instead, James blames the marriage's demise on Stacy's extramarital affairs. Conversely, Stacy asks the Court to affirm the chancellor's judgment. She argues that there is substantial evidence to support the chancellor's finding that James's drug use was habitual, excessive, and harmful to the family. Stacy also contends that the effect of marijuana is much like the effect of opium and morphine; thus, it is an "other like drug" for purposes of the statute.

* * *

Habitual and Excessive Use of Opium, Morphine, or Other Like Drug

Mississippi Code Section 93–5–1 (Rev.2004) lists "habitual and excessive use of opium, morphine, or other like drug" as a ground for divorce. A grant of divorce on this ground requires the plaintiff to establish that the spouse's drug use was (1) habitual and frequent, (2) excessive and uncontrollable, and (3) that involved opium, morphine, or drugs with a similar effect as opium or morphine. *Ladner v. Ladner*, 436 So.2d 1366, 1375 (Miss.1983).

Habitual use is established by showing that the spouse customarily and frequently used drugs. Stacy presented evidence that James began smoking marijuana at the age of fourteen, and his use continued until the age of fifty-five. James concedes that his drug use was habitual and frequent, testifying that he had used marijuana almost daily. As a result, we find substantial evidence in the record to support the chancellor's finding that James's drug use was habitual and frequent.

Excessive drug use requires a showing that the offending spouse abused drugs. The offending spouse "must be so addicted to the use of drugs that he cannot control his appetite for drugs whenever the opportunity to obtain drugs is present." *Ladner*, 436 So.2d at 1375. James argues that his drug use was casual, it relaxed him, and he was not dependent on it. The evidence shows the contrary. Stacy and James testified that James had attempted to stop smoking marijuana several times, quitting for weeks at a time. But, as James stated himself, he always went back to it. James argues that his drug use was not as serious as that of the spouses in *Ladner* and *Ashburn v. Ashburn*, 970 So.2d 204, 212 (Miss.Ct.App.2007). * * * The extent of James's addiction may not be as drastic as that of the spouses in *Ladner* and *Ashburn*, but it is obvious that James had a problem. Quitting for weeks at a time but then always going back to achieve a high is the nature of addiction. Like the spouse in *Ladner*, James abused the drug almost daily for years-approximately forty years in James's case. This is evidence that, at the time, James could not control his appetite for marijuana. Also, the chancellor found that James's marijuana use negatively impacted his interaction with his family, work productivity, and the family's financial stability. There is substantial evidence in the record to support the chancellor's findings. Thus, we hold that the chancellor did not err by finding that James's drug use was excessive and uncontrollable.

Opium, Morphine, or "Other Like Drug"

Next, James argues that Stacy failed to prove that marijuana is an "other like drug" similar to opium or morphine. In Section 93–5–1, the language "other like drug" does not mean a drug similar in chemical makeup to opium or morphine. Instead, it refers to drugs with similar adverse effects. In *Ladner*, the Court set forth factors to consider, along with other relevant circumstances, to determine whether a drug is an "other like drug" for purposes of Section 93–5–1:

> [S]uch factors as the guilty spouse's inability to support his wife and family or to properly attend to business should be considered. Additionally, the guilty spouse's incapacity to perform other marital duties or his causing the marital relationship to be repugnant to the innocent spouse are equally important.

In this case, the chancellor determined that James's marijuana use had isolated him from the family and had caused him to botch a costly printing job. Consequently, James was demoted, and the chancellor determined that this had negatively impacted the family's finances.

James points out that neither party cited a decision in which a divorce was granted based on marijuana use alone. We are not convinced that the absence of such a decision has any bearing on this case. James argues that no credible evidence supported the chancellor's finding that his marijuana use interfered with his ability to support and interact with his family and that his marijuana use caused the marital relationship to be repugnant to Stacy. Instead, James maintains that the evidence shows that Stacy sexually withdrew from him, pursued her own activities, and engaged in extramarital affairs. But the chancellor is the finder of fact, and the assessment of witness credibility lies within his sole province. The chancellor resolved any conflicts in the evidence in favor of Stacy, and the evidence supports his decision.

The evidence shows that the family's financial problems were due mainly to James's layoffs. But by smoking marijuana, James, at least once, affected his work productivity and lost his bonus pay. In addition, he continued to purchase marijuana during the family's economic troubles. James maintains that his marijuana expenditures were minimal and did not affect the family's income. But he cannot escape the fact that spending money on illegal drugs is wasteful, especially when the family is suffering financially. According to Stacy, James's drug use created a routine in their marriage by which he would work, come home, use drugs and then sit on the couch or stay on the computer all night. Perhaps he did not isolate himself from his children, but he definitely isolated himself from Stacy. Stacy was worried that James would get arrested for possession of marijuana. And although Stacy did not give James an ultimatum, she was exasperated over his failed attempts to remain clean, causing her to file for divorce.

The evidence supports the chancellor's finding that James's marijuana use had a like effect to the use of opium or morphine. James evidenced an inability to support his family and to properly attend to business. This made the marriage repugnant to Stacy. Accordingly, we hold that the chancellor did not err by finding that James's drug use involved opium, morphine, or a drug with a similar effect.

CONCLUSION

Stacy was entitled to a divorce based on James's habitual and excessive use of marijuana. James conceded that his drug use was habitual and frequent. Evidence that James continuously used marijuana for approximately forty years and continuously failed at sobriety supports the chancellor's finding that James's drug use was excessive and uncontrollable. Furthermore, evidence that James's marijuana use caused him to isolate himself from the family and affected his work productivity, which impacted the family's finances, supports the chancellor's finding that

James's marijuana use was similar in effect to opium or morphine. As a result, we affirm the chancellor's judgment of divorce.

AFFIRMED

CARLSON, J., dissenting.

The Hancock Country Chancery Court granted Stacy Carambat's divorce from her husband, James Carambat, on the ground that he was a habitual and excessive user of opium, morphine, or other like drug, where the drug in question was marihuana. This Court has never found this ground for divorce to be satisfied by marihuana use alone; nor, indeed, has any appellate court in the United States. It is my opinion that granting the divorce on this basis will dramatically expand this ground for divorce far beyond the language of the statute, effectively legitimizing divorce based on the use of any illegal drug. Because I believe that the majority's opinion goes far beyond the intent of the Legislature and creates new law, I must respectfully, but fervently, dissent.

I.   Nature of the Appeal

James argues that marihuana is not a like drug to opium or morphine. There is no relevant caselaw from Mississippi granting a divorce on this ground for the abuse of marihuana alone. Indeed, both parties, as well as the judge, conducted searches for persuasive precedent from all U.S. jurisdictions. Their research, and my own, indicate that no appellate court in the United States has ever granted a divorce based on marihuana use alone, or indeed has ever faced this question. This is a novel issue, and one that the chancery court specifically intended for us to consider. Accordingly, I respectfully believe we must thoroughly address this issue.

The chancery court in the initial case adjudicated that marihuana was a like drug to opium and morphine, but granted James leave to petition us for an interlocutory appeal. The chancellor explained that the relevant substances were alike in that they were habit-forming, mood-altering or hallucinogenic, and illegal. * * *

This Court must consider whether marihuana is a like drug to opium and morphine. In construing the statute, it must be given its ordinary meaning. Mississippi Code Section 1–3–65 (Rev.2005) provides that "all words and phrases contained in the statutes are used according to their common and ordinary acceptation and meaning."

In *Lawson v. Lawson*, 821 So.2d 142, 145 (Miss.Ct.App.2002) the Court of Appeals held that, in determining whether a drug is an "other like drug" under Section 93–5–1, "[so] far as the kind of drug is concerned, chemical content is not important, but effect caused by use is the test." *Id.* at 145. In *Ladner*, this Court set forth factors to consider: "[S]uch factors as the guilty spouse's inability to support his wife and family or to properly attend to business should be considered. Additionally, the guilty spouse's incapacity to perform other marital duties or his causing the marital relationship to be repugnant to the innocent spouse are equally important." *Id.* at 1375.

* * *

Effect of the Drug

I first wish to address the effect of marihuana usage, which, this Court has held to be the key determinant in finding that a drug is sufficient for this ground for divorce. While the chemical content of the like drug is irrelevant, I would hold that the physical or physiological effect of the drug was meant to be considered in the *Ladner* effect test.

In *Ladner*, this Court found "a physical effect [on the husband] similar to morphine or opium." *Ladner*, 436 So.2d at 1375. Furthermore, if "effect" and thus "like drug" mean no more than work productivity, marital duties, and repugnancy of the marriage, the term would become synonymous with the "excessive" standard already incorporated into the test. As a result, I have analyzed the physical effects of marihuana and find it to be unlike opium and morphine as a matter of law.

For information on the effects of marihuana, and of the most commonly utilized opiates, I consulted the Research Report Series of the National Institutes of Health's National Institute on Drug Abuse.

Marihuana, per this resource, is ingested to cause the user to feel a euphoria or "high" by stimulating brain cells to release the chemical dopamine—a phenomenon also associated with most drugs of abuse, as well as alcohol, tobacco, chocolate, and sexual activity. Acute dangers associated with marihuana intoxication include short-term memory loss, impaired attention and judgment, increased heart rate and blood pressure, decreased coordination and balance, and occasionally feelings of anxiety, distrust, or panic. Cumulative use may lead to addiction, though it is considered less addictive than "hard" drugs.

The following information is also gleaned from the Research Report Series of the National Institutes of Health's National Institute on Drug Abuse. The most commonly used opiate in the United States today is heroin. Heroin is severely addictive, and withdrawal can cause painful physical symptoms, including vomiting and bone pain. Since users are typically unaware of the amount and purity of the drug they are using, the drug can lead to nearly instantaneous death upon use. In the brain, the heroin converts to morphine and binds rapidly to opioid receptors, triggering a surge of pleasurable sensation called a "rush." Several drug analogs to opium have been produced, some by pharmaceutical companies for medical reasons, but others, known as "designer drugs," by illegal laboratories. This latter category may be more dangerous than the original compound. Several of the most abused prescription drugs are also opioids, commonly prescribed because of their pain-relieving properties. These opioids, such as OxyContin, also produce euphoria as a side effect.

Withdrawal leads to the same physical symptoms caused by heroin withdrawal, and a large enough dose of these drugs may lead to death.

The effect of marihuana is unlike the effect of opiates. The only real similarities between the drugs appear to be the euphoric rush or high associated with their use, and the addiction. Neither of these features is alike in degree. Marihuana, according to the Research Report Series of the National Institutes of Health's National Institute on Drug Abuse, never leads to immediate death, lacks physical withdrawal symptoms, and is much less addictive than opium. While this resource indicates that marihuana clearly leads to decreased activity in the abuser, holding that marihuana is like an opiate on these grounds is analogous to holding that caffeine is like cocaine.

Our state's caselaw on this issue, scant though it is, has been dominated by the abuse of prescription drugs including opiates, and without exception, a divorce has been granted only when individuals were much more severely incapacitated than James was in this case. With this caselaw in mind, in today's case, James was able to function on a relatively normal level while abusing marihuana, hardly a behavior associated with abusers of drugs as depicted in the cases cited. In addition, given the unfortunate prevalence of marihuana in American society, it is a dangerous precedent to allow divorce for marihuana use alone. As already revealed, marihuana is considered to be a relatively mild drug, and remains the least regulated of all illegal drugs in the State of Mississippi. Marihuana is less addictive, less immediately dangerous, and less incapacitating than the major opiates, and indeed than most other illegal drugs. Allowing a divorce based on marihuana abuse will effectively hold that divorce is available for the abuse of any drug—which is not a natural reading of "opium, morphine or other like drug."

To be sure, marihuana abuse, like alcohol abuse, has the propensity to destroy a marriage. However, the Legislature has not seen fit to provide for divorce on such grounds, and it is not this Court's responsibility to create new grounds for divorce ex nihilo. In my opinion, the natural meaning of "opium, morphine or other like drug" is not so broad as to cover marihuana. Accordingly, I would find that the chancery court erred in granting a divorce on the ground of using "opium, marihuana or other like drug," where the sole drug habitually and excessively used was marihuana.

* * *

Here, even assuming arguendo that marihuana is not an unlike drug to opium and morphine as a matter of law, the effect of the marihuana abuse was minimal. In my opinion, the chancellor abused his discretion in finding that James was a habitual and excessive user of opium, morphine, or other like drug, thus justifying granting a divorce to Stacy on this ground. The evidence indicates that marihuana usage at worst marginally affected James's business life and did not substantially harm James's relationship with his children. While James's relationship with his wife Stacy sharply declined, the evidence does not indicate that James's marihuana usage was responsible for this deterioration.

Marital Duties and Repugnance

As the majority recognizes, James's marihuana abuse was in no way comparable to the facts of *Ashburn* or *Ladner*. James did use the drug almost daily for more than forty years. Stacy testified that James's routine was to come home from work, smoke marihuana, and wait for her to prepare dinner. He would then isolate himself on the couch or in the computer room and sometimes come to bed late after staying awake to use the computer or watch television. James testified that he withdrew from his wife because she had withdrawn from him sexually after their children were born, in 1999, ten years before this divorce action was filed. Stacy admitted that she had withdrawn from James on an intimate level at that time.

Stacy testified that James had remained involved in their children's lives, taking them to church, helping them with their homework, and participating in their social activities, particularly fishing, sporting events, and shooting "bb" guns. Stacy complained that he came to only a few school activities, such as parent-teacher conferences. James did attend events with his wife's family less frequently and with Stacy's mother, Barbara Ruth in particular, stating that he became disinterested in these family events about three years before these proceedings began. James testified that this was because he did not like his wife's family.

On the whole, James's relationship with his in-laws is far less significant in divorce proceedings than his relationship with his children and with his spouse. The evidence is clear that James's relationship with his children remained strong and healthy. In contrast, his relationship with Stacy clearly declined. However, this decline was due to reasons other than the marihuana abuse. James testified, and Stacy admitted, that she had withdrawn from him sexually ten years prior, when their children were born.

Stacy testified that she began dating a man named Tom Henry before filing this divorce. James suspected or became aware of Stacy's adultery, and this affected the relationship between them. James also testified, and Stacy agreed, that Stacy never specifically asked James to stop smoking marihuana, though she claimed that his continued use exasperated her. The evidence is uncontroverted that Stacy was aware of James's marihuana habit two years before they married. While James failed to timely plead the affirmative defense of condonation, this testimony can hardly be irrelevant to our analysis. Since Stacy married James with the knowledge that he was a heavy abuser of marihuana, and never asked him to quit, in my opinion, it was unreasonable to conclude that James's marihuana abuse made the marriage repugnant to her.

James did stop performing certain marital duties, though there is no evidence that this was due to incapacity to perform them. The marriage obviously did become repugnant to Stacy. However, since Stacy had withdrawn from James sexually, engaged in an adulterous affair, and was aware of James's marihuana use even before marriage but never asked James to quit using it, the chancellor, in my opinion, abused his discretion by holding that marihuana abuse was responsible for this state of affairs.

Support of Family and Attending to Business

There was minimal evidence that James's marihuana use substantially affected his earning capability. Trial testimony showed that James worked every day of the marriage except for brief periods of time when he lost employment due to his job being discontinued or, in one case, his company going bankrupt after Hurricane Katrina. As the majority notes, the Carambats' financial difficulties were primarily caused by these layoffs. Stacy was able to argue only one instance in which marihuana use affected James's job performance: an instance where James was demoted for botching a printing job. Stacy testified that James had told her that his drug use played a part in this incident.

On cross-examination, Stacy was impeached with her deposition, in which she was questioned about the demotion. Stacy admitted that, to her knowledge, James's demotion was not caused by, and was never connected to, James's drug use. When specifically asked whether this work incident was due to a mistake or a result of James's drug use, Stacy answered that it was a mistake. The evidence does not show that, by smoking marihuana, James's work productivity was affected. The majority finds that James's marihuana use did affect his work productivity, but solely based on James's demotion, which the evidence does not show was based on James's marihuana usage. A statement by Stacy, later contradicted on cross-examination, that James had stated to her that his demotion was based on his drug use, is insufficient to show that James's drug use caused him to fail to attend to his business or support his family.

Stacy admitted that James's expenditures on marihuana were a minimal portion of the family income—approximately $300 annually out of a combined annual income of approximately $70,000. James's expenditures on marihuana may have been wasteful, but a $300-a-year habit for a family with an annual income of $70,000 is hardly grounds for a divorce.

James's abuse of marihuana was heavy, but there is minimal evidence that his family or work was impacted. James's admittedly wasteful spending on the marihuana was minor, and only one incident was reported indicating that James had failed to attend normally to business as a result of his drug use, and the only testimony concerning this one incident was successfully impeached by prior testimony. There was also uncontested evidence that the main cause for the decline in the family income was linked to events outside James's control, as the majority opinion concedes.

After consideration of these factors, I conclude that it was an abuse of discretion for the chancellor to find that James's use of marihuana met the effect test as a like drug to opium and morphine.

Suggested Disposition and Future Proceedings

For these reasons, I respectfully dissent from the majority and would reverse and remand for further proceedings. I recognize that remanding this case after a divorce has been granted would be an unfortunate step. The obvious effect is that James and Stacy would continue to be bound together, unhappily, in matrimony. However, from the record before us, it is abundantly apparent that, on remand, the parties would have alternate grounds for divorce to consider. Admittedly, this Court is not in the business of issuing advisory opinions, so I go no further as to what might or might not happen if this case were remanded.

However, in sum, I conclude that it was error for the chancery court to find that James was a habitual and excessive user of opium, morphine, or other like drug. If the Legislature wishes to provide for divorce on the grounds of abusing any illegal drug, or any dangerous drug, it of course may do so. To date, however, it has not. What the Legislature has provided is that parties may seek a divorce on the grounds of "[h]abitual and excessive use of opium, morphine or other like drug." Miss. Code Ann. § 93–5–1 (Rev.2004). Because marihuana is unlike opium or morphine, both in physical effect and in its effect on family life, I would reverse and remand. Because the majority finds otherwise, I respectfully dissent.

NOTES AND QUESTIONS

1. **Addiction and abuse.** The question of marijuana's potential for addiction and abuse is at the heart of the *Carambat* case. In the first part of this chapter, we saw that most courts do not view marijuana use by itself as sufficient grounds for a fault divorce or loss of custody. Mississippi law does not mention marijuana, but Mississippi Code Section 93–5–1 (Rev. 2004) lists "habitual and excessive use of opium, morphine, or other like drug" as a ground for divorce. How then does marijuana fall into the category? Is it a drug that is capable of habitual and excessive abuse and addiction? As it is a Schedule I controlled substance, the federal government maintains that marijuana has a "high potential for abuse," 21 U.S.C. § 812(b)(1)(A)–(C), and is liable to psychic or physiological dependence. § 811(b)–(c). But if marijuana does not in most cases lead to severe dependence, can it really be considered an "other like drug" to opium and morphine? And even if marijuana did have a high potential for abuse and addiction, would it be sufficient to satisfy Mississippi Code Section 93–5–1 to show merely that the spouse consumed marijuana? Or must the spouse consume marijuana habitually and excessively? Does there need to be an independent ground for divorce, like adultery or neglect of marital and familial duties caused by the marijuana use?

2. Quitting use. In assessing habitual and excessive use, the Court held that the spouse "must be so addicted to the use of drugs that he cannot control his appetite for drugs whenever the opportunity to obtain drugs is present" and that "quitting for weeks at a time but then always going back to achieve a high is the nature of addiction." But is persistent use by itself a sign of abuse and addiction? Would we say that someone who cannot control an appetite for snack foods or lottery gambling is showing abuse and addiction? How much does the nature and voluntariness of the activity count in assessing abuse and addiction? Didn't the offending spouse in *Carambat* quit for periods of time and claim that he consumed marijuana not out of addiction but enjoyment?

3. Statutory language. What statutory language is more suitable for assessing marijuana's possible dangers: whether marijuana has a high susceptibility to abuse and dependence, or whether it is susceptible to habitual and excessive use?

4. The dissent. The lengthy dissent seems to conclude that the defendant spouse did not abuse marijuana. Is that because the dissent finds that marijuana cannot be abused in a manner similar to opium and morphine, or that the evidence shows that marijuana was not so abused by this spouse?

5. Floodgates. The dissent suggests that if this divorce is permitted on the grounds of the use by this plaintiff, the floodgates of divorce would be opened in Mississippi. What reasons are given for that conclusion?

6. Scientific criteria. The dissent also cites a Research Report Series of the National Institutes of Health's National Institute on Drug Abuse (NIDA) to show that marijuana is significantly less addictive than opium. The most recent report of the National Academies of Sciences, Engineering, and Medicine, *The Health Effects of Cannabis and Cannabinoids: The Current State of Evidence and Recommendations for Research* (2017), discussed in chapter 18, does not seem to find marijuana to be highly addictive, at least in the manner of narcotic drugs. Should that determination be dispositive for Mississippi law?

PROBLEM 20-3

The Mississippi law of divorce cited in the *Carambat* case—Mississippi Code Section 93–5–1 (Rev. 2004)—lists "habitual and excessive use of opium, morphine, or other like drug" as a ground for divorce. Under this section, and the precedents of *Carambat* and the cases cited therein, Husband sues for divorce on the grounds that his wife is addicted to smoking marijuana and abuses the drug. The evidence shows that the offending spouse used marijuana on a daily basis for the length of their thirty year marriage. However during this time, Wife also stopped marijuana use periodically, for example, during her two pregnancies. Wife testifies that she smokes marijuana for its calming effect, it helps her with sleep deprivation, and softens the depression that she is susceptible to. Wife claims that she can stop consuming marijuana at any time, and her resumption of use shows not that she is addicted but that she has choice in the matter.

The uncontested testimony is that the Wife spends a sizeable portion of her discretionary income on marijuana and secludes herself in her room when she smokes. But there are no allegations of gross neglect, such as withdrawal from spousal companionship or child or spousal abuse. Wife admits that she has turned down promotions at work because the added duties would burden the free time she uses for consuming marijuana, and the increased visibility might expose her to possible criminal liability. Both spouses have engaged in adulterous affairs which they now regret; Husband admits however that he has fallen in love with another person whom he wishes to marry.

Is Husband entitled to a Section 93–5–1 divorce on the grounds of habitual and excessive use of an "other like drug" to opium and morphine, to wit, marijuana?

E. ADOLESCENT USE

Marijuana is the illegal drug most likely to be used by adolescents in the United States. Recent studies have shown that almost half of the nation's adolescents have tried marijuana at least once in their lives and about 6 to 8 percent are frequent users; 80 to 90 percent of high-school seniors report that marijuana is easy to obtain. See e.g. Jonathan P. Caulkins, Beau Kilmer, Mark Kleiman, *Marijuana Legalization: What Everyone Needs to Know* (2d ed. Oxford Press 2016), pp. 166–68. Yet numerous studies have shown marijuana use harmful to the developing adolescent mind, cognitively and socially.

Both opponents and proponents of marijuana legalization agree that it should be a goal to decrease adolescent use of marijuana. Opponents of legalization argue that a complete ban on marijuana most effectively keeps marijuana away from minors. They claim that marijuana legalization leads to a decrease in the perceived risk of using marijuana and an increase in teenage marijuana use. Likewise, if legalization reduces the price of marijuana, it will be more affordable to minors. Plus, edibles and aggressive advertising targeted to adults will inevitably spill over to underage consumers.

Proponents of legalization argue that education campaigns reduce teenage use of marijuana, as education campaigns have done for tobacco use. As with alcohol and tobacco, a regulatory framework can make marijuana available to adults and reasonably restrictive for minors. In addition, while marijuana will inevitably fall into the hands of some minors under either an illegal or a regulatory scheme, regulation will reduce teenage contact with drug dealers and the black market.

Although these arguments have been largely theoretical, with the advent of state legalization, empirical data are now becoming available.

Following is an excerpt from an empirical study of hospital visits for marijuana use by adolescents in Colorado.

> Despite national survey data suggesting no appreciable difference in adolescent marijuana use, our data demonstrate a significant 10-year increase in adolescent marijuana-associated ED/UC [emergency department/urgent care] visits in Colorado, most notably in the years following commercialization of medical (2009) and recreational marijuana (2014).

George Sam Wang et al. *Impact of Marijuana Legalization in Colorado on Adolescent Emergency and Urgent Care Visits,* 63 J. Adolesc. Health 239 (2018). In light of this increase in marijuana-related visits in a state that has legalized marijuana, the authors recommend comprehensive marijuana prevention programs for youth, especially for youth exhibiting other drug use or psychiatric illness.

NOTES AND QUESTIONS

1.   **Increased marijuana-related ED/UC visits.** While this empirical study in the official publication of the Society for Adolescent Health concludes that "marijuana legalization has impacted our adolescent population by an increase in marijuana-related ED/UC visits," it also cautions that "ED/UC visits are just one aspect of adolescent health." The study recommends that Colorado implement comprehensive marijuana education and prevention programs directed at youth. Based on its data, should it recommend a reversal of Colorado's legalization instead?

Although several studies have found an increase in marijuana-related ED/UC visits, one explanation may be that state statutes require reporting any mention of marijuana use, even if it is not the primary reason for the visit. In addition, patients may be more willing to divulge marijuana use, when not faced with punishment thereby.

2.   **Decreased marijuana consumption.** Other studies have found a decrease in marijuana use in Colorado among adolescents since legalization. For example, the National Survey on Drug Use and Health found that a little more than 9% of Colorado teens age 12 to 17 consumed marijuana monthly in 2015 and 2016. This represents a significant drop from the period prior to legalization and the lowest rate of consumption since 2007 and 2008. https://www.samhsa.gov/data/sites/default/files/NSDUHsaeShortTermCHG2016/NSDUHsaeShortTermCHG2016.htm.

3.   **Unchanged marijuana consumption.** A *Prevention Science* study published in July, 2018 found that after retail legalization of marijuana in 2014, there was not a significant change in marijuana use by Colorado high school students. The study did however find significant decreases in both frequent use and use on school grounds. The researchers hypothesized that these decreases might be related to the public discourse around marijuana policy leading up to and following the passage and enactment of Colorado's

recreational marijuana law. Finally, the study found significant decrease in perceived harmfulness of marijuana use among adolescents. See Scott Harpin, et al., *Adolescent Marijuana Use, Marijuana-Related Perceptions, and Use of Other Substances Before and After Initiation of Retail Marijuana Sales in Colorado (2013–2015)*, 53 Prevention Science 451 (2018). For additional studies, see Lloyd Johnston, et al., *Monitoring the Future: National Survey Results on Drug Use, 1975–2017: 2017 Overview Key Findings on Adolescent Drug Use* (Ann Arbor: Institute for Social Research, The University of Michigan, 2018); Mallei Paschal, et al., *Medical Marijuana Legalization and Marijuana Use Among Youth in Oregon*, 38(3) Primary Prev. 329 (June 2017).

4. **Contrasting data.** These studies, and others, find somewhat conflicting data on adolescent marijuana use by Colorado adolescents after legalization, ranging from an increase in hospital visits for marijuana-related problems, to little change in marijuana use, to a decrease in marijuana use and perceived dangers of marijuana. To some extent these differences can be accounted for by different methodologies, difference in variables studied, and differing population groups, time periods, and samples. But given the differences, what lessons can policy-makers draw with regard to use of marijuana by adolescents in regulatory states?

5. **College-age consumption.** The annual national Monitoring the Future Panel Study found that college students' use of marijuana in 2016 and 2017 was at the highest level in the past three decades. In 2017, 38 percent of full-time college students aged 19–22 reported using marijuana at least once in the prior 12 months. In the same year, 41 percent of high school graduates, not in college full time, aged 19–22, reported using marijuana at least once in the prior 12 months. However, daily or near daily use of marijuana was at 4.4 percent in 2017 for college students, down from a recent peak of 5.9 percent in 2014. Lloyd Johnston, et al., *Monitoring the Future: National Survey Results on Drug Use, 1975–2017: Volume II, college students and adults ages 19–55* (Ann Arbor: Institute for Social Research, The University of Michigan, 2018).

CHAPTER 21

MARIJUANA IN SOCIETY

■ ■ ■

The debate over marijuana regulations extends beyond legal questions, and beyond the medical questions we considered in Chapters 18 and 19, and the social issues in Chapter 20. Marijuana legislation is also shaped by political, economic, sociological, criminological, and cultural perspectives. The pros and cons of marijuana regulation have been debated in the halls of government and in the public arena. We touch on some of these questions in this chapter. In Section A, we look at the intersection of politics and marijuana crimes in the historic case of *People v. Sinclair* (1972). In Section B, we look at another case involving a more famous cultural figure, John Lennon, not for the marijuana crime itself, but for the collateral consequence—deportation—that exemplifies the manifold civil sanctions that attach to marijuana convictions. In Section C, we look at the 2018 change in marijuana enforcement policy, promulgated by Attorney General Jefferson Sessions, as a window into political and public policy questions underlining the marijuana debate. These public policy considerations include questions of economic, criminological, sociological, environmental, and cultural import.

A. MARIJUANA AND POLITICS

Marijuana is always a political issue but perhaps was never more so than in the late 1960s and early 1970s, when marijuana became popular with middle class youth, and a symbol of the counter-culture and political protest. The following case involves the marijuana arrest of a political activist, John Sinclair, in which questions of the classification of marijuana, severity of marijuana penalties, government crackdown on dissent, personal autonomy, and public protest, came to the fore. It was controversial enough that the majority of members of the Michigan Supreme Court issued individual opinions to support the per curiam decision. Two questions run through the various opinions. First, was Sinclair's arrest motivated by political considerations? Second, in this high-profile prosecution, did the judges take into account popular reaction, and especially public protest? Excerpts from the opinions of several of the justices follow.

PEOPLE V. SINCLAIR

Supreme Court of Michigan
387 Mich. 91, 194 N.W.2d 878 (1972)

PER CURIAM:

For the reasons set forth in our several opinions, the judgment of conviction of defendant Sinclair is reversed and set aside and the defendant discharged.

SWAINSON, J.

Defendant, John A. Sinclair, was arrested on January 24, 1967, and charged with the unlawful sale and unlawful possession of two marijuana cigarettes. Defendant was convicted by a jury in the Recorder's Court for the City of Detroit of unlawful possession of the two marijuana cigarettes, on July 25, 1969, and on July 28, 1969, he was sentenced to 9-1/2 to 10 years imprisonment. During the 2-1/2 years between his arrest and trial, defendant was free on bond in the amount of $1,000, and never failed to appear when required to do so.

Prior to the trial, a special three-judge panel of Recorder's Court was convened to consider the constitutionality of the Michigan statutes prohibiting sale or possession of marijuana. On April 17, 1968, the panel upheld the statutes against the contentions that they violated the equal protection of the laws; denied defendant due process of law; violated rights of privacy retained by the people; and that the penalty provisions imposed cruel and unusual punishment. Judge Robert J. Colombo, a member of the three-judge panel, in a concurring opinion stated that he personally believed that there was a question of whether defendant had been entrapped. The trial judge (Hon. Robert J. Colombo), on June 23, upon motion of defense counsel, dismissed the count for unlawful sale on the ground that the sale was entrapped by the police officers. Defendant was thereafter convicted of the unlawful possession of marijuana based on the two cigarettes introduced into evidence. The Court of Appeals affirmed the conviction. 30 Mich App 473. We granted leave to appeal. 385 Mich 786.

The Detroit Police Department Narcotics Bureau had instructed Patrolman Vahan Kapagian and Policewoman Jane Mumford Lovelace to assist in an investigation of illegal activities involving narcotic violations in an area surrounding Wayne State University and, in particular, an establishment known as the Artists' Workshop which was located at 4863 John Lodge, in the City of Detroit. Defendant Sinclair made his residence above the Artists' Workshop, at 4867 John Lodge.

In pursuance of this assignment, Patrolman Kapagian grew a beard and began to let his hair grow long, in late August 1966. On October 18, 1966, using the aliases of Louis Cory and Pat Green, the officers commenced their assignment. They continued working until January 24, 1967, on this particular assignment. The officers assisted in doing typing and other odd chores at the Artists' Workshop, including sweeping floors and collating literature. They sat in at communal dinners and provided the food for one of these dinners. They joined a group called LEMAR, which advocated that marijuana be legalized. They listened to poetry and helped in the preparation of certain literature. Patrolman Kapagian visited the shop and saw defendant approximately two or three times a week until the defendant's arrest. As part of the assignment, Patrolman Kapagian took a job at the Candle Shop. Patrolman Kapagian was equipped with a porta-talk radio transmitter which allowed him to keep in contact with other police officers stationed outside and nearby.

Patrolman Kapagian testified at the preliminary examination that on two occasions prior to December 22, 1966, during the investigation, the police officers asked defendant for marijuana. He denied this at the trial, despite the fact that his testimony to that effect at the preliminary examination was read to him from the transcript. Policewoman Lovelace stated that she had asked defendant on previous occasions to obtain marijuana for them.

Officer Kapagian testified that on December 22nd, at about 7 p.m., defendant appeared at the Workshop and following an exchange of greetings, defendant asked whether they had received any marijuana the previous night. The officers responded affirmatively and stated that they were looking for some more. At approximately 8:55 that evening, Kapagian told the defendant that they had to leave and defendant asked them to accompany him upstairs to his residence. Once inside the residence, the officers were seated at the kitchen table. Defendant went to a shelf and removed a brown porcelain bowl which he set down on the table before him. Defendant took some cigarette paper and from the contents of the bowl rolled a cigarette, which he gave to Kapagian. Kapagian handed this cigarette to Lovelace, who inserted it into a partially filled Kool pack. Defendant then rolled a second cigarette, lit it, and handed it to Kapagian. The officer said he did not want to smoke it then because he had to drive and the cigarette would make him dizzy. Kapagian gave the cigarette to Lovelace after defendant Sinclair had butted it. She placed the cigarette in the same Kool pack. At that time they said they had to leave, and departed. Sinclair was not arrested for committing a felony in the officers' presence because, as Kapagian stated, he did not want to tip his hand since numerous arrests were to be made as the result of this investigation.

At the trial, the only witnesses were the two police officers. No corroborating evidence was introduced. Although officer Kapagian was equipped in a manner to enable the transmission of his conversation to other officers, no arrangements were made to tape the conversations, which allegedly occurred between defendant and the police officers. In addition, officer Kapagian testified that he did not preserve his log book for the year 1966 because he decided that it was not worth saving. He did admit that if the log book had been preserved, the presence or absence of entries relating to the transactions of December 22nd and all previous transactions during the investigation, would either confirm or disprove his testimony. Prior to trial, the defendant made several motions to quash the information and to exclude the marijuana cigarettes from evidence. These were denied by the trial court.

Defendant raises ten issues on appeal, and the prosecutor lists five. We will deal with two of these:

1)   Whether the classification of marijuana as a narcotic under MCLA [Michigan Compiled Laws Annotated] 335.151 violates the equal protection of the laws under the US Const, Am XIV, and

2)   Whether the two marijuana cigarettes should have been excluded from evidence on the ground that they constituted evidence obtained as the result of an illegal police entrapment?

I.

It is not denied that the State of Michigan has the power to pass laws against the sale and use of marijuana. Rather, the issue is whether marijuana may be constitutionally classified as a narcotic drug if, in fact, it is not a narcotic. * * *

We now turn to a comparison of the properties of marijuana and the other drugs classified as narcotics under MCLA 335.151 et seq.; MSA [Michigan Statutes Annotated] 18.1121 et seq.

Comparison of the effects of marijuana use on both the individual and society with the effects of other drug use demonstrates not only that there is no rational basis for classifying marijuana with the "hard narcotics", but, also, that there is not even a rational basis for treating marijuana as a more dangerous drug than alcohol. This is not to say that our scientific knowledge concerning any of the mind-altering drugs is at all complete. It is not. Even our society's vast experience with the mind-altering effects of alcohol has not led to complete scientific knowledge of that drug, as the Canadian Government Commission of Inquiry pointed out:

"Little is known as to the specific mechanism by which alcohol produces its psycho-pharmacological action. As with most drugs, alcohol effects, especially those resulting from low or moderate amounts, depend to a large extent on the individual and the situation in which the drinking occurs. A drink or two may produce drowsiness and lethargy in some instances, while the same quantity might lead to increased activity and psychological stimulation in another individual, or in the same person in different circumstances. Furthermore, a dose which is initially stimulating may later produce sedation."

Despite our lack of complete knowledge though, we do have sufficient scientific knowledge to categorize drugs according to their relative level of danger to both the individual and society. Proceeding to a comparison of marijuana with other mind-altering drugs, we find marijuana is a euphoria producing, mind-altering drug, whose effects are generally obtained by smoking, but can also be obtained by oral ingestion of the drug, usually mixed with other food or drinks. Coming from the hemp plant, cannabis sativa, the psychoactive strength of the drug varies greatly with the part of the plant used, quality of the seed stock, and the growing conditions.

The psychoactive ingredient of cannabis sativa has been isolated as two isomers of tetrahydrocannabinol (THC, although additional active ingredients of cannabis sativa may be discovered and isolated in the future). Thus the strength of any given amount of marijuana depends primarily on the amount of THC it contains. The ordinary street form of marijuana, commonly available and used in the United States, is composed of the leaves and flower clusters of the female plant, which are dried and crushed to make up the variable strength mixture. The resin from the flowering tops of the mature female plants is known as hashish (*charas* in India) and is apparently the strongest form of the naturally occurring drug because it contains the highest concentration of THC. Hashish is as much as eight times as strong as ordinary marijuana.

Consideration of the scientifically observed physical and psycho-motor effects of marijuana indicates that it is overall, the least dangerous mind-altering drug. Observed physical effects of marijuana use include dryness of mouth and throat, slight increase in pulse rate, and slight conjunctival reddening of the eyeball. No known tolerance develops to marijuana, in fact negative tolerance has been observed, that is, a decreased amount of the drug taken on subsequent occasions produces the same level of physical and euphoric effect. No physical dependency is produced by use of the drug and, hence, there are no withdrawal symptoms or "abstinence syndrome" when the drug is unavailable to the user.

No lethal dose for marijuana has been established. The lack of harmful physical effects from marijuana use has been well summarized by Dr. Grinspoon in *Marijuana Reconsidered* (Bantam ed., 1971), p 60:

> "What is so striking about the pharmacology of cannabis is that it has such limited and mild effects on human nonpsychic function. This is consistent with the equally striking observation that there has never in its long history been reported an adequately documented case of lethal overdosage. Nor is there any evidence of cellular damage to any organ."

Both the opiates and alcohol provide a dramatic contrast to the lack of physical harmfulness of marijuana. With the opiates high levels of tolerance develop, severe physical addiction results from repeated use, and deaths resulting from overdosage also occur. Occasional social use of alcohol in moderate dosage as a mind-altering drug has few deleterious physical consequences. However, tolerance does develop in alcohol use and the drug is subject to a great, acute and chronic abuse. Acute alcohol abuse can lead to death from overdosage. In addition, chronic alcohol abuse leads to alcoholism where a clear withdrawal syndrome is observable (an easily discernible physical shaking and later delirium tremens), and death of brain cells, mental deterioration, and cirrohsis of the liver may occur.

Damaging effects of alcohol on psychomotor coordination are so well known as to need no documentation. The President's Commission on Law Enforcement and Administration of Justice, Task Force Report: Drunkenness, commenting on alcohol, observed that: "There is probably no other area in the field of drug research and related dangerous behavior where the role of a drug as a precipitating factor in dangerous behavior is so clear." On the other hand, the evidence available concerning marijuana's effect on psychomotor functions seems to show very little impairment, at least in experienced users.

Psychological Effects: Marijuana is a mild hallucinogen, which in view of its lack of any other harmful effects, leads us to conclude that there is no rational basis for penalizing it more severely than the other hallucinogens (MCLA 335.106; MSA 18.1106). Indeed, mild hallucinogenic effects are reported almost exclusively from use of more potent hashish type preparations and rarely, if ever, from the use of ordinary street variety marijuana. * * *

The murky atmosphere of ignorance and misinformation which casts its pall over the state and Federal legislatures' original classification of marijuana with the hard narcotics has been well documented in the 250-page article by R. Bonnie and C. Whitebread, II, *The Forbidden Fruit and the Tree of Knowledge: An Inquiry into the Legal History of American Marijuana Prohibition*, 56 Va. L. Rev. 971 (1970). We can no longer allow the residuals of that early misinformation to continue choking off a rational evaluation of marijuana dangers. That a large and increasing number of Americans recognize the truth about marijuana's relative harmlessness can scarcely be doubted. The truth compels us to conclude at the minimum that marijuana has been erroneously classified with the opiates, and thus it is clear that based on current scientific knowledge, marijuana is not a narcotic drug.

Indeed, the Michigan legislature has recognized the erroneous classification of marijuana as a narcotic by its passage of the "Controlled Substances Act of 1971" (1971 PA 196; MCLA 335.301 to 335.367; MSA 18.1070[1] to 18.1070), effective April 1, 1972, which classifies marijuana as a distinct type of substance and provides drastically reduced penalties for its sale and possession.

We agree with the Illinois Supreme Court in *People v McCabe*, supra, that marijuana is improperly classified as a narcotic and hold that MCLA

335.151; MSA 18.1121, in its classification of marijuana violates the equal protection clauses of the U.S. Const. Am XIV and Const. 1963, art 1, § 2.

II.

[In the remaining part of the opinion, Justice Swainson holds that the police entrapped Sinclair into selling marijuana.]

WILLIAMS, J. (for reversal).

This is an opinion concerning a problem whose time has come. The name in the entitling is happenstance as the defendant could have been any mother's son or daughter.

The specific issue this opinion will consider is whether the categorization of marihuana in 1929 PA 310 along with the "hard drug" narcotics such as heroin, cocaine, and opium with the same penalty is denial of equal protection of the law because of unreasonable classification. The defendant raised other issues such as entrapment and cruel and unusual punishment but inasmuch as the issue of equal protection is dispositive of the case neither those issues nor the factual details supporting them will be here considered. My Brother T.E. Brennan's opinion concerning the issue of cruel and unusual punishment is well-reasoned, and I am in agreement with it as far as it goes, but it goes only to the length of defendant's sentence, not to his conviction.

For the purposes of this opinion the facts of the case are that the defendant prepared two marihuana cigarettes from a jar in his private quarters and handed them to two undercover police personnel. The defendant was subsequently charged on separate counts with sale and with possession of marihuana, the charge of sale being dismissed by the trial court because of entrapment. Defendant was tried, convicted, and sentenced to 9-1/2 to 10 years in prison.

The Court of Appeals affirmed the defendant's conviction in *People v Sinclair*, 30 Mich App 473 (1971). This Court granted the defendant's application for leave to appeal on September 1, 1971. * * *

[T]he classification of marihuana as a "hard drug" in MCLA 335.151; MSA 18.1121, constitutes a violation of the Equal Protection Clause of the United States Constitution. Such a classification is irrational in view of the present evidence which exists concerning marihuana. This is particularly true since other hallucinogenic drugs such as d-lysergic acid diethylamide, peyote, and mescaline are grouped together. (MCLA 335.106; MSA 18.1106). The penalties for the use of these drugs are less severe than those for the possession of the narcotic drugs with which marihuana is included. This classification promotes no "compelling governmental interest". Therefore such classification of marihuana deprived the defendant of his constitutional right to equal protection of the law.

The Supreme Court of the State of Illinois recently considered this same issue in its review of a case involving an Illinois statute classifying marihuana with narcotic drugs. In *People v McCabe*, 49 Ill 2d 338; 275 NE2d 407 (1971), that Court stated, "Marijuana, in terms of abuse characteristics, shares much more in common with the barbiturates, amphetamines and, particularly, the hallucinogens than it does with the 'hard drugs' classified in the Narcotic Drug Act". 49 Ill 2d 338. The Court concluded that the grouping of marihuana with narcotic drugs was irrational and violated the Equal Protection Clause.

It is of interest to note that the Michigan legislature itself has decided that the classification of marihuana with narcotics and other so-called "hard drugs" is not rational in the light of present scientific knowledge. The legislature has removed marihuana from the category containing "hard drugs", and has lowered the penalties for the marihuana crimes. The legislature also has recognized the problem arising from the fact that the Controlled Substances Act of 1971 may only be applied prospectively. Aware of its inability to pass a retrospective law, the legislature has wisely called for a committee to review the sentences of those individuals presently incarcerated for drug offenses. Such a committee can make recommendations concerning the commutation of sentences to the Governor. Unlike the legislature, however, this Court does have the authority to apply its decisions retrospectively. Justice demands that we so apply this decision. * * *

Reversed, defendant discharged.

T.M. KAVANAGH, C.J., concurs with WILLIAMS, J.

T.G. KAVANAGH, J.

John Sinclair was convicted of the crime of possession of marijuana contrary to the provisions of MCLA 335.153; MSA 18.1123, and was sentenced to serve 9-1/2 to 10 years in prison therefor. I agree with my Brother Brennan that a minimum sentence of 9-1/2 years for the possession of marijuana is cruel and/or unusual punishment prohibited by the US Const, Am VIII and the Const 1963, art 1, § 16, for the reasons he states. I also agree for the reasons he states, that in the discharge of our duty we have the power to review sentences. I do not agree that the other issues urged on appeal here were adequately treated by the Court of Appeals or that on the basis of their reasoning or any other that the conviction can stand.

My Brother Swainson has written that the police procedure followed in this case was tantamount to entrapment and does not meet a standard of practice which we can countenance. I agree with him in this for his stated reasons. Here because of the way it was obtained, the evidence should have been suppressed for all purposes, so defendant's conviction based upon it was improper.

My Brothers Williams and Swainson, however, both write to the effect that our statute denied the defendant equal protection and due process of the law on account of its classification of marijuana with heroin and other "hard narcotics", prescribing the same penalty for their possession and use. They demonstrate that the overwhelming weight of scientific opinion today is that marijuana is not a narcotic at all, but rather a mild hallucinogens which should, with propriety, be treated with other hallucinogens. They hold that classification of marijuana with the "hard" drugs is wholly unreasonable and unconstitutional.

Although I am persuaded that our statute is unconstitutional, I cannot agree that my Brothers have ascribed the correct or even permissible reasons for this conclusion. The testimony and data upon which this legislation was based may indeed be out of date and of exceedingly doubtful validity today, but I do not perceive it the prerogative of a court to substitute its assessment of such testimony and data for that of a legislature. Rather I believe our duty is to determine whether what the legislature *did* conformed to constitutional limits.

I find that our statute violates the Federal and State Constitutions in that it is an impermissible intrusion on the fundamental rights to liberty and the pursuit of happiness, and is an unwarranted interference with the right to possess and use private property. As I understand our constitutional concept of government, an individual is free to do whatever he pleases, so long as he does not interfere with the rights of his neighbor or of society, and no government state or Federal has been ceded the authority to interfere with that freedom. Whatever the validity of the concept that *traffic* in marijuana is freighted with a proper public interest, it is extending the concept entirely too far to sanction proscription of possession and private use of it. Although it is conceivable that some legitimate public interest might warrant state interference with what an individual consumes, "Big Brother" cannot, in the name of *Public* health, dictate to anyone what he can eat or drink or smoke in the *privacy* of his own home.

In my view when the legislature proscribed the possession and private use of marijuana as a Public health measure it did so unconstitutionally.

John Sinclair's conviction should be set aside and the prosecution dismissed.

BRENNAN, J., concurring.

Defendant was convicted of possession of two marijuana cigarettes in violation of MCLA 335.153; MSA 18.1123.The offense occurred in the defendant's home, and in the presence of two police officers whose identity as such was unknown to the defendant. Defendant did not testify at his trial. On July 28, 1969, defendant, in the company of his attorney, appeared before the trial judge for sentencing.

The following is a transcript of that hearing:

* * *

MR. RAVITZ [attorney for defendant]:

"* * * In America, which has never known anything but the history of racism, and in America which practices those imperialistic and those brutalistic and inhumane wars in Asia and elsewhere around the globe, and in America which sends a man to the moon while millions of its citizens starve, John Sinclair is brought before this Court and he is said to be a criminal. He isn't a criminal. He isn't a criminal at all. The criminals with respect to this law, are the doctors, the legislators, the attorneys who know, who know, because they have knowledge that these laws are unconstitutional. That these laws defy all knowledge of science. That this sumptuary legislation, like its predecessors and like other forms of sumptuary legislation, are on the books to go after and to oppress politically unpopular people and groups and minorities. That's the only reason they are on the books.

Persons brought before the bar of the Court aren't the middle-class, aren't the popular, they are the oppressed. They are the unpopular. It's a terrible law, it's a criminal law. * * * What I really hope the Court recognizes is that other judges and other persons of this society charged with responsibilities, come to recognize is that America cannot single out unpopular leaders and go into their arsenal of over-kill, be it through stone or rifles or highly punitive sentences and think that the problems in this country can ever be solved in that fashion. Yet all around this country, we see political prosecutions. We see the Tom Haydens, we see the Huey Newtons, the John Sinclairs singled out. And somewhere in the warped minds of those so-called leaders, they think that they are going to cure the generation gap. They think that they are going to stem the tide of revolution by picking out leaders."

* * *

The legislature has no power to invest a court with discretion to violate the Constitution. This case of Sinclair has been given much notoriety. Defendant and his supporters have used his conviction and sentence as a vehicle to attack the wisdom and efficacy of the marijuana laws. We have declined to enter into that controversy. The judicial fact-finding process is not adaptable to finding mixed questions of fact and policy.

But we do note that the possession of narcotic drugs is a crime *malum prohibitum* only. This is particularly apparent in the case of marijuana. The statute prohibits possession of any part of the cannibus sativa plant. Possession of a natural growing plant can hardly be *malum in se*.

As officers sworn to uphold the Constitution we recognize with understanding, the action of the learned trial judge. The attitude of hostility and remorselessness displayed by the defendant and the disruption of orderly proceedings by his supporters surely combined to tax the patience of the court. And certainly if rehabilitation were the sole purpose of sentencing, the measure of the imprisonment would be more the posture of the defendant than the gravity of the offense.

But rehabilitation is not the only function of punishment. It is not even always possible. Where the defendant is recalcitrant, whether from principle or out of sheer meanness, the law cannot, in a free society, disregard the nature of the offense and address itself only to the character of the offender.

Where a minimum sentence is imposed which is demonstrably and grossly excessive, in the light of the depravity of the criminal as shown in the commission of the act and in light of the usual and customary disposition of those convicted of like conduct, such minimum sentence violates the constitutional prohibition against the inflicting of cruel or unusual punishment, and is illegal and void.

ADAMS, J., concurred with T.E. BRENNAN.

NOTES AND QUESTIONS

1.   **Political activism.** John Sinclair was a political activist in Detroit in the 1960s; he was also a poet, managed rock bands, wrote for underground newspapers, and founded the Detroit Artists Workshop. In 1967, he moved to Ann Arbor, living in what was described as a "hippie commune" of about 35 people. In 1968, he co-founded the White Panther Party to support the Black Panther Party. After his arrest, Sinclair and his supporters launched a freedom campaign on his behalf. After sentencing, Sinclair circulated manifestos from his prison cell, claiming that he was a political prisoner, and that because the police could not arrest him for his political views and activities under the First Amendment, they entrapped him into a marijuana crime, and the courts imposed the harshest sentence possible for this minor offence.

2.   **"Ten for Two."** Ten for Two—ten years in jail for two joints—became the rallying cry of the freedom campaign. Its climax was the John Sinclair Freedom Rally, a protest and concert held in Crisler Arena at the University of Michigan, in Ann Arbor on December 10, 1971. The musicians who performed included John Lennon, Yoko Ono, Phil Ochs, Commander Cody and His Lost Planet Airmen, Bob Seger. Archie Shepp, and Stevie Wonder. The speakers at the rally included Bobby Seale, Jerry Rubin, Rennie Davis, Allen Ginsberg, and Sinclair himself, by phone. *Ten For Two* is a documentary film of the concert and rally. The highlight of the concert was John Lennon singing "John Sinclair," which he wrote for the protest.

It ain't fair, John Sinclair
In the stir for breathing air

Won't you care for John Sinclair?
In the stir for breathing air
Let him be, set him free
Let him be like you and me

They gave him ten for two
What else can the judges do?
Gotta, gotta, gotta, gotta,
Gotta, gotta, gotta, gotta,
Gotta, gotta, gotta, gotta,
Gotta, gotta, gotta set him free

If he'd been a soldier man
Shooting gooks in Vietnam
If he was the CIA
Selling dope and making hay
He'd be free, they'd let him be
Breathing air, like you and me.

3.　　**Per curiam.** This is a per curiam opinion, in which the entire Court concurred in setting aside Sinclair's conviction and vacating his sentence. The judges wrote separate opinions to state that classifying marijuana as a narcotic violated the equal protection clause and that Sinclair's sentence constituted cruel and unusual punishment. For a discussion of the precedential impact of this per curiam decision, see *People v. Waxman*, 41 Mich. App. 277, 199 N.W.2d 884 (Mich. Ct. App. 1972). Do you get a sense from the opinions that the motivating factors in reversal reflected: a judgment on marijuana as a narcotic; on constitutional factors; on the harshness of the penalty; the belief that this was a politically motivated prosecution; the recently amended Michigan marijuana statute; or the pressure of the Free Sinclair Campaign?

The opinion of Justice Swainson focuses on comparing marijuana to other narcotics and alcohol to show that there is no rational basis for classifying marijuana as a narcotic. As Swainson does not define what is a narcotic drug, are these comparisons sufficient to show that the legislature could not so classify it? Also, Swainson declares that Sinclair's sentence violates the equal protection of the laws. What is the precise basis of this equal protection argument? Is it that all marijuana users be treated alike? All drug users? All defendants, regardless of their political notoriety?

Justice Williams begins by stating that this is "a problem whose time has come. The name in the entitling is happenstance as the defendant could have been any mother's son or daughter." Why is this the opportune time to vacate the marijuana law? Is it, as implied by the judge, that the middle class is now facing for the first time marijuana use and thus drug penalties that could imprison their children, as opposed to those at the margins of society? Justice Williams also cites *People v. McCabe*, 49 Ill 2d 338, 275 N.E.2d 407 (1971), as did Justice Swainson in his opinion. We discussed *People v McCabe* in Chapter 19. Why did these justices look to this out-of-state precedent as one of the bulwarks for their opinions?

Justice T.G. Kavanagh joins the court in finding the Michigan marijuana classification unconstitutional, but disagrees with Swainson and Williams for undertaking their own assessment of the characteristics and effects of marijuana, as it is not "the prerogative of a court to substitute its assessment of such testimony and data for that of a legislature." Is that correct in the circumstances of this case? Justice Kavanagh instead finds the marijuana prohibition to be an unconstitutional intrusion on the right to liberty and private property. Justice T.G. Kavanagh's opinion would be cited for this proposition in the historic case of *Ravin v. State*, 537 P.2d 494 (Alaska 1975). See Chapter 4.

Justice Brennan, in his concurring opinion focuses on sentencing, quoting the argument by Sinclair's lawyer at sentencing that this was a political prosecution of leaders of revolutionary movements. Was it an effective trial strategy for Sinclair's counsel to categorize Sinclair with revolutionaries such as Tom Hayden and Huey Newton? On appeal, what are Justice Brennan's reasons for finding the sentence excessive?

4.   **Entrapment.** The Court finds that Sinclair was entrapped into selling two joints. We have omitted from the opinions most of the explanation of the criminal law of entrapment. Even apart from the legal consequences of an entrapment defense, the facts seem to indicate the extraordinary lengths the police undertook to snare Sinclair. Would this seem to confirm that this had the nature of a political prosecution? On the other hand, should political notoriety exempt someone from the consequences of violating criminal law?

5.   **Reclassification.** Perhaps as a result of the Free Sinclair campaign, the Michigan legislature, on December 9, 1971, the day before the Crisler Arena Rally, reclassified marijuana under the Michigan Controlled Substances Act of 1971, effective April 1, 1972, to reduce penalties for its sale and possession. In a sense, the opinions of the judges that the classification of marijuana as a narcotic was unconstitutional had been rendered moot. As the legislature made provisions for review of those sentenced under the older, more rigorous schedule, can the vacating of Sinclair's sentence be seen as applying the statute retroactively to Sinclair's particular case, as suggested by Justice Williams?

6.   **Aftermath.** After Sinclair's conviction was reversed, the Ann Arbor City Council in September 1972 decriminalized marijuana. In the following years, eleven states and numerous municipalities, in part due to the *McCabe*, *Sinclair*, and *Ravin* decisions, decriminalized marijuana.

PROBLEM 21-1

State X is a traditional prohibition state which has not legalized marijuana for any purpose. Under State X Controlled Substances Act, the weight of marijuana for purposes of sentencing for the crime of possessing resinous extractives of cannabis" (hash oil) includes "adulterants and dilutants." Thus for marijuana edibles, the aggregate weight of the baked goods, rather than the net weight of the THC or hash oil contained therein, is the sentencing weight. A 19-year old, first-time Defendant is arrested in possession of a pound and a half of hash brownies that exceeds a 400 gram level for hash concentrates under X law. The prosecutor thus is authorized to, and does charge Defendant with a narcotics felony, subjecting him to a possible sentence of ten years to life. An outcry erupts, Defendant's parents appear on television, Defendant's supporters deliver a petition with a quarter million signatures to the District Attorney's Office requesting that the charges be reduced, a protest concert is organized, and the charges are denounced by a local congressman. What weight should the prosecutor give to this outpouring of protest in deciding what offence to charge Defendant? If Defendant is convicted for the maximum charge, how much consideration should the sentencing court give to the public outcry? Should the protests and public opinion be taken into account by an appellate court in reviewing the conviction and sentence? [Based on the 2014 Texas case of Jacob Lavoro, who after the charges were reduced, pleaded guilty to a second-degree felony charge of possession of tetrahydrocannabinol in exchange for a sentence of seven years' probation.]

B. PROTESTING A COLLATERAL CONSEQUENCE

John Lennon, the Beatle, was the most famous musician to appear at the Free Sinclair Rally. Like Sinclair, he was also known for his political activism and protest of the Vietnam War. Based on Lennon's obscure British conviction for marijuana, the U.S. Government persuaded an immigration court to deport him. The appellate court again had to deal with the political ramifications of a marijuana possession charge. Just as importantly, the court has to address the situation where a marijuana conviction gives rise to a drastic collateral consequence that outweighs any criminal sentence imposed.

LENNON V. IMMIGRATION AND NATURALIZATION SERVICE (INS)

United States Court of Appeals, Second Circuit
527 F. 2d 187 (2nd Cir. 1975)

KAUFMAN, C.J.

We have come a long way from the days when fear and prejudice toward alien races were the guiding forces behind our immigration laws. The Chinese exclusion acts of the 1880's and the 'barred zone' created by the 1917 Immigration Act have, thankfully, been removed from the statute books and relegated to the historical treatises. Nevertheless, the power of Congress to exclude or deport natives of other countries remains virtually unfettered. In the vast majority of deportation cases, the fate of the alien must therefore hinge upon narrow issues of statutory construction. To this rule, the appeal of John Lennon, an internationally known 'rock' musician, presents no exception. We are, in this case, called upon to decide whether Lennon's 1968 British conviction for possession of cannabis resin renders him, as the Board of Immigration Appeals believed, an excludable alien under § 212(a)(23) of the Immigration and Nationality Act (INA), 8 U.S.C. § 1182(a)(23), which applies to those convicted of illicit possession of marijuana. We hold that Lennon's conviction does not fall within the ambit of this section.

I.

To provide the necessary context for decision in this case, an overview of the factual background is appropriate. On October 18, 1968, detectives from the Scotland Yard drug squad conducted a warrantless search of Lennon's apartment at 34 Montague Square, London. There, the officers found one-half ounce of hashish inside a binocular case and thereupon placed Lennon under arrest. Lennon pleaded guilty to possession of cannabis resin in Marylebone Magistrate's Court on November 28, 1968; he was fined £150.

On August 13, 1971, Lennon and his wife Yoko Ono arrived in New York. They had come to this country to seek custody of Mrs. Lennon's daughter by a former marriage to an American citizen. It was at this point that the Lennons first met with the labyrinthine provisions of the Immigration and Nationality Act which were to result in the deportation proceedings which we review. Accordingly, a brief description of the relevant portions of that Act is here in order.

INA § 212(a), 8 U.S.C. § 1182(a), lists thirty-one classes of 'excludable aliens' who are ineligible for permanent residence, and, indeed, are (with the exception provided by § 212(d)(3)(A)), unable to enter this country at all. This portion of the Act is like a magic mirror, reflecting the fears and concerns of past Congresses. Among those excludable is "any alien who has been convicted of a violation of . . . any law or regulation relating to the illicit possession of . . . marihuana (§ 212(a)(23))." Section 212(d)(3)(A) permits the INS, in its discretion, temporarily to waive excludability and to admit the alien under a temporary non-immigrant visa. When this visa expires, the alien must leave or face deportation. § 241(a)(2). At any time after admission, however, the alien may petition for permanent resident status. § 245(a). This classification can be, in effect, a challenge to his classification as an excludable alien.

Since Lennon's conviction appeared to render him excludable, the INS specifically waived excludability under § 212(d)(3)(A). The Lennons were then given temporary visas valid until September 10; the INS later extended the expiration date to February 29, 1972. The day after Lennon's visa expired, March 1, Sol Marks, the New York District Director of the INS, notified the Lennons by letter that, if they did not leave the country by March 15, deportation proceedings would be instituted. On March 3, Lennon and his wife filed third preference petitions. In response to these applications, the INS instituted deportation proceedings three days later. The INS, for reasons best known to them, did not act on the applications, and the Lennons were therefore unable to apply for permanent residence. After waiting two months, the Lennons filed suit in the Southern District for an injunction compelling the INS to rule on their petitions. *Lennon v. Marks*, 72 Civ. 1784. At oral argument in that case, Marks advised the judge that the INS would consider the applications; they were approved within the hour.

In March, April, and May, 1972, deportation hearings were held before Immigration Judge Fieldsteel. On May 12, 1972, ten days after the INS finally approved their petition for third preference status, the Lennons applied to the Immigration Judge for permanent residence. During the hearing, letters from many eminent writers, artists, and entertainers, as well as from John Lindsay, at that time the Mayor of New York, were submitted to show that, were the applications approved, the Lennons would make a unique and valuable contribution to this country's cultural heritage. The Government did not challenge Lennon's artistic standing, but instead contended that his 1968 guilty plea made him an excludable alien, thus mandating the denial of his application. Lennon countered by arguing that he was not excludable under § 212(a)(23) since he had not been convicted of violating a law forbidding *illicit* possession. Under British law, Lennon urged, guilty knowledge was not an element of the offense. Lennon further argued that, by commencing deportation proceedings while he was seeking custody of his wife's child, the agency had violated its hitherto invariable practice and therefore had abused its discretion.

The Immigration Judge filed his decision on March 23, 1973. Since Yoko Ono had obtained permanent resident status in 1964, he granted her application. But, because he believed that Lennon was an excludable alien, the Immigration Judge denied his application and ordered him deported. The Immigration Judge also held that it was not within his province to review the Director's decision to begin deportation proceedings.

Lennon sought review of the Immigration Judge's decision before the Board of Immigration Appeals. He also began a collateral action in the Southern District in which he sought to enjoin his deportation. He was deserving of this relief, he contended, since the District Director and the Immigration Judge had prejudged his case. The INS had, he said, instituted deportation proceedings because they feared he might participate in demonstrations that would be highly embarrassing to the then-existing administration. In January, 1975, Judge Owen denied a government motion for summary judgment. *Lennon v. United States*, D.C., 387 F.Supp. 561 (1975).

Meanwhile, on July 10, 1974, the Board filed its decision. The Board conceded that § 212(a)(23) does not exclude aliens convicted of possession under laws which made knowledge immaterial to the offense. However, the Board concluded that "a person who was entirely unaware that he possessed any illicit substance would not have been convicted under the

(British) Dangerous Drugs Act of 1965." The Board also held that it was without jurisdiction to consider Lennon's claim that he was improperly denied nonpriority status. Accordingly, the Board concluded that Lennon was ineligible for permanent residence and affirmed the Immigration Judge's deportation order.

II.

It is within the context of these issues that we must decide the merits of this appeal. INA § 212(a), 8 U.S.C. § 1182(a), provides:

> (T)he following classes of aliens shall be ineligible to receive visas and shall be excluded from admission into the United States. . .(23) Any alien who has been convicted of a violation of, or conspiracy to violate, any law or regulation relating to the illicit possession of or traffic in narcotic drugs or marihuana. . . .

The Immigration Judge and the Board of Immigration Appeals believed that Lennon's 1968 conviction made him excludable under this section. We are of the view that it did not. We base this result upon our conclusion that (A) Lennon was convicted under a law which in effect makes guilty knowledge irrelevant and that (B) a foreign conviction for possession of marijuana under such a law does not render the convicted alien excludable.

A.   Lack of Knowledge Requirement under British Law in 1968

The language of the British statute under which Lennon was convicted is deceptively simple: 'A person shall not be in possession of a drug unless . . . authorized . . .' But around this concise provision, judicial interpretation has created a scholastic maze as complex and baffling as the labyrinth at Knossos in ancient Crete.

The most authoritative judicial pronouncement on the knowledge requirements of the British act is *Warner v. Metropolitan Police Commissioner*, (1969) 2 A.C. 256, (1968) 2 All E.R. 356. The facts in that case were relatively simple. The luckless Warner was stopped by police while he was driving his van. Inside a box in the back of the vehicle, police found twenty thousand amphetamine tablets. Warner claimed ignorance; he had, he said, been given the parcel by a friend who had told him that it contained perfume, which Warner sold as a sideline. The House of Lords was called upon to decide whether Warner would be guilty of amphetamine possession even if he did indeed believe that his package held perfume.

Each of the five Law Lords delivered a separate opinion. All save Lord Reid agreed that, once possession was proven, liability was absolute and mental state irrelevant. They felt that, to require the prosecution to prove full mens rea would, in Lord Guest's words, create a 'drug peddlar's charter in which a successful prosecution will be well-nigh impossible.' The Lords recognized, however, that it was unfair for a person to be held criminally liable if it appeared that the drugs had, for example, been 'planted' by an enemy. The Lords sought a halfway house between equity and efficiency that would permit many if not most blameless defendants to go free without allowing the guilty to escape in sheep's clothing. To do this, they resurrected a hoary line of cases which had held, in the context of larceny statutes, that some knowledge must be proved to establish *possession*.

The peers' progress up to this point was relatively straightforward. But the question of how much knowledge should be required for possession precipitated a verbal Donnybrook Fair. From the ensuing tangle of rhetoric, two conclusions emerged. First, four of the Lords adopted the conclusion of the Queen's Bench Division in an earlier case, *Lockyer v. Gibb*, (1967) 2 Q.B. 243, (1966) 2 All E.R. 653, that a person who is aware that he has a substance possesses it even if he is mistaken as to its qualities. The grave import of this holding is made clear by the striking example used by Lord Pearce: "Though I reasonably believe the tablets which I possess to be aspirin, yet if they turn out to be heroin I am in possession of heroin tablets. This would be so I think even if I believed them to be sweets." (1969) 2 A.C. at 305, (1968) 2 All E.R. at 358.

The second holding which may be gleaned from Warner deals with the so-called 'package cases'. In these cases, the defendant possesses a box or container but is either mistaken as to its contents or thinks it empty; the package in fact contains drugs. Three of the Lords held that such a person would be guilty if he had a chance to open the parcel, the right to do so, and (perhaps) some indication that the package was not empty; that he never availed himself of the opportunity to open the container would be of no importance. Under British law, as Lord Pearce stated, "a man takes over a package or suitcase at risk as to its contents being unlawful if he does not immediately examine it (if he is entitled to do so)." A.C. at 306, All E.R. at 389.

We conclude from this analysis of British law as it existed in 1968 that Lennon was convicted under a statute which made guilty knowledge irrelevant. A person found with tablets which he reasonably believed were aspirin would, under the Warner holding, be convicted if the tablets proved to contain heroin. And a man given a sealed package filled with heroin would, if he had had any opportunity to open the parcel, suffer the same fate—even if he firmly believed the package contained perfume.

B.   Knowledge Requirement of INA § 212(a)(23)

Any analysis of § 212(a)(23) must find its starting point in the statute's plain language. That language provides compelling evidence of a knowledge requirement, for it renders excludable 'any alien who has been convicted of a violation of . . . any law or regulation relating to the *illicit* possession of . . . marihuana.' (Emphasis added)[1] * * *

---

[1]   We note that if 'illicit' merely meant 'unlawful', it would be redundant.

Deportation is not, of course, a penal sanction. But in severity it surpasses all but the most Draconian criminal penalties. We therefore cannot deem wholly irrelevant the long unbroken tradition of the criminal law that harsh sanctions should not be imposed where moral culpability is lacking.

We are now called upon to decide whether the exclusion of convictions for possession obtained under laws imposing absolute liability would significantly impede the enforcement or undermine the purpose of the Immigration and Nationality Act. If we find that it does not, then we cannot, in the light of these firmly established precepts of statutory construction, conclude that Congress intended to include such convictions within the ambit of § 212(a)(23). The general purpose of § 212 is, of course, to bar undesirable aliens from our shores. There is also, we note, some indication that Congress, in enacting § 212(a)(23), was far more concerned with the trafficker of drugs than with the possessor.

We do not believe that our holding will subvert these Congressional ends. Virtually every undesirable alien covered by the drug conviction provision would also be barred by other sections of the statute. Thus, the statute makes excludable "any alien who the consular officer or immigration officers know or have reason to believe is or has been an illicit trafficker in ... drugs." § 212(a)(23). Moreover, addicts are barred by § 212(a)(5). Finally, our holding will not, of course, give any comfort to those convicted in the United States of drug violations.

Given, in sum, the minimal gain in effective enforcement, we cannot imagine that Congress would impose the harsh consequences of an excludable alien classification upon a person convicted under a foreign law that made guilty knowledge irrelevant. We hold that it did not. We base our decision in this appeal solely upon our interpretation of § 212(a) (23) of the Immigration and Nationality Act. We deem it appropriate, however, to add a brief word on Lennon's contention that he was singled out for deportation because of his political activities and beliefs.

Although the Board rejected Lennon's selective enforcement defense as beyond their jurisdiction, we do not take his claim lightly. This issue, however, is not presented to us for determination. At oral argument, Lennon's counsel agreed not to press this point unless we found Lennon to be excludable under § 212(a)(23). We note, nonetheless, that if Lennon's application for permanent residence should be denied for discretionary reasons after our mandate is received, Judge Owen will proceed expeditiously to hear Lennon's claim and accord him the relief to which he may be entitled. The courts will not condone selective deportation based upon secret political grounds. It would be premature for us to be more specific, since the facts underlying Lennon's claim of selective prosecution have not been developed sufficiently for appellate review.

Before closing with the traditional words of disposition, we feel it appropriate to express our faith that the result we have reached in this case not only is consistent with the language and purpose of the narrow statutory provision we construe, but also furthers the intent of the immigration laws in a far broader sense. The excludable aliens statute is but an exception, albeit necessary, to the traditional tolerance of a nation founded and built by immigrants. If, in our two hundred years of independence, we have in some measure realized our ideals, it is in large part because we have always found a place for those committed to the spirit of liberty and willing to help implement it. Lennon's four-year battle to remain in our country is testimony to his faith in this American dream.

Accordingly, the denial of Lennon's application for adjustment of status and the order of deportation are vacated and the case remanded for reconsideration in accordance with the views expressed in this opinion.

MULLIGAN, J., dissenting.

As the majority opinion observes, Lennon's claim that he is the victim of selective prosecution is an issue not before this court but rather is sub judice in the Southern District, and therefore we cannot appropriately discuss its merits. The sole issue before us is whether Lennon is an excludable alien under INA § 212(a)(23).

That statute would exclude any alien who has been convicted of a violation of any law or regulation relating to the illicit possession of narcotic drugs or marihuana. Since the statute applies to any alien it makes no difference whether he be John Lennon, John Doe or Johann Sebastian Bach. Great Britain has made the possession of cannabis resin (marihuana) without authorization illicit (§ 3, Dangerous Drugs (No. 2) Regulations, under the Dangerous Drugs Act 1965). It is further conceded that Lennon pleaded guilty to the possession of that drug on November 28, 1968 and was fined £ 150. From these premises one would logically conclude that Lennon should be excluded from the United States.

The majority argues however that § 212(a)(23) should not be interpreted to exclude from this country those who are innocently in possession of an illicit drug. I agree but I cannot agree that Lennon was convicted under a statute which imposes 'absolute liability' and makes the knowledge of the defendant 'irrelevant.' The five opinions in *Warner v. Metropolitan Police Commissioner*, (1969) 2 A.C. 256, (1968) 2 All E.R. 356, which interpret the British statute, are hardly as clear as a mountain lake in springtime but there is a consensus on basic principles.

Lennon claims here that the drugs were concealed in a binocular case in a closet of his apartment and that he had absolutely no idea of their presence. There is the further suggestion that they may have been 'planted' by the arresting constable who it is alleged was at the very least overzealous in prosecuting rock musicians. Assuming that Lennon's version of the facts is accurate, it is my view that he could not have been properly convicted in Great Britain of the offense charged.

In *Warner* Lord Pearce clearly held the view that the Parliament did not intend to impose absolute liability in the Drugs Act of 1965. 'It is conceded by the Crown that these words (have in possession) do not include goods slipped into a man's pocket without his knowledge.' (1968) 2 All E.R. at 386. It must be further observed that this was the interpretation given to *Warner* in later English opinions. Lennon's position has been either that the cannabis resin was planted by the police or that in any event he was totally ignorant of its presence in the binocular case. His counsel must also have so read *Warner* since as the opinion below reveals his solicitors told him after his arrest that he stood a good chance of acquittal at trial.

In light of this discussion I cannot accept the majority view that Lennon was convicted under a law which imposed absolute liability and eliminated mens rea. If ignorant of the drug's presence he would not have had possession under English law and could not have been properly convicted. The undisputed fact however is that Lennon did plead guilty to the possession of cannabis resin, and while this may have been convenient or expedient because of his wife's pregnancy and his disinclination to have her testify in court, it is elementary that we cannot go behind the plea. Since Lennon was convicted under a statute which did not impose liability absolutely but required knowledge on the part of the defendant where the contraband is secreted in a container, I cannot concur in the result reached by the majority.

The majority here further concludes that a foreign conviction for the *possession of marijuana* under the British statute or any similar foreign law does not render the convicted alien excludable. They argue that the Congress was more concerned with trafficking in drugs than in possession and their opinion does not cover the trafficker who obviously is fully aware of the nature of the business he is pursuing. The statute (INA § 212(a)(23)) however bars the possessor as well as the trafficker. If there were no users there would be no trafficking.

Great Britain bars the unauthorized possession not only of cannabis resin but raw opium, coca leaves (from which cocaine is extracted) and other substances as well. Congress has also barred from this country those aliens who have been convicted of the possession not only of marihuana but other illicit drugs. Although the majority limits its holding to a marihuana conviction under the British statute or any foreign counterpart, its reasoning would compel the same result if the drug at issue were heroin or cocaine. It must also be emphasized that the vast majority of those who are arrested with illicit drugs in their homes or on their persons are users who are fully aware of their presence and their properties. It is the unusual case where contraband such as this is surreptitiously planted in one's reticule or blue jeans pocket. Yet by disregarding convictions under the British statute or any other foreign counterpart, the majority would admit to the United States those who knowingly possessed any illicit drugs. This holding seems to me to conflict with INA § 212(a)(23) which plainly bars those who have been convicted of a violation of 'any law or regulation relating to the illicit possession of . . . narcotic drugs or marihuana'. Lennon's guilty plea here puts him within the statute.

The holding here will undoubtedly and unfortunately result in the abandonment of Lennon's claim of selective prosecution now pending in the Southern District Court. If others found guilty of the same crime have been permitted entry and Lennon has been barred because he is John Lennon, the jongleur, and not John Doe, then that contention should be litigated not only in the interests of Lennon and INS but the public as well.

NOTES AND QUESTIONS

1. **Political protest.** It was widely believed that John Lennon was selected for deportation because of his political activism and especially his outspoken opposition to the Vietnam War. His supporters reacted with a "Let Them Stay in the USA" campaign. His cause was taken up by artists and politicians such as musicians Joan Baez, Leonard Bernstein, Bob Dylan; writers Joseph Heller and John Updike; artist Jasper Johns; and New York City Mayor John Lindsay. In a strategy that combined marketing with politics, the 1972 Lennon-Ono album "Sometime in New York City" included a petition to the INS in support of Lennon.

2. **Selective prosecution.** The majority decisions and dissent take opposite positions on the question of selective prosecution. To the majority, Lennon is entitled to special status in immigration decisions as a cultural asset, long a positive consideration as to who to admit into to U.S. and to whom to grant citizenship. Judge Kaufman implies that Lennon was the subject of selective prosecution and threatens to initiate a judicial action to investigate. The dissent on the other hand, claims that all aliens should be treated equally in immigration decisions, and "it makes no difference whether he be John Lennon, John Doe or Johann Sebastian Bach." Which approach is correct in this case? In general? Was Lennon being favored or disfavored in his battle to remain in the United States and become a U.S. citizen?

3. **Deportation.** Judge Kaufman writes that "Deportation is not, of course, a penal sanction. But in severity it surpasses all but the most Draconian criminal penalties." As we saw in Chapter 14, the collateral consequences for drug convictions in the U.S. can be grievous. For many aliens, none is more so than deportation, which can be triggered by a relatively minor marijuana conviction. Under present law, drug offenses can render non-citizens, including those with permanent residence, deportable, 8 U.S.C. § 1227(a)(2)(B)(i)–(ii), and can bar their reentry into the United States, 8 U.S.C. § 1182(a)(2)(A)(i)(II), (a)(2)(C)(i). However there is an exception for a "single offense involving possession for one's own use of 30 grams or less of marijuana." § 1227(a)(2)(B)(i). Would Lennon have been eligible for this

exception? The U.S. Supreme Court has decided a trio of cases involving questions of deportation for marijuana crimes. *Padilla v. Commonwealth of Kentucky*, 559 U.S. 356 (2010); *Carachuri-Rosendo v. Holder*, 560 U.S. 563 (2010); *Moncrieffe v. Holder*, 569 U.S. 184 (2013). See Chapter 14.

4.   Foreign marijuana conviction? Much of this case revolves around an abstruse analysis of British law as to Lennon's conviction for possession of cannabis resin in Marylebone Magistrate's Court, Great Britain on November 28, 1968. Judge Kaufman describes this British law as "a scholastic maze as complex and baffling as the labyrinth at Knossos in ancient Crete." Judge Mulligan describes it as "hardly as clear as a mountain lake in springtime."

Why is it crucial to decide whether under British law guilty knowledge is an element of the offense for which Lennon was convicted? Does it matter whether Lennon actually knew of the presence of marijuana in his apartment? Which judge, Kaufman or Mulligan, seems to conduct a more accurate analysis of British law? What are Judge Kaufman's arguments against finding that this conviction satisfied the deportation requirement of INS (§ 212(a)(23) that "any alien who has been convicted of a violation of . . . any law or regulation relating to the illicit possession of . . . marihuana (§ 212(a)(23))"? What is the dissent's argument that Lennon's British conviction did satisfy the requirement? Is it sensible for U.S. judges to write short treatises on foreign law? Were they equipped to do so in this case? The difficulty is compounded by Lennon's contention that a British expunction statute (1974 Rehab of Offenders Act) had wiped out his conviction for purposes of § 212(a)(23).

5.   Any law? Neither judge discusses the extent of the "any law" INS requirement that a conviction of any law relating to the illicit possession of marihuana renders an alien deportable. Is there a fair reading that "any law" refers only to U.S. law? If it does refer to foreign law, does it refer to any law anywhere in the world, regardless of consideration of the nation, locale, jurisdiction, or court? What if the conviction is imposed by a nation that is not recognized by the United States, or labeled by the State Department as a nation that supports terrorism or commits human right abuses?

6.   Guilty knowledge. How convincing is Judge Kaufman's analysis that Lennon was convicted under a British statute which made guilty knowledge irrelevant." Kaufman contrasts the statute with U.S. law, writing:

> Any analysis of § 212(a)(23) must find its starting point in the statute's plain language. That language provides compelling evidence of a knowledge requirement, for it renders excludable 'any alien who has been convicted of a violation of . . . any law or regulation relating to the illicit possession of . . . marihuana.'

Kaufman notes in a footnote that "if 'illicit' merely meant 'unlawful', it would be redundant." Is this sufficient to show "compelling evidence of a knowledge requirement" under § 212(a)(23)?

7.   Guilty Plea. What does the dissent mean that "it is elementary that we cannot go behind the plea"? Why is that an important issue to resolve for this case?

8.   **Marijuana and politics. The Inside Story.** An anecdotal account of this case is *John Lennon vs. the USA: The Inside Story of the Most Bitterly Contested and Influential Deportation* (2016), by Leon Wildes, Lennon's lawyer during his deportation contests.

9.   **Collateral Consequences.** This case demonstrates that a minor marijuana offense, even a foreign one, can have significant collateral consequences. Drug offenses, including marijuana offenses, can trigger numerous civil repercussions, some of which are listed in the CSA itself (see e.g., 21 U.S.C. § 862). The civil sanctions that attach to criminal convictions are an important element in the debate over marijuana legalization. We looked at two significant collateral consequences (housing and immigration) in depth in Chapter 14. For legalization advocates, the collateral consequences that attach to marijuana convictions damage the lives of numerous defendants arrested or convicted of minor marijuana crimes. Opponents argue that civil penalties attached to criminal convictions are necessary to protect society and prevent recidivism.

According to information collected by the National Inventory of Collateral Consequences of Conviction, about 48,000 federal and state laws apply legal sanctions and restrictions to persons with criminal records. About 641 federal laws apply specifically to nonviolent drug offenders, including those with marijuana offenses. Collateral consequences that apply to a wide range of criminal convictions, and sometimes with special force to drug and marijuana convictions, include:

- *Bans on employments.* The greatest number of sanctions relate to employment, including revocations and bars on federal and state occupational licenses, ineligibility for federal grants, contracts, loans, and exclusion from management and operation of regulated businesses. See e.g. 21 U.S.C. § 862(a), (b), (d)(1).

- *Public assistance.* Depending on the state, can include denial of cash assistance, food stamps, and Supplemental Security Income (SSI), Social Security Disability Insurance (SSDI), home loans, small business loans, veterans benefits, and other payments. See e.g. 13 C.F.R. § 124. 108(a)(4)(ii) (2016).

- *Domestic relations.* Restrictions on family relationships and living arrangements, including foster care adoption, and child custody. 42 U.S.C. § 671(a)(20)(A)(ii).

- *Public housing.* Denial or eviction from federally assisted housing. 42 U.S.C. § 1437d(l)(6); 42 U.S.C. §§ 13661–13662; 24 C.F.R. § 996.4(l)(5)(i). See Chapter 14, *Forest City Residential Management, Inc. v. Beasley*, 71 F.Supp.3d 715 (E.D. Mich. 2014).

- *Student financial aid.* Denial of federal assistance to higher education students. 20 U.S.C. § 1091(r)(1); 26 U.S.C. § 25A(b)(2)(D).

- *Firearms.* Prohibitions on obtaining or using firearms. 18 U.S.C. §§ 922(g)(1)(3), 929 (a)(2); 27 C.F.R. § 478.11 (2016). See Chapter 8.

- *State driving licenses.* Depending on the state, suspension of driving licenses. 23 U.S.C. § 159.

- *Denial and revocation of passport for international drug crimes.* 22 U.S.C. § 2714(a)(1); (b)(1)(2).

- *Five years supervision and residency requirements.* 18 U.S.C. § 3583.

- *Disenfranchisement.* Several states bar persons with criminal records, including marijuana convictions, from voting, which can have significant effect on elections, given election patterns. In 1976 about one million people were disenfranchised; currently about six million voters are disenfranchised. It is estimated that approximately one in thirteen African-Americans is prohibited from voting; in several states it is as high as one in four. Nevertheless, such laws have been upheld by the U.S. Supreme Court, *Richardson v. Ramirez*, 418 U.S. 24 (1974), except if the legislature explicitly stated that the law was enacted to establish white supremacy, *Hunter v. Underwood*, 471 U.S. 222 (1985). For a comprehensive discussion of felony disenfranchisement, see Jeff Manza and Christopher Uggen, *Locked Out: Felon Disenfranchisement and American Democracy* (Oxford University Press 2008).

For articles on collateral consequences, see Nora V. Demleitner, *"Collateral Damage": No Re-entry for Drug Offenders*, 47 Vil. L. Rev. 1027 (2002); Gabriel J. Chin, *The New Civil Death: Rethinking Punishment in the Era of Mass Conviction*, 160 U. Pa. L. Rev. 1789 (2012).

C. MARIJUANA PUBLIC POLICY

As has been noted earlier, on January 4, 2018, the Department of Justice issued a memorandum on federal marijuana enforcement, reversing the policy of the Obama administration as enunciated in its Department of Justice guidance memoranda. According to the Justice Department, Attorney General Jeff Sessions in his memorandum directed the U.S. Attorneys to enforce the CSA so as "to reduce violent crime, stem the tide of the drug crisis, and dismantle criminal gangs." Department of Justice Office of Public Affairs, *Press Release 18-8*, January 4, 2018.

MEMORANDUM FOR ALL UNITED STATES ATTORNEYS

Department of Justice, Office of the Attorney General
January 4, 2018

JEFFERSON SESSIONS, ATTORNEY GENERAL.

In the Controlled Substances Act, Congress has generally prohibited the cultivation, distribution, and possession of marijuana. 21 U.S.C. § 801 et seq. It has established significant penalties for these crimes. 21 U.S.C. § 841 el seq. These activities also may serve as the basis for the prosecution of other crimes, such as those prohibited by the money laundering statutes, the unlicensed money transmitter statute, and the Bank Secrecy Act. 18 U.S.C. §§ 1956–57, 1960; 31 U.S.C. § 5318. These statutes reflect Congress's determination that marijuana is a dangerous drug and that marijuana activity is a serious crime.

In deciding which marijuana activities to prosecute under these laws with the Department's finite resources, prosecutors should follow the well-established principles that govern all federal prosecutions. Attorney General Benjamin Civiletti originally set forth these principles in 1980, and they have been refined over time, as reflected in the U.S. Attorneys' Manual. These principles require federal prosecutors deciding which cases to prosecute to weigh all relevant considerations, including federal law enforcement priorities set by the Attorney General, the seriousness of the crime, the deterrent effect of criminal prosecution, and the cumulative impact of particular crimes on the community.

Given the Department's well-established general principles, previous nationwide guidance specific to marijuana enforcement is unnecessary and is rescinded, effective immediately.[2] This memorandum is intended solely as a guide to the exercise of investigative and prosecutorial discretion in accordance with all applicable laws, regulations, and appropriations. It is not intended to, does not, and may not be relied upon to create any rights, substantive or procedural, enforceable at law by any party in any matter civil or criminal.

NOTES AND QUESTIONS

1.   **Marijuana Public Policy.** This memorandum (Sessions Memo) represents the latest Department of Justice policy decision as to marijuana enforcement. The Obama administration memoranda did not change the law,

---

[2]   Previous guidance includes: David W. Ogden, Deputy Att'y Gen., Memorandum for Selected United States Attorneys: Investigations and Prosecutions in States Authorizing the Medical Use of Marijuana (Oct. 19. 2009); James M. Cole, Deputy Att'y Gen., Memorandum for United States Attorneys: Guidance Regarding the Ogden Memo in Jurisdictions Seeking to Authorize Marijuana for Medical Use (June 29, 2011); James M. Cole, Deputy Att'y Gen., Memorandum for All United States Attorneys: Guidance Regarding Marijuana Enforcement (Aug. 29, 2013); James M. Cole. Deputy Att'y Gen., Memorandum for All United States Attorneys: Guidance Regarding Marijuana Related Financial Crimes (Feb. 14, 2014); and Monty Wilkinson, Director of the Executive Office for U.S. Att'ys, Policy Statement Regarding Marijuana Issues in Indian Country (Oct. 28, 2014).

see e.g. *United States. v. Washington*, 887 F. Supp. 2d. 1077, 1094–98 (D. Mont. 2012), but stated policy guidance for law enforcement. The Department of Justice in promulgating the Sessions Memo stated that by revoking the earlier memoranda it was "return[ing] to the rule of law." Department of Justice Office of Public Affairs, *Press Release 18-8*, January 4, 2018. Why does the Justice Department assert that the Sessions Memo represents a "return to the rule of law?"

2. Congressional role. The Sessions Memo reverses the enforcement policy of the Obama Administration, which had issued memoranda that reflected a change from Bush Administration policies. What role should Congress play in determining enforcement policy of the CSA? Does congressional enactment of the Hemp Pilot Program, Section 7606 of the Agricultural Act of 2014 (legalizing the growing and cultivating of industrial hemp for research purposes in states where such growth and cultivation is legal under state law), and annual passage since 2014 of the Rohrabacher-Farr Amendment (which forbids Department of Justice from using funds to prevent states from implanting medical marijuana laws), signify an intent of Congress that is opposed to the public policy indicated by the Sessions Memo?

3. Take Care Clause. How much discretion can the Department of Justice exercise in enforcing the CSA. Under the Constitution, the president is required to "take care that the laws be faithfully executed." U.S. Const. Art. II, § 3. Can the executive branch decide that the CSA will not be enforced in legalizing states? Can it decide to enforce the CSA to its maximum extent, even if this reverses long-standing practice? How much discretion is allowed by the CSA itself, in the following provision?

> The Attorney General shall cooperate with local, State, tribal, and Federal agencies concerning traffic in controlled substances and in suppressing the abuse of controlled substances. To this end, he is authorized to* * *cooperate in the institution and prosecution of cases in the courts of the United States* * * notwithstanding any other provision of law, enter into contractual agreements with State, tribal, and local law enforcement agencies to provide for cooperative enforcement and regulatory activities under this chapter.

21 U.S.C. § 873(a). See Sam Kamin, *Prosecutorial Discretion in the Context of Immigration and Marijuana Law Reform: The Search for a Limiting Principle*, 14 Ohio St. J. Crim. L. Rev. 183 (2016).

4. Public Policy Considerations. Public policy considerations as to marijuana law reflect a wide variety of views of marijuana in society. In the notes that follow we address the public policy debate over marijuana from economic, criminological, sociological, environmental, and cultural perspectives.

5. Economy. The debate over the economic effects of marijuana is particularly heated—and particularly difficult to assess. That is in large part because of the different ways of measuring economic effects. On the one hand, there is little doubt that legalization has added significant revenues to state coffers. For example, in 2017, Colorado collected $247 million in marijuana taxes, licenses, and fees on medical and recreational marijuana. California is estimated to collect about $630 million in marijuana excise taxes in the 2018–19 fiscal year. The *Annual Marijuana Business Factbook* (6th ed. 2017) states the economic impact of legal marijuana sales in 2016 at $16 billion. Opponents, however, claim that these revenues are more than offset by increased consumption of marijuana, leading to higher healthcare costs, more motor vehicle accidents, expenses due to widespread criminal activity, and loss of worker productivity. See, e.g. Kevin Sabet, *Reefer Sanity: Seven Great Myths About Marijuana* (Beaufort Books 2013), pp. 123–132.

6. **Criminological.** The United States has one of the highest incarceration rates in the world. According to Bureau of Justice Statistics, in 2016, there were approximately 2.2 million prisoners in the United States, representing an incarceration rate of 860 people for every 100,000 adults. It is difficult to assess the rates of marijuana incarceration in part because marijuana arrests are often associated with other drug crimes, and the majority of drug sentences represent plea deals reduced from initial charges. Opponents of legalization point to the low incarceration rate for everyday marijuana users. Legalization proponents point to the nearly 600,000 people arrested for simple possession in 2016 (in the decade between 2001 and 2010, there were 8.2 million marijuana arrests, 88% for simple possession), entangling them in the criminal justice system, regardless of the eventual disposition, and the collateral consequences that flow from drug convictions.

Other points of debate as to the criminal justice system are the effect of legalization on the black market for marijuana, the high potency of street marijuana as compared with that of previous decades, whether legalization will increase or decrease marijuana consumption, or consumption of other dangerous substances, and how it will affect the control of organized crime and international drug cartels over marijuana supply and traffic. For an in-depth study of issues relating to criminal enforcement of marijuana laws and other contemporary public policy issues, see Lisa Sacco, et. al., *The Marijuana Policy Gap and the Path Forward*, Congressional Research Service (CRS) Report Number: R44782 (March 10. 2017).

7. **Sociological.** Marijuana as a social artifact has been studied by sociologists. In 1953, Howard Becker wrote a trilogy of innovative articles arguing that marijuana use is a social process characterized by three stages in which the user learned from peers to overcome restrictions and social opprobrium due to its illegal status: first, the technique of how to smoke marijuana properly; second, to perceive intoxication; and third, to treat marijuana intoxication as pleasurable. Becker was analyzing the sociology of illegal marijuana users. Sociologists are now applying Becker's theories to legalized marijuana. One of the questions that has arisen from this research is: If marijuana relieves pain and provides pleasure, why should society value and allow relief of pain but devalue and forbid providing pleasure? A recent sociology article asks whether prohibiting marijuana is only "to ensure social rectitude and demarcate those who choose a lifestyle unlike our own." See

Nicholas Athey, Neil Boyd, Elysha Cohen, *Becoming a Medical Marijuana User: Reflections on Becker's Trilogy—Learning Techniques, Experiencing Effects, and Perceiving Those Effects as Enjoyable.* 44 Contemporary Drug Problems 212 (2017).

Empirical studies differ as to whether marijuana is a gateway drug to illicit substance use. This is a notoriously difficult assessment to make, given all of the variables that account for substance abuse. For example, one study estimated that approximately 40% of individuals with lifetime cannabis use progress to other illicit drug use. Roberto Secades-Villa, et. al., *Probability and Predictors of the Cannabis Gateway Effect: a National Study.* 26 Int'l J. Drug Policy 135 (2015). In contrast, another recent study found that alcohol consumption in youth was the leading gateway drug to illicit substance use. Adam Barry et al., *Prioritizing Alcohol Prevention: Establishing Alcohol as the Gateway Drug and Linking Age of First Drink With Illicit Drug Use*, 86 J. of School Health 31 (2016).

As to changing social views on marijuana legalization, a 2017 Pew Research Center poll found that 61% of Americans support marijuana legalization, with the greatest support from younger voters. This contrasts sharply with 16% of Americans favoring legalization in 1990, 31% in 2000, and 41% in 2010.

8. The Environment. A modern debate is the effect of marijuana cultivation on the environment. Certainly the widespread manufacture of marijuana has a significant environmental impact. Indoor grow operations use a massive amount of energy in terms of high-intensity light bulbs. It is estimated that indoor operations may account for as much as one percent of total electricity use in the United States. Outdoor growth also uses an enormous amount of water, pesticides, and fertilizer, and has been blamed for deforestation in California. Advocates claim that legalization of marijuana will allow for environmentally-friendly regulations and controls.

9. Experience of Legalized States. Advocates have traditionally argued that legalization will reduce crime rates, bolster traffic safety, and improve public health. Opponents argue that legalization will spur marijuana and other drug use, increase marijuana consumption, increase crime, increase motor vehicle accidents, endanger public health, and reduce teen achievement. An empirical study of the effects of adult legalization in Colorado, Washington, Oregon, and Alaska, found these claims for both sides overstated. The authors compared pre-and post-legalization data from all four states as to marijuana use, other drug or alcohol use, marijuana prices, crime, traffic accidents, teen educational outcomes, public health, tax revenues, criminal justice expenditures, and economic outcomes. Their conclusion is that "state-level marijuana legalizations to date have been associated with, at most, modest changes in marijuana use and related outcomes." Specifically they found at most minor or insignificant changes in:

- Marijuana consumption
- Marijuana prices

- Suicide rates

- Crime rates

- Highway fatalities

- Housing prices

- GDP per capita

- Employment rates

As could be expected, there was a sharp increase in state tax revenue. Angela Dills, Sietse Goffard, and Jeffrey Miron, *Dose of Reality: The Effect of State Marijuana Legalizations,"* Cato Institute, September 16, 2016. http://www. cato.org/publications/policy-analysis/dose-reality-effect-state-marijuana-legalizations.

10. Marijuana and Culture. Marijuana is unique among controlled substances because of its long and significant cultural connections. Its use in prevalent in almost all of the world's cultures and has historic and religious associations. Cannabis is a unique plant. It is the most widely used illicit substance in the world. It grows easily, is hardy and is available in most parts of the world. It does not require much processing and can easily be home-grown or purchased cheaply. It has been a staple of many cultures for millennia, for alleged medical benefits, and for the euphoric effects it produces, without obvious side effects or overpowering intoxication.

In the United States, marijuana law has always been intertwined with broader cultural trends, at no time more so than the counter-culture and protests movements of the late 1960s and early 1970s. In *Lennon v. INS*, Judge Kaufman refers to marijuana as a "magic mirror," which can reflect the fears and concerns of society. Attitudes about marijuana can transcend the cannabis plant itself and become symbolic of political, religious and social beliefs.

When marijuana use first became prevalent in the United States in the early 1900s, its source was Mexico and its prohibition connected to anti-Mexican feelings and opposition to immigration. In the 1930s and 1940s, it was associated with African-American music, especially jazz and blues musicians. In the 1950s, marijuana use was advocated by Beat Generation poets. In the 1960s marijuana flourished with rock and roll musicians, hippies, and the protest movement. This was perhaps the most important cultural shift because marijuana use became widespread among broad segments of the young population, and its use was seen as a protest against society's mores and the Vietnam War. It has been argued that the crackdown on marijuana users was to deter public protest.

In some ways, the debate over marijuana legalization may be at its heart a cultural one, reflecting demographics, social status, and attitudes toward the role of law and medicine in society. Certainly this would go a long way to explaining why alcohol is a legal substance and marijuana is not. The debate over recreational marijuana reflects one's view of the role of government in regulating lives of its citizens, and preventing harm to marijuana consumers and ancillary effects on others. The debate over medical marijuana reflects differing cultural views of medicine. Some proponents argue that tradition and personal testimony demonstrate the medical uses of marijuana; that the choice of what kind of medicine to use should be essentially a personal choice; and that the marijuana plant is nature's beneficial method of obtaining the health effects of cannabis, as opposed to single-molecule pharmaceutical cannabinoids. Opponents argue that medicine is most safely used when approved by the FDA; that only carefully regulated cannabis substances can be consumed safely, and not in smokeable form; and that such substances have already been approved by the FDA in the form of dronabinol (Marinol and Syndros), nabilone (Cesamet), and a purified cannabidiol extract (Epidiolex), obviating the need for any kind of whole plant legalization.

For a comprehensive history of marijuana in cultural life, see Emily Dufton, *Grass Roots: The Rise and Fall and Rise of Marijuana in America* (New York: Basic Books, 2017).

PROBLEM 21-2

Does the Sessions memo represent the correct public policy as to federal enforcement of marijuana laws, especially as compared to the Obama era memoranda? If you were tasked to draft Department of Justice policy as to marijuana law enforcement, what policies would you propose?

PROBLEM 21-3

What legislation, if any, should Congress enact to clarify public policy as to marijuana law? Should Congress enact amendments to the CSA, and if so which ones?

PROBLEM 21-4

You have been asked to arrange a debate at a local university on marijuana legalization. Regardless of your personal positions on marijuana law, what would you outline as the strongest policy arguments for and against marijuana legalization?

APPENDIX

MARIJUANA LAW BY JURISDICTION

■ ■ ■

As of December 2018

Category	Number of States
Illegal	4
Cannabidiol Only	13
Medical	23
Adult Use	10

ILLEGAL[1,2]				
Jurisdiction	Amount	Incarceration	Fine	Statute
Federal	Any amount	1 year	$1,000 (minimum)	21 U.S.C. § 844
Idaho	3 oz. or less	1 year	$1,000	Idaho Code § 37–2732
Kansas[3]	Any amount	6 months	$1000	Kan. Stat. Ann. § 21–5706(c)(3)(A)
Nebraska[4]	1 oz. to 1 lb.	3 months	$500	Neb. Rev. Stat. Ann § 28–416(11)

---

[1] Although marijuana use is restricted in every state, these jurisdictions allow almost no exceptions.

[2] Shows maximum penalties and fines for simple possession for personal use, first offense.

[3] Allows CBD, Kan. Stat. Ann. § 21–5701(j)(3), as long as product does not contain THC, Kan. Stat. Ann. § 65–4105(h)(1).

[4] Less than 1 oz., $300 citation, drug abuse course. Neb. Rev. Stat. Ann § 28–416(13).

South Dakota[5]	2 oz. or less	1 year	$2000	S.D. Codified Laws § 22–42–6

LOW THC, HIGH CBD (CANNABIDIOL) ONLY[6]		
Jurisdiction	**Conditions Covered**	**Statute**
Alabama	Chronic conditions producing seizures	Ala. Code § 13A–12–214.3
Georgia	16 conditions	Ga. Code Ann. § 31–2A–18
Indiana	Medical recommendation not required[7]	Ind. Code Ann. § 24–4–22–1
Iowa	9 conditions including any terminal illness	Iowa Code § 124E.2
Kentucky	If recommended by a publicly affiliated physician	Ky. Rev. Stat. § 218A.010
Mississippi	Epilepsy	Miss. Code Ann. § 41–29–136
North Carolina	Intractable epilepsy	N.C. Gen. Stat. § 90–113.101
South Carolina	Intractable epilepsy	S.C. Code Ann. § 44–53–1810
Tennessee	Medical recommendation not required	Tenn. Code Ann. § 39–17–402
Texas	Intractable epilepsy	Tex. Occ. Code § 169.001
Virginia	Any, as approved by physician	Va. Code Ann. § 54.1–3408.3

[5]   Allows FDA-approved CBD. S.D. Codified Laws § 34–20B–1(12).

[6]   Other than authorized CBD use, penalties are similar to states in the "illegal" category. MS, NC have decriminalized (no incarceration, fine) possession of small amounts.

[7]   Some jurisdictions do not have a medical CBD program, but have excluded non- or low-THC cannabidiol from the statutory definition of marijuana in the penal code.

Wisconsin	Any, as approved by physician	Wis. Stat. Ann. § 961.38
Wyoming	Intractable epilepsy	Wyo. Stat. Ann. § 35–7–1901

MEDICAL[8], RESTRICTION[9,10]			
Jurisdiction	**Restriction**	**Estimated No. of Registered Patients[11]**	**Statute**
Arkansas	No home cultivation	5,936	Ark. Const. Amendment 98, § 2
Connecticut	No home cultivation	26,323	Conn. Gen. Stat. § 21a–408
Delaware	No home cultivation	3,274	Del. Code Ann. tit. 16, § 4902A
Florida	Non-smokeable	111,970	Fla. Stat. Ann. § 381.986
Guam	No home cultivation	N/A[12]	10 GCA § 122503
Illinois	No home cultivation	21,800	410 Ill. Comp. Stat. Ann. 130/10
Louisiana	Non-smokeable	N/A	La. Rev. Stat. Ann. § 40:1046
Maryland	No home cultivation	20,157	Md. Code Ann., Crim. Law § 5–601

---

[8] Qualifying conditions in the "medical, restriction" category can be similar to those in the "medical, broad" category. See footnote 13 for a list of common qualifying conditions.

[9] Jurisdictions may be classified as "medical, restriction" because the law places restrictions on the types of medical marijuana available to patients, or prohibits home cultivation.

[10] Other than authorized medical use, penalties are similar to states in the "illegal" category. CT, DL, IL, MD, NY, NH, OH have decriminalized possession of small amounts.

[11] States with active medical marijuana programs publish statistics with varying regularity. Some of these numbers represent program statistics as of 2018, some as of 2017.

[12] Jurisdictions with "N/A" number of patients have enacted medical marijuana laws, but have yet to begin administration of a medical marijuana program.

Minnesota	Non-smokeable	8,075	Minn. Stat. Ann. § 152.22
New Hampshire	No home cultivation	3,493	N.H. Rev. Stat. Ann. § 126–X:1
New Jersey	No home cultivation	17,806	N.J. Stat. § 24:6I–3
New York	Non-smokeable	61,699	N.Y. Pub. Health Law § 3360
North Dakota	Smokeable form requires further certification from physician	N/A	N.D. Cent. Code § 19–24.1–01
Ohio	No home cultivation	N/A	Ohio Rev. Code Ann. § 3796.01
Pennsylvania	Non-smokeable, vaporizing OK	25,508	35 Pa. Stat. Ann. § 10231.103
Puerto Rico	Non-smokeable	28,108	24 L.P.R.A. § 2621
Utah	No home cultivation	N/A	Utah Code Ann. Title 26, Ch. 61a
West Virginia	Non-smokeable, vaporizing OK	N/A	W. Va. Code § 16A–2–1

MEDICAL, BROAD[13],[14]			
Jurisdiction	Chronic Pain Permitted as a Qualifying Condition[15]	Estimated No. of Registered Patients	Statute
Arizona	Yes	158,654	Ariz. Rev. Stat. § 36–2801
Hawaii	Yes	21,004	Haw. Rev. Stat. Ann. § 329–121
Missouri	Yes	N/A	Mo. Const. Art. XIV
Montana	Yes*[16]	25,725	Mont. Code Ann. § 50–46–302
New Mexico	Yes	54,857	N.M. Stat. Ann. § 26–2B–3
Oklahoma	Yes	N/A	63 Okl. St. § 420
Rhode Island	Yes*	18,728	21 R.I. Gen. Laws § 28.6–3

[13] Jurisdictions with "medical, broad" marijuana laws permit a broad array of qualifying medical conditions. The most common are: Alzheimer's, cancer, Crohn's, epilepsy, glaucoma, HIV, Parkinson's, PTSD, and multiple sclerosis. These states also permit smokeable forms of marijuana and home cultivation for medical use.

[14] Other than authorized medical use, penalties are similar to states in the "illegal" category. MO, RI have decriminalized possession of small amounts.

[15] States that permit "chronic pain" as a qualifying condition generally have the greatest percentages of qualifying patients.

[16] Jurisdictions marked with "Yes*" in the "chronic pain" category permit chronic pain as a qualifying symptom, but require that the pain be debilitating and/or unresponsive to previously prescribed medication or surgical measures.

ADULT USE		
Jurisdiction	**Maximum Amount[17] (Personal Possession)**	**Statute**
Alaska	1 oz.	Alaska Stat. § 17.38.020
California	1 oz.	Cal. Health & Safety Code § 11357
Colorado	1 oz.	Colo. Const. Art. XVIII, Section 16
D.C.	2 oz.	D.C. Code § 48–904.01
Maine	2.5 oz.	Me. Rev. Stat. tit. 28–B, § 1501
Massachusetts	1 oz.	Mass. Ann. Laws ch. 94G, § 7
Michigan	2.5 oz.	Mich. Comp. Laws Serv. § 333.27955
Nevada	1 oz.	Nev. Rev. Stat. Ann. § 453D.020
Oregon	1 oz.	Or. Rev. Stat. Ann. § 475B.337
Vermont	1 oz.	Vt. Stat. Ann. tit. 18, § 4230
Washington	1 oz.	Wash. Rev. Code Ann. § 69.50.360(3)

---

[17] Possession of more than maximum amount subject to sanction.

INDEX

References are to Pages